Producing Great Sound
for Film and Video

Producing Great Sound for Film and Video

Expert Tips from Preproduction to Final Mix

Fourth Edition

Jay Rose

Focal Press
Taylor & Francis Group

NEW YORK AND LONDON

First published 1999 by Miller Freeman Books

This edition published 2015
by Focal Press
70 Blanchard Road, Suite 402, Burlington, MA 01803

and by Focal Press
2 Park Square, Milton Park, Abingdon, Oxon OX14 4RN

Focal Press is an imprint of the Taylor & Francis Group, an informa business

Cover image: Production Mixer G. John Garrett, Cinematographer
Peter Hoving, and Director John Angier interview biologist John H. Hobbie
near Toolik Lake, Alaska, for an episode of Scientific American Frontiers.
Photo courtesy G. John Garrett, CAS.

Notices
Knowledge and best practice in this field are constantly changing. As new
research and experience broaden our understanding, changes in research
methods, professional practices, or medical treatment may become necessary.

Practitioners and researchers must always rely on their own experience and
knowledge in evaluating and using any information, methods, compounds, or
experiments described herein. In using such information or methods they should
be mindful of their own safety and the safety of others, including
parties for whom they have a professional responsibility.

Product or corporate names may be trademarks or registered trademarks, and
are used only for identification and explanation without intent to infringe.

Library of Congress Cataloging in Publication Data
Rose, Jay.
   Producing great sound for film and video: expert tips from preproduction to
   final mix/Jay Rose. — Fourth edition.
   pages cm
   ISBN 978-0-415-72207-0 (paperback)
   1. Sound—Recording and reproducing—Digital techniques. 2. Digital
   video. 3. Television soundtracks. 4. Film soundtracks. I. Title.
   TK7881.4.R67 2014
   777'.53—dc23
   2013050015

ISBN: 978-0-415-72207-0 (pbk)
ISBN: 978-1-315-85850-0 (ebk)

Typeset in Palatino and Frutiger
by Florence Production Ltd, Stoodleigh, Devon, EX16 9PN

Printed and bound in the United States of America by Sheridan Books, Inc. (a Sheridan Group Company).

To CR, who taught me whimsy,
and to GT, who keeps me sane.

Contents

Acknowledgments

This book is now in its fourth edition. It wouldn't have gotten anywhere without a lot of help. I'm particularly grateful for the interviews, deep technical advice and in-the-field tips supplied by production mixer G. John Garrett, boom operator Chris O'Donnell, re-recording mixer Marti Humphrey, PBS narrators Wendie Sakakeeny and Don Wescott, custom and library composers Doug Wood and David Grimes, producer/director Steve Stockman, processing expert Denis Goekdag, late and much-missed editing consultant Bob Turner, audio guru Richard Pierce, and Grammy-nominated engineer and educator Dave Moulton. Many thanks to sound designer Randy Thom for the phone conversations we've had about feature film tracks, and his letting me include parts from some of his essays. And I'm in debt to the more than 100 other working professionals who let me bother them with specific questions. Thanks to all of you.

Engineer/educators Vic Costello, Christopher Anderson, John Hodges, Mike Michaels, and Justin Davis went through my initial proposals for this edition, and offered suggestions to make them more useful. Mike Duca at Talamas Broadcast Equipment and John Rule at Rule Boston Camera provided the cameras I tested in Chapter 8.

While all these fine people made valuable technical contributions, any mistakes in the text are my own fault. If you find one, please let me know.

I owe a lot to the professionals at Focal Press who turned my jottings into a usable book: acquisitions editor Emily McCloskey, project manager Peter Linsley, production editor Denise Power, and e-book manager Gareth Jarrett. And a deep note of thanks to freelance copy-editor Victoria Chow, who not only fixed my typos and grammatical errors, but also let me know when technical explanations needed simplification.

This book was also shaped by readers of my old column at *DV* magazine and the current tutorials on my website, members of the online forums at jwsoundgroup.net and gearslutz.com, email correspondents, and all the Amazon customers who posted comments of the first three editions. Your suggestions and complaints helped make this a better work.

While I created the accompanying audio and video files in my own studio, some of them use content graciously supplied by Bluestar Media, Jetpak Productions, Captains of Industry, Don Wescott, and the Omnimusic library. This material is protected by copyright, but you may copy it to your computer for the book's tutorial exercises.

And lastly: it's customary for authors to thank their families. I've been very lucky with mine. My late wife Carla, who wrote some 32 successful books about computer graphics during her career, taught me the practical realities of getting a manuscript out the door. My son Dan, a patent attorney and former broadcast engineer, remains my anchor to all things technical and legal.

Introduction

FREQUENTLY ASKED QUESTIONS

There's a good chance you picked up this book because you're working on a project and having trouble with its sound. So we've included a chapter of Frequently Asked Questions at the end of the book: common film and video sound problems, and either how to fix them or—if the fix is complicated—where in this book you'll find the answers.

This section is set apart on gray pages. Turn to them if you have to put out fires in a hurry.

But read the rest of this book if you want tracks that are truly hot.

I'm going to try to guess some things about you. You may have taken some film or video courses, but a lot of your production knowledge is self-taught. You improve your skills by watching projects you've produced, seeing what you don't like, and changing it the next time. You look at still frames—your own and those of master filmmakers—to analyze lighting and composition. You compare your own editing techniques with what you see on TV and in theaters. Since you're primarily an artist, your eyes are your guide. When you're working on the pictures, you can see what you've done wrong.

I'll make one other guess. You've discovered it's almost impossible to teach yourself sound that way. There are too many variables. If a finished mix has hard-to-understand dialog, there's no intuitive way to know whether it's because the boom was placed badly, levels weren't set properly, or it was mixed on the wrong kind of speakers. Sometimes, trying to fix one sound problem makes some other aspect of the track worse!

Even if you play a musical instrument, your taste and judgment don't bail you out when the track isn't working. There's a reason for this:

- Good soundtracks aren't just a question of art.
- You also have to understand the science.

In this book, we cover both.

IT'S NOT ROCKET SCIENCE

Don't be scared about the science part. The math is mainly stuff you learned in elementary school, and the physics is common sense.

Don't be scared of the art, either. This isn't about aesthetics. There are plenty of essays and theories of sound design, but they're irrelevant to what we're trying to do here. This book is about the technique and tools for delivering a message to a viewer. What's *in* the message is up to you.

And don't be scared of me or my colleagues. The heart of this book is the tricks, shortcuts, and industry practices developed over nearly a century, since the beginning of radio and talking pictures. In the 40-some years I've been at this, I've worked on tracks ranging from sales videos to theatrical features, engineered every kind of facility from local stations to large post houses, helped design some of the industry's standard pieces of digital audio gear, and seen my projects win Clios, an Emmy, and hundreds of other awards. I've learned a lot, and had a lot of friends help me. This book is an attempt to share as much as I can.

HOW THIS BOOK IS ORGANIZED

The first section of this book is an explanation of how sound works. It covers the physics of sound in space and the technology of digital recording. I've put this material in front because it's important. I've also put it in plain English, without jargon or complicated formulas, and with plenty of drawings and examples. It shouldn't take more than a couple of evenings to read.

The rest of the book is practical advice.

First, pre-production: how to plan the track, figure the budget, and pick the location.

Second, acquisition: how microphones work and are affected by acoustics, how to use mics on location and in the studio, how to get the best sound from cameras and recorders, and how to work with the people and things that make sound.

Finally, postproduction: editing voices, adding and editing music and effects, processing for the best possible sound, and mixing for various viewing situations.

There are also some 80 audio and video demonstrations, diagnostics, and exercises that friends and I have created to illustrate specific concepts. They're identified in the text with links like this: **Sound 13.2**. If you're reading this as an e-book on some systems, you can click the links to hear the files. Otherwise you can audition them from any Web browser: just go to the book's website, GreatSound.info, and log in using a password you'll find buried in these pages. The files are also downloadable so you can hear them on your best speakers and load them into your own editing software. They're protected by copyright, but you're free to use them for the book's exercises.

Do it yourself?

There are a couple of simple projects in this book, for building helpful tools that aren't commonly available off-the-shelf. They require a little bit of soldering but no other special techniques. If you don't want to tackle them, ask a local high school hardware hacker or amateur radio enthusiast. I've chosen parts that should be available at any electronics store or website. I've also included Radio Shack part numbers for ordering convenience. Parts from other sources will work just as well.

ABOUT THIS BOOK AND *AUDIO POSTPRODUCTION*

The first edition of *Producing Great Sound* sold well enough that my publisher asked for an additional book, with much more detail about the postproduction process. That book, *Audio Postproduction*, goes much deeper. It has almost 150 pages just about processing: tutorials, explanations, examples, practical tips, and specific recipes for equalization, compression, and the other processes necessary to build a good mix. There's a full chapter on removing noise from bad recordings. That book has long sections about editing, postproduction sound and music sources, debugging sync and NLE problems, and soundproofing and wiring an audio post setup. It comes with almost a full hour of new audio diagnostics, examples, and tutorials aimed at postproduction. But it doesn't cover any aspect of location sound at all.

Since *Audio Postproduction* covers that side of the process so fully, I felt free to expand the production side of *Producing Great Sound*. The book in your hand has sections on choosing locations and microphones, proper handling of boom mics and mounting of lavs, and both the technical and legal aspects of wireless mics. There's coverage of techniques used in creating a feature film Hollywood-style, shortcuts and timesavers that are often used on smaller productions, and how to pick the best from both. There's a chapter on getting the best results with in-camera sound and with separate audio recorders, including specific measurements and tips for some popular camera models.

There's also plenty about post in *Producing Great Sound*. You'll find enough information to round out your filmmaking skills and create a fully polished track: working with audio in your computer; editing voice, music, and effects; processing; mixing for various media including broadcast and theatrical. This book is a guide to the entire production process.

Some parts of the two books necessarily overlap. The basics of sound, digital recording, accurate monitoring, and editing belong in both books. But I've written about them differently in each, to give you a better chance of understanding these important concepts.

In other words, it's entirely reasonable to own both *Audio Postproduction* and this edition of *Producing Great Sound*. But if you can get only one:

- Choose this book for an overview of the entire audio process, with a strong emphasis on sound at the shoot;
- Choose *Audio Postproduction* for a complete discussion of turning that sound into a polished, finished soundtrack.

What's new in the fourth edition

Many aspects our art have changed radically in the past few years.

- DSLR cameras were just starting to appear when I wrote the last edition; now they're an accepted part of filmmaking.
- Tapeless workflows are now the norm for both low-end corporate productions and Hollywood blockbusters.
- US and European regulations have changed how we use wireless mics. They also set completely new rules for controlling loudness in broadcast projects.
- There's a new category of processing plug-ins, using neural network principles to do things that were previously impossible in desktop computers.
- And there have been lots of smaller changes in the filmmaking process, thanks to more efficient technologies.

I needed to cover these topics in some detail, and wanted to include tips based on how we're actually using these new tools in productions. I also re-wrote many of the technical explanations to make them more understandable, based on feedback from readers of past editions. The result was a lot bigger manuscript.

Even though I deleted some obsolete topics,[1] it was too much book for Focal Press to publish at a reasonable price. So we compromised: they gave me more pages (this is the biggest *Producing Great Sound* ever), and I moved one whole chapter to the book's website. Chapter 9, covering recording for ADR, voice-overs, and sound effects, now lives at GreatSound.info. The site will ask for a passphrase buried in this book. Then you can read the chapter online or download it as a pdf.

Staying up-to-date

Styles evolve, but the techniques behind good audio remain constant. The physics of sound won't change without a major overhaul of the universe. You should be able to hang onto this book for a while.

---

[1] Such as analog workflows and processing, or DAT and MiniDisk techniques. That material still lives on my hard drives, though. If you need it, drop me a note.

My intention is to share the what and why, as well as the how. While I talk about how to get the best from today's cameras and equipment, I also explain the principles involved so you'll be ready for next year's gear. The step-by-step instructions don't require a particular system or platform.

I used a large range of programs for the screenshots, and even created my own generic program screens when it would make something easier to understand. So if you see specific software in these pages, it doesn't mean that's the *only* program to use. The techniques in this book work with almost any software. Use them with tools you have now, and keep using them when you upgrade.

For the most current information, check the online resources at the end of this book. Or ask a friendly professional: we're not territorial, and are usually willing to share ideas and information.

Jay Rose
Boston, February 2014
jay@dplay.com
www.dplay.com

How to Create a Great Soundtrack
(in a Quarter of a Page)

Here are the rules:

- Know what you're doing before you start.
- Plan the sound as carefully as you plan the picture.
- Get good elements.
- Treat them with respect.
- Do as little processing as possible until the mix.
- Listen very carefully while you mix.
- Follow the tips in this book.

The rest is just details.

Section I

AUDIO BASICS

These three chapters are the technical stuff: How sound exists, what happens when it gets to your brain, how it can be turned into electronic signals, and how those signals can be carried over wires. It's the foundation for everything else in this book.

I've avoided complex math. If you made it through grade school, you'll be able to understand these concepts. I've also used visual analogies as much as possible . . . my thinking is that if you're making films, your visual sense is probably fairly sharp. So we'll let it help you learn about sound.

But these chapters *are* technical, and I don't want anybody fainting or running from the room.

- You can skip these technical parts—if you must—and go directly to the practical tips and techniques that fill most of this book.
- But I promise that if you *do* read it, the whole book will make a lot more sense.

These chapters might even make your life easier. You'll know how sound actually works, so you'll get better tracks without having to memorize meaningless rules.

And that gives you more time to concentrate on the fun stuff.

CHAPTER 1

How Sound Works

MUSIC-SICLE?

"Architecture is frozen music." When philosopher Friedrich von Schelling wrote that, he was being poetic. If there were such a thing as frozen music (or any frozen sound), it would be *pressure*. It would also be unlistenable, because humans can't perceive pressure as sound. What we hear are *changes* in pressure, not the pressure itself. If pressure hasn't changed in the past fraction of a second,[1] we don't hear anything at all.

The process is fairly easy to understand:

Something—a drum skin, human vocal cords, a loudspeaker's cone, or anything else that makes noise—starts vibrating back and forth. As its surface moves towards us, it squeezes nearby air molecules together. As it moves away, it pulls the molecules apart.

---

[1] Pressure has to change in 1/20th of a second or faster to be heard as sound.

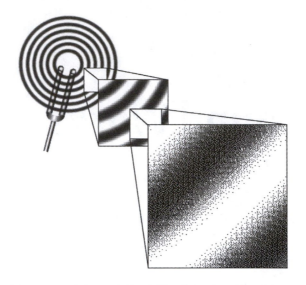

Figure 1.1 If we could see sound, it would look like this. Air molecules are squeezed together and pulled apart by the vibrations of the tuning fork.

This motion bumps from one molecule to another and the sound moves. The movement is like billiard balls on a table: each molecule pushes the molecules around it, not necessarily in a straight line. Eventually the bumping air molecules carry the sound to our ears.

They don't have to be air molecules, by the way. Almost any kind of molecules will do. Some molecules carry the vibration better than others. That's why movie heroes put an ear on the tracks to listen for distant trains . . . steel is a very good conductor of sound.

But most of the time we're dealing with sound as it moves through air. If we *could* freeze sound in air and see its individual molecules, it would look like Figure 1.1.

Think of Figure 1.1 as a snapshot of a single moment in the life of a sound. Air molecules are represented as tiny black dots. As we enlarge sections of the picture, we can see individual molecules.

The life of a sound

The tuning fork vibrates back and forth. As its metal surface moves towards nearby air molecules, it squeezes them together.

Push the molecules . . .

Those compressed molecules push against some a little farther from the tuning fork, squeezing those farther molecules together.

They then push against some even farther, and so on. As the squeezing spreads out to successive layers of molecules, the pressure spreads out. The pattern is something like ripples on a pond when you throw a stone into the water.

This doesn't happen instantly. It takes a moment for each air molecule to move toward its neighbor, and those tiny delays add up. That's important to remember, as you'll see later in this chapter.

. . . and pull the molecules . . .

While this is happening, the tuning fork continues to vibrate back and forth. So while those air molecules are bumping each other outward, the fork's surface starts moving back in the other direction.

This frees up a tiny space between its surface and those nearby molecules that had been squeezed, and the slight vacuum pulls the molecules back. This very slight vacuum—engineers call it *rarefaction*—pulls on the next layer of molecules, separating them. And the process repeats to successive layers.

. . . both movements continue to spread out

Eventually the cycles of pressure and rarefaction reach our ears. The eardrum gets pushed and pulled in response, and that vibration is carried across tiny bones to a part of your inner ear that's filled with nerves. Different nerves are more sensitive to vibrations at different speeds, and so a specific group of nerves are triggered and send a message to your brain. Your brain interprets them, and decides the vibrations' speed and strength. That's what we hear as sound.

Everybody feels the pressure

As you can imagine, pent-up molecules try to push away from what's squeezing them together. Unlike ripples on the surface of a pond, however, sound doesn't push along a flat plane. Molecules can bounce all over the place, so the *sound spreads in all directions*.[2] Remember that part in italics, because it means:

SOUND IS MESSY STUFF
- Sound spreads in every direction, until something stops it.
- You can point a light, but you can't point a sound.
- You can aim a lens to avoid something out-of-frame, but you can't effectively aim a microphone to "miss" a distracting sound.

---

[2] It doesn't necessarily spread in a perfect sphere; other factors influence how the sound travels. Unfortunately, you can't control most of them on a movie set.

FREQUENCY: IT MATTERS HOW OFTEN YOU DO IT

Since sound is changes of pressure, its only characteristics can be how much pressure exists at any moment, and how the pressure changes. Let's deal with the "how it changes" part first.

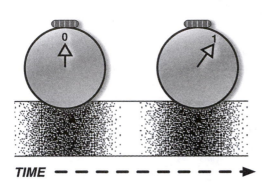

Figure 1.2 Timing from one pressure peak to the next.

Think back to the imaginary world of Figure 1.1, where we could see individual molecules. If we stand in one place, waves of pressure and rarefaction would go past us. With an imaginary stopwatch, we could measure the time from the densest part of one wave to the densest part of the next. This would tell us how quickly the tuning fork is vibrating.

Figure 1.2 shows two density peaks that are one second apart. If the vibration continues at this rate, we'd say it's "vibrating with a frequency of one cycle per second." That's a mouthful, so we use the term Hertz—named after a nineteenth-century physicist—or its abbreviation Hz instead.

Fast pressure changes are heard as sounds

In Figure 1.2, our imaginary stopwatch is vibrating at 1 Hz . . . which, incidentally, is too slow for our ears to pick up.[3] Another measurement—kiloHertz, or kHz—represents 1,000 cycles per second, which is friendlier to our ears.

Frequency ranges

It's generally accepted that humans can hear sounds in a range between 20 Hz and 20 kHz. That's a little like saying, "Humans can run a mile in four minutes"—maybe some humans can, but I certainly can't. A few exceptional humans can hear up to 20 kHz, but even the best hearing deteriorates when you get older. Fortunately, very few useful sounds extend to these limits. If all you consider are basic vibrations:

- The highest note of a violin is about 3.5 kHz.
- The highest note on an oboe is around 1.8 kHz.
- In fact, of all the instruments in a classical orchestra, only the pipe organ can vibrate faster than 5 kHz.

Figure 1.3 shows the basic vibration frequencies of various instruments.

---

[3] I don't care. It was an *imaginary* sound wave.

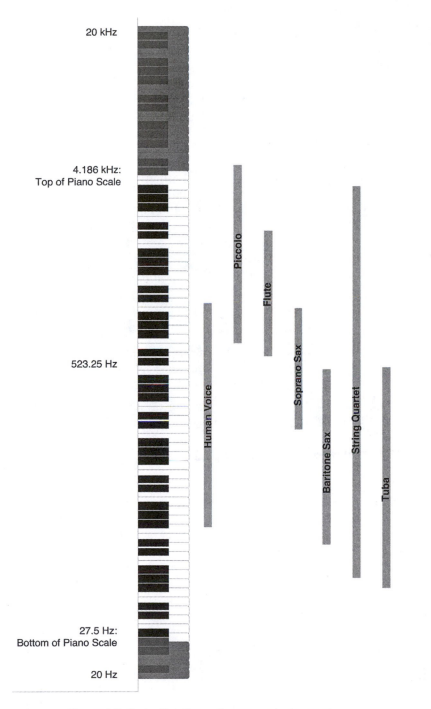

Figure 1.3 Basic vibrations of common instruments.

Harmonics

The fastest that a violin string or oboe reed can vibrate is considerably less than 5 kHz. But frequencies higher than that are still important. To see how, we need a closer look at the pressure waves.

As you know, a microphone converts sound vibrations into varying electrical voltages. If we connect the microphone to an oscilloscope—a device that draws a graph of voltage changes over time, such as a video waveform monitor—we can see the wave with considerable detail. Figure 1.4 shows how an ideal wave looks, photographed on my oscilloscope. **Sound 1.1** lets you hear that wave.

Positive pressure generates a positive voltage, forming the peaks. Negative pressure generates negative voltage, forming the valleys. The two voltage peaks A and B are like the two pressure peaks we measured in Figure 1.2.

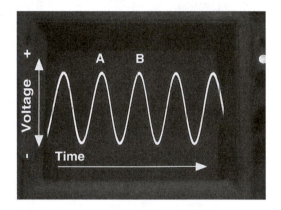

Figure 1.4 A pure wave on an oscilloscope, with some letters and arrows added for explanation.

But this is a pure wave, also known as a *sine wave* from its mathematical function.[4] In the real world, most things don't have this simple, symmetrical back-and-forth vibration. Different parts of the object vibrate at different speeds, so other smaller wiggles get mixed with its main one.

The basic back-and-forth movement is called the *fundamental*. It carries most of the energy and is what we hear as the pitch of a sound. The smaller wiggles are *harmonics*. They take the form of softer, higher-frequency waves superimposed on the fundamental. The shape of an instrument, what it's made of, and how it's played determine which harmonics we hear.

Harmonics are what make the difference between two instruments playing the same pitch. You can see the difference in Figures 1.5 (an oboe) and Figure 1.6 (a violin); you'll hear it on **Sound 1.2** (oboe) and **Sound 1.3** (violin).

---

4 This is the only time you'll see the words "mathematical function" in this book.

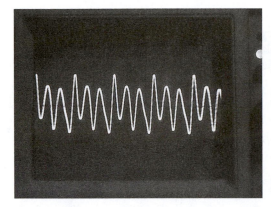

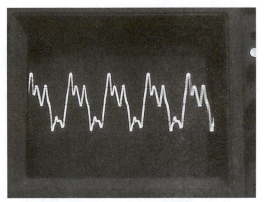

Figure 1.5 An oboe playing an A . . .

Figure 1.6 . . . and a violin playing the same note.

Notice how every third wave of the oboe is stronger than the others. This is the fundamental frequency of its reed. The smaller peaks are a harmonic, three times as fast. The violin's fundamental is exactly as far apart as the oboe's in these photos, because they're both playing the same note. But violins have a more complicated mixture of harmonics, ranging from two to eight times higher than the fundamental. Their combination is what we hear as "a violin sound." Harmonics are the main way we tell a *toot* from a *squeak* on the same clarinet, or even an *ooh* from an *aah* by the same singer. They might be making their sounds on the same musical note, but harmonics let us tell them apart.

 Just for fun, here's the same note on a trumpet: a stronger fundamental with a very complex harmonic pattern (Figure 1.7 and **Sound 1.4**).

Want proof that fundamentals make this much difference? Sounds 1.5 through 1.8 are the four waves you've just heard, but passed through a sharp filter that eliminates

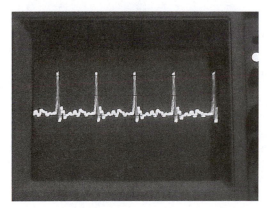

Figure 1.7 A trumpet's A shows a very different pattern.

harmonics. Listen to all eight on a good stereo or home theater: you'll find it's easy to tell them apart with the harmonics, but very difficult when the harmonics are cut off. Try the same tracks on a low-quality speaker—perhaps the one in a tablet or smartphone—and you'll find it's hard to tell a violin from an oboe, even without the filter!

Source	With harmonics	Without harmonics
Sinewave	**Sound 1.1**	**Sound 1.5**
Oboe	**Sound 1.2**	**Sound 1.6**
Violin	**Sound 1.3**	**Sound 1.7**
Trumpet	**Sound 1.4**	**Sound 1.8**

✍ TRY THIS

Say what?

Human speech has highly complex harmonic patterns. We control them by changing the shape of the mouth. Try singing "eee," "ooo," and "aah" on the same note, paying attention to what's going on with your tongue and lips. The fundamental pitch stays the same for each . . . but the harmonics—and the vowel—change as your mouth moves.

You'll notice that the filtered instruments—Sounds 1.6 through 1.8—are considerably softer than the unfiltered ones. That's because most of their energy is carried in the harmonics. (I didn't change any volume settings while making these files.)

Unpitched sounds

Many sounds don't have regularly repeating waves at all. You can't pick a frequency in Hertz for an explosion or rustling leaves. They're caused by random movements, with no organized pattern of repetitions: instead of any particular pitch, these sounds have bunches of pitches. However, their frequencies usually fall within certain limits: when we talk about a high-pitched noise (such as a hissing air) or a low-pitched one (like thunder), we're really describing which group of frequencies is most prominent.

Human speech is a combination of pitches with harmonics (the vowels), unpitched noises (about half of the consonants), and noises simultaneous with pitches (the other consonants). Remember that fact. It'll be important when we get to dialog editing.

The myths of frequency response

One way to rate the quality of a sound system is to measure the highest frequency it can carry. For a system to be considered good quality, we usually expect it to handle harmonics up to 20 kHz. But in a lot of cases, this much range isn't necessary.

- The upper limit for conventional FM stereo in the United States is 15 kHz.[5] Frequencies higher than the limit cause problems with the broadcast system, so they're generally cut off at the transmitter. But nobody says a good FM station is particularly "low-fi."

- Most films made before the 1970s—including all those great Hollywood musicals— carried harmonics only up to about 12.5 kHz. Theater sound systems weren't designed to handle much more than that.
- We don't need high frequencies to recognize voices or understand speech. Telephones cut off at 3.5 kHz . . . but most people would describe a telephone as lacking bass notes, not high ones. Syndicated radio talk shows, even on FM stations, are often limited to 7.5 kHz to save transmission costs.
- Even most home theater systems don't reach that full bandwidth. While it's easy to build an amplifier with 20 kHz response, very few speakers can handle those high-frequency sounds accurately.

The next section will let you test this for yourself.

A diagnostic: Test your own equipment (and ears)!

The next set of audio files will help you understand how well your own systems handle highs. We took a musical selection with reasonable high frequencies, as you can see from the spectrum display in Figure 1.8.[6] While it's playing, we switch a high-cut filter in and out at various frequencies. If you can hear the filter as changing the sound, then you've been hearing the highs. If you can't tell when the filter is working, then you weren't hearing those frequencies in the first place . . . probably because your speakers are doing the same filtering, all the time (but possibly because your ears have lost high-frequency sensitivity).

You can visualize how the filter works. Imagine a pianist playing the piece in Figure 1.9.[7] Right in the middle—where the drawing says *Filter: ON*—we'll grab some of the pianist's fingers! The high notes in gray don't get played, but everything else stays the same. When the filter is off, those fingers go back to work and we hear those upper notes. This music, with our hand grabbing the pianist's fingers, represents the test file.

---

[5] That was also the limit for US television, up until the digital changeover of 2009.

[6] The web versions of these files have *not* been processed with any kind of lossy compression. None of the highs are being lost by the Internet.

[7] It's a section from *Jeux d'eau* by Maurice Ravel. But you don't need to read music in order to understand the example.

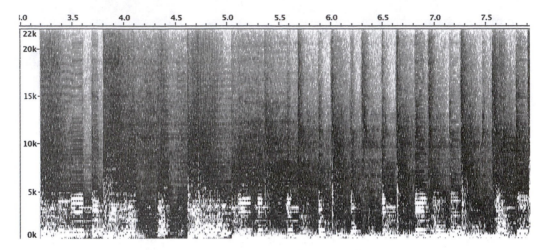

Figure 1.8 Typical spectrum of the music[8] used in Sounds 1.9–1.14. This spectrogram is calibrated in time across the top (about four seconds' worth), and frequencies on the side (between 0 Hz and 22 kHz). Where it's darker, there's more energy in the music. You can see how there are rhythmic high frequency peaks at 3.4 seconds, 3.8 seconds, 4.2 seconds, and so on. Listen to the first eight seconds of **Sound 1.9** to get a better idea of how they all fit together.

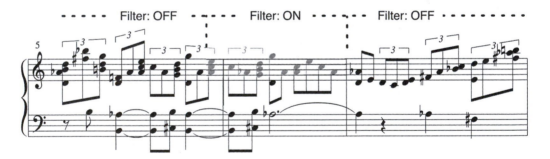

Figure 1.9 Visualizing what our test filters do to the music.[9]

---

[8] Excerpt from "Sock Hop Swing" (Doug Wood), from the Omnimusic library and used by permission. This versatile library graciously provided all the musical examples in this book. They're protected by copyright so you can't use them in your productions, but you can load them into your own computer if necessary to do the tutorials in this book. You can also purchase reasonably priced licenses to use them in films, TV shows, websites, and other projects. Investigate the whole library at www.omnimusic.com.

[9] The notes in this graphic aren't what's being played in our test files. That would make it too easy (assuming you can read music). This is a test of your speakers and ears, not your ability to read a score.

Now imagine if the piano had been broken before this test, and none of the keys above D^{10} worked at all. If that were the case, it wouldn't matter if we'd grabbed the pianist's fingers or not . . . no matter what we did, there'd never be any high notes. You could listen as hard as you wanted, but would never be able to tell when we were grabbing fingers. The broken piano, in our visualization, represents the speakers you're testing.

Sound recordings can work the same way. If your speakers (and ears) are capable of handling the highest tones, you'll notice a distinct difference when the filters are switched on and off. But if those frequencies wouldn't make it through your system anyway, the filters don't have any effect.

✍ TRY THIS

Sounds 1.9 through 1.14 are a simple way to test your own equipment, to find out exactly how many of the highest harmonics in a track are actually getting through to you.

Listen to the test sounds in order, starting with **Sound 1.9**. If you don't hear a filter switching in and cutting the highs, then switching out so you can hear the highs, move on to the next test sound. When you *do* hear the filter working, you've found the highest frequency that your speakers and ears transmit.

To make things easier, the filters switch in and out three times during each test file, always in the same places.

The filters are set like this:

Test sound	Filter frequency
Sound 1.9	18 kHz
Sound 1.10	15 kHz
Sound 1.11	12 kHz
Sound 1.12	9 kHz
Sound 1.13	6 kHz
Sound 1.14	4 kHz

Most people won't hear any difference when the 18 kHz, or even the 15 kHz filter, is turned on. Depending on age and other factors, many won't hear a significant loss with a 12 kHz cutoff.

---

[10] That's a dot hanging right below the treble staff (the top set of five parallel lines).

Try downloading these files and playing them at your editing station as well. Put them on your laptop or tablet. You might be amazed how much you're missing through typical multimedia and personal monitoring speakers.

A few notes on these tests:

- Even with the 4 kHz filter switched in, the music remains mostly listenable. That's because I used a very sharp filter, so at least one harmonic of most instruments remained.

- Remember that you're testing your own ears, as well. Results can be different if you have a cold, or you've have been in a very loud environment recently. If you think that's affecting your results, try again in a few days.

- If you want to duplicate this test with your own music files, I suggest you get the free Audacity software (described fully in Chapter 10) and use its low-pass filter set to 24 dB per octave. Audacity will also let you draw spectrograms, so you can prove visually that the filters are working.

- One reader suggested I start with the lowest frequency filter and work upward, because the changes can be hard to hear. I'd like to oblige, but doing it my way makes it less likely you'll fool yourself into imagining things your ears aren't actually picking up.

SOMEWHAT SLOWER PRESSURE CHANGES ARE HEARD AS ENVELOPES

We know that fast pressure changes—above 1/20th of a second or so—are heard as sounds. But if we compare the peak pressure of one wave to another, there can also be slower changes over time. This is the sound's *envelope*, how it varies between loud and soft over a period as short as a fraction of a second. Figure 1.10 shows the envelope of about a second of dialog. It's too long a period to display on an oscilloscope, so I'm using a screenshot from an audio-editing program instead. But the information displayed is the same as a scope: the vertical axis is sound pressure translated into voltage, and the horizontal axis is time.

If you look closely you can see individual waves (I drew arrows to a few on them, on the bottom of the figure). But if you look at the larger picture—which I've traced with a heavy gray line—you can see the slower changes of volume that make up the envelope.

Speech envelopes are very seldom related to individual words, because people tend to elide words together: We. Don't. Talk. Like. This. The voice in these figures is saying "Oh yeah, that's great. Thank you" (**Sound 1.15**), but it's difficult to correlate those sounds with the peaks of the envelope unless you've had a lot of editing experience. I've done it for you in Figure 1.11: note how some peaks are shared by more than one word, while some words have more than one peak.

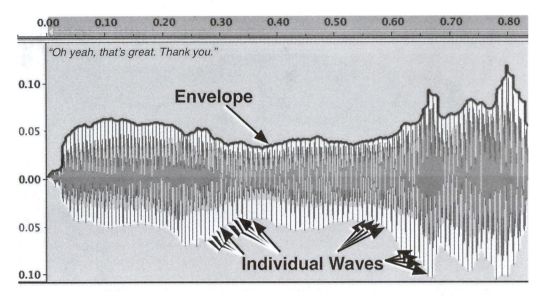

Figure 1.10 Envelope of a human voice.

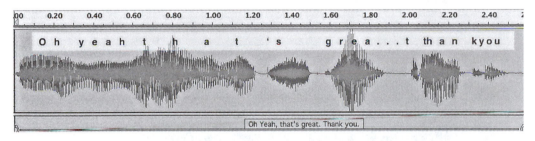
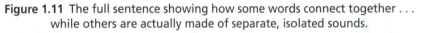

Figure 1.11 The full sentence showing how some words connect together . . .
while others are actually made of separate, isolated sounds.

This suggests two rules:

☞ ROSE'S RULES

- You don't edit words in a soundtrack. You edit envelopes
- Unless you're doing the most rudimentary cutting—moving whole paragraphs that have big pauses between them—it's impossible to mark edits just by examining what an envelope looks like. You have to listen.

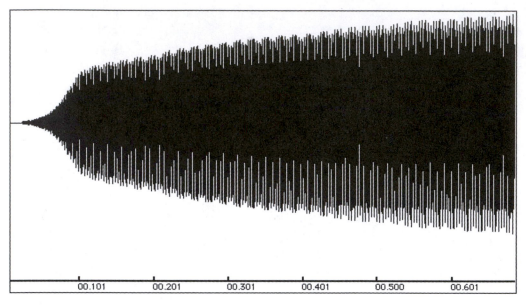

Figure 1.12 Clarinet envelope.

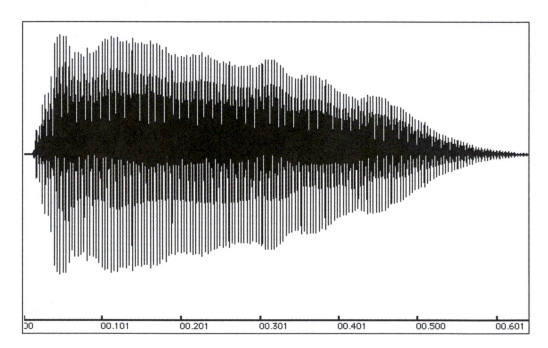

Figure 1.13 Trumpet envelope.

Obviously, envelope plays a large part in how we understand speech. But it's also important in how we differentiate musical instruments. Compare the clarinet in Figure 1.12 with the trumpet in Figure 1.13: The clarinet starts its sound slowly, as the reed's vibrations get reinforced by the resonance of its long tube. The trumpet starts with a burst as the player's lips start vibrating from built-up air pressure. (This sudden burst is characteristic of many brass instruments, and is often called the *brass blip* by people who design synthesizers.)

In Chapter 16, you'll see how devices like a compressor can manipulate the envelope to make a sound stronger—or completely change its character.

When envelopes and frequencies overlap

The time scale in the previous screenshots is calibrated in seconds. If you look closely at Figure 1.13, you can see that the "blip" takes about .03 second—roughly the length of one video frame. But we've already learned that frequencies higher than 20 Hz—or .05 second per wave—are audible. So is the blip part of the envelope or a sound by itself?

In this case it's part of the envelope. That's because the repeating wave is a lot faster: 0.0038 second (261 Hz), corresponding to C4 on the piano. But the issue becomes important when you're dealing with predominantly low-frequency sounds, including many male voices, because the equipment can't differentiate between envelopes and waves unless you adjust it carefully.

SLOW CHANGES OF PRESSURE ARE LOUDNESS

You can play that trumpet note through a clock radio at low volume, or blast it out of a giant stadium sound system, and it'll still sound like a trumpet. The overall range of sound levels we can hear is amazing:

> **A jet plane landing is about *ten trillion times* more powerful than the quietest sound doctors use to test your ears.**

Our brains can handle such a wide range of pressure because they deal with volume changes as *ratios*, rather than absolute amounts. We're constantly adjusting what we think is loud or soft, based on what came before. A sound that would be absolutely jarring in a quiet setting is practically ignored in a noisy one. (A crying baby is a major distraction in a public library—but put that baby in a noisy factory and you won't hear it at all.) The standard way to think about loudness ratios is to use decibels. Here's how they work.

The need for a reference

Since our brains hear loudness as ratios, we can't describe how loud a sound is unless we relate it to some other sound. Scientists have agreed on a standardized reference

✔ TIP

Comfort-zone warning

This section contain some math. It's simple math, but it's numbers nonetheless. If that scares you, just skip down to the box labeled "Bottom line."

sound, nominally the softest thing an average healthy person can hear. It's often called the *threshold of hearing*. A quiet living room may have a sound pressure level about a thousand times the standard. The level at a busy city street is about five million times the standard.

So far, pretty simple. But adjusting a sound's volume—the most basic operation in audio—means multiplying its pressures by a specific ratio. Since the original volume was measured as a ratio to the threshold of hearing, the new volume is the product of both ratios combined. You start with the ratio between the original sound and the standard, and then multiply it by another ratio that represents the volume change. These ratios are usually fairly complex (rather than something easy, like the ratio of 3:1) so the math can get messy.

The logarithm

✔ TIP

"I don't want to learn logarithms!"

You don't have to. Just remember two rules:

- Any logarithm is a ratio or fraction, but expressed as a single number. The ratio "three to one" is the log ".477". Nobody remembers all the logarithms; you look them up or use a spreadsheet program.
- If you have to multiply two ratios, just add their logs. If you have to divide two ratios, subtract their logs. Complex problems—with multiple ratios— become simple addition or subtraction.

Here's an example of how logarithms save you time: A voice-over announcer, standing one foot away, will generate sound pressures that are about 350,000 times the threshold of hearing. (That might look like a big number, but not when you consider some of the ratios in the previous paragraph.) Suppose we have to make that voice twice as loud. Loudness is influenced by a lot of subjective factors, but if we're considering just sound pressure, we'd want to multiply it by two.

Sound pressure is the product of two factors: power and the area it occupies. To give something twice as much pressure we either have to double both factors, or double one of them *twice*.

So we have to multiply the ratio of the announcer's voice to the threshold of hearing, times two, and then times two again. On a piece of paper it would look like

$$
\begin{array}{ll}
\text{ratio of one to} \quad 350{,}000 & \text{(original volume)} \\
\times 2 & \text{(volume change)} \\
\times 2 & \text{(pressure change)} \\
\hline
\end{array}
$$

equals one to 1,400,000 [11]

However, if we express that 1:350,000 ratio as a logarithm, it's the much simpler 5.5. And the 2:1 volume ratio becomes log 0.3.[12] That makes the job a lot easier:

$$
\begin{array}{ll}
5.5 & \text{(log of original volume)} \\
+\ 0.3 & \text{(log of "two times")} \\
+\ 0.3 & (\text{"}) \\
\hline
6.1 &
\end{array}
$$

This means if we turn up an amplifier so this voice is mathematically twice as loud as it was before, the result is log 6.1 times as loud as the threshold of hearing. For short, we could call it "just about log 6." Hold that in your head for a moment.

The decibel

The engineering name for the logarithm of any two acoustic or electric power levels is called the *Bel*, in honor of the fellow who invented telephones.[13] A decibel is actually 1/10th of a Bel, which is why it's abbreviated dB. We use a tenth of a Bel because it multiplies the log by ten, making it easier to think about (logs can be funny that way). So the announcer's voice at one foot had a sound pressure level with a ratio of 55 dB to the standard reference, commonly written as 55 dB SPL (*Sound Pressure Level*).

The neat thing about logs and decibels is not just that they make the math easier, *they also reflect how we hear!*

---

[11] You might be able to do that math in your head, but it's still a lot of zeroes to whip around. And we picked some very easy numbers for our example. Announcers can talk at any loudness, and volume knobs are continuously variable, so real-world numbers are never this convenient.

[12] I've rounded both these logs to the nearest tenth. They're actually a few thousandths different from what I've written . . . but it's certainly close enough for audio purposes.

[13] I have no idea why Bell Labs decided to spell Alexander Graham's name with only one L. Or why they chose a unit so big that it's always cut down to one tenth.

Think of two babies crying simultaneously, instead of just one . . . and then two jet planes instead of one. We'd hear both increases as "twice as loud," even though the extra jet added a lot more sound pressure than the second baby. Our ears listen to ratios and fractions, rather than absolute numbers.

☛ ROSE'S RULES

Bottom line

The software and equipment you use to manipulate sounds works in terms of voltage, representing pressure. So to double an electrical volume, we turn its knob up 6 dB.

Absolute volume vs. absolute loudness?

A paradox: Two sounds can have the same peak level in decibels, yet one may be much louder than the other. That's because loudness is a subjective thing. It depends on more than just the voltage or sound pressure involved.

This paradox used to annoy TV viewers. Even though stations controlled their signal using volume meters, commercials often seemed much louder than the programs they interrupted.[14] In the United States, the CALM Act (Commercial Advertisement Loudness Mitigation Act of 2010) was designed to fix this problem. There's more about loudness standards, and how to deal with them, in Chapter 17.

It's also why inexperienced filmmakers often find that their mixes seem much softer than they expect, even though their NLE[15] is displaying proper levels.

Our brains decide whether something is loud based on its frequency and its density, as well as its absolute sound pressure.

Frequency is important because we evolved to hear mid-range sounds—between about 2 kHz and 4 kHz—much better than very high- or low-pitched ones, and this difference changes depending on the overall loudness. It can be as much as 75 dB, for deep bass in a very soft passage. It's about 20 dB across normal speech frequencies at dialog levels. Most volume meters can't take this into account.

Density—or how long a loud sound has lasted, compared to silence or soft sounds—is important for many reasons. If a sound lasts less than a second, our impression of its loudness gets distorted by its length. The perceived loudness of longer sounds can depend on the loudness of any sounds a second or two earlier.

---

[14] Advertisers paid people like me to make this happen.

[15] Nonlinear editor, or basically any piece of software used to edit video. Media Composer, Premiere, and Final Cut Pro are among the most popular NLEs.

On top of that, average volume over several minutes contributes to our sense of a film's loudness: a scene with a single very loud gunshot surrounded by soft sound effects will seem softer, overall, than a scene with continuous music that's actually a tiny bit softer than the gunshot.

It's not hard to build a meter that takes all these factors into account. Having this kind of tool is definitely necessary if you're mixing for network television. There are some downloadable versions discussed in Chapters 12 and 17.

If you're not worried about meeting network specifications, just an occasional glance at a conventional meter can be adequate. Mix by ear! Of course you'll have to calibrate your monitors, since perceived loudness also depends on absolute sound pressure levels. But that's easy and just requires a $50 tool from an electronics chain store; instructions are in Chapter 11.

THE SPEED OF SOUND MAKES A BIG DIFFERENCE

Sound pressure travels through the air, as one molecule bumps the one next to it. This takes time: roughly a thousandth of a second to go one foot. (In non-rough numbers, 1,087 feet/second at 32° Fahrenheit, speeding up as things get warmer.)

A thousandth of a second might not seem like much when you're producing a movie.[16] But it adds up: it takes about one frame for sound to reach us from just ten yards away. This can be critical if you're shooting events with a long lens and a camera-mounted mic, because the image won't be in sync with the sound. That's made worse by moviemaking conventions: we expect to hear sound effects exactly in sync with the picture, no matter how far away they're supposed to be. The noise from an explosion 100 feet away, placed realistically, strikes most viewers as being three frames late. Science-fiction adventure films carry this to extremes: you can blow up a planet thousands of miles away and hear it explode instantly. (Not only that, but the sound has travelled through the vacuum of space. You know better: if there aren't any molecules to move, there can't be any sound.)

Echoes and colorations

The speed of sound also determines how we (or our microphones) hear sounds in enclosed spaces. Vibrating air molecules can't relieve the pressure by moving a wall or ceiling, so they bounce off these hard surfaces and spring back in the opposite direction. The reflected waves mix with the original ones.

If we hear the reflection a tenth of a second or more after the original sound, it's perceived as an echo. If the sound keeps bouncing between hard surfaces you can get many echoes, randomly spaced. That's heard as reverberation.[17] But almost any enclosed space—not just cathedrals and courtrooms—will have some echoes.

---

[16] If a 90-minute feature film cost $50 million to make, each millisecond cost only about ten bucks.

[17] To a sound designer, there's a very real difference between echo and reverberation. See Chapter 16.

Echoes in small rooms

We're usually not aware of how sound bounces in small spaces like offices or editing rooms, because the reflections arrive very quickly, and our ears and brain learn to filter them out. But a microphone doesn't have that advantage, and the result interferes with intelligibility. It's one of the main causes of amateur-sounding tracks in bad videos. We'll devote a lot of pages to its cause and cure in later chapters. It also affects critical monitoring, since these echoes can color even the best speakers and fool you into making mistakes in a mix.

The problem is how the echoes combine with the original sound. Think of a sound's compression-rarefaction cycle like the phases of the moon. A moon goes through continuous cycles from dark to bright and back, just as a sound wave cycles between pressure and partial vacuum. If there were two moons in our sky and each was in its full phase at the same time, we'd have a very bright night. But if one moon was new while the other was full—if their phases didn't match—it wouldn't be as bright.

When two sound waves are in the same phase, they add together the same way. Figure 1.14A shows how this works with our familiar pressure-over-time graph. When both waves are positive, the result is twice as much pressure; when both are in a negative phase, we have twice as much vacuum.

But while a new moon doesn't suck light out of the sky, sounds in rarefaction draw pressure from around them. Figure 1.14B shows what happens if our two sounds aren't perfectly in phase. Where the top sound has pressure, the bottom one is almost at its strongest vacuum and absorbs the pressure. Where the bottom one is pushing, the top one is pulling. The two forces cancel each other, leaving very little sound. Since

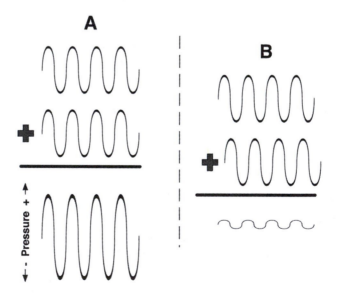

Figure 1.14 Sounds add differently depending on their phase.

both sounds are at the same frequency, this cancellation continues for each wave.

This is more than just an academic exercise. These cancellations happen all the time in the real world. In Figure 1.15, our listener hears both a direct sound from the tuning fork and a reflected one from a nearby wall. Unfortunately, since the reflected path is a different length than the direct one, the reflection takes longer to arrive and is at a different phase when it gets to the listener. The reflected sound is compressing while the direct sound is in rarefaction. The two paths cancel each other's sound.

If you moved the listener's head in the drawing, the relationship between direct and reflected sound would be different. At some positions the waves reinforce; at others, they'll cancel.

Figure 1.15 A reflection can arrive at a different phase from the original sound. The magnified section shows how they cancel at the listener's head.

If you want to actually hear this happening, grab a hard-surfaced object like a clipboard or a notebook. Then play **Sound 1.16**: a steady high-frequency tone (7.5 kHz) recorded on one channel only. Set it so the sound comes out of one speaker at a moderately low volume, and get three or four feet away from the speaker in almost any room. Move your head a foot or so in either direction, and you'll hear the sound get louder and softer. Or hold your head steady with the reflecting object facing your ear and about a foot away, then move the object. You'll hear the sound change volume as you do.

This works best when you're in a normal room with hard walls and surfaces like a desk that can reflect sound. If you're outdoors or in a very large space with no nearby walls, or in a room with acoustic padding on the walls, you might not hear the effect at all. That's why sound studio walls are padded.[18]

The situation gets worse when you start dealing with complex sounds. Different frequencies will be at different phases, depending on how far they've traveled. So when the direct path's sound mixes with its reflection, some frequencies will cancel, but others will reinforce. In Figure 1.16, a loudspeaker generating two tones replaces the tuning fork.

Over the direct path, the high frequency (closely spaced waves) and the low frequency (waves are farther apart) both happen to be compressing when they reach the listener. When the reflected low frequency reaches the listener, it also happens to

---

[18] It has nothing to do with our sanity as sound engineers.

🔊 TRY THIS

Sounds 1.16 and 1.17 are simple tests you can do at your desk, to show how important reflected sounds are in the real world.

be compressing: the two paths reinforce each other. But when the reflected high frequency reaches the listener, it's in rarefaction. It cancels the direct path. As far as Figure 1.16's listener is concerned, the sound has a lot less treble.

Sound 1.17 demonstrates this, with a 400 Hz low frequency added to the 7.5 kHz high one. Play it like you did Sound 16, get at least four feet from the speaker, and start moving your head around. Unless you're in a room with very few reflections, at some positions you'll hear the high frequency predominate. At others, the lower frequency will seem louder.

Real-world sounds have a lot more frequencies, and real rooms have lots of reflecting paths. Full and partial cancellations occur at random places throughout the spectrum. So what you hear at any given point in the room depends a lot on the size and shape of the room. Ever notice how the inside of a small car sounds "boxy" when you talk? That's why.

We get used to rooms very quickly (as soon as you're into a conversation with a passenger, you forget how boxy the car sounds). That's because we use our eyes and ears together to correlate the sound of a room with its shape.

But put a microphone in one room, and then listen to the playback somewhere else, and the cancellations become more obvious. And if the characters are moving around as they talk, the cancellations are constantly changing — just as they did when you moved around the room while listening to Sound 17. The result is a distracting hollowness or boxiness.

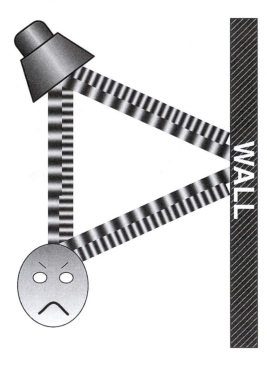

Figure 1.16 Different frequency sounds get canceled differently by their echoes.

Bad filmmaking 101

There it is, in a nutshell:

The way sound moves in an enclosed space is the reason many amateur soundtracks sound so bad.

Not the microphones used, the recording techniques, or the editor's skill (though those all have some effect). It's mostly that someone was ignoring the physics of sound.

The Inverse-Square Law

Fortunately, physics is on our side here. As sound spreads out from a source, the pressure waves have to cover a larger area. But the total amount of power hasn't changed, so the pressure at any one point is less. Light works the same way: as a spotlight projects its beam farther and farther, the size of the beam increases but its brightness diminishes.

Figure 1.17 As you get farther away, the pressure gets less intense.

In fact, under ideal conditions (a nondirectional sound source and an echo-free listening environment) the intensity of a sound diminishes with the square of the distance. This is called the inverse-square law. Figure 1.17 puts it in graphic terms.

Since decibels compare the loudness of two sounds, and they use logarithms to make things like squares easier to compute, the result of the inverse-square law can be very simply stated:

So if a microphone hears an instrument as 58 dB SPL at one foot, it'll hear it as 52 dB SPL at two feet, or 46 dB SPL at four feet.

Each time you double the distance from a sound source, its sound pressure becomes 6 dB less.

The inverse-square law applies to ideal conditions, with a non-directional sound source and no surfaces that stop sound from spreading. Most sources are directional at some frequencies, and anywhere you shoot is going to have hard surfaces. But the law still holds up fairly well in the real world:

☞ ROSE'S RULES

Rule 1: If you can get closer to a sound source—and farther from interfering sounds or reflective surfaces—you'll record it better.

Rule 2: Read rule 1 again! It's the best and easiest way to improve your soundtrack.

If we take our bad-sounding setup in Figure 1.16, but increase the distance to the wall, the inverse-square law reduces the amount of cancellation. Figure 1.18 shows how this works.

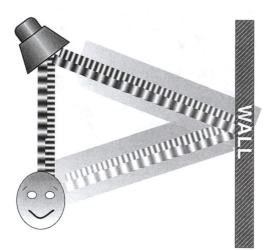

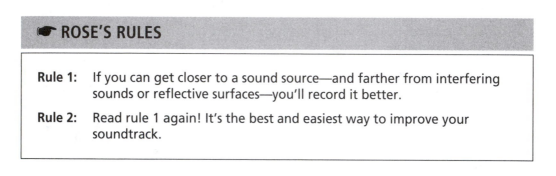

MAKING THE INVERSE-SQUARE LAW YOUR FRIEND

- Try to place a microphone at least three times closer to the sound source than it is to any source of interference.
- If you have to listen to a playback in a less-than-perfect editing room, get at least three times closer to the speakers than to any reflecting walls.

Figure 1.18 When we get farther from a reflecting surface, there's much less cancellation.

The first point explains why camera-mounted microphones rarely do a good job of rejecting interference or echoes. The camera is usually too far away from the sound source.

The second point is the principle behind the "nearfield" speakers that sit on the console of just about every recording studio in the world.

"Soundproofing"

The wedge-shaped foam panels, special tiles, or tuned cavities you see in recording studios aren't there to stop sound from entering or leaving the room. They're to reduce reflections by absorbing sound energy and turning it into mechanical motion. Sound studios also frequently have rigid curved or sculpted panels along one wall, to diffuse the reflections so cancellations don't build up at a particular frequency.

Later in this book, we'll discuss specific ways to use absorption and diffusion for better sound when you're shooting, recording voice-overs, and mixing.

We'll also discuss the use (and limitations) of portable sound barriers and how to take advantage of existing building features to block sound. But true soundproofing—stopping outside noises from getting into a room, or keeping a loud mixing session from disturbing the neighbors—requires special construction techniques and belongs in a different book. You'll find some explanations in my book *Audio Postproduction*, in the section on building a new studio or editing room. (Details about the book and other information about practical acoustics are at my website, www.dplay.com.)

✳ TIDBIT

For the practical filmmaker, the best soundproofing is understanding:

Know how to avoid situations where reflected or incidental sounds will interfere with what you're trying to do.

DIRECTIONALITY

Humans evolved to use both ears as an accurate directional gauge, to let us know where predators are coming from. Obviously, a growl coming from your left will be louder in your left ear than in your right. But our hearing system examines more than just volume. There are tiny timing differences when a sound comes from the side, because of the few extra microseconds it takes for a sound to travel the width of your head. And the folds and convolutions of your outer ear affect the timing of sounds from your front differently than those from behind or above. Our brains learn to interpret these differences, and when outdoors can paint a very accurate picture of exactly where that tiger is. (Things get more confusing indoors, because of sound bouncing off walls. Fortunately, early humans didn't worry about indoor tigers.)

Stereo

We can simulate the left-right aspect with two speakers. A sound that's supposed to be exactly between them is carried equally by both. A sound that's fully on the left, obviously, comes out of the left speaker only. By varying how much of the sound goes to the left or right, we can swing it across an imaginary plane between the two speakers. The two speakers create an aural illusion of a continuous space. We call that stereo.

For the illusion to work properly, the speakers have to have identical characteristics and be symmetrical around the listener, and the room can't have interfering echoes. But that's fairly easy to achieve in most listening setups.

Symmetry is harder to achieve in a movie theater, because exhibitors like to sell all the tickets. Inevitably some seats will be closer to one side than to the other. This could be distracting, since inverse-square dictates that a speaker on that side of the auditorium will seem much louder than the one on the other side. Things the director wanted to be centered on the screen, like dialog, would get pulled to the louder side for those side-sitting patrons. So the dialog in a movie usually gets anchored by using a third speaker, centered in the middle of the screen.[19] This has been the standard since movies first went stereo.

High-frequency sounds have shorter distances from one pressure peak to the next, so they're more affected by ear convolutions and room acoustics. This is why you heard them varying, in the exercises using Sound 16 and Sound 17. Very low frequencies have much wider waves, making them less directional. That's how a subwoofer, tucked into a corner, can fill a room with satisfactory bass.

Surround

Any two symmetrical speakers can create the illusion of a full soundstage between them. By setting a speaker in each corner of a room, you can move sounds in a full circle: the front speakers take care of left-to-right movement in front of you; the front and rear ones on the left play front-to-back movement on that side; and so on. Quad sound, popular in the 1970s, used this effect for music recording.

Movie theaters have three speakers in front, so when you add the two surround speakers you get five-channel sound. The subwoofer carries only a tenth of the normal frequencies—just the lows—so its channel is called "point one." That's why we talk about "5.1 sound."[20] Other formats add channels above, around, or completely encircling the audience.

Binaural

Those ear convolutions can also let us create the illusion that sounds are moving completely around you—front and back, above and below, as well as left and right— using just two speakers. But this effect is very fragile, and most listening situations don't support it accurately. On the other hand, headphones bypass a room's acoustics

---

[19] That speaker is almost always reserved exclusively for dialog. See Chapter 17.

[20] Movie surround usually puts the "rear" speakers along the sides of the auditorium, so each seat gets more consistent coverage.

and couple sounds directly into your ears. *Binaural* recordings, using two matched microphones surrounded by ear-shaped reflectors, and heard via headphones, can be very convincing.

If you don't mind the effect of room acoustics, you can process a stereo sound to be "almost" surrounding. That's how a laptop's startup sound can seem larger than the computer it's emanating from. There's more about this processing in Chapter 16.

Two tracks doesn't mean stereo

Stereo, binaural, and surround depend on different information coming out of each speaker. Otherwise *every* sound just ends up centered between the speakers, or what we call *monaural* or mono.

Most cameras and many NLEs will route a single microphone to two adjacent channels, even though the channels are carrying the same signal. This presents a tiny advantage in overcoming electronic noise, but is mostly for convenience: with modern equipment, the noise advantage doesn't justify the doubling of storage space or download time. It also can cause problems in postproduction, if you're not aware that the dual-waveform signal isn't stereo. There's more about this in Chapter 17.

VERY SLOW CHANGES OF PRESSURE ARE WEATHER

Barometric pressure—the stuff reported on The Weather Channel—is exactly the same kind of molecular pressure as sound, only it's much larger and changes over hours instead of milliseconds. I include it here for the sake of completeness; to suggest there's a continuum that links all things; and because after a chapter like this one, you might want some comic (or cosmic) relief.

CHAPTER 2

How Digital Audio Works

WHY DIGITAL?

Sound, when it's vibrating through the air, is definitely not digital. Pressure varies smoothly between compression and rarefaction; it doesn't have steps that can be turned directly into digits. Or to put it another way, Figure 2.1A couldn't happen. The tines of a tuning fork can't click instantly between –1 and +1, with nothing in between. They go through a smooth movement between the two extremes, like Figure 2.1B.

Sound is a continuous variation between positive and negative air pressures. A microphone reads that sound as a continuously changing voltage.[1] Often, we'll store these voltage changes for later playback:

---

[1] Sound as a voltage is usually referred to as *audio*.

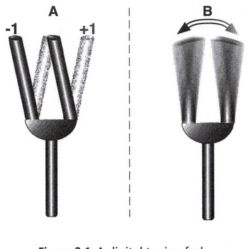

Figure 2.1 A digital tuning fork —if there were such a thing—could instantly click between two positions (A). But real ones (B) move smoothly between the extremes.

- We can use them to wiggle a needle and cut grooves in a moving phono disk.
- We can use them to wave a shutter and cast shadows on a moving film track.
- We can send them through a coil and write varying magnetism on a moving tape covered with iron particles.

Then we can reverse the process, create a varying voltage from what we've stored, and send it to a speaker. The speaker's diaphragm pushes or pulls the air, and recreates the sound.

What we've really stored is a mechanical, optical, or magnetic *analogy* of the sound. And while all three of the above examples are obsolete for mass media, they were the primary way to capture sound for most of the last century. Analog recording is mature, most of its problems have been solved, and it works pretty well.

So why complicate matters by turning the sound into computer data?

We don't use digital audio because it's nonlinear; we use it because it's robust

The nonlinear revolution primarily affected video production. Movie film and audio tape have always been nonlinear: you could open any scene or sequence, any time, and trim or add a few more feet of film or tape. Computerized editing may be faster or less messy than splicing (in a few cases, it's slower), but that's not why professional media adopted digital.

Historically, creating media involves a lot of copying. Pieces of movie film are copied onto other pieces of film for special effects, composite masters, and release prints. Analog videotape was edited by copying individual shots from one video deck to another. Most music originates as multitrack recordings, and has its tracks copied in various combinations onto a stereo or surround master; the master is frequently copied a few more times before reaching a format that consumers can play.

Traditional movie tracks went through at least six generations of copies between the shooting stage and the theater. In fact, the room where critical movie sound decisions are made—even in today's digital world—is called a *dub stage*. The person who runs it is the *re-recording engineer*.

But analog doesn't copy well. When analog film images are copied, grain builds up and subtle shadings are lost. A similar thing happens when you copy analog video or audio: noise builds up and high frequencies or fine details are lost. Then, each time you play an analog tape or film, it wears out a little more and gets a tiny bit worse.

Digital data doesn't deteriorate this way. When you copy a number, you get exactly that number—never a little more or less. You can store the data, play it countless times, manipulate various aspects of it, transmit it across great distances, and it'll always be the numbers you expect. Digits are ideal for the "copy-after-copy" style of media production.

Figure 2.2 shows a simple visual analogy. If we photocopy the cat (an analog process), and then copy the copy, we start to lose details. After a few generations, all that's left is a blob with whiskers. But if we invent a digital code for the puss—say, the three letters CAT—we can make as many copies as we want. The letters don't identify our exact kitty as well as the photo does. But with enough digits, we could spell out every one of his feline details.[2]

Step 1: Original   **Step 2: Copy of Step 1**   **Step 3: Copy of Step 2**   **Step 4: Copy of Step 3**

Figure 2.2 A multigenerational cat. Analog copies on top, and digital ones on the bottom.

---

[2] In fact, that particular kitty has a chip behind his shoulder. A vet can read it, identify me as owner, and access the cat's medical history . . . and it's all digital.

Digital audio hides its mistakes

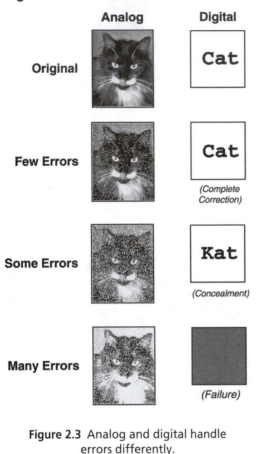

Analog   **Digital**

Original

Few Errors   Cat   *(Complete Correction)*

Some Errors   Kat   *(Concealment)*

Many Errors   *(Failure)*

Figure 2.3 Analog and digital handle errors differently.

If one of our analog cat pictures got scratched before its copy was made, we'd be stuck with the scratch in every subsequent copy ... but we'd still recognize our furry friend. If that copy got scratched, *its* copy would be even worse.

Digital audio handles data loss differently:

- Small data errors are reconstructed perfectly. The system uses checking digits to find out what the missing data should have been, and recreates it. If the scratch was a minor data error on a picture file, a copy of the file would be scratchless!
- Medium data errors can be hidden. The checking digits let the system know that *something* is missing, but it doesn't have enough data to make a perfect reproduction. Instead, media players guess the missing data by interpolating from numbers they know are good. In almost every case, the repair is transparent.
- If a big scratch represented so much damage to the data file that it couldn't be reconstructed, the system could blur over it instead. Details would be missing, but it's unlikely we'd notice the scratch.

This error-concealment process is used in real-time media like audio CDs, DVDs, and HD radio. Computer media, including hard drives and files on CD- or DVD-ROM, and Internet packet transmissions, often skip the concealment; if the system can't recreate the data perfectly, it tries again. If the data is completely lost, it lets the user know.

In an analog system, even slight problems cause noise or distortion. But humans are very good at guessing what should have been there, and noisy or distorted signals may still be recognizable. In a digital system, the small problems go away, but the big ones can be catastrophic. Figure 2.3 shows this difference with our cat pictures.

Those catastrophic failures may be rare, but they do happen. As with any other data, it's just common sense to make backup copies of any video or audio material you might ever want to keep.

Digital media can be copied very quickly

When I wrote the first edition of this book, digital audio and video recording used rotating heads writing slanted tracks on moving magnetic tape. The systems were finicky and often fragile, but worst was the fact that it was almost impossible to make high-speed copies or fast transfers. Getting material from the camera to the editing system required a real-time digital copy.

That problem went away. Today's hard drives can transfer data at around one Gigabit per second, and a Thunderbolt connection is about ten times that fast. Tomorrow's drives and wiring are sure to be even faster.

For reference: high quality stereo audio needs about two megabits per second . . . so with today's best drives, a 90-minute stereo track can transfer in about 12 minutes. Theatrical tracks use data compression, so they'd transfer even faster.

Some processes can eliminate transfers entirely. In television news, it's routine to pop a solid-state drive out of the field camera, plug it into an editing computer, and then upload the finished story to the station's server.

Digital storage is incredibly cheap: Compared to analog, it's virtually free

Like almost anything else that's related to computers, storage keeps getting more capable and less expensive. As of this writing, a writable DVD disc costs less than 25¢ in quantity, and holds 4.7 gigabytes. A plug-and-play USB hard drive with 1,000 gigabytes of storage costs less than $100. Plug the drive into most routers, and you can create a "Personal Cloud": any computer on your local network can save or retrieve files.

Or use the vast Internet Cloud instead. Google now gives you 8 gigabytes of storage for free; all you need is a free Gmail account to access it from anywhere in the world. If you need more space, they'll sell you 100 gigabytes for $5 a month. Competition means they and other services will soon be offering even better deals.

If you want to compare that to the cost of analog media, I'll get you started: An hour of two-track audio mastering tape is between $60 and $120, depending on the quality standard you choose. A well maintained analog deck to record or play that tape will set you back at least a thousand bucks . . . if you can find one.

TURNING ANALOG TO DIGITAL

Digital circuits are immune to gradual noise because they ignore ambiguity. A digital bit is either zero or one. If a signal falls between those two values, the circuit picks one and ignores the difference. But remember: sound is *continuous changes* of pressure, so the voltage that represents it never stays at one precise number. To take advantage of the digital process, we have to change these smoothly varying, often fractional voltages—perhaps representing our continuously moving tuning fork—into unambiguous digital-friendly values.

We do this by taking a snapshot of the voltage at a particular moment, measuring and reporting the voltage, and then taking another snapshot.

Each snapshot is called a sample.

- How often we take these snapshots is the *sample frequency*.
- How precisely we measure the voltage is the *sample depth*.

Those two qualities—sample depth and frequency—get chosen by the user for the specific purpose. They represent a trade-off between how much data is generated (and needs to be stored), and what the theoretical maximum accuracy of the recording can be.[3]

Sample depth

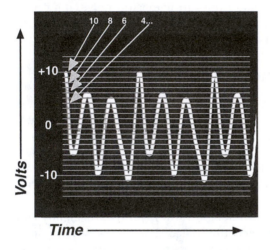

Figure 2.4 An oscilloscope displays voltage over time.

We used an oscilloscope in Chapter 1 to show sound waves. This analog gadget displays varying voltages along the vertical scale, and ongoing time along the horizontal. Aside from being a vital piece of test equipment, it's handy for visualizing audio processes.

In Figure 2.4, I've drawn horizontal lines across the oscilloscope to represent voltage levels. The numerical units I've assigned are completely arbitrary, but, for the sake of simplicity, we'll call them volts. The signal is an oboe, amplified to approximately +10 volts at its highest compression and −10 volts at its deepest rarefaction. The arrows show how the waveform reaches different voltages at different times.

Now we have to keep track of those voltages. It's very easy to build an electrical *comparator*, a circuit that turns on only when an input is above a particular level. If we fed our analog signal into a bunch of comparators, each set to a slightly higher voltage, we could turn the analog voltage into a digital one. All we'd have to do is see which is the highest-voltage comparator that's turned on. It would work like Figure 2.5.

If you want more accuracy, add more comparators. Figure 2.6 shows how this works. It's a close-up of the wave in Figure 2.4. The value at sample A is 6 volts. But what's the value at sample B? Five and a half volts isn't allowed in a system that requires whole numbers. The comparators would say it's 5 volts, but they'd be wrong.

---

[3] The *minimum* accuracy, unfortunately, is determined by the system's designers. Cheap components and engineering shortcuts can make any digital recording sound awful, no matter how good the sample rate or bit depth look.

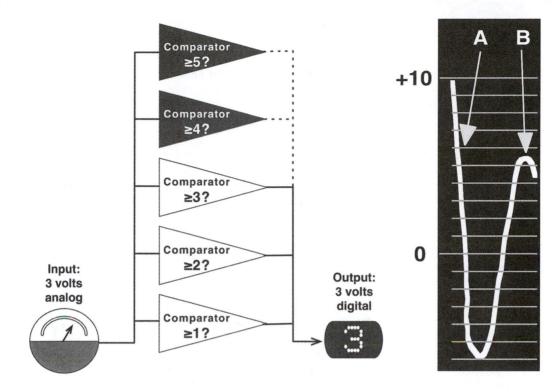

Figure 2.5 A simple digital measuring circuit. The highest comparator that's turned on is set for 3 volts, so we know that's the input level.

Figure 2.6 An ambiguous voltage at B.

Figure 2.7 Our 2-bit cat *(upper left)* has only black, white, and two grays. But our 4-bit cat *(lower right)* has 14 grays, for much more detail.

The solution is to use a lot of comparators, spaced very closely together. To keep things manageable, their outputs are combined into binary numbers. Each time you add another bit to a binary number, it doubles the possible values that can be represented. So adding a few bits—doubling, then doubling again, then doubling *that* a few more times—makes a big difference.

Figure 2.7 shows the advantage of this binary doubling. It's our cat in both 2- and 4-bit versions. The upper left version uses two bits, for four possible values: black, white, and two grays. Note how a lot of details get lost in the same color gray blob. But the four-bit version on the lower right has 16 possible values: black, white, and *14* different grays. The usual minimum for computer photos is 8 bits, or 256 gradations, per color . . . a very accurate kitty indeed. The first standard for desktop computer audio was 8 bits as well; today, it's often 24 bits . . . or about 65,000 times more resolution than that original standard!

Bits don't have intrinsic value

It's wrong to think of one bit as representing a specific brightness, voltage, or sound-pressure level. Digital systems don't care what you assign to a single bit. In a vending machine, it could be a nickel or a penny or a quarter. In a traffic control system, it could be a car. The very first video games assigned the simple presence of light on a pixel to a single bit, or 1 volt sent to the monitor. A modern video game has tens of thousands of color choices; for an analog display, that means less than a millivolt (1/1,000 volt) per bit.

Bits can also express multiple choices, instead of continuously increasing values. Teletypes used 6 bits to carry 64 different characters for news bulletins or telegrams.[4] Early computer communication protocols used 7 bits to represent 128 possible ASCII characters, including both upper- and lower-case letters and a lot more punctuation; an eighth bit was reserved for signaling and reliability. Today's word processors devote 8 bits for each letter, with 256 possible values, enough to cover typographic symbols and even some simple graphics.

A little historic note: radio and TV news used to be transmitted from press associations via 6-bit Teletype. News stories were printed by the machine in all-caps because lower case letters weren't possible. They were given to the newscaster that way, and read on the air. Somehow this turned into a tradition that *all* scripts have to be upper-case, which is just plain silly when you're writing on a computer (or even a typewriter). Countless studies have shown that words with lower case letters are easier to read.

The 16-bit solution

The minimum standard for professional digital audio is to use 16 bits, representing 65,536 possible different values for each sample. In terms of sound, that's a pressure

---

[4] Twenty-six upper-case letters, the numbers, some punctuation, and a few system functions like ringing a bell.

change of about 0.00013 dB.[5] Real audio circuits round up as well as down, so the worst error will occur when an analog signal falls precisely between two of those tiny slices: the digital value will be wrong by exactly half a slice, or less than 0.00007 dB.

Trust me: an error that tiny doesn't matter in media production.

The error can get worse, however. Once you've digitized that signal, you'll probably want to do things to it: change the level, or equalize it, or add reverb, or try other processing. Each time you do, the system has to perform math, usually division (*very* long division), on its numeric values. There's a good chance the right answer will include fractions between two sample levels, and have to be rounded off. This isn't just mathematical nit-picking. The resulting rounding errors generate random noise, and the noise gets worse with each subsequent operation.

Professionals avoid noise by working at 24 bits or higher,[6] for a possible error of roughly 0.00000026 dB. As far as I'm concerned, an error of a quarter-millionth of a dB is pretty accurate. The software I use every day does its math with a minimum of 32 bits; often more. Don't ask what the precise decibel error is in my system; my calculator can't handle fractions that tiny.

Bits as dynamic range

You can also look at bit depth another way. Each bit doubles the possible values for a sample. We know from the previous chapter that doubling a voltage means increasing it just about 6 dB.

So it's reasonable to say each bit represents a 6 dB range between the lowest and highest level the system can handle. (If you try to record more than the highest possible level, you get horrible distortion. If you try to record less than the lowest possible, the signal gets buried by ambiguous noise.) An 8-bit signal has a 48 dB maximum range, which is similar to the range for analog AM radio or 16mm film.

A few older prosumer cameras have a 12-bit mode, letting them record four simultaneous channels. Using this mode for field recordings is almost always a mistake: the 72 dB dynamic range either won't leave a safety margin for loud dialog, or will add too much noise.

A 16-bit signal has a much better range of 96 dB (16 × 6 = 96). This is considerably better than FM radio, and close to the limits of human hearing. A 24-bit signal has 144 dB maximum dynamic range, well beyond the limits of even the most golden-eared listener. Those extra bits provide a margin for calculation errors.

[5] How can a bit have a precise decibel level, when we just finished saying bit values are arbitrary? It's because decibels are ratios, not absolute values of sound pressure or voltage (see Chapter 1).

[6] Unfortunately, no practical camera or field recorder can capture sound with 24-bit accuracy. Their analog circuits just won't perform with that kind of precision. Pro recorders rated "24 bits" usually achieve about 18 bits' worth of accuracy. Cameras and consumer gear rated "24 bits" seldom give you more than 14 bits' performance. There's a lot more about recording accuracy in Chapter 8.

☞ **ROSE'S RULES**

Practical bit-depthery

- If your camera or recorder does 24-bit recording and you've got enough blank memory to store all you're shooting at that mode, use it. With some equipment this won't make any difference in recording quality, but it will save a step later.
- If your camera or recorder does only 16-bit recording, or media storage and transmission are at a premium, feel free to use that lower mode. Just be careful about setting levels (Chapter 8). And bump the files up to 24 bits before mixing or processing.
- If your editing system doesn't support 24 bits, don't worry . . . but if you want the highest quality, restrict your editing to cuts; they don't require rounding. Before you do crossfades, equalization, or any other processing, move the files to a good audio program.

Of course we're talking about *maximum* and *potential* ranges, because recording circuits are often limited by their analog components. Even the best pro sound recorders can't give you the 144 dB theoretical range of a 24-bit signal. Most "24 bit" cameras have about 15 dB of audio resolution, once you get through their analog circuits.

But after a signal has been captured, it makes sense to bump the file up to a higher bit depth before processing or mixing. Converting a recording to a higher bit depth doesn't make it sound any better, but does leave more of a margin for rounding.

You can hear the effect of different bit depths. **Sound 2.2** is a 16-bit recording of music and a narrator. **Sound 2.3** is the same material, truncated to 8 bits. **Sound 2.4** reduces the original to 4 bits. All were re-encoded at 16 bits and saved in a high-quality compressed format, so additional quality doesn't get lost by your playback system.

Decibels and digital

While bits don't have intrinsic value, one number always exists in any digital system: *full scale*, when all the bits are turned on. A digital signal just can't get any bigger than full scale, because there aren't any more bits to represent it.[7]

Think about it. What would happen if you had a recorder where 1 volt turned all its bits on . . . and you fed it 2 volts? The comparators would all get turned on, just as they would for a 1 volt signal. So one volt is what would get recorded. If you fed

---

[7] It's possible to accurately record a specialized test signal at +3 dBFS, but it wouldn't make a very interesting soundtrack.

100 volts to that recorder the result would still be 1 volt. (The recorder would probably also catch fire, but that's not the point.)

It doesn't matter whether the equipment uses 8 bits, 16 bits, or dozens. Full scale is unambiguous: it refers to just one specific level, no matter what digital circuit is looking at it.[8] Adding more bits just lets you cut full scale into smaller slices, for more precision.

When a recording reaches full scale, the waves get distorted out of shape. Instead of reaching a gradual peak and falling back towards lower voltages, you get a flat top as in Figure 2.8. It's as if the original vibrating element suddenly stopped, breaking the law of momentum.

Because of this, digital signal levels are always described as dBFS: *decibels referred to full scale*. Audio level meters on digital recorders and cameras are usually calibrated this way, with zero at the very top, and negative numbers representing decibels below it. This is different from analog metering, which can be calibrated any way the designer wants. (Analog audio meters usually have their zero placed about 85% of the way up, with positive numbers above it. But that's a matter of custom and standards rather than physics or math.)

Depending on the equipment, the results of trying to record louder than full scale can be anything from unintelligible to downright ugly: **Sound 2.1** plays some examples. First you'll hear the properly recorded original music and voice, then digitally boosted with peaks trying for +12 dBFS, and then with peaks attempting +24 dBFS. I did these examples entirely in the digital domain because analog circuits add their own unpredictable damage. I also lowered the files' level back to something that would be playable on your equipment . . . but by then, the digital damage had been done.

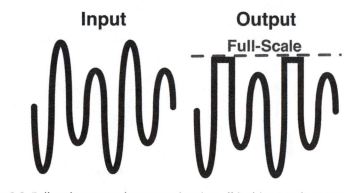

Figure 2.8 Full scale means the system is using all its bits. Louder waves get their tops chopped off, and sound pretty awful.

---

[8] Analog designers are free to assign any voltage they want for full scale. But that's outside the digital domain. It has nothing to do with the digital numbers you've recorded in a file, or any distortion or noise from digital problems.

✳ TIDBIT

Are you reading digital or analog meters?

- Digital meters are calibrated in decibels relative to full scale, with values ranging from around –60 at the bottom, to zero at the top. You can't record a digital signal louder than zero on a proper digital meter. (You can try, but all you'll get is very ugly digital distortion.)
- This is not the same as analog recording and metering, where signals louder than zero are common and most meters extend to +6. Music studios often push signals past +6 on their analog tape recorders, because many pop producers like the distortion that causes.
- A few programs have digital meters calibrated to look like analog ones: they have a zero point *near* the top, with some decibel or VU values above zero. This is the worst of both worlds, since there's no way of knowing what the programmer considered zero.

Don't let these differences get you into trouble.

An analog myth

You'll find this on the Internet: "Analog audio is inherently better than digital. That's because digital is 'steppy', with pre-determined voltage levels. But some of the signal you're recording will fall between the steps . . . and get lost!"

While the logic is right, the underlying assumption is wrong. All analog systems have continuous random background noise, something that doesn't exist within the digital parts of a signal chain. In a very good analog system, this noise may be negligible—but it's there.

Continuous noise in analog systems, and the stepping (or *quantizing error*) in digital systems, have almost exactly the same effect. They make it impossible to tell exactly what the signal is. There's going to be ambiguity, either because the analog noise has buried the smallest details or because the quantizing error lost them. In a 16-bit signal, that error happens 96 dB below full scale; there are no smaller steps. In a decent analog system, there might be exactly 96 dB dynamic range between noise and maximum output;[9] anything softer is lost behind noise.

The result is the same in both systems: you've lost the smallest details. It's like trying to see something in a picture, when it's smaller than a digital snapshot's single

---

[9] For more technical readers: I'm assuming an 80 dB s/n, and 16 dB headroom above nominal before the signal gets clipped.

pixel, or smaller than a chemical photograph's film grain. Despite the TV cop cliché of "Computer: Enhance," it just can't be done without guesswork.

Are some analog systems worse than 96 dB dynamic range, and others much better? Of course. You can also record audio with 8 bits or 24 bits. But then it becomes a question of design and component quality, not the underlying technology. You aren't asking "which is better—digital or analog?" now; you're asking "which is better— Prius or Humvee?"

Dither: Making the most of those bits

Even with the best digital systems, you'll eventually encounter some quantization error at the tiny level represented by only 1 bit. The error is small—it takes trained ears and excellent monitors to hear it in a 16-bit system—but it can be ugly. That's because it creates a distortion that follows the signal but isn't harmonically related.

The solution is to add the same stuff that causes so much trouble in analog circuits: random noise. Digital designers add a tiny amount of noise, at a level about one-third what a single bit represents. When this noise has a positive voltage, it pushes the signal up to where the smallest comparator sees it as *one*. When it's negative, it pulls the details down to *zero*. Since this happens totally randomly, the error occurs across the entire band . . . it's not trying to follow the desired signal. The ear is good at picking up sound patterns when they're obscured by random noise, something you've probably noticed if you've ever followed a conversation at a noisy cocktail party. So the process— called *dithering*—not only reduces perceived errors at low levels, it even makes it possible to hear some details that are smaller than the lowest possible value!

It's easy to understand dither with a visual analogy. Hold your hand in front of this page (as in Figure 2.9), and some of the words are obscured . . . just as if they'd fallen below the lowest level of a digital signal and were zeroed out.

Now start waving your fingers rapidly side-to-side (Figure 2.10). The fingers didn't go away—they still cover as much of the page at any one time—but your mind can pick the meaningful words out from the randomly obscuring fingers.

Dither is best used when going from a high-resolution format to a lower one. Well-designed professional systems apply it during the initial quantization, and on the output of high-bitrate processes. Most desktop video editors never reach this kind of precision, and dither isn't available. Either way, you usually don't have to make decisions about its use.

But if a program gives you the option of dither when converting 16-bit files to 8 bits for older multimedia systems, turn it on. As 24-bit digital audio equipment becomes more common in production, you'll want to use dithering whenever you move to a lower bit depth. Just remember:

- Don't reduce the bit depth until you have to. If you've shot 24 bits and are editing on a system that can handle it, stay at 24 bits.
- If you've shot 16 bits or are doing any mixing in a system that supports 24 bit files, convert files to the higher standard.

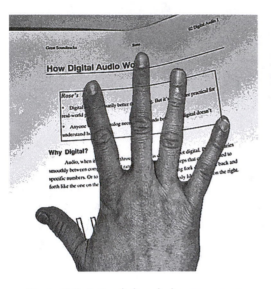

Figure 2.9 A steady hand obscures some of the page . . .

Figure 2.10 . . . but when the hand moves rapidly, you can "see behind it."

- If you've edited or mixed at 24 bits but need a 16-bit version for distribution, use dither if it's available. (If it isn't available, consider moving the 24-bit files to other software for the conversion. Dither is worth the effort.)
- Never dither unless you're lowering the bit depth. Otherwise, it just adds noise.

Levels and loudness

Decibels are great for measuring sound pressure levels, but don't predict loudness. What we think is "loud" depends on two additional factors: frequency and context.

The sensitivity of our ears varies with frequency. Humans evolved with better hearing in the middle of the range, because that's where other humans (and predators) make meaningful sounds. For quiet sounds, we're most sensitive between about 700 Hz and 5 kHz, with particular emphasis around 2 kHz. The difference becomes less for louder sounds, but it's always there.

Sound level meters—gadgets used to determine industrial noise exposure, and also to calibrate monitor speakers—almost always have a switch to compensate for this. *A-, B-,* and *C-weighting* are attempts to match the meter's sensitivity to our ears. The differences are primarily related to how loud the measured signal is.

K-weighting was developed by the European Broadcast Union as a standard for media sound, and takes loudness into account. It's a newer method and requires more sophisticated processing, so isn't usually seen on sound level meters. We'll talk more about this kind of loudness measurement in Chapter 17.

Two other factors influence how we'll hear a signal as loud or soft:

- Our *physical ability* to determine a sound's loudness depends on what sounds occur a fraction of a second before and after. Standard analog volume meters had mechanical damping to partially simulate this.[10] Most of the digital meters in today's desktop video software don't.

- Our *psychological perception* of loudness is influenced by any other sounds we've heard recently in the same context, such as dialog in a continuous scene of a film. Over the past few years, research has attempted to set formulas for this factor. The results have been standardized for broadcasters in the United States (CALM Act) and Europe (EBU R128), usually using *LKFS*[11] measurements. Dolby further refined the system into *Dialnorm*. This encodes the producer's intended loudness so sophisticated home viewers can recover it, while giving broadcasters a way to keep commercials and programs at approximately the same loudness. There's more about these measurements—and how to use them on broadcast mixes—in Chapter 17.

Sample rate

Bit depth is only half the equation. Since audio is changes of voltage *over time*, you can't record it unless you're measuring the voltage at multiple times. This means multiple measurements; the more often you measure, the better you can reproduce its changes.

We'll start with another scope photo. In Figure 2.11, I've added eight vertical lines spaced evenly apart. The scope's display sweeps at a controlled speed, so each vertical line can mark a different time in its sweep. For simplicity, we'll say the vertical lines are one millisecond apart.

At the start of this section of sound, the signal is 9 volts. A millisecond later, it's 4 volts. And a millisecond after that, it's 4 volts again. These are the first three *samples*, the data a digital system would store at this sample rate. Since the samples are one millisecond apart, we say "this system has a sample rate of 1,000 times per second" (usually written as 1 kHz s/r).

On playback, the system smooths these values to produce an output like the gray line along the top of Figure 2.12. This output doesn't look very much like the input, and it wouldn't sound like it either. Obviously this is a bad recording (1 kHz s/r is a ridiculously low rate for digital audio).

---

[10] The "VU Meter," used in professional broadcasting and recording for most of the last century, smoothed out its reading over roughly one-third of a second. Unfortunately the cheaper voltmeters supplied with consumer audio (and pro video) gear generally lacked this feature, even if they were marked in decibels or volume units.

[11] Loudness, K-weighted, in decibels relative to Full Scale.

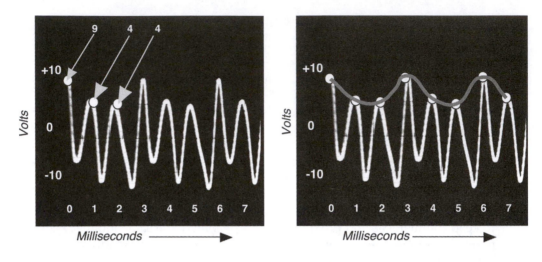

Figure 2.11 Sampling over time, at a low sample rate.

Figure 2.12 Badly recreated signal from a very low sample rate.

But suppose we speed up and check the voltage *twice* each millisecond. This raises the sample rate to 2 kHz, doubling the amount of data generated (Figure 2.13).

When we smooth these samples, we get a somewhat more accurate result (Figure 2.14). Still not perfect, but better.

As you add more samples, you get a better representation of the sound. An older multimedia computer system might be standardized at 22,050 samples per second, or

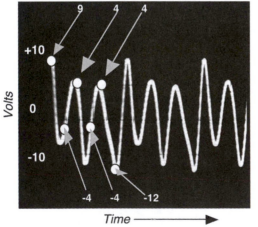

Figure 2.13 Doubling the sample rate gives us more data.

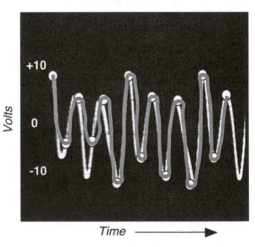

Figure 2.14 With more samples, we can recreate the signal more accurately.

a sample rate of 22.050 kHz. Compact discs double that, for a sample rate of 44.1 kHz. Professional broadcast formats operate at 48 kHz s/r, and DVDs are capable of 96 kHz (though most don't take advantage of it). Some pro audio equipment records with 192 kHz sampling. Whether these super-fast rates actually add anything of practical use is open to debate, but there's a definite relationship between sample rate and potential sound quality.

The Nyquist limit and aliasing

In the 1920s Harry Nyquist, an engineer at Bell Labs, proved mathematically that the highest frequency you can faithfully reproduce has to be less than one-half the sample rate. Since U.S. FM analog stereo doesn't carry audio higher than 15 kHz (to protect other parts of the broadcast signal), the Nyquist theorem says broadcasters can work at 32 kHz s/r without losing any signal. A few years ago U.S. television had the same 15 kHz limit, so some TV equipment ran at the same 32 kHz.

Unfortunately, audio sources often extend beyond the Nyquist limit. Many good analog recordings carry sound above 17 kHz. When frequencies higher than Nyquist reach a digitizing circuit, strange things start to happen. The signal gets combined with the sample frequency, and the circuit kicks out data that implies additional signals based on the two. These are *aliases*, other waves that could fit the same samples. The output circuit of the digital device doesn't know which wave matches the original, so it creates them all. The result, with a single wave going in, is a very unmusical trio.

A complex musical signal, with lots of harmonics, can have thousands of aliases. The playback system turns them all back into analog audio, creating a combination of squeaks and whistles accompanying the high frequencies. It isn't pretty, as you can hear from the example on **Sound 1.5**.

The solution is to use an *aliasing filter* before you sample: a circuit that absolutely blocks any frequency higher than half the sample rate, and doesn't affect any frequency below it. Such a filter would let you record perfectly, without any aliases.

The only problem is that a perfect filter like this can't exist. You can't design a filter with infinite cutoff at one frequency and absolutely no effect on frequencies below it. Any real-world hi-cut filter has two characteristics:

- A slope between what passes through and what's blocked. As the frequency rises, the volume is slowly turned down—not instantly turned off.
- Some degradation to signals below but close to the cutoff frequency. Even though those lower-frequency signals are passed, they get distorted.

Early digital devices were designed with a safety margin—usually around 10% of the sample rate—to allow for that first characteristic. The first compact disc recorders started their filters sloping slightly below 20 kHz, so they could achieve a reasonable cutoff by the time they reached 22.050 kHz (half the 44.1 kHz sample rate). Manufacturers would often tolerate some aliasing as a compromise, so there wouldn't be too much high frequency loss. Many computer sound cards, consumer recorders, and even prosumer cameras are still designed the same way.

But there's no way to compensate for the second characteristic. The sharper a filter gets, the more it affects sounds below its nominal cutoff frequency. You can put multiple filters in series, or use other techniques to sharpen their rejection, but this inevitably adds distortion as sounds approach the frequency limit. And affordable analog filter components lose their calibration as they get older, further compounding the problem. So it was fairly common for early digital devices to suffer high-frequency distortion. Between this and the "tolerable" aliasing that designers would allow, early digital earned a reputation for having poor high frequency sound. That's where most of the analog-is-better myths come from.

Oversampling

Modern professional equipment solves both these problems by using an initial sampling frequency many times higher than the desired one, digitizing at two *million* samples a second or more. This raises the Nyquist limit so very gentle, super-high frequency filters can be used, which have no effect on the desired audio. The initial high sample rate signal is then filtered using digital techniques, which are more accurate than analog ones, and down-converted to the desired rate. A similar scheme is used on the output.

Oversampling presents other advantages as well, in that digital artifacts can be spread across a much wider band and not affect the audio signal as much. It's more expensive to design and build circuits that use it, because the high data rates require

---

✳ TIDBIT

Be rate-wise

In the analog world, high frequency losses are cumulative. For best results, each analog generation has to be as wide-range as possible. Master recordings were often done at a much higher tape speed than the release cassette or broadcast master, to preserve highs.

That's not how digital works. If you keep everything digital, you can go many generations—theoretically, an infinite number of them—without damaging high frequencies.

Higher digital rates improve frequency response, but only if the analog components support the improvement. Most analog recorders use the same filters for both 48 kHz and 44.1 kHz, so the higher rate doesn't give you any advantage. With some portable recorders, even 96 kHz sampling doesn't have significantly better high frequencies.

Upsampling—recording at one rate, and then converting the signal to a higher rate—doesn't improve the sound. It can't recreate frequencies that weren't in the original recording.

very precise timing. But the necessary chips are getting cheaper, and newer portable digital audio recorders often include oversampling.

Working with sample rates

Broadcast digital videotape and digital film soundtrack formats use a sample rate of 48 kHz, so if your project is destined for that kind of showing, it makes sense to keep your equipment at that setting. But if all of your sound sources are at 44.1 kHz (such as CDs and converted mp3, or low cost digital recorders), or you're intending Internet delivery only, it makes the most sense to keep your NLE at that rate as well. Depending on your software, it can save a lot of rendering time.

Some NLEs don't allow a sample rate choice, and some projects may be destined for both Internet and broadcast or DVD. So don't obsess about choosing a rate. The differences in sound quality are negligible, and modern software does a good job of converting rates.

There is one rare exception to that last rule. *Harmonic enhancers* are processors that change the timbre of a sound, brightening it by creating artificial harmonics at frequencies an octave higher than the original recording. A very low sample rate recording may be subjectively improved by converting it to a higher rate and then using an enhancer. But this requires special software—a standard equalizer won't do the job.

AUDIO DATA REDUCTION

If the goal is simply to reduce storage space or Internet bandwidth, there are better strategies than lowering the sample rate or bit depth. Audio data reduction or compression relies on statistical and psychoacoustic principles to squeeze a lot of sound into the smallest number of bits. While most compromise the sound quality— and are often referred to as *lossy compression*—they don't damage it as much as equivalent lowering of the sample rate or bit depth. In fact, these compression techniques are considered so benign that they're built into digital TV, digital theatrical film surround, and DVD . . . and nobody considers those media to be low-fidelity.

✔ TIP

As good as lossy data-reduction techniques get, they're not perfect. And subsequent mixing, editing, and re-reduction make the sound a lot worse. So if you're using them, be sure to keep an uncompressed version on a backup tape or disk.

Standard redundancy-compression methods like PKZIP and Stuffit aren't much good for audio. They rely on finding repeating patterns in the data, and normal audio is just too random—in a numeric sense—to have these patterns. The best they can do with a typical track is only a few percent reduction.

Delta encoding

Fortunately, most sounds do have one predictable element: from one sample to the next, the incremental change isn't very great. Figure 2.15 shows how this works, using a 16-bit recording of a piano.

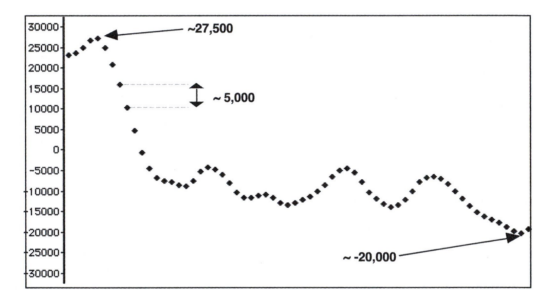

Figure 2.15 Individual sample data in a 16-bit recording of a piano.

A 16-bit digital word represents about 65,000 voltage values, half positive (representing compression in the original sound) and half negative (representing rarefaction). This particular slice of piano—a bit more than one millisecond's worth–has values from about +27,500 to about –20,000. It takes all 16 bits to represent it accurately. But from one sample to the next, the biggest difference is never more than about 5,000 values, and is usually a lot less. We need at most 13 bits to record the biggest jump, and most of the jumps could be recorded with only a few bits.

"Delta" is math-speak for "difference," and this *delta encoding* records just the difference from one sample to the next. It's the basis of QuickTime IMA, one of the first popular multimedia compression methods and still found on many editing systems. It can cut files down to a quarter of their original size without seriously affecting the audio quality.

Delta coding has the advantages of easy math, could be played back or recorded on early low-power desktop computers, and doesn't add much distortion to most well-recorded speech or music. But it can't cope with very sudden changes: beeps, clicks, and sharp sound effects can be surrounded by noise.

Lossless encoding

Delta's limitations can be eliminated by using more powerful math in more modern desktop computers. Today's *linear prediction* stores the exact difference from one sample to the next, no matter how big the jump. A Zip-like algorithm then simplifies the predictions further, saving data on continuous tones and silences. Depending on the content, linear prediction can shrink a file between 40% and 60%—it's about half as efficient as delta, but the restored file has absolutely no distortion: *lossless* data compression. Every bit of the original is retained in the decoded copy. With linear prediction, you don't need to keep an uncompressed backup copy.

Linear prediction guesses the size of the next jump based on what's gone before, tests its guess, and then guesses again if it was wrong. This takes a lot of calculations, but nothing unreasonable for modern computers. The savings in file size make it worth using, particularly when shipping large audio files across the Internet. Decoding doesn't require much math at all, and can be handled in real-time by most modern audio software. Unfortunately, some NLEs don't handle it well and require lengthy rendering for lossless formats. If you encounter that, save some time by moving the file to an audio utility and saving in an uncompressed format.

Linear predictive delta is the basis for:

- **FLAC**, the Free Lossless Audio Codec, a cross-platform open-source implementation at http://flac.sourceforge.net.
- **Apple Lossless**, an implementation within QuickTime for Macintosh and Windows. Most software that plays QuickTime will play Apple Lossless files; encoding may require Apple's $30 QuickTime 7 Pro application. Since QuickTime is also a standard for video interchange, we've used Apple Lossless for the high quality diagnostic files on this book's website.
- **Windows Media Lossless** can be encoded or decoded in current versions of the Windows Media Player. While WMA is ubiquitous, the Lossless version isn't seen as much as FLAC or Apple Lossless. Still, it's perfectly appropriate for internal workflows.

Perceptual encoding and masking

As we discussed earlier, our ears aren't very sensitive at the extremes of the audio band. Figure 2.16 shows a typical threshold of hearing curve, though the details vary depending on the listener. The curved line shows how a sound at 20 Hz has to be at least 70 dB SPL in order to be heard, while a sound at 3 kHz merely has to be at 0 dB SPL, the nominal "threshold of hearing." Sounds softer than the curve—within the gray area—disappear for most listeners. A relatively soft sound at 1 kHz (the gray bar) is perfectly audible because it falls above the curve. But at other frequencies, the threshold rises, and equally soft sounds at 500 Hz and 15 kHz (the black bars) aren't heard.

There are actually a bunch of threshold of hearing curves, because relative sensitivity to different frequencies depends on a sound's loudness. But in almost every case, your ears will be the most sensitive within the speech range of around 350–3,500 Hz. Most people can hear more than 16 bits' worth of detail in that range. At 50 Hz, many people hear only about 6 bits' worth of detail. At 18 kHz, 2 bits may be sufficient.

Figure 2.16 is a static threshold with sounds superimposed on it. Real-world thresholds are constantly shifting, based on both the current and previous sounds. A loud sound raises the threshold around its frequencies, as shown in Figure 2.17. The signal at 1 kHz (gray bar) stops you from hearing slightly softer signals at 700 Hz and 1.5 kHz (black bars).

My drawings are slightly exaggerated to highlight the effect, and the actual amount of masking varies depending on individual hearing and how carefully it's been trained. As a practical example, consider the case of a large orchestra playing a full chord, with one instrument slightly out of tune. It's unlikely than anyone other than the conductor and a few music critics will notice.

Layer 3/mp3

It takes sophisticated processing to predict how various threshold shifts will mask specific sounds. But once the masking is calculated, you can save a lot of data by removing the sounds that are hidden. One popular way to do this was standardized by the International Standards Organization's *Moving Pictures Expert Group* [ISO/MPEG] in 1992. Its most complex implementation, Layer 3, uses 576 separate frequency bands to analyze the sound. Stereo tracks are further processed to find the details that are identical on both channels and encode them only once. The resulting sound stream not only uses fewer bits because masked or redundant sounds are eliminated, it's also more predictable, so pattern-saving algorithms like Zip are effective with it. You've probably already guessed: ISO/MPEG Layer 3 usually is abbreviated as *mp3*.

Layer 3 is scalable depending on how much detail you're willing to sacrifice. Broadcasters use it carry high-quality audio in real time over ISDN and Internet with data about 12% of its original size. Casual music listeners are usually happy with well encoded mp3 files at 4% of their original size. Voice tracks can remain intelligible when as small as 0.5% of the original.

How bad is mp3?

There are many reasons for mp3's bad reputation. It's often encoded with badly written shareware and very little care, so there's plenty of bad-sounding mp3 on the Internet. Attempting to remix or otherwise 'improve' an mp3 file makes it worse: the original has to be decoded before manipulating it, and then the result gets re-encoded. Since details have already lost by the first coding, the re-encoding does even more damage.

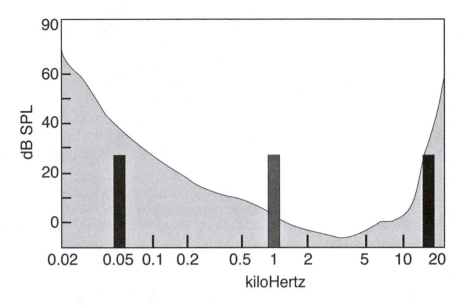

Figure 2.16 The threshold of hearing changes with frequency.

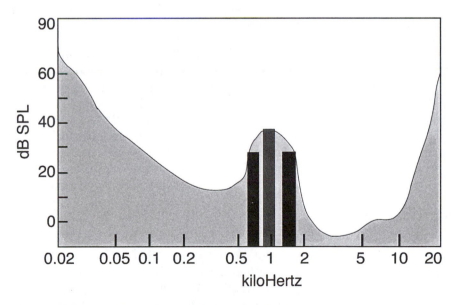

Figure 2.17 Louder sounds raise the threshold around them.

The truth is, mp3 compression can sound fine when done right. It's used in many professional applications.

Yes, the compression throws away details. But it's easy to demonstrate exactly how insignificant those details were, by mathematically comparing an mp3 song with its original, and listening to just the differences. You can do this on your desktop with any multitrack software, including the free Audacity (page 260):

1. Load the original onto one set of tracks; load the MP3 version onto another.
2. Manually align the two, so they start at exactly the same time.
3. Flip the mp3 version's polarity (with the software's *Invert* command) and mix the two together.

What's left will be any sound that was in the original, but didn't make it to the mp3 version. I do this comparison from time to time. You can hear the results at various mp3 settings, and read further details about the procedure, at www.dplay.com/tutorial/squeeze.

Other encoding standards

A less complex cousin than mp3, Layer 2, uses fewer bands and masks fewer details. It became popular because it could be implemented on simpler processors, and is still preferred for high-bandwidth applications like satellites and hard-disk audio storage systems.

It takes the ear a few milliseconds to recover from loud sounds, so threshold shifts continue even after the masking sound has ended. Layer 3 takes some advantage of this as a side effect of its very sharp filters. The Advanced Audio Coding (AAC) algorithm, used in MPEG4, exploits this further and even eliminates sounds that occur slightly *before* the masking signal. AAC files can be some 30% smaller than similar sounding mp3 versions. AAC files are often designated .m4a, though that extension can also be used for Apple Lossless (the playback software chooses the proper decoder).

MPEG and AAC are open standards, supported by many manufacturers. Macromedia Shockwave and Microsoft ASF also use the MPEG Layer 3 algorithm, with some additional non-audio data functions. You may also encounter older standards such as mu-law encoding (the Internet .au format), developed for telephone calls. And there are proprietary schemes promoted by companies including Dolby and APT, which may find their way into broadcast, DVD, theatrical, and Internet standards.

Metadata

Play almost any song from a commercial download source, on almost any music player, and the display can show a lot more than just the filename. You might see the name of the artist, the lyricist, album information, publisher and copyright information, or about sixty other categories of information . . . plus the song lyrics and album art. This *metadata* is encoded in the mp3 file along with the music. Similar schemes exist for other file formats including QuickTime, WAVE, and FLAC; each has a wide selection of pre-defined slots where you can store useful information about the file.

With appropriate software, you can search or manipulate metadata-equipped files like any other data. For example, iTunes lets you sort a music library by artist, composer, album name, genre, year recorded, and some other useful categories. Broadcasters put metadata on news clips, so they can find the ones relating to a particular politician or issue quickly. In filmmaking, metadata can tag each file of production sound with information about the scene shot; sound effects editors also use it to find just the right effect out of tens of thousands in their libraries.

Free metadata editors are available for just about every operating system and media type. Check your favorite shareware source.

Copy protection

Since digital files can be copied easily with no errors or generation loss, large copyright owners such as record companies tend to worry about unauthorized copies affecting their profits. They've been able to convince manufacturers and Congress to protect their interests. Whether this is fair, legal, or even good business practice is a topic for some other book . . . but it is a fact of life.

Digital Rights Management (DRM) schemes appear in a lot of perceptual coders, as encrypted data in the bitstream that tells the player how many times a file can be played or how a user can make copies. Software manufacturers agree to respect these schemes, as part of their license to decode the algorithm. But DRM isn't a necessary part of encoding, and shouldn't be confused with it. There is nothing about just making a file smaller that makes it hard to copy.

Watermarking is a variation on DRM which doesn't prevent copies, but makes it easier for copyright holders to prove that a piece of sound was originally theirs. It can take the form of relatively inaudible signatures spread across the spectrum of the original sound, or a seemingly random tone that can't be removed without the right equipment and a cryptographic key.

You can copy the contents of any file that can be played, whether or not it's protected, by playing it and re-recording the result. This may require multiple generations of coding and decoding, transfers to the analog domain and re-digitizing, or steep filters to remove watermarks—all of which can hurt the sound quality. How secure a DRM method is, how hard it is to defeat, and the legal status of everyone involved is a constantly changing landscape; check the Web for up-to-date reports.

From a producer's point of view, DRM doesn't matter: virtually every piece of recorded music is protected by copyright, whether or not it's digitally locked. Chapter 14 covers ways to use music legally.

CHAPTER 3

Audio on
a Wire

In most professional facilities, high-resolution audio exists primarily as high-speed data or instantaneous transfers. Dialog that was recorded to hard disk or other media on the set is opened as files in the editor, with no transfer time; audio and video workstations pass content back and forth via Ethernet; client copies are sent to servers over the Internet. The data is usually packets of sample values, assigned through routers, and distributed via Internet Protocol. We take advantage of computer technology every way we can.

But the old-fashioned idea of varying voltages on a cable—the way just about every signal was wired in the twentieth century—isn't obsolete. At the shoot, we send analog microphones to a camera or recorder, headphones, and possibly a mixer. In even the simplest editing suite, audio travels from NLE to monitor speakers. More complex video and audio post setups can have hardware-based processors, patchbays, voice-over mics, and sometimes even audio or video tape decks. Almost all of these connections use analog wiring.

Digital audio is often transported as voltages as well, as real-time serial streams using direct connections, over cables that look a lot like analog mic or video wires. It's definitely digital, but addresses and routers aren't involved. It's more like the

RS-232 data that used to flow between computers and modems, with outputs connected directly to the inputs they feed.[1]

Maybe some day computers will take over all our information handling, and every signal will be addressable packets. Until then, signals need to travel as voltages or serial streams on a cable. As a filmmaker, you should how to do this without losing signal quality.

ANALOG WIRING

When the phone company made up the rules for audio wiring, more than a century ago, most devices were powered by the audio signal itself. Audio levels had to be measured in terms of how much power they had available, as decibels related to a standard wattage.

Transferring this power efficiently meant paying attention to both voltage and *impedance*, a measure of how much current a device needs to work properly. Get either one wrong, and the result was bad signal levels and distortion.

This idea of power coupling, and paying attention to power and impedance, persisted for decades. Until the mid-1970s, stations and studios were wired using principles developed for hand-cranked phones.

Impedance is still important today, though nowhere near as much. That's because the analog equipment we use is designed differently. Modern circuits use just a tiny amount of current from the input signal, and react to its voltage instead. This makes life a lot easier, and lets you do things like splitting a signal to two or more different devices with a simple Y-cable. Connections are about as complicated as Christmas tree lights.

However, current and impedance still matter for some equipment. Headphones and conventional speakers need power from the signal, and should be somewhat matched to the amplifier output. Connecting more than a couple of them to a single amplifier channel often degrades the signal quality, and may damage the amp.

Microphones are a special case, depending on their type (see Chapter 6 for more about this). Most of the mics used for dialog pickup have internal power supplies and work as voltage-based devices. Impedance is still somewhat important, because the voltages are so tiny, but minor impedance mismatches don't cause problems. Other types of mics—including popular ones for voice-over and music recording—turn sound power directly into electric power. Power transfers are critical for them, and you must pay attention to impedance.

Digital connections also usually require matched impedance. That's not because of power issues. It's because the very high frequencies involved are subject to reflections within the wiring itself. It's the same effect as acoustic waves bouncing off a wall and cancelling each other, which we talked about toward the end of Chapter 1.

---

[1] Even SDI video, the high definition standard in modern TV facilities, works this way.

Ohm's Law

I was an electronics geek in high school. Plaid flannel shirt, heavy-framed glasses, and even a slide rule at my belt (well, it was the 1960s). That slide rule helped me solve problems in Ohm's Law and its derivations, an essential set of formulas predicting how electrons move from one place to another. Take any two electrical characteristics such as voltage or resistance, and these equations let you determine things like wattage and amperage. Impedance behaves like resistance, and follows Ohm's Law.

While the Law has many permutations, they're easy to remember if you think of the triangles in Figure 3.1. The letters stand for Volts, Amps, Ohms (Ω), and Watts. To remember the equation for one value on a triangle, check the locations of the other two. If they're both on the bottom, multiply them. If one's on top, divide. So volts = amps × ohms, and amps = watts/volts.

Figure 3.1 The easy way to remember Ohm's Law. Engineers use different letters, but the meaning is the same.

It gets useful very quickly. Want to plug three 750 watt lights into a 20 amp generator? Well, the three lights want 2,250 watts total. On the right triangle, we see watts is at the top. We know volts, since it's standard 110 volt wiring. So we divide 2,250 by 110, and get an answer of 20.45 amps. It's close enough that the generator would probably work.[2]

Watts, of course, are the measure of electrical power—the stuff that gets things done. This is as true in audio as in lighting. When I was in high school, almost all recording used dynamic or ribbon mics, which convert the movement of air molecules directly into electricity. Molecules are small, so the resulting tiny signal was measured in millionths of a watt. Even the mixers and preamps that boosted the mics' output dealt with only around a thousandth of a watt. To use these tiny signals efficiently, you had to connect to inputs with the right number of ohms. It was common to have a transformer or a resistor network between audio gear, just to match the impedance and power.

Fortunately, that's mostly ancient history. With most modern equipment, impedances just have to be in the same range. But another leg of Ohm's Law, the voltage, still has to match. Ancient history has a lot to do with the voltages we choose.

Analog's strange standards

There are two voltages you should remember when working with today's analog audio wiring. They're not intuitive.

---

[2] But remember, the lamps draw a little extra current when they're first turned on. And the generator will definitely be running at its maximum. So Murphy's Law suggests the whole thing will blow out in the middle of an important take. Make one light smaller, or get a bigger generator.

✳ TIDBIT

Where the silly numbers come from

Nobody ever said "let's make pro level equal 1.228 volts, just to confuse people." Those analog standards began life as the very friendly "1 milliwatt" for pro gear, and "1 volt" for consumer. Then things got strange.

About a century ago, the phone company decided that the power level on an audio cable should be 1 milliwatt nominal. Since they owned most of the audio cables in the US, it was easy to establish this as the standard. They called it 0 dBm, where the *m* meant *1 milliwatt*. Since decibels are ratios, any audio power from the tiniest microphone signal to the biggest amplifier output could be specified in decibels referred to that milliwatt.

It's difficult to measure wattage on an audio cable, but very easy to measure voltage. Phone lines were always 600 ohms impedance, and Ohm's Law says 1 milliwatt at that impedance equals .775 volts. They built voltmeters with a handy zero on the scale at that point, and marked the rest of the scale in decibels above and below that voltage (Figure 3.2). You could look at one of those meters and see if the lines were running properly.

Figure 3.2 A modern analog audio level meter. The upper scale is marked VU (Volume Units), but it matches the phone company's original meters.

Broadcasters rented phone company lines for everything from transmitter links to elaborate country-wide networks, so stations adopted the 0 dBm standard as well.

Or at least, they tried to. Problem was, components in the phone company's meters actually added distortion to the signal they were measuring. It wasn't enough distortion to disturb a phone call, but the broadcasters didn't like it. Rather than invent a new meter, they isolated the components with a resistor . . . solving the problem, but also lowering the readings by –4 dB. So they compensated by raising their standard level to +4 dBm. On a 600 ohm line, that equals 1.228 volts.

Of course, Ohm's Law insists that +4 dBm—a level in milli*watts*—can equal a precise voltage only at one impedance. So two other standards evolved. In the United States, the National Association of Broadcasters took just the voltage part of the phone company standard and called it 0 dBu—the "u" stands for *unterminated*: an open circuit with no impedance. Modern pro gear is often specified as "+4 dBu" . . . which means 1.228 volts, as measured on the old-fashioned broadcasters' meter.

That irrational number irritated Europeans, so their International Electrotechnical Commission picked a much simpler reference: for them, 1 volt would equal 0 dBV (decibels referred to a volt), and this was their standard for professional equipment. It turned out that tubed hi-fi equipment worked best with an input 10 dB below this reference, or .316 volts. Low-budget studios adopted this equipment, so −10 dBV became the "professional/consumer" standard—what we call *prosumer.*

- Professional equipment usually has a nominal line level[3] of 1.228 volts—roughly, a volt and a quarter. This is what you'll find at the line output of most mixers, or what you should feed the line input of some cameras, recorders, and powered loudspeakers. It usually appears on XLR or ¼" TRS phone connectors.
- Prosumer and consumer gear usually likes a nominal line level of .316 volts— call it a third of a volt—which is what you often find on *phono* or *miniplug* connectors.
- There are different nominal levels for various microphones, discussed in Chapter 8.

These are important voltages to remember. If you plug a 110-volt lamp into a 220-volt socket, the results will be disastrous. Similarly, if you plug a pro analog output into a phono or miniplug input, you'll probably ruin the signal with distortion. Going in the other direction (consumer output to pro input) usually has a lot of electronic noise. Either of these conditions pollutes your track with problems that can't be fixed later.

You can't solve the problem with a simple XLR-to-miniplug adapter. Pro and consumer gear requires some other accessories before it can be cross-connected successfully. Details start on page 88.

Fortunately, dBm and dBu are functionally equivalent in most modern equipment other than microphones. So we really have only two standards to worry about. Since they're all based on the same rules of physics and math, they're easily related (Table 3.1).

Fortunately also, this problem doesn't exist with digital wiring. In the digital world, voltage levels don't change depending on the signal, and having the wrong voltage won't give you noise or distortion.[4]

---

[3] Nominal levels are what you can expect as the long-term average on a fully produced show, and are the levels you'd see on the tone at the front of a tape. See page 337. "Line" means we're measuring the output of a mixer or recorder, as opposed to much smaller "mic levels."

[4] Instead, it'll either be perfect—because the equipment has compensated for the voltage differences—or you won't hear anything at all. This doesn't mean there aren't other problems, but we'll get to those in the section on digital wiring.

Table 3.1 Voltage compared to dBV and dBu

	Level in dBV	Voltage	Level in dBu (or dBm across 600 ohms)	
	+6	2.0	+8.2	
	+4	1.6	+6.2	
	+1.78	1.228	+4	(Pro standard)
	+0	1	+2.2	
	−2.2	0.775	0	
	−6	0.5	−3.8	
	−8.2	0.388	−6	
(Consumer standard)	−10	0.316	−7.8	
	−20	0.1	−17.8	

Nominal levels

Analog equipment is designed to be adjusted for "zero level," where the VU meter shows a zero somewhere near 2/3 of its scale. This is the steady operating voltage that results in the best compromise between noise and distortion. Digital equipment calibrates its meters differently, putting zero at Full Scale (page 40) and the nominal level somewhere between −24 dBFS and −12 dBFS (see Chapter 17).

But audio is a constantly changing voltage, not a constant tone at a particular level. The actual range any piece of analog equipment can handle may extend from greater than +12 dB above zero, to around 80 dB below it. At the lowest levels, signals compete with internal noise. At the highest, there's too much distortion.

"Too much distortion" is completely subjective, of course. With analog gear, you can redefine the standard level depending on how much noise or distortion you want to tolerate. Figure 3.3 shows how this could work. Dialog is recorded at a relatively low average level, to avoid having distortion build up over multiple generations. Symphonic music is recorded a little louder, since distortion is harder to spot on orchestral instruments than in voice. Rock music is recorded with a high average level; many pop producers go out of their way to add analog distortion to their songs.

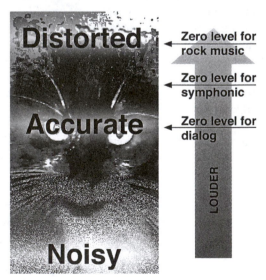

Figure 3.3 In the analog world, zero level is arbitrary. It depends on how much distortion you can tolerate.

☞ **ROSE'S RULES**

Numbers don't make it professional

+4 dBu and −10 dBV are just voltages. There's no physical reason why one should sound any better than the other.[5] However, the higher voltage standard is usually used in higher-quality equipment. That's a marketing decision, not physics.

Equipment manufacturers make similar choices. They'll specify a higher level if they want to brag about low noise, or a lower one so they can brag about low distortion.

In theory, digital recording eliminates these decisions. Noise is determined by the number of bits in the signal, and there's no distortion until full scale. But all-digital recording exists only in theory: sooner or later, there's going to be an analog microphone or speaker involved. So the same level considerations apply.

Cross-connecting −10 dBV and +4 dBu equipment

If you plug the output of a consumer-level mixer into a professional recorder or camera, you may get a usable signal. As Table 3.1 indicates, a consumer mixer's idea of zero level output is only about 12 dB lower than a pro recorder's input. But since the signal will be that much closer to the recorder's noise floor, the recording will be about 12 dB noisier—that's four times the noise voltage. The best solution is to put a small amplifier in between the units, converting the mixer's −10 dBV output to +4 dBu.

If you plug the output of a professional-level mixer into most computer inputs or prosumer camera line inputs, it'll be four times as much voltage as expected. You'll probably hear bad distortion. This distortion occurs in the input stages, so lowering a software volume control won't help. You need a network of resistors between the two units to lower the voltage.

Some high-end pro equipment uses transformers at the input or output. These solve a lot of problems and can contribute to better sound, but need to see a proper impedance as well as level. They also might need a slightly different connection than non-transformer gear; it depends on the design. Check the manual, and follow the tips in Chapters 8 and 11.

Avoiding noise with balanced wiring

While the idea of impedance matching has mostly been abandoned, another telephone-company idea is still very much with us. Phone calls travel over hundreds of miles of

---

[5] Until you get down to the level of molecular thermal noise, which really isn't important in the kind of signals we're talking about.

low-quality wire, often near power lines and other interference sources, without picking up too much noise. The phone company's secret? *Balanced wiring.* It's used today by professional broadcast and sound studios for the same reason.

Professional mics are almost always balanced, because the tiny mic signal is easily damaged by noise pickup. But editing and dubbing setups often aren't, and can be plagued by noise, low-frequency hum, and zaps or buzzes that appear related to nearby lamp dimmers or electric motors. Here's what's really happening inside your equipment:

The sensitive circuits in audio amplifiers and processors need a reference they can be sure is zero volts. They compare the input signal to this reference, amplify and process as necessary, and generate an output signal that's also compared to the reference. Designers designate one point within a piece of equipment, usually connected to an external ground screw or the grounding pin of the power plug, and call it "ground": this is zero volts,[6] and all voltages within the equipment are referenced to it.

That's fine for a single piece of equipment. Problems arise when you try to connect equipment together. All the pieces have to agree on a reference zero. But if current is flowing on a wire between one reference point and another, Ohm's Law insists there will be a voltage difference between those points, because of the wire's resistance. That voltage is where noise enters the system. It's picked up magnetically.

In any editing room or shooting stage, there's a lot of magnetism being generated by high-current AC wires going to wall outlets and lights. Inside the equipment, the reference point keeps moving in response to the power line frequency. It also reacts to any glitches in the electrical system, from things like motors and circuit breakers. That's where the hum and noise comes from.

The signal wire itself also acts as an antenna, picking up interference. You can eliminate some of this by wrapping a shield around the signal wire, and analog audio cables almost always include a copper braid or metal foil for this purpose. The shield is connected to ground and shorts out the interference before it can reach the signal wire. But for that to work, ground has to be the same on both ends of the wire. Otherwise, it makes an even more efficient loop antenna. Figure 3.4 shows how this mess can happen.

 Sound 3.1 lets you hear a typical result, as it might get mixed with dialog. The noise is a complex signal with lots of harmonics. You can't remove it without damaging the underlying recording.

These ground "loops" are difficult to predict, and can appear even in very simple installations. In a practical studio, there are lots of places ground loops can form: the grounding in on power cords, and the shields on unbalanced audio and video wiring, computer FireWire or USB, RS-422 control, and even cable television.

---

[6] The concept of zero volts isn't related to the nominal levels discussed above. Levels are long-term averages. Zero volts happens when the sound it represents is halfway between compression and rarefaction, so nearby molecules are at their original position.

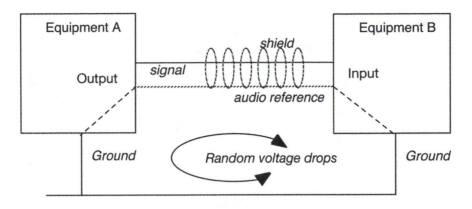

Figure 3.4 What does "zero voltage" actually mean in this circuit?
A ground loop in action.

Balanced wiring

Professional equipment solves this problem by using two closely spaced conductors twisted together. The audio is balanced equally between these wires, flowing in a positive direction on one wire and simultaneously in a negative direction on the other. Instead of comparing incoming voltages to a reference zero, the equipment merely looks at the voltage difference between the two wires. Figure 3.5 shows the basic setup.

The two conductors in a balanced wiring scheme are often labeled + and – for convenience, but they're not strictly positive and negative. Analog audio is an alternating current, with electrons flowing back and forth depending on whether the original sound wave was in compression or rarefaction, so either wire might carry a positive voltage at one moment and a negative one the next. What's important is that the other wire has the same voltage but of *opposite polarity* at that same moment.

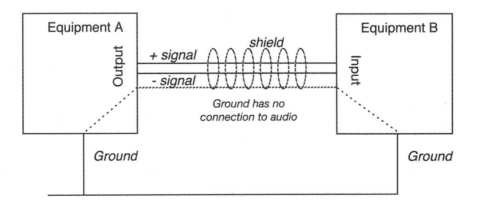

Figure 3.5 Balanced wiring eliminates ground loops.

The two wires are twisted closely together in a single cable, so any interference radiated into the cable gets picked up equally by both wires. Since subsequent circuits look for voltage differences between the wires, the noise is ignored.

Figure 3.6 shows this happening in a balanced circuit. In part A, the top wire carries 1 volt positive while the bottom one carries 1 volt negative. The difference between them is the audio signal of 2 volts. In part B, a volt of noise is also picked up by the cable. The top wire gets one additional volt and now carries 2 volts positive. The bottom wire also gets an additional volt, which adds to its negative signal for a total of 0 volts. The difference between the wires is still exactly 2 volts.

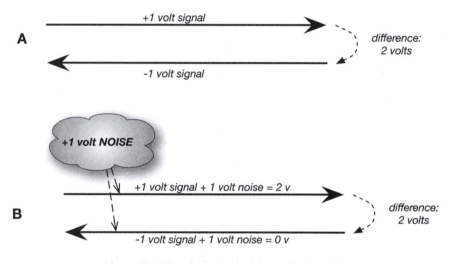

Figure 3.6 How balanced wiring rejects noise.

☞ ROSE'S RULES

When you can ignore balancing

- In a simple studio setup, with only a few pieces of equipment and short cable lengths, noise pickup may be so low that balanced wiring isn't necessary for line-level signals.
- If you do hear ground loops in a simple unbalanced setup, the easiest cure might be to break the loop. See Chapter 11.
- Microphone signals are much weaker than line level, and more prone to interference. Balanced wiring is almost always necessary for microphones. The only common exception is the very short cable from a camera-mounted mic or XLR adapter to the camera itself.

There are many different ways to build a balanced input or output circuit, and some are more successful than others at rejecting noise. But balancing will always add to cost and complexity, so it's often omitted in prosumer or music-industry audio equipment. That equipment is called *unbalanced*, or occasionally *single-ended*.

You can't tell a wire by its connector

Balanced wiring is sometimes mistakenly called "XLR wiring." That's because it matches the plugs and jacks introduced by connector manufacturer Cannon in their XLR series (Figure 3.7). But it's dangerous to assume that any XLR plug or jack is balanced. While most manufacturers reserve these connectors for balanced circuits, there are some exceptions. Check the spec sheet to be sure.

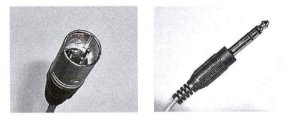

Figure 3.7 XLR-style male connector.

Figure 3.8 Three-conductor phone plug, sometimes used for balanced signals.

You can also get into trouble assuming that other kinds of connectors *aren't* balanced. Some manufacturers save money and space by putting balanced signals on three-conductor phone jacks. From the front panel, these jacks look identical to unbalanced two-conductor ones. But if you connect a three-conductor phone plug—known as *tip-ring-sleeve* or *TRS* and also used for stereo headphones (Figure 3.8)—you can access the balanced circuit. Again, check the specs; some equipment uses TRS jacks as a way to simultaneously connect an unbalanced input and output to external processors.

⚠ **WARNING**

Y? Not!

The worst thing you can do to a TRS balanced output is use a stereo Y splitter cable to feed both channels of a stereo device. This kind of cable has the tip of the TRS plug going to one phono plug's tip, and the ring of the TRS going to the other.

If you use it this way, you will hear a signal on each end of the Y. If you listen to the result on stereo speakers, you'll probably hear the track.

But the left and right channels will be of opposite polarity, because they were originally one balanced signal. If the channels are combined—which can happen easily in broadcast, home video, or Web use—they cancel each other and the track disappears!

Cross-connecting balanced and unbalanced wiring

You can plug a balanced output into an unbalanced input or output without damaging the signal, but this unbalances the entire connection. The connecting cable loses its noise immunity. (If the wires are short or in a benign environment, this may be perfectly acceptable.)

To make this cross-connection work, you have to make sure that both devices see the signal path they've been designed for. The best way to do this depends on how the balanced circuit was designed. Tables 3.2 and 3.3 are intended just as a starting point for systems using modern video equipment and might not always yield the best noise performance. There are tips for debugging these connections in Chapter 11.

The best way to hook balanced and unbalanced equipment together is not to attempt a direct connection, but to use a separate balancing transformer or electronic interface at the unbalanced end. This lets you use balanced wiring, with its inherent noise immunity. It can also provide a necessary voltage conversion as well, since unbalanced devices are usually designed for –10 dBV and balanced ones are usually +4 dBu.

Prosumer digital cameras often have unbalanced microphone inputs. While unbalanced mic cables can be used for a few feet, realistic distances between subject and camera are too long for this kind of wiring. A transformer or electronic adapter, or most mixers and preamps, will let you use balanced connections. Mic to camera hookups are described in Chapter 8.

Table 3.2 Directly connecting unbalanced sources to balanced inputs

Unbalanced output	Balanced input		
	Conductor	XLR	Phone
Signal	+	Pin 2	Tip
Ground	–	Pin 3	Ring
(no connection)*	Shield	Pin 1	Sleeve**

* If you hear excessive hum, try connecting the unbalanced ground to this point as well.
** Some balanced phone-plug inputs are designed so that you can plug an unbalanced two-conductor plug directly into them.

Table 3.3 Directly connecting balanced sources to unbalanced inputs

XLR	Balanced output		Unbalanced input
	Phone	Conductor	
Pin 2	Tip	+	Signal
Pin 3	Ring	–	(no connection)*
Pin 1	Sleeve	Shield	Shield

* Some transformer-balanced outputs won't work unless you connect pin 3 to the shield.

Other cable types

Internet audiophiles sometimes write about the need for special oxygen-free cables, often with patented braided construction or solid-gold connectors, or ones that get "broken in" by playing specific music for a certain time. These hookups allegedly have a unique sound that only people with golden ears can appreciate. They certainly add a unique, gold-like price tag to the installation.[7]

Nobody has been able to show me or my speaker-designing friends evidence that these cables make any measurable difference, when compared to much cheaper wires with similar electrical specifications. There isn't even a body of repeatable studies suggesting *non-measurable* differences that are identified by trained listeners. I believe the people who make these things should be forced to spend time in special oxygen-free listening rooms.

However, two other cable developments with esoteric names are worth considering for analog hookups: Star-Quad and Category-5 Ethernet cable. They're also both much cheaper than the fancy audiophile cables, and well within the budget of any filmmaker.

Star-Quad

Balanced cable typically has two conductors loosely twisted within a shield. If noise attacks both conductors equally (Figure 3.9A), a balanced input will be able to reject the noise completely. This is how pro mics are able to avoid all the radiated junk from lamp dimmers, HMI ballasts, computers, and other noise sources on a film set.

But if noise attacks from the side of a twisted pair (Figure 3.9B), the distance from the noise source to each wire will be slightly different, because of the thickness of the cable itself. Each wire will pick up the noise at a slightly voltage or phase. When this happens, the balanced input circuit can't reject it as well.

When two wires are carrying the same signal and very close together, they act like a single antenna centered between them. Star-Quad puts balanced wiring on four

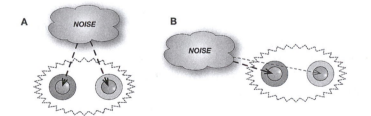

Figure 3.9 Geometry makes a difference. If two wires receive noise equally (A), balanced circuits can reject it. But if noise reaches each wire differently (B), rejection won't be as good.

---

[7] As I write this, Amazon.com sells a few brands of 20′ speaker cable at $48,500 for a stereo pair. I can think of a whole lot of other things I'd rather get from Amazon for that money.

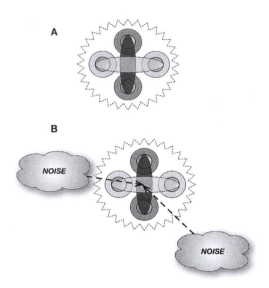

Figure 3.10 Star-Quad has four conductors, two for each leg of the circuit. When combined, they pick up noise equally for better rejection.

individual conductors, wrapped around each other, with a pair carrying signals in each direction. This makes the pairs act like two antennas sharing the same center. Figure 3.10 shows how it works. The ovals between the wires in part A are the virtual antennas; part B shows how no matter where the noise comes from, it gets picked up equally by both.

The basic principle was invented in early telephone days, and popularized some years ago by wire-maker Canare. They didn't trademark the name, so Star-Quad is now available from a number of companies. It's also known as *double-balanced* wiring. It adds about $10 to the cost of a 50' cable, and is easily worth the price for microphone connections. Since line-level analog is stronger and more immune to noise pickup, and digital interconnections aren't subject to this kind of noise at all, it's not needed for non-microphone signals.

👆 TRY THIS

Do it yourself

If you're soldering your own Star-Quad cables, you'll notice that the wire has two pairs of conductors of the same color—usually one pair blue, and one white. You must connect same-colored wires together at both ends. With XLR connectors, standard practice is to connect both white wires to pin 2, both blue wires to pin 3, and shield to pin 1.

If you don't do this—or use the four conductors for two separate signals—the cable loses its noise-rejection benefit.

Category-5 for audio

Balanced wiring achieves most of its noise rejection through its dual conductors, rather than its shield. So does a lot of computer wiring, which might not be shielded at all. Standard Category- 5 cable (also known as UTP, and used for Ethernet) has four pairs of balanced twisted wires with no shield.

High-quality Cat-5 cable (like Belden's Mediatwist) is built to very rigorous balancing standards, usually much higher than ordinary audio cable. It can be perfectly appropriate for line-level audio in electrically quiet environments. In fact, the balancing can be so good that different signals can be carried on different pairs in the same cable, without significant crosstalk. Since there's no shielding, you might not want to bundle it with sources of high-frequency noise (like video or timecode). Mic-level signals are a little bit too delicate for unshielded wire. But +4 dBu line-level signals from tape decks, mixers, and effects can be carried perfectly. Even though data cables are built to higher specs than most audio ones, economies of scale often make them cheaper.

Category-5 can introduce losses, compared to a more standard wire. You want a cable with low capacity between conductors, so high frequencies aren't lost. This is a matter of design and what the insulation is made from. There can also be a tiny voltage loss, since the conductors are slightly thinner than most audio cables—but it's negligible because there's so little current flowing. You should also pay attention to mechanical issues: audio cables with stranded conductors and thicker insulation can take stress better than thin solid data cable. Cat-5 is designed to be crimped into RJ-45 Ethernet connectors, not stripped and soldered to an XLR, and won't stand up to repeated bending.

As you can guess, Cat-5 won't give you any noise protection on unbalanced signals. It may not even be appropriate for low-cost balanced gear that might not have good common-mode rejection. Furthermore, classic transformer-coupled equipment might not like its 110-ohm characteristic—though that probably isn't significant for short runs. *Balun* transformers (the name comes from "balanced/unbalanced") are available to solve these problems: they have appropriate connectors for audio or even video on one side, and RJ-45 connectors on the other. While these transformers can cost a few dozen dollars for each end, using them with low-cost and easily available Ethernet cables is cost-effective in some applications—particularly where there are long runs, or in situations where the cable is subject to damage and may need frequent replacement.

Radio Systems, Inc. sells pre-built cables and adapters for use with Ethernet. Their StudioHub+ system is a range of reasonably priced XLR and other adapters, balancing adapters, mic preamps, headphone amps, and other accessories, all with RJ-45 connectors for Category-5 or better cable. It's designed for studio installations, but can be handy for ad-hoc shoots and editing or viewing setups. StudioHub+ dealers like <u>Markertek.com</u> and <u>BSW.com</u> also carry shielded Ethernet cables for even more noise immunity.

DIGITAL WIRING

Since digital audio cables carry only ones and zeroes, they're unlikely to be affected by noise and ground loops. However, digital audio uses very fast signals. Individual bits are sent serially in bi-phase format, so a 48 kHz s/r signal can have frequencies higher than 6 *mega*Hertz!

At these speeds you're not dealing with audio any more. You're in radio land. The construction of the wire itself, along with the impedances of connected devices, becomes significant. Even if a cable successfully carries the high frequencies, unmatched impedances can cause reflections within the wire itself. These can destroy the signal.

Impedance matching is simply a matter of using cables rated for the particular kind of digital signal, rather than just grabbing something with the right connectors. Termination usually occurs automatically in digital equipment, but can be ruined if you try to route a digital signal using analog wiring techniques. Ordinary patchbays, switchers, and splitters can cause drop-outs.

☞ ROSE'S RULES

- Always use a cable matched to the impedance of the digital audio signal.
- Make sure cables are properly terminated.

Linear audio vs. Packet audio

Until recently, digital audio was sent as a continuous stream. Cables go from the output of one device to the input of the next, just like they do with analog. This is still the simplest and most reliable way to get high-quality audio from one place to another, so we'll address it first.

There are also emerging standards that break audio signals into addressable packets, and then route them like computer networks. Standard computer routers and switches are often employed, and in many cases the audio signal can plug directly into the network interface RJ-45 of a computer.

Linear digital audio wiring

Mono or stereo digital audio wiring almost always follows one of two electrical standards.[8] These standards have been around for more than two decades, and are supported by almost every piece of pro digital equipment. There is absolutely no difference in sound quality between them.

Both channels of a stereo pair are carried as a single, interleaved data stream. Signals travel from output to input, just as they do with analog wiring. There are status bits to identify sample rate and other signal characteristics, and error detection bits to verify connections. But there is none of the handshaking or data exchange used in most computer connections.

---

[8] There are also two data formats, professional and consumer, but for practical purposes the data formats are identical.

Audio levels are implicit—signals are referenced to zero decibels Full Scale (dBFS), where every bit is turned on—rather than depending on particular voltages.

AES/EBU

This standard was set by the international Audio Engineering Society and the European Broadcast Union, and is found on virtually all professional digital audio equipment. The signal is electrically similar to RS-422 computer data, and to TTL logic levels, using 5 volt balanced signals with 110 ohm impedance.

AES/EBU usually terminates in XLR connectors, looking like standard balanced analog audio.[9] However, you should use 110 ohm cable designed for digital audio.

Or use Ethernet connections. RJ-45 jacks and Category-5 cable are close enough to the desired impedance and will work perfectly. You might need to solder XLR connectors onto the cable, which can be tricky because Cat-5 is a thin solid wire with little flexibility. Plan for some strain and vibration relief. Or use crimpable XLR connectors, or XLRs with RJ-45 jacks, available from electronics suppliers.

S/pdif

This standard was invented by consumer audio manufacturers (Sony/Philips Digital Interface Format) and adopted by electronic manufacturers' associations in Europe and Japan. It's also known as *coaxial* digital, and occasionally as IEC-958.

S/pdif is electrically similar to composite video, though at a lower voltage. It puts a half-volt signal on 75-ohm coaxial cable, terminating in either phono or BNC video connectors. Standard RG-59 analog video cables, available from electronic chain stores, are perfectly acceptable for s/pdif.

Toslink

The two-channel linear digital data standard also often appears in an optical version. Toslink, invented by Toshiba, turns s/pdif's squarewave voltage into flashes of light from an LED and carries it on optical fibers. Toslink is frequently found as the main digital connection on computers and consumer equipment, including DVD players and home theater amplifiers. Its advantage is that the fiber can't act as an antenna or ground loop path, so transmission is noise-free and doesn't cause problems with connected analog equipment. The disadvantage is physics: because of light loss, fibers must be much shorter than AES/EBU or s/pdif cables. While optical cables as long as 50' are available, most connections are in the order of a few feet. Low-cost active adapters to convert between Toslink, AES/EBU, and s/pdif are available from most pro supplies.

Toslink connectors are designed to assure good light transfer (Figure 3.11). Toslink equipment often ships with plastic plugs blocking the jacks, to protect the components

---

[9] Some multi-channel gear puts AES/EBU on smaller connectors to save space. Adapters are available.

> ⚠ **WARNING**
>
> ## Don't let the connectors fool you!
>
> - AES/EBU connections look like standard mic jacks. But even high quality mic cable doesn't have the necessary impedance characteristic, and data echoes can destroy the signal.
> - S/pdif phono connections look like standard unbalanced analog wires. But analog phono cables are also the wrong impedance and can hurt the signal.
>
> In both of the above cases, use cables rated for digital audio. They're usually not much more expensive than the analog ones.
>
> - S/pdif on either phono or BNC jacks also looks like a video connection. Surprise: standard video cables work perfectly with s/pdif!

and curious eyes. These blocking plugs look like square pegs sticking out of the jack (Figure 3.12); just pull them out when you want to use the connector.

Some laptops and a few portable recorders have optical digital connections as part of their analog stereo line connections, on combination mini-jacks that look like an ordinary headphone jack. They switch to digital when they sense the proper connector. Toslink-to-mini cables and adapters are available from electronics suppliers.

Home theater equipment also often uses Toslink to supply multichannel Dolby or DTS sound for home theater receivers. The data format is different, so the equipment usually provides a software selection to choose which will be active.

Figure 3.11 Toslink jack and plug for optical digital.

Figure 3.12 If a Toslink jack has a square peg sticking out, just remove it.

⚠ **WARNING**

Beware of combination analog/digital mini-jacks

Making an optical input or output as part a conventional headphone or mic jack shows considerable ingenuity, and certainly saves money and panel space for manufacturers. But it doesn't work well.

The problem is tiny pieces of dirt, carried into the jack when you insert a plug. The electrical parts of the connector can push the dirt aside, so mics and headphones work reliably. But the dirt inevitably gets shoved into the bottom of the connector, right in front of the optical data components. After a few dozen connections, you have to blow dust out. After a few dozen more, the connector's springs can't hold the optical plugs in place and things stop working entirely. These connectors are usually machine-soldered onto the motherboard, making replacement a very expensive repair.

On the other hand, the optical version of computer audio input or output sounds a lot better than the motherboard's analog i/o. So it's worth maintaining those connections:

- Insert short miniplug optical cables when you first unpack the equipment, and tape them in place! The other end of the cables can be re-plugged as needed, particularly if they have more reliable Toslink connectors.
- Label the connectors as "optical only." Each time you put an analog plug into one of them, you're increasing the likelihood of failure.

MADI

The idea of carrying just two channels at a time is *so* twentieth century! When the standards were developed in 1985, they were the most that you could put into an affordable cable or interface device. But modern computer chips can handle a lot more data, and have been adapted for multichannel digital audio.

MADI (Multichannel Audio Digital Interface) uses video cables or glass fibers to carry as many as 64 simultaneous channels, combined into a single data stream. It's supported by dozens of manufacturers, and is often used to replace complex wiring around multichannel audio software and mixing consoles. Many film and video record-ists use the system to simplify multi-mic setups for performance and sports shoots, and for reality programming where lots of wireless receivers have to be located far from the mixing position. MADI-equipped remote mic preamps, recorders, and adapters are available from large film sound rental companies.

While MADI uses computer technology, it's not networking. Cables are run from a single multichannel output to the appropriate input; there are no addresses or routers to deal with. Figure 3.13 shows a typical MADI setup. A standalone converter, which

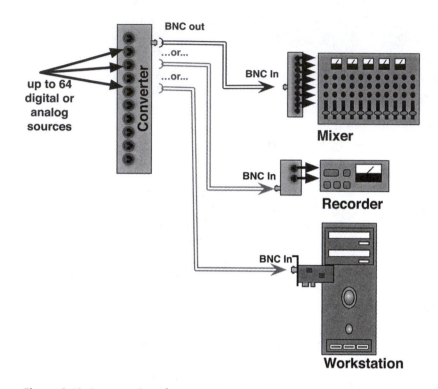

Figure 3.13 Some options for a MADI setup. Only one of the cables shown can be used at any one time.

may include mic preamps and analog converters, shuffles the digital audio streams onto a single BNC (professional video) connector. A video cable then carries the signal to an output converter, which sorts the signals out again and sends them to a mixer . . . or possibly a recorder . . . or possibly a multichannel MADI input card in a computer. The "*or possibly*" wording is because only one of those functions can exist at a time. And if you want to send a signal from the device back to the source, you'll need another cable and set of converters.

While MADI isn't as flexible as packet-based systems like Dante (discussed below), it's a lot simpler and more reliable. It doesn't need programming, just plugging. And if something stops working, chances are you just need to change the cable. Some MADI equipment accommodates dual cables with automatic switchover in case of failure.

AUDIO AS IP

We're used to media streaming over the Web. Requests begin as packets at your computer, get carried to a nearby router, then jump to the World Wide Web. Addresses on the packets help them find their way to an appropriate server. Then, if all goes well, the server starts sending packets of information (or movies, or music) back. Those returning packets also have addresses, which let them find the way to your local computer. Meanwhile, a planet full of other users are sending and receiving similar packets with other music, emails, software, and sometimes soft-core. It's really a miracle of modern technology.

Since the Web already has standards to handle media streams, and competition has driven down the price of the necessary equipment, manufacturers have adapted the technology for smaller networks carrying higher-quality audio. A handful of proprietary systems are used in broadcast studios and large concert sound systems, and on shoots. Each adds refinements for their specific application, but that also makes them incompatible unless you can find licensed translation software. Eventually there'll be open, free standards that all manufacturers adhere to. For the meantime, Dante[10] is the popular current choice in our industry.

Dante uses standard Gigabit routers and Cat-5e Ethernet cables to carry up to 1,024 audio channels—certainly more than any film or video setup would require— along with control and other data. Packets travel bi-directionally, so a single cable can send multiple mics from a shooting area to the mixer, while simultaneously carrying a reference mix back to the director and cue channels for talent and boom operators. Control software lets you route individual signals to specific inputs on mixers, and a "virtual soundcard" app lets standard audio workstations record or play back through the network using the computer's built-in Ethernet jack. Figure 3.14 shows a typical network.

Dante networks are often set up for specific shoots with dedicated cables, but the system can also piggy-back on existing business or campus networks with a slight sacrifice in channel count and latency.

The biggest downside of Dante—or any other audio-over-IP network—is setup and debugging. Unlike linear audio systems, including the multichannel MADI, you can't just plug a cable into a monitor box and listen for signals. Even if the hardware is behaving properly, there's no sound until each source and destination has been identified and assigned in the control software. Other network traffic, user errors including multiple Ethernet paths, and similar gremlins can disrupt the audio. Keeping a complex network running can require IT skills as well as audio ones.

Other audio wiring

USB

This computer connection standard is used by a lot of audio input/output devices, and can be the best way to connect audio devices to your computer. USB boxes are available with balanced mic- and line-level connections and with Toslink or s/pdif digital audio. Some also include mixer or jog-wheel remote controls that can be recognized by audio software. Audio-to-USB input cables are also available—they

---

[10] A product of Audinate Pty, Ltd (Australia).

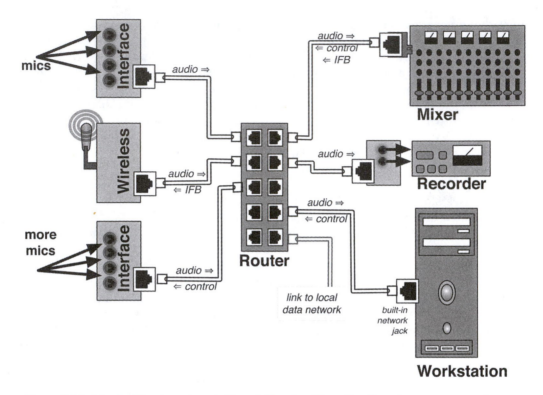

Figure 3.14 A typical Dante network. Signals flow in either direction, from any source to any output.

have the same digitizing circuitry as the boxes, but it's buried in their connectors. You can even get USB microphones, which have digitizers built into the mic body and connect with computer cables.

USB audio devices come in a variety of styles and price points. Some meet the highest professional standards; others are barely adequate for voice conferencing. While USB may be the most convenient way to deal with audio in a computer environment, merely having that kind of connection doesn't guarantee quality.

USB 3.0, the latest version, is much faster than its two predecessors: it really speeds up connections to hard drives and other bulk data transfers. But it presents no real advantage for real-time audio, and there are reports of driver issues when using older interface boxes with new computers. If you hear crackles or similar problems, look for updates at both the audio manufacturer's and operating system publisher's websites.

FireWire

This connection standard, also known as IEEE Standard 1394 and iLink, was designed to let computers transfer large amounts of data quickly. It was adopted by digital video camera manufacturers to send audio and video simultaneously to an editing system, but can also be used for AES/EBU-format audio transfers.

However, FireWire is much more complicated and expensive than is needed for simple two-channel audio interconnections. FireWire audio adapters are often used in music production to get multitrack signals in and out of a computer in a single pass.

Thunderbolt

This standard, designed by Intel and Apple, is replacing FireWire on newer systems. At present there are only a few high-end audio and video interfaces available, and there's no real advantage to using them for production sound. The situation was similar in the early days of USB and FireWire, and eventually we'll see a whole infrastructure.

SDI

Modern large video facilities are often wired using Serial Digital Interface, which carries uncompressed digital video over coaxial cables. The SDI standards allow up to 16 channels of embedded audio in the bitstream, though many installations carry their audio separately. Adapters to convert SDI to AES/EBU, MADI, and Dante are available from broadcast suppliers.

HDMI

This video connection standard can support up to eight channels of high-resolution digital audio, though not all HDMI connections are equipped for sound. Its primary use in a film/video environment is carrying audio along with HD picture, from an optical player or similar source to a video monitor or flat-screen TV. The TV often directs the audio signal to a dedicated digital output, where it can be sent to a home theater receiver. HDMI to SDI and AES/EBU adapters are available, but at present nobody seems to be making dedicated audio equipment with this connector.

Multitrack

Small multitrack digital recorders often use proprietary data formats. Two of these recorders have become de facto standards: the Alesis ADAT (eight channels optical on a Toslink connector) in music studios, and the Tascam DTRS (eight channels electrical on a DB-25 connector) in film and video. Cables and adapters are available from broadcast suppliers.

Dolby E

This format carries up to eight digital audio channels in a single AES/EBU bitstream, used in very large facilities to simplify wiring and allow surround sound on stereo digital recorders. While it's compressed, Dolby claims up to ten encode/decode cycles are possible without noticeable deterioration. It requires special converters, available from Dolby.

Cross-connecting digital formats

The most common cross-connections are between s/pdif coax, Toslink, and AES/EBU. Since the impedances, balancing, and voltages are different for s/pdif and AES/EBU, you can't plug one into another with a standard audio adapter. Transformers and electronic adapters designed for this purpose are available from pro dealers. And while most equipment is tolerant of the tiny data differences between professional and consumer digital audio streams, some gear is picky. An adapter that works well in one situation might not work in another.

Toslink and s/pdif coax use similar data streams. Simple adapters are available from electronic suppliers.

It used to be common, in large facilities, to use a transformer to convert AES/EBU signals to unbalanced 75 Ω so they could use video cables and patchbays. This setup has been mostly replaced by SDI, which is a lot more flexible.

Digital audio errors

If you don't treat digital audio properly, it may jump up and bite you. Some of the ways include:

- Data errors, resulting in dropouts or loud, sporadic popping. Check the cables. Chances are an AES/EBU signal is running through a microphone cord, or an s/pdif signal through an analog phono cable.
- Timing errors, heard as periodic clicking in the sound or sometimes no sound at all. This can happen when a digital input isn't in sync with a device's internal clock, and usually can be fixed by changing the equipment's settings. Sound studios often distribute a separate digital audio sync signal, called Word Clock, to all their equipment. Every audio signal is then aligned to this clock.
- Many professional digital video recorders require that digital audio signals be related to the video frame rate. In most cases this means your key audio components will also have to accept black-burst, and you'll have to give them the same signal that locks your video equipment.
- A few consumer digital camcorders use slightly off-speed digital sampling internally. This results in an insignificant pitch shift when their tapes are played, but can cause sync errors in an NLE. See Chapter 12.

Another kind of digital audio error, jitter, has gotten a reputation for causing subtle problems with stereo imaging and compatibility. But almost all modern equipment re-clocks the incoming signal to eliminate this problem.

Section II

PLANNING AND PRE-PRO

When I was a kid, some friends and I decided to build a playhouse in one of our backyards. Since my father was an accomplished carpenter and had a successful business building new homes, I figured we'd have an easy time obtaining the necessary materials.

Dad asked what we'd need.

"Well, a couple of pieces of plywood and some two-by-fours, and maybe some shingles for the roof. Oh, and red paint. What do you think, Dad?"

"I think you forgot the paper and tape."

I wasn't figuring on any fancy flooring that would require rosin paper, fiber house-wrap paper hadn't been invented, and I *knew* nails would hold it together better than duct tape. Then he handed me a tape measure and some graph paper.

"Plan first. Measure the area, and make scale drawings. Do up a bill of materials. Until you know what you're trying to accomplish, the details are just guesswork."

This from a guy who could stroll into a lumber yard, point at materials seemingly at random, and then throw together a complex cabinet or a room partition from a sketch on a napkin.

* * *

Years later, I realized that Dad really did work from elaborate plans. But they were in his head. The napkin was just a reminder.

After a while, you'll be able to produce most of your soundtracks the same way . . . and discover favorite ways to plan and manage the really complicated ones, like feature film tracks. Until then, you can rely on the next two chapters. Chapter 4 describes the thinking that goes into an effective soundtrack, in terms of both creative design and basic storytelling. You'll learn the various elements go into an effective track for any kind of show, why they're appropriate, and probably some options you haven't thought of. Chapter 5 tells you how much all this cost in time and cash—it might be less than you think—and what to look for when scouting locations.

CHAPTER 4

Planning for Sound

THE NEED FOR SOUND

Many filmmakers approach their projects as a chance to shoot interesting pictures and string them together in an effective way. Sound is secondary: after all, film and video are "visual media."

But communication isn't a visual-only phenomenon. Psychologists estimate that more than two-thirds of everything a person knows was experienced through their ears. Sound surrounds us and can manipulate our primitive emotions better than a framed image. You can't blink or look away from a sound: your ears are always turned on and processing.

Obviously, early motion pictures had no sound. But producers were quick to realize the benefit of adding music, often sending suggested scores—with sound effects —to be played on piano or organ while the film was projected. It was a live performance, not a soundtrack, but it functioned the same way.

Today, network television is almost entirely driven by dialog. Try to imagine any popular program without sound. The most immediate and compelling use of pictures—breaking news events—is accompanied by voice-over and surrounded by talking heads. When they don't have anything to say, most correspondents keep talking anyway. And there's even less visualization in sitcoms, game shows, soaps, and late-night talk shows; most of those dialog-driven shows would need only minor adjustments to work on radio. Even visually rich documentaries primarily use pictures to illustrate a soundtrack, and talking heads to narrate a story. See any recent animated cartoon shows? They still have visual jokes . . . but most of the humor, and usually all of the plot, is carried by dialog.

Good sound is more than just dialog. Dialog is the first thing you've got to get right, and that's what a lot of this book is about. But getting a good balance between picture and the *combination* of dialog, music, and effects, is vital to reaching your audience. That's what this chapter is about.

Thinking about sound while planning the shoot should be a no-brainer. But it goes against Hollywood tradition. Even during the early days of talkies, when the sound engineer could stop the action if dialog wasn't being recorded to his standards, sound was considered a technical function.

✔ TIP

Are you throwing away half your film?

I don't mean half the footage should end up in the trash.[1] But filmmakers often claim "sound is half the film" . . . and then ignore the things sound can do for their film, until it's almost time to mix.

Production is picture-centric. The visual "half" is harder, and much more expensive, than the track. So that's where the most attention is paid during pre-pro and shoot. The mistake is when you turn sound into an after-thought, instead of giving it a small but necessary part of your attention while planning and shooting.

I'm not saying you have to hire a big-name sound designer to rework your script or storyboard. Your film will benefit just by talking over the scenes with somebody who's sound-oriented, and who can suggest tiny things you can do during shoot or edit that let sound help get the message across. This can be as simple as choosing your audio post supervisor now, while planning the shoot, and asking their advice.

If you can't find somebody like that, at least read this chapter and take it to heart. You'll make a better film, with both halves of it working together.

---

[1] Even though that's often good advice for editing.

Today having the sound recordist call "cut!" is a major faux pas. No matter what noises or other disasters start ruining the track, the mixer and boom operator are supposed to keep going . . . and then discreetly tell the assistant director, after the fact. This even makes sense, when you consider that the director might have been planning to use that take's visuals without sound, or didn't want to break the actors' concentration while they were still developing the characters. But it reinforces the idea that sound is technical, not creative.

I believe part of the reason is the decline of radio. For the first half of the twentieth century, Americans grew up listening to the family receiver. It was the mass medium, and figured into the plot and design of many movies. Early RKO talkies were sold as "Radio Pictures." Radio's influence in Orson Welles' (and some lesser directors') movies is obvious. Even after TV came along, radio remained a strong inspiration; many film schools were teaching radio drama well into the 1960s.

But today radio is a marginalized generic jukebox; the commercial mass media demand visual glitz to capture distracted eyeballs. For today's filmmakers, sound isn't an important consideration in their media environment. There are still a few excellent sound designers in the industry, with enough credibility to actually make a difference . . . on a few projects. But most mainstream films still treat 'sound design' as something added in post, if at all. Many directors act like the musical score is the only creative part of the soundtrack, and sound effects are just punctuations for on-screen objects.

A few directors suddenly get religion . . . they realize a scene isn't working, and demand continuous loud sound effects to make up for a lack of excitement. You can do better. Your films will be more effective, go together more smoothly, and possibly cost less if you let sound contribute to the creative vision. It should start long before the cameras roll.

You can also do worse. In Hollywood, at least, there's usually money to hire good technicians. If you're working on smaller projects and are tempted to let sound be an automatic function of the recorder or camera, or run by an untrained production assistant,[2] you may seriously hurt an otherwise good film. There's a reason for that:

People are conditioned to expect good sound

No matter what your budget, your efforts will be compared—at least subliminally—to every other film and video that's ever been released. Maybe you think you're just shooting a training film or mumblecore short for the Web; your audience *knows* they're watching a movie. People watching don't have your commitment to the message, and don't know what compromises you made during production. The only yardstick they have for your project is what they've seen in professional media.

The people who make a living doing shows and commercials (myself included) know their crafts, and the production process is well-defined. Got a story you want

---

[2] There's nothing wrong with having PAs or even unpaid friends run sound while shooting a low-budget film. But you have to give them some advance training (Chapters 7 and 8). It's not intuitive, and you don't want them guessing how to do their jobs while the camera is rolling.

to turn into a film? I'll call a bunch of my colleagues and we'll put together a darned good one. Of course, you'll have to pay us.

That may not be an option for your production. There often just aren't the resources to hire specialists for every job. You may end up being scriptwriter, director, camera and sound crew, and eventually editor and mixer. This high distraction level means that sound will be neglected unless you plan for it.

Invest time to save money

Even if you don't have deep pockets, you can still have a good track. Just don't expect sound to magically happen, no matter what equipment you've borrowed for the shoot or software you'll use for editing. "Automatic" recording controls, self-editing music software, or preset mixing has to be designed for foolproof operation on any production ... at best, these features are uncaring robots; at worst, they push your production down to a level of mediocrity.

These functions aren't rocket science. If you or your volunteer production assistants have average intelligence and a cooperative attitude, they can learn how to gather and edit sound that's appropriate for your film. But it will take some knowledge of the fundamentals—this book or some other training resource—along with adequate time to practice the techniques.

Of course if you do have a few dollars to bring in someone with experience, you'll get a better track. And instead of taking time to train them, you can take advantage of their knowledge while planning the film—often, without paying any extra. Check with your sound crew before production to make sure locations, equipment, and shot plan won't fight the dialog. Talk to your post sound supervisor or designer while planning the shoot or storyboards: often, a tiny adjustment in the visuals, accompanied by the proper creative sound, can make any film more effective.

The need for early collaboration

Many beginning directors think of film production as a straightforward process of *A to B to C*. Prepare to shoot, then shoot, then edit and finish. This approach probably dates from Hollywood's early studio system, where so many films were being turned out that an assembly-line workflow was necessary. Not only were technical functions standardized, even the creative ones were. Directors seldom got to edit their own films; they were off shooting something else while the film got finished.

This approach, still taught at many schools, divides filmmaking into isolated functions of production and post (Figure 4.1). Ideas can flow from left to right ("there'll be a dissolve here," or even "this shot isn't working and there isn't time to change it, so we'll fix it in post"), but not the other way (you won't hear "editorial says we need one additional angle to make the fix work," or "the sound department says you can't match this dialog with ADR, so record a couple of wild lines while we're still on the set").

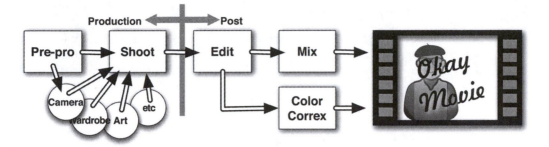

Figure 4.1 Traditional workflow splits filmmaking into isolated parts, with a logical progression from pre-pro to finished movie.

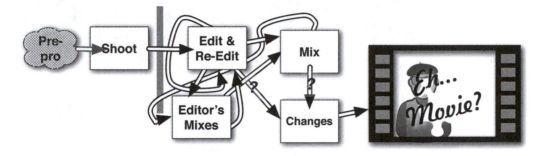

Figure 4.2 What happens when tradition meets today's reality.

It worked for studios with assembly lines and strict release schedules. But today's directors want to edit their own movies, refining the vision—and often rewriting the script—in a lengthy cut-and-review process. Temporary mixes are necessary to support the reviews, so they're done in the edit suite. And since you can never finish "making a movie better," there are lots of re-edits . . . even after the film has been sent to audio post. The workflow starts to look like Figure 4.2.

This hurts the budget, the track, or both. (It hurts other departments as well, but this book is about sound.) A tiny picture edit involving just a few frames—a keystroke or two in an NLE—can have lengthy ripples across the soundtrack. Not only does sync have to be adjusted, but also music and effects have to be changed to fit.

This also means people get used to picture *and sound* before the film is even seen by people who can offer the best creative options for the track. Audio decisions are often made on the spur of the moment by the director and editor—neither of whom has the equipment or training to explore better solutions—and get locked in.[3] The film suffers.

---

3 Last year I worked on a network documentary using a lot of amateur folk music recordings, all of which needed special treatment to be listenable. At one point I suggested extending a song: after we saw the singer

Forget "workflow" and think "thought flow"

A wise filmmaker gets post involved before the shoot. It's still the director's film and vision, but now decisions can be based on the most informed creative contributions. Production goes more smoothly, and post gets exactly the best pieces to work with. Figure 4.3 shows how it works. An emailed script and quick phone call is all you need to get started.

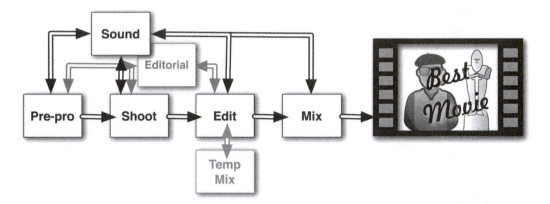

Figure 4.3 Let the post departments talk to each other and to you before the shoot, and you'll get a better movie.

☞ ROSE'S RULES

Four rules

- Start prepping the track while you're still developing the script and budget. Know what it'll sound like, how you'll get the necessary elements, and what resources you won't be able to live without. If this isn't your strong point, talk things over with somebody who is sound-oriented.
- Verify that the location and equipment you're planning to use will support the track you want. If they don't, now's the time to make changes: if you can't modify the budget, simplify the script or shots.
- Make sure you'll have the skills you'll need. Don't expect to pick up competent sound people a few days before the shoot, unless you've also got money to pay them.
- **Absolutely don't expect to point a microphone and get lucky, and don't expect that whatever you record will be fixable in post.**
  The former never happens, and the latter can be expensive . . . if it's possible at all.

HOW A GOOD SOUNDTRACK CAN HELP

Good sound adds believability

We spend our lives hearing the sounds around us. We've learned what conversations should sound like in different environments, and what kind of noises everyday objects make. But for good technical reasons,[4] a microphone doesn't hear the world the same way. Unless you're careful, what a mic picks will be a constant reminder that what we're seeing isn't real. This takes viewers "out of the film," making it harder to identify with the character or buy into the message.

Sound often has to be more realistic than picture. Very few people look at a screen and assume it's a window into another world. We're aware of camera movement and editing, reminding us that a director has defined reality for us; that's what dramatists call "the willing suspension of disbelief." But in a properly created soundtrack, the only unbelievable element will be the music. When sound professionals do our jobs right, most of the time you don't realize we've been there at all.

❋ TIDBIT

As technology gets better, maintaining the illusion becomes harder

The earliest adventure films seem crude by our standards. But when the first audiences saw them, they thought they were real.

When TV was black and white and the sound came out of a tinny speaker, it was easy to accept its technical limitations. We knew that Lucy's hair and Ricky's skin weren't really gray, but we didn't care. Or we filled in the red and tan ourselves.

Color television made it harder to suspend our disbelief. While gray hair was acceptable for Lucy, bright orange wasn't. Lighting and makeup became much more important. A few years ago, as local stations were making the transition to live HDTV news, they also had to adopt better makeup skills for their anchors' faces.

The same thing happened to sound. The increased audio clarity of digital broadcasting, better speakers and amplifiers in TV sets, and the prevalence of stereo and surround conspire to let us hear more of the track. Since it's no longer obviously canned, it has to be right.

---

on-camera, the music would continue under a few paragraphs of relevant narration. The director told me "We already spent time arguing about that in the edit. The editor couldn't make it work, and I don't want to waste time re-litigating the decision." So I asked if I could play "friend of the court," and give him just a quick demo of how the music could go. Happy ending: when cut and processed properly the music fit fine, and turned it into a unified scene. Moral: you can't solve sound problems in a picture environment.

[4] See Chapter 7.

Or look at it this way: You can build a small bedroom set in a corner of a giant warehouse, and shoot an intimate and romantic scene. We may be intellectually aware there were camera, lights, and a lot of people around; but while we're watching, we accept the actors' reality and get wrapped up in their story. However, the moment their voices sound like they're in a warehouse, the illusion is shattered.

As budgets go down, spend proportionally more on sound

Sound is more cost-effective than picture.[5] Good audio doesn't need elaborate sets or locations, its mics and recorders cost less than similar-class cameras and lenses, and it takes less time to put together. It can add a professionalism you might not be able to afford with images.

- Voice-overs are cheaper than on-camera spokespersons. The money saved here can buy you a more experienced (and convincing) actor.
- A small buyout score for a non-theatrical film can cost as little as $10 a minute. Even a full symphonic score, played by a world-class orchestra, can cost less than $50 a minute (Chapter 14). It's the cheapest high-class effect you can buy.
- Sound effects cost virtually nothing and can add realism. A few well-placed actors backed up by a crowd recording costs less than shooting a room full of extras. Or take the noise of an explosion, a flashing light, some smoke and a few thrown debris, and a horrified on-camera reaction . . . that's a lot cheaper than blowing up a building, even if you use CGI.

I worked on a theatrical feature recently that had big ambitions and big-name stars, but not much money. The director said he didn't want it to sound like a low-budget film. Since he was hiring an experienced crew who could record the dialog properly, I asked what he meant. For this director, the difference was that low-budget film soundtracks were "sparse." You could understand the characters, but their worlds were empty. He knew the answer wasn't a lot of loud noises, but a complex acoustic mixture that sounded like real life but never distracted from the story.

☞ ROSE'S RULES

Take your pick
- You can plan properly and train the people you work with.
- You can hire professionals to worry about sound for you.
- Or you can have an echoey, muffled track that says, "This film isn't any more important than most of the stuff shot with phones and uploaded to YouTube."

---

[5] It has to be. Our "half" of the movie often gets by with much less than one-tenth of its budget.

THINK ABOUT THE OVERALL TRACK

A track is more than the sum of its sounds. If this idea appears strange to you, you're not alone. Some mainstream producers' idea of sound design is a track with nonstop gunshots, car crashes, explosions, and alien growls. They worry that if nothing is happening on the track, the audience might forget the story. But this isn't interesting; it's just loud. After an initial adrenaline reaction to extreme volume wears off, it isn't even exciting.

Using a lot of sound effects doesn't necessarily equal a lot of effective sound. On the other hand, well-chosen sounds—including pauses and ambiences as well as hard effects—can almost become another character: the track builds a world around your actors and helps the viewer believe the message.

Start with the script

Many producers believe that creative sound happens in postproduction. *Good* sound begins when you first start writing the script. This doesn't mean typing Crash! and Zap! into the descriptions—most scripts have no place for that, and I wish none did—but thinking about the *sound* of the story. A couple of techniques can help.

Listen to the words in your mind

Hear the script in your head while you're writing it. Don't just type

```
Sfx: phone rings
Sue: Hello? George! I've been waiting to hear from you ...
```

That's not what's going to happen on the screen. Instead *hear* the sequence from Sue's point of view. You'll realize that what actually happens is

```
Sfx: phone starts to ring
Sue looks at phone, reaches toward it, picks it up
Sfx: ring is interrupted
Sue picks up the handset
Sfx: soft clattering sound of handset being picked up
She holds the handset, talks into it
Sue: Hello?
Sue pauses, then reacts to voice
Sue: George! I've been waiting to hear from you ...
```

You won't type all that on the script, of course. But hearing it in your head makes you realize how much this simple action affects the pacing. The scene plays slower than you might have originally thought. (If you're writing a commercial, this can be critical.) And it can reveal what Sue is already thinking: does she pick up on the first ring, because she's really eager to talk to George? Does she put away other things or close windows on her screen so she can concentrate? Or does she grab the phone while finishing the email she's typing?

Thinking this way lets you explore other sound options. What about backgrounds? If Sue is watching TV when the phone rings, what happens to the TV's track? Is she in an office, but the ambience gets softer because she's paying attention to George? Or are people still shouting off-screen—or maybe talking directly to Sue—to tell us her busy life isn't on hold.

How about her emphasis? It can totally change the meaning:

- "I was *waiting* to hear from you," says Sue was eager to talk to George.
- "I was waiting to hear from *you*," suggests other members of her workgroup have already chimed in.
- "*I* was waiting to hear from you," suggests she's the only one left in the group who cares.
- And "I *was* waiting to hear from you," tells us she'd just about given up.

These are soundtrack decisions that affect meaning. If you leave them entirely up to the actors—who might not know Sue's back story—you could be throwing away part of the film. If you don't address them until post, you might be stuck with a meaning you didn't want to convey.

Now think about music . . . is there any under previous dialog or as a transition into this scene? Ending that music on the first ring will have a very different effect than waiting until Sue recognizes George's voice.

This is real sound design. The thinking can apply to any kind of movie, from a dramatic or comedy feature to a re-enactment in a training film or documentary. It doesn't add much time to the writing or planning process, and you'll have a much better movie.

Sounds often need a reference

Often, a sound that makes sense in the script can become "widowed" in the track, because it's hard for the viewer to identify. Many sounds aren't obvious unless there's a visual or verbal reference to them.

Imagine a film noir sequence in a cheap hotel room on a rainy night, with the sound of a neon sign flashing. Any realistic recording of rain through a closed window could be mistaken for static. The rhythmic *bzzap* of a neon sign only adds to that confusion. You can solve this sound problem with an establishing shot, perhaps a point of view looking out through the window to see rain splashing on the glass and part of the sign. If that's too expensive, you could have a character comment on the weather while you rhythmically flash a red light onto the set. Either way, the sound is established. After that, you're free to block the rest of the scene any way you want; viewers will remember that the noises mean rain and neon.

Now's the time to also think about how music will work, rather than waiting for a spotting session after the film is cut. Dramatic scripts usually don't include music descriptions, but it'll help you as a director to know which scenes are getting scored and where there might be transitions. Corporate and sales scripts often do include music notes on the script, but don't just write "music fades up." Specify what the music is trying to convey, in terms of emotion or attitude as well as style. Not only will this influence pacing while you're directing or editing; it'll also guide the composer in postproduction, or—if you're using library music—help you find appropriate pieces faster.

Sound design after the script is written

If you're creating the script, you've got a great opportunity to write for sound. But if you're shooting someone else's script, you must still go through the process of hearing it in your head, marking sound cues, and possibly opening things up to make room for audio. It's the best way to assure that the track will go together smoothly and predictably.

Mark the script for sound

Walk through the script in your head, hearing every scene. Pay attention to who each scene is about—it's not necessarily the star of the movie—and whose point of view we should be following. Then make notes about possible sound treatments. It's usually easiest to make these notes on the script itself, since there probably will be a lot of them referring to specific actions. If the script is on a computer and you don't want to print it out, see whether your software supports sticky notes. Figure 4.4 shows the notes for an early minute in a drama.

Some of those notes are reminders of things to do in post, both real-world sounds and textures, and special effects that might be worth trying. Others are things that should be decided before the shoot, so actors can perform or react to them. These notes will also often suggest extra sounds or wild lines you can grab quickly at the shoot (and a lot more cheaply than trying to recreate them later). They may also uncover some audio conflicts that can be resolved before you roll camera.

Mark the camera shots for sound as well

While you're deciding shots and angles, leave some room for sound as well. A little visual obscurity can tease the viewer's eye while involving their ears. This helps bring them into the characters' world.

The script in Figure 4.4 starts with a disorienting shot of a man's face, sideways, discolored and distorted as if it's squeezed against something. There's a quick flashback, and then back to the man. Then a flight attendant wakes him up. We realize he'd been sound asleep, leaning against the window of an airplane in flight, and our camera was looking in through the window. He's tired and disoriented.

What a great opportunity for sound! When I first saw the script, I suggested to the director that we start with a disorienting drone—something that could be a machine, or could be electronic—growing out of the main title music and swirling around the surround speakers. As viewers, we'd be as disoriented as the passenger. The flight

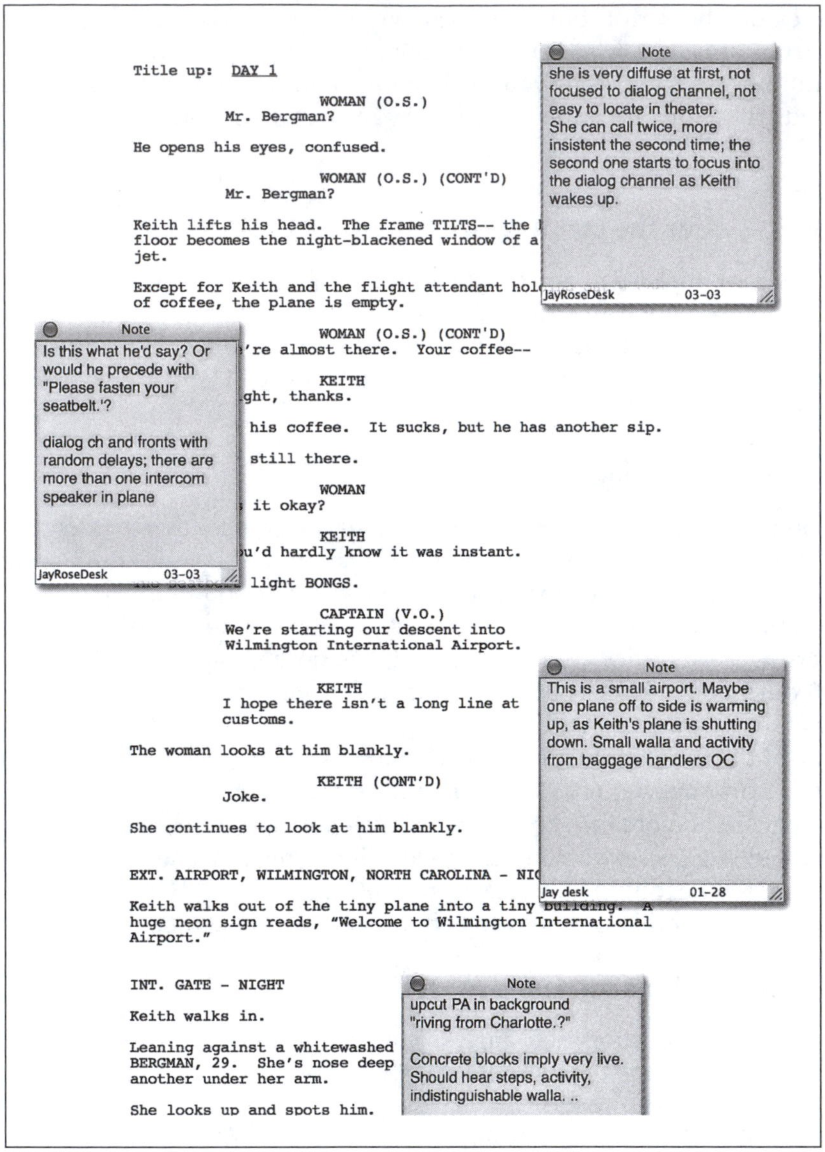

Title up: DAY 1

                    WOMAN (O.S.)
          Mr. Bergman?

He opens his eyes, confused.

                    WOMAN (O.S.) (CONT'D)
          Mr. Bergman?

Keith lifts his head. The frame TILTS-- the
floor becomes the night-blackened window of a
jet.

Except for Keith and the flight attendant hold
of coffee, the plane is empty.

Note

she is very diffuse at first, not focused to dialog channel, not easy to locate in theater. She can call twice, more insistent the second time; the second one starts to focus into the dialog channel as Keith wakes up.

JayRoseDesk   03-03

                    WOMAN (O.S.) (CONT'D)
          're almost there. Your coffee--

                    KEITH
          ght, thanks.

his coffee. It sucks, but he has another sip.

still there.

                    WOMAN
          it okay?

                    KEITH
          u'd hardly know it was instant.

light BONGS.

Note

Is this what he'd say? Or would he precede with "Please fasten your seatbelt.'?

dialog ch and fronts with random delays; there are more than one intercom speaker in plane

JayRoseDesk   03-03

                    CAPTAIN (V.O.)
          We're starting our descent into
          Wilmington International Airport.

                    KEITH
          I hope there isn't a long line at
          customs.

The woman looks at him blankly.

                    KEITH (CONT'D)
          Joke.

She continues to look at him blankly.

EXT. AIRPORT, WILMINGTON, NORTH CAROLINA - NIG

Keith walks out of the tiny plane into a tiny building. A
huge neon sign reads, "Welcome to Wilmington International
Airport."

INT. GATE - NIGHT

Keith walks in.

Leaning against a whitewashed
BERGMAN, 29. She's nose deep
another under her arm.

She looks up and spots him.

Note

This is a small airport. Maybe one plane off to side is warming up, as Keith's plane is shutting down. Small walla and activity from baggage handlers OC

Jay desk   01-28

Note

upcut PA in background "riving from Charlotte.?"

Concrete blocks imply very live. Should hear steps, activity, indistinguishable walla. ..

Figure 4.4 Notes on a feature film script.

attendant's voice initially would be processed to be equally distorted and disorienting. Then, as he wakes up and we reveal more of the airplane interior, the voice becomes clearer and becomes conventional dialog, while the background resolves to an aircraft cabin.[6]

A couple of seconds on the screen, and a window into the character's fatigue and mindset.

Genius-level sound designer Randy Thom suggests some other ways to tease the eye while giving the ear time to listen, in his essay *Designing a Movie for Sound*:[7]

1. Use very long or very short lenses
Randy quotes the opening sequence of *The Conversation*, where we see people in San Francisco's Union Square through a telephoto lens. The narrow depth of field and squeezed perspective of that lens forces a very subjective point of view. "As a result, we can easily justify hearing sounds which may have very little to do with what we see in the frame, and more to do with the way the person ostensibly looking through that lens *feels*."

2. Use dutch angles and moving cameras
Shoot from floor or ceiling, rotate the camera's horizon a few degrees off horizontal, or rotate the camera around the action. It puts the audience into unfamiliar space, rather than just depicting the scene. "The element of unfamiliar space suddenly swings the door wide-open to sound."

3. Put darkness around the edge of the frame
This is a mainstay of film noir. Not everything in the characters' world (or ours) is brilliantly lit or easy to understand. "Get the point across that the truth, lurking somewhere just outside the frame, is too complex to let itself be photographed easily. Don't forget that the ears are the guardians of sleep. They tell us what we need to know about the darkness, and will gladly supply some clues about what's going on."

---

[6] The film is *Two Weeks* (MGM, 2006), starring Sally Field and Ben Chaplin, written and directed by Steve Stockman. Steve had me execute that opening sequence for the first versions of the movie . . . but the scene and its track were totally deleted from the final released version, as were a lot of other nifty ones. Great ideas frequently end up on the cutting-room floor; that's part of how movies are made. (Which is not to say this idea of mine was particularly great.)

Stockman is also author of *How to Shoot Video that Doesn't Suck* (Workman Publishing, 2011). While he specializes in reality programming now—and has a couple of series on the air—there are great production tips for any kind of shooting at his website, SteveStockman.com.

[7] Randy has recorded, mixed, or designed sound for almost 100 mainstream films, starting with 1979's *Apocalypse Now* and still going strong with 2014's *Rio 2*; he's had 14 Oscar nominations, and won for his work on *The Right Stuff* and *The Incredibles*. He is Director of Sound Design at Lucasfilm's Skywalker Sound, and has collaborated with top talents including Coppola, Lucas, Spielberg, Lynch, Murch, Zemeckis, Howard, Burton, Waters, and Mel Brooks. The entire essay appears at http://filmsound.org/articles/designing_for_sound.htm, © 1999 Randy Thom, and is quoted by permission.

4. Compose extremely tight or long shots

Extreme close-ups of hands, clothing, and other details can make us feel that we're experiencing a scene through someone's point of view, whether they're the main character of the scene or somebody watching that main character. Similarly, extremely long and wide shots give us an opportunity to hear the fullness or emptiness of a vast scene. Randy refers to *The Black Stallion* and *Never Cry Wolf* as two films, both directed by Carroll Ballard, that use wide shots and extreme close-ups coupled brilliantly with sound.

5. Use slow motion

"*Raging Bull* and *Taxi Driver* contain some obvious, and some very subtle uses of slow motion. Some of it is barely perceptible. But it always seems to put us into a dream-space, and tell us that something odd, and not very wholesome, is happening." A version of slow motion where selected frames are repeated, giving a stepped motion without changing the overall length, is often used in documentary re-creations for the same disorienting reason.

The point behind all of these "camera tricks" is that they take us away from being passive viewers of a scene. We start seeing a world that's been distorted through the character's eyes and emotions, so we can start listening to that world as well.

Letting sound design reflect the character's point of view isn't new. In 1935, *Top Hat* introduces the romantic conflict between Fred Astaire and Ginger Rogers by having us hear things from her point of view. Fred is happily dancing by himself in a hotel room. The camera pans down through the "floor" of the hotel . . . where we see Ginger being kept awake by his footsteps. He dances some more, she gets more annoyed, and eventually she decides to confront the noisy monster in person. Hijinks ensue, and 90 minutes later they dance into the sunset.

Sound design after the shoot

Once editing has started, sound notes are still important, particularly on film-length projects where audio post can last weeks or more. But once editing starts, the script might become irrelevant: While shorter projects are usually pretty good at sticking to the script, long form documentaries and narrative films often get rewritten during the edit. I've found the best way to keep track of notes on long post jobs is with a spreadsheet, organized by timecode. Start a couple of columns for minutes and seconds, and one for hour or reel if it's a long show. Then watch the edit. When you hear something that could be improved, stop and note its location, its cue or dialog, and what you want to do. Go through the film more than once, but don't worry if the notes aren't in order—it's easy enough to sort by time when you need to. Don't worry either if a note doesn't have a particular code location: leave those columns blank, and the note will fly up to the top of the page when you sort.

You can also add columns to identify a note dialog or effects, what kind of work is needed, which characters are involved, and even the director's responses. It'll all save time when you're actually doing the work. Figure 4.5 shows how it all works.

◇	A	B	C	D	E	F	G	H	I	J	K	L	M	N	O
1	reel	min	sec	cue	scene	by	done	dia	efx	foley	special	char	note	decision	
2	0	0	0	Nintendo							1		**replace all. John will be getting the a**	process to remove music c	
3	1	0	0	main title			1		1				clock ticking under open?	steve says try it	
4	1	0	0	**You're just going to (Keith overlap)**	2	j		*1*				**A**	Fixed - j		
5	1	0	52	**Voicemail calls: Script not finalized**	0	s	1	*1*				**K E B M**			
6	1	1	4	Main title			1						song exists can can be cut in	Guster: Lost and Gone For	
7	1	1	4	1M1 Main Title			1				1		**ends with last leaf hitting pile**		
8	1	2	28	**Voiceover: Ready Mom?**	1	s	1	*1*				**K**			
9	1	2	28	**Interview questions**	2	s	1	*1*				**K**			
10	1	3	14	airport interior					1				quiet activity and little walla. Maybe a floor polisher off.		
11	1	3	28	just before suitcase appears (dock isnt on camera yet) Loud buzzer from big luggage carousel. Don't do anything else... just keith's case's nat sour											
12	1	3	37	**pilot cabin announcement**	3	s	1	*1*				**Pil**	re-record with "north carolina"		
13	1	3	53	airport int					1				luggage offscreen but add buzzer		
14	1	3	53	**Welcome to Wilmington Intl airport..."**			1	1			1		**PA system**		
15	1	3	55	ext			1		1				start outdoor tone. dx traffic. maybe some dx jet whine. no steps or		
16	1	5	0	Anita's room			1				1		**clock ticking**		
17	1	5	0	**tv sounds**			1	1					announcer: Jay to temp		
18	1	5	38	**re-voice or get licensed source**	7	s	1	*1*				**Ne**	Do we need this? Check with John		
19	1	5	48	**em: fck you**			1	1			1		**Steve: is this saved enough? NEED TV**		yes
20	1	6	20	**DAY 2**				*1*	1			**E**	Birds, kids playing (or should they be in school... day 2 is weekend.		
21	1	6	33	barry disconnects call					1				Do we want tiny beep as he folds phone? Will this help in airport? (N		
22	1	6	39	**Interview questions**	8	s	1	*1*				**K**			
23	1	7	16	"We're playing your song"		j	1				1		**move puking so it doesn't sound cued**		
24	1	7	45	K moves IV tree			1			1			wheels (try to match 10_2 prodn sound		
25	1	8	12	tie into pan						1	1		**slosh noise**		
26	1	8	38	sheet snap						1			foley		

Figure 4.5 Notes for the same film, after it's shot and editing has begun.

Make room for sound

Real people stop talking every now and then. When they do, we hear the world around them. As a filmmaker, you can help this along by avoiding dialog over noisy actions: Sue shouldn't be talking to another character while she hangs up the phone. It complicates mic placement and makes a good mix more difficult.

Even if a sound effect will be added in post, leave room for it in the dialog. Characters shouldn't start screaming at the same moment there's supposed to be a car crash or explosion—that just detracts from both sounds. Let them scream in anticipation as the car careens towards the wall, or react after the explosion settles.

Since different sounds have different frequency ranges, consider how their ranges might conflict. The metallic crunch of car against wall has a similar timbre to an adult male shouting, so you might not hear both if they're happening at the same time. But substitute breaking glass for the metal, or a child's scream for the man, and they'll coexist together.

This also affects how you specify the music. Good scoring composers are very aware of how instrumental timbres fit in the overall track. When John Williams orchestrated the rolling rock in *Raiders of the Lost Ark*, he relied almost exclusively on high, staccato strings. That way the rumbles of the rock itself could show through. The low notes of his theme for *Jaws* aren't just ominous; they also leave room for the ocean and seagull effects. Even if your budget is limited to library cuts, you can use the same kind of thinking. Solo brass and winds occupy the same range as the human voice, so avoid that lonely sax player in the window if there's simultaneous dialog.

Sound and picture also have to make room for each other. If you want viewers to follow complex visuals, lighten up on the track. Consider the classic recapitulation at the end of many mysteries: as the detective finally describes what really happened, we see a montage of flashbacks showing the murder . . . but the sound effects in that montage are almost always underplayed. We may hear a gunshot and body fall, but that's about it.

Bear this in mind while you're editing as well. Corporate and commercial pieces are often cut with wall-to-wall narration. This is fine for one continuous message, but if you want logical breaks or chapter headings, leave some pauses for music or effects.

Provide texture changes

When people know what to expect, they stop paying attention. At the subtlest level, that's why we tend to ignore normal room reverberation and background sounds in daily life, even though the mic hears them clearly at a shoot. But this affects scriptwriting and planning as well.

Long dialog sequences with static actors get very boring acoustically, even if the words themselves are interesting. Let the characters move around the room, so we can hear differences as their voices bounce off different surfaces. Move some of the dialog into a hallway or another room with different acoustics. Or let them continue some of the conversation outdoors or in their car. If your budget is limited to a single setup, at least give the characters a chance to stop talking and react to an off-camera sound. Instead of just walking a new actor into the scene, let everyone else react as we hear the earlier off-camera sounds of a car stopping, a door slam, and footsteps.

Music helps break up boring sequences, but may become a cliché. A stab after a dramatic line can give a soap-opera feel to a scene . . . but make it more subtle and it could be just what's needed to let us think about a dramatic point. If a sequence is light on dialog, try specifying an underscore instead of matched sound effects to fill the pauses. If your video has a lot of music, leave some scenes unscored to make them stand out.

Remember the medium

A business or event video's track will usually be a lot more limited than a theatrical film's. That's not only because theatrical films have bigger budgets, or because you can usually take more time building their tracks; it's also because theatrical films have surround sound and much wider frequency and dynamic ranges to play with, plus the emotional effect of a big screen in a darkened, quiet room. Business videos often have to play on a conference room TV and sometimes on a laptop; wedding videos usually end up on a home TV but might even be seen on a cell phone. And realistically, your first narrative film might see its only audience on YouTube. So if your project relies on the slam-bang sound effects or stirring music you saw in the latest adventure thriller, you'll be disappointed at the result.

Sound can be most ambitious in projects that will be shown only under controlled circumstances. If you know a sales meeting film or festival entry will have high-quality digital or playback, in an auditorium with a good sound system, you can rely on stereo or surround, and differences of loudness and texture to help carry your message. It's reasonable here to think in terms of five or more layers: dialog, up-front effects, effects that aren't sharply on-camera, ambiences, and music. The stereo field and high playback quality help the viewer sort things out.

Broadcast sound is a lot less flexible. Even though most stations transmit in surround, many satellite networks are squashed to mono by the local cable system, to save money. Even if a viewer has a surround set, it's likely to use a limited-width "sound bar" and be off to one side of the room. Unless you're sitting right in front of it, the speakers are too close together to project a realistic field. That goes for stereo sets as well, and many of the smaller sets from chain retailers don't even have stereo circuits feeding the two speakers in front. With more and more people watching their "broadcast" TV on laptops and tablets, the situation is even worse. Broadcasters also deliberately limit their dynamic range, so viewers can hear normal dialog without having to constantly compensate for screaming commercials. Don't count on more than three layers in a broadcast track, and pay careful attention to what's on them so dialog and foreground effects don't conflict.

DVD players are almost all capable of surround . . . if they're properly hooked up to a surround set, and their menus are set correctly. And of course the set's speakers have to be properly positioned. Otherwise they'll play in stereo or worse. If you want to be safe, you should think of home DVD tracks like you would broadcast TV.

The most limiting medium is Web audio. While some viewers use streaming devices to route YouTube and other sites into their home theater systems, most playback will be on tiny speakers in noisy rooms, or handheld devices with earbuds or tiny speakers in even noisier surroundings. Internet compression techniques further muddy the sound. In these situations, even voice and music can fight each other.

Planning and the bottom line

Planning a track long before production will save money you can spend elsewhere in the video.

- If you know what sounds you'll need, you can get them at the shoot. It's a lot cheaper to grab an off-camera line, crowd walla, or a specific prop noise when you've got the actors, extras, and props already there.
- If you know what you won't need, you don't have to waste time recording it.
- If you think about the final track while you're shooting, editing will be smoother because you won't be trying to fudge existing footage to make room for audio.

ELEMENTS OF THE SOUNDTRACK

It's standard practice, after mixing a film or TV show, to give the producer files with three separate mixes or *stems*, each devoted exclusively to voice, music, or effects. This simplifies the process of creating foreign-language versions and allows additional

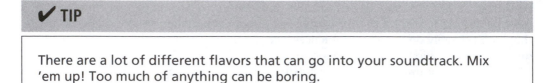

✔ TIP

There are a lot of different flavors that can go into your soundtrack. Mix 'em up! Too much of anything can be boring.

freedom when cutting promos or lifts. Professionals also generally organize their work and responsibilities by those three categories: on a big feature, separate specialists edit dialog, sound effects, and music; when it's time to mix they worry about dialog first, then add the sound effects, and finally bring in the music.

But don't let those categories fool you into thinking there are only three kinds of sound. Within the broad areas of voice, music, and effect are enough subcategories to satisfy the most ambitious sound designer. If you train yourself to think in terms of these subcategories, rather than just "we'll use a voice," you can create more interesting tracks and do a better job of engaging the viewer.

SPOKEN WORDS

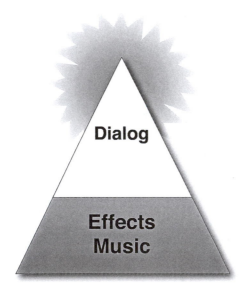

Figure 4.6 The Soundtrack Pyramid: Music and sound effects provide the base, but dialog is most important.

Video is driven by the spoken word. It affects the visual editing rhythm and style as well as the choice of shots. Marti Humphrey, a 33-year veteran re-recording mixer and owner of The Dub Stage in Burbank, likens the finished soundtrack to a pyramid (Figure 4.6): Dialog is most important and occupies the top of the pyramid. Music or sound effects may take the second place, depending on the scene, but both of them exist to provide an emotional base, supporting and subordinate to dialog.

Remember: Dialog is King. It has to sound natural and right for the character or situation. Specifics on how to record it, edit it, and process it make up more than half of this book. But you've got a lot of freedom where that dialog comes from, and how you'll control it.

On-camera dialog

This is the primary way to get words across in dramatic films, many corporate pieces, and some commercials. Obviously, on-camera voices are recorded while you're shooting picture; in a lot of productions, they're recorded on the same tape or file. But that doesn't mean they have to stay together forever.

You can often improve a track by breaking the link between on-camera faces and the voices that were recorded at the same time. It's common practice in Hollywood to use voices from a close-up against pictures from a long shot, or even to re-record dialog after the shoot.

Modern audio workstations let you take the process even further: I'll frequently use words from a discarded take to fix sound problems in the performance that was actually used, even if the shot is fairly tight on the actor's face. I'll also take individual syllables to fix a word that might have been mispronounced or clipped by the video editor. I believe it's more important to have dialog that's understandable and expressive, than to have every frame be in perfect lipsync. If sync is close, you've got a second or two before fine errors become obvious. You can add a lot of expressiveness in those 50 or so frames, and nobody will be the wiser.

If your editing skills aren't up to replacing individual words against picture (you'll get plenty of practice in Chapter 12), there's still lots of freedom to edit the on-camera voice during cutaways. Any time we're not seeing the characters' lips, you can make their voices do anything you want. Feel free to grab a better reading from an alternate take, or to edit out long breaths. Use time compression to pick up the pace slightly so there's room to hear other sounds. Or use time expansion to stretch individual words for emphasis. The only limit is that you be back in sync within a few frames of cutting back to the actor's face.

> ✔ TIP

> ### Editing tip
> The easiest way to mess with words during a cutaway without risking sync errors during on-camera segments is to split the voice onto two separate tracks in your editor. Keep on-camera segments on a track that's linked to picture, and use a temporary work track for the highly edited stuff. After you're sure it all works together, move the edited version back to the main track and discard the temporary one.

On-camera dialog and on-camera narration have different sounds

We usually think in terms of characters talking to each other on screen because that's what we see most often in movies and episodic TV. But occasionally in movies, and frequently in corporate and commercial projects, the actor talks directly to camera. This affects the texture of the sound as well as the writing and performance.

Dialog in a dramatic scene requires a sound that matches the environment where we see the actors. If they're in a normal room, they'll usually be boomed from slightly above their heads, so the mic also picks up some room reverb. If it's a long shot in a very big room where booming is impossible, they're probably wearing radio mics only a few inches from their mouths. Very little of the room is picked up when the mic is this close, so artificial reverb is added to match the shot. The idea in both cases is that we're eavesdropping on the conversation these people are having, so the room they're in becomes a natural part of the sound.

But if a spokesperson is in a normal room and talking directly to camera, we— the viewers—become part of the conversation. The real room where we're sitting is as much a part of that conversation's environment as the shooting stage. In that case, it can be appropriate to have less reverb, or move the boom much closer to the actor so it hears less of the set's acoustics.

If a spokesperson is in front of a drape or in limbo, there isn't any "room" at all. Any reverb would sound unnatural. This also applies to highly staged settings that aren't trying to be real-world rooms, such as a typical news set with desk, station logo, and monitor wall or chroma key. We're perfectly comfortable with the close lavaliere sound of the evening newscast or talk show, because the performers are talking directly to us.

Vérité audio

Documentaries and some commercials often depend on ad-lib comments, directed to an interviewer who's very close to the camera lens. The texture of these voices can be very different from a trained actor or spokesperson, lending additional interest to the track. Because these people aren't polished performers, their voices are often weaker and need to be miked with a very close boom or a lavaliere that rejects most of the room sound. This is entirely appropriate: since they're essentially talking to camera, the environment works like it would for a spokesperson.[8]

Remember the room

Staying aware of the presumed acoustic environment of on-camera dialog can help you avoid conflicts where sounds don't match their apparent location, or where insert shots don't match the master.

---

[8] By the way, it's almost always a mistake to ask a vérité subject to deliver a spokesperson's scripted selling line. Nothing destroys a commercial faster than having an allegedly real customer shout into the camera, "I love the variety and selection!" That's not how humans talk.

In his seminal book on sound design, *The Responsive Chord*, Tony Schwartz pointed out how early versions of Johnny Carson's *Tonight Show* used a close desk mic for Johnny. An overhead boom picked up the guests, plus quite a bit of the studio's natural reverb. For this reason, Johnny always sounded more intimate and closer to the viewer than sidekick Ed or the guests. (Later incarnations of his and many other talk shows kept the desk mic as an iconic prop, but put lavalieres on everybody.)

Even modern, technically sophisticated shows have to pay attention to these issues of perspective. Just a month before writing this, I was mixing network promos for *Sesame Street*. One of the Muppet characters had to interact with a child, a fairly common situation on that show. The puppeteer stood beneath the counter where the child was seated, and held his hands overhead to work the puppet. He wore a head-mounted mic so he'd have freedom of movement, and it picked up his voice from an inch away. But the child's voice was on an overhead boom, at least a foot above his head.

The kid sounded like he was in a real room. The Muppet sounded like he was in an echo-free announce booth. This made it hard for viewers to believe the child and the Muppet were sharing a moment. I had to split them to separate tracks, then add enough artificial reverb to put the Muppet back in the same room with the child.

Historic audio

Documentary producers can take advantage of almost a century of historic audio available from archives, stock footage sources, and the Library of Congress. Some of it has accompanying video or film. If you're planning to use historic sound with sync pictures, plan for a few still photos of crowd reactions as cutaways. This kind of sound almost always needs a lot of editing, both to fit the story, and—if lipsync isn't an issue—to pick its pace up to modern expectations. Of course it also needs processing to enhance intelligibility and bring the sound as close to modern standards as possible; that's in Chapter 16.

Crowd voices

If dialog is shot where there's a crowd, it's almost universal practice for the extras playing the crowd to mime their conversations, moving their lips but not making any noise. This is the only way to get a clean, editable recording of the principal dialog.

Appropriate crowd sounds or *walla* is then added in postproduction. Walla can be recorded at the shoot, after the scene is shot but before the extras go home, but this is seldom necessary or economical. Sound effects libraries have multiple discs of crowd backgrounds and reactions in every possible setting; if you don't have such a library, you can sneak an audio recorder into a crowded restaurant or building lobby and grab what you need. If the crowd has to have unique reactions or say particular key phrases, you can simulate a large crowd with four or five people ad-libbing conversations in different voices. Record this small group in a quiet studio, so you can run two or three separate ad-lib takes simultaneously without noise buildup. Then mix the result with prerecorded walla from a library.

⚠ WARNING

Guerrilla no-go

You can't walk into a working bar or restaurant, freely shoot your actors while regular patrons are eating or imbibing, and expect to get good dialog. It won't happen, no matter what you think you've seen in mainstream films. It certainly won't happen if you're using concealed cameras and their built-in mics.

If you're willing to equip the actors with head mics (Chapter 7), position everyone carefully, and block the scene so they're seen only in profile from the non-mic side, you can get reasonable dialog without telling everybody else in the room to be quiet. But this will mean serious compromises in the look of the film, so you probably don't want to use the technique for extended scenes.

In other words, don't bother. Instead, tell the venue you'd like to shoot there, work out at time when it's closed to regular patrons, and bring your own extras.

Voice-over narration

In most commercials, corporate or educational videos, and documentaries, we never see who's doing most of the talking. A voice-over exists in limbo by definition; there shouldn't be any background ambience or room reverb around it. With nothing to suggest any distance between us and the narrator, it can become the most intimate part of the track and interpret the rest of the video for us.

Narrations should almost always be recorded in a sound studio designed for voices, or in an isolated space with plenty of absorption (see Chapters 6 and 9). If an actor is going to appear both as an on-camera character and a voice-over talking to the viewer, don't expect to record the voice-over the same way you shot their scene. You'll pick up extra noises and ambience cues that will limit your editing options later.

The idea of an intimate announcer is a relatively modern concept. It seems to have grown out of the one-on-one style of pioneer television talk hosts like Jack Paar and Arthur Godfrey. Voice-over announcers in films prior to the mid-1950s usually had formal "speaking to the masses" deliveries and were often mixed with reverb. You may want to experiment with this style of narration as yet another texture, one that evokes a nostalgic or historic feel.

Voices are almost always mono

In a broadcast or theatrical mix, dialog—whether it's from characters, interviews, or narration—is almost always mono and appears to come from the middle of the screen. If multiple mics are used, they're routed to the center during the mix. Other than for

☛ **ROSE'S RULES**

Shooting silence isn't golden

There's a temptation, if you know a scene will be accompanied by narration, to shoot it without sound. This is almost always a mistake. Even if there's no dialog, point a mic at the scene. It doesn't cost any extra to record sound in a video camera, and the ambience and action noises you pick up can add another texture to the mix—or at least provide a guide track if you later want to add cleanly recorded effects.

This is also one of the few times when a camera-mounted mic can be useful in dramatic production.

Of course if you're shooting old-fashioned film this becomes a bigger decision, since sound does cost extra. In these situations, shooting *MOS*[9] may be reasonable.

---

special effects like rapid motion or off-screen characters, no attempt is made to make characters voices match their positions on the screen.

Part of the reason is economic. Dialog usually carries the plot, so it's important that everyone in the theater hears it well. You don't want to sacrifice the story for people on the left side of the auditorium, just because a character is standing on the right side of the screen. This applies to broadcast as well, because people seldom design their living rooms to put the TV directly on-axis with all the seating. You want everybody to get hooked on the story. That way they'll stay hooked for the commercials.

But there are also aesthetic reasons. We accept the concept of picture editing, where our point of view constantly shifts from wide to narrow, and from groups to close-ups. But the ear can't get used to sudden changes in level and direction. If we tried to match a character's location—on the left side in a two-shot, then suddenly centered and louder when we cut to a close-up—it would be distracting and take away from our involvement in the story.

Protect the center

In theatrical films, dialog is almost always carried on a separate channel and played back through a speaker behind the center of the screen. This *center channel* rarely carries

---

[9] Pronounced "M-O-S" and meaning *shot as picture-only*. The basis for this acronym is lost in history, but theory is that it was an instruction to early sync operators to start the nearby camera motor without alerting the distant sound recorder, or as a "Motor-Only Shot." On the other hand, Hollywood tradition is that a German-speaking director asked for a scene "Mit Out Sound." (Current Hollywood joke is that it stands for "mixer outside, smoking.")

background sound effects or solo musical elements, even if they're supposed to sound like they're coming from the center; instead, those elements are often routed equally to the left and right speakers and mix psychoacoustically in the theater. (This psycho-acoustic mixing, to form a *phantom center*, takes place in good stereo setups as well. That's how your favorite musician can be in the center of a mix on a stereo CD playing through two speakers . . . or even in the center of your head when you're wearing a pair of earbuds.)

Keeping the dialog on its own center channel in a theatrical mix helps guarantee it'll stay intelligible, no matter what else is going on. But even if your film or video will never be played on systems with more than two speakers, you should still try to reserve the center—or at least the phantom center—for dialog.

- Beware of musical solos under dialog. In most music mixes, the vocal soloist is centered. If your score will have a vocal while somebody's talking, try to get it remixed so the vocal is off to one side. If that's not possible, consider editing the music so an instrumental bridge is playing during dialog (music editing isn't difficult; see Chapter 13).
- This applies to solo instruments as well, if their frequencies compete with voice. An acoustic guitar or alto sax can have a lot of energy in the same range as dialog. Treat it as you would a vocal.
- Remember that anything carried equally in both the left and right stereo speakers will appear to be coming from the center. If a sound effect is supposed to be *big*, start with a stereo source rather than just putting the same thing on both left and right. Or use a trick like echo or delay to make the channels slightly different (see Chapter 15). Loud and wide is bigger than loud and in the middle, and leaves room for dialog as well.
- Obviously, you don't have to worry about protecting the center when there's no dialog.

MUSIC

It may seem obvious, watching the latest Hollywood blockbuster with a wall-to-wall orchestral score, that music can play an important part in a production. But many producers don't do anything with music until the end of the editing process, and then simply add an opening and closing theme for a corporate piece, or leave everything up to the composer in a narrative film.

Music can be an important element throughout a production. Aside from the obvious title and end credit theme, it can be used to explain settings, tie scenes together, emphasize emotions, call attention to important plot or visual elements, or even be an additional character with an attitude of its own. In any film or video, music can be everywhere.

Source music

The most obvious place to consider music is when it's a sound effect—something we can see happening on the screen. If the characters are at a parade, we must hear a marching band. If we see someone put a CD into a player, we should hear music come out of the speakers.

Other kinds of scenes imply music even though we can't see the source. A school dance should have rock and roll, sounding either live or played by a DJ depending on the school's budget. But don't forget other places where canned music will make a scene more realistic: restaurants (particularly if you want to establish an ethnic flavor), shopping malls, and—though often played for humor—elevators.

Source music—sometimes called *diegetic music* by film theorists—is an excellent way to build another layer into your soundtrack, since it occupies a place between the up-front dialog and any background scoring. The trick is that it has to sound like it's really there. You can't shoot the scene with the music playing because that would make voice pickup difficult and editing impossible. So a separate music track has to be heavily processed with echoes and equalization to put it in the same environment as the dialog. If the characters are hearing the music from a loudspeaker, remember that the viewer is hearing *the entire scene* from a loudspeaker: the music has to be extra processed, so it sounds even more canned than the dialog.

Source music also has to be chosen for musical and production values that match the scene. Background music in a supermarket or elevator should be appropriately insipid. If the characters are listening to a pop radio station or jukebox, the music should be an authentic pop style, probably a vocal. This becomes most critical in cases like that of the school dance with a live band: a five-piece garage group will have a thinner sound and more inept playing than anything you're likely to find in a studio recording. Chapter 13 has some tips for getting source music.

Scoring

The kind of continuous underscoring found in theatrical films can be too expensive for smaller projects, but it still helps to think about music the way they do in Hollywood. Once you know exactly what the music is trying to accomplish, it's easier to find what you want in a library or hire a composer to create a few short affordable cues.

Aside from the title and end credit sequences, there are three major ways scoring can be used in your project.

Music as an emotional statement

There's no question that sad, anxious, or romantic music, riding under the dialog, affects how we perceive a dramatic scene. But music can convey emotions even when there is no dialog. The pounding score under a car chase or fight scene, and the whimsical ditty under a comic montage, are both filling the same purpose: to help shape the viewer's reaction to what's on the screen. By extension, a montage of widget manufacture in a corporate video can use music the same way. Rather than settle for a background track, think about what the scene is supposed to convey: Is Widgetronics including this sequence to show off their precision, or their efficiency, or their power, or the human way they care about every widget that comes off the line?

The classic film scores of the past were composed in the European tradition of *program music*, where events in a story were linked to parts of the composition. They developed along musical lines, while still being timed to important emotional moments in the scene. These days, it's equally common to match every action to an appropriate chord or shimmer and then fill in the notes between (musical development may be an afterthought, if the composer even has time to deal with it), or to use a piece of music that wasn't necessarily written for the scene and add occasional punctuations in sync with the picture. While these two conventions may represent a decline in the art of classical Hollywood scoring, they're a blessing for video producers: the matched-chord-and-shimmer approach can be executed economically on electronic keyboards, and even if you can't afford any original music, library cuts can be edited seamlessly to fit this occasional-punctuation style.

In its sparsest incarnation, this kind of scoring can punctuate dialog with just a few notes. A quick broken piano chord might be all you need to highlight a conflict; a string stab can call our attention to a dramatic foreshadowing. Even a few whimsical notes under some vaguely humorous action can help add texture to an otherwise static scene. The important thing when using music this way is to plan for it, leaving appropriate pauses during the shoot or creating them in the edit.

Music to identify a character or plot development

John Williams used motifs in the score for *Star Wars*: every major character had a unique theme, and these themes would interact and develop as the characters played out the plot. But he also used motifs in the score for *Superman*, linked to plot developments instead of characters. Whenever Superman went to fight villains, the score was based on the march music from the main title. But when he and Lois had a romantic moment, we'd hear a snippet of their love song (oddly reminiscent of Richard Strauss' 1898 orchestral suite *A Hero's Life*).

You can do the same sort of thing when scoring a smaller film. Recurring themes—even ones chosen from a library—can be used whenever a particular kind of plot development takes place. Using music this way isn't limited to dramatic videos: for a History Channel documentary about a citywide construction project, I used timpani-heavy variations of an orchestral theme under the heavy-equipment sequences, an electronic piece reminiscent of the theme when we were seeing the high-tech control rooms, and classical instrumentations of the main theme during history and archeology scenes. And it all came from library cuts.

Music to set a scene

There is no faster way to establish an ethnic or nostalgic setting than to use appropriate music. Any good music library will have plenty of cuts designed for this purpose, and most composers welcome the challenge of working their music into a different style.

But scene-setting music doesn't have to be a caricature. You can use more mainstream styles to mark the passage of time, or a jump from one locale to another. You can also join two pieces of music that are related in key and texture, but different in tempo or dynamic, and use this new cue to show an abrupt change in mood.

The pitfalls of popular music

It's common practice in mainstream films to include a number of pop songs either as source music or underscoring montages. These songs might be newly created for the film, be classic recordings, or be new covers of pop standards; no matter where they came from, they're sure to receive lots of attention and be highlighted in the film's promotion.

There can even be artistic justification for using the songs, if they're tied to emotions in the story, and over the sweep of an hour or longer they can provide a textural element . . . particularly in sections where there's no dialog. But there's also financial incentive to use these songs: a best-selling "soundtrack" album can contribute to the producers' and musicians' income stream. (I put "soundtrack" in quotes because these albums seldom have much to do with the film's track: they often include songs heard only peripherally in the film, and covers by big-name artists that weren't part of the track at all. It's a certainty that very little of the film's actual underscore will be included.)

This Hollywood practice may tempt you to use popular songs in your video the same way. If so, remember two things:

- If you don't have a slew of permissions—at least two different ones from the people who wrote or published the music, and two more from whoever owns the recording—you're running the risk of major lawsuits. The fact that a video may be nonprofit, educational, or nobly intended is not a defense. Unless you're willing to risk your production business or personal savings, talk to a lawyer before you consider breaking this rule. I've heard of record companies putting wedding videographers out of business, because of an unlicensed pop song in some couple's precious memories. There's much more about licensing and copyright in Chapter 14.
- Even if you have permission to use an existing song, your viewers have already linked it to events and feelings that may have nothing to do with your video. Once you start playing *their* music, you don't control their experience any more. While there may be emotional justification for hearing "Can You Feel the Love Tonight" when George first tells Sue how he feels, do you really want to remind a viewer about her own breakup with an ex-boyfriend who liked that song . . . or have her start thinking about animated jungle animals?

Pop music sound-alikes are available from bigger music libraries, can be fully licensed to avoid lawsuits, and carry less emotional baggage.

SOUND EFFECTS

There's a rule in Hollywood: if you see it, you should hear it. While it's true anything that moves air molecules quickly enough will make a noise, features and episodic television have taken this to extremes. I'm sorry, folks: no matter how good the action hero is at karate, his hands don't go "whoosh" when they fly through the air. And the *Enterprise* won't move air molecules as it swoops past us in the vacuum of space.

Low-budget producers often err in the other direction. Both documentary and dramatic videos can suffer from a silence that never occurs in the real world. (Take a listen while you're reading this ... there's probably a symphony of muted traffic noises, distant conversation, and small machines like clocks or computer fans. Even in the quietest library reading room, you'll hear footsteps and pages turning.)

Use sound effects to add richness and believability to your track.

Sound effects categories

As you're thinking about sounds in your video, you can break them into three categories.

Hard effects

The most common film definition of a hard effect is any noise that's linked to an on-screen action and must stay in sync with it. This includes the tiniest footsteps as well as gunshots and car crashes. In smaller productions, many of the smaller sounds may not need to be in perfect synchronization. If a project will be shown only on the Web or small screens in an office, the medium will forgive some lack of precision. Budget realities can also force you to paint with a broader brush. So I prefer to use "hard effects" to refer to sync effects that are big, obvious, and usually help the plot; of course, this includes the car crashes and gunshots, but also Sue's telephone or the crunch of a briefcase hitting the desk.

Natural sounds

This is a subcategory of what a Hollywood sound editor would consider hard effects. Feature films make a point of giving them their own track during a dialog edit, and then usually add more in *foley* recording sessions where specialists walk, move props around, and fake fist fights to mimic the on-screen actions.

In smaller productions, I prefer to use this term to denote the smaller sounds that add realism to the scene. They may be foleys, but they're more likely to be lifted from the production tracks or edited in from an effects library. Many times they're created by making small edits in a stock background or ambience track so that loud sounds happen around the same time as on-screen actions. These natural sounds might not match the video perfectly, but—as in the case of most clothing rustles, footsteps, or automobile passbys—they only have to *appear* to be in sync.

By the way, TV editors often refer to any incidental noises that were recorded with the video as "Nat Sound," including hard effects and even on-camera interviews. Their Nat Sound tracks can be an excellent source for natural sound in a scene.

Backgrounds and ambiences

Traffic, crowds, or random interior and exterior noises may be recorded at the shoot, but are more often lifted from a sound effects library or specially recorded by the sound editor.

Backgrounds usually aren't added until just before the mix because one of the purposes of these tracks is to smooth over dialog edits with continuous sound. Fading in the background a few frames earlier than a scene starts, and holding it a few frames after the scene's end, can also help smooth over visual transitions.

SILENCE

Walter Murch's track for *The Godfather: Part III* ends with Michael screaming when he discovers his daughter has been shot. But at first we don't hear the scream; we see Al Pacino's open mouth with nothing coming out. Murch deleted the scream during editing, to add that extra tension.

In *The Artist*,[10] "negative silence" becomes an element. The film takes place in the silent film era, and we get used to hearing only a score. There are no sound effects; when characters speak we see title cards instead of hearing their voices. But talkies are on the way, and silent movie star George Valentin has a nightmare about his future. In his dream we hear a glass clink and a dog bark—just two tiny sounds, but they're the first sounds in the movie, and they shake us up as much as they scare him.

SPECIAL EFFECTS AND PROCESSING

Don't forget that creative editing and technical manipulations can create additional types of elements for your soundtrack. Ideas like these might be too avant-garde for a corporate video, but certainly are appropriate in other films:

- Repetitive sound effects can be slowed down to a small fraction of their original speed and serve as the bass line of a piece of music.
- Musical elements can be used as sound effects. Try placing a cymbal crash or drum hit on the same frame as a hard effect, to thicken the sound. If the score uses similar cymbals or drums, it'll tie the music and action together—even if the action is nowhere near a musical beat.
- Tightly edited off-camera voices can serve as a rhythmic element that complements or replaces music. Tony Schwartz's track for the Academy Award-winning animated short *Frank Film* used a rhythmic montage of individual words in the animator's voice, as a quasi-musical element under the animator's own voice-over. And that was done long before digital editing and looping was possible.

---

[10] Winner of the 2012 Academy Award for Best Picture. You haven't seen it?

- Processed off-camera voices can serve as an additional layer in the track. Ken Nordine pioneered the idea of running his own voice through a telephone filter, and mixing in the result as parenthetical comments in commercials he created; this is now common practice in radio station promos. Other techniques, including diffusion and delays, can help viewers get into a character's mindset or point of view. The most common example—reverb when a character is thinking—is almost a cliché, but can still be effective. More creative solutions just require a willingness to play with sound.

THE LAYERS OF A TRACK

There's a definite order of importance of the various elements in a soundtrack. Understanding this can help you plan the track better; assembling the track in this order can be the most efficient way to work.

- Dialog and narration come first. They have to be edited smoothly and stay in the foreground of the mix. In a theatrical film, dialog editors will spend weeks working just on the words, and then their edits will be processed in a separate *dialog pre-mix*.
- Hard effects, if any, come second. They advance the plot and lend realism.
- If you're doing a low-budget project, music may come third. This is contrary to the way feature films are often built, but your resources may be more limited. A well-chosen and edited piece of music can eliminate the need for backgrounds and natural sounds.
- Backgrounds should be chosen and placed before worrying too much about natural sounds. Often, random noises in a prerecorded background will appear to be in sync and can serve the same purpose.
- Natural sounds should be finally added to scenes that don't have music or much of a background, or where an action definitely appears to be missing audio.
- In a feature film or other large project, music is often treated separately. A composer writes and records the score while the rest of the track is being developed and mixed. The music then gets added as the last step in mixing.

CHAPTER 5

Budgeting, Scheduling, and Pre-production

☞ ROSE'S RULES

- Sound is faster and cheaper than picture to create. But it's not instant, and it's not free. Having the right resources can change your film from embarrassing to elegant.
- Professional sound people are a bargain when you consider their skills and experience, and how that makes your production go faster and turn out better.
- Beginning sound people and volunteers can be a bargain, but only if you provide the time and training for them to do a good job.
- When you're scouting locations, remember you're making a talkie. A location that sounds bad can kill your film or its budget, even if it looks good . . . unless you plan for it before you shoot.

Digital camcorders and desktop video systems are enormously capable, but they're not magic. If you want a good-looking movie, you do much more than point the camera and hope for the best. If you want a good track, you have to do more than simply point a camera-mounted microphone. (In fact, the camera mic is usually the *worst* way to record a track. Chapters 6 and 7 tell you why, and show you the right way.)

A proper soundtrack requires a commitment of time and money. This is merely a small fraction of what you have to set aside for visuals, but it's still a commitment you have to make. In many cases, you can trade sound resources: spend a few dollars more and you'll get more convenience and a faster workflow; or work a little harder and save some money.

There are only a few basic tools you need to record dialog properly, and they're available for rent or purchase around the world. The more important decision is who's going to run them.

- If your project has a real budget,[1] hiring the right pros will save you money and aggravation, and give you more creative options.
- If you've got only a few dollars but a great script or compelling message, it may still be possible to get experienced professionals . . . if you go about it the right way.
- If you don't want to spend any money but are willing to spend some time, you may be able to attract talented beginners. But if you want a good track from these beginners, you'll have to make sure they're properly trained, and that they have time at the shoot to solve problems that an experienced pro would take in stride. You can save some time ahead of the shoot, by planning very simple shots.
- If you don't have any money, refuse to compromise the vision, and just want to start shooting . . . go for it. Your production tracks won't sound too good, but that's the risk you took. You won't be able to fix them in post without spending money you didn't have in the first place. Call the whole thing a learning experience—you'll have learned plenty—and move on to the next project.[2]

These decisions can be made on a task-by-task basis: it might make sense to get a professional sound operator for the shoot, but plan to edit the music track yourself.

To make these decisions efficiently, you have to know how much time or money each aspect of the track will cost. The Golden Triangle of production (Figure 5.1) applies to sound, just as it does to the rest of our business. Pick any two sides. You can have fast and cheap (but mediocre), good and cheap (but slow), or fast and good (but not cheap). You can't have all three.

Figure 5.1 The Golden Triangle: Pick any two sides.

---

[1] We're not talking millions, or even dozens of thousands. Even those cheap in-house training films and low-budget Public Service Announcements can get good professional sound, if you approach them right.

[2] I'm not being sarcastic. This is a perfectly valid way to learn filmmaking. Just temper your experience with books like this one, and don't expect Tour de France race results while you're still biking with training wheels.

BUDGETING FOR SOUND

I'm assuming you already have picture editing software and know how work it, or will be working with an experienced editor. So we won't include any costs for basic dialog assembly while you're building the show. (On the other hand, the techniques in Chapter 13 will make this part go faster and better.)

But you must budget for basic dialog recording. It doesn't just happen by pointing a camera's built-in mic at the actors. Expect to spend a few dollars for crew and the right equipment. And it helps to have a few dollars ready for postproduction sound: many producers find outside scoring, sweetening, and mixing services a bargain compared to the time and equipment necessary to do these things properly on their own. If a film is headed for broadcast or theatrical exhibition, they know they'll save a lot of disappointment, embarrassment, and even anger by having an experienced professional refine the track with a calibrated monitoring and metering system.

Here are some of the personnel and equipment costs you can expect. They were accurate when I wrote this (early 2014) and had been stable for years. Barring major technology or economic changes, they should be accurate for a long time to come— or if the economy does change, you'll at least be able to use them as a guideline.

The prices are based on nonunion corporate, feature, or documentary film and video in major production centers. Smaller towns are apt to have personnel with less experience or who split their time between audio and other gigs; they usually charge less. Union rates are similar but based on a fixed-length day, so overtime can get expensive. Advertising shoots are often more demanding, and personnel expect to be paid more for them.

Production costs: Crew

Audio mixer/recordist

Experienced operators who bring their own equipment for miking or recording the shoot may be the best investment you can make. (They're called *mixers* for historic reasons, even if they're holding a boom instead working a mixing panel.) That'll let you concentrate on getting good pictures and performances, while they guard against the acoustic and electronic problems that plague so many amateur productions. Plan on a pre-production meeting where you can fully describe the project and the location to the mixer; ideally, the head of every major department should be in on this meeting.

Most pros have invested tens of thousands of dollars in portable recording gear, know how to get the best performance from it, and have customized some of it for their working style or unique shooting situations. So they'll expect to get paid for their equipment, over and above a daily fee for their time. Rates are usually about the same as you'd pay at a rental house, so it's just a question of who you pay rather than how much.

If you already own the necessary equipment, of course, you can save on rentals. But don't expect anyone to do a good job with un-maintained equipment or the wrong gear for a specific project, just because you already own it and it was adequate for some other project.

For many video productions, there's no need to have the sound recordist actually use a sound recorder; they'll give you a proper audio feed to record in your own camera. Check Chapter 8 for guidelines. Some video cameras aren't capable of theatrical quality recording—this includes some of the highest-end cameras used in theatrical features—so a separate *double-system* recorder may be desirable. It's also common to record one or two mixed dialog tracks on the camera, while isolated mics and higher quality mixed tracks go to a separate recorder. The camera tracks are used for review and editing, with the isolated mics' tracks being edited along with them or applied as needed in audio post (these tracks are often called, simply, *iso*). The mixed track can also be fed to headphones for the director or clients at the shoot.

Of course, conventional film cameras require double-system because they don't record sound. (The few film cameras that did record sound were built for early television news. You might come across one in a rental or school inventory. A few models were capable of very good 16mm pictures, but none of them had good audio.)

An experienced mixer brings more than equipment to your project: you can rely on their skills for mic placement, acoustic concerns, boom and level control, and the setup of electronics and wireless mics. During the pre-pro, make sure they're familiar with the video camera you'll be using and its audio specifications; if they're not, plan for some compatibility tests before the shoot. Even the pros get blindsided by some of the compromises in prosumer equipment.[3]

Experienced mixers are often the most technically trained people on a set, even in Hollywood, and may be able to help you diagnose non-audio problems as well. Of course, sound has to be their first priority: Don't expect a mixer to do the job of a Digital Imaging Technician (DIT), who supervises the video equipment on complex feature shoots.

✔ TIP

It only looks simple

Don't assume that a boom operator is merely someone strong enough to hold a pole with a mic at the end. Aside from the physical endurance required, there's a lot of skill involved in pointing a mic accurately and quickly enough to cover back-and-forth dialog, while aiming the mic to avoid noise sources and changing its distance to compensate for the actors' delivery.

If you must use an inexperienced boom operator, make sure they read Chapter 8 and have a chance to practice with the equipment before the shoot.

---

[3] The same warning goes for your picture editor or the software you'll be using. Make sure the video workflow actually works, before you start shooting.

Depending on experience, figure $350–600/day. Experience, in this case, refers specifically to working on films or videos.[4] You'll also be expected to pay overtime after ten hours, and provide appropriate meals and breaks.

Boom operator

If only one mic boom is needed and it won't be actively mixed with radio or other mics, the location mixer will usually handle it. But if the mixer has to be constantly balancing multiple mics, or you need more than one boom, get an additional experienced operator. Figure $200–350/day.

✔ **TIP**

Nothing matters as much as experience

A young location mixer asked an experienced pro why the pro's daily rate was higher: "We use the same equipment, and do the same basic work. Why do producers call you first, even though you're more expensive?"

The answer? "Producers pay me for *mistakes I've already made*. They know I've already learned from those mistakes, so I won't be making them again when I get to their shoot."

Finding a good sound crew

If you're looking for an experienced sound pro, ask an experienced producer in your area. Or ask postproduction houses to tell you which mixers give them the best tracks. If you don't have those resources available, try the Web: sites like ProductionHub.com and Mandy.com act as clearing houses for film professionals in every category, and crewing agencies keep a stable of pre-qualified pros available.

Feel free to ask a prospective mixer what they've worked on, and cross-check their references. You may be able to verify their credits on IMDB.com, but don't be alarmed if they're missing: that site is geared toward Hollywood-based features, and a lot of experienced television, documentary, and corporate professionals slip beneath its radar. Don't ask for samples or a composite reel the way you would with an actor or director. There's no way to tell from a reel what the mixer was up against at the location, or how much fixing was done before the final mix.

---

[4] Experience with live sound, broadcast, and studio music recording is nice, but they use different techniques and have different philosophies. So don't expect a brilliant résumé in music to automatically mean skill with film dialog.

One excellent writer/producer/director[5] told me he tries to find out what else a prospective crew member does, apart from the job they're applying for: "We look for people with multiple abilities. Right now I've got a mixer who's also a great still photographer. He doesn't take pictures on our show, but it shows that he thinks creatively and in terms of a story. The technicians who keep their heads down, stick to their area and protect its turf, are the ones we don't want . . . regardless of how well they do their jobs."

Hiring a pro strains your budget?

In general, you get what you pay for. But if you can't afford a full-priced pro, it's still worth asking one or two. Some mixers are willing to do discount work for students or low-budget projects when they've got the time and are intrigued by the film. Or they might know a talented beginner who needs more experience.

But if you're not paying your mixer more than they'd make flipping burgers[6] —or maybe not paying them at all—skip the pro sites. You'll only be laughed at. Try Craigslist.org or a school's bulletin board instead. For best results, keep your posting real:

- Don't talk about "Sundance" or "network broadcast," unless you've personally had similar shows accepted there in the past.
- Don't promise money on the back-end, or that you'll hire them for big bucks after you get famous. Experienced crew members know both these things are usually illusions.
- Don't ask for specific equipment if you don't know exactly why that particular gear is appropriate. Don't expect professional equipment when you're paying hobbyist wages.
- Don't ask them to share your passion, even if you believe this is The! Greatest! Movie! Ever! Remember, at the end of the day it's *your* movie and vision. Even if they agree with your opinion, being sound mixer is just a line on the end credit.
- And please, never brag about the great camera you've rented, when you're not willing to pay for sound.

Contracts and deal memos

Unless you and a crew member have worked together before, some negotiation will be necessary. You must spell out at least a few things:

---

[5] Steve Stockman, who shows up in this book a couple of times. He's produced and directed everything from an MGM feature starring Sally Field, to weekly reality shows, with a lot of ads and music videos in between. He also wrote *How to Shoot Video That Doesn't Suck* (Workman, 2011).

[6] I've seen ads on Craigslist for "professional mixer with gear, $750/week" . . . and then listing a bunch of wireless mics and other gear the mixer is expected to supply. Figure five ten-hour days, the necessary self-employment taxes and insurance, and financing an equipment package and you end up with less than minimum wage.

- Dates of the shoot, agreed rate or total price for those dates. Unless it's an hourly rate, exactly how many hours make up a "day" and how overtime hours get treated.
- What equipment, expendables, and media will be provided, along with who's providing it. Also, who is responsible for loss or damage to equipment during the production.
- Agreed provisions or allowances for transportation, housing, and meals.
- Who owns the finished product and under what circumstances. Obviously the production wants all rights to use the recordings in any way. But are you insisting that rights transfer instantly, or does the sound mixer own the sound rolls until they've gotten paid?

That last item gets into the choice between hiring crew as employees or contractors. If they're employees, you're also responsible for reporting and paying the employer's share of their taxes, workers' compensation, or other legal requirements. If they're contractors you don't have to worry about these things, but they'll have to charge more to cover their own responsibilities. If a production is being made with state film incentive money, there may be strict rules about employment.

You can hire a production staffing company to sort this all out, pay the crew and required fees, and present you with a single invoice. Find them on the Web or ask your state's Film Bureau for recommendations.

Semi-formal agreements

None of this requires a lengthy document. Even a simple email conversation can be sufficient to cover the details. Even better is to gather all the details from that conversation into a simple letter and have both the producer and the crew member sign it. One common arrangement is the *Deal Memo*, a semi-standardized form including the above provisions plus such things as overtime, cancellations, screen credits, confidentiality, or anything else that might be important to a specific show. There are plenty of simple one- and two-page Deal Memo templates on the Web; they're all slightly different, so search and download a few.

No matter how you're handling the work arrangement—email conversations, a pdf Deal Memo, or even face-to-face—it's important that both parties okay the terms. Simply telling someone "this is how I work," without their acceptance, leaves you in a much weaker position if anything goes wrong.

The phrase "work for hire" is often tossed around when hiring crew, but be careful; this has specific legal meanings that aren't obvious to us non-lawyers, and the IRS has tax rules for judging when it applies. I always insist on deleting that provision when I'm crew, and never ask for it when I'm producer. I figure it's better to spell out exactly what we're agreeing to, and leave the legalisms to attorneys.

And obviously, I'm not an attorney. Lawyers are specially trained not only to know the law, but also to analyze how it applies to your specific situation. The good ones keep tabs on everything that can affect our industry. Consider these pages merely general advice, based on what colleagues and I have learned in our careers. Because another thing professionals learn is that there are times when it's worth hiring a lawyer. If you need advice for a specific situation or there's lots of money at stake, this can be one of them.

Production costs: Equipment

The mixer may supply an equipment package as part of their basic fee or charge a nominal amount for its use. If not, you'll most likely need to rent an appropriate sound kit. Professional gear is rented on a daily basis; many rental companies price their weekly rentals at three or four times the daily rate, and allow extra time for shipping to out-of-town customers.

All of the equipment below is described in the next three chapters, along with directions on how to use it. Here are some usual daily rates:

- Lavaliere mics (non-wireless): $10–15.
- Lavaliere mic systems (wireless analog): $45–80.[7]
- Lavaliere mic systems (wireless digital): $75–150.
- Shotgun and hypercardiod (boom) mics: $25–50.
- Microphone booms: $10–15.
- Microphone mixers: $35–60.
- XLR transformer adapters for DV and SLR cameras: $5–20.
- Basic portable digital file recorder: $25–40.
- Professional portable digital file recorders (non-timecode): $60–100.
- Professional portable digital file recorders (timecode and multitrack): $100–175.
- Bundles including recorder, boom and mic, wireless lav and receiver, spare power sources and over-the-shoulder bag: $175–600.
- High quality wireless link from mixer to camera: $75–150.
- Wireless cueing/monitoring system: $75–125 plus ~$25 per additional receiver.
- High-quality headphones: $5.

Of that list, the last item is not only the cheapest but the most important. You can't count on good sound unless you're absolutely sure of what you're recording. Walkman-style phones aren't appropriate: you need a set that will isolate you from the outside world, so you can hear how room acoustics are being recorded and if there's any noise on the track. If you're using a boom mic, the boom operator should also have a set of headphones and—depending on your camera setup—may also need a separate headphone amplifier ($10/day).

Rental equipment usually comes with adequate cables for basic hookups; additional cables are available at trivial cost. Sound absorbing blankets or movers' pads are often thrown in for a few dollars, but you can buy them so cheaply that many producers don't bother renting.

---

[7] If you're renting older wireless systems, make sure they're still legal at the location where you'll be using them. See Chapter 7.

While I've included digital file recorders on this list, they may not be necessary: choosing the right audio setting and adjusting things carefully can give you adequate sound, with many cameras, for most non-theatrical purposes. You may also be able to use low-cost consumer file recorders, or even a laptop. Specific information about these options is in Chapter 9. Remember, how you use the microphone—not what you record it on—can have the biggest effect on a track's quality.

If you're doing a multi-camera shoot that relies on timecode and double-system sound, or plan to use multitrack recording to catch ad-libs on multiple wireless mics, hire a pro who can also specify the equipment. There are too many ways an inexperienced operator can ruin this kind of shoot.

✔ TIP

Compare rental rates

Film sound rental houses usually charge less than companies specializing in video gear, because they understand how good audio equipment, when treated properly, will be serviceable for a long time.

Video rental companies expect all equipment to become obsolete as quickly as digital cameras do, so they frequently charge more than the film houses for the same sound gear.

Expendables

Many wireless transmitters use a standard 9-volt alkaline or lithium batteries, but burn through them quickly: to be safe, allow three battery changes per mic per day. Wireless receivers use one to three batteries each; change them once a day. While 9-volt batteries are available almost everywhere, it's important to use fresh ones. Batteries from an electronics store are usually better because they haven't sat on the shelf as long as those from a supermarket or drug store. Long-life batteries are available from film sound suppliers.

Most of the wired mics used in video production also require power, but don't consume very much. Prosumer mics often have a small battery in their case; one battery every day or two should be sufficient. Most professional and some prosumer mics can also run on *phantom power* supplied by the mixer or camera. See Chapter 6 for details. A few consumer mics use *plug-in-power* provided by consumer cameras … but wiring issues can make these mics hard to use on a boom or as a lav, and it's almost always a mistake to record dialog with a mic mounted on the camera.

Other handy sound supplies include non-allergenic paper surgical or makeup tape (for mics and wires hidden on an actor's body), safety pins (for the ones hidden in clothing), alcohol prep pads (for cleaning skin when mounting mics), rubber bands of various sizes, felt pads for noisy footsteps, pony-tail holders (the ball-and-elastic type are great for keeping cables neat), anti-static spray (for carpets and clothing), and gaffer tape (for just about everything). Condoms can protect small mics from water while only slightly muffling the sound, and I'll let you make your own jokes about their use.

Unless you're using older equipment, you won't need to worry about bringing tape. These days, sound recordings are delivered on DVD-ROM, compact flash, or conventional and solid state hard drives. Check with the production to decide what format will be the most acceptable and who's supposed to supply it, and with your equipment manufacturer to make sure a particular solid-state storage unit is fast enough. It's fairly common for a mixer to own multiple portable drives, lending or renting one to the production each night for transfers, and then taking it back later and recording new material on it. Of course there should always be a backup medium as well.

Sound logs—pre-printed pads for keeping track of audio takes and technical conditions—used to be essential for shoots. But this chore is now often done in the recorder itself, becoming a pdf file that goes along with the media.

Special shooting situations

Performances and sports or special events present their own problems. Large numbers of wired and wireless mics are often used. Multichannel mixers send a stereo track to the camera, an encoded surround mix for live broadcast or reference, and individual iso tracks for future remixing.

Musical and some stage events will mic the performers, and it's reasonable to borrow those mics' signals at the house sound system. But pre-pro is important here: you'll need a way to tap each mic without disturbing the house sound, which may be a jack on their mixer, or might require an isolation box (about $5 per mic to rent); plus permission to mess with their equipment. Permission isn't automatic and is more a question of the company's or touring act's policy than any technical consideration.

It may be tempting to just grab the house system's stereo mix: many house mixing consoles even have handy jacks for this purpose. But their mix is designed to combine with drums and amplified instruments to excite a crowd in the auditorium, and almost never works for a soundtrack. That's why you want to get isolated feeds from each mic, ideally going to a multitrack recorder for your own mix after the film is edited. Also, the amplified instruments, crowd responses and room acoustics probably aren't being miked by the house system, so they'll need extra mics and channels for the film track.

Theatrical performances can use multiple mics spaced around the stage apron. Panel discussions and legal proceedings may use separate mics for each participant. While there might not be more than three or four mics for either of these setups, they have to be actively controlled during the event to prevent noise and echoes. If you're not able to do this live, or can't record iso tracks for postproduction, then rent an automatic mixer ($75–250, depending on number of inputs).

Reality programming

This popular TV style presents unique sound challenges to the producer. Full-budget network shows often have two or more cameras rolling on each interview to provide reverse angles for editing, and might have another camera (or many) simultaneously covering action elsewhere. There are a lot of wireless mics, not only fed to appropriate cameras but also to individual channels on a recorder. The sound mixer has to make sure all those mics are properly routed, the recorder is functioning properly, timecode is going to cameras and slates as needed ... and still mix the primary scene in real-time, while paying attention to a producer or story editor who's trying to coordinate everything on the fly. It's a job for a pro with very good equipment.

Of course you can also shoot reality shows the way you would a single-camera documentary. It takes longer, and you'll probably miss some stuff, but it's simpler and cheaper, and conventional techniques apply.

Voice-over recording

The acoustics of the room become very important when recording narration, so unless you have a space specifically built for this purpose, it's best to hire a studio. Look for a studio that does a lot of spoken word; the acoustics and techniques for music recording are different. If a studio is completely out of your budget, plan to spend a few dollars on the sound-control techniques in Chapter 9.

In large cities, a good studio with an experienced engineer will cost between $125 and $300/hour, plus stock. The difference often has do to more with market dynamics and other services offered, rather than recording quality. The amount of time a session takes depends on the talent's experience, how much jargon is in the script, and your own directing style. If you're efficient, you should be able to record 20 minutes' worth of material in an hour.

Most studios will normally record directly into a computer, possibly with a separate drive or optical recorder as simultaneous backup. Make sure they'll deliver a format you can use. AIFF or .wav files at 48 kHz sampling are the most universal; higher sampling rates like 96 kHz have no advantage for voice recording. Standard 16-bit files are fine for professionally recorded voice-overs, though some studios prefer to record 24-bit files; again, there's no real advantage for narration recordings if they're using good equipment. You can get the files on optical media, USB flash or portable hard drives if you need physical media, or they'll send via one of the many Web delivery services. If storage space or upload time is a consideration, they can compress the voice tracks using Apple Lossless or Free Lossless Audio Codec (FLAC). Make sure the studio keeps a backup, at least until you've copied your version onto two separate drives.

DAT and other digital tape media are now obsolete for professional production, and many studios no longer have the equipment to deal with them. Analog media (¼" tape, or 16mm and 35mm magnetic film) are so ancient that you probably won't even be able to find blank media, other than through specialty suppliers at very high prices. These changes have been meteoric—DAT was common less than ten years ago, and analog well into the late 1990s—so some schools may still be using the older systems. Presumably they'll have a source for stock as well.

Long-distance recording

Dial-up ISDN lets you walk into a local studio and record an announcer from a distant city, hearing them with perfect fidelity and even playing voice or music references, or cueing a video playback in front of them. The sound is carried real-time in compressed format (see Chapter 2) and recorded locally. Aside from a slight delay introduced by the encoding system, it's exactly as if they were in the next room.

Depending on the compression system used and the studio's policies, this service will add between $75 and $300/hour to the local studio's charge. The distant studio will, of course, add their own charges. They may also ask if you want them to record a backup tape, but this is seldom necessary (if there's a problem, you'll hear and fix it immediately).

ISDN is also quickly becoming obsolete. It's limited to 128 kbps for a standard connection, a fraction of the speeds now standard with cable or fiber Internet. You can record an Internet session virtually in real-time, using high-quality compression; all that's needed is a fast connection and compatible software at both ends. The software is a minor expense for the studio, and may even be built into the multitrack program they already use, so most studios don't charge extra for this service.

Or you can direct the talent via Skype, Google Chat, FaceTime, or similar. The quality isn't wonderful, but you can have the studio send high-quality files immediately afterwards.

You might not need to pay a studio at all: Many professional narrators now have their own studios with good acoustics, professional equipment matched to their voices, and fast internet connections. Most will throw in studio services as part of their talent fee. Voice-over talent costs are described in Chapter 9, along with how to pay voices without getting into trouble with the talent unions.

Postproduction costs

Budgeting for music

Now we get to some real variability. Here are some guidelines for a corporate video shown to an internal audience. Commercials, theatrical films, broadcast programs, and videos for sale or public exhibition are more expensive: see Chapter 12 for a full breakdown.

Stock music: $15–100 per selection, between $75 and $350 for unlimited scoring in a ten-minute video. The lower end covers buyout music, typically basic arrangements on electronic keyboards. The higher end covers needle-drop libraries that use top film composers and arrangers, and record using top session players, vocalists, and full orchestras when appropriate.

Original music will cost between $200 and $1,000 per screen minute, depending on how good the composer is and how quickly you want it. At the higher end, it usually includes a mix of live instruments and high-quality samplers and can sound excellent.

While music prices have remained stable over the years, technical advances in the music industry keep raising the quality standards for both library and custom music. Shop around: you may find some incredible music for the money.

Sound effects

If you gather them yourself, or use some of the tricks in this book, sound effects are free. You can also download high-quality ones from the Internet, for license fees of a few dollars per minute. Most audio post facilities have immense stock sound libraries with computerized searching; depending on studio policy, the cost may range from nothing to $15 per effect. You can purchase libraries of sounds in a specific category (jungle animals, footsteps, sports, cars, etc.) from online sources and have them ship CDs for $50–75 each. Once you've purchased a sound this way, it becomes yours to use in any future productions. All of this is covered in Chapter 15.

Postproduction audio studio

A good studio that specializes in editing and mixing corporate or broadcast video sound, fully equipped and with a large stock library, will cost between $150 and $300/hour in major production centers. Studios that specialize in advertising sound are more expensive, because of the more intense client services and glitziness expected.

Theatrical sound editing and mixing

If you're working on a large theatrical project, it's wise to split the audio editing and mixing. Freelance editors can handle editing chores, often with very simple equipment and sometimes on their kitchen table. All they're paying attention to is dialog continuity and sound placement, and they can do that on a laptop with headphones. Then you take their pieces to a big calibrated studio for processing and cleanup, and for the final mix.

Sound editors can cost between $250–600 per day, depending on the market and their experience.

Theater-sized re-recording rooms, with surround monitoring (often calibrated to THX or Dolby specifications), and personnel experienced in film mixing: $250–1,000 per hour depending on equipment and experience. If you want your film to carry a Dolby logo—considered essential for theatrical release—be prepared to pay a few thousand dollars more depending on your film's budget. That covers their technical supervision and the legal license to use their name and logo.

How many hours will you need in a post studio, editing station, or re-recording room? The studio or editor will be glad to help you estimate, and some general guidelines appear below.

ALLOW TIME FOR SOUND

Again, I'm assuming you're already familiar with your editing equipment. Otherwise, all bets are off: you can waste hours rendering or processing sequences only to discover that the sound is damaged or out of sync because of a simple mis-set switch or a system conflict. Problems that are specific to particular brands or versions of editing systems are beyond the scope of this book, but there's some trouble-shooting information in Chapter 18.

Pre-production time

It won't take more than an hour to go through all the planning and location audio considerations in this chapter. Now is also the time to line up a location sound crew if needed, and also start thinking about postproduction audio resources: sources for music, voice-over studios, and—if you're going to use one—a mixing facility.

If you're using an experienced sound operator at the shoot, spend at least a quarter hour on the phone with them describing the location and setup. If it's a complex production, it's a good idea to schedule a full pre-pro meeting with the videographer or director of photography, set designer, sound mixer, wardrobe supervisor, and any other department that will have a major role at the shoot. The best pre-production meetings also include postproduction specialists, who can suggest things for the shoot that'll save time or money later on.

Have your meetings with the people who will actually be providing the services, not an agent or studio's booking manager. The former are involved in day-to-day problem solving; the latter just want to book as many days as possible.

☞ ROSE'S RULES

A half day practicing with a boom mic or mixer?

Yes.

Production sound is critical to the success of any dialog-driven project. The person responsible for sound has to know how to record a voice cleanly while compensating for room acoustics. This book explains the procedures, but hands-on—and ears-on—experience is essential.

If you can't afford the time to learn how to do this correctly, hire a professional. While almost any other kind of audio problem can be repaired (or resurrected) in postproduction, bad production sound will haunt your video forever.

Training time is an important resource

If you're running sound yourself, or assigning the job to a production assistant, allow enough time to get used to the equipment. I'd suggest at least a half day, doing actual recordings in similar circumstances. You may need to enlist a colleague to serve as temporary talent during practice sessions with a mic boom. Read Chapters 6–8 to learn what you'll have to do.

Time requirements at the shoot

If you've hired an experienced mixer, sound shouldn't take up much extra time during the shoot; most of the setup will take place while other people are worrying about sets, lights, makeup and camera. While it's fairly common to hear "waiting on sound" at a shoot, usually that's not because of problems with the sound recording itself. The waiting is for trucks or airplanes to pass and the set to get quiet: it's a location problem, caused by the producer's decision to shoot there. To keep sound most efficient, let the crew see any on-set rehearsals and keep them informed about blocking changes: this way, they'll know when to expect characters to talk or move.

Concealing a wireless mic on the talent can take a few minutes each and should be coordinated with wardrobe and makeup. If you're running sound yourself, don't assume a wireless mic will work before shooting anything important. Record a test first, and make sure both mic and camera are set up properly.

If you're using a boom mic with an inexperienced operator, the mic will dip into the scene or cast a bad shadow. It's inevitable. Allow time for extra takes. This is better than telling the operator to keep the boom high, where it might be safely out of the camera's way but won't get good dialog.[8]

If you don't have a separate audio operator and are using a simple setup with one or two wired lavs, allow an extra quarter hour to get things right. If you're using wireless mics in a steel-framed building or a location you haven't tested, make it at least a half hour. Count on a few extra takes when you notice, on playback, that a battery was running down.

If you're renting sound equipment, allow enough time to test it thoroughly. Allow even more time, before and at the shoot, if you're unfamiliar with that particular model.

Be realistic about ADR and noise reduction

Some locations have too many problems to allow successful dialog recording, and a dialog replacement session may be the only way to get an acceptable soundtrack. ADR (automatic dialog replacement, but it isn't really automatic at all), also known as looping, is an accepted part of Hollywood filmmaking. So are budgets that reach a hundred million dollars.

---

[8] Even experienced pros may dip into a scene once or twice, as they try to get the mic in that golden spot where it's close enough for good sound but out of camera range. Having a good working relationship between camera and boom operator will minimize this.

ADR is expensive, exacting, annoys the actors, and seldom gives you a wonderful performance or perfectly matching acoustics. It's frowned upon by the feature-film sound community. But some Directors of Photography will suggest it, when they feel they've waited too long for a set to get quiet or don't want to change the lighting to accommodate a boom mic. When a DP says "you can loop it later," sound designer Randy Thom often replies, "That's not fixing it; it's replacing it." In a production sound newsgroup, mixer Jon Trebilcock points out: "If you bring your Mercedes for a repair, and the next day they give you the keys to a Ford, would you say you got your car fixed? No, you had it *replaced* with something inferior. It runs, and will get you from point A to point B, but it's not what you originally bought. That's why the *R* in *ADR* stands for 'replacement,' not 'repair.'"

ADR should only be considered as a last resort in production; often, compromising slightly on the choice of location will yield a better overall project. If you must use it, *plan ahead*:

- Long shots are easier to loop than close-ups, because lip-sync errors aren't as obvious.
- Quick cuts with lots of cutaways are easier than longer takes, for the same reason.
- Short phrases are easier to loop than long speeches.
- Every word counts. The less dialog in a scene, the faster you'll be able to fix it.

The decision to use ADR doesn't absolve you of the responsibility to record sound. Your actors will need a guide track to work efficiently, and some of the original dialog or effects may be salvageable.

Be even more wary if the DP—or anyone else who doesn't deal with audio post—listens to noises on the set and says they can be cleaned up electronically with software. Many times, their ideas of what these tools can do are a mixture of wishful thinking, advertising hype, and urban legend. Noise reduction tools work pretty well for certain noises, under certain circumstances. But they're not magic—most rely on psychoacoustic tricks to hide the noise, not remove it—and can hurt the dialog quality. They're also not automatic and usually require time-consuming adjustment in post. See Chapter 16 for more on what they can and can't do.

Bottom line: Clean location dialog is best. ADR and noise reduction are occasionally effective workarounds, but always involve compromises.

The actual techniques for ADR are discussed in Chapter 9; noise reduction in Chapter 16.

Postproduction time

Ingest and syncing/conforming time

In the Bad Old Days (circa 2005), videographers couldn't start editing until they'd played location tapes in real time, and re-recorded them into their computers. At least they could do it digitally, a significant advantage over the Badder Older Days (circa 2000). Back then, most editing systems had only analog inputs.[9]

These days life is a lot simpler: you either pop a camera's memory card into a computer or copy it via a high-speed connection. This is the same as copying any other large file, but in the video world it's called *ingest*.

There's no extra expense and negligible extra time required to ingest audio that's been recorded along with video. Unless there's something wrong with your setup, it'll arrive in perfect sync. Transferring double-system audio from a separate recorder doesn't add any real expense either; editing systems can copy audio files much faster than video ones.

Of course the double-system files aren't in sync until you match them against picture. If you've recorded timecode on the camera and recorder, the editing system might do this automatically. Or it might not: there are still incompatibilities and bugs, even with professional equipment. It's standard to back up the timecode recorded on video with a human-readable visual slate: this is a conventional Hollywood-style "clap the sticks together" slate, with an added illuminated display locked to the sound recorder's timecode. Productions will shoot the display in close-up, so an editor can freeze the video and slide the sound so its timecode matches. If a production isn't using timecode, they record the same dialog on the camera's track and the double-system recorder and use the camera track as a sync reference.

Manual syncing takes time. Each time the camera stops and starts, files have to be located and slid together. This usually takes about twice the running length of the takes, but can be a lot more or less depending on the length of each take, skill of the editor, and luck.

As an alternative, you can use software like PluralEyes. It lets you load all the camera and sound takes onto a timeline, pairs up their names and then slides each pair to match, and then exports files in sync. It's incredibly fast compared to manual syncing, but does require a little thought and preparation while shooting. Details are in Chapter 13.

A traditional slapped slate is almost always shot and recorded as a backup for double-system sound. It's synchronized the same way they did it in Hollywood half a century ago, matching the still frame against the clapping sound. No matter how the matching is done—automatically or manually, using timecode or sound as a

---

[9] I first cut magnetic film tracks in college, in 1966. That technology was slightly less than 20 years old then, but not much different from the optical film recording developed in the 1930s. It remained the standard into the 1990s . . . So for 60 years, the industry was making sound recordings on magnetic or optical stuff that looked and felt like 35mm movie film. Since then we've moved from recording on DAT to hard drive to magnetic/optical disc to removable memory, and I've also had to learn at least four new and totally different methods of joining two sounds together.

Two take-aways. First, the basics haven't changed at all: how you place a microphone or adjust levels, or where you make the edits so nobody can tell they're there, are still the same. Other than the medium, we're still using—and building on–techniques people were developing 80 years ago. And second, I'm not complaining. Today's gear is cleaner, sounds better, and weighs a lot less.

reference—precision crystals in the camera and recorder will keep digital files in sync for the length of a take. (For very long takes or complex setups, you can replace the crystals with a common wired reference.)

We don't need no stinkin' sync?

It may be tempting to skip the process entirely, edit picture based on the reference audio track, and plan to sync the double-system recording before mixing the track. This certainly means you'll start editing faster. But be warned: Syncing is many times slower after the picture is cut, because the slates have been discarded and takes have been sliced into multiple pieces which must be synced separately. It can add extra days and thousands of dollars to the production.

There are post-edit conforming systems that are supposed to do this job automatically, but don't assume they'll work. Unless everything is perfectly coordinated —the shoot, the sound recording, the brand and model of editing system, the audio software, and the editor's technique—they're not very reliable.

Audio postproduction time

I can knock off a 20-minute spokesperson show for a corporate sponsor in about a day, including dialog repair, music scoring, sound effects, and mix. A one-hour documentary for one of the arts or science cable channels—some 42 minutes of material—takes about a week, because there are more diverse sources and the standards are higher. So when I did my first theatrical feature, I figured "It's only 90 minutes on the screen. What can it take? Three weeks?"

I should have known better. I used to mix national TV commercials, 30-second small-screen epics where the financial stakes are so high that there would often be four or five executives from the ad agency in the room. One of those spots could take a day or more, depending on how much the various players wanted to tweak and second-guess. And then they'd call a week later with changes.

I learned that sound for a 100-minute theatrical film is as complex as 200 national spots, and takes about as long.

This isn't because theatrical films have steep technical requirements; it's that the expectations are higher. When you're dealing with an emotional story going on a large screen in a darkened room with excellent sound, you want everything to be perfect. You'll want to try things, be a bit cleverer in the design, and fix tiny clicks or slightly odd timings that nobody would notice in a TV show.

This is the main reason why the credits at the end of a feature film are so long: those hundreds of people each had something to contribute. A mentor once told me, "Nobody ever finishes a movie. It just gets taken away from you." Since this was the director who'd hired me for that first feature, and we were making tweaks in the track almost up until the day the distributor took it away to run in theaters, he probably had something there.

When you're figuring your time budget, use the following section as guidelines only. Some simple videos may go faster. And depending on your commitment to the project, you might want to spend a lot longer.

Editing/mixing in an audio post suite

This is the standard for smaller projects, including many TV shows and almost all corporate or special-interest films. Everything is done in one room equipped with a combination of audio editing and mixing software, a medium-sized control console (perhaps eight or 16 hands-on faders), calibrated monitoring speakers and acoustics, and a medium-sized picture monitor (maybe 50″ or so). The emphasis is on efficiency: both the room and the operator can do audio chores faster and more accurately than they'd be in a video editing suite. For example, replacing a single word of on-camera dialog may take five minutes or so in a frame-based NLE, but the same edit could take less than 30 seconds for an experienced sound editor with a high-end audio work-station.[10] The workstation's mix automation lets you fine-tune levels with more flexibility than an NLE, controls special processing like noise reduction or room simulation, and can generate voice-, music-, and effects-only mix stems[11] with a single command.

The time needed to fine-tune and pre-mix the dialog depends on program length and the quality of the original recordings. You can start by figuring half a day for a well-recorded half-hour TV episode (about 20 minutes of new recordings, after you subtract for commercials and the show's standard open and close) or similar length from a dramatized corporate piece, but it'll be faster for a piece with a lot of voice-over narration, and slower if you've got a lot of noisy recordings. The other factor is how much you want to chase perfection: a tiny click from a radio mic, or slight difference in dialog texture between shots, might be acceptable in a weekly TV show. But if the piece is heading for theatrical exhibition or will be shown every hour in an important museum, you'll take the time to fix those things. Even playing the mix "just once more" to make sure you're happy can eat up a significant fraction of an hour.

Sound-effects placement is easier to predict. Adding one or two hard effects and a couple of backgrounds to a five-minute scene shouldn't require more than 15 minutes, assuming you already have the effects in a well-indexed library or are willing to buy them from an online source. If you have a library management program like SoundMiner it'll go even faster. But don't expect to achieve the deeply layered richness of a feature film: Hollywood sound cutters allow a week per ten-minute reel.

Finding library music is a major variable. If you have a large library on hand or online, and use the tips in Chapter 14, plan on spending five to ten minutes per cue. Picking music for a one-hour, densely-scored project should take about a third of a day. This is often best done outside the post studio, since all you need is simple software to play the scene and prospective music at the same time.

Using the music also takes time. Figure two to three times the running length of the music to download the cues, place them against picture, and check the result. Fine-tuning stock music to match the length of a sequence depends on your skill as an editor; maybe ten or 15 minutes per scene.

---

[10] Of course, they'd be using the tips in Chapter 13 to do the job faster.

[11] Usually required by TV networks and theatrical distribution companies, and a good idea for any complex soundtrack.

Editing and mixing theatrical films

Bigger films almost always break editing and mixing into separate functions, mostly for economic reasons. A theatrical mixing suite is expensive, and the giant screen and calibrated surround monitoring is overkill when all you're doing is putting takes together and cutting out noises. That's why the editing is farmed out to freelancers (page 268).

How long a dialog editing job will take depends on its complexity, but a good editor should be able to cut a 20-minute segment of a well-shot dramatic film in about a day.

For theatrical mixing, figure three days per 20-minute segment as a minimum, but it often takes much longer. Add about a day for mastering and outputting the final version. TV and corporate projects go much more quickly, though in most markets they're mixed in the smaller postproduction audio suites.

CHECKING LOCATIONS

If you're producing an action film for theatrical release, you can choose locations based on how they look. If they're also good for sound, that's great; if not—or if special effects machines will be noisy—you'll replace the dialog later. (And if replacing the dialog means a more stilted performance, who cares? It's an action film.)

For most other projects, dialog replacement isn't a good option: it costs money, wastes time, and usually results in a less believable film. So the location has to sound as good as it looks . . . which means scouting with your ears as well as your eyes.

If you know in advance how locations affect sound, you can prepare efficiently for the shoot and be ready to fix problems as they occur. If a location is just too beautiful to pass up but sounds awful, try rewriting the script so there isn't so much spoken dialog there.

Potential problems

I live in New England, where autumns are particularly spectacular. You can point a camera almost anywhere and get a wonderful shot . . . unless you're shooting dialog. Even the prettiest location can have audio problems that cost time and money to fix.

The laws of acoustics are in full force every day of the year, indoors and out. There are only three things you have to ask to know if a location is sound-worthy:

- Is it quiet enough for dialog?
- Does it have the right acoustic properties?
- Will you be able to use equipment without interference?

There are other location issues—access, electrical power, legal clearance, and so on—but they also affect picture, so you'll probably be checking them anyway.

Noise in exteriors

The microphone is a lot less selective than the lens. A city park may look as bucolic as a medieval pasture, if you avoid shooting the tall buildings behind the trees. But you can't avoid traffic and crowd noises; once they're on your track, you can't get rid of them without starting from scratch. It may be obvious you can't record dialog for *Robin Hood* in Central Park, but other conflicts aren't as obvious. You have to visit the location, stand where the talent will, and listen. Whatever you hear will be part of your finished track,[12] unless you're willing to spend extra time and dollars in post. Here are some ways to avoid unpleasant surprises with exteriors:

- Scout at the same time of day you're planning to shoot. A suburban park that's quiet at nine o'clock may be very noisy when school's just gotten out. Traffic and crowd patterns change depending on the time of day, and major streets have been known to attract radio station helicopters during rush hour.

Figure 5.2 That shack in the woods would make a great rural setting—
but the apartment house behind it (inset) reflects traffic noises all over the "farm."

---

[12] Old joke: Director of a Civil War epic asks, "Will that jet plane overhead hurt our sound recording?" Sound mixer replies, "Not at all, sir. We'll get a perfect recording of a jet plane."

- Try moving ten or 15 feet in various directions while listening to the background noise. One side of an open field might be a lot noisier than another, without any visually obvious reason. On the other hand, low-frequency sounds aren't as directional: if there are a lot of trucks on a nearby highway, their sound will infect the whole location.
- Watch out for very large buildings in the middle distance, like the apartment house peeking over the trees in Figure 5.2. Those buildings don't make noise themselves, but mid-and high-pitched noise from nearby traffic or factories can bounce off them and into your shot. This is worst when a building's surface is mostly glass and it has two wings at an angle: they act as a corner reflector, focusing the sound right at you.
- Be aware of airline flight patterns. Some times of day have more flights than others, and runways change from one day to the next. Ask neighbors what their experience has been.
- If you're using generators, make sure they can be positioned far enough away to be quiet; ideally behind some solid structure to block the sound. Bring enough high-current extension cable to run between generator and set.

Noise in interiors

Interior locations have fewer variables, but you still should listen at the same time of day you'll be shooting. Pay careful attention to windows: do they overlook a potential noise source, such as a loading dock or trash compactor? Can you get these operations shut down while you're shooting?

If a window leaks a small amount of traffic noise even when it's tightly shut, try hanging sound-dampening blankets over it. If the window is part of the shot and can't be covered, cut down its transmission by sealing a piece of thick Lexan or Plexiglass to the frame. If all else fails shoot a point-of-view through the window, showing the traffic, or have a character remark on how many cars are on the road today. Include it early in the edited sequence so the viewer at least has a reference for the sound.

Check every opening into the room. Standard office doors aren't very good at stopping sound.[13] If there's a potentially noisy work area or hallway on the other side of the door, make arrangements to keep it quiet while you're actually shooting. Pay attention to conference room media walls as well: these are often openings to another potentially noisy room.

A common practice in office buildings is to build partial walls that stop at the suspended ceiling. The area above the ceiling is an open plenum—sometimes extending completely across the building—where ducts and cables can be run. It's also an open path for sounds to pass from one room to another. To check if this is the situation at

---

[13] A solid-core door makes a fairly good barrier by itself. But it's almost never installed with tight seals on all four edges, so sounds are free to go past it. A typical closed office doorway is almost as sound-transparent as an open one.

a proposed location, pop a tile near a suspect wall and take a look. But you can sometimes tell just by following the ceiling grid as it approaches a wall. On a proper wall, the grid terminates at an angle bracket (Figure 5.3A). But in some cheaper construction, they hang a continuous suspended ceiling over the entire space before they break it up into rooms. The walls extend just up to the tiles, so the grid disappears above them (5.3B).

There are special fiberglass ceiling blankets to absorb some of the noise from an open plenum, available from acoustic suppliers and installed by laying them over a room's entire ceiling. They're not expensive, but installation is difficult and they're not wonderfully effective. If you absolutely must shoot in a space with an open plenum above, you may have to shut down nearby areas or wait until after the building closes.

Air-conditioning systems can be particularly troublesome at interior locations. Listen carefully for sounds they make, remembering that the microphone will hear them louder than you do. Fortunately, a lot of the noise from HVAC systems comes from the grilles themselves! The stamped metal louvers bounce air molecules to direct

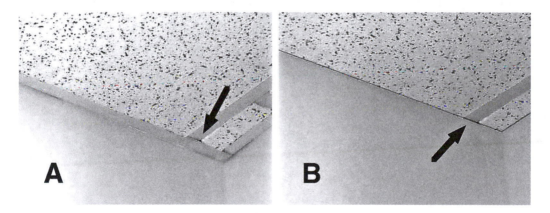

Figure 5.3 If a suspended ceiling grid disappears (arrow on right), it means the wall doesn't go all the way to the true ceiling.

✔ TIP

Hush that heater!

If you can't shut an HVAC system off, grab a screwdriver and take off the grille where air enters the room. You'll often eliminate more than half of its noise that way!

them into the room, and moving air molecules *are* noise.[14] Office buildings often have adjustable dampers built into the grille to control air flow; these contribute a lot of noise as well.

HVAC noise can also come from poorly chosen or routed ductwork, or nearby fans and compressor motors, so turning the system off is always the best solution. This kind of noise is one of the hardest to treat in a mix, so anything you can do to control it at the shoot will help your film.

The worst situation is an HVAC system that turns on and off automatically and can't be manually controlled. When some shots have air noise and others don't, it's very distracting to cut between them. Be sure to record additional room tone with the air conditioner running, and place it only under the quieter shots. This is a compromise solution, of course, degrading good recordings to match the bad ones.

Even with the system turned off, ducts are still sound paths to other parts of the building. If there's another vent in a noisy hallway, you may hear the hallway's conversations and footsteps on your set.

There are also noisy motors in refrigerators, water coolers, ice makers, large computers, and even fish tanks. The best solution is to turn them off while you're rolling. As with air-conditioning systems, watch out for ones that turn on and off automatically.

✔ TIP

A key trick

If you're turning off a refrigerator, put your car keys in it first. You won't be able to go home without being reminded to turn the fridge back on. (I wish there were a similar reminder to make sure you turn on a fish tank's circulator after a shoot. Fish probably wish the same thing.)

Acoustic problems

Even if you've found an incredibly quiet interior location, you still have to deal with room acoustics. You don't notice all the reverberation in a room while you're having a conversation. Microphones pick it up, and can make a recording sound boomy or hollow.

While some new software can actually lower this reverb at the mix, it's not perfect. The best solution is to quiet those echoes before you shoot. This needs a combination of added absorption, often provided by sound blankets or fiberglass panels,

---

[14] They can also be music or dialog, as you'll remember from Chapter 1. But in this case they're purely noise.

and keeping the mic close to the talent. It's counterintuitive, but larger spaces can be less of an echo problem. They let you place the action in the middle of the room, far from reflective walls. There's more about reverberant rooms in the next chapter.

Reverberation is seldom a problem with exteriors, unless there's a large building nearby to reflect sound. If there is, it'll probably be in the shot, so viewers will expect to hear some slap from it.

Electronic interference

Wireless mics are subject to interference from television stations, police radios, video monitors, neon lights, bug zappers, and virtually anything else that relies on sparks or electronic circuits. Over the next few years, these problems will get even worse as new consumer electronic devices crowd the frequencies normally used by mics.

The problem is that a transmitter tiny enough to hide in somebody's sock or the small of their back isn't going to be very powerful. Also, wireless signals are reflected by a building's steel framework, nearby cars, or even large lights; this can cause radio cancellations similar to the acoustic ones in hard-walled rooms. Newer all-digital wireless rigs are less subject to noises from sparks or zaps, but can be more sensitive to radio echoes from metal in the building.

Check Chapter 7 for tips on getting the best results from a wireless rig. And always bring a wired backup, or adapters to use the wireless mic's pickup element with ordinary cables.

Wireless can also be affected by those rectangular cell phone antennas planted all over the place (Figure 5.4). While the phones themselves currently work on different frequencies than a wireless mic, the signals from the relay station can mix together in low-cost receivers to create unpredictable interference.

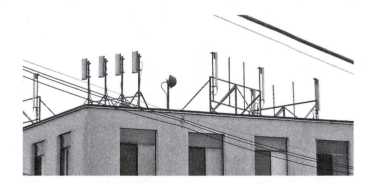

Figure 5.4 Those ubiquitous cell phone antennas can radiate combinations of signals that interfere with wireless mics.

Some locations even cause noise in wired mics. High-voltage transmission lines, power distribution transformers, medical equipment, and even lamp dimmers can radiate interference that's distributed by the building wiring and picked up by the mic. If you're at a location where this may be a problem, try a test first. Balanced wiring with Star-Quad (Chapter 3) really helps—but only if your mixer or recorder has true balanced inputs, usually on XLR connectors. If your mic plugs into a mini-jack on the camera or is otherwise unbalanced, you'll also need a transformer adapter (Chapter 8) to get Star-Quad's noise immunity.

Noises made by the production

Even if a location is quiet when you scout, the crew and equipment make noise. Personnel can be told to shut up, but they're still going to breathe and move . . . and whisper, hoping it won't be heard (it will be). Better to provide a workroom away from the set, where talent, makeup, and other folks who aren't involved in the current shot can prepare for the next one. Generator sounds carry for long distances outdoors, so you should plan to locate them at a distance and if possible, on the other sides of buildings and solid walls. Even some pro video cameras make noise with fans and lens motors: if the camera is close to talent for an intimate scene, you'll hear it in the track. These motors can have temperature sensors that make them go faster when the camera heats up, meaning the noise can vary during a scene. See if there's a menu setting to turn off the fans or at least keep them at a constant speed, and let the camera cool off between takes.

Remind everybody who's staying on the set that "Turn cellphones off" means *off* . . . not "silent." Vibrating phones can be picked up on your track (particularly if they're touching something solid that can resonate). And even a truly silent phone will make somebody start moving around, rustling clothing and clicking buttons, when there's a call. Turn the things off. If someone insists on merely setting theirs to silent, make them wear a sign, "My personal business is more important than your shoot!"

Be aware, even if your perfectly behaved crew is being quiet, their breathing and subtle movements will get into a dialog track. This probably won't be a problem while you're shooting, but you'll miss their quiet rustle if you edit with roomtone that wasn't recorded until everybody went home. For the best roomtone, ask the entire set to stand still and hold for 30 seconds, right after the last shot of a setup. Record roomtone for that setup. Then they can strike and move the camera.[15]

Location considerations for special situations

Voice-overs

If a character or spokesperson is seen on camera and then intercut as a continuing off-screen voice, the reverberation should match or the edit will be distracting. Best to record that voice-over at the same location as the on-camera shot. Obviously, you should use the same mic at the same distance as the character's on-camera dialog.

---

[15] C'mon: 30 seconds in the service of a better sounding movie? Producers might complain that it's a waste of time, but you're probably spending a lot longer than that adjusting each light.

If there's a lot of material to record this way and it can't be scheduled during down-time at the location, come back when the location is free. If that's going to be impossible, record in a studio. But choose one with excellent acoustics and no natural reverb of its own. A studio is essential for this kind of matching: every location has its own unique sound, and trying to match a real-world shoot with a randomly chosen room near your office—even if it's roughly the same dimensions, carefully isolated with blankets—is seldom successful. Recording continuing off-camera lines in the star's trailer only gives you temporary dialog for editing, no matter how good they are as actors. You'll have to re-record in a studio later.

The studio engineer will need to know how the microphone was set up at the location and should have a sample location track as a guide for processing. Hearing a location track will also help the talent match the original speaking style.

Actual narration, where the character or spokesperson is talking directly to us as viewers, is a different story. The acoustics should be different. Ideally they're in a kind of limbo with no acoustic of its own, so the character's voice seems to be in our own viewing space. This is best done in a studio. If there are only a few lines and time or budget is a major concern, use a folding portable sound booth made of absorbing panels that snap into a frame. They don't provide any isolation—the area around the booth has to be kept quiet—but can control reverberation. In a pinch, you can assemble this kind of booth on the spot: create a frame with light stands, and hang sound blankets around its perimeter and across the top.

Industrial locations and other noisy places

If you have to interview a manager at a construction site or inside a busy office, intelligibility is more important than looks. Get the mic as close as possible—even if it's in the shot—and hope for the best. If you have to shoot dramatic dialog at a noisy site, a miniature lav as close to the mouth as possible—taped to the glasses or peeking out from a shirt collar—may be adequate if they're speaking loudly. But it's better to shut down most of the operations while shooting. A dialog replacement session (Chapter 9) may be the only cure.

Very wide shots

Since there's no place to put a boom, you have to use lavalieres. Wired is always better than wireless, but will restrict the actors' movement. Wireless mics work best when they're close to the receiver, so if a very wide shot means you can't get the sound cart close to the action, try hiding the wireless receiver behind some object on the set and run a cable to the mixer. If that's not possible, you can conceal a small recorder in the character's costume. Zaxcom makes digital wireless transmitters that include a timecode-capable recorder in the tiny body packs. It works as a conventional wireless when close, and provides a time-stamped digital recording when wireless isn't feasible.

On-set playback

Some sequences require that talent lipsync or dance to a previously recorded track. If you don't intend to record dialog or footsteps during these sequences, the audio setup is simple: all you need is a stable playback medium (portable CD, mp3 player, or even a laptop); speakers close enough so that talent isn't confused by room echoes; and a feed from the playback to your recorder for sync reference. It's helpful to use a medium that can be cued quickly to a specific point, for shots that don't start at the beginning of the song. Prepare a special playback disc or files with separate sections for each shot. Talent often likes to hear a bar or two of countdown before the shot starts, in a rhythm that matches and sets them up for the music to come. Your composer or post studio can prepare these tracks for you.

These sequences are often more effective if you're also recording natural sounds, dialog, or live singing in sync with the music track. This requires pre-production planning; if you play back the music track while they perform, their mics will pick up echoey and hollow-sounding music from the speakers along with their voices. Mixing will be virtually impossible. To shoot this kind of scene properly, have an experienced production mixer help you sort out the options:

- **Soft foldback:** This is the simplest kind of playback. Small speakers are used with just enough volume for the talent to hear the cues. Mic placement is critical to minimize pickup from these speakers, or else there'll be problems when the mic is mixed with the original recording.
- **IFB:** Small radio receivers, with tiny earpieces, are hidden on the talent. The cueing signal is transmitted to them. Mic placement is less critical, but the individual receivers can get expensive if you have to equip a large cast, the earpiece may show in very tight shots, and active movement—such as dancing—can shake the whole thing loose. An alternative scheme picks up audio frequencies from a large loop of wire running around the shooting area. It's cheaper and simpler than radios, but you still have to worry about visible earpieces.
- **Thumper:** The lowest rhythmic notes of a piece of music are played on special speakers and conducted through the floor. Miking is very flexible; any thumps that make it to the soundtrack can be filtered in postproduction. Dancers literally "feel the beat," but singers might need additional coaching right before the shot to make sure they stay in the right key.

If your project uses both film and video in the workflow, such as filmed scenes that will be delivered on videotape or DVD (or high-def video that'll be burned to 35mm film for foreign distribution), there will be subtle speed shifts that can affect sync (Chapter 12). This also requires pre-production planning. Sound and camera crews have to be aware of the workflow and make subtle adjustments to their equipment. Editorial and audio post will also be players, but taking care of this with everybody involved will eliminate major (and expensive) headaches.

If your project uses film as part of a video scene—perhaps because a character is watching a movie and we see the screen—or a video or computer screen appears in a scene shot on film camera, careful planning is also necessary. Fortunately for this book, those are camera issues. Play the movie silently or mute the computer, and add their sounds at the mix. If the on-screen movie's sync is critical, record a couple of seconds of its track while everything is rolling but before you call "action." This will serve as a sync reference in post.

Section III

PRODUCTION SOUND

Enough theory and planning. Here's where we get to practical realities.

This section is about production:

- Chapter 6 discusses how to choose the right kind of microphone, and how to deal with location acoustics. It's slightly technical, but it's definitely real-world. The concepts in this chapter are as important and necessary as pointing a light or focusing a lens. Get them right, and you've got a good chance of getting a great track.
- Chapter 7 teaches the techniques of production sound. There are long sections on holding and manipulating a boom mic, where and how to hide a body mic, and how to get the best results from a wireless rig. It won't turn you into a professional sound recordist overnight, but it does cover all of the basics you need to record professional quality dialog.
- Chapter 8 details the actual field recording process: capturing the signal from the mic with a minimum of noise and other problems. It includes advice for specific cameras and shooting situations, information you won't find in manufacturers' manuals. It also includes when and how you should record in something other than a camera.

Those three chapters are some of the longest in the book, because getting good sound at the shoot is critical, and there are a lot of things to consider.

- Chapter 9 explains how to record additional voices and effects after the shoot is over—the techniques are different from those in Chapter 7. It also has sections on how to record synchronized dialog for existing picture, and good ways to direct a voice-over performer. These techniques aren't used on every film, and this is also a long chapter. So to keep the length manageable (and save a few trees, on the print edition), we posted Chapter 9 at www.greatsound.info. You'll want a copy of this book handy, the first time you go to the website, to look up a password.

Okay: Let's shoot a movie.

CHAPTER 6

Microphones and Room Acoustics

☞ ROSE'S RULES

- What you hear isn't what you get. Mics and acoustics conspire to make any recording seem different than reality.
- It's not hard to choose the right mic for your budget and location . . . if you remember a few simple physical facts.

We listen to the world through rose-colored ears (though mine are sort of pink). Within a few minutes of entering a room, most people start to ignore its acoustics. The hum of machinery and computer fans that normally surrounds us seems to disappear when start paying attention to something else. It's no problem to pick out your child's voice in a crowded schoolyard or your friend's conversation at a noisy cocktail party. Our brains use subtle timing and level variations between what each ear actually hears, and rely on the convoluted shape of outer ears to affect sounds from different directions differently. Our eyes, and even our memories of being in different spaces, help focus our hearing even further.

This is not the real world. Our perception of the sounds around us is much more detailed than a simple measurement of vibrating molecules. We evolved this way to avoid predators, and it helps us modern humans cross the street safely and find our friends in a bar.

A microphone isn't that smart. It merely captures sound waves. When you shoot a home movie[1] with a camera mic, all the spatial and off-screen visual cues get lost.

---

[1] I'm using home movie as an example, but you can find plenty of similar tracks on YouTube as well. Chances are your first attempt at a no-budget narrative film, shot after school with some friends, had the same problem.

Play back that scene and your brain doesn't get the data it uses to perform perceptual magic while you're shooting. You become fully aware of the noise and reverb . . . they were there all along, but you ignored them while shooting.

To put it another way, reality makes the track sound awful. The only way to avoid this is to take special care when you choose and set up the mic.

ABOUT MICROPHONES

A camera's lens defines a precise rectangle. Point it in the right direction, and you'll frame a shot with only what you want the audience to see. Everything else is out of camera range.

A camera lens can take a basic two-shot (Figure 6.1) and zoom in on the dotted lines, eventually framing just our horn-playing trickster. After zooming, his bear friend is completely gone (Figure 6.2).

Figure 6.1 A basic two-shot before you zoom.

Figure 6.2 A longer lens lets us focus on just one character.

A mic doesn't work that way. When we talk about a mic's pickup pattern, we're merely indicating where the mic is slightly more sensitive. It always hears things from all around the room; it's just that sounds from some directions are softer than sounds from others. There is no such thing as "just out of microphone range."

Figure 6.3 is a visual analogy of what a good shotgun mic will hear, focused on just the Kokopelli doll.

Three aspects of Figure 6.3 make this a very good analogy:

- A directional mic makes sounds coming from the front seem slightly closer. That's why our horn player is slightly larger, compared to the bear, in Figure 6.3.
- It does this by lowering the volume of sounds from other directions. That's why the rest of the scene is darker.

Figure 6.3 Unfortunately, the mic isn't as discriminating. Even the most directional shotgun can't exclude the bear.

Figure 6.4 Real-world mics continue to pick up, far beyond where we think they're pointing.

- A directional mic also *changes the timbre of sound* coming from other directions. It adds a coloration that emphasizes some frequencies and lowers others. Notice how the bear's colors are distorted, compared to Figure 6.1.

The more directional a mic is, the more you hear both these effects. Better quality mics will have less of the off-axis coloration than cheaper ones of the same directional pattern, but it will always be there.

✍ TRY THIS

Hear for yourself

Take your best directional microphone, camera, and good headphones. Turn on a good mono radio or other system with a single speaker, playing music at conversational volume, in an average room of your house or office.[2] Stand about two feet away from the speaker, and listen to it through the mic.

Now turn the mic 180°, so its back points to the radio. Listen again. You'll still hear the radio. But it'll be a little bit softer and not sound as good.

Now try the same thing at six feet instead of three. There won't be as much difference between front and back . . . but that's because they'll both sound equally bad.

---

[2] We're trying to simulate a single on-camera talent. If your playback system has two speakers the experiment will be weaker because the mic will pick up from multiple directions. We're using music rather than speech because it's easier to hear the effects on a wide-range source.

Actually, Figure 6.3 is a simplification. What that directional mic *really* hears is more like Figure 6.4 . . . except the mic's pickup is three-dimensional. It continues beyond the photo, picking up me, my camera, and the room behind me.

Types of microphones

A microphone is just a pickup element, converting sound pressure into electrical voltages, mounted in a box. The construction of the pickup element determines how it translates pressure into electricity. While there are many different kinds of elements, only two—dynamic and condenser—are appropriate for video production. We'll cover those in a few pages.

What's much more than the element is how the microphone treats pressure from different directions. This is usually determined by the shape of the box, its vent holes, and internal baffles; occasionally there's also an accessory element and circuits to sort the two out. But it's also influenced by frequency: sounds of different frequencies work their way through those holes and baffles differently.

The shape, venting, and baffles are designed into the mic; you can't control them. The frequency issue is influenced by the room's acoustics and how you position the mic: How you deal with these two factors makes a big difference on your track.

Microphone directionality

Polar patterns

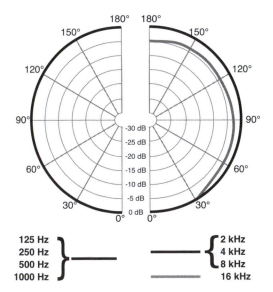

Figure 6.5 A graph of the polar response of a good omnidirectional mic.

Mics have different sensitivity from different directions. This is easy to measure. Manufacturers put the mic in a room without echoes, walk around it with a tone generator, and read the output from different frequencies and directions. They plot this on a circular graph like the one Figure 6.5. Directly in front of the mic is considered 0° on the graph, at the bottom of the figure. The voltage for sounds coming from the front is considered 0 dB. As the voltage drops for sounds from different directions, it's plotted on the inner circles. Multiple plots in different colors show how the mic reacted to different frequencies. The graph is split in half to show multiple frequencies while saving space on the page. Mics are symmetrical, so you can assume there's a matching half circle in the other direction for each side. All the patterns in this section are based on actual measurements of some highly-regarded pro mics, re-drawn for clarity.

Figure 6.5 shows the polar pattern of an *omnidirectional* mic. On the left, you can see that the mic is equally sensitive from any direction, for any frequency between 125 Hz and 1 kHz. On the right, it's also equally sensitive from any direction between 2 kHz and 8 kHz. The gray line on the right shows how this mic becomes slightly directional at 16 kHz. Sounds at that frequency coming from the rear are picked up –5 dB softer than those from the front. This is caused by sound waves being blocked by the shape of the mic itself. Since the mic is small, only the shortest waves (representing the highest frequencies) are affected. The difference shows on our graph, but at 16 kHz it's insignificant for most purposes.[3]

Omnidirectional

Omnidirectional mics (or *omnis*) have a solid box around the element's side and back (Figure 6.6). There's often a tiny hole in the back, just to equalize barometric pressure. Air-pressure waves strike the front of the element and generate a signal. The air inside the box acts as a spring to push the diaphragm out when the sound wave is in rarefaction. Sound waves coming from the back refract around the mic and hit the element from the front as well. Since their path is only an inch or so longer than the front sounds, their volume is essentially the same. Omnis are sometimes called *non-directional* for this reason.

Since an omnidirectional mic is mostly a sealed box, it's less sensitive to wind noise than other designs. This kind of mic is also sometimes called a *pressure mic* because it reacts to any changes in sound pressure, anywhere around it. Lavaliere microphones are often omnis because this design can be made very small. Since lavs are mounted on the actor's body, rather than hanging in the air, they can be closer to the actor's mouth than a boom mic. So even though they're not directional, the inverse-square law means a properly mounted lav will pick up lots of voice with very little reverb or noise.

Full-size omnis are often used in studio recording and as handheld vocal-performance mics, but their major use in video is as handheld-close-up interview mics in windy exteriors. They can also be used for recording background ambiences, when you want to pick up a diffuse impression of everything going on in a space.

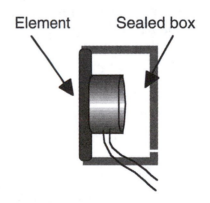

Figure 6.6 Omnidirectional mic.

---

[3] Critical measurements in a sound lab's echo-free room often use very thin omnidirectional mics, sometimes just looking like a small stick, so there isn't much of a shadow effect.

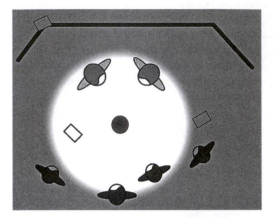

Figure 6.7 Omnis pick up everything around them. But read the text—their pattern isn't exactly like the drawing.

For visual reference, an omni's pickup pattern looks like Figure 6.7. The mic is the black circle in the middle. I've emphasized the shape of the pickup in all of these drawings to make them more understandable. In reality, there's a smooth and gradual falloff of sensitivity around the shape, more like the retouched photo in Figure 6.4. In other words, all four of the dark gray crew members around the bottom of the picture will be recorded at about the same volume as the two actors at the top, because they're all at about the same distance. When you're looking at these drawings, remember it doesn't make any difference whether a sound source is precisely inside or outside the white circle; all that matters is about how far a source is and in what direction.

Boundary mic

The boundary mic is a variation on omnidirectional mic design, which can be very useful in video production. It was originally developed by Crown International as the Pressure-Zone Microphone, and boundary mics are still referred to as *PZMs*. A very small omni element is mounted a fraction of an inch above a large rigid plate (Figure 6.8), which is then taped to a wall or other flat surface. Sound waves can reach it from only one direction, so there's less of the interference caused by reflections coming from multiple paths. Because of their low profile, boundary mics can be concealed on the walls or floor of a set (placing a mouse pad between the mic's plate and the floor will help isolate it from footsteps). They're also useful when you have to record in a reverberant space and can't get close enough to the source. The reverb is still there, but it doesn't color the sound as much. Some lavalieres come with mounting adapters to use them as boundary mics.

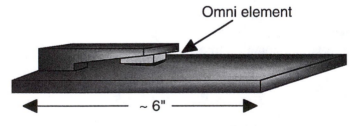

Figure 6.8 A boundary or PZM mic.

Cardioid

Cardioid mics are named for a sort of heart-shaped pickup pattern. You might hear claims that this rejects sounds from the rear, and accepts them only from the front and sides. Figure 6.9 shows how their pattern really works: It's reasonably heart-shaped for mid frequencies (black lines), though rear rejection in the mid-band is only about –15 dB ... about a third as loud as sounds from the front. But low frequencies (gray line on the left) are only reduced –7 dB from the rear. And high frequencies (gray lines on right) are barely down –5 dB.

So despite the claims, sounds from the rear aren't really rejected. Instead, they're a little softer—and because of the frequency differences, much tubbier sounding—than those from the front.

This kind of microphone, also known as a *unidirectional*, often looks like an elongated omni with a few large holes or slots in its sides (Figure 6.10). When a sound comes from the rear (top path in the drawing), it enters the hole and strikes the back of the element. It also refracts around the mic and strikes the front of the element. Since these paths are about the same length, the front and back versions are the same volume and cancel each other out.

Figure 6.9 A cardioid mic's polar response.

125 Hz, 250 Hz, 500 Hz, 1000 Hz, 2 kHz, 4 kHz, 8 kHz, 16 kHz

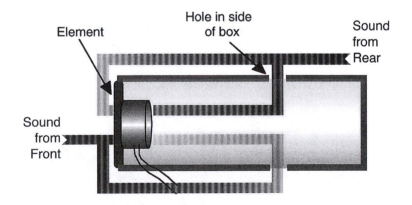

Figure 6.10 Cardioid microphone with sound coming from two directions.

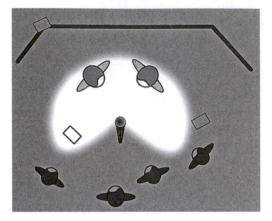

Figure 6.11 Cardioid pickup pattern.

A sound coming from in front of the mic (bottom path) can also reach the back of the element. But in order to do so, it has to travel the length of mic to the hole, and then back again to the element. By that time, it's considerably weaker than it is at the front and doesn't cancel itself.

Figure 6.11 is a visual reference of how a cardioid mic performs. The mic is the black cone in the middle, parallel to the floor and pointing to the actors. The actual pickup pattern is mostly circular for three-quarters of the way around the mic and tucks in at the back. Viewed from above, it's sort of heart-shape . . . hence the name. Of course, the warning about Figure 6.7 also applies here: all mic patterns are much more gradual than I could ever show in a printed diagram.

This directionality makes cardioids more useful on the video set. They can be aimed so their front is pointing to the actor, while the rear is pointing to a noise source or reverberating surface. The difference between front and back sensitivity decreases as the frequency goes down, and, at very low frequencies, the design is almost omnidirectional.

☛ ROSE'S RULES

Use the hole mic!

The holes in the sides of a directional mic are a critical part of its design. If you block them by grabbing the mic around its middle or gaffer-taping it to a support, you can seriously hurt the sound. It's counterintuitive, but cupping your hands around the end of most microphones—the way you'd cup them around your ear to concentrate on a sound—makes them less directional.

Hypercardioid

A hypercardioid is a variation on the cardioid design. It's about the same size but with multiple holes in the side of the box, tuned for different frequencies. This makes it more directional, and a good hypercardioid will have very little side or rear coloration except at the highest frequencies.

Figure 6.12 shows the polar pattern of a top-quality hyper. It's a Schoeps MK41, a favorite Hollywood boom mic at about $2,000 with its powering module. The heart

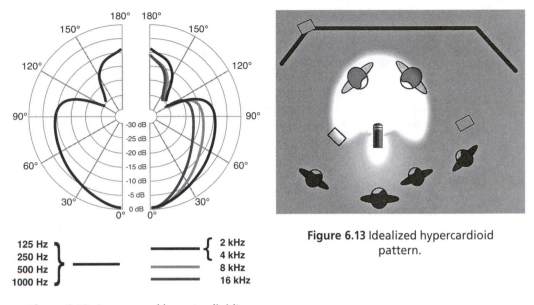

Figure 6.13 Idealized hypercardioid pattern.

Figure 6.12 A very good hypercardioid's polar response.

is tucked in under 4 kHz, with side rejection –15 dB and down to –25 dB at 120. There's a rear lobe, typical of very directional mics, of only –10 dB. At higher frequencies, the mic gets more directional, with about –5 dB more rejection for each octave up. Sounds from the sides will be just a bit duller than those from the front, but this effect doesn't really kick in at dialog frequencies.

Lesser hypers, such as the AKG C1000 (about $250), exhibit the same tucked-in pattern but with about twice as much coloration from the sides and rear above 4 kHz and below 250 Hz. There are other differences between those two mics as well, of course, including the smoothness of the pattern and how much noise and distortion the capsule generates. The AKG is a good mic. But these factors—the smooth pattern, low noise, and low distortion—are why Hollywood mixers pay eight times more for the Schoeps.

Figure 6.13 shows a visual reference. The hypercardioid is the short cylinder in the middle.

Shotgun

You can make the mic even longer, with more carefully calibrated holes and the element at the back. You can also add a few calibrated tubes so that sounds entering from the sides travel multiple paths of different lengths, canceling themselves when they arrive; sounds from the front have a straight path back to the element. Now your mic is much more directional across more frequencies. It's called an *interference tube* mic, or more commonly goes by the nickname *shotgun* (Figure 6.14).

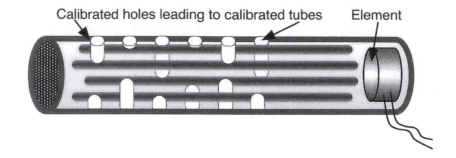

Calibrated holes leading to calibrated tubes   Element

Figure 6.14 A shotgun mic with internal interference tubes.

Short shotgun mics are used frequently on DV shoots. Figure 6.15 shows why their results might not be what a videographer expects. The mics are reasonably directional, losing 15 dB or more from the sides. But side rejection varies greatly with frequency: it's almost 30 dB at 125 Hz, around the vowels of most male voices. It's just 15 dB at 2 kHz, at the consonants. Anything coming from the side—this can be off-mic voices, or echoes of the main voice bouncing off a nearby ceiling or wall—will have a breathiness or other strange effect.

Furthermore, rejection from the rear isn't as much as from the sides . . . something new users seldom realize. The rear of a short shot is only about 5 dB down for low frequencies, and 10 dB down at the mids. That's much less rejection than you get from the sides. If the mic is on a camera while you're interviewing a subject four feet away, your voice will not only be louder than theirs, but also a little tubby sounding.

The graph in Figure 6.15 is from a well-respected, high-priced short shotgun; cheaper ones are even more irregular. But all shotguns, long or short, have this issue: less rejection from the rear than from the sides. Figure 6.16 shows their idealized

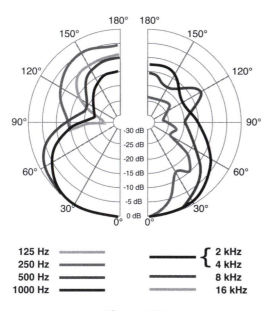

Figure 6.15
Short shotgun polar response.

125 Hz		{ 2 kHz
250 Hz		{ 4 kHz
500 Hz		8 kHz
1000 Hz		16 kHz

pickup pattern. Notice the little wings of extra sensitivity at about 30° from the rear; you can also see this in Figure 6.15. All interference tube mics have these *lobes* to some degree. It often affects boom mics held near a low, hard ceiling and pointed slightly down to the talent: the bounce from talent to ceiling to lobe is loud enough to mix with the direct path from the talent, and it causes hollowness.

Shotguns come in varying lengths, with longer ones having narrower pickup angles (and more coloration from the rear and sides). Short shots are useful on booms in rooms without much echo, or outdoors. They can be handheld for interviews, or

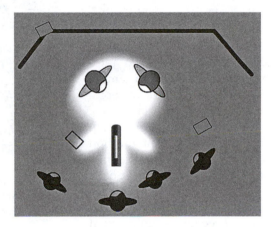

Figure 6.16 Short shotgun pickup. No matter how good a mic you use, some of that side and rear pickup will always exist.

✔ **TIP**

Hyper or gun?

Shotgun mics are more directional than hypercardioids. Besides, they *look* impressive, with their long barrels and calibrated slots on the side. Many filmmakers assume, because of this, that they're the ideal mic for all booming situations. But if you're shooting in a normal-size room with untreated walls, or there's a hard ceiling close to the boom mic, the side slots can pick up some serious echoes. Since directionality varies with frequency, the echoes' timbre gets changed before it reaches the mic element. The result can be an unnatural hollowness to the voice.

A hypercardioid must be placed a little closer than a gun, but in most interiors it will sound better. They're the best choice for most indoor location shoots.

used for close-miking announcers or sound effects in rooms with less-than-perfect acoustics. (While these rooms will have reverb, inverse-square law says the echoes won't be loud enough for the mics' coloration to matter.) Long shotguns are generally reserved for exteriors or large, well-treated studios, where reverb isn't an issue.

Zoom mic

Figure 6.17 is the best illustration we could find for this kind of mic.

It's relatively easy to make a mic with selectable directionality, and large studio mics frequently contain multiple elements and simple circuits to let you switch between omni, cardioid, and hypercardioid. It's a little harder to make a mic with continuously variable directionality, but it can be done with something like an M/S configuration (discussed in a few pages). But a true "zoom," behaving the way your camera's lens does? Snake oil.

The mics sold as zoom are a marketing myth. They're typically not very directional—going from somewhat omni to somewhat hypercardioid. Worse, they're usually mounted on a camera, which limits their usefulness to capturing events or ambiences ... no way they'll be able to zoom in to dialog, in any environment less than a lab's echo-free room. These typically low-end consumer devices, with their dual elements, also contribute additional noise.

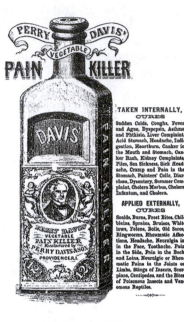

Figure 6.17
A "Zoom" mic won't be much more effective than this stuff.[4]

About "reach"

If you study the pattern drawings, you'll notice that directional mics don't hear any farther into the set than the omni does. The difference is in how they reduce pickup from the sides or back. Because this tends to lower noise and reverb, we can use an amplifying circuit to hear comparatively more dialog. But the extra reach is being provided by the preamp or mixer, not by the mic. When film sound mixers talk about the reach of a directional mic, they're mostly referring to how much electronic noise it contributes. If there's less noise, you can amplify it more before the noise becomes annoying.

---

[4] Library of Congress image.

☛ ROSE'S RULES

By this point, I hope you've got the message
- There is no such thing as a telephoto mic.
- All microphones are wide angle and have to be brought close to the subject.
- Some mics have wider angles than others.

The best directional mics reject off-axis sounds by about 30 dB at mid and high frequencies. This is a significant amount, but certainly nothing like total rejection.

There are only two exceptions in common use. Some mics are coupled with a parabolic reflector, a large circular disk that gathers sound pressure from a specific area and focuses it in towards a small mic. Parabolics sacrifice frequency range for sensitivity, so they don't sound good for film recording. But they can be useful where intelligibility is more important than natural sound, particularly where you can fill in unfocused lows with another mic. They're also sometimes used in nature recording and surveillance.

Array mics use multiple directional elements, and then circuits that combine the signals in various ways. They can provide amazing results, but only in limited circumstances. A directional array for dialog is the Audio-Technica 895, no longer on the market but available from some rental companies. While the manufacturer didn't publish a polar graph, I found incredible rejection from the rear and sides. It can be great for sports coverage or on-the-street dialog: relatively noisy exterior situations. Unfortunately, the circuits get confused by room echoes, and all those elements add hiss: indoors, the thing is no better than a $100 short gun. Other array mics are used for surround ambiences, and (at considerably lower quality) to pick out nearby voices in smart phones.

Increasing your microphone wisdom

Why take the time to explain polar graphs in a book for film and video producers? Two reasons. First, I wanted to make sure you absolutely understood how a mic's directionality also colors the sound. More directional equals more coloration, if two mics are otherwise of the same quality.

But second, you now know how to judge those mics' quality. You can read a polar graph and understand both directionality and coloration. All good mics come with this kind of information. If you can't find it, suspect that the manufacturer either doesn't understand the technology or was ashamed of the results.

Mics also should come with frequency response graphs, showing relative sensitivity across the band for sounds coming from the front. Without these two graphs, there's no way to tell how good a mic is. Claims like "acceptance angle 70°"

or "frequency range 80 Hz–18 kHz" might sound technical, but they're as useful as that bottle of patent medicine.

An excellent source of mic specs can be found at microphone-data.com. This site is maintained as a public service by Rycote, a top manufacturer of windscreens and boom shock mounts for professional sound production. They don't do their own measurements, but have gathered manufacturer's published data on hundreds of mics and organized it for easy comparison. Along with the specs, you'll find polar and frequency response graphs for most professional mics.

Directional mics in use

With nothing but patterns of holes and hollow tubes to work with, it's amazing that microphone designers can make their products as good as they are. But even the best of them are subject to physical limitations:

Off-axis response

The holes and tubes cause cancellations and reinforcements depending on frequency. Sounds from the rear and side will have their timbre affected. The more directional a mic is, the more pronounced this effect.

Sounds 6.1 through 6.6 let you hear on- and off-axis response for different kinds of mics. All were recorded in the same typical large office, using the same talent, at the same distance:

- **Sound 6.1** is a full-size omni (not a lav), facing the talent.
- **Sound 6.2** is the same omni, facing 180° away from the talent. She sounds the same in terms of echo and coloration, just a little softer.
- **Sound 6.3** is a cardioid facing the talent. She has much less echo now, so she sounds closer. Remember, each of these examples was recorded in the same position; we didn't move the talent or the mic stand.
- **Sound 6.4** is the same cardioid facing 90° away from the talent. She sounds even further away now, and has a metallic tinge. This is the side coloration in a cardioid.
- **Sound 6.5** is a short shotgun facing the talent. She's closer now, with just a little warm echo behind her voice.
- **Sound 6.6** is that shotgun at 90°. It's more reverberant than the cardioid was, even though the mic is more directional.

My 90° placement simulates the reflections when a mic is pointed to the talent but near a wall or ceiling. It doesn't sound very good. **Shotguns have to be placed precisely: 1) fairly close and 2) pointed to the talent, and 3) not too close to other surfaces**. A camera-mounted gun will give you item 2 and usually item 3, but fails miserably on item 1. A handheld gun can catch all three, but only if there's room to hide someone just above or below the frame line. (Frames are rectangular, so you can usually get closer from above or below than from the sides.) A boom is usually the best and most flexible solution. But your operator has to know how to point and move it properly. There are some tips for learning the skills in the next chapter.

Proximity effect

Directional mics emphasize bass notes as you get closer to them. Radio announcers frequently take advantage of this, working close to the mic to make their voices appear deeper. This also means that directional mics are more sensitive to "popped Ps": an overload caused by the sudden blast of air from a plosive consonant spoken too closely to the mic. At normal operating distances, the proximity effect shouldn't be a problem.

Wind pickup

Directional mics are more sensitive to wind. That's because they have so many openings along their sides. Any air movement will be heard. You almost always need to use a windscreen with them, except if the mic is perfectly still and indoors. The foam windscreen supplied with many short shotguns doesn't provide enough protection for exteriors or even fast-moving booms indoors; a zeppelin-style hard windscreen, often with a furry cloth cover, is preferred.

Lack of low frequencies

It's difficult to make a very directional mic directional on bass notes, so manufacturers often limit a shotgun mic's low-frequency response. The frequencies involved are too low to be of much concern for dialog, but you should be aware of this if using a shotgun for music or deep sound effects.

Stereo mics

A few manufacturers make dual mics in a single housing, designed to pick up stereo. Stereo mics can be useful for backgrounds, large sound effects, and music recording. They're seldom used for dialog, however. Even large-screen features record the actors in mono. No matter where the actors are on the screen, their voice usually comes out of a center speaker. If some sense of direction is needed for a special effect or a distant character, the mono recording will be placed in a specific position at the mix.

Stereo mics usually come in two configurations: X/Y and M/S. In an X/Y mic, two separate cardioid elements are positioned with their fronts very close together and at a 90° angle. Their outputs are fed down a single multi-conductor cable and terminate in either a stereo mini-plug or dual balanced XLRs.

A minor problem with X/Y miking is that it's not truly mono compatible. Sounds coming from the side may combine strangely when the channels are mixed together, causing colorations similar to the multiple acoustic paths discussed in Chapter 1. You may think this doesn't matter because your film will be released in stereo or surround . . . but you'd be wrong. Film dialog is almost always mixed in mono—even in blockbuster surround features—and directed to a single channel behind the screen. Your dialog recordings have to work in this format. And if you're recording music or sound effects that won't go to the dialog channel, you still have to think about people who'll be watching your film in mono on their computers, tablets or phones, and many cable hookups.

An alternative scheme, M/S (for mid/side) miking, uses a cardioid mic pointing forward, with a *bidirectional* mic close to it and pointing to the sides. Bidirectionals work like dual hypercardioids, back-to-back, but have a single element. Because of this, pressure coming from one side of the element will create a positive voltage, and pressure from the other side will create a negative voltage. In effect, the mic works equally well for both sides, but one side has its polarity reversed. The two mic signals are routed down one multi-conductor cable, but the cardioid output is considered *middle* and the bidirectional is *side*.

A circuit then adds the two outputs, as shown in Figure 6.18, to create left and right outputs. Since the cardioid (light gray in the drawing) is facing the performers, it picks up the right and left side of the stage equally. The bidirectional (dark gray) is facing the left, so sounds from the left side of the stage reach the front of its element, with positive pressures producing a positive voltage. Sounds from the right side of the stage reach the back of its element, so positive pressures from that side produce a negative voltage. Its signal consists of +Left combined with –Right, often referred to as *left minus right*.

If the two mic signals are mixed normally, the positive and negative right sides cancel out, and you get the left side of the stage only. But if the bidirectional's signal is inverted before they're mixed, it consists of –Left and +Right. Mixing the two mics together now means the positive and negative left sides will cancel, and you get only the right side of the stage.

This may seem like a lot of work—it's really not—but it pays off when somebody listens in mono: when you combine the derived left and right outputs, the bidirectional mic completely cancels itself out! You're left with nothing but the cardioid's signal, and absolutely no coloration caused by time delay.

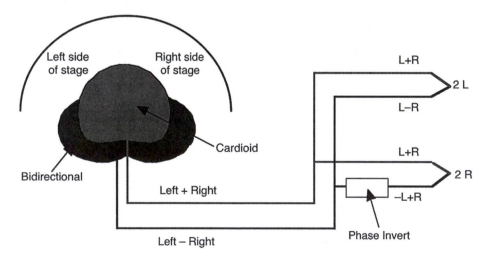

Figure 6.18 Mid-side miking to preserve mono compatibility.

As a matter of fact, this same scheme is at the heart of analog stereo FM and TV. Using electronic inversions rather than a bidirectional mic, the left and right channels are combined into a main mono signal. This is what's broadcast in the usual band, and mono listeners hear it with no trouble. The "side" signal is broadcast in a slightly higher band that stereo receivers can get. The receiver then performs a similar translation, recreating left and right.

You can create your own M/S rig with two microphones, closely matched for sound quality. One should be an omni or cardioid for the middle, the other a bidirectional. Bidirectional (also called *figure-8*) mics are so rare in film and video production that most catalogs don't list them. You'll have to get them from a music studio supplier. Many multi-pattern studio mics also have a bidirectional setting.

Place the microphones as close together as possible, with the omni or cardioid facing the performers. The bidirectional mic should be aligned sideways, so that its front is facing the left side and its back is facing the right. Since the mics are close together, the time delay between them is very slight.

Stereo on a boom

An alternative, sometimes used in documentary production (favored by the BBC, but rarely heard in the US), substitutes a short shotgun or hypercardioid for the cardioid. The two mics are wired as in Figure 6.18.

This configuration is useful if the subject is in an interesting-sounding place, and isn't moving. Its advantage is that, for mono listeners, most of the room disappears. Instead of an echoey sound with background noise, they hear the tighter sound of a normal boom mic. Stereo listeners hear the subject centered but with a good sense of the room's background and reverb coming from the sides.

Ambient (www.ambient.de) makes an *Emesser* miniature bidirectional mic, designed to fit on the shockmount of a conventional hyper or shotgun, so you can create your own. It's available from film sound specialty shops.

Stereo booming usually isn't appropriate for dramatic shoots or any situation where the boom isn't in a fixed location, because the stereo image swings around unrealistically as the mic moves.

Camera mics

The mics built into most cameras are awful. They're included because amateurs expect their camera to have mics, but there's no reason for manufacturers to spend much effort or expense to make them sound good. Unless you're shooting from a foot away or have ideal acoustics, even an expensive mic won't do a good job on dialog. Save the camera mic for birthday parties where you don't care about sound.

Even placing a high-quality mic on the camera isn't a very good solution. Four inches from the lens is a terrible place to put a mic, too far from dialog and too close to camera (and camera operator) noises. Save this configuration for breaking events, where it's impossible to get a mic closer, or for the kind of close-camera shouted interviews sometimes done at wedding receptions. And if you absolutely have to use

☞ ROSE'S RULES

In the first edition of *Producing Great Sound*, I wrote the following:

> Are you using the camera's built-in mic? If so, you haven't been paying attention to my words. So for you, here's a better way to use this book: take it in one hand and *WHACK THE MIC OFF YOUR CAMERA!*

I'm older and mellower now. And I do acknowledge that for things like B-roll with no dialog, a camera mic is better than silence. But otherwise, the principle stands.

a camera-mounted mic, use an adapter that lifts the mic as far above the camera as possible. Inverse-square law will reduce camera noise while not lowering the dialog level, and it also keeps longer mics out of the lens's way during wide shots.

Types of pickup elements

So far, we've spoken about a microphone's pickup element but haven't explained how they work. Here's how a mic converts varying air pressure to a changing voltage.

Dynamic mics

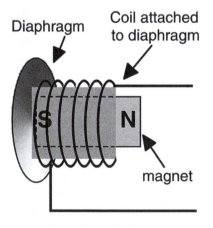

Figure 6.19
Dynamic microphone.

The simplest pickup element has a coil of wire attached to a plastic or foil diaphragm, suspended in a strong magnetic field. Air pressure waves make the diaphragm vibrate, and, as the coil vibrates along with it, the magnetism creates an electric current (Figure 6.19). This is the same principle as an electric generator, except the ones in a power plant use turbines to continually rotate the coil instead of letting it just vibrate. In both cases, they turn physical movement into electricity.

Since a dynamic mic's voltage is directly generated by sound pressure, it takes a relatively large amount of pressure to get a usable output. An internal transformer is used to raise the output voltage enough so that it can be carried on a cable cleanly. Dynamic mics are not as sensitive as condenser mics, particularly at high frequencies. On the other hand, the simplicity of design makes them very rugged, and the lack of electronics in the mic itself means it can handle louder sounds than a condenser.

On the other hand, since dynamics convert sound directly into electricity, they can have very low distortion and don't contribute any electronic noise. Many announcers prefer their sound, and full-sized dynamics like the Electro-Voice RE-27 and Shure SM-7 have been staples in the pro studio for years.

Performance mics, such as the classic "ball on a cone" Shure SM-58, have low-sensitivity dynamic elements designed to work best when they're very close to an instrument or vocalist's mouth. They are not suitable for dialog, unless they're being used as a practical musician's or stand-up comic's mic on the set.

Dangling a musician's mic like an SM-58 over the actors might give you understandable dialog. But it won't sound good, and—if you care at all about the project—is hardly worth the effort. If the only way you can get a boom mic for your shoot is to borrow an SM-58 or similar from a band, consider using lavs instead.

✳ TIDBIT

Talking mics

A dynamic mic's construction is very similar to a headphone. Back when I was a radio station engineer, I'd occasionally fuddle announcers by connecting their mic to an intercom output, so it worked like a speaker. As they were about to record a commercial, I'd whisper into the 'com. Their mic—now working as a headphone—would say "Eww. You had garlic for lunch!"

Don't try this stunt unless you thoroughly understand the engineering risks involved. And the physical risks, if your announcer doesn't have a sense of humor.

Condenser mics

A condenser mic doesn't turn sound directly into output volts. A metalized plastic diaphragm is mounted close to a rigid plate, and an electric charge is applied to it. As sound pressure waves move the diaphragm closer or farther from the plate, a tiny but varying stream of electrons can jump across. This stream is just a few electrons, so it's too weak to send to a recorder—even a few feet of extra cable will damage the signal. Instead, a preamplifier is built inside the mic body (Figure 6.20). The preamp uses an external voltage to boost the signal to usable levels. The voltage can come from an internal battery, or be supplied by the mixer or recorder.

Most of the mics on a film or video set are condensers. Since they don't use a magnet, they can be smaller and lighter—an advantage for both booms and lavalieres. High-quality condensers can be more sensitive than dynamics. Even cheaper condensers

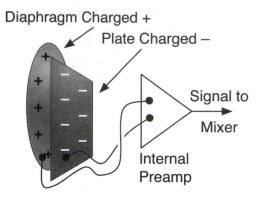

Diaphragm Charged +

Plate Charged −

Signal to

Mixer

Internal
Preamp

Figure 6.20 Condenser microphone.
If the output is balanced, there'll be another
component to provide the second wire.

will sound better and can be smaller than similarly priced dynamics.

The best professional condenser mics are *externally polarized*. The diaphragm is polarized with a couple of hundred volts, stepped up from the preamp's power supply. This means they can be highly sensitive (or create very little electrical noise of their own, which amounts to the same thing), so this design is preferred for high-quality studio and boom mics.

A simpler condenser design uses a permanently charged diaphragm, made with a chemical process similar to the one used for static-charged dust mops. The result is the ubiquitous *electret* condenser, found everywhere from cell phones to mid-priced shotguns. This is the technology used in most sub-$400 studio mics. While the best of them are almost as good as externally polarized mics, they can't be as sensitive, so their internal amplifiers generate comparatively more noise. However, the lack of a high-voltage supply means they can be smaller and less expensive.

Condenser mics also lend themselves to modular construction. The pickup element and whatever arrangement of ports and tubes that give it directionality can be one module. The preamp can be another. They connect with screw threads or a bayonet arrangement.

Modular systems let the user can carry multiple heads for different miking situations, while having to pay for only a single preamp. Accessories like filters or short extension cables can be inserted between the head and preamp for special

---

✳ TIDBIT

A mic's "preamp" isn't a preamp

The preamp part of a modular condenser mic is designed to bring the tiny output of the head up to normal mic levels (and power the element, if needed). It's often called a *powering module* instead. It isn't like the preamps used to bring mic outputs up to line levels.

In Chapter 8, we talk about some cameras doing a better job of recording if you feed them a line-level signal rather than mic-level, and recommend a preamp or mixer to achieve this. That's a different kind of preamp . . . the ones supplied with modular condenser systems won't do the job.

situations. It's a little like a photographer carrying multiple lenses and filters with a single camera body. Modular design is used in the Sennheiser K6/ME66 short shotgun popular in video production ($500), the Schoeps CMC5/MK41 found on most feature shoots ($2,000), and other mics of varying quality.

Very cheap electrets—costing less than a dollar each—are found in toys, telephones, and multimedia computers. Don't expect the mic that came with your computer or sound card to be any more than a toy.

All condenser mics require some form of power supply:

- Very cheap electrets are usually powered directly from the circuits they're built into.
- Electrets designed for mounting on prosumer cameras use *plug-in-power*, a low voltage applied to the mic jack.
- Full-sized electrets with XLR connectors are powered either by a small battery in their bodies or via phantom powering (see below). Externally polarized condenser mics require phantom power. Some classic older ones might be wired for T-power, which isn't directly compatible.
- High-quality music studio mics that use vacuum tubes often require dedicated power supplies, and multi-conductor cables.
- The tiny electrets used as lavalieres are powered by batteries in their plugs or by phantom powering. If they're part of a wireless mic system, they'll get power from the transmitter's battery.

☞ ROSE'S RULES

Dynamic or condenser?

- Choose a condenser mic when you can for video and film; the extra sensitivity translates into a better-sounding track. Use an externally polarized mic, if possible, for tracks that are intended for theatrical playback. The reduced noise is worth the extra expense.
- If the mic is going to be subject to humidity or physical abuse, or if you're planning to record very loud sounds, choose a dynamic mic.

When power is first applied to a traditional condenser microphone, it may produce a loud "thunk" as the plate charges. Electrets may make clicking or popping noises when they're powered. As a general rule, leave a condenser mic's volume turned down when you change the battery or plug it into a phantom supply.

Other microphone types

Ribbon

Ever notice the large jellybean-shaped mic on some talk hosts' desks? It's a classic RCA 77DX, one of the all-time greats for making a voice-over sound both warm and natural. The 77DX and other *ribbon* mics use the same basic principle as dynamics, but without a diaphragm. Instead, a delicate foil strip is vibrated by the sound waves, while suspended in a very strong magnetic field. This produces a tiny electric current. Because the foil has so little mass, a ribbon can be extremely accurate—particularly on relatively loud sounds that lack extreme highs, like the human voice—and is often preferred by announcers.

Ribbon mics are great in the studio. Unfortunately, their giant magnets make them big and heavy, and the tiny ribbon is physically fragile. These factors make them unsuitable for location film shoots.

Ceramic and crystal

These used to be the cheapest mics available for home recording and two-way radio. Their quality was never very good, and they were easily damaged. Unless you want a deliberately bad sound (which is easier to accomplish with processors), there's no reason to use one of these . . . if you can even find one. These days, electret condensers are cheaper and better.

Digital mics

All condenser mics require internal electronics to condition the signal. Almost all mic setups then send an analog signal to a mixer or recorder, where ADC chips[5] convert the signal to digital. So it makes technical sense to put those ADC chips right into the mic's electronics, and send digital data back to the mixer. Digital wiring isn't subject to the noise or hum problems of analog, which can be a major issue with all the power cables on a film set. This scheme also eliminates some of the active analog components on both ends of the long cable, which means it has lower inherent electronic noise.

Digital film mics

As of this writing, high-end manufacturers Neumann and Schoeps offer digital versions of hypercardioids and short shotguns using this principle. They can plug directly into suitable digital recorders. They really do offer those digital advantages, along with some remote controls over the mic cable and, in the case of the Schoeps, internal signal processing to improve the pickup pattern.

There are trade-offs, of course. Like any condenser mic, they need power— 48 volt standard phantom doesn't appear on AES/EBU inputs, but the newer AES-42 standard does provide power and has started to appear on high-end recorders. If your

---

[5] Analog to Digital Converters. Microchips that, with a few extra components, do all the sampling chores we discussed in Chapter 2.

recorder or mixer doesn't meet this standard, you'll need an external power adapter. They also require 110 Ω cable, which isn't any more expensive than Star-Quad, but is much harder to find in rental inventories.

Neumann's digital mics cost about the same as their equivalent analog versions (about $1,600 for their short gun). The Schoeps is about $4,500 (compared to $2,500 for their analog mic using the same configuration), but that includes digital signal processing inside the mic.

This is definitely the way mics will be wired in the future, so more units will surely be coming from other manufacturers. If you're buying new mics, check the websites and magazines for the latest information.

USB voice-over mics

There are dozens of low-cost electret mics on the market that can plug directly into a computer's USB port, get power from it, and show up in the computer as a sound device ready to record. They're designed primarily for podcasters and bedroom musicians, and are perfectly fine for that application. USB doesn't like long cables and computers don't mix multiple USB mics,[6] so they're really not suitable for a film shoot.

These are not the best voice-over mics, in terms of sound quality or polar pattern. Manufacturers have no incentive to add USB to their higher-end products, since studios and other professionals aren't able to use that connection. But they're cheap, don't sound any worse than similarly-priced analog mics, and are certainly easier to set up and use. If you've got good acoustic surroundings, they can be fine for a low-budget film narration.

Powering a mic

Years ago, condenser mics were the only kind that required power . . . not just to polarize their elements, but also for the tubes that lit up inside their internal preamps. They required large AC power supplies that usually sat on the floor near the mic, and were connected with multi-conductor cable.

While tubed condenser mics are still used in music recording because of the unique distortion they add, modern mics use a lot less power. It can be provided by internal batteries or supplied by whatever recorder or mixer the mic is feeding. A few dynamic and ribbon mics also have internal preamps to make hookup easier; these are powered the same way.

Phantom power

Balanced wiring, discussed in Chapter 3, uses a positive audio signal on one wire of a two-conductor cable with a matching negative signal on the other. This way, it can reject noises that are picked up equally on both wires. A metallic shield is usually

---

[6] Readers may feel free to extend USB cables with powered adapters or buffers, and hack some way to mix unsynchronized multiple USB devices for recording. It's certainly possible. I'm not going to bother.

provided for additional noise protection. This scheme is used by all professional microphones that have to drive long cables.

When solid-state microphones started replacing tubed units for production, engineers realized the balanced cables could also carry power without contaminating the audio signal. A positive current is applied to *both* wires of a balanced cable, with the current's negative side returning through the cable shield. Since this causes no voltage difference between the two signal wires, the audio circuitry totally ignores it.

In most equipment, phantom power is applied with a pair of precision resistors so the voltage is equal on both wires. A pair of capacitors keeps the voltage from affecting the audio circuits, since capacitors block DC voltages (Figure 6.21). This is the most common arrangement for professional cameras with XLR inputs, and small mixers. If a device has an input transformer, the phantom voltage is applied to the microphone's side of the transformer and capacitors aren't needed (DC can't jump from one side of a transformer to the other).

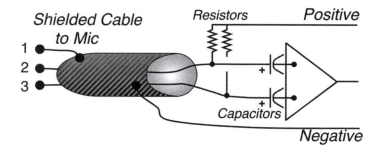

Figure 6.21 Simplified drawing of a phantom power input. Numbers on the left refer to standard pins on an XLR jack.

At the microphone end, a center-tapped transformer is usually used to gather the DC voltage from both wires (Figure 6.22). Transformers can be sensitive to AC hum in the vicinity, so some microphones use capacitors instead to sort out the phantom power.

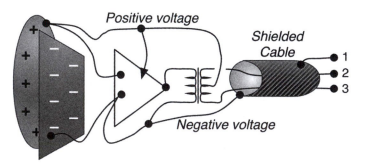

Figure 6.22 Simplified wiring inside a phantom powered mic.

The voltage is called "phantom" because if a mic doesn't look for it, it disappears. For example, the output transformer of a dynamic mic (Figure 6.19) is never connected to the cable shield. So even if it's plugged into a phantom input there won't be a complete circuit. No power will flow through the microphone itself.

All phantom-powered mics operate with 48 volts supplied over the audio cables, and most professional mixers and preamps supply this voltage (often called *P48*). A few mixers and cameras supply lower phantom voltages, and some mics work fine with them. Many electrets can use a phantom as low as 9 volts, and even some high-quality externally polarized mics will boost a lower voltage as needed. But voltage specs vary, and can't be generalized. Unless you're sure a supply provides 48 volts, it's a good idea to check the manufacturer's specs to make sure a particular combination will work.

T or Simplex powering

Before phantom power became a standard, some popular film mics were powered with a positive voltage on one of its balanced wires and a negative voltage on the other. It didn't work as a phantom, wouldn't disappear for dynamic mics, and required additional components in the audio path that could compromise the sound. The scheme is now obsolete, but some classic high-quality mics in rental inventories or on eBay may be wired this way. Some older analog recorders and mixers in film schools might still supply this power rather than phantom.

⚠ WARNING

Beware the phantom!

Phantom power works well in most professional applications. However, using it improperly can damage the microphone or mixer:

- If an unbalanced microphone is connected to a phantom supply, voltage will either be applied across its element, or shorted out by the XLR adapter. You'll get extra distortion, damaged equipment, or both.
- Ditto damaged cables or jury-rigged adapters. They can short things out the same way.
- If a balanced line-level signal is applied to a balanced mic input that has phantom power, the voltage will usually cause distortion and can also damage the source device.

On the other hand, phantom power lets you run wired condenser mics all day without worrying about changing batteries. If your microphones and cables are in good shape and need the voltage, leave it on. Otherwise, turn phantom power off.

Third-party T-power supplies or phantom converters are available from film sound suppliers.

ROOMS AND RECORDING

I have an actress friend who used to dub the muttered dialog during steamier scenes of Swedish sex films. When she told me about it, I topped her: I've done *my* job under blankets in a hotel room, in the back of a limousine, and with a professor inside a world map. The search for good acoustics on a location can make you do strange things, but the right technique makes a big difference in your finished track.

That's also the reason for foam tiles on a sound studio's walls. They're not part of the soundproofing—foam doesn't have much mass, and it has too many holes to stop airborne noise. Their purpose is to absorb reflections, since sound bouncing around a room can make a voice sound tubby or hollow (see Chapter 1).

Testing the space

It's not practical to put up foam tiles when you're shooting, but you can still use a piece of foam to find out if there will be echoes. Stand at the talent's position, facing where the camera will be. Hold a square of foam—or a folded towel, couch cushion, or anything else absorbent—about two feet in front of your face and sing "ahh" at a fairly loud volume. Then take the absorber away and keep singing. If you hear any difference in the sound of your own voice, it's caused by reflections.[7] They'll hurt your track.

You can sometimes lower the reflections by moving the talent's position slightly, or by facing a different direction. If the sound can bounce at an angle, the reflections follow different paths each time, and the hollowness gets smoothed out. Sound studios often have non-parallel walls to spread and randomize reflections. You probably can't push the walls away where you're shooting, but you can do the next best thing by keeping the talent at an angle to any reflective surfaces.

Both the distance and the angle between talent and wall are important. Walk around the room while you're doing the sing-into-the-foam test. If light or props mean that you have to place the talent in a less-than-ideal position, try rotating the setup a few degrees so the voice strikes reflective surfaces at an angle. Figure 6.23 shows how changing the talent's position can make a big difference in a finished track.

The drawing shows a typical conference room with drapes and a bookshelf. Actor A is in the worst position, facing a wall (and close to any noise from the hallway). Actor B is better because the angle gives echoes a longer path and the drape absorbs some of the sound. Actor C is in the best position, taking advantage of distance, absorption, angles, and the way an uneven surface like a bookshelf breaks up the reflections.

---

[7] With experience, you can learn to hear the echoes without using an absorber. I'll still sing a little (or bark like a seal, so I can also hear the echo's decay) when testing a new space.

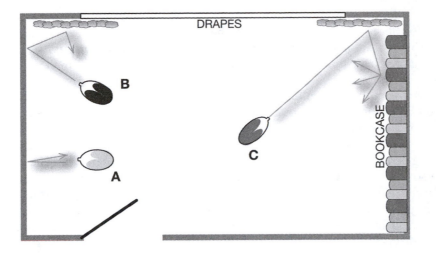

Figure 6.23 Where the talent stands in a room can make a difference.

Obviously, shooting those three positions will give three totally different looks to the scene. But even subtle changes can improve the sound of a room. If you consider reverb when you're first scouting or planning an interior, you may find a position that provides both good pictures and good sound . . . which will result in a much better film.

Cutting down reflections

The reflections that really matter are the ones the talent is facing into—usually from the wall behind the camera. Since that wall isn't in the shot, you've got more options for lowering reflections without worrying about how they'll look. The most common solution is *sound blankets*—heavy, padded cloths about six feet square, available from film and video supply houses. Furniture-moving pads are a close equivalent, though with a little less absorption. Hang them from the offending wall, at about the same height as the talent's mouth. Hanging a few on the sides of the room can also cut down the parallel wall problem. You can boost their echo-cutting ability by hanging them from a light stand and boom instead of directly on the wall. A couple of inches between wall and blanket lets it trap more sound.

Sound blankets can be folded up and stored when they're not in use. A less flexible alternative (literally) but with better absorption is Owens-Corning type #703 fiberglass. This is a specially compressed version of the fibers used for house insulation, designed specifically for acoustics. It's yellow rather than pink, and comes in lightweight 2′ by 4′ panels, two inches thick and weighing about half a pound per square foot.[8]

---

[8] Other sizes are available, but this is the most convenient one for quieting a set's echoes and for building a studio or post suite.

It can be found at acoustical ceiling supply companies and bigger home-improvement centers for about $12 per panel. Wrap the panels in an old bed sheet or something similar to keep the fibers from irritating your skin. The panels are rigid enough to be leaned against a wall and light enough that they can be hung from standard picture hooks.

If you can't use sound blankets or #703, you can at least partially treat a reflective surface by closing drapes, moving a sofa, or even lining up a row of heavily dressed production assistants against it.

But there's another technique—diffusion—that can also conquer many of the offending echoes. That's because the biggest problem with a hard wall is that it reflects all the sound back in the same direction. If you can break up the surface so some of the reflections go elsewhere, there'll be less noticeable echo. If you don't have a bookshelf handy, try stacking up some road cases and equipment boxes at random angles, behind the camera. The round tubes used to ship tripods or light stands—or any large rounded objects—are particularly helpful since they diffuse sound in all directions.

If a room has a high reflective ceiling, you can provide both absorption and diffusion by filling the ceiling with helium-filled balloons. Yes, people might call you a clown when you try to buy the balloons . . . but it's an accepted technique on film shoots. It's sometimes the only way to get usable dialog from rooms with a domed ceiling, because the dome can focus all the echoes right back at the actors.

Be flexible

Keep trying different placements and angles within a room—and other recording spaces—until you get a sense of how walls affect sound. Some zero-budget filmmakers record voice-overs in a closet stuffed with winter coats (the coats absorb sound). It's also how I got into some of the weird places referred to at the start of this section. The blankets in the hotel room were, of course, sound blankets. The limo was parked in a dealer's showroom—but the room itself had gigantic glass windows and an opening to their machine shop, so we moved an interview into the limo to gain isolation and absorption. The map was the kind with heavy paper hanging from an easel; we were recording voice-over inserts in an echoey classroom, so we held some of the pages out to improvise a tent. I put the professor inside of it.

CHAPTER 7

Production Mic Technique

No part of production seems to cause more trouble for self-taught producers than dialog recording. If you don't believe me, listen to almost any amateur video on YouTube. You'll hear hollowness and noises that at the least, say "this is not worth your attention" . . . and at the worst, make it nearly impossible to understand.

The problem isn't YouTube's streaming software. Clips posted by broadcasters and other professionals sound fine. So do amateur videos set to music recordings. Besides, the problem exists beyond YouTube or even data compression: you'll hear similarly awful tracks on public access cable channels, and on many school videos.

The problem isn't lack of money. You can record better dialog with a $15 mic than with one built into a $3,000 camera, if you know what you're doing. And it isn't rocket science. Once you understand some basics about handling a boom, rigging a lavaliere, or using a wireless rig, the rest is just common sense. You don't need a Hollywood mixer on your staff, just someone who's willing to take the steps necessary for good sound.

This chapter will tell you how to do those things. But first, a few definitions:

In this book, *dialog* refers to human speech. If you're writing or producing a film the term *dialog* may be more specific, and not refer to spontaneous interviews, narrations, or recognizable phrases added to enrich a crowd recording. But we'll use it to refer to all human speech captured for a soundtrack, because the basic process stays the same.

Boom, of course, is the pole holding something over the actors' heads. It can also be an adjective (a *boom* mic on the pole, or a *boom* track in a mix) and a verb (you need someone to *boom* your film).

Lav or *lavaliere* is a tiny mic that can be mounted near a subject's mouth, and the track that results.

Don't confuse lav with *wireless*.[1] Lavs are small mics, usually mounted on the body. Lavs can be wired to a mixer or camera, or use a wireless radio link. Similarly, boom mics can be wireless or wired.

A wired connection will always sound better than a wireless one for the same mic.[2] Lavs should always be wired unless the cable limits the actors' movement, or will be seen in a wide shot. Don't use wireless just because "we've always done it that way," or you don't have convenient cables. This applies particularly to sub-$1,000 wireless rigs; they will affect your track, in ways that can't be fixed in post.

WHICH MIC SHOULD YOU USE?

Hollywood is a boom town.

In dramatized feature films, there's a definite hierarchy to miking methods. In order of preference:

1. Use a hypercardioid or shotgun on a boom,[3] over the actor's head and just out of camera range. If that's not possible . . .
2. Use those mics on a boom, but from underneath and pointing up to the actor. If you can't boom . . .
3. Plant a cardioid, hypercardioid, PZM, or shotgun on the set where it'll cover dialog. First choice is wired; wireless if the cable would be seen by the camera. If there's nowhere to hide a full-size mic . . .
4. Plant a lavaliere on the set. They're small and easily hidden. If a plant mic will be too far or pick up unevenly when the actor moves . . .
5. Put a lav on the actor, and run the cable out the back of a jacket or down a pants leg. If that puts the cable in the shot . . .
6. Use a wireless lav, and hope that radio problems don't ruin the take.

---

[1] In productions, *using a wire* usually refers to using a wire*less* lav. It's not very logical, and probably comes from the dialog in cop shows and noir films.

[2] Unless you're using one of the newer $3,500 all-digital wireless rigs. While their price has stayed stable for the past several years, competition will probably make them more affordable in the future.

[3] Chapter 6 helped you decide which of those two mics to use for a particular kind of shot.

In feature films, boom mics are preferred because they sound better. Since they're bigger than lavs, they can have better low-frequency and noise performance. They're also free from clothing rustles (as are planted mics) and the wired ones don't get radio interference.

But Hollywood's choice of boom mics is also artistic. Because of where they're placed, overhead mics pick up the natural ambience and perspective of a scene, much more than body mics can. These subtleties help the illusion that we're overhearing the characters' real life rather than a performance. Of course, most of what they do in Hollywood is narrative: scripted or directed ad-lib films, telling a story about peoples' lives.

Documentaries, training films, and commercials can have other priorities, and lavs can be more appropriate. Because of their closeness to the mouth, they pick up the performer's voice more than their environment. This helps create the illusion that a person is talking directly to us. For this reason, they're often the best choice for tight shots of a spokesperson, demonstrator, or interview subject: the sound matches the visual perspective of a person talking to camera.

In Hollywood, boom mics usually sound technically better than lavs, with lower noise and better bass. That's because feature film boom ops usually reach for a very high quality mic like the $2,000 Schoeps MK41. If you're using a lower priced electret hypercardioid or gun, the technical differences between it and a lav won't be as noticeable.

Please note that "use the built-in camera mic" doesn't appear anywhere in this section. The mics supplied with most cameras are pretty poor. You can fix that by buying a better mic and mounting it on the camera, *but it'll still sound bad in most applications.* That's because the camera is usually too far from the subject to get good sound. You'll get mostly noise, and (if you're indoors) annoying room reverb. Professionals use camera-mounted mics only for breaking events when there is no time to rig something better, for in-your-face interviews where both camera and mic are close to the subject, or for footage where they know the track will only supply background atmosphere and not dialog.

☛ ROSE'S RULES

Professionals have a simple rule for how close a mic should be:

Unless the talent can reach out and touch the mic comfortably, it's too far away.

These are technical and practical realities. Your own artistic sensibilities and shooting situations may outweigh any hard-and-fast rules, and reasonable directors may disagree. However, I'll go on record as saying the worst tracks I've ever had to rescue were shot with camera mics. Choosing a particular kind of mic for artistic reasons is one thing. But choosing one just to save time or money can destroy your film.

You can hear the difference

Here are eight clips that let you audition boom, lav, and camera mics in a variety of shooting situations. They're grouped so you can compare different mics with the same subject and setting.

The first two are a master shot of an actor delivering formal lines, while a student reads to himself on a tablet. On **Clip 7.1**,[4] he's being picked up by a very good mic mounted on the camera. Because it's an exterior without large nearby buildings, there's none of the echo that haunts camera mics indoors. You can hear the director and background outdoor tone, but this was a controlled shooting situation, so you don't hear other voices or noises. This recording is just on the edge: an audio post expert with proper software could make it usable in a mix, but it'll never sound good.

Clip 7.2 is the same camera take, but dialog is from a wireless lav on the actor. The sound is clean and noise-free, though you can hear the director's voice very softly at the head. It's also a little muffled, both because of the wireless link and the fact that the lav is buried under his cravat. While some of that can be fixed in post, there'll always be a little distortion from the analog wireless.

Clip 7.2 is actually *too* noise-free. It sounds like the actor is talking in a quiet studio, rather than outdoors. And even though the student is visually closer to us, we don't hear any of his movements. So I've included **Clip 7.3** for comparison. It's the edited and mixed sequence that used this master shot.

Sound 7.1 is a camera mic in a quiet, well treated office, at about 4' distance. While this is a reasonable quality, multi-thousand-dollar camera from a major manufacturer, their brochure makes no claims about the mic's quality or appropriateness for actual shoots. You can hear why. While we're not too concerned with room noise and there's not much electronic hiss, the mic picks up almost as much reflected voice as direct signal. Our actress sounds like she's in a tiled locker room.

Compare it with **Sound 7.2**: the same camera mic and actress, at the same distance, but in a well-treated sound studio with lots of absorption on the walls. She still sounds distant, and probably wouldn't match the shot, but at least most of the reverb is gone. Unfortunately you'll seldom get to shoot in this kind of room.

Sound 7.3 moves us back to the office setting, but with a short shotgun on a boom, at about 2'. The better position (only two feet closer than the camera mic demo) cuts the reverb considerably. The more directional mic, with a better element, gives us much cleaner sound. A few inches closer would make it even better, but you could conceivably use dialog like this in a film.

Sound 7.4 is the same actress in the same office, but with a lav concealed in her shirt collar. All we hear is her, with essentially no room reverb or ambience. Many

---

[4] *A Tale of Two E-Readers*, produced for Eink and courtesy of Captains of Industry. You can see the whole thing at www.dplay.com/movies/EinkAgcy.mov, or in a more compressed version on YouTube.

people would consider this too tight a sound, though you hear it on TV shows every night. (I'd probably add both reverb and roomtone in the mix.)

Because dialog quality is so dependent on room acoustics, we also did an interview in a typical apartment setting. All three mics—lav, boom, and camera— were recorded to separate tracks. Figure 7.1 shows the setup.

Clip 7.4[5] switches between the three mics in a single take, to let you hear the differences while looking at the talent. Even though we used a professional camera, the camera mic's pickup is clearly unacceptable for any professional purpose. The lav is usable, but the sound is almost too sterile for the setting: it doesn't sound like we're in someone's den. (A little

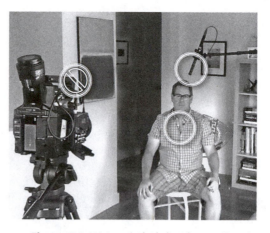

Figure 7.1 We've circled the three mic locations for this interview. Please don't use the one on the left.

reverb, along the necessary equalization, could be added in post.) The boom sound clean and realistic, and is ready to mix into a finished video.

You can also use traditional handheld or stand-mounted mics if you don't mind them being in the shot. This is common in news reporting, where the goal is to get

---

✔ **TIP**

There's another factor in the *boom vs. lav* decision if you're producing for broadcast commercials. TV is a very processed medium, and advertisers add lots equalization and compression (Chapter 16) to make their commercials sound louder. Recent laws attempting to control loudness haven't really stopped this; they've just moved the target a little.[6]

All that processing tends to emphasize the acoustics of the room. What was a reasonable, clean sounding location in the mixer's headphones can become an airplane hangar in the mixing suite. I'd rather start with production tracks that have very little reverb, do the processing that producers demand, and add high-quality artificial reverb to the mix if it's needed.

---

[5] Director Mike Kuell, courtesy JetPak Productions LLC.

[6] Those of us who mix commercials have already come up with ways to make our spots remain loud and up-front . . . as you can hear, any time you watch network TV.

the mic as close to a subject as possible without wasting time on setup. Non-news shows usually don't show the mic, except for scenes of musicians or other performers. In fact, sometimes what you see in a film or on a talk show is a prop mic. The actual voice pickup is from a lav or boom.

A good way to assure clean dialog from a single performer is to use both a boom and a lav, plugged into separate tracks in the camera or recorder. But don't mix them. When you edit, keep both in sync. When you mix, choose the one most appropriate for the shot. If that's the boom, save the lav for when talent turns off-mic or a prop makes too much noise. If you've chosen the lav, keep the boom as an alternative during clothing noises or momentary radio problems. Since you're using these alternate tracks for only a syllable or two, a little equalization (plus some reverb, when lav is replacing boom) is usually all that's needed to make the sound quality match.

⚠ WARNING

Make sure of your workflow

The dual mic, isolated track strategy requires coordination with the postproduction team. If you're shooting and editing yourself, just remember to keep the tracks separate until the show is cut, and then choose the best one. Don't mix them, unless you're sure of what you're doing and have an excellent monitoring environment. Mixing them to "sound best" on most editing setups' speakers usually gives you something worse than just keeping a single track.

If you're shooting material that'll be edited by somebody else, make sure they're expecting isolated tracks. If the editor mixes boom and lav together before cutting, they can't be un-mixed.

If you don't know how the show will be edited and can't confirm instructions with a postproduction supervisor, the best strategy is to supply a single track. Multiple mics can be carefully mixed on the set, fading one mic up while another comes down, but only if your sound person can concentrate on what the mix sounds like. Don't expect them to do this if they're also holding a boom or doing other duties.

Multitrack recording

Multitrack recorders are now common on professional productions, keeping a separate track for each microphone, usually called *isos* for *iso*lated mic. A single mixed track is also sent to the camera. The mixed track is usually from the boom, but lavs and plant mics are subtly brought in when the boom can't reach a character.

This adds expense, of course, since a separate recorder has to be rented and someone has to control the mix. But it saves money for the production, because takes can be used that otherwise would have to be either thrown out or require ADR. Dealing with the additional tracks doesn't cost the production extra, if the editor ingests all of the tracks (Chapter 12) before editing. The editor then works while listening only to the mixed track, but edits all the tracks simultaneously. These multiple tracks are sorted in audio post. Doing it this way—cutting all the tracks at the same time you're dealing with picture—is far cheaper than trying to re-sync isolated mics after the edit,[7] and gives the sound department the most flexibility for refining the track.

USING BOOM MICS

The downside of boom mics is that they require an operator. Sound mixers who aren't too busy worrying about multiple mics may be able to double on boom. Otherwise, you need a separate boom op. Good ones cost a few hundred dollars a day, a worthwhile investment if you want high-quality sound.

If you can afford only one professional, hire an experienced mixer instead of an experienced boom op. Mixers have to deal with the entire mic-to-camera-or-recorder process, and can bring more to your production.

If you can't afford trained personnel at all, you'll have to designate a production assistant or someone else on the crew, or find an intern or film student. *But this only works if you give them enough support to do the job right.* That costs money, too, but far less than an experienced operator. It also requires a time investment from both of you. Don't expect to train them on the day of the shoot, and don't expect them to pick up the skills by guesswork or magic, or even by reading Wikipedia the night before. You have to either pay for experience, or take the time to make sure your sound crew has it.

There's another alternative: You can point to an enthusiastic volunteer at the shoot, hand them a boom, and tell them to deal with it. Even if you've relieved them of other responsibilities like changing lights and getting coffee, you'll still get a track that's echoey and uneven, harder to edit and very difficult to mix. Your whole film will seem more amateur.

Choose boomer and boom

Let's assume you've picked the middle ground, and want to use inexperienced personnel but still get the best sound possible. You'll have to find the *right* inexperienced person:

- Someone with the physical strength and endurance to hold a long, unbalanced pole over their heads during a long shoot day . . . but also with the agility to

---

[7] It's expensive even in those rare cases where timecode works properly for this purpose. If you're syncing with any other method, each edit may need to have its isos matched by ear after the picture has been cut. That takes a good ear, and can bust any budget.

make tiny movements and keep themselves in an awkward position for the length of a take.

- Someone who can hear subtle differences in sound through their headphones.
- Someone with an alert attitude. They have to pay attention during the rehearsal and the take. They have to learn how the actors will exchange lines, and good boom operators usually memorize cues from the dialog. They should also pay attention to the actors' body language, to anticipate their movements. The point is having the mic in position *before* the actor begins a line. If the mic is in the wrong place, moving after the line starts can sound awful.
- Someone who doesn't have anything else important to do at the shoot. Wardrobe or makeup personnel are theoretically free to hold a mic during takes, but their distraction levels will be too high. If they even manage to start worrying about mic placement, they probably won't be able to do their own jobs as well.
- **Someone who has at least half a day to practice with boom and mic before the shoot.** You may need to pay for their time, and you'll definitely need the full sound package for this session, as well as somebody else to play "actor." But this is an absolutely necessary expense. Booming is a physical skill. You can't learn it just by reading a book. If you don't provide this practice session, be prepared to throw away most of the first day's shooting. That's where the practicing will take place.

You're also going to need some equipment.

Gear for booming

Microphone

The most critical part of a boom rig isn't the boom; it's the mic. Professionals describe boom mics in terms of "reach"—a combination of how much noise the mic itself generates, and its directional characteristics. Low self-noise is essential so the signal can be amplified without losing any subtleties. For film and HDTV, or videos using separate recorders and destined for theatrical projection, it's worth using an externally polarized condenser element (see previous chapter). Good electret condenser mics are quiet enough for broadcast or streaming.

Too much directionality may be as bad as too little. As discussed in the last chapter, very directional shotguns suffer from uneven response along the back and sides. If a mic is close to the ceiling, reflections from that surface will color the sound. Professionals working on theatrical films in location interiors usually choose a relatively small high-quality hypercardioid like the Schoeps MK41. This mic can also be used successfully outdoors, but at greater distances a short shotgun like the Sennheiser MKH416 is often used. It's worth getting one or both of these for an important shoot.

If you're aiming at broadcast or lower-quality media, you can use the fairly good electret short shotguns from Audio-Technica, Beyerdynamic, Sennheiser, and Sony selling in the $500 range. Aside from differences in noise level—which translates to how close they have to be to a performer—these mics are more sensitive to reflections and noisy crew members then their higher-priced cousins. But if you use them carefully, you can get a decent track. No matter what quality of mic you choose, the techniques for using it will be the same.

While you're picking a mic, get an appropriately sized windscreen. You'll need a hard mesh windscreen, with a porous cloth cover if it'll be outdoors. A set costs about $350, but they're very cheap to rent (and occasionally thrown in as a boom/mic/windscreen kit). The foam windscreen that came with the mic is useful only indoors, in situations where the boom won't be moving through the air much.

Pole and shockmount

Of course, you'll also need a boom pole. You really will: a lightweight paint-roller extension or plastic broom handle just isn't worth the money you save.

- Professional boom poles are incredibly rigid for their weight. They won't droop because of a microphone on their end, and your operator won't droop from holding up a heavy handle. A nine-foot Gitzo metal boom weighs less than two pounds. A nine-foot Van den Bergh carbon fiber boom weighs 13 oz!
- The clutches on a professional boom lock securely when the boom is extended. This is important. Nobody cares if a paint roller or broom creaks when you move it, but the slightest squeak or rattle in a mic boom will be recorded with the dialog.
- Booms are usually matte black. Lighting a set is hard enough, without a shiny piece of metal or plastic over the actor's head.
- The shockmount is important if you're going to be moving the boom. Otherwise, even the movement of a rigid boom can turn into rumbles on the track.

Good boom poles aren't expensive when considered as long-lasting professional investments. The ones mentioned sell for between $300 and $500 and there are cheaper pro alternatives; add about $150–200 for a good shockmount. Because these tools last so long, rentals can be a real bargain: boom, shockmount, and cable go for as little as $10–15/day.

Necessary accessories

The other items you'll need might not be obvious:

- Monitoring. Even experienced boom operators don't rely on their eyes to tell when the mic is perfectly positioned. Headphones are essential for the amateur. You'll also need some way to power them: a separate cable from the mixer or recorder, or an inline headphone amp like the Shure FP-12 (rentable for under $10).

  European boom operators sometimes pride themselves on their ability to get by without headphones. In the US, that's considered too risky; professionals always use phones. Amateurs need them even more, since they have no experience correlating mic position and sound. Don't depend on earbuds or flimsy Walkman-style foam bubbles. You'll need a reliable isolating phone, designed for voices. The standard on film and video shoots is the full-size but folding Sony MDR-7506 (about $100, rentable for under $10/day).

A few boom operators like a video monitor as well, and may even wear LCD screens on their chest. This helps them see if the mic gets in the shot—something even an experienced operator will occasionally do. They'll still have to glance at the real-life scene to see body language and other important cues that might not be in the frame.

- You'll need some way to get the mic's signal into your recorder. See the next chapter for details about adapters, mixers, preamps, and other accessories.
- You'll want thin cotton gloves. The $5 kind sold for gardening are fine. Choose the ones without rubber grips, and clip the fingertips off so you can manipulate clutches and other small items quickly. The cotton palms pad your hands, so you can slide the pole without making noise.

Figure 7.2 Hairballs!
Also known as Goody Ponytailers;
you won't find anything better for keeping
wires clipped to a boom.

Figure 7.3 A caribiner clip,
available from theatrical rigging and rock-
climbing suppliers.

- You might also want a few pony-tail holders, about $2/dozen in drugstores. I'm not kidding. The plastic balls with elastic between them (Figure 7.2) can be opened or closed with one hand, and are ideal for holding hanks of cable or keeping mic wires from rattling when you move the boom. Goody Products' Ponytailers are so useful that many operators affectionately call them "hairballs," and keep some on hand at all times.
- A rigger's caribiner clip (Figure 7.3) or Velcro strap with clip, about $10. Attach it to your belt to keep a loop of excess cable handy without letting it fall noisily to the floor.
- A small, directional flashlight. This is not just so you can see in shadows on the set. You can attach it to the boom, in place of the mic, for practice sessions in darkened rooms. Enlist a friend to be the "actor," and try to keep the light focused on their mouths while they move around. Once you get the hang of that, graduate to mic and headphone.

The bargain-basement solution: Mini-recorder on a stick

One low-budget solution has become popular among the no-budget crowd: take one of the $100–300 flash recorders with built-in mic, and somehow mount it to an improvised pole. Most of these units have a standard ¼"–20 camera mount socket on their back. Figure 7.4 shows a Tascam DR-07, on an adjustable camera mount taped to a bulb-changing pole from a hardware store. The adjustable mount lets you aim the recorder's mics down toward the talent. This is a compromise—heck, it's laughable by any professional standard[8]—

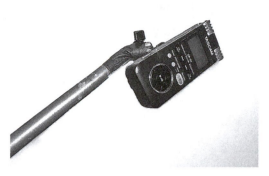

Figure 7.4 A very low budget boom setup. Don't expect great sound, but it might be usable.

but at least it keeps the mic close to the action, and gives you better sound than a mic at the camera.

The compromise isn't the recording circuits. When set to full quality, these units can make a recording that's at least as good as the multi-generation analog tracks Hollywood lived with for decades.

One compromise is the mic built into these recorders, usually low-cost electret elements that can generate hiss. Worse, they can't have the full-size acoustic design of even mediocre hypercardioids or shotguns. Often they're barely cardioid, with two mics contributing to a mono cardioid pattern. (Good luck improvising an effective windscreen.)

The other compromise is the controls: they're at the wrong end of the boom. It takes lots of trials—and a bit of luck—to find a record volume setting that works for your actors' delivery. In most cases you're forced to use the recorder's Automatic Level Control to avoid distortion or electronic noise; this *increases* apparent noise pickup from the set, because the ALC brings things up whenever the actors pause.

At least the speed of these recorders is usually very stable. If you sync your takes with a slapped slate, they should stay synchronized for at least 20 minutes at a time. You'll probably have to record at a 44.1 kHz sample rate, the maximum available on most pocket recorders. Some video editing software has a hard time dealing with that rate, or requires lengthy rendering for it. If so, you can save some time by converting to 48 kHz in an audio program before you start the edit.

A better solution, but still a money-saver, is to take that same recorder and move it to the base of your improvised pole. Then plug a good directional mic into it, and mount the mic at the far end.

---

[8] We call the arrangement "Zoom on a Boom," after one brand of pocket recorder.

The art of going boom

No matter what kind of mic and pole you use, the basic concept is simple. Hold things so the mic is above the actor, slightly in front of and pointed towards the mouth. Make it as close as physically possible without being in the frame. Thirty inches from the actor can be too far away, unless you're in a well-designed studio or quiet outdoor setting. Use your earphones as well as your eyes for this placement: since you're most likely coming at the actor from a sharp angle, you won't be able to see when the tip of the mic is pointing off to one side instead of directly in front.

Closer is always better. Too close is impossible. On some sets, a difference of a couple of inches can turn usable dialog into something that has to be replaced in post. Some Hollywood mixers feel their boom operators aren't doing their jobs unless the mic dipped into the frame on at least a couple of takes. As a general rule, the mic should at least be close enough that your actors can reach out and comfortably touch it.

Keep the mic pointed at the mouth at all times. You should be able to draw an imaginary straight line, through the center of the mic and right to the talent's lips. Otherwise, as the actor drifts into areas of the pickup pattern that aren't perfect, the quality of their voice will change. This may require adjusting the angle of the shock mount, so the mic stays in the right direction for the way you're holding the pole.

Boom mic locations

Overhead booming provides the most natural sound for dramatic dialog. Since the mouth is closest to the mic, voices are emphasized—a good thing—while the downward angle picks up prop noises and footsteps to a lesser extent. But remember that highly directional mics change the timbre of sounds coming from the back and sides. If the ceiling is too close to the mic, echoes from it may color the dialog.

In his book *Sound Man*,[9] experienced mixer Richard Patton suggests waving the boom around the acting area, before the take, and looking at the shadows. Get used to where you can put the mic safely, so as not to cast a distracting shadow while panning from one actor to another. Patton recommends sighting along the pole when you find that position, and mentally marking where it points to on the set—a prop, decoration, or even marks on the wall—so you can get back to that position quickly when you need a safe place again.

Patton's advice continues:

- If there are many lights, you may be able to plant an opaque object to cast a deliberate shadow. These *flags* can blend in with the set lighting, giving you a larger area to move the boom. But at many shoots, getting one is as much a

---

[9] Published by Location Sound Ltd, 2010. It may be hard to find, but definitely worth reading if you're going to spend any part of your life gathering sound for movies. The title isn't sexist, by the way; it's autobiographical.

political challenge as a technical one. On a professional set, anything to do with lighting is the responsibility of the grips. You can't touch the flags or lights, so you have to convince them to.

- If you can't avoid shadows, find a place where you the boom casts a soft shadow that blends in with the set somehow. Then don't move during the take: a moving shadow will call attention to itself.

Patton passed away in 2012, after a long career that included mentoring and supplying equipment for other sound people as well as working on major shoots. His contributions certainly live on.

If the ceiling is too short or the shot requires a lot of headroom, booming from below is often an alternative. But it requires more cooperation on the set. Prop noises and footsteps will be louder, so lines have to be delivered without too much movement. If you can, stage the shot with characters sitting down: their mouths will be closer to the mic. There's a tendency to tilt the camera down as a shot gets wider, so the camera operator will have to warn the boom op before zooming out.

If two characters are close together, you can often position the mic between them— either above or below—and just rotate it slightly as they exchange lines.

Booming from directly in front, with microphone parallel to the floor, is seldom a good idea. Echoes and noises from behind the actor will be picked up almost as loudly as the voice. Mouth noises and sibilance are generally projected forward, so a close frontal mic will pick up more of them.

✔ TIP

How to stay out of the shot
- The boom operator wants the mic as close as possible. The director of photography wants total freedom composing the shot. A reality check is always necessary, and—unless you have a video monitor available—you'll have to count on the camera operator to tell you during setup how close you can get.
- You could start with the mic high and gradually lower it until someone says "any lower and you'll be in the shot." But that almost always results in too much safety margin, and more mic distance than is necessary. A foot of extra distance to protect the frame doesn't look any different than an inch or two, but sounds a lot worse. It's better to start with the mic in the shot and gradually raise it until it can't be seen any more.
- Some boom operators put a piece of white camera tape on the end of their windscreen, so it'll be immediately obvious in the viewfinder if the mic dips too low during a take. Others feel this compromises the sound.

Two-shots

If there'll be more than one actor in the scene, things get complicated. You have to move between them in the pauses between lines, stay approximately the same distance from each, and end up in the same place each time. For occasional step-ons, when you can't swing around in time, it might sound better to stay with the first speaker rather than move during the second one's line; depending on the mic, moving during the line can be very distracting. If there are a lot of step-ons, have a production conference: something—the quality of the track, the director's vision, or the ability to use a boom at all—is going to have to be compromised. The everybody-talking-at-once scenes pioneered by Robert Altman used lavs on each actor, often recorded to individual tracks so they could be sorted in postproduction. Booming that kind of scene is almost impossible.

Stretching the distance

The reason you need to be close, is to get as much of the actor's voice as possible. Competing noises are all around the shooting set, even if you're not aware of them during the take. The mic also hears prop noises and footsteps, background traffic rumbles, and reflections of the dialog off nearby surfaces (because of the delay, these reflections muddy up the voices instead of reinforcing them). Sounds fall off rapidly with distance, so by getting closer to the actor you'll hear proportionately less of the junk.

A few tricks will let you get farther away without hurting the sound:

- Soften the set. Reflections are the biggest problem, particularly when you leave the well-designed spaces of a studio and move to real-world locations. There are tips for cutting reflections at the end of Chapter 6.
- Keep things quiet. Get rid of as many environmental noises as possible. This may mean turning off HVAC or computer systems during the take, or moving generators to another location. It also means cutting down on prop noises and footsteps. Throw a sound blanket on the floor, or moleskins on the soles of actors' shoes, if they have to walk around (particularly important when booming from below). Put a piece of foam-core on the desk if the actor's going to be putting something down.

Be aware of electronic noise as well; it also competes with dialog.

- Get a better mic. All mics generate some internal noise, and electrets are noisier than externally-polarized condensers. But cheap electrets are invariably noisier than good ones. Often, the amount of noise is almost directly proportional to how much you thought you saved when you bought the mic.
- Use Star-Quad cable (Chapter 3) if the mic is any distance from the recorder or mixer. This cheap enhancement lowers electronic noise pickup from lamp dimmers, video wiring, and high-current lighting cables.

- Depending on how you're recording the sound, it can help to use an external mixer—even if there's only one mic and you're not really mixing anything. Most cameras add electronic noise to the track when you plug a mic directly into them, and generate less noise with line-level signals.

Controlling perspective

As a shot gets wider, you'll have to move the boom out so it won't be seen. This changes the ratio of direct to reflected sound, so the mic will pick up relatively more room reverberation. A small amount of this is not only acceptable, but appropriate: wide shots make the actor appear farther from us, and in real life we expect to hear more echo from a distant voice than a close one (even across a small room). The converse is also true: as the shot closes in, you have to move the mic in to pick up less echo.

If a shot is framed very wide but without much headroom, you might want to deliberately pick up more echo. Raise the mic slightly higher than usual, or point it more toward the floor. Don't do this trick unless you're absolutely sure of things. While it's easy to add room reverb in post, it's very difficult to make it match the visual setting. While it's possible to partially reduce some kinds of reverb in post, using very new software, the process is as likely to make things worse as to make them better.

Three tricks will help you keep mic perspective in, uh, perspective:

- The effect must be subtle. Once we're aware of changes in reverb, they become distracting. Early talking pictures changed the mic perspective with each edit: the effect was horrible, and sound operators quickly learned to leave their mics relatively stable.
- Each character's volume should stay constant during a scene. Since moving a mic farther away means less of the voice is picked up, you have to compensate by raising the recording level . . . simultaneously raising the background noise.
- Leave difficult decisions for postproduction. If you're not sure, stay close.

Operating the boom

It's no problem to work a mic boom. You just have to be strong enough to hold your arms up for long periods of time. But it's not intuitive. The next few pages explain the technique.

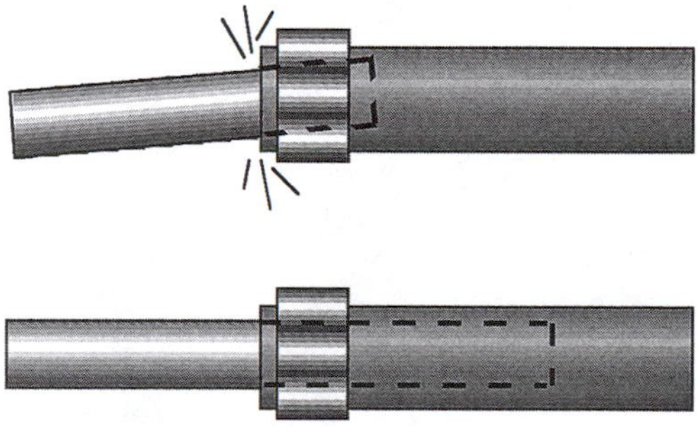

Extension

After you extend each boom section as far as it'll go, collapse the joint slightly so the pieces overlap a couple of inches. This will make it sturdier and less likely to creak at the joints. Figure 7.5 shows the

Figure 7.5 If a boom section is extended all the way *(top)*, it won't be as strong as if it overlaps *(bottom)*.

wrong (top) and right (bottom) way to extend. It's better to extend three sections part-way than two sections all the way.

The clutch that locks the sections of a boom when they're extended can wear out and become difficult to use. A layer of plumber's Teflon tape around the threads usually fixes things. Sometimes sections of a collapsed fiber boom can get stuck together, particularly if it was moist when stored. Gentle heating in an oven can usually get things moving again.

Good boom poles have plastic bushings inside them, to keep one section from hitting another. If an older pole makes noise when you move it, chances are the bushings have worn down. A strip of female Velcro—the loop part—usually has the right thickness and "give" to serve as a replacement.

When you're finished using a boom, wipe it down as you collapse it. This will keep dirt from working its way inside, where it can damage the clutch or bushings.

Boom handling

Holding a few pounds of metal and plastic over your head might seem trivial at first, but can get very heavy as the day wears on. Avoid holding the arms in a wide Y position (Figure 7.6); instead, stand like the letter H (Figure 7.7) with the arms as straight up as possible. This is a matter of physics, not aesthetics. When the arms are spread at an angle, you're supporting the mic with your muscles . . . which will get tired. When the arms are vertical, the weight of the boom and mic is carried straight down through your bones. If you're moving the boom around, the outside arm should be slightly bent for control (see Figure 7.9).

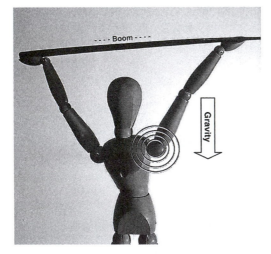

Figure 7.6 Extending your arms
to the sides puts the full weight of the boom
on your muscles . . .

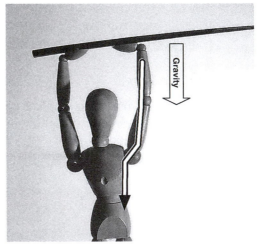

Figure 7.7 . . . while keeping arms
straight and vertical lets your bones carry
most of the weight.

Figure 7.9 How to hold a boom properly, overhead.

Figure 7.8 Don't hold the boom like a flagpole.

It may be tempting to hold the boom like a flagpole at a parade (Figure 7.8), but this gives you less control over how the mic is aimed. Also, since the pole itself will be at an angle coming from below, it's more likely that it'll cross into a corner of the shot.

If you don't need the full length of the pole to reach the actors, hold it a foot or so in toward the middle rather than at the very end. This way part of the boom will act as a counterweight, and you won't be stressing your wrists as much.

It takes a human model to demonstrate additional details, so we'll use Christopher O'Donnell.[10] Note in Figure 7.9 how he keeps his inner arm—his left, in this photo—straight and rigid. It's not directly overhead, because he doesn't need the height, but vertical enough that his bones provide most of the support. The outside arm is at the end of the boom, slightly bent so it can move easily. This gives control without being tiring.

This is also a flexible position for documentary boom ops, letting you rest one end of the boom to free a hand while operating shoulder-bag equipment. Figure 7.10 shows busy production mixer G. John Garrett[11] boom-and-bagging a shot of a dolphin and its trainer: his right (inside) arm supports the weight straight down, while his left hand steers. He can concentrate on the shot while occasionally glancing down to read his equipment's meters.

---

[10] Not the model-turned-actor with a similar name, but an excellent feature film boom operator.

[11] His IMDB listing stretches back 20 years, and includes work for Disney and other major networks as well as lots of PBS documentaries.

Figure 7.10 The same technique is adaptable while working with bagged equipment, even in slightly more challenging environments.[12]

Figure 7.11 Booming at chest level: the arms still have the same functions.

If you're tall, you can hold the boom at chest level for some shots. This position is less tiring than overhead. In fact, many boom operators bring an apple box or step ladder to get some extra height, no matter how tall they are. But the strategy is still the same. Chris demonstrates in Figure 7.11: he keeps the inside arm rigid, bearing most of the weight straight down; his outside arm does the steering. Both arms are still mostly vertical.

Check the positions of the hands in those three figures as well. The inner hand is *under* the boom to act as a pivot. The outer hand is wrapped around the *top* of the boom, because the supporting hand's pivoting action makes this end push up.

In Figures 7.9 and 7.11, O'Donnell holds the cable tightly at the end of the boom instead of letting it flop. Cable management is important, because a section of wire hitting the pole will make noise. That's also why there are a couple of loops at his belt: he can move the boom suddenly, and the loops prevent cable from dropping or rubbing against the floor.

The wire spirals around the pole in the O'Donnell photos, a common practice outside of Los Angeles. Some boom designs let you run wires inside the pole, as Garrett's does in Figure 7.10; this seems to be the preferred Hollywood method. It doesn't make any difference which you choose, so long as the cable is kept tight and can't swing or bounce when you move the boom. If you're using inside wiring, wrap a couple of turns of cable around your finger where it exits the boom, so you can keep tension on the wire to stop it from swinging around inside.

You also have to secure the cable at the mic end, both to keep it taught and to provide a strain relief that protects the connector. Figure 7.12 shows the end of

---

[12] Photo courtesy Chedd-Angier Production Company.

O'Donnell's boom, with a couple of hair-balls doing that job. Common practice, here in New England, is to mount the Ponytailers with "balls in back." facing the rear end of the mic. This way, you can glance at the entrance to the windscreen and see which way the mic, inside, is pointed. (You can also use tape to secure the cable.) If the cable is inside the pole, add a small loop of wire at the mic end; it protects the mic and connector if something snags the wire between takes.

Figure 7.12 Hairballs in use. Not only do they keep things neat; they also let you know that this mic is pointing down.

The voice, and just the voice

With the boom pointing down from above, it can be hard to avoid picking up actors' footsteps as they move around the scene. This is a problem, since steps should be treated differently from dialog in postproduction. The techniques that make a voice crisp and understandable can make footsteps unnaturally sharp. Besides, steps are often added to or moved, depending on how a scene has been edited. Footsteps *in the clear*, while the actor is pausing, can be moved to a separate track. But those that occur during lines—if the actor is "walking and talking"—cause trouble.

- The first defense against footsteps is to get the mic as close to the actors' mouths—and as far from the floor—as possible. If you can hold the boom so its least sensitive side (usually about 120° off axis) is toward the floor, even better.
- If that's not enough to do the job, get the actors to take off their shoes. If they refuse, lay some extra carpet down for them to walk on.
- If stocking feet or extra carpet will ruin the shot,[13] you'll have to treat the actors' shoes. Foam-covered moleskin and similar stick-on pads from film sound suppliers can help a lot. At a minimum, get them to wear softer-soled shoes for the scene.

Two more tips

Booming requires strength and agility. You can build up the arm muscles necessary with pull-ups and overhead weight presses. You can strengthen your hands and fingers—just as important—with squeeze balls.

It also requires skill and talent, and frequently luck. Even the most experienced operators occasionally get into trouble with noises. If at all possible and you're dealing with just a single actor, run a lav on a second track. Or actively mix multiple

---

[13] That is, the precise shot where dialog occurs. There might be a wide shot to establish the scene, but that doesn't mean you can't control foot sounds for the mid-shots and close-ups while the actors are talking.

lavs for that track. Just don't mix lavs and boom together; that limits your options in post-production.

In *Soundman*, Richard Patton points out that good boom operation is as much about the camera as about the actors. Good communication is essential. "Experienced boom ops spend most of their day hanging out next to the camera. When the next shot is being discussed between the camera operator and the director, the boom op is right there, listening."

LAVALIERE MICS

A lav works by being close to the source of sound—the actor's mouth—so that the inverse-square law (Chapter 1) assures a clean pickup with very little room reverb or natural noises. For dramatic dialog, this frequently is *too* clean. Don't try to compensate by moving the mic farther down the actor's body; all you'll gain is extra clothing noise. Instead, use a second mic for room ambience. Point a shotgun away from the actor or put a boundary mic on the floor near a wall. If you can, record it to a separate channel and mix them in post; otherwise, just mix a tiny bit of the room mic in with the lav.

Types of lavs

The first lavalieres, in the early days of television, used dynamic elements. They were so big and heavy they had to be worn on a lanyard around the neck—hence the name. (Louise de La Vallière, a girlfriend of Louis XIV, liked to suspend pendants from a gold chain around her neck. Never thought you'd find that in a book about digital sound, did you?)

Figure 7.13 Nobody would ever notice the Countryman B-6 peeping out from this collar. You can barely see that mic in the enlarged inset.

Today, lavs almost always use electret condenser elements (Chapter 6), and they range in size from about a third of an inch diameter by half an inch long, to smaller than the head of a match (Figure 7.13).

While the smallest mics are easier to conceal, as the element gets smaller it intercepts fewer moving air molecules. This generates less voltage, so electronic noise from the mic's preamplifier becomes more significant. As a general rule, smaller mics generate more self-noise, but today's mic manufacturers have learned how to make even the better subminiature mics quiet enough for professional use.

The preamps are powered by a small battery in the XLR connector, phantom voltage on the audio line, or a special multi-pin connection to a wireless transmitter. The internal batteries are usually good for at least a day or two's worth of shooting; when they get weak, you'll start to hear distortion or extra hiss. If you've got a source of phantom power, it's more reliable for wired lavs and you won't need to bother the talent for battery changes. Batteries in a wireless transmitter don't last more than a few hours.

If you're buying a lav to use with a wireless, specify what kind of transmitter you have. The connectors are different. If possible, get an adapter that'll let you use a standard XLR connector as well. That way, you can use the same mic when interference forces you to use cables.

Lavs are sometimes described as having "reach," with some being better than others for distance miking. Actually, the main difference between them is how much noise their preamps make—quieter ones can be amplified more, so you record more details of the scene—and how evenly they pick up different frequencies. A mic with more bass is often considered a close-up mic and can be appropriate on a spokesperson or demonstrator who's talking directly to camera. Mics with less bass are better matched to the sound of boom mics and can be intercut more easily in dramatic scenes. Some lavs have a "presence" peak around 3 kHz to pick out the voice better when an actor turns slightly away. A few deliberately boost all the high frequencies to compensate for the muffling effect of clothing. While any of these characteristics can be desirable on their own, they make matching with other mics more difficult.

Almost all lavs are designed as omnidirectional, but when you place them on an actor or on a wall of the set then one side gets blocked. Some lavs have their element pointing towards the top of a cylindrical case, while others point toward the side. This makes no difference in the pickup pattern, though it does influence the shape and thickness of the mic. All lavs have a pattern of holes or a grill either on the top or side where the sound enters; be careful not to block it when mounting the mic.

A few directional lavalieres are available. They're difficult to hide in clothing because they have to be precisely pointed, and because the tape used to mount a hidden mic blocks the holes that make them directional. However, they can be handy as plant mics.

Mounting lavalieres

Decide whether the mic can be visible in the shot. A lot of times there's no need to hide a mic, either because the talent is obviously a spokesperson or because a shot is wide enough that a tiny dot on the lapel won't be noticeable. It's always easier, and always sounds better, to have the mic outside the clothing. Sometimes, all you need to do is wrap some paper tape around the mic and clip, and color it with a felt-tip pen to match wardrobe.

Clip-on visible lavs

Lavs come with a variety of mounting clips and tie tacks to make the sound operator's job easier. Choose an appropriate one for the clothing, and you're almost all set.

The mic should be as close to the mouth as possible. A shirt collar or high up on a jacket lapel is always preferable to the middle of a necktie. If talent's head will be turning during the shot, choose the side that'll be favored—usually the side facing the interviewer or camera.

If the mic comes with a foam windscreen, you may want to use it to prevent popped Ps. You'll seldom need to use the wire mesh windscreen supplied with some mics, except in windy exteriors.

Don't let the wire dangle from the lavaliere. You need to provide some kind of strain relief. If the mic is wired to the camera, accidentally pulling on the cable can un-mount the mic, or even damage it. Even if the cable just goes a few feet to a transmitter in the talent's pocket, the strain relief will protect the mic from cable-borne noises. If you're using a clip, loop the wire up through the clip and into the clothing (Figure 7.14A). Then grab it from behind with the clip's teeth (Figure 7.14B) to hold the loop in place. This sometimes means the mic looks "upside down." Since most lavs are omnidirectional, it doesn't matter. If the fabric is too flimsy to keep the mic steady, try adding a small piece of flat plastic—such as half an old credit card— behind the fabric as a stiffener.

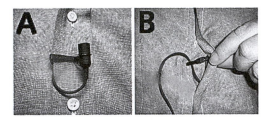

Figure 7.14 Loop a lav's cable up through the clip (A). Inside the shirt (B), grab the cable with the clip's teeth.

An alternate for mics mounted on clothing is the "vampire" clip. Instead of alligator teeth, it has two short pins that can be stuck through an inner layer of cloth. They cost about $10 at film sound suppliers. If you're using one or a tie-tack mount, make a loop of wire as a strain relief and hold the loop in place with tape. It will be similar to the strain relief shown in Figure 7.15.

Hidden lavs

Lavs are frequently hidden between layers of clothing, high up on the chest or under a collar. The preferred mounting method is to take two pieces of one-inch tape and fold them into triangles, like folding a flag, with the sticky sides out. Put these half-inch sticky triangles on both sides of the mic, and stick the mic to the inner layer of clothing with one. Loop the cable below the mic as a strain relief, with a piece of tape or thread to hold the loop loosely enough that there's some play if you tug on the wire. Tape the cable down below the loop. Then press the top layer of clothing onto the other sticky triangle, holding it in place so it can't rub against the mic. Figure 7.15 shows the completed assembly, as it would look under the top clothing layer.

If talent is wearing only one layer of clothing and you have to mount the mic directly to skin, use non-allergenic surgical paper tape. Wipe the skin with an alcohol prep pad first to remove grease and perspiration. The tape and pads are available at drugstores.

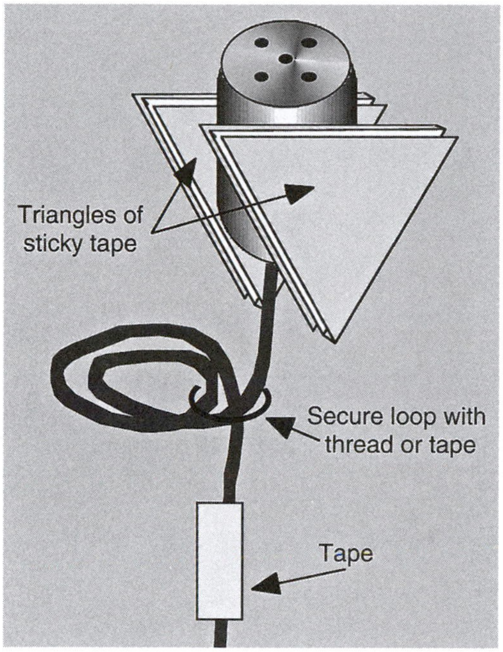

You can use similar mounting methods to hide a mic under long hair, the bill of a hat, inside a woolen cap, or even—with a very small mic—on an eyeglass frame. One favorite trick is to hollow out a pen and cut a hole in the top, place the mic inside, and stick the pen in a shirt pocket. That pocket can be a reasonable place for a lav, and you don't have to worry about clothing noises. You'll have to make a small hole in the pocket for the wire, but presumably your video has some budget to repair wardrobe.

Hair mics can be secured with spirit gum, used by makeup people to attach mustaches. They usually don't need a windscreen, even outdoors—the hair itself acts as a screen. Mount them as low on the scalp as possible. If the hair is worn long, just under the ear can be a good place. Bangs will let you mount a mic on the forehead. Long beards let you mount the mic right under the chin.

Triangles of sticky tape

Secure loop with thread or tape

Tape

Figure 7.15 Taping a concealed mic in place.

Body-hugging T-shirts or other very tight clothing presents a special problem, in that you don't want the lump of a microphone or its cable to show. A couple of suggestions:

- Use a miniature lav like the one in Figure 7.16. Tape it right behind the collar, which is usually thicker cloth than the rest of the T-shirt. Then run the cable around the collar and down the back.
- Wrap two layers of an elastic bandage around the talent's chest. Put the mic between them, with its element just sticking out, in the depression in the middle of the breastbone.

Invisible lavs

The smallest lavs are about an eighth of an inch in diameter. They look like a blob of glue on the end of a particularly skinny mic cable. (Don't believe a mic can be that small? Figure 7.16 is a close-up of a Countryman B-6, the same mic that disappears in figure 7.13.) Despite the mic's tininess, it sounds just like a Sony ECM-55, a full-size lav and broadcaster's favorite, shown in Figure 7.13.

Figure 7.16 That blob on the end of the wire is really a full-quality professional mic.

Mics this small can peek above the collar, or be poked through a buttonhole or between the weave of a loose sweater, and secured from the back with tape. (There can be a problem with through-the-weave rigging, if an over-eager wardrobe person mistakes the mic for a piece of lose thread and clips it off. Friends have reported this actually happening on their shoot. So if you're using a mic this small, warn the other departments.) The mics come in colors, or with colored caps. If you choose a color that's close to the wardrobe or skin, it will be invisible in all but the tightest shots.

Pin-Mic

Another alternative is the Pin-Mic, introduced by Ricsonix and now sold by Rode. It mounts on the front of wardrobe without any visible wires. Three small pins protrude from a wired disc inside the clothing, and the mic attaches from the front like a piece of jewelry. The pins hold it in place and carry the signal to the disc, which is then wired to a transmitter or XLR connector.

While not quite as microscopic as the B6, Pin-Mic is small: the part that lives on the outside is about ¼″ in diameter and ⅛″ high. It can be easily concealed behind a logo pin, tie tack, or other accessory.

Cable termination

If talent is wearing a wireless transmitter, hide the transmitter somewhere on their body and you're done. Observe the precautions about wireless antennas in the next section.

A wired connection is more reliable, so cable is usually run down a pants leg. But don't let the mic's XLR connector dangle: this puts extra strain on the thin mic cable, and if the character moves around during a shot, the connector will make noise hitting the floor. Instead, loop the excess cable and secure the connector inside the pants. Then run a heavier standard-gauge mic cable to the mixer. You can use a rubber band and safety pin to attach the connectors to the inside cuff, or an ace bandage or ankle warmer to wrap it to the talent's leg.

As the talent moves around, an assistant crouched at the side of the set can adjust the cable slack.

If the character will be seated, you can run the wire out the back of their shirt or under their jacket. Stuff the XLR connector into a back pocket and secure it with a rubber band and safety pin. Between takes, all the talent will have to do is reach up and unplug. Then they'll be free to roam around without you having to unrig them.

Coverage and multiple lavs

If two performers are going to be very close together, miking just one of them may be sufficient. In fact, wedding videographers frequently mic just the groom or minister (the bride would never stand for anyone messing with her gown). This picks up the entire ceremony.

If the performers are going to be apart for some of the scene, you'll need to mic them separately. But don't just combine their mics together; this increases noise pickup.

Use a mixer and actively bring up just the person who's speaking at the time, or route each mic to a separate channel on the recorder and take just the active one while you're editing.

If performers are on separate mics and then come together for intimate dialog, each mic will pick up both voices. The effect can be muddy or hollow sounding if both mics are mixed. **Sound 7.5** demonstrates this happening: two actors are lav'd for a soap opera close-up, but their mics are mixed together. Compare that with **Sound 7.6**, the same take but with only one mic turned up at a time.

In very noisy environments—particularly if the noise is mostly low-frequency—putting two identical lavs on the same actor can sometimes help control things. Mount one as closely as possible to the mouth and the other at least a few feet away. Inverse-square will mean that both mics pick up about the same amount of noise, but the close one gets a lot more voice than the distant one. Invert the polarity of the distant mic, and its signal will cancel part of the close mic's noise when you mix them together. Monitor as you adjust the two mic levels, to hear when things are at their quietest.

Newscasters frequently wear dual lavs on their lapel or tie, and some alligator-clip mounts are designed to take two mics at once. This redundancy is insurance against failure during live broadcasts, and not—as some people claim—so that polarity inversion can be used. (The mics are too close together for that trick to work.) Only one of those mics should be on-air at a time.

Avoiding noise in lavalieres

All other things being equal, a lav is usually electrically noisier than a shotgun. This is a function of the smaller element, and there's nothing you can do about it. If you turn the mixer or preamp all the way up, you may hear some hissing. Fortunately, a lav is almost always closer to the sound source than a shotgun; it picks up more sound pressure and generates more voltage from the voice, so you don't have to raise the recording volume so high that you'll hear the hiss.

Mechanical noise is a bigger problem, but easy to control. If you've mounted the mic properly, there shouldn't be any clothing rubbing directly against it. Clothing can also rub against the mic's cable, and the noise will be transmitted up the wire. If this happens and the strain relief isn't enough to keep the mic from hearing it, tape the wire somewhere it'll be protected. Some mics have special fiber inserts in their cables so they don't transmit as much noise.

Clothing can also rub against itself, and the mic will pick up the rustling sound. It may take some detective work to isolate the exact area where the rubbing is taking place. Once you do, use triangles of tape to hold clothing in position. Anti-static spray, sold to avoid thin clothes from clinging to the wearer, will soften crinkly layers of clothing near the mic. If a shirt has been heavily starched, spray water where appropriate for some local de-starching.

Coordinate clothing choices with the wardrobe department or talent. Cottons and woolens will always be quieter than synthetics or nylons. Corduroy should be avoided.

Headworn mics

In particularly noisy environments, it helps to put the mic right at the actor's mouth. This doesn't have to be the kind of golf-ball-on-a-stick that some singers wear at concert performances; Audio-Technica and Countryman make subminiature head mics. They include stiff wires that hook behind the ear and are bent to hold the element at the corner of the lip. They don't block the mouth from view, and while they're visible, they're also unobtrusive. They look like thin, skin-colored lines drawn from the ear to the mouth (the mics are available in a variety of skin tones), and often can't be seen on long shots. If the actor is facing sideways to the camera, operating a computer or driving a car, the mics can be kept on the unseen side of the face.

The big advantages of head mics are that they're so close to the mouth that room noise and acoustics are seldom a problem. I've used them to record noisy product demonstrations, and singers in front of bands, with almost perfect isolation. They also keep a constant distance from the mouth, no matter how much the performer turns and twists—which was handy when I had to record a yoga trainer.

Planted mics

Because they're so small, lavs are often used as plant mics. But their higher self-noise means they have to be close to the sound source. If you can hide a full-size mic in the same place, you'll find it usually sounds better.

If you're planting a lav at a desk or table, hiding it in a pencil jar or flower pot may pick up echoes. Depending on how the talent sits while they're talking, their voices might be directed at the table surface and bounce back to the mic. If the mic is a third of the way between table and mouth, these reflections can be almost as loud as the direct sound. To avoid this, use a directional lav, or mount the mic to some surface that can block reflections (such as the hidden side of a telephone or a computer monitor).

Watch for hidden low-level noise sources when you're planting a mic. A computer, for example, will radiate electronic hash while it's turned on. Electret lavs are usually immune to this, but a mic with a transformer may pick it up. A potted fern can be a good place to "plant" a mic, but its leaves will get noisy if there's a breeze.

Dialog in a car

The common way to pick up voices in a car is to clip a cardioid mic to a sun visor or headliner just above the front window, for front passengers. Rear passengers can be covered with a second mic attached to the back of the front seat, though if the road and car is quiet the front visor mic might be able to cover them. As an alternative mounting, place a hypercardioid under the dash, sticking up between two passengers. If only one person is talking, you can use a short shotgun there.

Unless you've got an electric car, the engine will make noise. And unless your passengers are wearing head mics, it'll be louder than you want on the dialog track.

Hollywood's usual solution is to turn off the engine, put it in neutral, and tow it from another car in front. (The tow car is also a good place to put the sound recordist and equipment.)

If the script will at all tolerate it, close the car's windows. Road noise, and normal outdoor backgrounds, can also pollute a track.

Avoid using body-mounted mics other than headworn in a car shot: shoulder belts can rub against them, making noise.

CONTROLLING WIND NOISE

An electronic filter can reduce the rumbling noise of a very light wind—the kind that would barely ruffle a flag—but anything else requires a mechanical solution as well.

Shotgun mics should always have a windscreen. The holes that make them directional will also pick up wind noise. Even swinging the mic back and forth on a boom, indoors, can create enough wind to be a problem. Low-cost foam windscreens that cover the entire mic should be adequate for interiors if the boom isn't being moved, and on wind-free days may be usable for closely miked handheld interviews outdoors.

If the wind is strong enough to feel, or you're whipping a boom around indoors, you'll need more protection than a foam windscreen can provide. Hard windscreens, consisting of a wire or open plastic frame surrounded by fine mesh, work by creating a low-turbulence area around the mic and can be very effective. They're often called *zeppelins* because of their shape. You can see one in Figure 7.9. For extra protection, a layer of furry cloth can be wrapped around the windscreen; it makes the assembly look like a small animal, but it does cut down on noise (see Figure 7.10). If you're using a zeppelin, a foam windscreen on the mic itself may also help. However, there must be at least a half inch of airspace between the windscreen and the interior of the zeppelin for it to work properly.

The tiny foam windscreens that come with lavalieres can reduce popped Ps, but don't provide any protection against outdoor wind. A metal mesh windscreen designed for the mic can help, using the same principle as the zeppelin on larger mics. If you don't have one of them available, try using a combination of these sound recordists' tricks:

- Pull the foam tip off a video head-cleaning swab.[14] It's often just the right size to fit over a lav.
- With the swab in place over the mic, wrap a couple of layers of cheesecloth around it.
- Snip the fingertip off a child's woolen glove (remove the child first), and fit the tip over the cheesecloth for extra protection. This also gives you the opportunity

---

[14] Remember when video used tape, and the heads had to be kept clean? You can still get these long wooden sticks with foam swabs at some electronics dealers. As an alternative, look for printer cleaning swabs.

to choose a glove color that will match the talent's overcoat, so you can leave the mic outside their clothing without it being too obvious. Putting the mic under the talent's heavy overcoat will definitely protect it from wind, but cuts the voice down too much.

If you're shooting in a howling wind-storm, the noise *will* get into the mic. The most you can expect from a windscreen and filter here is to reduce low-frequency sounds that can interfere with the recording. Get the mic as close to the speaker's mouth as possible, or wait for calmer weather.

⚠ WARNING

Nothing can control airplane noise

If there's a plane flying overhead, some of its noise will be picked up. It might not be enough to obscure dialog *in that shot*, but when you edit to it from a different take, there'll be a distracting shift in the background sound.

- If you want good sound, wait until the plane passes.
- If you absolutely must shoot while the plane is overhead, grab some matching airplane noises immediately before or after the dialog. They'll be handy for fading in and out, to smooth over edits.

USING WIRELESS

Don't let the name confuse you. A "wireless mic" is actually two different systems: a microphone to turn sound into electricity, and a radio link to get the mic's signal back to the recorder. Many filmmakers concentrate their efforts on making sure the mic can't be seen. But to get a consistently good soundtrack, you also have to pay attention to the wireless part.

Wireless used to be a fairly scary way to do things, with battery-hogging transmitters and receivers that were prone to interference. But new technologies have made even low-cost wireless systems a lot more reliable. That's good, because there are times you just can't use a wire:

- Wide camera angles and some lighting situations can force the boom too far from the actor for successful pickup. You have to use a lav. If the shot is wide enough that we see the floor, or the talent has to do fast moves, a mic cable won't be practical.
- Actors often turn from the camera and deliver a single line into a doorway, open window, or some other spot you can't reach with a boom. Plug a PZM or small cardioid mic into a wireless transmitter, and you've got a plant mic that can be

hidden on the set. Record it to a separate track, or bring it up for just that line, so it doesn't contribute extra echo and hiss.

- You can also plug a boom mic into the transmitter. Wireless booming combines the sound quality of a large condenser boom mic with the flexibility of radio. Modern digital wireless systems let you do this without sacrificing quality, and can also provide a separate wireless return, so the operator can check placement and hear cues from the mixer.

- Blocking may make booms impractical, perhaps because the talent walks into another room while talking, and a wired lav would leave a cable trailing in the shot. (A higher quality alternative might be two booms, one on each side of the doorway, with the second boom's cable routed where it won't be seen.)

- Booming often isn't possible at event or documentary shoots. A wireless rig on an athlete at a sporting event, or on the groom at a wedding, can capture sounds that would be lost otherwise.

- If a location has a lot of video or computer wiring, or is near a radio or TV transmitter, interference can be radiated into mic cables. Star-Quad (page 69) might be able to fix things. So might mounting a mixer or mic preamp much closer to the action, so the mic cable is very short, and then running a line-level cable to the camera or recorder. The higher voltage on the longer cable would be less prone to interference. But if those solutions aren't practical, a wireless right *might* be able to ignore the noise.

Multiple wireless mics, or a wireless on one character while a boom follows another, is often the only way to record complex dialog where the actors are moving around. They can also give the actors flexibility to ad-lib and overlap: if the mics are recorded to separate tracks, important lines can be brought up in postproduction. While there are a few multichannel receivers available, they're not the highest quality. Use multiple systems, tuned to different frequencies, instead. You can rent "quad boxes," multi-mic systems that combine four receivers into a lunchbox-sized pack, with circuits to share the antenna and power supply.

While wireless gives you exceptional flexibility, it has its own drawbacks. Good sound quality and reliable transmission aren't possible unless you adjust the transmitter and place the antennas properly. In some situations, you can do everything right and still suffer horrible interference. But if you want to do wireless right, the biggest drawback will be the cost.

Buying wireless

Wireless is one of the areas where there's a direct relationship between how much you spend and how reliable the system will be. The high frequencies require precision design and components, and that doesn't come cheap. Budget systems, costing $200–300, might be adequate for your production. But if you're unhappy with the results, know that higher priced pro systems—at three to five times more—really do sound better and offer more features. And know that Hollywood recordists will pay as much as

$5,000 for a pro system,[15] which might also include monitoring channels back to the talent or boom op, internal backup recorders for when there's too much distance or interference, and networking so you can control the mic from the mixer. These are the rigs to use if you're shooting for theatrical release, where dialog is exposed and played loud.

NEWS

Wireless in Wonderland

Sometimes it seems we live in a fantasy world. Every time I've written a new edition of this book, the future of wireless mics has gotten more surreal.

First, it was "what will we do if TV ever goes digital?" Analog TV left some frequencies unused within each broadcast channel, and pro wireless mics would take advantage of them.

But Congress mandated that every TV station had to convert to digital, which uses the whole channel and leaves no room for wireless. While most of our equipment would have to be converted, nobody was sure how or when: Congress kept delaying the conversion, years at a time, because broadcasters complained there weren't enough digital viewers.

Then, Congress set a firm date. They insisted that broadcasters get digital transmitters, often moving to different channels in the process, and offered $40 coupons so home viewers could buy converters if needed (cable subscribers could still use their analog TVs). Low-cost flat-screen LCDs then flooded the home market, and they were all equipped for digital. The conversion left a few frequencies for wireless mics, so filmmakers converted most of their older equipment or traded it in.

Except now there were fewer frequencies available and a lot more wireless mics in use. The explosion of cable networks and low-cost filmmaking meant lot more people were shooting. Churches and convention centers started equipping their auditoriums. Stage shows got into the habit of miking every performer: a typical Broadway musical might have 60 separate transmitters on different frequencies!

The FCC is responsible for regulating frequency use, so they came up with a registration system (page 208). It's cumbersome and slow, and pretty much leaves filmmakers out of the process. But at least it's something . . . for now.

Never underestimate the power of politicians and lobbyists to muddy the waters. As of this writing, Congress wants to auction big chunks of the spectrum to businesses, for an immediate cash infusion to the budget.

---

[15] That's just for a transmitter and receiver, without the mic. It's an expensive business.

Electronics companies want that space for wifi- and Bluetooth-like devices yet to be invented. Cellphone companies want it so they can sell data services, both for today's smartphones and for tomorrow's dream of a totally wireless Internet. Police, fire, and other public safety services want specific frequencies reserved for emergency management.

In this noisy environment, wireless mic advocates—including the manufacturers, film and TV companies, churches, theaters, and everybody else—barely have a voice.

Some compromise will eventually be reached. Will we have to get new mics, get licensed and have our equipment registered, or learn to rely on tiny body-mount recorders? There's no way to tell, right now. Check the manufacturers' websites or your equipment dealer for the latest update.

All this—and other mentions in this chapter about what's legal or illegal with wireless mics—applies only to the United States. Things might be easier if you're somewhere else . . . check with your local dealer, or search your local equivalent of the FCC's website.

Digital

Digital wireless can sound as good as a wire, and can offer options like letting the receiver control the transmitter, the ability to string up multiple receivers to cover a large area (the receivers constantly poll each other to select the best signal), and AES/EBU output. Like all things digital, prices for basic systems keep coming down. One disadvantage of digital wireless systems is that they're trying to pack more information into the same radio bandwidth, so the signal isn't as robust over long distances. Of course, price is still a factor in this: better quality digital will have a longer range than cheap analog.

Another disadvantage is processing delay. It takes time to digitize a signal, do the math necessary for processing, and then convert it back to analog at for the camera or recorder. These delays aren't significant in terms of lipsync, but can cause a metallic effect if digital rigs are mixed with analog wireless or wired mics. Good digital field mixers and recorders frequently have compensation built in, to delay analog mics to match.

Fully digital wireless is now available from a number of manufacturers, in a fairly wide range of prices. All of these systems digitize the sound and send binary data through the air. When done right there's no companding or pre-emphasis, which means the signal has none of the inherent (but subtle) distortions of conventional wireless. High-end units, like the Zaxcom TRX900 series, use professional wireless bands for the main signal. There's also often a return signal for monitoring and remote control, along with features like stereo within the same channel for feeding cameras, and internal full-quality recorders inside the transmitter for backup.

Digital hybrid treats the signal digitally for best analog transmission, and then sends it as analog FM through the air. The combination means less delay, while avoiding the problems of conventional companding and pre-emphasis. The digital processing can also emulate some analog signals for compatibility and emergency use with older systems. Friends who have compared them say the analog radio signal from a hybrid is more robust than one from the fully digital systems, and can cope with long distances and reflections better.

Since the actual transmission is analog and one-directional, some of the features of fully digital rigs—including remote control and talent cueing—aren't available in digital hybrids.

Mid-priced alternatives

If professionals are paying as much as $5,000 per mic for the wireless they use on feature film shoots, what can you expect from systems costing far less? Sony, AKG, Sennheiser, Shure, and Audio-Technica sell wireless combos in the $1,000 range, including microphone, that are good enough for television and can be used in low-budget features. Azden, Nady, and Samson offer combos in the $300–500 range that are fine for corporate and event productions. What you're giving up is how natural the voices sound: as price goes down, bandwidth and dynamic range shrink, making dialog seem more "canned."

Shure, Audio-Technica, Line 6, and others have digital systems in that same price range. They have fewer sonic disadvantages than low-cost analog, but often can function only over short distances. They also usually share frequencies with computer wifi and may be subject to interference.

If you want to hear how these price differences actually affect your track (or don't like the idea of paying more for a mic than you paid for the camera), consider renting. Larger rental companies will have a variety of brands to choose from, and they'll help you choose frequencies that will avoid interference at your shooting location. They'll also be on top of any changes to wireless operation while our legal and regulatory system tries to sort out all the conflicting demands on a limited number of frequencies.

Whether buying or renting, there are a few features you should definitely look for. They add to the cost, but are worth the investment:

Ultra-high frequency

Originally, wireless mics ran in the upper part of the VHF TV band, using standard broadcast channels 7 through 13. At the time it was very difficult to build small, reliable equipment for frequencies higher than that. TV channels were used—even if a local station broadcast on the same channel—because wireless mics could squeeze into the hole between analog television's separate audio and video signals. A lot of other services also use VHF frequencies, so interference was often a problem on that band.

Fortunately, modern circuits can easily handle the UHF range above TV channel 14. It costs a little more to build equipment for that part of the spectrum, but it's less crowded up there—for now—and each channel can support more individual wireless signals. The higher frequency means that manufacturers can use broader audio channels for better fidelity. UHF uses a smaller antenna, so it's easier to wire the actors, mount a receiver on the camera, or build special directional antennas for difficult pickups.

The disadvantage of UHF is that the signal is more fragile: it can bounce off light stands and girders in the walls, and even be absorbed by cast and crew on the set. There's no danger to the humans involved, but if things or people move around during a take you might hear sudden dropouts.

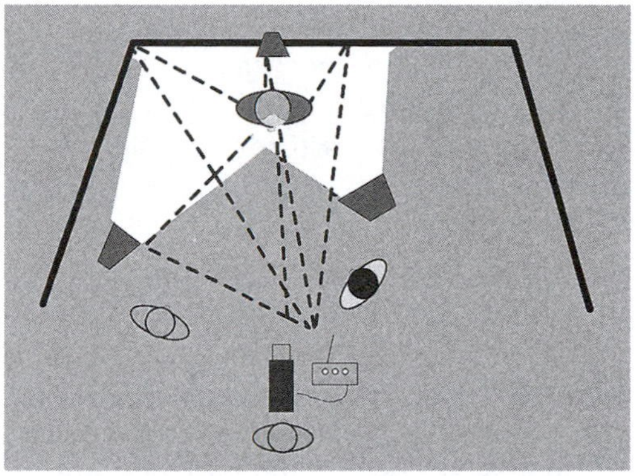

Figure 7.17 Wireless signals can reflect off metal objects, and the pattern changes when anything moves.

Diversity reception

UHF's tendency to bounce off metal objects can present a problem when using wireless. Figure 7.17 shows how it could arise, even on a very simple set. One dashed line represents the main signal path between an actor's transmitter and the camera's receiver. But note the bent path—a signal bouncing off a nearby light—which is almost as strong. Depending on the distances involved, the bounced signal may reinforce or partially cancel the main one. If anything moves, including the actor, these distances change and so does the cancellation effect. It will also change if the right-hand crew member steps forward and absorbs some of the signal. The other dashed paths start to show how complicated it can get at a shoot: if anyone moves, the signal may fade in or out.

In this case, diversity truly is strength. Diversity receivers actually have two spaced antennas with separate radio-frequency circuits. They constantly compare signals and use whichever antenna is getting the best one. Because real-world paths are so random, it's highly unlikely both will be fading at the same time. Both VHF and UHF systems can use diversity reception, but UHF's higher frequencies mean the antennas don't have to be spaced as far apart and the receivers can be smaller. Digital wireless systems, which operate in the UHF range, include diversity and also have the polling option described above.

Frequency agility

Until recently, wireless equipment used fixed frequencies. Transmitters were controlled by stable crystal oscillators. Receivers used similar crystals along with carefully tuned resonant circuits. Changing the frequency required a trip to the service shop, but the spectrum was less crowded in those days so the trip was seldom necessary.

Then things got busy. More feature and corporate crews started using wireless, often requiring frequencies for multiple mics. Breaking stories started attracting news crews from around the country, and a city's wireless-mic population would swell by the hundreds overnight. If you count all the media, event staff, team and official uses, a planned event like the Super Bowl can have 1,000 separate channels of mics and communications systems.

Just like an agile athlete, frequency-agile wireless rigs are flexible and can change direction quickly. Instead of crystals, they have precisely controlled oscillators that can be set to several different operating frequencies. Good ones let you select among a few dozen, and the best offer more than 100 frequencies spread over a number of UHF channels. They're a lifesaver if you're shooting near other crews. During the DTV transition, they were the only wireless mics you could rely on.

Limiting and companding

All wireless mics should include some form of limiter. It saves very loud sounds from being totally lost, at the cost of some distortion, and prevents the transmitter from interfering with adjacent frequencies. The limiter is preceded by a volume control, so the transmitter can be adjusted for a particular mic and acting style. If it's not adjusted properly, either there'll be too much electronic noise or the limiter will be constantly on, distorting the dialog.

Most analog wireless rigs also use *companding*, a system that uses a volume compressor on the transmitter, precisely matched to an expander at the receiver. This yields more effective dynamic range with less noise, for a better overall track. The downside is that very fast sounds might have a little extra noise or some variation in level, if either end of the companding system drifts out of calibration.

Physical form

Wireless transmitters designed for dialog usually take the form of body packs, slightly smaller than a wallet. There's a connector for the mic to plug into, which also provides power for the mic's internal preamp. Professional systems may be supplied without microphones; users usually order their favorites from other manufacturers, customized to plug into the transmitter. Low-cost systems often come with low-quality generic lavaliere mics, which are sometimes soldered directly into the transmitter.

Transmitters can also be built into small metal cans with full-size XLR jacks, as *plug-on transmitters*. These are handy for plugging onto the end of a shotgun or the end of a boom cable, or for connecting to a standard mic for hiding on the set. Handheld wireless mics, with transmitters built into their bodies, are designed for stage vocal performance and rarely used in film or video.

Wireless receivers used to be fairly large boxes, but have shrunk to cigarette-pack size. Those with diversity reception tend to be slightly larger, to accommodate the extra circuits and spacing between antennas, but can still be small enough to mount on a camera.

Reach

Depending on its design, a wireless transmitter may radiate between 10 and 250 milliwatts of electrical power. But while that number lets you predict how fast the battery will wear down, it doesn't say much about how well the system will perform in the field. Some of the best professional systems radiate less than 100 mW, and many digital systems let you adjust the transmitter power, saving battery life when high power isn't needed for shorter range pickups. Also, some power ranges are available only to licensed users (see Finding a frequency below).

You can usually ignore a manufacturer's "range" specification, particularly if it's linked to a boast about power. The actual usable distance also depends on the quality of the receiver, the frequency, reflective and absorbing surfaces on the set, and how you place the antennas. That's why it's important to learn how to use a wireless properly.

Pre-emphasis

Analog wireless systems boost high frequencies before transmitting, then reduce them in the receiver; this lowers any noise picked up by the link itself. But it also means that loud high frequencies may distort, even when the transmitter's volume is set properly.

Experienced operators check wireless system quality with the "key test": they jangle their car keys in front of the microphone, and listen to how clean the received signal is. In a very good system, it'll sound something like keys. In a poorer one, there's so much pre-emphasis that you get mostly hash and static. But a system can fail the key test and still be usable for non-critical productions, since dialog is mostly lower frequencies.

Buying used wireless

The government has changed what bands are available for wireless and which channels are available in different locations. For example, transmitters in the formerly popular 700 MHz band became illegal in the United States in 2010: their use might interfere with public safety equipment, and can be subject to criminal penalties (eBay warns against buying or selling them through their service). Of course, the government might change things again, or pack so many other signals into a formerly desirable frequency that it becomes useless.

For this reason, it's not a good idea to buy used wireless now . . . unless you're dealing with a reliable film sound supplier, who also guarantees you'll be able to use the system where you'll be shooting.

Using a wireless

Hiding a mic on an actor is only half the battle. You also have to adjust the transmitter, and rig it and its antenna properly.

Finding a frequency

Almost all wireless systems sold today are tunable, so you can choose frequencies that won't conflict with other users at your location. Since "other users" includes TV stations as well as permanent installations like churches and shows, this can get complicated.

If you're renting equipment, let the rental company know exactly where you'll be shooting. Ask them to make sure the rig can be tuned for use at that location, and make sure they tell you the appropriate channel or setting.

If you're using your own equipment, check one of the websites that offer searchable databases. You'll need the street address or zip code for each location. High-end mic manufacturers often have online tools on their sites that are customized to their specific models; these are probably the easiest for a novice to use. Spectrum Bridge has a free full-service database[16] and also offers interactive maps, iPhone and Android portable apps, and a lot of information on current regulations. Figure 7.18 shows the open channels they found for downtown Boston.

Broadcasters and legitimate film or video producers can also register with the FCC and get priority on the frequencies that are available. This registration is also necessary if you want to use the highest transmitter power settings. I can't say whether authorities will go after you for an unlicensed high-power use, but if they do, they can charge you a serious fine and jail you for up to a year! The FCC forms don't require a lawyer, but they are complicated, so at least one broadcast engineer has set up a service to do the paperwork.[17]

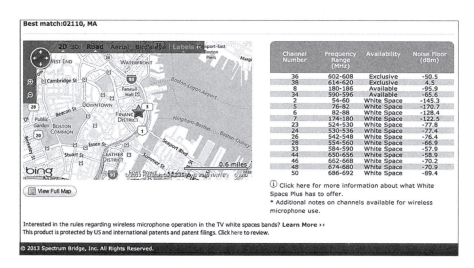

Figure 7.18 Spectrum Bridge's free service will help you locate available frequencies in your area. Be aware they're available to other users as well, unless you've registered with the FCC for priority.

---

[16] http://whitespaces.spectrumbridge.com.

[17] Forms are currently at http://transition.fcc.gov/Forms/Form601/601.html. Completing-it-properly service is currently being offered by billruck@earthlink.net. Fees are currently $145 for the government, plus $100 for Bill to take care of the details. Any of this may have changed by the time you read it.

Volume adjustment

Most transmitters have a small volume adjustment screw with a LED or meter to indicate when the limiter is activated. After the mic is in place, ask the actor to deliver a few lines in the voice they'll be using. Adjust the volume so the limiter just starts to turn on at the loudest part of their speech. If that results in too soft a signal at your camera, turn up the receiver's volume control or add some extra gain in a mixing board. Cranking up the transmitter won't make things any louder; it'll just add more distortion.

A few digital wireless systems let you adjust this from the receiver while you're shooting. That's much easier.

> **Don't ignore this step!** With most rigs, you don't have any control over the transmission after the talent walks away. While you can turn the record volume up or down at the camera or mixer, this doesn't help if a badly adjusted transmitter is causing noise or distortion.

Transmitter and antenna rigging

Transmitters usually have belt clips so you can hide them on an actor's back, if they're wearing a jacket or won't be turning away from the camera. A jacket or pants pocket can also work, though it might require cutting a small hole in the cloth for the cables. If you want pockets without the pants, audio supply houses sell little pouches with elastic or Velcro straps. These can be used to hide the transmitter at belt, thigh or ankle level. In a pinch, you can tuck a transmitter into a dancers'-style ankle warmer or wrap it to a leg with an elastic bandage.

The mic cable absorbs radiation and should be kept as far away from the antenna wire as possible. In extreme situations, putting those wires together can feed some of the radio energy back into the system and cause bad distortion.

VHF transmitters have long wire antennas that should be extended in a fairly straight line. While you can dress an antenna into the actor's waistband, it's often better to let it hang down inside a dress or pants leg. A long rubber band, tied and taped to the end of the antenna and then safety-pinned to a stocking, can keep the antenna straight while providing some strain relief and flexibility. Some recordists assemble custom antenna stretchers for this purpose, with a small alligator clip and a length of elastic ribbon. The clip pulls on the end of the antenna, and the ribbon is tied around the leg.

UHF antennas are short and stiff, making them much easier to rig. Just try to keep them away from the mic cable. If a UHF antenna sticks out so much that it shows when the actor turns, use some paper tape to attach it to the costume where it'll be out of sight. It's always better to attach antennas to wardrobe, rather than place them directly against an actor's skin. This isn't because of health hazard—a wireless transmitter's power is so small it won't hurt you, but it's also so small you can't afford to squander any. People absorb radio waves, and perspiration makes the situation worse. If signal is being absorbed by the actor, it isn't going to the receiver.

Some transmitters don't appear to have an antenna at all. They actually use the mic cable as an antenna (a few extra components keep the radio signal from interfering with the audio). This limits your options: while the antenna wire should be straight, the mic wire often has to take a winding path from mic to transmitter. If you're stuck with this kind of system, use long loops in the mic cable instead of abrupt turns. Never coil the wire to eliminate slack.

Receiver placement

Reception is always best when the transmitter and receiver have a line-of-sight path and are close together. Mounting a receiver on the camera can satisfy the former, but a long shot may keep the units too far apart. This gets worse if there are things around that reflect or absorb radio waves. In most cases, you'll get a more consistent pickup by taking the receiver off of the camera and putting it on the floor, just out of camera range. Or mount the receiver high up on a ladder or grip stand near the talent. Higher is better, because it usually provides a good line-of-sight path without too many reflections. If the actor is moving around, have a production assistant carry the receiver—keeping their body away from the antenna—just out of camera range.

A single antenna on a non-diversity receiver should be oriented the same direction as the transmitting one: for example, if the transmitting antenna runs down the leg of a standing actor, the receiving one should also be vertical. Single antennas work best when they're parallel to each other. If you're using a diversity receiver, angling the two antennas 90° can help you compensate for reflected signals. Try it with one antenna horizontal and the other vertical, or the two in a V configuration.

Low-cost receivers often have short cables with unbalanced mini-plug outputs, designed to plug directly into a prosumer camera. Extending these cables can lead to noise and hum problems. If you want to move one of these units closer, plug it into a nearby mixer. Then run a balanced cable from the mixer's output to a transformer-coupled adapter (Chapter 8). Of course, the cost of mixer and adapter may be more than you saved by choosing a cheap wireless.

Professional-quality UHF receivers usually use removable short metal or rubber antennas with standard radio connectors. These can be unplugged and replaced with more powerful antennas for better pickup.

When wireless goes bad

If you follow the tips in this section, and are in a location without too much interference, a wireless rig will give you decent pickup most of the time. But because they're more complex than a simple piece of wire, things can go wrong.

If audio starts sounding funny in any way at all, check the batteries first. Depending on the model and the shooting situation, weak batteries will result in distortion, low volume, intermittent interference, noise, or other gremlins. Since you can't predict which symptom will appear, change the transmitter battery whenever you hear any problem with a system that previously worked. If that doesn't help, change the receiver battery as well. Always use high-quality, fresh alkaline or lithium batteries.

If it's not the batteries, look for user errors. Even audio professionals have been caught by receiver output levels that don't match the camera, mics that have come unplugged, or actors who've fiddled with transmitter controls. Then look for radio-frequency problems: many receivers have a meter to let you check the signal strength. If it's suddenly dropped and you know all the batteries are good, check to see if a mic cable has gotten wrapped around an antenna, a large reflecting object has moved near the set, or a performer's wardrobe has gotten wet.

Occasionally, two wirelesses won't work properly where one will. If you're using multiple systems for different characters, make sure they're on different frequencies. But also be aware that each *receiver* radiates a tiny signal of its own, which can interfere with other receivers nearby: try separating the units a few feet.

While some mics are rated as water-resistant, all of them rely on very tiny amounts of static electricity to turn varying air pressure into voltage. Excessive humidity, as well as downright dunking, can interfere with this. Moisture around the transmitting or receiving antenna will also cause problems. Most transmitters and receivers can survive normal on-set banging around, but physical shock can damage the crystal or knock fragile tuned circuits out of alignment.

Watch out for anything that can generate interference on the set—neon lights, electronic dimmers, generators, even coils of powered cable. Video cameras, recorders, and monitors can also generate local interference that can be reduced by moving away from them. Cellphones don't work at the same frequencies as wireless mics, but nearby cellphone antenna installations—often found on the tops of office buildings—may be powerful enough to harm a wireless signal anyway.

And always bring a backup wired connection, whether it's another mic or an adapter to use the wireless rig's mic with a standard cable. Sometimes the voodoo doesn't work.

A wireless alternative

Some situations are just not conducive to wireless use, because of interference, large amounts of metal in the building, large distances between performer and camera, or restrictions by the venue (some churches won't let wedding videographers use wireless). In that case, a portable digital recorder can provide a bail-out. These can fit in a performer's pocket, and—when used properly—provide excellent sound for dialog. Since the recording isn't on the videotape, it's essential to provide some form of sync reference so you can put things back together in your NLE; there are tips in the next chapter.

You may have to train the performer to start and stop the recorder. Some units revert to automatic level control each time you stop them. If you're using manual volume control, it may be better to pause instead of stop between takes.

ROOMTONE

Every acoustic space has its own sound. This isn't just a combination of air-conditioners, distant traffic, and other machinery coming through the windows, but also how the size and shape of the room itself modify these sounds. We're almost never aware of this sound, but if it goes away—perhaps because a line of dialog has to be opened up to accommodate a cutaway—we can tell that it's missing.

It's common practice in features, after all the shooting at a location is done but before equipment is struck, to record a minute of "roomtone": just the sound of the room itself, with the same general mic placement and volume settings as were used for dialog. Then in post, if a production track has to be muted or replaced with a studio version, the roomtone is mixed in for acoustic continuity. Roomtone is also used to replace on-set noises, or to smooth over edits between takes.

The practice is often ignored in low-budget video production. Since television sound is broadcast through noisy channels, and played back at low volumes in home systems, it's thought that roomtone won't be missed on a video. Obviously, I don't agree. If you're telling a story or doing an interview that'll require a lot of editing, record some tone. You'll need it.

On the other hand, if you're doing a fast-paced sequence or a commercial, it may be possible to skip this step. A good sound editor, using a modern workstation, can usually pull enough tone from between words or at the heads and tails of takes to satisfy any dialog fixes in this kind of project.

CHAPTER 8

Production Recording

☞ ROSE'S RULES

- Today's cameras give you great pictures for the money, but that doesn't mean they'll give you great sound. Most full-size cameras—even the $80,000 ones used for features—don't deliver feature-film sound quality.
- You can get broadcast- or Web-quality recordings in most mid-size or larger cameras . . . if you set them up properly.
- It's even possible to get adequate dialog recordings in some DSLRs. But you have to be very careful . . . there isn't much margin for error.
- But if you want quality tracks that'll sound great in any situation, and that'll give you lots of flexibility for processing and editing in post, you need a separate recorder. Fortunately, there are good choices for any budget and shooting situation.

WHERE'S THE TRACK?

In terms of audio capability, movie cameras haven't changed much since the silent ones used for Clara Bow and the Keystone Cops. Image registration, film, and lenses got much better over the years, and the cameras got quieter with better speed regulation so they'd be friendlier to sound. But they never became sound recorders. With very few exceptions, any sound for theatrical features has always been captured on separate machines.

Of course, video cameras do record sound. Some[1] are good enough for almost any purpose, if you're careful with setup (and ignore the built-in microphone). But projects that demand quality are almost always recorded on separate recorders. And today's recorders also have the flexibility of multiple tracks to isolate individual mics, many can function as mixers to create a working dialog track for the editor, and some act as network centers to control wireless mics and communication on the set.

Shooting sound and picture on separate devices is known as *double-system*. The term started with the projection end of the process: some of the earliest talkies had their sound on a separate phono record, as opposed to *single system* where an optical soundtrack was printed on the same film as the picture. (Single-system soon became the preferred way to distribute soundtracks with a finished film: it's cheaper, more convenient, and more reliable.[2])

Hollywood's choice of double-system for filmmaking isn't just a case of "we've always done it that way." You could get single-system 16mm Auricon cameras as early as 1931: the process offered convenience and low cost, but didn't have the quality or flexibility needed for feature films. On the other hand, Auricons were used by Army cinematographers in World War II, and then adopted—in both optical and magnetic sound versions, along with competing models from other makers—by television stations for nightly news stories.

Then came video.

So . . . should video be shot with single- or double-system?

If you're using most modern full-size cameras, you do have a meaningful choice. (If you're using an older camera or most DSLRs and want a professional track, the choice is already out of your hands. Some of those cameras just aren't capable of good recording. See page 230.)

Choose single-system for:

- **Simplicity**, particularly when it comes to logging shots and editing them. Each picture file has a soundtrack already attached. As soon as you ingest the file to your editing system, it's ready to use: no searching for a matching sound take, and no worrying about sync.
- **Slightly lower cost**: Quality tracks still need careful miking and someone to control sound during the shoot. But at least single-system saves you the cost of a separate recorder.

---

[1] Specific recommendations start on page 235.

[2] Release prints had single-system tracks through most of the twentieth century. DTS digital sound—introduced with *Jurassic Park*—went back to double-system for release prints, with multichannel sound on a separate synchronized CD-ROM. Now that theatrical films are transitioning to Digital Cinema on hard drive, the issue becomes irrelevant for distribution. But it's still an important decision when shooting the movie.

Choose double-system for:

- **Flexibility**: Multichannel recorders let you keep isolated tracks for each mic. This can often save shots that would otherwise be lost or require ADR.[3] It can give you more editing options for a scene. It's almost essential for reality projects, or scripts that rely on ad-libs. Having a separate recorder also makes it simple to grab extra dialog lines and sound effects while the camera is being set up.
- **Reliability**: Cameras are not built for sound recording. Connections can be fragile, critical audio adjustments can be hidden or unavailable during the shot, and even some feature-film cameras are notorious for dropouts on the track. Besides, putting both sound and picture in the same device invites human error: a camera operator has enough to do without worrying about the recording.

✔ TIP

Two channels, single-system

- Productions that are limited to single-system can still add a little flexibility to their audio setup. Send your two separate mics to separate channels on the camera. This can be two lavs for an interview shoot, a boom and a lav to cover an actor, or even a single dialog mic on one channel with the camera mic on the other for ambience.
- Keep the channels separate while editing. Put off the choice of which to use and how to process each until you're mixing, where there is a better environment for listening and the scene can be viewed in context.

Any project shot on DSLR usually requires double-system, because the audio circuits in those small cameras just aren't going to be comparable to their excellent picture quality.[4] A $100 pocket digital recorder or even a laptop can be an improvement over a DSLR's sound. Along with better audio circuits, you'll also get more flexibility and the ability to adjust the recording while shooting—something very difficult on most DSLRs.

Bigger projects that use multiple mics, or are serious about theatrical release, should always use double-system. You'll need a sound recordist anyway, and they'll need some gear to control and mix the mics. Spend a few dollars more and they'll be able to record a high-quality track on a separate recorder, while sending a mix to the

---

[3] Automatic Dialog Replacement. It's not automatic and it's not an exact replacement, but you can read about the technique in Chapter 00.

[4] At least, not according to lab tests that I've run. Maybe a new camera will appear with good internal sound, but I don't expect it for at least a few years.

camera for reference and sync. If you lock these double-system tracks to the reference track before you start cutting, the time and cost of *conforming* (matching original sound to the edited picture) goes away.

The result of this minimal investment? More options at the mix, a better chance of capturing subtleties in your actors' performances, and a film that seems a lot more professional.

Choosing a recorder

When I started in this business, anything important was shot on film and recorded on a Nagra, a particularly rugged and good-sounding portable tape recorder designed for sync dialog.[5]

Today even digital tape is obsolete. DAT recorders that were standard less than ten years ago are gathering dust. They sounded great, but were never as reliable as the good old Nagra. (DAT recorders had to pull 4mm tape along twisting paths. There were lots of motors and internal cogs and levers, just waiting to get out of alignment.)

Thankfully, for the past decade or so, audio has been able to ride on the computer industry's coattails. Advances in portable hard drives, large-capacity solid-state drives, and the chips used for processing have given us rugged recorders with more features and much better sound.

Ultimately the decision of how to record a track may depend on what's in your closet (or your company's or school's inventory). But stay aware that the choice between single- or double-system can have a direct influence on your film's quality—as much as your choices of actors or locations. And there are lots of options for double-system, making it easier to find a match for your budget and working style.

Pro-level field recorders

These units can be mounted on a portable cart or worn on a body pack, are powered by AC or batteries, may support timecode and can act as a master clock for cameras and slates, and have other handy features like built-in shot logging and test oscillators. They're robust and reliable for field use, include high-quality mic preamps with phantom power and switchable filters and limiting, and record to multiple media simultaneously (you can write a DVD or removable drive for the production at the same time you're writing a backup to hard disk). Many pro projects record on high-end laptop setups instead. They're less rugged, and their performance depends on external audio hardware. But they're still capable of first-class results, have film-oriented features similar to the all-in-one recorders, and are often the only choice when you've got lots of mics that need separate tracks.

---

[5] Before I went digital, I owned a Nagra III, a Nagra IV, and alternative film sound recorders made by Arriflex Camera and Uher. Those competing units, while good value for the money, just weren't in Nagra's league. The Nagra IV was a particularly elegant classic of audio technology . . . and I almost cried when it was time to sell mine.

Multichannel timecode recorders

Zaxcom and Sound Devices make excellent portable recorders with multiple analog and digital inputs. They have between four and 16 separate recording tracks with mic preamps and level meters for each input, may have internal compressors and equalizers to trim the sound,[6] and will act as sophisticated mixers with multiple outputs for the camera, director's monitor, boom op, and talent cueing. Both companies specialize in film sound. They both offer multiple versions, with various track counts and additional features. Some Zaxcom units will also act as central controls for their proprietary network of wireless mics, camera links, and talent cueing receivers.

The 16 track Zaxcom Deva shown in Figure 8.1 runs about $15,000 ... not an outrageous figure, when you consider that a pro will spend that much for three really good wireless mic rigs.

Figure 8.1 Deva portable with 16 separate tracks, full mixing capability, and a lot more.[7]

Two-track pro recorders

Sound Devices also has a line of two-track recorders with field ruggedness and features, including optional timecode. Their audio quality and controls are first-class, equal to the best studio music recorders. These are excellent choices for one or two mic setups or when your recordist might also be handling the boom. The Model 722 in Figure 8.2 doesn't have timecode (many workflows don't require it), but will record to three separate media simultaneously, in just about any format from 32 kb/s mp3 to 24-bit, 192 kHz WAV. It'll set you back $2,600, or can be rented for around $50/day.

---

[6] Professionals almost never do this kind of processing while shooting. Location recording is hard enough, without trying to make subjective decisions about a sound's texture while wearing headphones and trying to keep up with the director and rest of the crew. Compression and equalization are difficult, if not impossible, to undo in post ... so if you make a mistake, you're stuck with it. On the other hand, there may be fast-turnaround or non-film situations where processing in the field is necessary.

[7] Photo courtesy Zaxcom, Inc.

Figure 8.2 Sound Devices 722, a fully featured non-timecode two-track recorder.[8]

Laptop with additional stuff

The "stuff" includes both hardware and software, but it's certainly possible to record a fully professional track on a modern laptop. You'll need an external audio input device with enough inputs for the mics you're using, connected to the computer by USB or FireWire.[9] These devices are available at music stores for between $100 and $2,000 depending on features; I don't know of any in rental inventories. Read the specs carefully: many have line-level inputs that will require separate mic preamps, and some will work only with AC power. Or look for a small mixing board with multiple mic inputs and a computer connection; these are bulkier and always require AC power but can give you more features at a lower price.

And you'll need software. Since this section is about pro-level field recording, your options are Boom Recorder and Metacorder. These programs offer very high track counts (at least 24 simultaneous isolated record tracks at a time; more depending on CPU) along with timecode, built-in logging, and other features such as recording to multiple drives. Their main screen looks like a high-end multichannel field recorder. But their biggest advantage over generic recording software is reliability: they'll record instantly, without intervening dialogs or spinning cursors, and stories of them crashing are virtually nonexistent.

Boom Recorder (www.vosgames.nl and through the Apple App Store) costs $250. Metacorder (www.gallery.co.uk, at pro dealers) is, $1,800. Why such a big price difference? Ask on a film sound forum . . . or download the demo versions of each and try for yourself.

Conventional multitrack software can also be used for field recording. Programs like ProTools and Nuendo certainly offer a lot more studio features than field recording software, but more features means more complex operation and more chances of a

---

[8] Photo courtesy Sound Devices LLC.

[9] Mac users who need only two tracks can also use the s/pdif digital input on all of the current machines. Also, Thunderbolt devices are starting to appear on the market.

crash. On the other hand, those two programs are available for Windows as well as Mac laptops.

Semi-pro recorders

Tascam makes an eight-track portable unit, their DR-680. It's designed for music recording, and has fewer field-recording features and lesser audio specs than the pro units above. On the other hand, it sells for about half the price of eight-track Zaxcom or Sound Devices recorders. It's seldom found in rental inventories, and rental managers have told me it's not as rugged. But if the features are appropriate and you'll be taking care of it yourself, it could be a good solution.

Tascam has also introduced a brilliant four-track solution for DSLR sound. Their DR-60D (Figure 8.3) tucks under the camera, has two balanced mic inputs plus two channels of mini-jack input that match most camera-mounted mics, and can feed or monitor a sync reference track for the camera. Audio performance is much better than any DSLR I've measured; if set up carefully and you're using good mic technique, it'll be good enough for theatrical dialog. And it's only $350.

There have been reports that the DR-60, when mounted as intended, will radiate noise into certain popular cameras . . . polluting the cameras' recording circuits, and making the internal tracks usable only for sync reference. This appears to be an error or shortcut in the hardware design, not fixable by a software update. It's not as big a drawback as you might think. The DR-60 is a double-system recorder so the camera

Figure 8.3 Tascam DR-60, a four-track recorder specifically designed for use with DSLRs.[10]

---

[10] Photo courtesy Teac America, Inc.

✳ TIDBIT

Why the big price difference?

It may be hard to grasp why professionals happily pay $2,600 for a Sound Devices two-track recorder, when they can get the Tascam four-track for $350. Or pay similarly higher prices for top-notch boom mics and wireless rigs when there are plenty of much cheaper alternatives.

Of course the more expensive gear sounds better, but that's only part of the story.

- The pro equipment is better built. It's more rugged, lasts much longer, and rarely needs repair or re-calibration. The total cost of ownership can be less, particularly when a piece of gear is considered as a long-term career investment. And it's impossible to put a price on the security of knowing that a take—or a day's shoot, or an entire career—isn't likely to be ruined by a catastrophic equipment failure.
- The pro equipment is designed specifically for our industry. Its circuits and software have been finely tuned for the purpose, rather than been built to attract the largest market at a particular price-point. Manufacturers like Sound Devices and Zaxcom send test units to pros working on major features and TV projects, change the designs based on their feedback, and repeat the process until the pros are happy. The equipment works the way we want; with features we need, where we expect to find them. It also plays nicely with all the other equipment on a shoot . . . something manufacturers can't predict in isolation.
- The pro products stay current for much longer. Software updates are distributed frequently. There are upgrade paths if a manufacturer tweaks the hardware design. Users circulate tips in the online forums, with manufacturers paying attention and contributing, so a collective wisdom gets a chance to grow up around the equipment. A long product life also means a better resale value if our needs change.
- Compare that with mass market semi-pro gear. There's usually no budget for ongoing development other than bug fixes. Instead, competitive pressures push for new products every few years.

These reasons apply to rental houses as well as to working professionals who buy their own gear. That's why renting pro sound equipment is usually a bargain, compared to semi-pro. The rates themselves will be higher . . . but rental houses know the pieces will stay in their active inventory much longer, with fewer repairs, so rates can be a much lower percentage of the equipment's initial cost.

track's quality isn't critical. Using one of these merely as a mixer while you record single system on the camera is a terrible waste of its talents.

Consumer recorders

The music industry is a much bigger market than film sound, so there's a lot of mass-produced equipment available at good prices. Some if it can be used on a film set, if you're willing to forgo features and deal with inconveniences. None of these units support timecode, but low-budget projects rarely need it.[11] Most record to a single SD card; if you want the protection of multiple media, you'll have to then copy the card using a computer. Many include processing features like multi-band compression or guitar amp simulation, which may be great for the hit song you're also writing . . . but it's a bad idea to use these features at a film shoot.

Multitrack digital recorder

Samson's Zoom R-16 recorder has eight mic inputs and simultaneous recording tracks, for $400. It looks like a small mixing panel, which can be awkward unless you're sitting down to work it, requires AC power, and records only at 44.1 kHz sampling. (Depending on your NLE, you might need to convert its files to 48 kHz in an audio program before ingesting.)

Other consumer manufacturers including Fostex, Alesis, and Tascam used to have competing units, but they seem to have given up that market to concentrate on mixers and interfaces for computer recording. If you need multiple isolated tracks and your budget is really stressed, you might look for one of these used. Most had only a pair of mic inputs, so you'll probably need external preamps as well.

Portable two-track recorders

Samson Zoom, Tascam, Sony, Yamaha, and others make reasonable quality pocket recorders for a few hundred dollars. Most of the new units do a reasonably good job, and can sound better than the recording circuits in many video cameras. Most record mp3 as well as 44.1 kHz uncompressed audio; skip the compressed format and be prepared to convert the uncompressed one to 48 kHz. Unfortunately, none have balanced inputs. If you're going to use them with pro mics, you'll need an external mixer or one of the video camera adapters mentioned on page 223.

All of these recorders have built-in mics. They may be slightly better than the mics built into low cost cameras, but are far from ideal for dialog. On the other hand, they may be acceptable for zero-budget projects if you can get the recorder and mic very close to the talent; Figure 7.4 shows a possible configuration.

---

[11] There's no benefit to devoting a record track to timecode. This was how you maintained sync back in analog days, but today even consumer gear is stable enough that a slapped slate or even visual matching of waveforms should hold sync for all but the longest takes. More about this in Chapter 12.

Portable laptop solutions

There are plenty of low-cost USB or FireWire adapters that'll plug into your laptop and record to standard multitrack music software; some include a bundled simplified version of one popular program or another. Most are powered by the connected computer, or an active hub. Physical formats include desktop adapters, rack mount, and mixers; inputs range from two mini-jacks to eight balanced mics with phantom power. All do a credible job, and most support 48 kHz recording.

The downside for all of these is reliability. At the price, these units aren't particularly rugged. More importantly, they're using music production software and are often used with a general-purpose laptop: with more software features, or other installed programs and services in the computer, the chances for a user error or fatal crash are much greater. And while high-end software often has a way to recover files after crashes, these programs frequently don't. So you're taking chances.

How to choose? Check local and online music stores. New products keep being introduced, so keep checking for price and features that fit your workflow.

Ad-hoc recorders

Got a smartphone or tablet? You've probably got a recorder. Two-track recording software is available for most of the mobile operating systems, for just a few dollars; check your system's app store for something with meters and the ability to record uncompressed files. Personally, I wouldn't want to mess with a touch screen and notoriously distracted operating system while recording dialog, but this solution is definitely low-cost.

You'll need an interface with mic inputs, of course. It should have an input level control with its own meters (the software metering on the screen is useful while recording, but too late in the signal flow to correct for different mics and perform-ance styles), and with a headphone output so you can monitor mic placement. Almost all of the current USB interfaces sold for computer recording will also work with mobile systems, if you get an appropriate USB input adapter for your phone or tablet; just check the manufacturer's site or forums before buying. The cables sold for connecting still cameras to a mobile device usually work. Most of these interfaces also require power from the USB jack, so you'll likely need a powered USB hub as well. You can use both the interface and the hub in your edit suite, after you've finished shooting.

GETTING AUDIO INTO A RECORDER

XLR vs. mini-jack

Professional cameras (or recorders) will have balanced mic inputs on XLR connectors, with separate level controls and switchable limiters. Connecting them to a high-quality microphone should be simply a matter of plug-and-play. If your camera was built with those kind of controls and connections, skip to "Avoiding noise" in a couple of pages.

Consumer cameras and pocket recorders usually have mini-jack unbalanced inputs, which don't offer the noise immunity of balanced inputs when used with long cables. They typically supply a DC voltage to power consumer-level electret mics, which won't power a phantom mic and may cause distortion when used with self-powered pro mics. The most common way to deal with both these issues is a balancing adapter with XLR inputs. Or you can use a mixer or external preamp for this purpose, which gives you other advantages as well. If your mixer or preamp will be some distance from the camera, you may need both.

There is no inherent difference in sound quality between an XLR and a mini-jack mic input, other than the noise immunity mentioned above. XLR usually implies a better input circuit, but that's a marketing issue rather than a technical one ... it depends entirely on how much the manufacturer is willing to spend on design and components.[12]

Balancing adapters

Transformer adapters

This is either a small metal box that screws into the camera's tripod socket (and has its own tripod threads on the bottom), or a belt-pack that can be worn or taped to a tripod leg. Both have a cord that plugs into camera's mic input. It contains transformers to balance the mic inputs, and individual volume controls. Most also have switches to combine the mics to a single channel, and a line-level input. Some models also include phantom power supplies (which provide 48 volts for the microphone from a 9-volt battery), meters, or even small preamplifiers to improve the signal, since many cameras do a better job with a mic signal at –35 dBu rather than the more standard –50 dBu. These adapters let you use balanced cables and microphones, which are virtually immune to wiring noise. Non-powered ones cost between $170 and $225; the other functions can raise that to about $350. Figure 8.4 shows the BeachTek DXA-HDV ($300), a popular under-camera model with phantom and preamp.

Adapter caveats

Some belt-pack adapters just contain a volume control, DC-blocking capacitor, and XLR jack. There's no transformer or specialized circuit in them. This defeats the noise-immunity of balanced wiring. But they might still be useful: see the section on "XLR adapters that aren't balanced" (page 225).

Some adapters have a balanced mini-jack for line level signals that match a few wireless receivers, but it's not the normal configuration for this size jack. Because of the way they're wired, if you plug in a normal mono mini-plug (from a mixer or music

---

[12] A few "XLR professional" cameras have had notoriously poorer sound than cheaper mini-jack versions in the same product line. The manufacturer used the same basic recording chain with an additional circuit to provide balancing in the more expensive camera, and then skimped on that circuit to save money.

Figure 8.4 A typical under-camera balancing adapter, with phantom power and internal preamp.[13]

player) and the jack's ring conductor doesn't connect properly, the bass suffers horribly. If your camera can accept line-level inputs on its mini-jack, you'll get better results bypassing the adapter and plugging that kind of signal directly into the camera. A few wireless receivers—mostly from Sennheiser—have balanced mini-plug line-level outputs. You can use these safely with the adapter, or you can plug directly into the camera. If you go the direct route with a balanced plug, one channel will be out of phase with the other. You'll be able to record them and hear them on stereo headphones, but the signal will disappear in mono unless you discard one channel in post.

Always listen to the signal through the camera, on good headphones, to verify the connections are working properly.

Mixers and preamps[14]

If you've got a mixer with XLR mic jacks, you can assume it has transformers or op-amps and the inputs are balanced. One of these may replace the need for a balancing adapter.

If your camera has mini-jack line level inputs and the mixer has an RCA output, a simple adapter cable is all you'll need. If the mixer has an XLR output, you'll probably also need an *attenuator*: a few resistors hooked up to lower the voltage in a specific way. You can buy one or build it yourself for a couple of dollars; see page 245.

---

[13] Photo courtesy BeachTek.

[14] Unless you're using more than two mics, the usual function of a mixer will be to boost the mic level to something that the camera can record better. That's exactly what a preamp does, so for the rest of this chapter I'll refer to them both as mixers.

XLR adapters that aren't balanced

You can get low-cost XLR-to-mini cables, designed for use with prosumer cameras, at video supply houses. These contain capacitors to block the DC voltage, which otherwise could cause distortion in some microphones. But they defeat the mic's balanced wiring, which can increase noise pickup through the cable. So use these adapters only if the mic cable will be kept short, or if you're feeding the camera from a nearby mixer's mic-level outputs.

Build your own

If you're willing to do a little soldering, you can make a cable adapter for a few dollars. You'll need a female XLR connector for the mic (Radio Shack #274–011), a mini-plug to match your camera (#274–284), and a few feet of two-conductor shielded wire (#278–513). The secret is a small electrolytic capacitor (like the 220 micro-farad, 35 volt #272–1024) to stop the recorder's polarizing voltage from causing distortion in the mic. The capacitor barely fits inside the XLR shell, and might need to be outside the shell and wrapped with tape instead. But the rating isn't critical—anything over about 100 μf and 6 volts should be adequate—and you'll find smaller units at electronics suppliers. Figure 8.5 shows the capacitor mounted directly to the XLR.

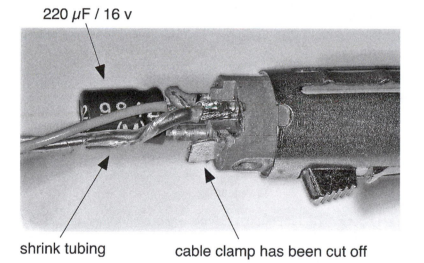

220 *μF* / 16 v

shrink tubing   cable clamp has been cut off

Figure 8.5 A small capacitor, hidden in the XLR connector, blocks DC voltage in this adapter.

Figure 8.6 shows how it's wired. The capacitor's polarity is critical: a white arrow indicates the negative side, which must go to the XLR. Also note how the cable shield is left unconnected at the mini-plug: insulate it with tape or shrink-tubing to prevent shorts.

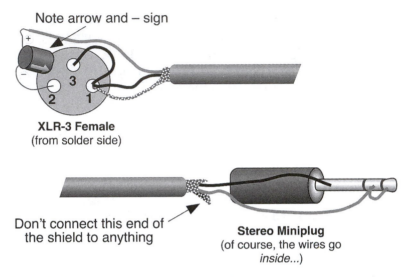

Figure 8.6 Wiring diagram for a simple XLR mic to mini-jack input adapter.

The circuit shown connects one mic to both channels of the camera. If you want stereo, wire two XLRs with capacitors the same way. Connect both shields and black wires together at the mini-plug, and wire them like the diagram. But connect the red wire from one capacitor to the plug's tip, and the other to its ring.

The circuit works with most dynamic and condenser mics, as well as with other portable recorders that have mini-jack mic inputs. But remember: this isn't a balancing adapter, and doesn't give you the noise immunity of balanced wiring.

⚠ **WARNING**

A bad idea

You can also get molded metal XLR-to-mini adapters for a couple of dollars at electronics chain stores. These don't block the DC voltage, don't provide balancing, may give you only one channel of signal, and their weight can stress a mini-jack. They shouldn't be used.

About mini-jacks

These connections are physically and electrically fragile. If there's a strain on the cable—even from the weight of a nearby XLR connector—they may unplug. If they're connected too many times, the jack's springs weaken and the connection becomes noisy. I suppose manufacturers choose them because they don't take up much room on a small camera and they're very cheap. Here's how to get the best from those little devils:

- Secure the cable plugs with a rubber band wrapped around the plug and camera, or with a piece of gaffer tape.
- If you're using adapter cables with XLRs or other heavy connectors on the other end, provide a strain relief by taping the heavy end to the tripod or camera.
- If you're using a camera-mounted balancing adapter, attach it to the camera before plugging in. If you're wearing a belt-pack, provide some strain relief. Don't walk away from the camera while you're plugged in.
- If you anticipate plugging and unplugging a lot, get a short extension cable, tape it to the camera, and leave it plugged in all the time. Wear out the extension cable's jack instead of the camera's.

Avoiding noise

Neither balanced nor unbalanced wiring is absolutely noise-proof. Mic signals are fragile, and cables can pick up radiated junk. For best results, use a balanced mic (virtually any mic with an XLR connector), and a balancing adapter or XLR inputs at the camera. You don't need audiophile gold-plated or pure copper wiring, but Star-Quad—discussed in Chapter 3—does make a difference. It adds about $15 to the price of a standard mic cable, and is worth the investment.

To chase down noise sources, wear good isolating headphones and turn up the volume. Listen for buzzes, hums, and clicks. You may also hear hiss, but that's probably coming from the camera itself; there are tips in the next section for keeping it at a minimum.

The worst electronic buzzes often come from electronic lamp dimmers. They convert relatively quiet 60 Hz AC power into a spiky mess with harmonics all over the audio band, which is then transmitted by the high current wiring from dimmer to lamp. If there are dimmers for the room lights where you're shooting, turn them either fully up or off to eliminate the noise. If you use dimmers to control set lighting, you can often eliminate a lot of electronic noise by using lower-wattage bulbs or neutral-density gels instead, or by switching to noise-free *autoformer* or *Variac* dimmers. One that'll handle a 1,000-watt light costs about $100, or rents for about $12/day.

Noise is also radiated by power, computer, and video cables. Run mic cables at least a couple of feet away from them. If a mic and a noisy cable have to cross, do it at a right angle for the least amount of pickup.

Clicks are caused when high-current devices are turned on. Their switches or relays make a spike that radiates through the power lines. Elevator and industrial motors are prime suspects, but the source could be something as small as a vacuum cleaner. Some older motors can also cause buzzing while they run. The usual solution is to use Star-Quad, and keep cables away from the walls. If that doesn't work, use a mixer near the mic and send line-level to the camera.

Impedance

When I first got into this business, Ohm's Law (Chapter 3) was an important consideration for connecting a microphone. Dynamic and ribbon mics generated very little power, and much of it would be lost to noise or distortion if they were plugged into the wrong impedance. So mics and inputs were standardized at various impedances, and we paid serious attention to that rating.

That's usually not the case today.[15] Cameras and recorders have input impedances ranging from 500 Ω to 2 kΩ, and mic outputs can be as low as 100 Ω. But don't go nuts trying to match them. These days, impedance is critical in only a few situations.

The medieval microphones I dealt with in the 1960s and 70s were driven by sound power. Today just about every mic used on a film set runs on either batteries or phantom, and has power to spare. They don't need the perfect current transfers that Ohm's Law guarantees. But the Law still applies to some mic connections.

- All lavs, and most other low- or mid-priced mics used on a shoot, are transformerless even if they're balanced. Their tiny built-in amplifiers are happy feeding a wide range of impedances, so long as it's significantly higher than the mic itself. A typical "500 Ω" mic may have an actual output of 200 Ω, and will work fine with inputs between 500 Ω and 5 kΩ. Transformer-based camera adapters have input impedances close to 500 Ω, and op-amp XLR inputs are usually around 2 kΩ . . . so if you're using this kind of setup, everything should be fine.
- Externally polarized condenser mics used for professional products, often costing in the $1,000 range, usually have internal transformers with 500 Ω outputs. An exact match isn't necessary, because the output power isn't generated by air molecules, but the anything over 2 kΩ might cause problems. Again, almost any XLR mic-level inputs qualify.
- Some excellent phantom powered mics have *impedance balanced* outputs. This circuit reduces the internal noise, but may cause periodic clicking when plugged

---

[15] Ohm's Law hasn't been repealed, but it's not enforced the way it was when I was younger.

into certain input circuits. I've seen this problem in studio setups, but never with the equipment used for field recording . . . but if things do start clicking, just grab a different mic or mixer. Nothing is broken, just incompatible; feel free to use the rejected device elsewhere in the setup.

- Don't worry about impedance when using mini-jack consumer electret micro-phones. The camera spec might be "high impedance" and the mic might be rated "low," but the actual impedances and voltages will be similar to XLR setups.

Bottom line: most of the mics and recorders you'll come across already know how to play nicely together . . . at least as far as impedance is concerned. There are only a few special cases where ohms and watts become critical:

- Most handheld performance and interview microphones are dynamic, and impedance can be important to them. They work best with transformer inputs, or with medium-to-low impedance transformerless ones. They also have less voltage on their outputs than condenser mics, so plugging them directly into most cameras will result in extra circuit noise. If you want to use one of these mics in a single-system setup, use a mixer or preamp between mic and camera.
- Ribbon mics, too fragile to use on a shooting location, are great for voice-over recording. Their impedances are similar to dynamics, but their lower output level requires a perfect match and extra sensitivity. If you have one of these mics, treat it to a good preamp.

✳ TIDBIT

An ancient impedance myth
- When I first learned this stuff, low impedance usually meant high quality. Pro mics used dynamic or ribbon elements and had 500 Ω transformer connections. Consumer mics used much cheaper crystal or ceramic elements: these didn't sound as good, but their high impedance—often tens of thousands of ohms—could connect directly to the input of an amplifying tube.
- These distinctions don't matter anymore. Today, everything from cellphones to the best boom mics use condenser elements, and they all run at about the same low to middle impedance. There are certainly differences between mics, but it's not because of how many ohms are shown on the spec sheet.

CAMERA SETTINGS

The advice in these pages is based on solid engineering, lab measurements I've done on cameras, years of field experience by colleagues and me, and lots of trying to help clients who couldn't understand why their tracks sounded so bad.

I don't guarantee this advice is best for every camera and shooting situation . . . but in most cases and with most cameras, it will give you the cleanest recordings.

There are actually two different challenges here: first, adjusting the camera for the best possible sound; then, making good artistic judgments about dialog levels. That first one is by far the greater challenge. Unfortunately, camera manuals aren't much help. Most seem to be written by video marketing specialists and are remarkably free of useful audio information.

Camcorder audio quality

The DV revolution changed the face of filmmaking. Anybody with a few dollars, a computer, and a little skill can make a film that looks good enough for broadcast. Even some $250 point-and-click still cameras will shoot tolerable HD video under the right circumstances.

Paradoxically, it's had a bad effect on sound.

Economics suggests this isn't likely to change. Since these cameras are aimed at mass market discount sales, they have to be built on a tight budget. Margins are so small that a few extra dollars cost can make a serious difference in a manufacturer's profit percentage. They believe people pay the most attention to picture when buying a camera—and are probably right—so they try to save money on sound.

This isn't just grousing by an audio curmudgeon. Go to an equipment dealer's website and you'll see what's considered important. The mixer and recorder pages brag about frequency response, harmonic distortion, and noise—things that indicate how good a circuit will sound. But if you look for audio specs on a camera page, all you'll find is something like "16 bit, 48 kHz sampling" . . . which says as much about sound quality as "16 × 9" tells you about the lens.

Years ago, when I was writing a monthly audio column for *DV Magazine*, I went looking for deeper technical details. There was nothing useful in the cameras' brochures or instruction manuals. When I asked the manufacturers directly, they said the information just didn't exist.

(I don't think anyone was deliberately hiding things from me. Camera audio circuits are often designed by outside consultants, and all the manufacturers care about is whether they work and can be manufactured at reasonable cost.)

So we began a project of measuring popular cameras and portable recorders with lab equipment.[16] Over the more than ten years we've been doing these measurements, we've seen some definite trends. While equipment comes and goes, the recommendations here will probably be valid for years to come.

How we did it, and what the numbers mean

We tested cameras and recorders with specialized audio analyzers and software, looking for three things: noise, distortion, and frequency response. Noise and distortion often depend on what kind of signal you're feeding the recorder, so our test tones matched the outputs from standard-level mics, "hot" mics (like the Sennheiser ME66), and portable mixers. We fed those tones into the devices' mic or line inputs, recording at the basic video standard of 16 bits, 48 kHz sampling, and then read the resulting digital tape or file directly into our analyzers. Wind filters, automatic level controls, and other options were turned off for the primary tests, though we examined those functions as well. Full details on the procedure and equipment used are at my studio's website, www.dplay.com. Figure 8.7 and 8.8 show both our earliest and most recent setups. Most of the original analysis hardware has been replaced by software, which I run in a powerful workstation computer.

Noise and dynamic range

The *signal-to-noise ratio* (s/n) is a measurement, in decibels, of how much hiss and other electronic junk a circuit adds to a recording. A higher s/n means less noise and a cleaner track. A proper s/n measurement includes a reference level, or "how loud is the signal we're comparing the noise to?" In digital recording, that's also the nominal or tone level, usually –12 dBFS for prosumer gear and –20 dBFS for professional. That 8 dB difference gives the cheaper gear an advantage when it's being measured. So to level the playing field, we express noise as *dynamic range* instead: the difference between the loudest signal a system can handle, and its electronic noise.[17] To convert it to s/n, just subtract the reference level. For example, a 90 dB dynamic range on a prosumer camera equals a 78 dB s/n . . . which is actually quite respectable.

If you're shooting for theatrical release or heavily processed broadcast, at least 72 dB s/n is desirable (that's slightly better than a typical feature film would get, back in the days of analog field recording and 35mm mag editing). Corporate and event videographers can work as low as 57 dB or so, if the voices don't have much dynamic range.

---

[16] "We" originally included *DV*'s publishers, my son Dan (then assistant chief at a major radio station), and feature film recordist John Garrett. *DV* no longer supports this research, but I've gotten a lot of help from Boston-based dealers Rule Broadcast Systems and Talamas Broadcast Equipment.

[17] You can't trust dynamic range numbers on an analog recorder, because "loudest signal" depends on how much distortion you're willing to tolerate. But digital recorders have an absolute maximum signal—Full Scale—so the measurement is appropriate for them.

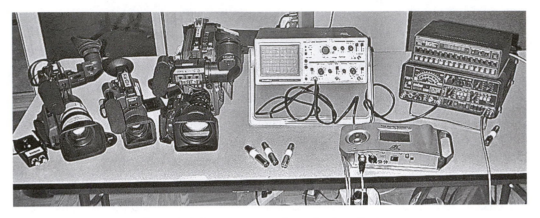

Figure 8.7 Our camera audio test setup, then . . .

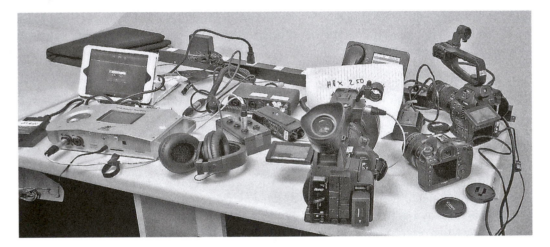

Figure 8.8 . . . and now.

Distortion

All recorders damage the waveform a little, adding harmonics (or worse, non-harmonic products) that weren't in the original signal. This is different from the constant noise discussed above, because this depends on what you're recording. Even-numbered harmonics can be tolerable in music production, but interfere with intelligibility on dialog. Non-harmonic aliasing distortion is a particularly nasty form caused by bad digital design; it can sound like intermittent whistling or screeching added to the signal.

We checked distortion by recording constant tones at mic and line levels, and then measuring everything in the recordings *except* those tones, figuring the result as a percentage: THD+N (Total Harmonic Distortion + Noise). The higher the percentage, the more junk a recorder is adding to a signal.

A THD+N of 1% used to be acceptable in pro analog recording. These days, 0.1% is considered reasonable in a music studio, and a lot of pro gear is better than 0.01%. But 1% is still adequate for dialog recording with today's all-digital setups. The multi-generation analog equipment and workflows of Hollywood's Golden Age resulted in many times more distortion than that.

Frequency response

Problems with frequency response result in a dialog track that might be called thin, dull, or canned . . . but never like we're listening to real slices of the characters' lives.

There's a lot of myth here. Manufacturers often quote limits or frequency ranges, which don't mean anything without a lot of qualifying data that they don't quote. At the very least, you have to know *how much* the device's sensitivity varies between those limits. For example, a specification of "20 Hz–20 kHz" by itself only says you can capture some fraction of the signal within that range, if it's loud enough. However, a specification of "20 Hz–20 kHz ± 2 dB tells you that system is equally sensitive at all those frequencies, within two decibels. So what you play back will have the same timbre as what you recorded.

For dialog, 80 Hz–15 kHz ± 2 dB is considered excellent; 100 Hz–12 kHz ± 3 dB can be adequate; and 150 Hz–10 kHz ± 3 dB is acceptable for basic news reporting. Music recording usually looks for wider response. But that can be another myth: while the audiophiles crowd insists you need 20 kHz, the human voice—and many acoustic instruments—has virtually no energy at those upper frequencies.

What we learned

A few of the units we measured are shown in Table 8.1. This is intended as a short summary to give you an idea of trends, not an encyclopedia. If you don't see a particular piece of gear here, it's because of lack of space, not necessarily because a product was unworthy. New cameras will also have been introduced by the time you read this.[18] But barring some major overhaul in electronics technology and marketing philosophy, this range of numbers is what you can expect from any camera.

Does all that seem too technical? There are practical recommendations after the table.[19]

---

[18] If you want me to test a specific unit and can get a sample to my studio in Boston, let me know. If it's interesting, I'll find time to do the measurements and publish the results on my website.

[19] See text for test levels, and converting these ranges to signal-to-noise ratio.

Table 8.1 A dozen years of actual camera performance. While the oldest units aren't up to today's spec, they do point out trends. And most recent cameras are perfectly acceptable (except for the smallest DSLRs, which should be used only for sync reference)

Camera or recorder	Dynamic range, dB19			THD+N			Response ± 2 dB unless indicated	Notes
	Mic	Hot	Line Mic	Mic (%)	Hot Mic (%)	Line (%)		
Arriflex Alexa	–	–	90	–	–	.001	20 Hz–20 kHz	
Canon GL2	72	81	–	4	.5	–	90 Hz–9 kHz	With Canon MA300 adapter
Canon XL1	53	67	–	1.2	.3	–	80 Hz–12 kHz	With Canon MA100 adapter
	62	66	–	2.5	.24	–	90 Hz–10 kHz	With BeachTek DXA–4c adapter
	–	–	73	–	–	.23	80 Hz–12 kHz	–30 dBV signal into RCA jacks
Canon EOS C100	88	–	91	.03	–	.01	25 Hz–19 kHz	
Canon EOS 5D Mark III	75	–	75	.05	–	.05	100 Hz–15 kHz	With BeachTek DXA–HDV adapter
JVC DV300	77	78	–	.15	.2	–	67 Hz–14 kHz	
Panasonic DVX100	70	70	72	.18	.16	.14	25 Hz –18 kHz	Line level –10 dBV
Panasonic HVX200	70	72	72	.09	.14	.02	25 Hz–19 kHz	
Panasonic HPX250	83	–	89	.01	–	.01	40 Hz–19 kHz	
Sony VX2000	63	66	59	6.5	1.4	.32	100 Hz–9 kHz	Using unbalanced inputs
Sony PD150	64	70	70	.5	.3	.3	160 Hz–9 kHz	Line level –10 dBV
Sony PD170	76	79	78	.1	.06	.05	125 Hz–20 kHz	Line level +4 dBu
Sony DSR570	72	85	88	.15	.1	.1	50 Hz–15 kHz	Line level +4 dBu
Sony HVR–Z1U	76	86	80	.09	.06	.06	30 Hz–19 kHz	Line level +4 dBu. 48 kHz 16bit. Measured saved file.

The recommendations

Sample rate and bit depth

Video usually runs at 48 kHz sample rate with 16-bit words. Some professional gear can use higher rates or deeper bit depths, but those settings aren't necessary for most field recording. In practice, higher settings might not do anything at all. The mid-price recorders we tested (but haven't listed in the chart) from Tascam, Edirol, and Fostex all advertised 24-bit recording, but their analog circuits weren't capable of much better than 16-bit dynamic performance. Unless you fed them a digital signal, the extra eight bits just recorded seven or more bits worth of noise.

Some prosumer cameras can also record with 32 kHz sample rate and 12-bit words. It's not a good choice. The low sample rate increases the chance for aliasing distortion. The fewer bits result in 24 dB more noise. Don't use this mode.

Volume controls, noise, and distortion

The challenge in any recording is to be loud enough that the signal isn't polluted by noise, yet not so loud that parts of it distort. It's a balancing act. Distortion that might be tolerable in some music recording can be a problem with dialog. Noise that's tolerable in a TV track can become overwhelming in a theater.

Manufacturers can trade noise for distortion when they design a circuit, as you can see by comparing some of the entries on the table. In general, you'll get the best noise and distortion performance from any camera, if you keep its meter peaking near the tone level for average spoken dialog. For prosumer cameras, that's –12 dBFS, and the camera's meter will have a mark at that level. Softer words will usually be a lot lower, and shouting or sudden sound effects somewhat louder, so judgment is required (that's why we use constant tones for objective testing). There's more about setting levels later in this chapter.

Input level is also a part of the trade-off. You can see from the chart that the stronger signal from a hot mic almost always results in a better recording than a standard mic, and that a line-level signal usually gets a better signal than either mic. Some very high end pro cameras are designed only for line-level from a mixer. Of course, those cameras are almost never used single-system.

Almost every unit we tested—cameras and recorders alike—performed best with signals that resulted in good meter readings when the volume control was around 50%. If an input level was so soft that the control had to be pushed up to two-thirds, there was usually a lot more noise. If it was so loud that the control had to be less than 33%, there could be distortion. Many combinations of equipment and performance work fine with the volume control around the middle, but if you find yourself going to extremes, consider the following.

Use a mixer for more signal

Boosting a mic's output in a mixer always sounds better than trying to boost it in the camera. That's probably because the mixer manufacturers pay more attention to their audio circuits. Plugging the mics to a mixer, and then the mixer's line-level output into the camera, will usually give you the best results ... particularly for marginal signals or soft performances.

Use an attenuator for less signal

In theory, turning down the volume control should make any loud signal soft enough to record properly. But most cameras and low-cost recorders have sensitive circuits ahead of that control, and a loud signal can get distorted, even when the meter shows a proper level. That's the reason for the "keep it above 33%" recommendation above.

Most cameras and recorders have a switch to select line- or mic-level signals, so that the line signals don't distort. Many also have a switch to select between hot mics or normal ones (marked MIC ATT, −12 dB, or similar). These are more than *attenuators* that just lower the voltage; they use other circuit tricks to reduce distortion and noise. That's why the specs for hotter signals are better.

If you have a MIC ATT switch available, use it ... but *only* if you're getting good meter readings with the volume control around 50% when the switch is on. If this function makes you raise the volume control too much to compensate, you'll get more noise than if you used the normal input mode.

Some units don't have that switch, and you need very low volume control settings to get good meter readings from a hot mic or mixer. In these cases you'll almost always get a better recording by putting an external attenuator between the signal and input jack. It'll let you use a higher volume setting. There's more about attenuators later in the chapter.

ALC

You'd think the answer would be to turn on the Automatic Level Control, a feature on most prosumer cameras. These circuits constantly adjust the volume to get the best recording. But they're not very smart. If the dialog pauses for a while, they'll turn up the volume looking for something else to record. As they do, any environmental or electronic background noise is boosted. When you play back the tape, you can hear noise rushing up during the pauses. If you cut two shots together, there may be an abrupt jump in noise level.

Turn ALCs *off* for any serious shooting. Some cameras turn it back on whenever you power up or change the tape or battery, so keep checking to make sure things are staying the way you want.

Low-end cameras often don't have an obvious way to turn ALC off. A few may have undocumented menu commands for this function; the best place to find out about them is from other users on Web forums.

If ALC absolutely can't be turned off, at least make sure you're sending the camera an appropriate level, that the signal path is very clean, and that the mic is close enough to the subject. And don't count on getting professional quality dialog recordings.

Limiting, which protects the recording from sudden very loud peaks, is often available on professional cameras. While it's similar in principle to ALC, it's faster and only triggers on the loudest sounds. When properly set up, it doesn't affect most of the dialog. If you have this feature, leave it on.

ALC defeat

Some under-camera balancing adapters have an ALC defeating function, which injects a high frequency signal that's theoretically loud enough to force the ALC to its lowest gain. Results with this feature have been mixed, depending on the camera and the audio being recorded.

I'm sometimes asked whether you could defeat ALC by mixing a loud low frequency tone with the mic signal, and filtering it out in postproduction. Unfortunately, low frequencies make ALC pump or otherwise modulate the signal and can't be filtered out.

In theory, you could use an expander (Chapter 16) as an "anti-ALC". But most cameras apply ALC non-linearly, and with unpredictable time constants. Unless the expander matches these characteristics perfectly, it'll just make things worse.

Mic noise reduction

A few cameras (mostly smaller, older Sonys) have a MIC NR setting in their audio menu. This is a simple noise gate that turns the input off when it falls below a certain level, to control hiss from inferior mics or very low-level environmental noise. It doesn't work very well, and can make a little "puff" sound after each word. Avoid this setting. You can do a better job in post, with the advantage of undo-ability if you don't like the result.

Bottom line on digital camcorders . . .

The technical discussions above are important if you want to get the best results from a setup. But if want to remember only a few rules:

- Use as little gain from the camera's internal preamp as possible. MIC ATT is better than MIC, and LINE is better than MIC ATT.
- But you'll get best results by keeping the camera's volume control around 50%. If you must choose between this rule and the one above, this rule wins.
- Keep automatic level controls and any microphone noise reduction option turned off. The former doesn't work well for dialog. The latter doesn't work at all.
- Be very careful of recording levels. One trick is to split a single mic through a mixer or transformer box, and then record it on both camera channels. Keep one channel set about 6 dB lower than the other. In post, choose the hotter channel for less noise or the quieter one for less distortion, and switch between them depending on the sound.
- Monitor with headphones while you're shooting, and play back important takes as well.

- Camera recording is designed for dialog, not music. We found serious aliasing distortion in earlier models, which affects music more than voice. Newer cameras have been better, but still aren't as good as double-system.

A sense of perspective

Sound in camcorders is far from perfect, compared to the gear that audio professionals use. But your final result can still be close to what was considered state-of-the-art a few decades ago. Traditional analog film production added distortion and noise with each subsequent dub in the process, and there could be six or more generations between the original shoot and the release print. If you're careful, digital production won't have these problems.

The worst part of analog soundtracks, *wow and flutter*,[20] was so prevalent that it's become a cliché: if you want to make a parody of an older soundtrack, add wow and flutter along with the noise and distortion. Digital doesn't have wow or flutter at all.

DSLR wisdom

Some network shows and mainstream feature films are now being shot on these cameras. Their large image sensors and ability to use high-quality lenses raised the standard for video-based production. Their low price has made this kind of picture quality available to business or event videographers and even hobbyists.

Unfortunately, their sound quality can be a major step backwards. Audio circuits are compromised. The lack of space in a tiny camera body means they use fewer and smaller electronic components, and can't have physical isolation from noisy computer chips. Their low selling price forces manufacturers to skimp on audio to make a profit: better pictures will sell more cameras; having better audio won't.

Here are some ways to get good sound when you're using a DSLR:

- First, don't think of a DSLR as a camcorder with better images. It's not. Think of it as a film-quality silent camera, that also captures a low-fi audio track for reference.

  Some of the DSLRs we've measured have had reasonable audio specs (others have been horrible), but none make it easy to get good sound. Menus are hidden; vital controls may be missing while others are locked while you're shooting; audio software can be full of bugs, some of which don't surface until you're editing.[21]

---

[20] Rhythmic variations in the speed, resulting in undesirable changes in pitch during sustained notes.

[21] One series of cameras turns on ALC when the camera powers up, even if it was off previously. If the camera has turned itself off because of inactivity or high heat, you have to go deep into menus to reset the ALC defeat . . . something that's not likely to happen during a production, when people are in a hurry to get the camera running again.

- Second, plan on recording double-system. Even a pocket digital audio recorder will be an improvement. Use the DSLR's track for sync when you first ingest files . . . after that, ignore the track. Better yet, sync the old-fashioned Hollywood way with a slapped slate.

  Some sound professionals I know refuse to send a mix to DSLRs. They record high-quality double-system, but insist you use the camera's built-in mic for any reference track. Their logic is that unless the DSLR's track is obviously bad, editors might take the shortcut and use it instead of syncing the better tracks.

  You don't even need a reference track. Hollywood-style slates are more accurate (see page 352), and just as fast to use. Most DSLRs and some camcorders record the sound a couple of frames earlier or later than picture, because of internal processing. The clip that the camera generates has a built-in sync error. This error can get worse if you're using the camera's mic to capture a reference track, because the camera is usually much farther from the actors than the lav or boom mic used for the main track. Matching a visual slate to a recorded slap sound eliminates these errors completely. Slates also carry important information about the scene and take number, making it easier to match sound and picture.

- You don't need timecode, unless you've got multiple cameras that are starting and stopping during the take and there's no opportunity to slate. If you're in that kind of situation but don't have timecode capability on the DSLR, put a *smart slate*[22] near the recorder. Shoot its numbers each time you start recording, and then focus on the scene. If you don't have a smart slate, point the camera at a timecode readout on the recorder instead. You'll be able to look at those initial frames in your editing software, read the code yourself, and match it against the track's timecode.

- If you're not using timecode at all, it can help to set the camera's internal time-of-day clock to match the recorder's timecode. These clocks don't have seconds and frames, so you'll be tracking to the nearest minute. But that can be enough to help you find matching takes if you discover a mistake on the camera log or file names.

DOUBLE-SYSTEM

Most features shot on video, and a lot of smaller projects, bypass the problems of camera audio and use a separate audio recorder instead. The process is known as double-system. It's the standard for features, since single-system was never available in high-quality film cameras. But it does take extra care to work properly.

---

[22] It looks like a traditional Hollywood slate and has a striped stick to slap, but it also has a timecode generator with a large readout. Its generator is matched to the sound recorder's timecode every few hours.

Videographers often look at double-system because they're unsatisfied with the sound from their camcorder. Try the tips in this chapter first. A balancing adapter or mixer, properly used, can produce usable tracks with most of today's cameras. It's how a lot of basic television and some low-budget features are shot, even when there's a professional sound crew.

For projects where dialog quality is critical, such as features that'll be projected in a theater, double-system has definite advantages. Even moderately priced, non-timecode audio recorders do a better job than most prosumer professional cameras. But it's always more work than single-system. Aside from the extra equipment, you have to deal with logging media, and take steps both when shooting and when editing to get things in sync.

Syncing double-system

The good news is you probably don't need timecode. Syncing is actually two separate functions. You have to make sure audio and video start at exactly the same time, and you have to keep both running at exactly the same speed.

Timecode

In the professional world, the first chore is usually handled by SMPTE timecode (see Chapter 12). Identical computer numbers are recorded on the audio and videotape, flashed onto the edge of a film, embedded in a file header, or shot from a human-readable slate. When playing back a tape, the audio deck looks at code coming from the picture, winds its tape to a matching location, then adjusts its speed until the two match exactly. Once the audio is synchronized, the deck turns speed control over to *house sync*, a video signal distributed to every device in the facility. When syncing digital files, the software looks at the file headers and aligns sound and picture so they both start together; after that, the picture's frame rate and the audio's sample rate are locked to the same computer clock so things stay together.

The double-system recorders used by professionals can cost more than many DV cameras. That money buys extremely high-quality audio, built-in mixers, and other production-oriented features along with timecode. Producers use timecode because it's a tremendous time-saver. But remember: Hollywood lived without it for half a century.

Non-timecode speed stability

Modern digital audio recorders have reliable internal crystals to keep their speed stable, often within one frame for as much as half an hour. Similar crystals are used in video cameras. There's always the possibility of two crystals slipping in opposite directions, one fast while the other is slow, but even then a well-maintained setup will stay in sync for at least 15 minutes. If a single shot lasts longer than that, you may need a recorder that can lock to video reference (see below). Or shoot some *B-roll*: shots that belong to the scene but don't show lips moving, such as audience reactions.

When sync drifts too far, cut to the B-roll for a moment while you trim a few frames in the master shot to match audio again.

Much older audio equipment has less accurate crystals. Analog cassette or open-reel tape recorders—even most professional ones—don't run at a constant speed and can't be used for lipsync. The Nagra portable open-reel recorder, a standard in film production for decades, used a special *pilot* track to control its speed.

Modern professional film cameras have internal crystals and run at a constant speed, just like videotape. If film is transferred properly, and the scanner is locked to a proper sync source, film on video will be just as stable. You may have to deal with pull-down (Chapter 12), but that's predictable and controllable. Older film cameras with battery or spring motors are notoriously unstable. The only way to achieve sync with them is to have a small generator, inside the camera, that creates a signal proportional to the camera speed. It requires special sound equipment to record that signal, and a transfer facility that knows how to handle it.

If you're going to be using an older film camera and transferring to video yourself, by pointing a camera at a projected image, forget about lipsync. Don't even count on replacing dialog later, since you won't have a reference track. This is a good time to think about telling the story in voice-overs.

Using a reference track for sync

The easiest way to get sound and picture moving together—at least within a couple of frames—is to record identical tracks on both.[23] Feed the recorder's audio output to the camera, and record it along with picture. Once everything's in your computer, slide the separate audio track until it matches the video's. You can do this visually by matching waveforms in an NLE's timeline, then checking sync by playing them together. When they match, you shouldn't hear an echo. Once you've got sync and checked it over the length of the take, you can delete the reference track and just keep the double-system one.

PluralEyes software does this for you, matching double-system audio files with reference tracks on similarly named video files, and then sliding them until they're in sync. It has some caveats, but if you have a lot of files and treat it properly, can be a real time-saver. See Chapter 12.

Manual and automatic sync gets harder when you can't feed the same signal to both recorders. A camera-mounted mic will hear more echo and noise than a properly positioned boom or lav, and matching will be more difficult. Camera distances can delay the video's track by more than a frame across a large room. If you can't run a cable, consider using a low-cost wireless rig between the recorder's output and the camera. Wireless problems—which could make a finished track unacceptable— don't matter to a reference track.

---

[23] This procedure might not be perfect because the camera can introduce delays to sound or picture.

Using a traditional slate

A basic Hollywood wooden slate—the kind with diagonal stripes on the top, emblematic of filmmaking—can give you more accurate lipsync than a reference track.

You can buy a slate for as little as $20 at a camera store, and a novelty one for about $5 at a toy store. Either will work. Or build your own with a couple of scraps of wood and a hinge. The important thing is having two parts that come together to make a sharp noise, and are painted so you can see them moving easily. Slap them together in front of the camera, while the sound is rolling, and let them stay together for a few seconds afterward. Make sure the mic isn't more than a few feet from the slate, so acoustic delays aren't a problem.

Writing the scene and take number is optional, as is announcing it verbally . . . but that information will bail you out if there's a problem. An additional slate, at the end of a take, can help diagnose speed problems. The usual practice, when marking the end of a take, is to hold the slate itself upside down.

Don't have a slate at all? Clap your hands together! Just place them so the camera sees both coming together, and keep them together after they meet. Don't let them bounce apart like you would when applauding; that makes it harder to spot the critical frame.

When it's time to sync, find the first frame of picture where the sticks or hands have stopped moving; usually that's the final frame where there's any blur from the motion. Line that up against the start of the sound, which you'll see on the waveform (and can also hear when scrubbing). That's it. You're done.

No sync reference?

Sound can also be matched to picture without any reference at all. This is time-consuming for professionals, and can be almost impossible for the beginner. There are some tips in Chapter 13.

Logging

The other responsibility when using double-system is keeping track of everything. That's why Hollywood slates are shot with the scene and take number written on them, and an assistant director calls out the same information so it's recorded on the track. At the same time, a camera assistant notes the information in a camera log, and the sound mixer writes it on a sound report . . . along with what kind of mic was used, how tracks were set up, and anything else that might be useful down the line. These logs accompany the project throughout its life. Small pads for sound reports are available at film sound dealers. Some field recorders and laptop software have built-in reporting and generate a pdf file with the necessary information. Most shoots involve multiple media—more than one tape, DVD-ROM, or solid-state drive is needed to hold everything—so the logs keep track of which scenes and takes are on which audio and video media.

Logging each shot isn't as important at spontaneous events, where you might be able to identify audio recordings by their content. But it's crucial when producing a dramatized film, since different takes of a scene will have the same words. It's also essential if there won't be reference audio on video or film.

MIXERS AND PREAMPS

The only serious functional difference between a mixer or preamp is mixing—combining multiple audio signals into a single channel. Otherwise, both can work as preamps to boost a mics to line level, which results in better performance with almost all cameras. Both almost always have balanced XLR inputs, eliminating the need for a separate balancing adapter if the unit is fairly close to the camera.

Preamps

Mic preamps designed for video use are small and rugged, and can be worn on the belt, slung over a shoulder, or fastened to the tripod. They're battery-powered, provide 48-volt phantom for the mic, and may have other specialized functions including:

- switchable filtering to eliminate low-frequency rumbles and some wind noise—most filtering should be put off until the more relaxed (and undoable) atmosphere of post, but wind and rumble filtering should be done in the field, because these frequencies can distort dialog in the recorder;
- switchable limiters;
- LED metering;
- headphone outputs;
- USB connections to record in a computer;
- transformer-coupled inputs and outputs—the input transformer provides the best cable noise rejection with the lowest self-noise, while the output one lets you run long cables to the camera (if it has balanced inputs), and prevents the possibility of noisy ground loops between preamp and camera.

Field preamps are high-quality, specialized equipment, usually costing around $350/channel. Preamps designed for music recording may cost less, but generally lack features and ruggedness. Some music preamps cost a lot more—into the thousands—but that kind of quality and specialized sound is lost in dialog recording.

Basic mixer

Mixers let you combine multiple mics into a single camera channel. In most multi-mic dialog setups, you have to constantly move the faders. Only one mic should be feeding a recorder channel at a time. Otherwise, room noise and reverb can build up. If two people are speaking simultaneously and going to the same track, both faders should be lowered slightly. You can't do this kind of mixing with the tiny knobs on a camera.

Small tabletop mixers, designed primarily for home music recording, can be used for this purpose. They lack features found in field preamps, aren't very rugged, and usually require AC power. Their specs are rarely as good as a field preamp, either. But they're certainly good enough for dialog, and if you can put up with the inconveniences can be a great bargain. Acceptable models, with two or four mic inputs, are often on sale at music chains for around $100.

On the positive side, most of these mixers have large knobs or slide controls that make it easy to make fine adjustments during a take. They also often have equalization controls, which should be set to neutral and ignored. Seriously: put gaffer tape over them, so you're not tempted to equalize in the field. They're designed for music recording, and are too broad for dialog and at the wrong frequencies. It's always better to leave equalization decisions for the calmer atmosphere, tighter controls, and better monitoring of postproduction. A bad decision in the field may be impossible to correct.

If a mixer or mic has a bass cut switch, you may be able to use it to cut wind noise and rumble. But check first; it might have a thinning effect on dialog.

If you're mixing between a boom and lav or plant mics, there will probably be some difference in their sound. Don't equalize the primary mic, but it's okay to use a tiny bit of equalization on the others—no more than 3 or 4 dB—to make them match. Of course, that's only if you're experienced with equalizing dialog, know the frequencies involved, and have very good headphones. And note what you've done on the script or sound log, so it can be undone if necessary in post.

Most tabletop mixers have small knobs near their XLR connectors to adjust each input's sensitivity. Be diligent about setting these to avoid noise and distortion. The general procedure is to set each of the volume sliders to a preset point (usually marked with a zero or U), point the mic at a typical source from a typical distance, and adjust the sensitivity so the mixer's meter reads 0 VU.

Field mixer

These units combine the ruggedness (and often, the high audio quality) of a field preamp with mixing capabilities. They have features designed specifically for film and video production, including most of the ones found on a field preamp.

These mixers typically have three or four inputs; in stereo mixers they're switchable between left output, right output, or both. They also usually include a tone generator and built-in mic for identifying takes. While their size makes them portable—they're typically worn over the shoulder or stuffed in a bag with wireless receivers—it also dictates small knobs that may be difficult to use smoothly during dramatic dialog. Depending on features, prices range from about $400 to quite a few thousand.

Many field mixers have *preamp gain* controls. They work similarly to MIC ATT on a camera: set them for the lowest gain that lets you get a good reading on the unit's meters. Unlike the volume controls in cameras, any good mixer's volume control won't generate hiss until you reach the very top of its range.

Some field mixers also act as hubs and controllers for proprietary networks of recorders and wireless rigs. Others are built into field multitrack recorders, like the Deva shown in Figure 8.1.

Matching a mixer or preamp output

Professional equipment line-level outputs are usually +4 dBu, balanced. DSLRs and camcorders with mini-jack inputs need –10 dBV unbalanced signals for best perform-ance. A few field mixers also have mini-jack outputs for this purpose; otherwise, you'll need one of the attenuators described below.

Connecting to the recorder

Field mixer outputs are usually switchable between mic and line level. If your camera can be set for line-level signals, that kind of output on the mixer will give you a better recording.

Some cameras accept only mic level. Don't try to reduce a mixer or preamp's line-level output to mic level by turning down its volume control; this just adds noise. But you might not want to use the mic-level output on a mixer either! That's because most mixers are built with a mic level of –50 dBu. A signal this soft can get noisy in DV cameras, if it makes you run the camera's volume control higher than about 60%. Instead, use an attenuator to knock the mixer's line-level output down to –35 dBu, and use the camera's MIC ATT setting. You might also need a capacitor to block DC voltage on the mic input, similar to the one in Figure 8.5.

You can also use a transformer adapter, described early in this chapter, to connect a mixer or preamp to a camera. Its volume controls function like an attenuator. But it does mean you'll be feeding the camera a mic-level signal.

Attenuators

These devices, also called *pads*, are simple resistor networks that lower the level of an audio signal. At the same time, they can connect a balanced source to an unbalanced input—though without the noise immunity of true balancing.

Attenuators are available pre-built in XLR male/female barrels, or as cables, for between $30 and $50 at broadcast suppliers. Many of the cable versions also include blocking capacitors.

Or you can build your own for a few dollars. There are three circuits for this, depending on how the equipment is balanced. The value of the resistors in each is determined by how many decibels of attenuation you need. Resistors don't have to be fancy: ¼-watt 1% film resistors, available from Radio Shack in packs of five for under $2, are perfectly fine. Or use ¼-watt 1% film or 5% carbon resistors from an electronics supplier. It won't make any difference in sound quality.

I've specified resistor values that Radio Shack sells, because they're easiest to get. This meant making some small compromises in the pads' designs, so they're not precise to the decibel. But they'll get a signal down to a level that your camera can record well. If you can't find resistors of these exact values, a few percent difference won't matter. Figures 8.9–8.11 show mono attenuators, but you can double them for a stereo mini-jack input: connect the output of one (marked "to pin or tip" in those figures) to the mini-plug's tip for the left channel, the other to the mini-plug's ring, and both grounds (from pin 1 on the XLR) to the sleeve.

If you're connecting an electronically-balanced output (most tabletop mixers) to an unbalanced mini-jack or RCA input, wire it like Figure 8.9. The two resistors marked R1 should each be 220 Ω, and R2 should be 750 Ω, to drop professional +4 dBu line level to consumer –10 dBV line. To drop pro line level to –35 dBu for a camera MIC ATT input, R1 is 590 Ω and R2 is 20 Ω. If you can't find a 20 Ω resistor, use two 10 Ω in series or two 39 Ω in parallel. If you're using the RCA inputs on an XL1 or similar Canon and want a –30 dBV signal, R1 is 511 Ω and R2 is 75 Ω (or two 150 Ω in parallel).

If the mixer or preamp has transformer-balanced outputs (most, but not all, field units), use the circuit in Figure 8.10. To go from +4 dBu to –10 dBV, all three resistors are 332 Ω. To bring +4 dBu down to –35 dBu, R1 is 590 Ω and R2 is 25 Ω. If you can't find a 25 Ω resistor, use two 49 Ω in parallel. Use the capacitor described in the previous paragraph for mini-jack mic inputs. To get –30 dBV for an XL1, R1 is 560 Ω (or two 1.1 kΩ in parallel) and R2 is 38 Ω (150 Ω and 51 Ω in parallel).

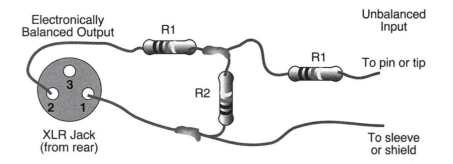

Figure 8.9 Use this circuit to plug a +4 dBu electronically-balanced output into a mini-jack camera. There are two resistors marked R1 because they have the same value; see text for details.

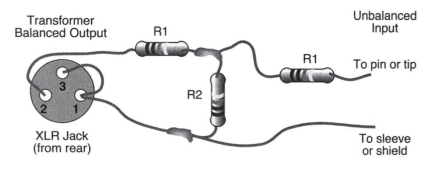

Figure 8.10 Use this circuit with transformer-balanced outputs.

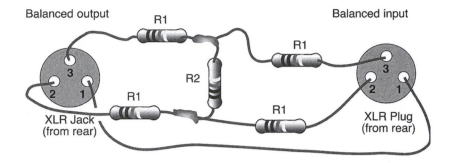

Balanced output

Balanced input

Figure 8.11 This circuit provides attenuation while keeping the signal balanced.

Figure 8.11 shows the circuit for an XLR-to-XLR balanced attenuator. It can be built into an empty male/female barrel, available from broadcast suppliers, but may be more convenient in a cable long enough to go from preamp to camera. To drop a +4 dBu signal to −35 dBu mic level, R1 is 301 Ω, and R2 is 15 Ω. It's important, in this circuit, that all four R1s be exactly the same value.

The XLR-to-XLR attenuator in Figure 8.11 can be used with long balanced cables. The attenuator should be at the camera, not at the mixer. (If you're building a cable version, put the resistors in the male end.) This keeps the signal at line level for most of the run, for better noise immunity.

ADJUSTING THE VOLUME

Shooting a dialog track that will be edited requires consistency, from shot to shot and from scene to scene. Otherwise the edited video will be full of distracting auditory jump cuts. These take a long time to correct at the mix.

A character's dialog level, as read on the record level meter, should stay consistent throughout a scene. Of course the volume may change if they shout or whisper, or if they're walking away from the scene, but that's related to what the character does on camera. We shouldn't be aware of any changes in their volume when you move the boom, or switch from boom to lav, because without any visual reference the shift becomes distracting. Since the electrical output of a mic varies both with the element type and distance from the speaker, the bottom line is you have to adjust the recording level when changing mics. It may even be necessary while booming.

Not all characters have to be at the same volume level. Differences in personality, or in their intensity during a scene, may mean that one voice is louder than another. But they should be fairly close—within 4 or 5 dB—or else the scene will be difficult to mix.

If you're using just one or two mics, it's easiest to route them directly to the camera. Set each for appropriate volume and record with a constant level, and make sure they go to separate tracks and aren't being mixed in the camera. Be aware that a character's volume will change if a boom operator can't hold a steady distance because of inexperience or how the scene is blocked and lit. You'll have to compensate while you're editing. If you have to raise part of a track by any significant amount, you'll also increase its noise.

If you're using more than two mics and don't have a good multitrack recorder, you must use a mixer. (Some cameras can record four simultaneous audio channels, but they sacrifice quality when they do. It's best to forget the manufacturer even provides this mode.)

Aligning the mixer's meters

Whether the analog mixer or preamp has VU meters with moving needles or a row of LEDs to indicate output level, it's set up as an analog VU meter. Camera meters are set up to read digital dBFS. These two ways of metering are not the same. Furthermore, what the camera records is influenced by its volume control, which comes after the mixer's meter. So you can't expect a mixer's meter to have anything to do with the camera's meter, until you've calibrated things.

The best procedure is to feed the camera some test dialog. First, adjust the mixer controls so that most of the peaks reach zero VU on the mixer's meter.

Then turn the camera's Automatic Level Control *on*. Note how the camera's meters respond to dialog: this is what the manufacturer calibrated the automatic controls to and is probably the best recording level for that camera. For most prosumer cameras, it'll be –12 dBFS; pro cameras usually work at –20 dBFS. Once you've got a feel for what the camera's meters do with ALC on, turn it off. Adjust the camera's manual controls for a similar meter reading. Note that you haven't touched the external mixer's controls at all during this paragraph.

From this point on, you should be able to rely on the mixer's meters. But check the camera's meters during the take. A meter designed for music recording can miss quick changes in dialog levels.

 TIP

The above procedure is best done with actual dialog, while the actors are rehearsing or with a friend talking at a constant level, rather than with a lineup tone. The relative response of analog and digital meters to tone is different from the way they respond to voice. Professionals use tone, but understand the differences involved.

Headphone amplifiers

If you're using a mixer or most preamps, you can use it to drive headphones for the boom and mix operators. But if you're plugging a mic directly into most cameras, you may need a separate amplifier. That's because small cameras seldom have enough headphone output to drive a set for the director or camera operator, and one for the boom operator.

One possibility is to skip the director's phones. But that raises the possibility of the director buying a take with problems that weren't heard at the camera position.

Headphone amplifiers, fed by the camera's headphone output and designed for three or more separate sets of phones, are a good solution. AC-powered units, intended for recording studios but usable in the field, cost about $150 at music stores. Rugged battery-powered ones, designed specifically for film and video, cost about $300 at broadcast suppliers. All will have separate volume controls for each output.

Or the boom operator can use a *bridging amplifier*. This is a belt-pack unit that passes a microphone signal through without affecting it, while tapping off some audio to drive a battery-powered headphone amp. About $350 at broadcast suppliers . . . though if you're considering this route, it makes more sense to give the boom operator a belt-pack mic preamp with headphone output, and send a line-level signal to the camera.

Another possibility is a small one-way radio system, often called a Comtek (after its manufacturer), that puts a transmitter at the mixer and gives a personal receiver to anybody who needs one. It's often found on advertising shoots, where agency executives and clients want to hear specific aspects of the performance while not being tethered to a cable. A basic system sells for around $1,500 or rents at about $200 per day, and has its own setup requirements. If you need one, ask your dealer for specifics.

No matter how you drive these phones, somebody must be listening specifically to the camera's headphone output; either the videographer, director, or mixer. Otherwise, bad connections and user errors might never be spotted.

Where's the next chapter?

- Chapter 9 deals with recording when the camera isn't rolling. That includes dialog replacement with and without video playback, narration and voice-overs, and sound effects. There are sections on synchronization and other technical aspects, suggestions for sound effects sources, and ways to get the best vocal performances . . . things rarely taught in film school. It's a lot of material, and the chapter is almost as long as the one you just finished.
- But many projects never need this kind of recording, and even without Chapter 9, this book is significantly longer than previous editions. So we put the chapter on the Web at www.greatsound.info. Keep this book handy when you go there; the site will ask you to enter a specific phrase from the text as proof of ownership.

Section IV

POSTPRODUCTION

One writer/producer I know loves every part of production except the last step: saying the film is done. He'd rather tweak edits and the track endlessly in postproduction, in search of absolute perfection. His clients and investors won't wait that long. He once told me, "A movie is never finished. It's just taken away."

This last section of the book is about getting the best audio in the least amount of postproduction time, so you can use whatever's left—before they take the project away—for additional creative tweaking.

The whole idea of "postproduction" originated in the glory days of Hollywood, where tasks were broken up so studios could crank out dozens of films simultaneously. Films were shot—that's *production*—and then edited and mixed in *post*production; then they were released from the assembly line.

These days post is anything you do after you've struck the set. It may include insert shots, new recording, computer-generated images, and a lot of other content creation. For some documentaries and commercials, the whole project is done with stock footage and computer graphics, so there's no production . . . only postproduction.

For many projects—and most feature films—postproduction consumes the most time, and it's usually the last chance for the filmmaker to exercise control. That's certainly true of the track: during production, it's hard enough just to capture intelligible dialog. Post is where you make that dialog sound natural, add the rest of the movie's environment, and put in the score.

This section includes chapters on the overall postproduction sequence, the hardware it needs, and the actual techniques involved for every step from digitizing to the final mix.

CHAPTER 10

Postproduction Workflow

ORGANIZING AND KEEPING TRACK OF AUDIO IN AN NLE

Very few films are edited "in the camera," taking shots that are just the right length and in the right order. There are a few kinds of video—such as legal depositions —that are shot in one continuous take with no editing at all. But every other project requires picture editing and soundtrack tweaking, and most of them involve quite a lot of it. When you have a good overview of this process, you can do it more efficiently.

Linear and nonlinear editing

The world is linear. Noon always comes one minute after 11:59 am. Productions are linear as well. Even interactive websites and menu-driven DVDs are built out of essentially linear sequences. Humans can't handle nonlinear time, so the very idea of nonlinear editing is an oxymoron.

The terms "linear" and "nonlinear" have nothing to do with whether a production is analog or digital. It refers to the timeline that a production is built on, and how much control we have over it. A few kinds of productions are handled better in a linear environment; most in nonlinear style. The decision of which to use has important implications for how sound is handled.

Linear editing

Linear editing was the standard for videotape production, until computers made it possible to edit full-resolution video on a hard drive.[1] In linear editing, the timeline is the master tape. Edits are made by playing precise sections of the original camera tape, while recording their picture in the right place on the master.

The timeline itself can't change: stuff at the two-minute mark always comes exactly one minute after the one-minute mark. (In nonlinear, you can pick up a sequence starting at 2:00, move it much later in the film, and make what *was* at 3:00 now happen at 2:00.) You can copy or erase things from the timeline and replace them with other shots from camera tapes, but you can't move pieces of the timeline itself.

Think of the images along the top of Figure 10.1 as the master tape, running from ten seconds to one minute, 50 seconds. We've copied a few scenes from the original location tapes along the bottom. We also left a space for a graphic title, between 40 seconds and one minute; we'll dub that when we get the title tape from the artist.

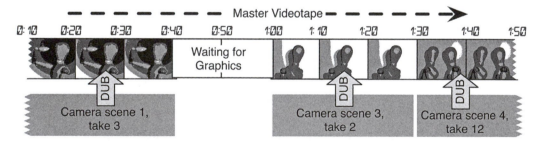

Figure 10.1 Linear editing: The show is assembled by dubbing scenes onto videotape . . . or by leaving precisely timed spaces where other scenes can be inserted.

---

[1] In the early days of nonlinear editing, hard drives weren't that big. So you made decisions while looking at low-res picture on a computer. Then went into an *on-line suite*, where you'd dub full-quality images from the camera tapes onto a master tape, using edit points you'd developed on the computer.

We can build a whole show this way ... and about for about 30 years that's exactly how we did, from the very first 2" black-and-white quad tapes[2] until computers got powerful enough to replace the process in the late 1990s.

The problem is that once something is on a linear timeline, it can't be moved. You can erase or record over a scene, but you can't nudge it a couple of frames without re-recording it. If everything in a show is perfect except the third shot is four frames too long, you can't cut out just those frames. You have to re-record the next shot four frames earlier, and—unless you care to lengthen something—you also have to re-record everything after it.

Analog audio for video was also usually linear. A timeline is one or two tracks on a multitrack tape, moving in lockstep with the video. Sounds are dubbed to the timeline from other tapes (or occasionally from other tracks on the same multitrack tape). Just like with linear video editing, you can dub to the timeline or erase pieces of it, but you can't move pieces of the timeline itself.

Nonlinear editing

Nonlinear revolutionized video production, starting with low-res systems in the late 1980s, but added only one new concept: the ability to pick up and move whole pieces of previously assembled timeline. This was a crucial difference.

In a *nonlinear editor* (NLE), all of the images are stored in a computer. While there's a timeline painted on the screen, the computer treats it like a database: an editable list that describes what part of the original scenes on its hard drive will be played back, and when they'll be shown. If you move scenes around, the NLE merely rearranges the database and repaints the timeline (Figures 10.2 and 10.3). Video isn't moved at all. Just a few bytes of data are involved, so it appears to happen instantly.

When the program is finished, complex effects are created by combining data from different places on the hard disk; then all the images are retrieved according to the database and either shown in real time and recorded to videotape, or rendered onto one large file.

The NLE's internal databases can even be thought of as linear: when you insert or rearrange a scene, the system copies part of the data list from hard drive, rearranges it, and then "dubs" it back. When you ask an NLE to print out an EDL (*Edit Decision List*), it's really just showing you a human-readable version of its internal database. There's more about EDLs at the end of this chapter.

---

[2] Quad tapes can be edited nonlinearly, with a razor blade and splicing tape, but it's enormously difficult, and most productions opted for building a show by dubbing onto a master instead. Quad was replaced by helical videotape in the late 1970s. It had a better picture, could do tricks like slow motion, and was both cheaper and more reliable. However, that format couldn't be edited with a blade at all, so people continued building their shows by dubbing. (*Quad* and *helical* are two very different ways of putting video information on a magnetic tape, but for editing purposes it boils down to what angle the head traces while writing or reading the signal.)

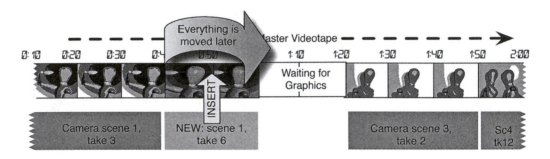

TIME	DATA	
00:00	Scene 1/3	frame 01
00:40	--	
01:00	Scene 3/2	fr
01:30	Scene 4/12	fr

Old database

New data inserted

TIME	DATA	
00:00	Scene 1/3	frame 01
00:40	Scene 1/6	frame 01
01:00	--	
01:20	Scene 3/2	frame 01
01:50	Scene 4/12	frame 01

Figure 10.2 Nonlinear editing is really just database management . . .

Everything is moved later

Master Videotape

0:10 0:20 0:30 0:4 0:50 1:10 1:20 1:30 1:40 1:50 2:00

INSERT

Waiting for Graphics

Camera scene 1, take 3

NEW: scene 1, take 6

Camera scene 3, take 2

Sc4 tk12

Figure 10.3 . . . though the result appears to be edited picture.

Nonlinear audio editing works just about the same way, with databases—often, one for each track—relating to sounds stored on hard disk. The counting system is more sophisticated than SMTPE frames, since most good systems count individual audio samples (at least 48,000 per second for video soundtracks).

In an audio editing system, effects such as reverb or compression can either modify clips on the hard drive while you're editing them, be noted with the clip for processing that clip during playback, or be noted for an entire track's worth of clips.

Linear versus nonlinear for video editing

The primary advantages of old-fashioned linear video editing are speed and simplicity. There's no time wasted on digitizing, file transfers, or rendering, so a long program with just a few edits can be put together in little more than the length of the show itself. The equipment is simple: all you need is one or more playback decks, a video recorder, and some way to control the decks and select the signal. The concept is even simpler—cue both decks and press Play on one while you press Record on the other[3]— even though it may take a lifetime to master the art involved.

---

[3] Okay, that's just the concept. To do this for real also involves preroll, synchronization, vertical-interval switching, and things like that. But an editing computer usually took care of this dirty work.

The primary disadvantage of linear editing *used to be* loss of quality. Each time an analog tape is copied, it picks up distortion and noise (see Chapter 2). But digital videotape and signal chains don't suffer from this. These days, the disadvantages of linear editing are the equipment cost and the time it takes to cue and record each individual edit.

Linear editing may be faster or slower than nonlinear. It depends on the project and the media.

- Linear wastes no time on "overhead." There's no need to ingest video, render, or dub a final project from the computer.
- But the edits themselves take place in real time, plus a few seconds each for cueing and locking.
- If a program is long and doesn't have many edits, linear editing will be faster. But if it's short and has complex sequences, nonlinear will be faster.

Linear's advantages on simple shows apply primarily when you're shooting and mastering on tape. The advantages tend to disappear if your entire workflow is totally file-based, slotting the camera's drives into the NLE, and delivering shows on DVD or the Web.

A form of linear editing is also used in live broadcasts of sporting events. Cameras are constantly recording to hard drive, and when there's an important play, that section of the drive is marked and played in slow motion. Even though this is done on a computer, there is no swapping or removing sections from scenes and the timeline stays intact.

The primary advantages to nonlinear video editing are that it's easy to make changes to a sequence, and the equipment can be small and inexpensive—all you need is a computer and possibly one recorder that will both play the original footage and record the finished show. (You also need accurate picture and sound monitoring, of course, for either linear or nonlinear editing.)

On the other hand, nonlinear systems have steep learning curves and are subject to setup and configuration troubles. Unless you're already an expert, or very lucky, or purchase a complete system with training, you'll find yourself facing mysterious blank frames, loss of lipsync, or other troubles—and you might not be able to tell whether it's your fault, the software's, or some incompatibility in the system.

Implications for audio

You have to pay more attention to audio during a linear editing session than during a nonlinear one.

- If dialog quality doesn't match across a cut, it may be almost impossible to correct later.
- Unless you have an automated mixer linked to the video editor, crossfades have to be done in real time by moving faders while you're watching the picture.
- Equalization and other corrections have to be applied on the fly, and you can't go back to change them without redoing the edit.

- You also need a clean audio path, with good wiring and a high-quality mixer. If there's a sound problem and you don't fix it immediately, you may have to live with it forever.

On the other hand, linear lets you hear problems as soon as they occur. And the most common audio problem with nonlinear editing—lost sync—almost never happens in a linear editing suite.

Nonlinear editing gives you more flexibility, but this can be a double-edged sword. While you've got the freedom to put off audio decisions during the visual editing process, this often translates to a carelessness regarding sound. There's a tendency for visually oriented producers to consider a project done when the pictures are finished, and blast through the audio mix without paying attention.

To make things worse, NLEs are often supplied with miniature monitors and set up in rooms with bad acoustics. Chapter 11 discusses some of the ways to help this, but with many NLE setups, the monitoring is so bad you couldn't do a good mix if you wanted to!

On the other hand, audio elements don't need to be copied or changed during the nonlinear process. There are fewer ways for their quality to be accidentally compromised. You have to get sounds accurately into the computer when you start the project (see Chapter 12); but once you've done that, you don't have to worry about them until it's time to concentrate on the track.

This means you can put off critical mix decisions until you have a chance to think about them, and you can move these decisions to a different editing station . . . or to a separate facility with good monitoring and control equipment.

AUDIO OPTIONS BEYOND THE NLE

Video-editing software is designed to manipulate pictures, and its audio capabilities— even on the big-name systems—are often minimal. You can add expensive processing plug-ins, but you'll still be limited by the NLE's software. Fortunately, the NLE keeps audio and video in separate files on the computer. Edited or raw audio can be exported in standard formats, and unless you've changed the volume or added effects, they don't lose any quality in the process. They can be processed or mixed elsewhere, and then get married back to the picture.

All this means you've got lots of choices for how to manipulate audio in a nonlinear environment.

Edit and mix within the NLE

This approach usually restricts you to editing on frame lines, which may be too far apart for precise audio edits. It also can limit what tools are available. NLEs come with a standard suite of equalizers, compressors, and reverb . . . but they're seldom as powerful as the ones that come in a *Digital Audio Workstation* (DAW), and their usefulness is limited by the NLE's clip-based architecture. Audio professionals also usually have large investments in third-party plug-ins, and big studios frequently have real-time rack equipment for manipulating sound.

On the other hand, keeping the audio inside the NLE is fast and simple, and you don't need to learn a new program.

Edit in the NLE's computer, but with a separate audio program

This choice gives you a lot more audio-editing power. It's also cheaper than buying a dedicated system: workable audio-only software costs just a few hundred dollars or may even be bundled with the NLE, and can share plug-in processors with it. Since both the audio editor and the NLE will be using the same drives, only a single set of files is necessary, and you don't have to worry about networking. Some NLE/audio combinations even have one-button transfers between programs.

However, both audio and video programs demand processing power and a lot of RAM, so it might not be possible to use them simultaneously. And using a separate audio program in your video-editing computer won't address problems you might have with audio monitoring and acoustics in a video edit room.

Edit/mix in a digital audio workstation

The *W* in DAW stands for workstation, which suggests there should be specialized hardware as well. Dedicated edit controllers with jog/shuttle wheels and buttons for common operations are available for most audio programs. More importantly, DAWs support multi-fader hardware surfaces for mixing. Having separate sliders for each of your important tracks is critical to a good mix, since you often need to have some fingers bringing tracks down while other fingers are raising different tracks, while you listen to how they all work in combination. You can't do this with a mouse, which only lets you move one control at a time.

High-end DAWs may also use dedicated, multiple digital signal processor (DSP) chips to do complex processing in real time. As host CPUs get faster this becomes less necessary, but some popular systems still require DSP to run their full version, and accessory DSP is sold to power effects processors in any system. At one time, the very best systems even had dedicated towers, running specialized operating systems that were essentially crash-proof. Competitive pressures forced most of these systems off the market—software that uses the buyer's general-purpose computer seems cheaper than software that requires you to buy a dedicated computer to run it—but that may have been a mistake. Most pro studios dedicate a computer (or two) to their audio editing anyway, and since the software-only systems run in general-purpose computer environments along with other programs, they're much more likely to crash.

Most professional DAWs can share file formats and removable drives with an NLE. In large facilities, audio- and video-editing systems are often networked together and communicate using Ethernet to a central server.

But the biggest advantage to working in a DAW may have nothing to do with the programs' capabilities. The major programs are expensive, require additional hardware for full operation, and can have a fairly steep learning curve. That might not sound like a benefit, but it means they're usually installed in rooms with good monitoring facilities and maintained by people who understand audio.

Free, or nearly-free, DAW options

Any filmmaker can expand their audio options with little or no investment. These two programs won't give you the capabilities of a good DAW (or even of the multitrack audio programs sometimes bundled with NLEs), but they are a significant improvement over doing audio in your video software. Both these programs run on Windows, Mac, or Linux.

Audacity (audacity.sourceforge.net, Figure 10.4) is a free, open-source multitrack editor. The interface can be confusing, it doesn't support video, and it takes longer to do some important operations . . . but you can't beat the price. It also does some useful things that most commercial software can't, including flexible handling of multichannel production audio files, and displaying waveforms in decibels or frequency as well as the standard envelope graphs. Everybody should have a copy.

Reaper (www.cockos.com/reaper, Figure 10.5) is a complete multichannel DAW with mix automation, sophisticated routing, video and MIDI support. It supports many of the features of a full studio DAW costing thousands of dollars, though some important ones require third-party additions or can be slow and hard to use. On the other hand, a full license costs as little $60 for non-commercial and low-budget film users, and $225 for everybody else. A 60-day trial is free: unless you've already got a DAW, it's definitely worth doing.

Moving your project between NLE and DAW

At their deepest level, virtually all NLEs and multitrack audio programs work the same: a database keeps track of clips, organized by tracks, in a timeline. Here's a quick review:

- A *clip* is usually a segment of a standard-format file on a local hard drive, identified as between two timecodes or audio samples. But it can also be a still image, or a title or effect rendered on the fly, or a combination of other clips. It usually appears on the screen as a row of still images or an audio envelope.
- A *track* is a subcategory in the database that shows clips in a horizontal row on the screen, and may be treated as a single source that can be routed to mixers or processors. Multiple tracks can play different clips at the same time. If there's no clip on the track at a given moment, it doesn't use any storage space and doesn't create an output. Tracks are usually used in NLEs just for organizing sources (multiple cameras, titles, inputs for keys, and so on). They're more powerful in DAWs, letting you assign groups of processors that will affect every clip on a track, and route to groups and submixes. They're also more prevalent in a DAW, where a single project might have 60 or 70 individual tracks.[4] While NLEs

---

[4] They don't all make noise at once.

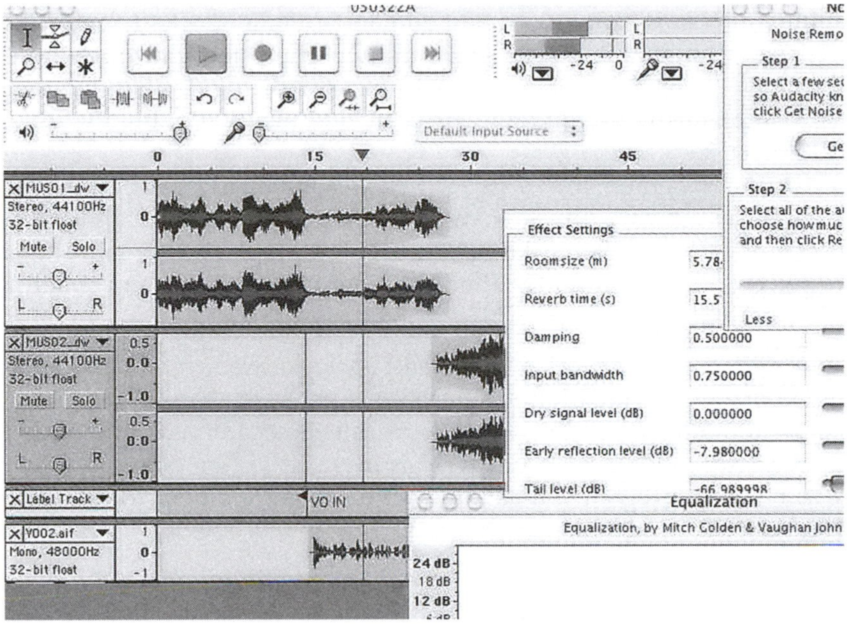

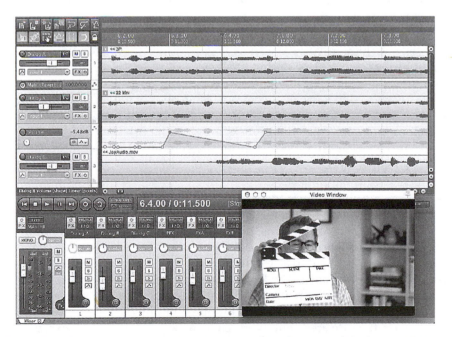

Figure 10.4 Audacity is a free, open-source audio editor that does a lot of sound chores better than your NLE.

Figure 10.5 Reaper manages to include many of the features of the biggest DAWs, for as little as $60.

usuallyapply crossfades between two clips on a single track, DAW users often spread crossfading sources across two tracks for control. A film's dialog might have more than a dozen tracks just for dialog, broken by character or technical treatment, even if only one character speaks at a time. More about this in Chapter 13.

- The *timeline* is a graph: tracks are stacked as horizontal bars of thumbnail images or audio waveforms; time—in timecode, musical bars, or other convenient measurement—runs along the horizontal. The graph is interactive, in that you can move clips around on the timeline. Your changes are immediately reflected in the database.

Clips might be called *segments* or *events*; some software refers to tracks as *lanes*; and the times actually recorded in the database might be in samples rather than what's displayed on the screen, but the point is that all these different programs organize their data in pretty much the same way. This means it's often possible to transfer the actual edits between programs. It can be a lot more flexible than transferring just the final audio or video product.

Importing by track

The most basic way to move a project from NLE to DAW is to render it out as finished picture and track in a standard file format. Just about every program can understand .avi or QuickTime for video, and .wav or AIFF for audio; there are plenty of translation utilities for the few that can't. Of course, if a project's track has already been rendered, there's not much about it that you can change or fix. It's far better to move individual tracks or clips, so long as you have some way to make sure the audio program keeps everything in the proper place on the timeline.

The most basic of these interchanges is necessary when the audio software and the video software don't speak a common language. Standard practice is to put a cueing mark (a flash-frame or beep) at the head of every track in the NLE, and then export each as a separate file. These tracks are then imported to the DAW as separate tracks, synchronized by their cues, and processed and mixed as desired. The mix is rendered as a single audio file with the beeps intact, which is then sent back to the NLE for inclusion in the project.

If the clips are slid on their tracks until all the beeps are in sync, the material will stay in sync unless there's a major error. This works even if the audio and video programs are on separate computers, in separate cities, running software from separate publishers. It works even if one of the computers' clocks is off-speed. That's because every piece of audio is timed to a specific number of samples, and every piece of video to a specific number of frames. We know how many frames or samples are in a single second, so it's easy to do the math that determines which chunk of audio will line up against which picture. That off-speed computer might play the entire film a little slower or faster than desired, but every element will be moved in exactly the same proportion.

If the audio and video files are going to be made or played in separate devices—perhaps a videotape or DVD for the picture, while the sound stays in a computer—timecode is used to make sure they start together. Audio is told to start playing its files on the exact moment when video reaches a specific frame. But timecode doesn't guarantee long-term sync.[5] Subtle variations in the machines' crystals can add up to large errors by the end of a show. In this case, it's necessary for both the audio equipment and the video equipment to share a common clock reference, which is usually either *blackburst* (a continuous stream of empty TV frames) or an *audio word clock* (continuous stream of blank audio samples).

A variation on this technique involves dubbing the picture to a videotape or DVD instead of rendering it to a file. This is handy for long projects, where a video file might be too large to conveniently handle, or in sophisticated audio facilities where video is often run from a separate tape deck or computer. In these cases, both timecode and blackburst (Chapter 11) will probably be necessary to keep things in sync ... though I'll admit at times I've been lucky and was able to sync computer files to a consumer DVD player and other non-stable sources.

While importing complete tracks as audio files has the advantages of being generally foolproof and universal, there are disadvantages. It can generate very big files, since the tracks require the same amount of data whether they're actually carrying sounds or being silent. (Lossless compression, discussed in Chapter 2, can resolve this problem.)

A bigger disadvantage is that edits from the NLE are locked when you render the audio file. Even though the DAW has finer resolution, you can't trim or move an existing edit point. Even though the DAW can adjust its own fades to last any length between a hard cut and any arbitrary number of samples, you're stuck with hard cuts or pre-built fades of at least one frame long. You can't move an edit a few milliseconds to where it's less apparent, and you can't grab roomtone from the parts of a clip that were thrown away in the video suite. These are fairly standard things to do when sweetening a soundtrack. Fortunately, they're supported by more standard ways of moving between NLE and DAW.

Interchange formats

Both the NLE and the audio software are actually just managing databases, so in theory you should be able to translate the data—and timeline—from one program to another. You could:

- Copy just the data, making a very efficient edit list that includes the track and frame number where a clip should be played, the source file and frame number within that file where it should start playing, and the length. Just a few kilobytes would describe a whole production, assuming that both the NLE and DAW had access to the same source files.

---

[5] It used to. When everything was analog, timecode was used to control the speed of the audio deck as well as its cueing and playback. Digital, unfortunately, doesn't allow that kind of control.

- Copy the data along with the source files, so they can be moved to another computer. This means a much bigger interchange file, but also makes the project completely portable.
- Copy the data with just the *relevant sections* of the source files. If part of an original take isn't being used in the final edit, it doesn't get copied. This is a good compromise between efficiency and portability. You can also specify that the source sections you're copying are a few seconds bigger than what's actually used, starting slightly before the in-point and ending slightly after the out-point. These *handles* can make it possible to refine an edit in the new software, or capture ambiences from before or after a line of dialog. With a sophisticated system, you can even specify that relative volumes or fades from the NLE get translated to the DAW. But they're done non-destructively, as instructions for the fade rather than volume changes within the file itself. This lets an audio operator change or extend the fades if desired. In many cases the DAW can also do a technically cleaner fade than the NLE, by using more bits in the math.

That, in a nutshell, is the basis of all current interchange systems. The advantages are obvious. The disadvantage is that things can go wrong:

- If the database isn't properly translated, you can lose sync between one program and another. Clips don't appear with the right picture, and clips that are supposed to play at the same time might be offset from each other. This can happen even in otherwise working interchanges, if the timecode formats don't match (Chapter 12).
- Since audio data is just being copied, rather than rendered or re-formatted, the target program has to understand the source program's formats. This isn't always automatic—some programs have different ways of handling stereo and multichannel audio, and some can't mix sample rates or formats the way others can. If one program also sends automation data for equalizers or other effects, the receiving program has to have matching processors; otherwise the result can be unpredictable.
- Something has to guarantee that all the files get transferred from one computer to the other, and that the necessary files can be found. An edited soundtrack can involve hundreds of individual files on the timeline, and filenames and paths are handled slightly differently in Mac and Windows, so there are places this can go wrong.

Consolidating solves this last problem by combining the database and all of the audio samples into one giant transfer file. These files can get very big—in the Gigabytes for a long or complicated show—so they might run into operating system or transfer restrictions. It's also inefficient to keep copying all the media every time there's an edit change in an ongoing project.

OMF, AAF, and their brothers
The most common interchange format between NLEs and DAWs is *Open Media Framework* (OMF; sometimes called OMFI; the extra letter stands for *Interchange*). It can

be used with consolidated media or with links to separately copied files. Most software also lets you specify handle length when making an OMF file, and whether other functions—such as fades drawn on the timeline—will get included on the database.

OMF was developed by Avid and Digidesign (now one company), but the details were published for other companies to use, and now most audio and video software supports this format. However, it is proprietary, and versions in different programs can have incompatibilities. Sometimes, manufacturers make changes in their OMF routines from one software generation to the next, so files or combinations of software that might have worked in one version don't work in the next. Recently Avid and Digidesign started promoting *Advanced Authoring Format* (AAF) as a more reliable interchange. While it's also published, it's also proprietary and subject to the same manufacturer's variations as OMF. Most of today's DAWs can speak AAF as well.

> Bottom line: even if two programs are OMF or AAF compatible, you should test the interchange with actual program material and edits before starting a big project.[6] Many audio post facilities also publish specific AAF or OMF instructions on their websites, or will talk you through the procedure.

There are also internationally standardized non-proprietary interchanges, such as *AES31* (from the Audio Engineering Society), but these aren't implemented by a lot of manufacturers.

AATranslator

Fortunately there's a Rosetta Stone: a translation program that converts one interchange format to another, or even turns obscure project files into something your DAW prefers. AATranslator is a fast and reasonably priced utility ($60–200, depending on which proprietary formats are included) that seems to accommodate every audio and video program released in the past ten years. Figure 10.6 shows part of a grid listing its current capability; the publisher, www.aatranslator.com.au, keeps up with manufacturer changes and issues frequent updates. If you work with a variety of editors or sound people, it's worth having around.

EDL

The most basic way of moving edit instructions from one system to another is the *Edit Decision List* (EDL). This is only data about which clips go where, in a text file that can be read by humans as well as by software, and doesn't include the actual source audio or video. In fact, EDLs grew out of the original online systems that put source material on multiple analog videotape decks, and reflect the way those systems' text-only displays looked to the operator.

---

[6] I insist on testing every time I start a new relationship with a picture editor, and whenever the editor has changed their software. These tests are important, and most professionals won't charge for the time it involves.

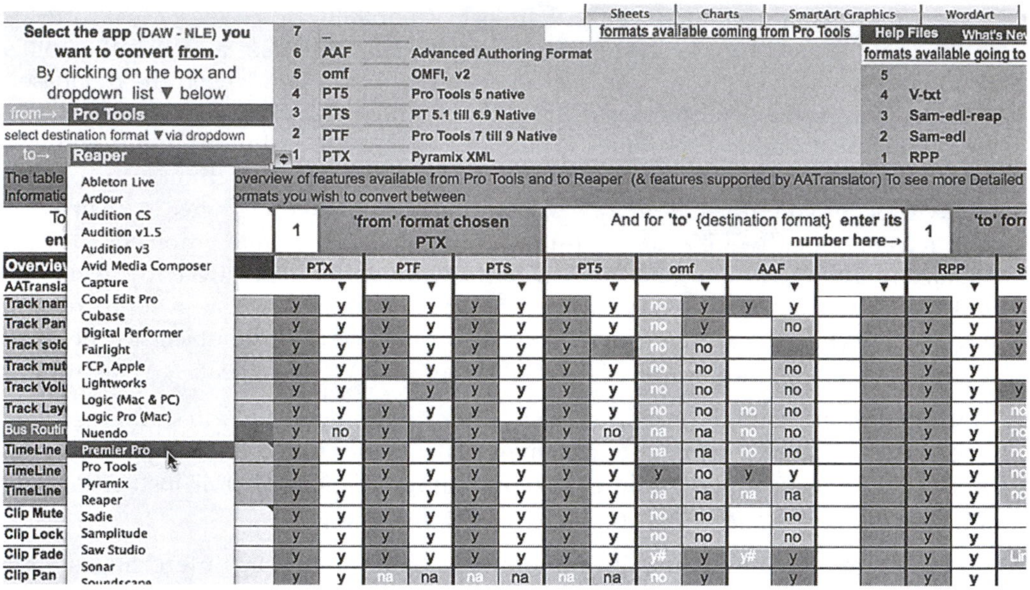

Figure 10.6 AATranslator handles proprietary audio and timeline interchange between most programs.

Most NLEs can generate an EDL. Because they are so basic and easy to understand, EDLs are often used as a reality check and debugging aid when more complicated interchange formats fail. Some software can also read an EDL and automatically assemble the edits it describes.

A typical entry in an EDL looks like this:

```
001 AX AAV C 00:00:00:00 00:00:44:07 01:00:07:04 01:00:51:11
* FROM CLIP NAME: TIM_OC_11.MOV
* COMMENT:
```

The first column (001) is the edit number, usually reading sequentially from the start of the timeline, but sometimes displaying the order in which the operator actually performed the edits. The next characters (AX) are the source of video in the edit, originally a videotape reel number; in modern systems it's usually AX for Auxiliary with the clip name appearing below. The third column (AAV) describes which tracks are affected; in this case, two Audio tracks and a Video track. The fourth column (C) is the type of edit: this entry stands for Cut; it could be D for Dissolve or other codes depending on the system.

The next four columns are timecode in hours:minutes:seconds:frames. In most formats, the first two are the in- and out- points where the clip will appear on the timeline; the second two are in- and out-points for what part of the clip is taken.

An EDL may look daunting at first, but after you've seen a couple they make perfect sense . . . and can occasionally be the best way to fix a bad edit or restore a garbled clip.

Film vs. video workflows

That subheading is misleading. Today there's very little difference between film and video production, other than how the image is stored. Major movies are shot and edited as high-definition video, and the overwhelming majority are now sent to theaters on hard drives or via satellite or fiber: *digital cinema*. Even features shot on film and released as prints are likely to have an electronic stage—*digital intermediate*—for effects and color correction. Just a few years ago one of the last manufacturers of 35mm film, Fuji, was running ads to insist certain scenes could be captured only on film: not necessarily their film, but just the idea of film rather than video. In 2013, Fuji announced they wouldn't be making movie film any more.[7]

(Exactly what is "film", anyway? Obviously, it's the flexible stuff with holes in the side that goes through a camera or projector. But consider this phrase from the previous paragraph: "Even features shot on film . . . " It could be written as "Even *films* that are *filmed* on *film*"—the first two uses of the word would still be correct for digital productions.)

While the physical medium is changing, many of the systems and workflows invented during 35mm's near-century reign as the serious way to tell a visual story are still used in this digital era. That's because, on a large project, they can make sense. Knowing how they work—and what you can borrow—can also make sense on smaller projects.

This was a revelation for me a dozen years ago, since I'm an East Coaster who normally works on TV shows and large sponsored projects; that is, "video." Then I had a chance to sound design a decently budgeted theatrical feature.

The team approach

In the video world where I grew up, it's not unusual for one person to handle almost every aspect of audio post—editing, sweetening, processing, and mixing (occasionally, that person is also director of photography and visual editor). But Hollywood sound evolved in a factory-like studio system. Hierarchies and strict job descriptions made sense in the assembly-line atmosphere of a large studio.

Even today, most audio post engineers in Los Angeles are extreme specialists. One person might be a dialog editor, while someone else cuts music. Some people just record foley; others are known for their narration recordings. King of the movie sound hill is the re-recording mixer, who's responsible for the ultimate balance and final

---

[7] There will always be a small quantity of 35mm film being manufactured, as long as some high-budget producers are willing to pay for it on certain features. What's significant is that the films' publicists now brag "we're shooting film!", the way they bragged about shooting high-def video a few years ago.

sound of a film. And even these mixers often concentrate on dialog, while assistants are mixing the music or effects.

In fact there may be platoons of people doing specific sound tasks on a big feature. With an army this big, predictability and order become important. The shortcuts you develop working by yourself in a New York studio might make perfect sense, save time, and result in a better track for less money. But they can be liabilities on a Hollywood feature . . . if the next person down the line can't figure out what you did.

For example, sound-for-video people often cut and tweak dialog linearly. If a phrase is garbled or badly read, you can reach for an alternate take or build one from syllables. If something wants noise reduction, it gets that processing immediately. If two shots have to be equalized to match each other, equalize and it's done. Add the music and effects, then move onto the next scene.

That's not the Hollywood way. First, dialog editors get tracks from the picture editor, as edit lists to be conformed or as digital audio files. But even though these tracks have already been cut to picture in an NLE, there's still a lot to do. A simple scene with three characters, filmed as a master shot with a couple of close-ups, will probably have a single dialog track in the NLE. The first thing the dialog editor does is break it up into three or more tracks, splitting by character or by camera setup, so that different room tones and voice characteristics are on separate channels and can be treated differently at the mix. Any problem with the dialog is noted, fixed using syllables from alternate takes if possible, or listed for consideration as ADR. Door slams and other useful noises recorded with the dialog are separated onto an effects track, to make mixing easier. Then each of these dozens of dialog clips is extended, with matching roomtone that was separately recorded or copied from pauses in the performance, so there are short overlaps between them. There's more about these techniques in Chapter 13.

Multiply this short scene by the length of a movie, and the dialog editor has a lot to do. But it's important, and producers are willing pay for this step, because prepping the dialog properly can make a big difference in how clean and professional it sounds in a theater. In fact, these same techniques can help difficult scenes in less ambitious videos.

Another advantage to the Hollywood workflow is that the dialog editors never deal with equalization, noise reduction, or overall levels. They don't need to spend money on high-quality monitors or advanced plug-ins. Even in one-person productions, treating dialog editing as a separate process means it can be taken away from the studio and done on a laptop with headphones, at the kitchen table or on an airplane.

On smaller productions, of course, it's often appropriate to do some processing to specific clips during the dialog edit. This can be the only way to hear if a noisy line can be cleaned up, or if borderline problems will require ADR. But if you find yourself doing this kind of pre-processing, take a tip from the people mixing Hollywood dialog: keep an unprocessed version of the same clip on a separate track, so the process can be removed or adjusted during the final mix. In fact, most re-recording mixers won't even work with dialog that's had processing, unless those unprocessed *mirror tracks* are also available.

ORGANIZING POSTPRODUCTION AUDIO

Polish the video first. It's silly to try to fine-tune a soundtrack if the picture isn't finished. Audio moves in continuous sweeps rather than individual images, so trivial picture edits may require large segments of track to be rebuilt. Audio edits can also help smooth over abrupt picture cuts. Ideally, you won't start on the track until the picture is locked.[8]

However, don't put off *thinking* about the soundtrack until after the picture is done . . . by then, it's too late to do a good job. There's a definite order to approaching a picture edit, if you want the best track with the least amount of bother:

1. Decide which visual sequences will be driven by non-sync audio, and make sure you have the necessary elements (music for montages, voice-over, and so on).
2. Edit the picture, along with its dialog or any non-sync audio that drives it. If you can't edit the sound smoothly, create your own handles in the NLE by putting the audio across alternating tracks and adding a few seconds of extra sound at the in- and out-points (Figure 10.7). These can be used later for correcting sound problems and fixing transitions.
3. Drop in any sounds that are necessary for plot development, such as phone bells, explosions, and off-camera dialog. Do this before committing to a final picture

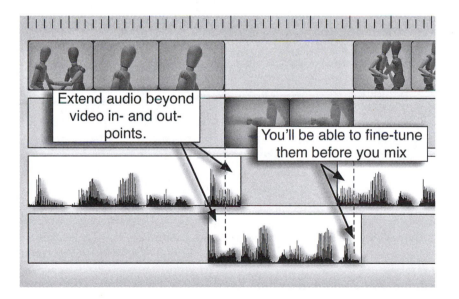

Figure 10.7 Create your own "handles" in the NLE, so you can manually improve an abrupt edit.

---

[8] Very few projects meet the ideal of a locked picture before audio post.

edit: these effects take time, and you might have to extend or shorten a scene to accommodate them. But don't obsess about sounds themselves. If something isn't perfect, use what you've got as a placeholder and plan to change it later.

4. Get the necessary approvals for the video, make any required changes, and lock the picture. Make sure everyone involved understands that from now on, any picture changes that affect timing—even by one frame—will also affect the cost or complexity of the track.[9]

5. Fine-tune the audio elements. There's also a definite order that makes this more efficient (see "Audio priorities" on the next page).

6. Mix the track and get it approved.

7. Finish the job: layback the track to videotape, add it to the QuickTime or .avi, or import it back to the nonlinear editor for final rendering in a file format.

Titles and other visual effects can be added at the same time the sound is being finished, if they won't have any effect on sync. Obviously, visual effects that are linked to sounds—explosions, flames, or a laser whoosh as the title is revealed—must either be in place before the final mix, or be animated to their sound.

Dealing with non-sync audio

It's important to have voice-overs and music available before you start cutting, because they influence how the picture is edited. But it's not important to have the same ones you'll use in the final mix.

Scratch tracks

Many producers prefer not to record the voice-over of a long project until the picture is fully cut, because any script changes may require another recording session. Sometimes you don't even know what has to be changed until the picture is edited.

But without a narration track, it's difficult to cut the picture. You have to guess how long each line of script will take, and edit in a sterile environment with no audio reference. This is extra work both for the video editor, and also for a narrator who'll then have to read each line to an arbitrary timing.

Instead, record a temporary narration track in your own voice. Quality isn't important—you can use a cheap multimedia mic, and record right at your editing station. What *is* important is that you speak slowly and meaningfully, simulating the pace you'll want from the professional narrator. Edit precisely to the scratch track, and feel free to place key visual cues and titles to fit your own reading. Chances are they'll still line up against the high-priced talent's version.

Besides, if your client approves a project hearing your amateur narration, think of how blown away they'll be when they hear a professional doing the job.

---

[9] All of the projects that don't meet the ideal of locked picture in footnote 8, end up paying for it here.

Temporary music

Hollywood editors often use a *temp track*: borrowing a piece of a pop song or even some other film score, and cutting montages and other music-driven sequences to it. When the final score is created, the composer or music supervisor uses the temp as a guide for tempo and feel. Occasionally a director falls so much in love with the temporary music that they buy the rights to it and use it in the finished film.

Unless you're dealing with Hollywood budgets, however, it's not a good idea to borrow copyrighted music this way. If someone falls in love with the piece, you'll have to tell them they can't afford the rights (copyright law doesn't forgive infringements just because "Hollywood does it"). More importantly, it's easy to get so used to hearing a particular piece of music that nothing else—no matter how good—will sound right.

Sometimes you can use a rough version of the actual music you're planning to use. If the video is going to have an original score, get the composer to throw together a demo of the scene's music. If you're buying library music, select the pieces for that scene before you start editing. Don't worry about the roughness of a demo or problems with specific aspects of the library cut; you can fine-tune after the picture is edited. In the meantime, you'll have the right feel and rhythm to cut against, and you won't have to worry about client disappointment in the final mix.

Audio priorities

Once the picture is cut, it's most efficient to approach the remaining audio operations in a definite order:

1. Edit the dialog first. It tells the story. Take advantage of cutaways and extreme wide shots, when lips aren't visible on the screen, to smooth out a performance or fit in alternates to garbled or badly performed words.

2. Edit the narration and voice-over—if there is any—second. It explains what we're seeing. If you've been using a scratch narration track, now's the time to replace it with the real thing. Chapter 13 has some tips on both narration and dialog editing.

3. Place any plot-critical sound effects, or replace any temporary plot effects that were added during the picture edit. Ignore smaller sync effects for now; you might not need to waste time on them after music and ambiences are in place.

Here the workflows for theatrical features and smaller video projects—even network documentaries—are slightly different. That's for practical as well as creative reasons.

4a. If this is a smaller project, insert the music now. If you're using library cuts, trim them to length. It doesn't take much effort or

4b. If this is a theatrical feature with a custom score, the music mix might not be finished until very late in the soundtrack process. But since

musical talent to stretch or shorten a piece of music seamlessly (Chapter 14 teaches you how).

the dialog and effects in a narrative feature are considered the characters' reality, it's appropriate to build those non-musical elements before the score. So skip directly to the next step.

5. Add background ambiences. On a smaller project or if time and budget are limited, don't do this until you've added the music. In a lot of films and videos, music can take the place of ambience.

6. Add whatever smaller sync effects seem to be missing. A lot of times, you'll find that a random noise from an ambience track can be nudged a few frames to take the place of a sync effect.

7a. If this is a very small project (say, a commercial or short Web piece), or one driven almost entirely by narration, mix the tracks into a single master. You might need to start and stop, or go back over certain scenes, but there's no reason not to handle voice, effects, and music at the same time.

7b. If this piece has dramatic elements or a lot of different voices (like a documentary), pre-mix the dialog first. Make sure it's smooth and natural, even in the transitions between voices.

   Then mix the sound effects so they belong to the characters' world, and add the music.

8. Review the mix! If possible, take a break—or even come back another day—and then play the entire film without interruption. Keep notes about things you might want to change in the mix, but don't stop the playback during this review. It's important to judge the entire project, top to bottom, the way an audience will see it. Then make any changes. Note that with most workstations, you haven't really created a mix yet. What you've done is programmed your fader moves, effects settings, and other audio options into an automation database. That's why you can still make changes in the mix easily . . . all you'll be changing is the automation values.

9. Render the automated mix to the final delivery format—usually an AIFF or .wav file—and dub to the delivery medium. Depending on the DAW and complexity of the mix, this might take as long as a real-time pass through the show.

10. Render *stems:* mixes of the show that have only the dialog, only the effects, or only the music. These will be handy if you have to make revisions later, and are required by many network and film distribution contracts.

Mixing and editing are separate functions

Modern DAWs can handle editing and mixing almost simultaneously. You can start mixing a sequence, notice a dialog glitch or misplaced effect and fix it immediately, and then continue mixing where you left off. You can also begin mixing a scene, decide that you don't like one particular crossfade or level, rewind to where the problem began, and start mixing again. The system will join the various parts of the mix seamlessly. These are great conveniences . . . but only if you don't take advantage of them too often.

While the computer lets you develop a mix in pieces, it's not a good idea from a human point of view. Audio develops over time. Your viewers will watch the scene as a continuous whole, and it's almost always best to mix it the same way. There's more about mixing in Chapter 17.

CHAPTER 11

Postproduction Hardware

☞ **ROSE'S RULES**

- The tools you use for editing video can permanently affect your sound. Don't try audio fixes in your NLE, unless you're sure the project will never go to a DAW.[1]
- When you set up an edit system, paying attention to detail is more important than spending a lot of money.
- The most important audio equipment you'll ever own is the monitor system. If you don't get this right, your film will suffer.

Want to buy some equipment? My studio has digital multitrack and DAT decks (all with timecode); racks of high-end analog and digital equalizers, noise reducers, compressors, and reverbs; three different kinds of broadcast video decks, including a hard disk video server; a 32-input digital console with extensive processing on every channel; and enough switching and routing equipment to build a small station. Ten years ago I used this equipment every day. Today, most of it doesn't even get turned on. I edit in a computer using a keyboard and mouse. I mix in the same computer using a fader panel that, as far as the computer is concerned, is just a few more specialized mice.

(I've also got excellent speakers and acoustic treatment, by the way. They're not for sale.)

---

[1] And even if you're sure, hold the audio fixes off until the last moment.

The point isn't that I make lousy investments.[2] It's that over the past few years, building a workable audio facility has gotten a lot easier. Of course the full-fledged theatrical mix suites still require major investments and racks full of specialized equipment. But smaller setups can get by with a lot less.

Just remember: you can't do it all with software. At the very least, you need reliable audio monitors and a way to calibrate them. If you're also going to use this system for input and output—that is, if you'll be bringing in some of your elements on tape or with a live mic, or delivering on some medium other than raw data—you may also need some decks, routing and control equipment, and audio wiring.

But even the simplest installation requires your attention. The time you spend here will have a direct influence on how good your finished film can be.

MONITORING

The quality of a monitoring system doesn't directly change anything in your soundtrack. Signals don't pass through your speakers on their way to a viewer. But they do pass through those speakers on the way to your brain ... which makes them the most important audio equipment you can own. The speakers you've chosen affect every other sound decision you make.

But before you buy new or better monitors, take a look around your editing room. The room itself can have as much of an influence on the sound as the speakers.

Editing room acoustics: When good speakers go bad

Figure 11.1 You wouldn't edit picture on a screen like this. Are you doing something similar to your sound?

You're ready to edit your magnum opus. You put up color bars and adjust the monitor so everything is mellow pinks or shocking green. Then you smear grease on the screen, splash some white paint around the edges, and—just for good measure—tilt it to catch the glare from a nearby window (Figure 11.1).

Maybe that's not how you work on pictures, but I've seen a lot of editing rooms where that's how they approach the track. Badly positioned speakers—in some cases, they don't even face the operator —interact with the room's walls. The combination actually blurs the sound. If any attention is paid to speaker choice

---

[2] Actually, all this equipment has paid for itself. I reserve my lousy investments for the stock market.

☞ ROSE'S RULES

Flattery, in a speaker, gets you less than nothing . . . it fools you into making bad decisions. Unfortunately, most consumer speakers are designed to be flattering rather than accurate.

at all, rather than just buying what's on sale, it results in units that *sound good* instead of being *honest*.

It's not hard to set up a good listening environment and choose good speakers. It just requires a little thought and some elementary physics.

As you learned in Chapter 1, echoes in a room interfere with a sound in ways that aren't immediately obvious. You don't hear them as reverberation, but they cancel and reinforce different frequencies in your mix, affecting its color or timbre. Furthermore, the effect can change drastically, depending on where you are in the room:

In many desktop environments, what you hear directly in front of the video monitor is different from what your client hears, sitting two feet away.

You can't fix this with an equalizer, since you can't equalize differently for every position in the room. You can't even equalize it for just the editing position: the affected frequencies are usually too close together for an equalizer to pick out, and moving your head six inches changes them.

Soft and hard

The best solution is careful room design. By calculating how different wavelengths will cancel or reinforce, you can plan room dimensions to smooth out the sound. If you're building a new studio from scratch, get a book on acoustics.[3] Learn how simple changes in the floor plan make tremendous differences to the sound.

But if it's too late to move the walls, you can still use basic acoustic science to correct a bad-sounding room. You've already learned some of the ways: the techniques in Chapter 6 that improve sound on location, also work for editing rooms. Substitute your chair for the microphone, and the monitor speakers for the actors. Of course, an editing or mixing suite is a bit more permanent than a shoot. So it's worth investing a little time in even better solutions.

Homemade sound eater

Luxury postproduction facilities have posh treatments and careful acoustic design. Even my mixing suite—a much more modest effort—boasts carefully chosen dimensions

---

[3] I recommend Mike Shea and F. Alton Everest's *How to Build a Small Budget Recording Studio from Scratch* (McGraw-Hill, most recently updated in 2012). Lots of practical ideas, not too much math.

and non-parallel walls. Unfortunately, the nonlinear editing suites in television stations, corporate environments, and kitchen-table production companies tend to be random rooms with mostly bare walls. Absorption is almost always needed to make these rooms sound good.

You can get studio-quality absorbers and diffusers from acoustic consultants. They'll measure your space, take careful acoustic surveys, and plan exactly what's needed in terms of stock and custom components to make the room sound excellent. It'll be expensive. Or you can spend a little less and get pre-assembled kits from studio suppliers: one of their clerks will put together a generic package of their stock products, based on dimensions you enter on a website. It'll probably be an improvement over what the room sounds like now, though in my experience, rooms treated this way never sound great.

Or you can build a set of efficient fiberglass absorbers for not much money at all, using only minimal carpentry skills, and put them up using some simple rules of thumb. Chances are it'll sound better than the generic package.

The key is to use the right kind of fiberglass. Owens-Corning type 703 is a semi-rigid yellow board designed for thermal and sound control. It's much denser than the fluffy pink stuff sold for home insulation. It's been the standard for professional studio construction for decades. A carton of 48 square feet, in 2′ × 4′ by 2″ thick panels, is about $70 at acoustic suppliers, ceiling contractors, and big online retailers. Three cartons should be plenty for a small editing room. (But before you place the order, do a sketch. Don't forget the lesson on page 81.)

Figure 11.2 shows the basic construction. The size of each absorber isn't critical, though of course it's easiest if you stick to multiples of 2′ × 4′ and don't have to cut the panels. Figure enough absorbers, next to each other, to make a stripe around the sides and rear of your editing area. The stripe should start a couple of feet below ear level when you're working, to a couple of feet above (if you edit sitting down, that's about 2′ 6″ to 4′ 6″).

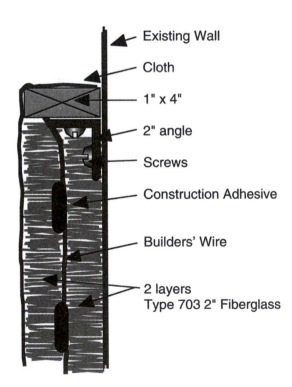

Existing Wall

Cloth

1" x 4"

2" angle

Screws

Construction Adhesive

Builders' Wire

2 layers
Type 703 2" Fiberglass

Figure 11.2
How a basic, low-cost wall-mounted absorber goes together.

Tiny scraps of fiberglass can fly around during construction, so wear long sleeves[4] while you do the following:

1. Build a rectangular frame out of 1′ × 4′ pine, cut to fit the wall area. Attach it to the wall using a couple of small angle brackets on each side.
2. Lay a piece of 2″ thick #703 inside, cut to fit the frame. Friction should hold it in place while you work. Secure the fiberglass with a few lengths of galvanized builders' wire stapled to the inside of the frame.
3. Stick another layer of #703 on top of the first piece. A few dabs of construction adhesive will keep it from sliding around.
4. Cover the whole thing with decorative cloth, burlap, or even brightly printed bed sheets. In commercial buildings, you'll want flame-retardant cloth, available from upholstery suppliers for a few dollars more per yard than the stuff that burns.

One-by-four pine is less than four inches wide—it's one of those ancient lumber-yard traditions—so four inches of fiberglass will be slightly thicker than the frame. If you don't like the way this bulges the cloth, use wood cut to an exact width. If you want a more professional appearance, replace the top layer of fiberglass and cloth with foam tiles.[5] The tiles don't absorb much better than the fiberglass does, but they look good, and their shape provides a tiny amount of diffusion at high frequencies. Figure 11.3 shows how it looks in my studio, with one tile removed so you can see the builders' wire and #703 underneath.

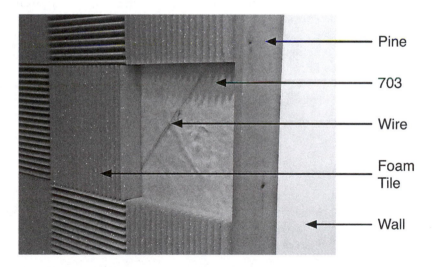

Figure 11.3 Absorber with one tile removed to show construction.

---

[4] If you're allergic, grab some eye protectors and a disposable breathing mask at your local drug store. I've never bothered with them.

[5] Available from audiovisual suppliers. I used 12″ × 12″ × 2″ fire-rated charcoal gray wedge tiles from Parts-Express.com, about $4 each.

Adding more diffusion to a room is even easier: a few shelves filled with random-size books or tape boxes does an excellent job.

The nearfield solution

The other way to conquer room acoustics relies on the inverse-square law: if a sound has to travel twice as far, it becomes four times softer. Make the speaker-to-ear distance significantly less than the wall-to-ear, and echoes will be less important.

That's the secret behind *nearfield monitors*, the square boxes you often see perched on top of the console in recording studios. These speakers are very close to the engineers' ears, so the engineer hears a lot more of them than of the reflections off walls. Nearfields have only a couple of problems:

- By definition, only a small area can be within the "near" field. So the monitors are effective in only one place. Unless you all sit very closely together, the producer, editor, and director or client will hear something totally different.
- It's next to impossible to get a good sound out of a box that's small enough to fit on the top of a console. Typical cube and small bookshelf speakers are notorious for distortion and limited bandwidth.

One high-tech solution is to integrate smallish speakers with a precisely calibrated amplifier. But it takes a lot of engineering and expensive components to do this right, and the professional versions that actually sound good can cost a few thousand dollars per pair, much more than equivalent full-size monitors. More modestly priced speaker/amplifier combos—those for a couple of hundred dollars—are often full of compromises that cause uneven response at various frequencies, and distortion at both ends of the band. Speakers like this aren't suitable for professional mixing. Low-cost amplified "multimedia" speakers, even those costing as much as $200 a pair, may offer pleasing sounds for gaming or listening to mp3s—but can lead to awful video mixes. And unless your viewers are listening on the same model speakers, the results will be unpredictable.

Choosing monitor speakers

If all you're going to do to your track is make straight edits, you can use just about any speaker. In fact, a lot of serious projects have been edited this way. But if you want to equalize the clip, add noise reduction, change its dynamics, or mix it with some other element—or even decide if a take is suitable for sound—you need to know exactly what your viewers will hear.

This means you don't necessarily want speakers that "sound good." Most people are partial to speakers with too much bass and a missing midrange, because it's flattering to a lot of popular music. Many manufacturers deliberately build their speakers this way. Speakers like this will lead you to bad decisions.

Fortunately, there are strategies to help find speakers that really are reliable. You can use them, even if you're not blessed with golden ears.

The theoretical case against small speakers

Some people claim you should always mix on tiny speakers because they represent a worst-case scenario: if a track can make it there, it can make it anywhere. But those speakers—even slightly larger ones, often bundled with editing systems—don't tell you anything reliable at all.

This is easy to demonstrate. Figure 11.4 shows the frequency distribution of a typical voice (black) and music (gray) track, as measured in Waves' PAZ psychoacoustic analysis plug-in. The relative heights show how much energy is in either track at any frequency. I've drawn the black box to indicate the accurate range of a typical desktop monitor—between approximately 200 Hz and 7,000 Hz.

If you look only inside the box I drew, the voice is louder than the music. Play a mix with these levels, on a speaker that can reproduce only what's in the box, and you may think it's fine. But look outside the box—or hear the mix played on a better loudspeaker—and you'll discover there's much more overall energy to the music. The voice gets lost on a good system. You'd never know it, if you approved a mix based on this small speaker.

Even if your viewers don't have the best of speakers in their televisions, this track is likely to find its way through a number of compressors and other level-control devices before it gets to them. Every time the music hits a loud note, these processors will squash the entire mix down—even if the note is in a range small speakers might ignore. (TV stations use multiband processors to reduce this problem, but many of

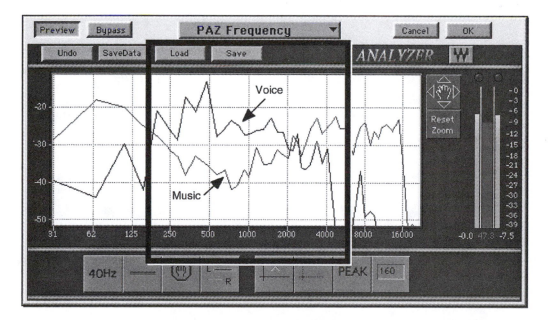

Figure 11.4 A small speaker can give you the wrong idea about voice/music proportions.

them also pass the signal through wide-band compressors with the same unfortunate effect. Cable networks, Internet broadcasters, and DVD-authoring stations usually have just the wide-band units. New legislation purporting to control commercial volume hasn't changed this.)

It's fine to check a mix on small speakers, but making decisions on them misplaces the track's priorities: you're sacrificing how things will be heard on better sets, to favor how music is heard on poorer ones. Film is a dialog-driven medium. If anything is at risk, it should be the music.

The real-world case against small speakers

So far we've dealt with small speakers in the abstract. But once you get to real-world examples, the problem isn't just the lost highs and lows—it's also what the speaker does to the middle.

Good full-size monitor speakers are accurate over their entire range. Mixes done on them sound right on any other good monitor, even in the largest theaters. They're also predictable on laptops, smartphones, and other tiny monitors. But mixes done on bad speakers are random; corrections that improve the sound on one may make it a lot worse on another.

For example, there's a small powered monitor that's been popular for years. It looks professional, has XLR connectors, and is often bundled with expensive dedicated nonlinear editors. It doesn't sound professional. A speaker-designer friend of mine tested one with lab equipment. I used what he discovered to retouch Figure 11.4. The result is Figure 11.5: the frequencies of a typical voice/music mix, as reproduced on

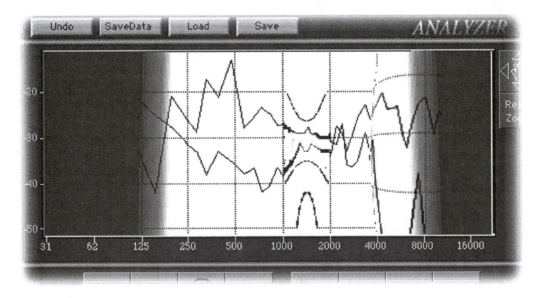

Figure 11.5 One popular small monitor is this sloppy, even on the frequencies it *can* handle.

this particular speaker. (Waves' PAZ will never look like this on your screen, but it does accurately depict how these speakers distort the sound balance.)

- The high and low ends disappear in the figure because they also do in the speaker. While the manufacturer claimed a low-frequency limit of 80 Hz, things got very quiet down there. In reality, the bass fell off drastically at 150 Hz, and was too soft to be useful by 100 Hz.
- The opposite happens to the highs: to reach a claimed 13 kHz cutoff, they applied a gigantic boost at 8 kHz . . . so these speakers tempt you to turn the mid-highs much lower than is appropriate!
- To top it all off, there's a major dip between 1 kHz and 2 kHz—probably to make pop music sound better on them.
- Nobody could do an accurate mix with this kind of frequency response. Worse, all that equalization adds significant distortion.

Things get worse in a different way, when a manufacturer tries to improve the sound by putting multiple small speakers into nearfield box. Along with the uneven response and distortion caused by equalization, the frequency response might not stay the same when you move your head! That's because the length of the path from each individual tiny speaker to your ear is slightly different depending on head position, causing random cancellations and reinforcements (see Chapter 1).

✳ TIDBIT

Deep woof

Don't confuse the concept of subwoofers with the *Low Frequency Effects* (LFE) channel in a film mix. LFE is the extra "oomph" in explosions, thunder, and other deep bass effects, along with some deeper notes in the music mix, playing simultaneously with the main channels. It's restricted to under 120 Hz, and usually set to play approximately twice as loud as bass in the main channels. (The extra volume is to help it compete with all the other channels.)

In a home theatre system, low notes from the main channels are often also directed to the LFE channel, without the extra volume, to compensate for low-frequency losses in the main speakers.

By the way, the "dot-one" in "5.1 sound" isn't just a cute marketing handle; it's a technical description. Since the LFE never carries anything above 200 Hz, the Nyquist limit says it can get by with a 480 Hz sample rate: exactly one-tenth the rate of the main channels (see Chapter 2). This reduced data makes it easier to fit on a film or DVD soundtrack, and requires less processing in the system.

Subwoofers

The smaller multimedia speaker systems often come with a subwoofer to provide some sense of bass. Don't confuse these subs with the powerful ones in a good 5.1 system. These are more like those in "satellite" systems sold for unobtrusive music listening. Bass notes aren't very directional and don't get affected as much as the treble ones by room reverberation, so a system like this has a lot of flexibility for placement.

Unfortunately, almost all of these systems split the band in the middle of critical speech frequencies, and distort or lose signal where you need the most accuracy. They're great for background music—they carry very little sound at dialog frequencies, so you don't have to shout to be heard over them. But not being very good at dialog is definitely *not* a good characteristic for a film mixing monitor. The only time these speakers are appropriate is when you know the viewer will also be using identical speakers—which might be the case in an interactive kiosk—and the track will never be played anywhere else.

Subwoofers, in and of themselves, aren't the problem. Theatrical surround-sound systems use them effectively. But they also use full-size speakers for the main channels. This way, the subs can concentrate on much lower frequencies than those in satellite systems. Critical sound in a theatrical surround system is carried by full-range, properly located speakers, and the subwoofer has its own channel for special effects.

You might conclude from all of the above that I think computer-store multimedia speakers are horrible for mixing film or video soundtracks. You'd be right.

✔ TIP

How about headphones?

Headphones can be helpful when editing, because they block out distractions and let you hear details of the dialog. But they're *too* detailed for mixing. Even ones with accurate sound will lead to a mix that's too subtle. You'll probably make sound effects or music too soft to compete with dialog, and subsidiary voices too soft to work with principal ones. Unless you're sure the audience will be listening with headphones, don't mix with them.

Choosing full-size speakers

If you want to know what you're mixing, you need real monitors. Your best source is a broadcast or studio supplier, or a high-end audio dealer, rather than a consumer electronics chain or home a/v store. Here's how to make an informed choice:

- Read the specs, but make sure they're real specs: it's a dead giveaway when a manufacturer brags about a speaker's frequency range, but doesn't say how much the sensitivity varies within that range. "30 Hz to 22 kHz range" doesn't tell you anything, other than somehow—with enough power and a sensitive enough meter—they managed to get some signal through the speaker at the extremes of that range. "50 Hz to 18 kHz ± 3 dB" tells you that every frequency in that range will get reproduced with about the same sensitivity. Or in other words, it'll accurately reflect the timbral balance on your track. Actually, a speaker with that second set of decibel-quantified numbers is probably better overall than the first one that just promises a "range."

- Watch out for specifications on speakers with built-in amplifiers. Some quote impressive numbers with decibels, and even supply a frequency-response graph . . . but if you look closely, you'll see the rating applies only to the amp. Specs don't mean anything unless they're for the system as a whole—amplifier and speaker—the way you'll be using it.

- Watch out for system specifications measured under unreasonable conditions, as well as the ones where measurement conditions aren't specified. One popular manufacturer released a speaker with "under 1% distortion." But the distortion graph showed they did the measurement at 40 dB SPL . . . meaning the speaker was about as loud as the background in a quiet library.

Yes, interpreting speaker specs can get a little technical. You might be able to enlist a friendly engineer to help. Or download some of the spec sheets from manufacturers of professional monitors—those costing some $750 per channel or more[6]—and compare them with the spec sheets (or lack thereof) from the cheaper manufacturers.[7] You don't have to *buy* the expensive speakers. Just look at the kind of information the manufacturers are willing to reveal.

- On the other hand, you can trust your muscles. Try to lift the speaker. Professional speakers use much heavier components, both for rigidity and to generate stronger magnetic fields. If an amplifier is built in, it'll have a large power transformer.

- Train your ears to know when a speaker is doing a good job (this will also help you do better mixes).

Enlist the aid of a friendly studio engineer, and listen to a good film or video mix in their studio. The dialog and narration should sound natural and close-up, with the consonants perfectly clear. The music should have a sheen or high-end sparkle. Listen for a full bass sound, but don't be swept away by thumping deep bass that might not make it to home viewers. Most importantly, get familiar with the relative ratio of voice to music, and male voices to female ones, on this mix. Then make a copy of it on an audio CD.

Then go to a dealer where you can audition different speaker systems simultaneously. Pick two stereo speaker pairs, adjust them to the same volume, and switch

---

[6] To get you started: www.jblpro.com, www.genelec.com, and dynaudioprofessional.com.

[7] You can find plenty of examples of these for yourself.

back and forth while you listen to that CD. Start with the best two pairs the dealer has to offer, and work your way down in quality (or price) until you notice that the disc doesn't sound like it did in the studio any more. Go back up one notch—that's the speaker for you.

If the speaker you choose is out of your budget, don't feel bad. It just means that your hearing is better than your bank balance. Settle for the best speakers you can afford, and try to stay aware of what's missing in them.

Be wary of dealers who don't let you do this test on your own terms. Here are a few ways a dishonest dealer will try to steer buyers to their most profitable speakers (rather than their best ones for the money):

- They don't let you switch quickly between speakers.
- They don't have a way to let you match the volume between different speakers (the speaker that's louder almost always seems better).
- They insist on using the manufacturer's CD rather than your own.

 TIP

No shortcuts here
- Relying on well-known manufacturers can help, but it's not infallible. One of the biggest names forbids its dealers from demonstrating their products alongside the competition.
- Besides, some reliable pro speaker lines have sold or licensed their names—or subtle variations—for consumer products that don't meet pro standards. A few even sell music-store speakers that look like small versions of their pro units, for what seems to be a bargain price. Until you look at the specs.

Separate amplifier or integrated system

An audio signal has to go through three different processes on the way from your computer's software to your ears. It has to be converted from the digital stream in your computer to an analog voltage, have its power boosted to the dozens of watts necessary to fill a small room, and have that power converted from electricity to vibrating air molecules.

These three functions have traditionally been handled by separate pieces of equipment, but they don't have to be. Putting them in the same box can have both advantages and disadvantages. It makes sense to look at the three functions individually:

Digital to analog conversion
Just about every computer has an analog output jack. It carries audio from any standard software running in the computer, and is usually sufficient to drive a headphone,

amplifier, or most amplified speakers. If you care about monitoring, this can be the worst way to get a signal.

The problem is twofold. Manufacturers don't invest much in these audio circuits, because their quality won't affect sales. But even if they used the finest components, the circuits would still be inside the computer and close to the motherboard. That's a horrible place to put an analog audio circuit. The CPU and its allied chips are generating all kinds of electronic hash, and it comes through as noise.

A separate audio card, located in a shielded PCI bay elsewhere in the tower, has a much better chance of giving a better signal. So do the analog output jacks on the video card you may have driving a high-quality picture monitor, and they also usually have the advantage of being built to stay in sync with that picture.

But the cleanest strategy is to stay digital until the signal has gotten outside the computer. Options for this include:

- video cards with digital SDI or HDMI outputs that also carry audio;
- internal audio cards with AES/EBU or s/pdif outputs;
- motherboard s/pdif optical outputs, standard on Mac computers;
- external USB or FireWire analog output converters;
- power amplifier with USB or s/pdif input;
- self-amplified monitor speakers with digital audio or USB inputs.

Assuming you buy reasonably reliable products, all of the above options should sound about the same. The first (having digital audio on the same wire as digital video) does present some advantages for simplifying wiring and holding lipsync. The last (choosing a speaker with digital inputs) can complicate the wiring, particularly if you want to switch multiple monitors or locate the speakers more than a few feet from the computer. But they'll all work.

I deliberately left "speakers with Bluetooth connections" off the list. Aside from the fact that I don't know of any with good audio specifications, there's the issue of what your system might be doing to squeeze a signal down to the most widely used Bluetooth data rates.

Power amplifier

Speakers are efficient machines, but they still need a bit more power than a headphone or line-level jack can provide. The amplifier boosts the signal from about a milliwatt coming out of the computer or sound card, to somewhere between 10 and 100 watts. The required amplified power might vary this much depending on both the speaker design, and how big a room you're trying to fill.

The power rating says how many watts an amplifier can pour into a speaker at the peak of the loudest wave, even though most of the time the amp is coasting along at about half that wattage. That maximum number is important because it's on those highest peaks that you'll hear the most distortion, possibly killing the intelligibility of your track. So, as you'd expect, some manufacturers manipulate that number.

Power rating is meaningless without a distortion percentage measured *at that same power*. Just saying an amp is capable of "100 watts on peaks" doesn't tell you anything at all. But "100 watts at 1% distortion" is tolerable in a basic consumer-quality amp; that same amp might reasonably claim "70 watts at .1% distortion," which is more likely how you'd be using it.

When looking at the specs for a powered speaker, ignore anything that pertains only to the amplifier. The important thing, along with overall system frequency response, is system distortion at a specified loudness and frequencies. Don't worry if distortion goes up on the deepest bass notes; the ear isn't as sensitive there.

For example, a good pro system might claim

- Distortion at 96 dB SPL:[8] 1.5% below 120 Hz, .5% between 120 Hz and 20 kHz.
- Distortion at 102 dB SPL: 1.5% below 120 Hz, 1% between 120 Hz and 20 kHz.

This means that in the nearfield, this speaker can be played at about twice as loud as normal theatrical dialog with almost no distortion at all. A speaker being used this way will likely carry only very short peaks, from loud drum beats or gunshots, so the speaker's higher distortion at louder levels won't last long enough to be noticed by the ear.

Separate amp or integrated speaker and amp?

The amplifier is often a separate rack-mount box in theatrical and high-end studio applications. This arrangement gives the most flexibility for switching and powering, and is easier to repair if something goes wrong. It's often a separate tabletop box in home stereos, and there's nothing wrong with using a consumer amp for your monitors . . . assuming it has good power and distortion ratings. Consumer amps also often include elaborate switching and control, an FM tuner, s/pdif and USB inputs, and—since they're not built to the same reliability spec as theater and studio amps—can be a bigger bargain.

The amp is also frequently mounted in the same box as the speakers. These integrated speaker-amplifiers—sometimes called *powered speakers*—can have the advantage of carefully chosen amp specs, designed to complement the specific speaker elements. (They can also have the disadvantage of amp specs that have been chosen to disguise low-quality speaker elements, as discussed above.)

Don't skimp on its wattage. Professional ported-design loudspeakers might need only 10 watts per channel for average speech-level mixing (sealed acoustic suspension designs are more power-hungry), but that's just the average. Peak requirements are many times higher, and an amp that can't handle the load will sometimes generate a form of distortion that actually damages the speaker elements. An absolute minimum per channel is 50 clean watts.

Building a good amp is a lot easier than building a good speaker, and higher-end amps from consumer-electronics stores can be perfectly adequate for driving your professional speakers—the only major differences between a top hi-fi amp and a studio one are ruggedness and reliability. Again, weight is a good guide: a decent amplifier

---

8 Usually measured one meter from the speaker. Remember the inverse-square law!

needs a good power supply and, in consumer amps, that always means a heavy power transformer. (Some music mixers prefer the sound of vacuum tube amplifiers. These will be even heavier because of their output transformers. However, tubes present absolutely no advantage—and a lot of disadvantages—in a digital film or video mixing suite.)

If you're buying the amp at a consumer retailer, check the volume control! The stereo image should stay absolutely stable as you raise or lower the volume control, and not drift from side to side. A cheap volume control won't have its channels matched properly across the entire range, and that can fool you into making bad balancing decisions in your mix. It also suggests the manufacturer might have cheapened things elsewhere as well.

✔ TIP

So which to choose?

Powered speakers:

- Take less thought to install: Run a USB cable from the computer, or an analog or digital one from its output device, plug in AC power, and you're good to go.
- Can require more expensive wiring: Long USB cables need built-in repeaters or intermediate hubs. Long analog or digital cables cost more than speaker wire.[9]
- Can give you more quality for the same money: A good manufacturer will carefully tune the amp to their speaker design.

Separate amplifier and speakers:

- Can give you more control, including multiple inputs and Dolby and other surround decoding.
- Are easier to fix or work around in an emergency, since you can substitute components without having to replace the whole system.
- Can give you better bargains, since you can shop for sales on individual components. Used or factory-second amplifiers are often just as good as new ones.

I've been very happy using both.

---

[9] 16 gauge two-conductor is perfectly adequate for almost every purpose, unless you're building a theater or high-end studio. Oxygen-free or special knitted cables aren't necessary. I usually use stuff from Home Depot, about $20 for a 100' roll.

Room equalization

Some professional studios have installed equalizers in their monitor amplifiers to boost or cut specific frequencies and smooth out the speaker's performance. Don't even think about trying this with the tone controls in a consumer amp. Their action is much too broad for this and will do more harm than good. In fact, most acoustic designers recommend against using equalization for all but the most subtle corrections: unless you've got very good speakers and carefully tuned acoustics, the equalizer will add its own distortion. And you can't do this kind of tuning by guesswork. You need precise test equipment and training to use it properly.

A few powered speakers come with a calibrated microphone and digital feature that measures the response in a room, and then applies the necessary correction. It's a cute feature, and actually doesn't cost the manufacturer too much extra if the units already have digital control. But again, this function should be saved for good speakers in well-tuned rooms. Otherwise even the automated equalization will add too much distortion.

Speaker setup

Once you've got the speakers, mount them rigidly—loose mounting can absorb bass notes. The tweeters should point toward your listening position and be about at ear level, because high frequencies are the most directional. There shouldn't be anything between the speaker and the listener; a computer monitor, part of a tower, or even a CD player can reflect high frequencies away from you.

One company sells resilient foam pads to put under desktop speakers, so the desk won't vibrate with loud sounds. They work as advertised, but also eat the bass from full-range speakers precisely because they're not a rigid mounting. (They're fine for small, limited-range speakers that don't have any bass in the first place.) If your desk is resonating, a better solution is to get a more massive desk. If you can't change your desk, add mass by gluing a large piece of ½″ or thicker plywood over the entire desktop, and mount the speakers to it.

One of the best arrangements for stereo speakers is an equilateral triangle, slightly above ear level and pointed down, as shown in Figure 11.6. That control room also uses absorption around the front and sides, has a bookshelf diffuser on the back, and uses another technique—splaying the side walls so echoes don't build up between them.

Monitoring for surround

5.1 surround can be very engaging when you're watching a Hollywood blockbuster on your home theater setups. But don't let it fool you into compromising the system where you mix your films. Dialog and up-front music and sounds are more important to a film than the surround channels. Good stereo monitoring will let you mix these elements properly. Typical surround-in-a-box systems won't. They'll give you five matched speakers and a subwoofer, but unless you're paying a few thousand dollars

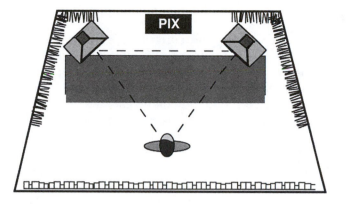

Figure 11.6 You and the speakers should form an equilateral triangle.

for the package, the five identical speakers can't be very high quality. Buying two very good speakers can be a lot cheaper.

(What about that third "dialog" front channel in a surround setup? A good stereo monitoring system will have a phantom center, in the middle of the screen, that translates dialog just as well. Unless you're mixing for surround release, stereo monitoring is perfectly fine.)

Surround needs a larger working area—and one with more symmetry across the room—than a stereo setup. Film surround uses a slightly different speaker configuration than music surround. In 5.1 films, the two surround channels extend along the sides of the auditorium rather than in the two rear corners.

Surround also requires a more complex monitor controller and metering. Professional setups let you monitor a left/right derived mix from the 5.1 channels, important for broadcast and home compatibility, and mute individual channels for calibration and problem solving. There will also be a reference encoder and decoder so you can hear how proprietary schemes like Dolby change the mix depending on the medium. You might find some of these features as part of your DAW software.

✳ TIDBIT

The easy way
Smoothing out the acoustics and buying a high-quality amp and speakers can be expensive. It may be more efficient to just keep the multimedia speakers that came bundled with your NLE—they're good enough for editing—and then rent time in a well-equipped sound studio when it's time to mix. Along with the improved acoustics and monitors, you'll probably also benefit from better processing tools . . . and an engineer who's experienced with film or TV mixing.

Monitor controller

Professional mixing facilities often have surround speaker controllers, costing at least $2,000 (and going much higher). They're overkill for video/audio setups, unless you're planning to spend many times more than that on the speakers and acoustics.

Music stores sell stereo monitor controllers for a few hundred dollars. These switch among multiple speaker systems, control monitoring in studios and isolation booths, and provide talkback—features missing from most music creation software. They can be handy for an audio post suite, but aren't much of a time-saver unless you're also recording voices or foley in a different room.

But they also provide a mono test switch, which is essential for broadcast, Internet, or home video projects. It combines the left and right channels electrically so you can hear if there are any phase errors that will affect mono compatibility. You can't take mono compatibility for granted: bad wiring, asymmetrical processors, and some "three-dimensional" effects can make a good stereo track sound awful in mono. A few stereo music synthesizers completely disappear when their channels are combined.

Mono switches used to be standard on home stereo amplifiers, but have mostly disappeared; the similar switches on most of today's FM receivers change the radio from stereo to mono, but don't affect the line inputs.

You can test mono compatibility by merging the file's channels together in an audio program, but using a switch is certainly more convenient. If you want to build your own, I've provided simple instructions at www.dplay.com/gotcha/02Gadgets.pdf. Some soldering is required, but nothing that would intimidate even an electronics beginner.

COMPUTER INPUT/OUTPUT

Most filmmakers now ingest files from their camera and recorder, or use FireWire to transfer audio and video digitally between camera and NLE. This is also an excellent way to get production dialog into a computer, or to lay a finished mix back to tape. If the only other sound sources in your production are already digitized as files, or are audio CD tracks *ripped* (converted to audio files) in the CD-ROM drive, you don't need any other input or output equipment.

But many projects need to add sound from microphones or other analog sources during postproduction. You could use your camera to digitize these signals, but camera audio doesn't live up to the quality of these other media (see Chapter 9). A low-cost analog video to FireWire converter box is going to be just as bad. These devices are not built to any higher audio standards than the cameras we measured.

Sound cards and converters

Almost all of the solutions for getting clean audio out of your computer—internal cards, external boxes, or motherboard s/pdif—will also work as analog inputs; see "Digital to analog conversion" on page 286.

Additional features

Most of the USB and FireWire devices can be powered directly by the computer, so there's one less wall-wart to worry about. This powering can be very convenient if you're recording on a laptop in the field, but be aware that extra current has to be supplied by the laptop's battery and will shorten the time between recharging.

Multichannel FireWire units are available that support eight simultaneous analog inputs and outputs—and a few have additional digital inputs—for isolating mics in the field or surround monitoring in the studio.

Both USB and FireWire units are available with extra control features, including jog/shuttle wheels or hands-on controls for your software's on-screen mixer. There's more about these features later in this chapter.

THE MIXER

Don't let the name confuse you:[10]

The mixer in an editing setup isn't much like a mixer you'd use in the field.

A lot of edit rooms have mixers that aren't used for mixing. They serve as selectors to capture and adjust one sound at a time, often with a digital connection to the computer.

Many mixing setups—including some top-notch re-recording suites used for feature film setups—don't have mixers at all. They have something that *looks* like a mixer, but is really just a sophisticated software controller. Individual tracks don't ever exist as signals to be mixed; instead, they're data streams that get added together inside the computer.

Mixer as selector and controller

It's fairly common to use a low-cost analog mixer as the input and output control in an editing room. It'll have mic preamps for narration, line inputs for video decks or other auxiliary sources, faders and meters for consistent operation, and controls for speakers and headphones. Many have USB or FireWire built-in, so they can send their mix to the computer and monitor its output.

Reasonable units range from the Behringer Xenyx (four rotary volume controls and USB, about $100) through the popular Mackie Onyx (eight sliding faders, internal multichannel routing, FireWire, $700) to some slightly more expensive and powerful Yamaha and Soundcraft units. All have good enough audio specs for most film and video purposes. Many have extra features built-in, including elaborate equalization, dynamics processing, and reverb. It's best to ignore those functions.

---

[10] To avoid further confusion: we're talking about hardware devices. There are also *people* called mixers, and their job in the field is also different from what they do in a postproduction setting.

✔ TIP

A mixer alternative

If you're mixing within your NLE still want some basic control over levels and equalization while digitizing from analog tape, consider a standalone equalizer instead. These provide finer control than the basic equalizer knobs on a mixer and are calibrated for easier resetting. A parametric equalizer—with knobs to control tuning as well as frequency—will let you hone in on offending noises without affecting too much else in the track. Hook up the equalizer through a patchbay, so you can bypass it when you want an absolutely clean connection. Processors, including equalizers, are discussed in Chapter 16.

The ability to manipulate a signal when you're digitizing is both a blessing and a curse. You can boost levels and reduce noise or add crispness quickly with analog controls, to take advantage of the widest digital range once the signal is in the computer. But if you're going to tweak a track before you digitize, you need some way to repeat those tweaks exactly if you have to redigitize part of a scene. You need a way to assure that good recordings aren't harmed by inadvertent tweaking. And—since it doesn't make sense to commit to any treatment other than initial level control until the track is fully built—you need a way to *undo* what you've done.

Mixing in the computer

At its heart, picture editing is just database management (Chapter 10), though modern NLE software does some amazing video transformations as well. But even basic sound mixing is more complicated.

- The computer has to keep track of how you've changed the volume for each track, smoothly raising one while lowering another.
- It has to multiply each track's sample data by a factor representing its volume change.
- It has to add the results of those multiplications together, combining volume-adjusted data from the dialog with that of music and sound effects, to create new sample data for the output signal.

A simple TV track might involve a matrix of a half dozen voice, music, and effects tracks that have to also be multiplied by the correct factors for left and right stereo outputs. A theatrical feature can have many dozens of tracks playing simultaneously, surround output channels, and voice- or effects-only submixes. There's a lot of math to take care of.

- It has to do all these computations for every element being mixed, in less than 1/48,000 of a second total. Then it has to do them again for the next set of digital samples.

And that's just the mixing. Equalization, compression, reverb, and other processes are also math, but are considerably more complicated than adjusting volume and involve many more computer calculations. It's not unusual for every track in a mix to have its own selection of processes, plus reverb and compression on groups of tracks, and some additional level control over the entire mix. Oh . . . and to keep up with current loudness regulations, you also need to do a sophisticated calculation on the mix's sample values, and then display the result on various meters.

Until relatively recently, desktop computers couldn't do it all. Mixing was either offline and slow, very limited in capability, or required cards full of *Digital Signal Processing* (DSP) chips to help the computer think. A decade or so ago, you could do more elaborate tracks on a $300 analog mixer than on a $3,000 computer.

Mixing in the box

Mixing has changed, because modern computers are smarter. Even complex mixes can be done without a mixing board. What *looks* like a big console in many dub stages is actually a hardware controller—a very specialized variation of mouse and keyboard—talking to one or more desktop computers that actually do the mix. There's no audio in that console at all.

In a few elaborate setups, those computers are running specialized mixing software. Console and software act together as a digital mixer, manipulating streams of digital audio from a device. But in many installations the mixing software is the same DAW, running in the same or similar desktop computer, that was used for building and editing the track. Engineers call this *mixing in the box.*

Two advantages are simplicity and cost. Big mixing consoles can cost more than $100,000 . . . and a lot of that goes into the expensive, custom analog circuits needed to handle the sound properly. (A third advantage—the ability to rehearse and refine an individual fader movement, or recall it months later to make a change—is also available on big analog consoles, but only if you add an expensive automation system.)

The primary disadvantage to mixing in the box is user interface. Mixing consoles evolved the way they did because they're easy to work with. The big consoles in Hollywood dub stages might look more complex than the cockpit of a jet plane, but they're mostly just the same basic controls repeated for a large number of tracks. Even the small analog mixers sold in music stores follow the same basic design. The most important controls are the volume sliders, one for each sound source; you move the slider away from you (or "up" on a slanted console) to turn the volume up, and pull it back toward you to bring the volume down.

On-screen mixers

What's needed for successful in-the-box mixing is a user interface. The typical rubber-band volume lines in an NLE (Figure 11.7) are too cumbersome: even a simple three-second fade—which would take exactly three seconds to perform on the sliders of a mixing console—requires placing a couple of points and drawing a line; if you want the fade to start slowly and then speed up, it'll take a lot of points to get the curve right.

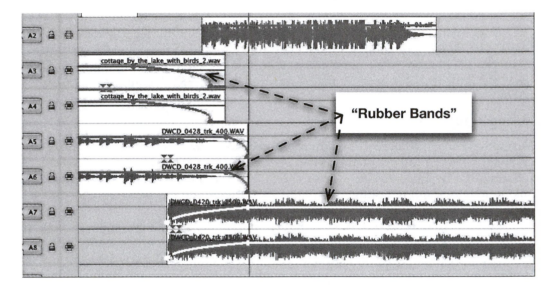

Figure 11.7 "Rubber bands" (darkened in this picture) to control volume when the timeline is played.

To make things easier, some years ago the multitrack audio programs started drawing pictures of mixing consoles on the screen. These on-screen mixers now appear in NLEs as well (Figure 11.8). They show the sliders and pan pots, and you can grab them with a mouse to move their knobs. When you do, the software automatically draws rubber-band lines to match those movements on the timeline. If your mouse is already on the right fader, any three-second fade—no matter how complex—takes just three seconds. If you then play the timeline, the on-screen fader follows the line, repeating your movement automatically. It's a vast improvement, but not enough to be practical for mixing a film.

The problem is that real-world mixes involve moving lots of faders at the same time, with some tracks getting louder while others get softer. If you want to cross-fade two sound effects with an on-screen mixer, you have to fade one effect down in real-time, then recue and position the mouse on the second effect's knob and push

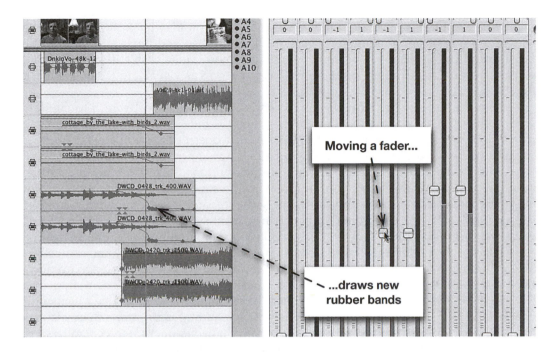

Figure 11.8 Many NLEs now have mixers like the one on the right side of this screenshot. When you move the on-screen fader, it draws a new rubber band on the timeline.

it up in real-time, and then possibly redo the first fade while you're listening to how the second effect actually sounds. Mixing a complicated scene this way is painfully slow.

Hardware controllers

While your computer has only one mouse, most of us have plenty of fingers. So manufacturers developed hardware controllers, with real sliders and knobs that can be moved by different fingers simultaneously. Figure 11.9 shows a simple one, a Behringer BCF-2000, sitting on a standard-size keyboard. It looks like a mixer, but the sliders and knobs are actually digital encoders. Each time you move one, circuits in the box send that movement to the computer via USB. The computer's DAW uses that information to move its on-screen faders, drawing

Figure 11.9 A simple hardware controller lets your fingers do the mixing.

appropriate rubber-band lines in the software. When you play back the timeline, the software sends position information back to the controller, and tiny motors move the faders, duplicating what you've done with your fingers. This doesn't affect the sound, since there's no actual audio in the controller, but serves as visual and tactile feedback for the user.

It may all seem complicated—box *A* sends commands to software *B* to emulate what was originally programmed as mouse action *C*—but it works just like an analog mixer, with all of the advantages of digital. And it doesn't have to be expensive ... the unit pictured in Figure 11.9 costs about $250.

Almost all controllers also include transport buttons for moving around on the timeline, and many also have a jog/shuttle wheel to save mousing while editing. Not every controller can talk to every brand of software, and some NLEs don't support the function at all—but drivers and protocols are downloadable from the manufacturers' websites for most popular combinations. USB is one common way of connecting these controllers; others include MIDI and occasionally RS-232 or Ethernet. Some controllers also include good quality multichannel audio input and output circuits—so you don't need a separate box for that function—and connect via FireWire.

Even many full-size controllers often have sliders and knobs for just eight channels. Expansion units are available as options, adding eight more channels at a time. Since a film mix can involve dozens of simultaneous tracks, the controllers are equipped with *bank switches* that assign the faders to different groups of tracks at a time. You can program all of the dialog fades, then move to another bank to adjust the sound effects or scoring. It's the modern equivalent of the old Hollywood practice of pre-mixing, where all the dialog tracks would be mixed to one piece of magnetic film and all the sound effects to another, to simplify the final mix. Except there's no quality loss from multiple generations, and it's easy to go back to change a things later.

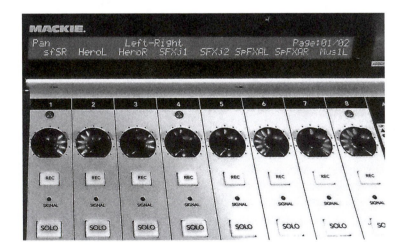

Figure 11.10 A readout above the faders lets you see which tracks will be controlled.

Switching controller knobs from one bank of sounds to another can get confusing, since you have to keep track of which track on the timeline belongs to which fader while you're mixing. More elaborate controllers include a text readout above each fader to report which track it's currently controlling, like the one in Figure 11.10.

A few companies make software to turn your iPad or other tablet into a controller, drawing faders on the screen and letting you adjust two or three of them at a time using multi-finger gestures. The tablet talks to your main computer's software via wifi or Bluetooth, either directly as data or through a server application in the main computer. It's a good idea, though some users report current versions can be sluggish or hard to use. Since the software starts around $10, it's certainly worth trying. Check your tablet's app store for the latest offerings.

There are also a couple of digital mixers on the market that use tablets for local or remote control, adding analog connections and digitizing for the computer via USB. This is an odd solution for a video editing room, but if you don't mix very often and already have a tablet, might be worth considering.

Audio sources and recorders

While a lot of your track will probably consist of dialog recorded in the camera, and then imported into an NLE from the camera or a separate video deck, you may also want additional equipment to play back non-sync elements such as music, sound effects, and narration.

Then again, maybe you won't. Chances are your NLE already has a provision for importing stock music and effects from audio CDs, and most sound studios and freelance suppliers can now provide narration and original music on audio CD, as files on CD-ROM and removable hard drives, or over the Internet. So consider all the equipment in this section optional.

CD players

Library music and sound effects are distributed on audio CDs, the same format as you'd play in a home stereo. These discs are readable in the CD-ROM drives supplied with virtually every computer, and software to convert the sounds to standard WAVE or AIFF files either came with your system or can be downloaded for free from the Internet.

There may be a few advantages to using a separate CD player with audio outputs and re-recording into your NLE. It can be faster to find specific sounds with a player, because discs load more quickly and the dedicated controls make cueing easier; some audio software makes you import the entire CD before you can play even a very short segment.

Reasonably priced professional CD players also offer features that may be impossible or require extra processing steps with a CD-ROM drive, including varispeed to change the tempo and timbre of a sound, the ability to cue directly to index points within properly encoded CD tracks, and—though I'm not sure why you'd want them for a film track—DJ-style scratching effects.

The best way to record audio from a standalone CD player is to use its digital outputs. Professional players come with s/pdif interfaces, which can plug directly into a properly equipped sound card. Good home players have Toslink outputs, and Toslink to s/pdif adapters cost less than $25. When you re-record audio through one of these connections, the signal isn't affected by noise or analog-conversion distortion. However, if you're using a digital connection, you may have to forgo varispeed or scratch effects; these change the sample rate to a nonstandard value, and most low-cost digital input devices can't deal with that at all.

You can also use a portable battery-operated CD player to import audio. Look for a unit with a line-level output on the back (many of them have one for connection to a hi-fi system), so you can avoid distortion and variations caused by the headphone amplifier and volume control. While the output converters on a portable player may not be as good as those on a studio deck, running the portable on batteries instead of its AC adapter will completely eliminate hum and ground loops from the power line.

DAT, MiniDisc, and MDM

When I wrote the first edition of this book, DAT tape was the only standard for interchange among audio studios. Narrations and original music were always supplied in this format and post audio facilities expected you to bring non-sync elements recorded this way. Timecode DAT, recorded on units costing many thousands of dollars, were the standard for professional video and film sound. This situation continued well into the mid-2000s.

What a difference in less than a decade! DAT is now largely obsolete, even for field recording, replaced by hard drive and flash RAM recorders. Most manufacturers don't even build DAT decks any more. My studio has gone from handling hundreds of those tapes a month to fewer than a dozen per year.

In the second edition of the book, I recommended MiniDisc for some field recording. The format's disadvantages, including sensitivity to shock during and immediately after recording, used to be outweighed by the fact that they were the only digital recorders that could be purchased for only a few hundred dollars and slipped into a pocket or concealed within wardrobe.

If your specific workflow includes DAT or MiniDisc, and you need to rent or buy a transport for feeding your NLE, look for one that can connect to your computer digitally—either via USB, or with an s/pdif or Toslink adapter. It makes a real difference to the quality of the sound, compared to using the analog outputs and re-digitizing. Don't be fooled by MiniDiscs that have "USB capability" but only for recording; some manufacturers deliberately hobble USB playback to prevent music piracy.

Modular digital multitracks (MDMs) used to be found in music studios for original recording and in high-end audio post facilities for interchange, but seldom find their way into an NLE setup. They've also been replaced by data on computer media. There are two competing and noninterchangeable formats, Alesis ADAT (used in music) and Tascam DTRS/DA-8 (used in postproduction), so check with the client or other studios you'll be working with before specifying one or the other.

Analog audio media

Forget about using audio cassettes in production, unless you're stuck with historic material in that format. Even the best analog cassettes don't have the quality or speed accuracy to be used with picture today.

Quarter-inch (and wider) audio tape is often used in music production to add "analog warmth"—a particular, pleasing form of distortion—but high-quality analog recorders are also mostly obsolete, and even the recording tape can be hard to find. A few non-Hollywood features may still be mixed from analog recordings on film-style perforated magnetic stock, but this is for operational reasons—some studios prefer to use the equipment they've always worked with, and that's already paid for—rather than any technical advantage.

Some historic documentary sounds, effects, and music may be available only on analog vinyl disks. If you have to play them, check with local studios and radio stations to find some way to transfer their sound to digital. (I still keep a turntable and preamp in the basement, wrapped in plastic, for just such occasions. Please don't ask if you can borrow them: I haven't unwrapped them since 2000.)

The best strategy with any of these analog media is to transfer to digital as soon as possible. Don't try to correct problems at this stage, unless they're being introduced by the playback mechanism—a badly maintained analog tape recorder will add hiss and lose high frequencies, and dirt or dust on a vinyl record can add noise. These problems can permanently damage your source material, so have them fixed before you continue with the transfer. Once the sound is in the digital domain, you can experiment with noise-reduction software and equalization and still be able to undo the effects.

Synthesizers and samplers

If you're a skilled musician, you might want to add music-making equipment to your NLE system. The technical requirements for this are documented in tons of books and magazines. They also tend to be somewhat different from the requirements for postproduction, so it might be more efficient to build separate setups and let two people play at the same time. Even if you're not making music, a small synthesizer can be helpful in the postproduction studio for laser zaps and other electronic effects.

Samplers—RAM-based digital audio recorders, with exceptional flexibility to warp the sound quality during playback—are often used in sound design. Both software-based ones and hardware samplers can be helpful in the postproduction suite for sound-effects manipulation—if you know how to work them.

OTHER HANDY GEAR

Software and hardware-based processors—such things as equalizers, compressors, and reverbs—are discussed in Chapter 16. But there's other hardware that can help you assure a good soundtrack.

Meters

The on-screen meters in many nonlinear editors range from deceptive to worthless. It takes computing power to make a digital meter that matches broadcast standards, but many programmers seem reluctant even to put calibrations on their nonstandard meters.

A proper meter should indicate both the peak level—bursts of sound that can overload a digital circuit, causing crackling noises—and the average level that a listener perceives. It should also be calibrated in meaningful units—in a digital studio, that would be decibels below Full Scale. Some programs have on-screen meters that are properly calibrated for digital with 0 dBFS at the top and –6 dBFS at some point higher than 75%; and that indicate peak and average levels as different colors, or with a bouncing line for peak. Figure 11.11 shows one such meter, from Premiere Pro CC.

If you're preparing material for broadcast, you probably should have a meter that shows LKFS, a long-term average level reading required by most US networks, or LUFS, a similar reading usually required in Europe. Software meters capable of this kind of measurement are included in many DAWs and are available as plug-ins; basic standalone analyzing software can be even cheaper. Figure 11.12 shows the Orban Loudness Meter, a free app that can monitor any signal playing through your computer, and displays the same audio in half a dozen different formats. Orban (www.orban.com/meter) manufactures the processor most stations use to control their transmitter levels, so they're well versed in this technology.

There's a lot more about these measurements in Chapter 17.

Hardware meters

If you're building a full broadcast facility, you'll probably want a comprehensive level and phase meter. It'll cost about $5,000. If you're building an audio mix suite, a digitally connected Dorrough Loudness meter is considered standard. Figure about $400 per channel. If you're not in that category, save your money: cheaper analog-connected meters will have bouncing lights and impress your clients, but will not give you much useful information.

Some people like the retro appearance of traditional swinging-needle analog VU meters. They are classy. But they also require precise ballistics and carefully designed electrical characteristics. These things have gotten so expensive that even

Figure 11.11
A software meter from
a popular NLE.

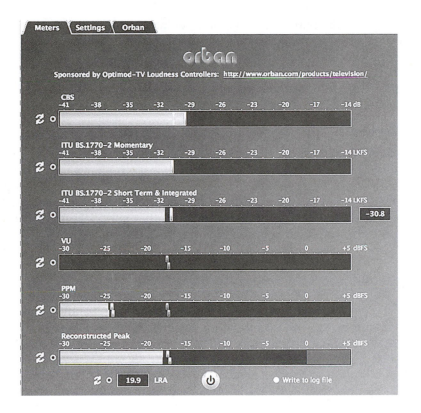

Figure 11.12 A comprehensive, but free, meter that reads
LKFS for broadcast projects.

large recording studio consoles don't have them anymore. The cheap voltage meters
sold as accessories for editing suites—and frequently included in analog broadcast
video decks—don't have the right response to audio waveforms and are too bouncy
to use as a reliable indicator while mixing.

There are some decent software meters in the next chapter. But they take system
resources, which can be a problem if you try to use them while actually mixing.

Tone oscillator

Even though a lineup tone isn't strictly necessary for digital videotape—the digits
themselves provide an unambiguous reference—it's still essential for making the digital-
to-analog leap in a dub house or broadcast station, and is required on the head of the
tape by most networks. A steady tone is also necessary for calibrating monitors, checking
stereo balance, and assuring that every device in a mixed analog/digital signal chain
is operating at its best level.

You can get a miniature test oscillator, built into an XLR plug, that uses phantom power and puts out a microphone-level signal. The units cost under $75 and are sold for checking PA systems in the field, and can be plugged into a mixer for postproduction use. But if you're don't need to test mic inputs in the field, you can get more flexible units with line-level outputs and a variety of test signals from B&K or Rolls for about the same price. One of these should be a part of any professional studio.

Most professional audio programs include a software-based oscillator that can generate these tones, either as needed or by creating clips for the head of a project.

A less flexible, but zero-cost alternative is included in the standard files with most NLEs. Or you can make your own in Audacity (Chapter 10): use the Generate:Tone . . . command and set the generator for a sinewave at 1,000 Hz, with an amplitude of 0.1. That'll match the –20 dBFS tone that's standard for broadcast and film.

Or use **Sound 11.1**: it's a 30-second tone at that spec. I've posted it as a .zip archive, since that compression format is very efficient on steady tones and doesn't corrupt the sound quality.

Phone patch

Sometimes you need to play a library cue or dialog edit to a distant client or director, just for content approval. You want to have a conversation about the piece while you're playing different options, so file transfers won't work; besides, you don't need that kind of quality . . . this is just for audition purposes.

You could hold a telephone handset up to a speaker, but the results are hardly professional. You can buy a digital hybrid, used in radio and TV call-in shows, for

---

✔ TIP

Playback through VOIP and cellphones

If you've got Voice Over Internet Protocol (VOIP, used in systems like Vonage.com) you may be disappointed when playing track samples on the phone. The compression schemes that squeeze a voice into Internet-friendly packets are optimized for speech. Depending on the scheme, music can get horribly mangled. Even voices can be a problem if there's music or sound effects in the background, or if two people are talking at once.

Similar compression schemes are used in modern cellphones. So even if you've got a standard analog phone line, check to make sure your client isn't on a cell when playing them music samples. Radio stations sometimes use hardware systems to feed higher quality signals over a cell connection, but this equipment is expensive and has to be installed on both ends of the line.

On the other hand, standard VOIP and cellphone connections can be fine for previewing dialog pacing or edits.

about $800. Or you can use the hybrid that's already built into most landline phones, tapping into it with a JK Audio Voice Path (jkaudio.com, about $110). JK makes other devices for recording and sending on cellphones, but I don't recommend cellphones for this purpose.

I used to include instructions for a $10 do-it-yourself phone tap in this book. It relied on a low-cost modem transformer that Radio Shack used to carry. Unfortunately, the Shack doesn't sell it any more ... but you might be able to find one on eBay, or adapt my instructions for equivalent parts. Read them at www.dplay.com/tutorial/archive/9809.

MOVING SIGNALS AROUND THE EDITING SUITE

The simplest wiring setup for NLEs is to have no wiring at all, other than the monitor speaker: ingest picture and sound from files, edit in an NLE, mix in a DAW, and lay the finished mix onto the finished video. A lot of small edit rooms are built that way.

It's also fairly common to use a video deck with a basic digital connection—FireWire, USB, AES/EBU, or s/pdif—between deck and NLE. You can import audio, edit and mix, and put the finished track back on videotape without worrying about the wiring compromising your signal.[11]

It's possible your setup will be as simple as this (Figure 11.13). If so, congratulations. Skip the rest of this chapter and start editing.

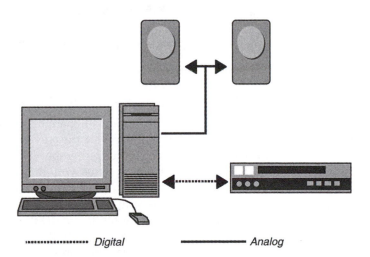

························ *Digital*   ———————— *Analog*

Figure 11.13 A simple edit suite doesn't take much wiring.

---

[11] Assuming you also set up the preference panels properly. There are still ways to subtly damage sound, even with a direct connection or file transfer. The most common is to choose the wrong sample rate, or with some software choosing the wrong frame rate or digital sync reference.

But if you're also using inputs and outputs for monitoring, voice-over, or using BetaSP, ¾″, or other archive media, things get complicated very quickly. You can run a wire from VTR output to editor input for digitizing, and from editor output to monitor to hear what you're doing . . . but once the job is edited, you'll have to rearrange things to get the signal from NLE back to tape and from tape to monitor.

If you add additional sources such as a mic preamp or CD player, the complexity grows geometrically. You need some way to choose which signal gets digitized, to dub between media, and to connect the monitor to the right output for each different function (Figure 11.14).

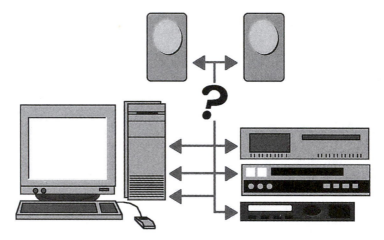

Figure 11.14 When you add more equipment, things stop being simple.

There are three different ways to deal with this web of connections:

1. You can reach behind the equipment when you want to change signal routing, find the right cords, and plug them into the right jacks for the current task. Aside from being inconvenient and confusing—you have to remember how things are wired before you can use them—this puts extra stress on the equipment's connectors and can lead to early failure.
2. You can use a routing device, which can be as simple as a low-cost patchbay or switch, or as complex as a microprocessor-based router, to handle the connections for you. It protects the equipment's connectors, and makes the whole process more straightforward. You don't have to do any reaching, and you can glance at the patchbay or switch to see how things are set up at any moment.
3. You can wire everything to a mixer, which then serves as your central audio control. This gives you other options for manipulating the sound, but may also subject your sound to unwanted changes.

The best solution—and the one applied in almost every professional studio—is to use both a patchbay and a mixer. The patchbay supplies flexibility and direct connections when you don't want the sound changed, and the mixer gives you control when you do.

The patchbay

Audio has been routed with plugs and jacks since the earliest days of the telephone, and a patchbay—with dangling cords, of course—seems to be in every photo of a recording studio.[12] There's a reason: patchbays make it easy to control where the signals go.

In its most basic form, a patchbay is simply a means to extend the jacks from the back panels of your equipment and group them in one convenient place. Even low-cost ones (starting around $50 for an eight-point bay) use ¼-inch phone jacks, which last longer and provide a better connection than the miniature or phono jacks on your equipment. Many models have jacks on both their front and rear panels, so you don't need to do any soldering to install them; just get cables with appropriate connectors for your equipment on one end and a ¼-inch plug on the other, plug them into the back of the patchbay, and forget about them.

Most preassembled patchbays have switchable "normals"—circuit paths that are activated when no cord is plugged in. Figure 11.15 shows how they work.

✔ TIP

Three into two!

Most patchbays available today have *tip-ring-sleeve* jacks. You can use them with either three-conductor balanced or two-conductor unbalanced plugs, depending on how your studio is wired.

You can also use them to connect balanced with unbalanced equipment. Just remember that the balanced gear works at a slightly higher signal voltage (page 62); and that when you add an unbalanced device, the entire connection loses the noise-rejection advantage of balanced wiring.

The contacts in a normalled jack are slightly bent. When there's no plug inserted (Figure 11.15A), they make contact with an internal jumper (gray circles). In this drawing, the jumper routes the signal to another normalled jack. This is known as a *full normalled* connection: when you plug a patchcord into either jack (Figure 11.15B), the contact is pushed away from the jumper.

---

[12] Go to my website's studio page (www.dplay.com/playroom), and you'll see a patchbay with colorful dangling cords on the extreme left of the photo.

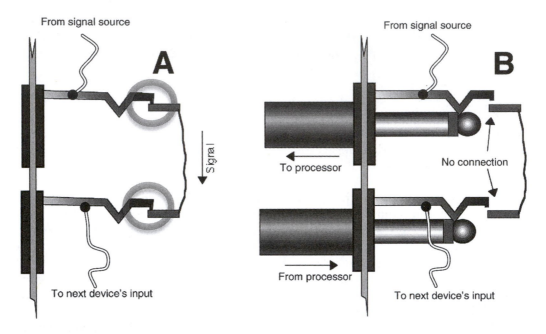

Figure 11.15 Normalled jacks provide a connection even when nothing's plugged in.[13]

A patchbay can also be *half-normalled*. Imagine taking the dark squiggly wire off the top contact and connecting it directly to the signal source. The white wire from the source stays connected. With this arrangement, you can plug into the top jack and tap the signal ... but it's still going through the normal and into the next device. If you plug into the lower jack, it completely breaks the normal and the next device hears only what's plugged in. Most patchbays today are half-normalled, to give you the flexibility of splitting signals easily. (Older equipment couldn't be split this way without lowering the signal, so older bays were usually fully normalled.)

Switchers and routers

While it's possible to route digital audio through an analog patchbay, it's not recommended. Ordinary patchbays aren't designed to handle the high frequencies of serial digital audio, and the connectors cause high-frequency reflections that interfere with the valid signal. Special patchbays that are designed for AES/EBU wiring, and broadcast-video patchbays, can handle the frequencies. But these are expensive solutions.

---

[13] I drew an unbalanced patchbay for simplicity. Balanced bays work the same way, just with twice as many sets of connections.

A few companies make electronic AES/EBU switchers. These route any input to any output—usually in an 8 × 8 or a 16 × 16 matrix—with additional buffering so that a signal can be sent to more than one device. Since they're driven by microprocessors, complex setups can be recalled quickly. Some of them also include reclocking and sample-rate conversion. While these routers are also expensive solutions—prices start around $1,000—they're the only efficient way to handle signals in a complex, all-digital facility.

Less-expensive switchers are also available for both digital and analog audio. The simplest of them are just mechanical switches in a box, but can be practical when you just need to select one of a few sources for an input. More elaborate ones can switch audio, video, and machine control simultaneously and are handy when your suite includes more than one video source.

Switchers are also available for USB and FireWire connections. Their mechanical switches let you connect only the selected device to the data bus, which generally results in faster transfers.

WIRING THE POSTPRODUCTION SUITE

The best, highest-quality way to wire your equipment together is to use equipment with digital inputs and outputs. Get appropriate cable for the high-frequency digital signal (see Chapter 3), and, if you have a lot of gear, use a digital mixer or routing switcher.

If you have to use analog connections, the best plan is to stick with balanced wiring (also in Chapter 3, along with some suggestions for when you have to mix balanced and unbalanced equipment). If everything in your facility is unbalanced and the cable lengths are very short, there's no point to using balancing adapters.

Practical ground-loop elimination

In Chapter 3 we talked about how a ground loop can form and produce hum or noise in a circuit, and how balanced wiring can eliminate almost all of the problem. Unfortunately, much of the equipment in the prosumer realm is unbalanced and not immune to ground-loop noise. It's also difficult to chase down loops, since equipment may be interconnected with video, machine control, Ethernet, and MIDI as well as audio cables and power-line grounds—and any of these can form an extra ground path. Finding and fixing a ground loop can be more voodoo than science.

Sometimes you can reduce the effect of a ground loop by tempting the circuit with an even better ground. Heavy-gauge wire has very little electrical resistance, so if you provide a ground path using thick wires, it can divert some of the ground-loop current from being carried on the signal wires. Get some heavy-gauge wire and run lengths of it from one piece of equipment to another—on audio equipment, there's usually a back-panel screw marked "ground" specifically for this connection; on computers, connect to the outer metal shell of a rear-panel jack. A good wire for this

✍ TRY THIS

Telescoping wiring

You can reduce noise pickup in unbalanced setups, if you're willing to do some soldering. This isn't as effective as balanced wiring, but can help lower the amount of radio or static pickup in an unbalanced wire.

1. Use the same kind of two-conductor shielded cable as you would for balanced wiring.

2. Connect the "hot" conductor—usually white—to the center pin of the phono or phone plug at each end, or to pin 2 of an unbalanced XLR.

3. Connect the other conductor to the sleeve of a phone plug, outer shell of a phono plug, or to pin 1 of an unbalanced XLR.

4. Now here's the trick: connect the cable's outer braided or foil shield to the sleeve, shell, or pin 1 **at one end only** (Figure 11.16). Use shrink-wrap or electrical tape to make sure the shield doesn't touch anything at the other end.

Solder shield to sleeve connection at this end only.

Make sure shield doesn't connect to anything at this end.

Figure 11.16 You can reduce noise in unbalanced circuits by connecting the shield at one end only (shown here with phone plugs).

5. Be consistent about which end of the shield gets connected: always connect the end at your patchbay and leave the equipment end floating, or always connect the end at the equipment and leave the patchbay end floating.

Do this only with two-conductor shielded wire, and with a definite ground connection through one of those wires. If you leave the shield disconnected with one-conductor shielded wire, you may get horrible hum.

purpose is 12-gauge electricians' type TW wire, available for about 15 cents a foot at building-supply stores, or 12-gauge automotive primary wire, which is slightly more expensive but also more flexible. You should hear the hum go down as soon as you make the connection. (You might also hear it increase, which means you're just making the ground loop worse. Like I said, sometimes it's voodoo.)

If you can't get rid of a noise-producing extra ground in a power or control cable (or even figure out which cable is the culprit), you can often reduce ground loops in unbalanced equipment by breaking the ground path that takes place across the audio cable:

⚠ WARNING

Don't do-it-yourself

If you can't find an exposed ground connection on a piece of equipment, *don't* go rooting around inside the cabinet. You might find dangerous voltages instead.

- Sometimes, just cutting the shield connection can help. Turn down the speakers; then pull a phono plug partway out, so its shell isn't contacting the jack. If your equipment has phono plugs, you can make up a special test cable where the sleeve isn't connected.

  Turn up the speakers *slowly*. Sometimes this fixes the problem, but other times it makes it much worse.
- You can isolate audio circuits completely by using a transformer. Small stereo-isolation transformers, prewired to phono jacks, are available at automobile sound dealers. Radio Shack's version (#270–054) costs about $20. If it fixes the problem but the Shack's transformer isn't good enough—you may notice a decrease at the extreme high and low frequencies—you can get a higher-quality unit from a broadcast- or video-supply company.

One special hum case occurs when a cable box is connected to a computer or audio equipment, or when cable TV is connected to a video monitor you're also using for editing. The cable company's wiring is a hotbed of ground loops (which don't matter to the high-frequency television signal). But once you complete the circuit to a piece of grounded audio equipment, hum develops. It won't go away when you turn off the cable box, but should disappear if you disconnect the television cable.

- If the humming connection to the cable box is via analog audio, use the Radio Shack transformer isolator mentioned above.
- It the connection is via digital audio, replace the RCA coax digital connection with an optical one. Most cable boxes support both, and optical wiring is totally free from ground loops.

If the hum is coming over an analog video cable (three-wire component, two-wire s-video, or one-wire composite), you can try inserting transformers. But it'll get expensive, about $75 per wire at broadcast suppliers. So try this alternative:

- High quality F-connector coax transformers can isolate your cable box from the street, and usually won't interrupt the signal (depending on how your cable system is built). Jensen makes a good one, VRD-1FF, about $60 at broadcast suppliers.

⚠ **WARNING**

BE CAREFUL: the ground loops in a large cable system can generate dangerously high voltages. Avoid touching other equipment or grounded objects while you're changing the street connection.

Wiring monitor speakers

Hi-fi enthusiasts claim great benefits to using special braided or oxygen-free cables between the amplifier and speakers. The physics behind these claims is doubtful. Ordinary 18-gauge "zip cord"—the stuff table lamps are wired with, available at any hardware or electronics store—should be sufficient for short speaker cables in a digital video studio. If wires are going to be longer than ten feet or so, you might want to bump up to 16-gauge zip cord, also commonly available. For longer than 30', use 14-gauge.

Two considerations are important when wiring between a speaker and amplifier, particularly if they have individual screw or pressure terminals.

First, electrical phase must stay consistent. Otherwise one speaker may be in compression while the other is in rarefaction: the result is that bass notes and centered dialog won't be heard at an accurate volume.

One screw or terminal at each speaker, and one on each channel of the amp, will be marked with a + sign or special color. One side of the cable will be marked, either by the color of the copper itself, or by a stripe or rib in the insulation. Use this marking to make sure both speakers in a stereo pair are wired exactly the same way.

Standard practice is to connect the copper-colored, striped, or ribbed wire to the + or red terminal on amp and speaker; and the silver colored (or unstriped, unribbed) wire to the – or black terminal. The important thing is that all of your speakers follow the same rule, so electrical phasing is consistent among them.

The second consideration has more to do with Murphy's Law than physics: fine copper wires that make up each conductor in the cable can become separated, and a tiny stray wire may bridge two terminals and cause a short. This may damage or blow a fuse inside the amplifier. If possible, tin the wires with a soldering iron to keep them together, or use a high-quality crimp- or screw-on lug or banana plug. If you can't terminate the wires this way, be extremely careful that *every* strand of wire is held in place by the screw or binding post.

MIXING –10 DBV AND +4 DBU EQUIPMENT

Even the most professionally wired postproduction suite may have some unbalanced –10 dBV equipment (see Chapter 3), and NLE setups are apt to have a lot of it.

Prosumer VTRs, musical equipment, and sound cards are likely to operate at the lower interconnect voltage. Consumer-grade monitor amplifiers may be totally professional in every respect except their input circuits.

There's no reason the two standards can't coexist in the same facility. Small buffer amplifiers, costing $50–75 per channel, are available at broadcast- and video-supply houses. They take a –10 dBV unbalanced signal and provide both amplification and balancing, turning it into +4 dBu balanced. If your facility uses balanced wiring, they can be mounted right at the low-level source to give you noise immunity as well as a voltage boost. If you need to integrate a high-level balanced input (such as on a broadcast VTR) into an unbalanced system, it's probably easiest to mount the booster right at the deck and consider it just another prosumer device.

If you have just a few high-level balanced sources and don't mind keeping your system unbalanced, you can build a simple resistive adapter for a few dollars. Instructions are in Chapter 8, in the section about attenuators. You'll lose the benefits of balancing at the professional devices, but it's no real loss since you're not using it anywhere else in the room. You may find it more flexible to build a variable version of this circuit using a 5 kΩ trimmer or variable resistor: Just substitute the three terminals on the trimmer for the three resistor connection points in the circuit, with the middle trimmer terminal going to the pin of the –10 device. Set it once for a proper level, then ignore it.

Impedance matching

Modern postproduction equipment is voltage-driven, and not subject to the impedance-matching rules that plagued us in the days of tubes and transformers (though those rules are still valid for dynamic and ribbon mics). In general, you don't have to worry about matching "high" or "low" impedance.

- Soundcards, miniDV decks, and most other unbalanced line-level equipment usually have outputs around 500 Ω, and inputs between 5 kΩ and 50 kΩ. The wide output-to-input ratio means you can feed multiple deck inputs from a single output. All you need is a simple Y-cord, or half-normalled patchbay.

  Higher input impedances can also pick up buzzing and other noises from electrical wiring; if this happens, try putting a 4.7 kΩ resistor in parallel with the input.

- Balanced NLE breakout boxes, mixers, and most high-end decks with XLR connectors follow the same impedance rules as unbalanced ones, even though they operate at about four times the audio voltage.

- Some of the high-end processing equipment in music studios has both input and output transformers. In most cases, these work fine with modern postproduction equipment. Sometimes they produce extra highs and hiss when connected to 5 kΩ or higher inputs: put a 680 Ω resistor in parallel, and the sound will smooth out.

There are only a few exceptions:

- Classic passive equalizers, like the blue-panel Pultecs that now fetch classic-car prices, are very sensitive to input and output impedance. If you're lucky enough to have some of this gear, treat it to transformers on both sides.
- The high-power connection between an amplifier and a separate speaker should be matched for a lot of reasons. But Ohm's Law also comes into play when choosing the cable: a high resistance, at these very low impedances, will cause serious signal loss. That's why lower-gauge speaker wiring is used in pro installations: the conductors are thicker, so there's less resistance.
- Digital audio signals require matched impedances, but not because of Ohm's Law. These signals operate at such high frequencies that the wrong impedance will send data echoes back down the line, possibly disrupting the signal. Even the wire has to be matched for impedance. AES/EBU digital audio (usually on XLR connectors) needs 110 Ω cable and inputs; s/pdif digital audio (RCA or BNC connectors) uses 75 Ω.

Nonaudio wiring

The digital video-editing suite is a complicated place, and some signals that have nothing to do with audio can still have an effect on your sound.

Digital sync

Digital audio is almost always handled in serial form: a string of ones and zeros is taken as a group, to represent one 16-bit (or higher) digital word. For this to work properly, the equipment has to agree how to find the start of each word—because if it can't, unpre dicta blethin gscan happ ento yourso und . . . like that. Each digital stream is self-clocking—a piece of equipment can look at it and determine where the word should start. But in a complicated facility, many audio signals may be moving simultaneously. If they don't all start their words at exactly the same time, the equipment won't know how to translate them. Audio/video equipment such as digital VTRs have the added burden of keeping the picture and sound words timed so they start together, so they can be recorded or processed predictably.

Word clock

In sound studios, digital audio is often synchronized by routing a separate audio sync signal. This "word clock" is wired like video, using 75 Ω cable and BNC connectors. One device is designated as the master clock, and every other piece of equipment is set to sync its own internal circuits to it. The advantage is predictable operation, particularly when multiple audio signals have to be mixed together. Many digital mixers don't need word clock and will buffer each input's data until all the timings match—but this adds another processing step, and another chance for the signal to get degraded.

Video sync

Equipment designed to handle audio in a video environment, such as professional DAWs and mixers, often gives you the option of synchronizing both their internal timing and their digital words to a video signal. This is the same blackburst, video sync, or "house black" that you should be distributing to your VTR and NLE already; all you have to do is extend it to the additional inputs. It's better than timecode for keeping internal timing in step, since it's more precise and not subject to audible variations.

Most audio equipment that can handle a video sync signal also provides a separate, synchronized word clock output. So you can use a blackburst generator for all your video equipment, route its signal to a convenient mixer or word clock generator, and then distribute synchronized word clock from it to any audio devices that don't accept video sync. This will keep all the timings accurate and assure the cleanest digital audio processing. You might not even have the choice whether to do this: some digital video devices won't accept digital audio unless it's also locked to blackburst.

Timecode

Even though it's not as good as video sync for controlling internal timing, SMPTE timecode is the standard for tracking individual frames of audio- and videotapes, and making sure shots and sounds start when they should. Its data format and standards are discussed in the next chapter, but it also has an implication on edit-suite wiring if you've got multiple video or audio-for-video devices.

SMPTE code is usually distributed as an unbalanced, audio-like signal. Its 1-volt square wave, right in the middle of the audible band, has harmonics that can leak into any nearby audio cables. The result is a constant chirping, very much like the sound of a fax transmission.

For best results, keep SMPTE cables far from audio ones. Don't run the two kinds of signals through the same patchbay. SMPTE is so likely to cause interference that it can even distort itself; if you run two different timecode signals on the dual shielded cables used for stereo wiring, the resulting cross-talk may make both unreadable.

Timecode information can also be carried over FireWire and RS-422 machine control wires. This kind of code can't radiate into audio cables in normal situations. Don't worry about it.

USB, FireWire, Ethernet, and the future

Thankfully, computer data connections are the same in a post suite as they are in a computer setup, and you can find lots of information about hookups on the Web or at your local computer dealer. The only audio-specific concern with them is the possibility that their shields and ground pins can cause ground loops, covered earlier in this chapter.

CHAPTER 12

Levels and Digitizing

If you've got new equipment and aren't trying to push the envelope, files on solid state hard drive or similar media may be usable all the way from original shoot to final delivery. Just ingest, make sure you've got backup copies, edit, render a final output, and transfer it to the delivery medium.

But there's still a lot of older gear out there, and there can be artistic or financial reasons why linear media (analog or digital tape, or even film) are chosen for acquisition or distribution. This means you'll need real-time transfers, rather than simple file copies. If your only transfers are to and from a camera or deck via FireWire, this is fairly simple. If you're using non-computer forms of digital audio, or analog connections, there are a few extra steps to take.

DIGITAL AUDIO TRANSFERS

When digitizing isn't

Editors often use the term "digitizing" to mean bringing sound or pictures into NLE, but the term actually refers to converting an analog signal to digital (Chapter 2). For a lot of today's projects, digitizing happens in the camera and never needs to be done again. The signal is already converted to ones and zeroes, and you just have to move the data.

Ingest

Most new cameras and audio recorders store their material as computer files, usually on solid state memory like SD or similar cards, or send a high-definition video signal to a separate recorder using solid state hard drives. The media can be removed from the camera or recorder, popped into an editing system, and you're ready for post-production. For some cameras, the file has to be copied before you can edit ... but that's often a good idea in every case. Either way, the process can be painless and quick: depending on the medium, computers can make their copies hundreds of times faster than real-time. The process is usually called *ingesting*.

It's not necessarily foolproof. File specifications keep evolving, and even standard ones might not be fully compatible between systems. In the audio world, a *.wav* (or *wave*) can be read by just about every system, regardless of age or manufacturer. But newer variations such as *.bwf* (*broadcast wave*) might include timecode information that your NLE ignores. Or it might contain multiple audio channels—one for each mic in a complex shoot, for example—that cause some NLEs to reject the audio entirely. Things get worse when data compression is involved, because not only the file type but also the codec have to be compatible, and newer codecs are constantly being introduced.

If files aren't compatible, translation software can usually be found. Low-cost utilities exist that can go from just about any standard format to any other; a Web search or trusted shareware source can usually locate what you need. Most standard formats, including multiple channel .bwf, can be opened and converted by the open-source Audacity software, discussed in Chapter 10.

If your system uses a proprietary file format, the manufacturer probably has downloadable translators available to convert the data to standard file. Or you can pay for professional software that processes entire directories of files in a single operation, or translates directly from one proprietary system to another.

But before you try any translation software, ask your NLE or DAW manufacturer about updates. Often, a file that isn't recognized in one software version can be opened in the next. Some version updates are free. Others may require a paid upgrade, new operating system, or even new hardware ... in which case, it can be reasonable to stick with what you've got, and use a translation utility.

Capture

In some setups, computer-style high-speed file copies aren't possible. This is the case with tape-based media such as miniDV and DAT: a camera or deck has to play the tape in real-time, and send its data to the editing computer where it's then written to files on a hard drive. Essentially, you're recreating the original signal and re-recording it elsewhere. This kind of *capture* takes time compared to file ingest, but it doesn't necessarily involve any loss of audio quality. (Loss of video quality can be a different story, depending on the codecs used.)

If the file's sample rate and bit depth matches that of the data stream, and you're not making any intentional changes to the sound, digital audio captures should be completely transparent. Sometimes it seems like a capture problem can be solved only by converting the camera or recorder's signal to analog, and re-digitizing it in the computer. This is seldom a good idea. Each analog/digital conversion—even with the best equipment—adds distortion and can make the sound muddier. If you care about quality, it's worth tracking down the digital problem and staying in that world.

This all-digital bias isn't the case in music production, where a certain amount of analog *warmth* may be preferred. Music mixers will run their computer-based creations through an analog processor or a generation of analog tape because of the pleasing distortion it can impart. But with the multiple generations of processing necessary for dialog-driven video, clarity is a lot more important than warmth.

☞ ROSE'S RULES

Debugging transfers

- If ingest isn't possible with your system, but you have the option of straight digital transfer—camera or deck to NLE via digital wiring, with no analog in between—use it.
- If a transfer isn't giving you any sound, or the sound has periodic clicks or bursts of static, there's probably a digital sync problem. Make sure the recording device is set to sync to its input, or that there's a common sync source. Verify that the recorder is looking for the same bit depth and number of tracks as the source material. Check equipment instructions or manufacturer's website for details.
- If a transfer sounds like the wrong pitch, it's usually a sample rate incompatibility. Make sure both devices are set to the same rate. For most film and video purposes, that'll be 48 kHz.

Years ago, some people recommended analog connections to solve these problems. Today, equipment is more flexible. Analog transfers degrade the sound, so it's a good thing that they're almost never necessary.

FireWire and other data transfers

The computer industry is way ahead of audio. If you're sending audio or file data over a connection designed for computing—such as FireWire, USB, or Thunderbolt—things will be relatively foolproof and work well. Or, when they don't work, diagnosing the problem can be easy.

FireWire/1394

FireWire is a high-speed data connection standard used for digital video with audio, multichannel audio, and computer peripherals such as hard drives and CD burners. In many devices, it appears as FireWire 400 on a six-pin jack (Figure 12.1A); cameras and other video devices usually put it on a four-pin jack to save space (Figure 12.1B). Only four of the conductors are used to carry data, so a simple adapter cable is all that's needed to connect one to the other. The other two wires are used to power some non-video devices.

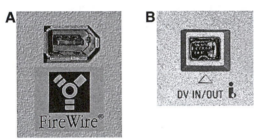

Figure 12.1 FireWire 400 connectors.

FireWire was developed by Apple. For at least a decade, they've made the name and Y-shaped logo available for any equipment that meets the standard. Sony adopted the same spec, but decided to call their system i.Link and use an i-shaped logo. The Institute of Electrical and Electronics Engineers, an international standard-setting organization, adopted it as IEEE 1394. Some filmmakers just call it the DV connection. All of these things refer to the same standard.

FireWire 800, also known as IEEE 1394b, is capable of even faster rates (slightly less than 800 megabits per second). This is more than digital video usually needs, but is included on new computers to use with fast removable hard drives or data transfers. FireWire 800 is backwards compatible, and can handle a FireWire 400 signal. Its nine-pin connector (Figure 12.2A) doesn't fit the older cables directly, but adapters are available (Figure 12.2B).

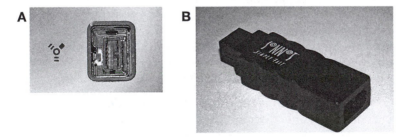

Figure 12.2 FireWire 800 jack and adapter.

✔ **TIP**

Playing with Fire(Wire)

FireWire is usually plug-and-play, but some gremlins can sneak in.

- Some third-party cards can have problems that cause loss of sync. This doesn't seem to be an issue with computers whose FireWire connectors are on the motherboard.

- Obsolete FireWire drivers can also cause loss of sync, as well as periodic clicking or dropouts. Check for updates.

- Dropped video frames often show up as a loss of *audio* sync. That's because an occasional one-frame jump in the picture is rarely noticeable, unless there's fast motion. But each jump knocks the sync out by one frame. If you're seeing strange sync errors, check the capture report for lost frames. Follow your NLE manufacturer's tips for reducing the number.

- While FireWire handles audio as data, your computer treats the incoming signal from a camera or other real-time device as sound. If the system-level record or input volume control isn't set to 0 dB, it may try to change the volume, increasing noise or distortion.[1] Files being transferred *as files* over a FireWire connection aren't affected by this. It applies only to real-time transfers.

- A few cameras use a slightly nonstandard sample rate. It's close enough to 48 kHz to sound okay, but can result in tracks that gradually slip out of sync over long transfers. You could fix this problem with an analog transfer—the computer would re-digitize at the proper rate—but you'd lose all the advantages of a digital transfer. It's better to tolerate the slowly drifting sync as long as you can, and then use a visual cutaway or find a pause in the track and trim a few frames to restore sync.

- Most consumer cameras don't lock the audio frames to video ones. This usually isn't a problem, but may cause trouble when dubbing to a more professional format. Your NLE might have a setting to restore the lock; or you might have to dub audio via analog. Since high-end video decks have decent analog circuits, this won't compromise quality when done properly.

- FireWire 800 doesn't provide power, so while it can be converted to the older six-pin standard, some peripherals will require additional power supplies. This isn't a concern with most video equipment and storage devices, which have their own supplies anyway.

---

[1] As you recall from the first chaper, 0 dB is a ratio of 1:1—often, the midpoint on a computer's volume control—and not tech-speak for "zero volume."

Both flavors of FireWire can be daisy-chained, with multiple devices hooked up in series on a single computer port. FireWire is hot-swappable, and usually plug-and-play. Get an appropriate cable, plug it into the camera and computer, and a few moments later the camera is available to the system. FireWire 400 standards call for a maximum cable length of about 15 feet, but that's to carry a full 400 megabits per second (MBPS) of data. DV uses only 100 MBPS, so longer cables can be successful. (Despite the data capacity of FireWire, DV tape transfers can't be faster than real-time; the transports and heads aren't quick enough.)

While FireWire devices are immediately recognized at the system level, most NLE software scans for the camera only on start-up. Plug in the camera, turn it on, and make sure it's in VTR mode before launching the program. NLEs can often control the camera's transport as well, and some perform automatic batch transfers. Since FireWire shows up at the system level, you can use a FireWire-connected camera as a source for recording in many audio-only programs as well. While FireWire can carry low-resolution four-channel sound from cameras that support 12-bit recording, most audio or video programs will record only two channels at a time. Select the appropriate pair in software before you capture or record.

FireWire connectors look something like the USB ones used for keyboards and other desktop peripherals, and the wiring scheme is similar, but they're not compatible.

Thunderbolt

Figure 12.3
Thunderbolt connector.

A relatively new contender to FireWire is Thunderbolt, introduced by Apple in their 2011 computers. Thunderbolt can handle almost any function that used to require an internal slot in the computer, is fast enough for Full HD 4k video, and simultaneously drives one or two computer monitors. Figure 12.3 shows the connector.

Its speed—about six times faster than the best FireWire—makes it ideal for solid state hard drives and multichannel audio. Thunderbolt can also be used to drive video, audio, and DSP cards ... probably its greatest potential for pro users. In non-Thunderbolt computers, those cards have to be installed on an internal PCI bus so they can communicate with the central processors efficiently. High-end users frequently run out of slots and have to relegate some functions to FireWire. They also have to worry about upgrading cards when tower configurations change.[2] A Thunderbolt expansion chassis lets you add cards outside of the tower, while still giving them full access to the central processors. It also means you can get away from towers

---

[2] My primary tower has four internal drives, and its slots are filled with pro audio input and output cards, graphics display card, and an additional FireWire bus card. I had to add that last function at the last upgrade, *downgrading* one of my critical audio processing subsystems from an older PCI format to FireWire, because the manufacturer didn't make a newer PCI card.

completely, using modern high-power laptops and mini-towers and running all your drives and processors externally.

Thunderbolt is just now coming into the market. As I write this, only a few high-end audio manufacturers make interfaces or DSP, with prices ranging between $2,000 and $6,000; audio is supported on a few video interfaces as well. Expansion chassis cost about $350 for each PCI card they support. FireWire was similarly high priced when it first appeared.

Will Thunderbolt eventually have the same acceptance (and competitive prices) as FireWire? Apple is the innovator, as it was with FireWire, and that counts for a lot . . . but it's hard to guess Apple's current plans for the pro video market. FireWire also got a big push when the camera manufacturers adopted it for real-time transfer; a function now standardized on HDMI. Check dealers and user groups to see how this plays out.

USB

This standard appears in almost all computers, most small audio/video gear, and a lot of other connected devices ranging from TV remotes to telephones. Its near-universality means it's robust, installs easily and usually without drivers, and devices using it don't have to be expensive.

Each iteration of USB has gotten faster, with USB 3.0 carrying a design speed twice as fast as the current FireWire.[3] Practical speeds tend to be a little slower, so USB audio devices usually have fewer channels than their FireWire cousins. The standard is downward-compatible, and most devices work fine at their original speeds when plugged into a higher-numbered jack: you don't have to worry about throwing away USB equipment with each new iteration.

USB may appear on three different standard connectors, plus a host of proprietary ones. The signal is the same, so simple adapters are usually all that's needed. Rectangular USB *A* jacks (Figure 12.4) usually appear on host equipment, like computers and hubs; many printers and other peripherals have cords that plug directly into them. Squarish USB *B* jacks (Figure 12.5) appear

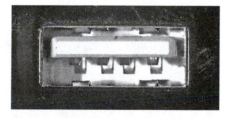

Figure 12.4 USB A jack, usually found on computers and hubs, but sometimes on power chargers (see tip).

Figure 12.5 USB B jack, reserved for peripherals like printers and audio interfaces with removable cords.

---

[3] Both are left at the starting gate by Thunderbolt: its design speed is about eight times faster than practical USB 3.0 chains.

✔ TIP

Where's my data?

USB provides 5 volts and is often used just as a power connector. USB A jacks appear on simple plug-in chargers—and sometimes on desk lamps, TV sets, and even adjustable beds—as a convenience for recharging the batteries in cellphones and other small gadgets. Manufacturers make charging cables with a USB A plug on one end and whatever's needed for the device (often USB mini-plug) on the other. These charging cables, however, often don't carry data and can't be used for syncing or downloading.

The problem is, you can't tell if a cable is for data or only for power just by looking at it. So if you've plugged a USB device into your computer but it's not being recognized, the first step is to try changing the cable.

Figure 12.6 USB mini-jack, functionally the same as a B jack but found on smaller gadgets like cameras and mini-recorders.

on peripherals with removable cords, or as the input jack on USB hubs, and are designed to plug into the host that controls them: a simple A to B cable is usually all that's needed to get things running. USB mini-jacks (Figure 12.6) appear on gadgets like phones that are too small to support a USB B jack, but work the same way.

Solid state USB storage devices—called *flash drives*, *thumb drives*, and similar names—look like elongated USB A plugs, and appear to your computer as a hard drive. They can hold more than 100 Gigabytes, though much smaller ones in the 4 to 16 GB range are more common. They're cheap and rugged, and have become an almost universal solution for carrying large media files of any kind, when networking is too slow or inconvenient.

Removable cards

Many cameras and multichannel portable audio recorders often use storage cards—effectively large flash drives with specialized and faster edge connections—instead of USB plugs. Wikipedia currently lists more than two dozen types, including three different sizes of Secure Digital (SD). Most can't be plugged directly into a computer for transfers.

The devices that use these cards frequently have built-in mini USB jacks for transferring the card's data, or adapters are available from the manufacturer. But it can be handier (and cheaper) to get a low-cost card reader. It'll save wear and tear on expensive field gear, and can be left plugged into the computer. When you insert a card, the computer sees it as a hard drive. The unit in Figure 12.7 costs about $80 and claims to support 19 different flavors of card—I haven't found one it has trouble with—though there are simpler and cheaper ones available.

Real-time transfers

Ingesting material as data directly from the camera or recorder's storage device is always better than playing it and re-recording into

Figure 12.7 A low-cost card reader like this can be better than trying to transfer files directly from the camera or recorder.

the computer. It can create an absolute clone of the data, bypassing (or postponing) error concealment schemes so you can archive it or fine-tune the processing, and is usually much faster than real-time recording. But it's sometimes impossible: older cameras and recorders use tape rather than nonlinear storage, and can play only at real-time speeds.

- MiniDV tape cameras often have FireWire jacks to facilitate the transfer, which can be plugged directly into the computer (though may require drivers). It doesn't usually result in an absolute clone of tape's data, because the camera does some processing on the way out. But it gives you a far better signal than using the camera's analog video output and re-digitizing in the computer, and it isn't any slower.
- DAT and MiniDisc recorders may have digital audio outputs, either s/pdif or AES/EBU. You can capture the signal with an audio card, or plug it into most Macs through a simple optical adapter. Again, this is processed and reconstructed audio rather than whatever is actually on the media, but is technically much cleaner than using analog.
- A few cameras have non-removable storage and play their internal memory through HDMI outputs. An HDMI input card on your computer—usually part of the same card that drives a high quality picture monitor for editing or mixing—will let you capture the signal digitally.

Dealing with digital audio

Digital audio wiring was designed to be more flexible than standard computer connections, so there's more room for user error. Setup problems can result in periodic clicking in the track, a low-level hiss that comes and goes with the signal, occasional dropouts, or sometimes a flutter or roughness to the high frequencies. But it's not hard to fix if you remember a few rules.

The following advice applies to *any* digital audio you might be moving around your edit setup. Follow these guidelines when connecting digital mixers and processors, as well as when you're feeding a digital source to a computer input.

Use the right cable

Generic hi-fi cables have the right connectors for s/pdif, but the wire itself can cause dropouts when used for digital connections. Old-fashioned modem cables look like they should be able to handle multitrack audio in TDIF format, but can damage the recorder. If you're not sure whether you've got the right kind of cable, check the manufacturer's instructions and Chapter 2 of this book.

Choose an appropriate sync source

Digital inputs rely on serial data, so they need synchronization to find the start of each word. Consumer gear synchronizes automatically to the input, so this may not be an issue. But professional equipment often gives you a choice of synchronizing to the input, a separate audio or video sync source (Chapter 11), or internal crystal. Some gear supports only external sync with certain inputs.

If your facility is wired with video or word-clock sync, use it whenever possible to prevent problems. You'll have to specify the sample rate or video format for it to work properly.

If you have to dub from a non-synchronizable source such as a CD player or portable DAT, you may have a choice: set the computer to sync from its input, or look for a setting to *reclock* (resynchronize) the input. Either will usually work. If the source has an unstable crystal, using the input as a sync source will often be cleaner. But if the source is intentionally out-of-spec—for example, if you've varispeeded a CD, forcing its sample rate to something other than 44.1 kHz—you *must* reclock the signal. If you don't, the effect of varispeeding will disappear when you play the transferred file at the normal rate!

Plan for as few sample-rate conversions as possible

It's probable that you'll have to change the sample rate of one source signal or another during production. CDs and consumer portable recorders run at 44.1 kHz. DATs can be 44.1 kHz or 48 kHz. Digital videotape is usually 48 kHz, but may be 32 kHz. Internet and multimedia audio might come through at 32 kHz or 22.050 kHz. Productions that involve 16mm or 35mm film usually require a 0.1% sample-rate correction in the US, and a 4% correction in Europe (more about this later).

A little planning here can make a world of difference. Figure out what your final sample rate has to be. If you're going to digital video or DVD, 48 kHz will be necessary. If you're mixing for CDROM or the Web, use 44.1 kHz. Set your NLE to this rate, and consider converting other sources before you import them. (While most NLEs can convert between 44.1 kHz and 48 kHz internally, it often requires an extra rendering step and many don't use particularly good-sounding or efficient algorithms for the conversion. Audio programs usually do a better job.)

✳ TIDBIT

Faster isn't necessarily better

When doing analog tape production, it makes sense to make working copies and mixdowns at their highest possible quality—15 inches per second or even faster for audio—and not slow things down until you make the final delivery tape. Each generation loses some quality, and higher tape speeds protect as much quality as possible.

But digital production doesn't suffer this kind of generation loss. While higher digital sample rates are directly equivalent to faster analog tape speeds, there's no advantage to dubbing to a higher rate than the original audio. It doesn't make the quality any better.

Keep the bit depth high

The minimum for professional production is 16-bit audio. Many NLEs will let you import 24-bit files, though they won't record or capture at that bit depth. Most good audio software supports 24-bit recording and mixing, and actually uses many more bits for processing.

Using 24 bits is theoretically always better than 16 bits, because it gives you more margin for error and lower noise. But the reality is that many NLEs don't fully support that bit depth—they'll import and edit files that were recorded at 24 bits, but don't make proper use of the extra data when mixing or processing. Many mid-price recorders that brag about 24-bit recording only achieve 16-bit performance from their mic inputs; the extra bits just waste storage space. On the other hand, most good audio software makes full use of 24-bit sampling, and may even use 32 bits or more for processing.

In other words: unless you're working with top-notch equipment, 16 bits is usually sufficient for recording and editing in an NLE. If you move your files to an audio program for final mix and processing, it can be worthwhile to set the DAW to 24 bits; it will convert the files to that standard when you move them from your NLE.

Never use eight-bit settings unless you've got a very good reason. Low bit-depth problems are cumulative over multiple generations. If you've shot 12-bit audio in the field—and you'd better have a darned good reason for using that setting—your NLE will convert it to 16-bits before editing. No quality is lost with this upward conversion, but none is gained either.

Normally, don't normalize until the mix is done

Normalizing is the automatic process of scanning a file, finding the loudest sample, and then amplifying the entire file so its maximum level reaches a preset peak. It's useful in some situations, but almost never for production tracks. That's because each clip of a scene may be amplified a different amount, depending on the loudest dialog in the clip. This changes the background level from clip to clip, making a smooth mix almost impossible.

If you have to boost a scene that was shot too softly, use a Gain or Amplify function instead, and apply the same amount to a copy of every clip. Most audio programs can do this as a batch process. Then check each of the new clips to make sure none of them reach 0 dBFS; if they do, go back to the originals and apply less gain.

After a project is mixed, you may want to normalize the entire track so it plays as loudly as possible. But making a mix sound loud actually requires proper processing and mixing, described later in this book. Normalizing a mix—particularly one intended for broadcast—can actually make it sound worse on the air, because stations have to go through extra steps to bring the program to the proper level for their transmitter.

There's a myth that normalization is necessary to get the best results from mp3 and other psychoacoustic compression (see Chapter 2). Strictly speaking, it isn't: the algorithm breaks the incoming audio into short chunks, normalizes each before encoding, and then applies a matching gain reduction on playback. Pre-normalizing the files won't make any difference to how the system performs.

Avoid data compression until the final step

You'll probably need to run the final mix through data compression for distribution. If so, keep an uncompressed version.

These processes are not reversible—decoding the compressed audio always results in some data loss—so you'll need the original if you have to re-edit or compress with a different algorithm. Besides, new processes are constantly being developed. Tomorrow's compression might be a lot cleaner, and you'll want to be able to take advantage of it without being stuck with yesterday's data loss.

Don't compress individual tracks, either. They'll just have to be decoded when you edit or mix—even if the software does this in the background, without telling you—and coding artifacts will build up when they're recompressed. Wait until you've got a mixed track, and then do the whole thing in a single pass.

Listen!

Whatever you do, keep an ear on what's actually coming out of your NLE or processor rather than on what's going in. If an element is being processed offline in software, play the whole thing back before proceeding. Most digital audio problems will show up on good monitors, if you just listen carefully, and can be undone if you catch them quickly enough.

Digital audio processors

If you need to tweak levels, equalization, or volume compression and you have a good outboard digital processor or mixer, it's acceptable (and certainly a time saver) to apply this correction while you're transferring from digital media. But keep things subtle;

it's a lot easier to add additional processing later than to compensate if you go overboard now. Make sure the source, processor or mixer, and recorder or computer are at the same sample rate. Be sure to store the processor's settings so you can reapply them if you have to retransfer.

No matter how good your digital reverb is, don't apply this reverb during the initial transfer stage. If a track seems too dry to match the picture—perhaps because a radio mic was very close during a long shot—cherish its purity; tracks like this are the easiest to edit. Once the show is completely cut, and you've also got music and sound effects in place, you can add appropriate reverb.

DIGITIZING ANALOG SIGNALS

Often, analog sources such as Betacam tapes or live mics have to be edited, or you're using digital sources like DAT or MiniDiscs, but your NLE isn't equipped for digital input. In these cases it's necessary to *digitize*, converting the analog signal to digital in the input circuits of the editing system. This introduces a whole new place for things to go wrong.

The problem is that analog audio can't be controlled with the precision or simple user interface of digital transfers. Until a signal is turned into ones and zeroes, your computer can't help. Using computer controls to compensate for badly-set analog equipment makes things even worse.

✔ TIP

The best way to avoid problems with digitizing is to not digitize at all. Connect digital sources like DAT or Flash RAM recorders through an s/pdif adapter if they won't plug directly into USB. Import CD audio by ripping it in the computer's CD-ROM drive, rather than playing the tracks on an analog-output player.

Most recording studios, announcers, and composers can supply elements as files or audio CD. Use this option instead of re-digitizing other media. Not only will the quality be higher; it's also faster to transfer a file than to re-digitize a real-time playback.

It takes some thought to set up a system for digitizing well, but, once you've done the preliminary work, things will go smoothly. The place to start is with the analog circuits in your edit suite, before the signal ever gets to the NLE.

Gain-staging

Everything in your analog signal path has a finite dynamic range. There's only a narrow window between too soft—when the signal is mixed with hiss and other electronic noise—and too loud to handle without distortion. Each piece of equipment has a specific range where it gives you the best performance. Gain-staging is the process of fine-tuning the volume as it passes from one piece of equipment to another, so that the signals always stay in that range. (This also applies to digital signals, but their dynamic range is wider, and you don't have to worry about recalibrating at every step—once a signal is digital, its level stays the same until someone deliberately changes it. So unless you're writing audio processing software, gain-staging is usually thought of as an analog concern.)

Figure 12.8 shows how things can go wrong in a setup with preamp, equalizer, and compressor. But the same problems can occur in a setup with just a preamp and computer input, between the input and output circuits in a mixing board, or any other time a signal has to pass through multiple stages . . . even if those stages are all in the same device.

Although both signal paths in the figure yield the same volume at the end, the top signal is distorted and noisy . . . and won't sound good in a mix. The problem is

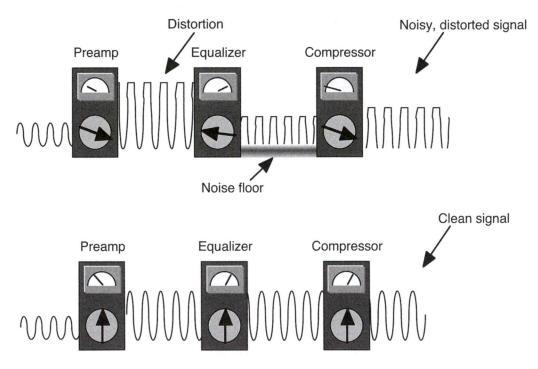

Figure 12.8 Both signal paths have the same final volume, but the bottom one will sound a lot better.

that the preamp was set for too much gain in the top path. This forced it to a higher level than its own circuits could handle, causing distortion on its output. It also meant that the equalizer saw too much signal, so its volume had to be turned down. But it was turned down too far, forcing its output down to where part of the signal is obscured by electronic noise. The input to the compressor was then turned up to compensate, amplifying both signal and noise . . . and doing nothing about the distortion.

In the lower path, the preamp is set to a reasonable amount of gain. Its output is just right for the equalizer, which puts out the right amount of signal for the compressor. The result is a signal that's just as loud as the top path's, but a lot better sounding.

Unfortunately, the nice meters and large calibrated knobs I drew usually don't usually exist in real life. Many consumer and semipro devices don't have more than a flashing overload light. The only way to tell if equipment is working in its proper range is to test a lot of different levels.

Here's a general procedure, though it's worth checking individual product manuals, since specific equipment may have other alignment procedures.

1. Start with the first item in your signal chain. Apply a normal signal, from the playback of well-recorded original track.
2. Raise the equipment's input volume until the overload light starts flashing; then lower it until the light flashes only on occasional peaks—no more than once every couple of seconds. If analog equipment has a bouncing meter instead of a flashing light, consider one or two units above the zero point—where the meter scale turns red—as the equivalent. If the equipment has an output level control, turn it to the midpoint or detent.
3. Now do the same thing with the next device in the chain. You should end up with its input volume control around the midpoint. If you have to turn it up or down a lot, there's either a mismatch between equipment at –10 dBV and at +4 dBu, or you've gotten microphone- and line-level connections mixed up. If it's the former case, you'll need a buffer or pad (see Chapter 11). If it's the latter, fix the wiring—anything else you do will sacrifice quality.

After you're sure that levels are being handled properly before the signal gets to your computer, you can start to turn the analog signal into data on a file. There are two potential trouble spots here: the quality of the NLE's digitizing circuit and how well the software's meters are calibrated. You can do something about both of them.

Getting better inputs

No matter how fast a processor chip is, or how many audio effects are supplied with the software, the ultimate limit on an NLE's sound is its analog circuits. Often, there's not much control over their quality. A lot of systems are sold by people who understand video and software, not sound. Some major NLEs have proprietary audio interfaces that were designed by independent contractors, and the manufacturer doesn't even know their basic specifications.[4] Software-only NLEs rely on the user's input device, which may not be particularly high quality.

Unfortunately, turning audio into digits is an exacting process, and it requires expensive components to do the job well. One good solution is to get a full-sized portable digital recorder. Use it at the shoot for double-system sound (Chapter 8), since the quality is usually so much better than most in-camera recordings. Ingest these tracks into your NLE or transfer them digitally. Then use just the portable in your edit suite to digitize mics and line-level analog sources—you may be able to leave its transport in pause, and feed its digital signal directly to your computer. These portables also have reliable metering and large analog volume controls, something you won't find with most other computer-input devices.

You need only one external converter to improve both digitizing and final output: while you're recording or editing, put the converter on the NLE's input and monitor via the system's built-in analog output. When you're ready to mix or send the finished track to analog tape, switch the converter to the output and use it in digital-to-analog mode.

Calibrating an NLE's meters

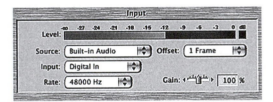

Figure 12.9 Record level meters in an NLE should be calibrated in dBFS, like this one.

Most NLEs these days come with audio level meters, calibrated in dBFS, looking something like the one in Figure 12.9. It's a welcome change; a few years ago, some popular systems left you guessing. But it's possible you're digitizing into an older system with sloppier metering . . . or it doesn't have a meter at all, and you have to use an external meter in a mixer or other device. In those cases, you'll have to go through some calibration steps. (An external meter might already be calibrated, but unless it's connected to your system digitally, the calibrations could be off.) Fortunately, the procedure is easy. You don't need any additional hardware or technical knowledge, and it'll remain accurate until you change the system.

Before you do anything else, check the system-level input volume controls (Figure 12.10). These take priority over any settings you make in software. They should be in their neutral position (shown) and left there for any audio operation.

---

[4] I've spent frustrating hours on the phone with product managers of a big-ticket editing system, trying to find out how their analog-to-digital circuit was calibrated. They offered to send me a schematic, but said nobody in-house could read it.

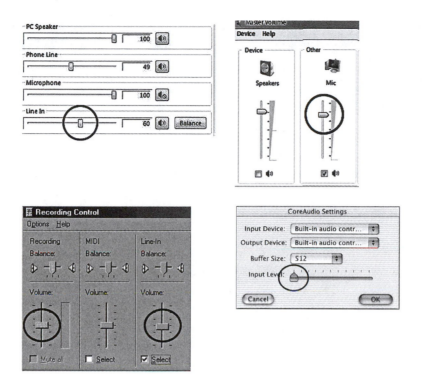

Figure 12.10 System-level input volume controls.
Make sure they're set to their neutral position.

1. Start by setting the program's input volume control (if it has one) to its nominal position. This is usually the default value and may be marked as 0 dB or 50%; in most situations, this results in the cleanest recording.
2. Adjust the *analog* equipment's output volume control for the next step. This is one case where analog is better than digital. If your analog equipment doesn't have an output volume control, or this procedure makes you turn that control below about 30% of maximum, you'll need an accessory attenuator like the one described in the next section. Without it, you'll never get the best digitizing level.
3. Find a well-recorded source tape. Play it and adjust the source's output (or accessory attenuator) so the recording meter comes close to the top on the loudest sounds, but never completely reaches the top. Don't pay too much attention to the average level for now, just the peaks.[5]

---

[5] The average level on a software meter can fool you. Some meters may show an average level that's only about 30% as big as the peaks; others might show an 80% average for the same material. It depends on whether the programmer knew that audio measurements are logarithmic. (You already know that, because you read Chapter 1 of this book.)

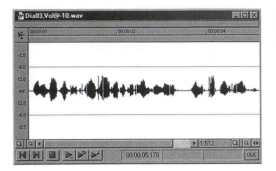

Figure 12.11 Save the file with a name that'll help you remember its level.

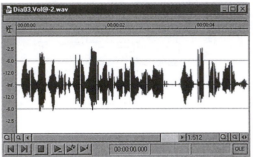

Figure 12.12 Good recording levels fill the screen without touching top or bottom.

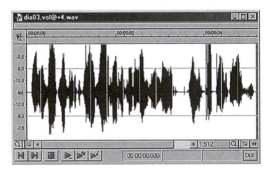

Figure 12.13 When the digitizing level is too high, tops or bottoms of waves will be flattened.

4. Once you've adjusted the volume, record about 15 seconds at that level and save the file. Use a name that'll help you remember the peak meter reading for that trial (see Figure 12.11). Now make two more recordings, one at a somewhat lower output level, and one somewhat higher. Note their peak readings also, and save them with appropriate names.
5. Open the three files and look at their waveforms. This is a little like Goldilocks and her bears, but you're looking for which file gave you the loudest recording without distortion. Figure 12.11 is too soft; the wave could be bigger and still look complete (as in Figure 12.12). Figure 12.13 is too loud: the waves reach the upper or lower boundary of the window or have flattened tops and bottoms; once this happens, the recording is distorted and can't be fixed.

Now just note the name of which file gave you the best looking waveform. That's your ideal peak meter reading.

It's unlikely your results will match mine on the first set of recordings. So repeat the process, making finer and finer adjustments centered around the best meter reading from the previous trial. In a few minutes, you'll find the ideal reading. It doesn't matter what the meter says in dB or percentage or arbitrary numbers, so long as you can repeat it. The next time you're digitizing, set the source's volume control so the meter reacts the same way. Dialog, narration, and different kinds of music can cause different meter responses, so you may want to repeat the calibration procedure with various audio sources.

Linear and "boosted"

Some NLE software lets you view an audio clip with a built-in visual distortion that boosts lower volumes so you can see them better. This affects how the softer samples will appear, but won't change the sound or what you're looking for: the best recording level will be the one that fills the window without touching the edges.

Accessory attenuator

If have to turn the source's output control very close to its lowest level to get a good recording, it's likely you'll be picking up extra noise from the source's output circuits. These usually follow the level control, so turning the knob all the way down has the same effect as bad gain-staging (as with the equalizer in the top of Figure 12.8). A better solution is to run the output device at its proper nominal volume, and insert an external volume control between its output and the digitizer's input.

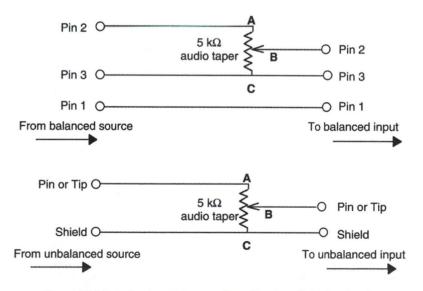

Figure 12.14 A simple attenuator for adjusting digitizing levels.

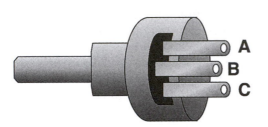

Figure 12.15 The letters refer to connections in Figure 12.14.

For some reason, nobody makes a reasonably priced plug-in volume control, but you can build your own for about $5. It uses a single 5 kΩ audio-taper potentiometer (Radio Shack #271–1720) and appropriate connectors. Figure 12.14 shows how to wire it for balanced and unbalanced circuits, and Figure 12.15 identifies the connections as they'll appear on most brands of potentiometer. You must use soldered connections to avoid noise, and may want to put the unit (or a pair of them for stereo) in a metal or plastic box with a large knob, so it's easier to check and restore the settings. If that's too much work, get a local hacker or repair shop to build it for you.

Diagnosing level problems

Bad digitizing levels can hide hum or noise in your audio chain. Once you've calibrated the system, digitize another test file at the correct volume. But this time, use a source tape that has some silence recorded on it as well as normal program material (unplug the mic or turn the record-volume control down when you record this part). Play back the file and listen very carefully to the silent part. If there isn't any noise, your system is properly calibrated, and you're done.

If there is noise on the test file, digitize that source tape yet again. But this time pause the source for a few seconds in the middle of the recording. Play back this file and listen to where you paused. If the noise stopped, it's on the source tape. You may be able to reduce it in software, but only at the cost of losing some of the desired sound. (Most "noise reduction" systems assume noise is most bothersome during pauses, and simply turn down the overall volume—or just the treble—when things get soft. But the noise is still there, lurking under the signal and ready to be emphasized by subsequent processors.) Some cameras generate a tiny amount of noise when the mic is unplugged. Others generate moderate amounts of noise at all times; read Chapter 8 for things you can do about it.

If the noise continues even when the source tape is stopped, it's being generated by the playback deck or digitizing hardware. Here are some steps for fixing it:

- Hiss is often a question of bad gain-staging.
- Hiss can also be caused by magnetized tape heads in an analog audio or video deck, or badly aligned analog equipment. You can get a demagnetizer with instructions at most electronics stores, but for anything else, you'll need the help of a technician.

- Random noises—snaps, crackles, and pops—are usually caused by loose connections or bad circuit components. Try cleaning the connectors (a rubber eraser works well, or you can get special cleaning fluids at electronics stores) or replacing the cables. If that doesn't help, it's time to take your equipment to the shop.
- Hum in desktop video setups is almost always the result of ground loops (see Chapter 11).

Once you've tracked down and fixed any noises or hum, make a final test recording at the ideal level you found, and look at its waveform. It's unlikely, but you may need to go through the calibration procedure again. Then relax, secure in the knowledge that your analog digitizing chain is properly set up.

METERING AND LINEUP TONES

Audio-level meters do more than tell you how loud a mix is, or when you're digitizing at the right level. Used with a lineup tone, they provide repeatability: you can digitize part of a scene today, re-digitize other parts of it next year, and all the audio should intercut perfectly. Meters and tone also assure consistency, so the dub house or broadcast station that gets your tapes will have some idea of what to expect for volume levels.

✳ TIDBIT

Tones-deaf

Experienced audio professionals usually take the lineup tone at the head of a tape with a grain of salt. We use it to calibrate gain-staging, and are rigorous about providing accurate tones on tapes we send out. But we've all been burned by badly applied tones on tapes we get, so we usually double-check the levels with actual program material before digitizing.

This means we sometimes get into the habit of ignoring tones when we get a digital tape. The levels recorded on the tape itself are unambiguous: they have a certain number of bits, which always means a certain level. Lineup tones aren't needed, because the digital signal provides its own constant calibration.

But once those digital tapes hit an analog connection, all bets are off. *That's* when we pay careful attention to lineup tones.

VU meters

The big Bakelite volume unit meter used to be a standard fixture on every piece of audio equipment. These were more than simple voltage meters; while they measured steady tones the way voltmeters did, they responded to quickly varying sounds like our ears do. Their ballistics were designed to smooth over very fast volume changes, so they correlated nicely with subjective loudness. Unfortunately, they also drew current from the audio line, loading it down, and their rectifiers added a subtle but audible distortion to the signal.

So much for nostalgia. Today there are so few true VU meters being manufactured that they're too expensive to include in most equipment. If they were included, they'd need separate overload indicators; their damped movements can't catch the sudden peaks that were tolerable in analog days but cause crackling with digital systems.

Analog voltmeter

Figure 12.16 The "VU" meters in most modern equipment are really low-cost voltmeters.

The things that *look like* VU meters (Figure 12.16) in modern analog gear are simple voltmeters and don't have the same calibrated dynamics. They're too fast to show average levels, but can't respond quickly enough for short transients. On the other hand, they're accurate with steady signals and can be used for lineup tones. If you have a true VU meter along with one of these voltmeters measuring the same signal, you'll notice that the VU is much easier to read because it's not jumping around as much. You'll also notice that if they're both calibrated to the same tone, sudden jumps to +1 on the VU meter might swing as high as +6 on the voltmeter.

Peak reading meter

Both digital and analog distort when a signal is too loud. But analog distortion isn't noticeable on very fast peaks, while some digital gear will make a horrible crackling noise if a peak is much longer than a thousandth of a second—the first split second of a gunshot, for example. Even a fast-responding analog voltmeter can't display peaks this fast, so electronic circuits are added to capture the loudest reading and hold it for a few seconds. These circuits can also determine the average volume and generate a voltage that makes a lower-cost voltmeter behave like a proper VU meter. (Building one of these circuits and calibrating it for a specific voltmeter mechanism is still an expensive proposition, however, so you rarely find them outside of recording studios.)

Microprocessors can also measure peak and average voltage. Some audio programs put a relatively reliable combination meter on the computer screen, though the CPU might be too busy during actual recording to respond to very fast peaks. The most accurate hardware-based audio meters today have dedicated circuit boards with their own processor chips and display both peak and average level, either on a row of LEDs or superimposed on the video monitor. If the circuit is fed with an AES/EBU or s/pdif digital audio stream, the meter is self-calibrating and absolutely reliable. Figure 12.17 shows one from my studio. It's a standard unit you'll find in studios everywhere, and is available from Dorrough Electronics.

Digital metering in software

I use that Dorrough meter because I want a standalone reference that's always available, no matter what the computers are doing or what part of the screen I've highlighted. It cost me about $800. But if you don't mind a software meter, you can get a lot more measurements for a lot less money ... and basic metering for free. The free digital meters can be just as accurate as the standalone expensive ones. That's because digital audio always includes a built-in reference to full scale, so any competently designed software can measure its peaks without calibration. If you have any interest in consistent audio, get one of these. You'll use it to check digitizing levels, make sure your program's built-in meters are accurate, and verify that mixes won't cause problems on the air or during duplication.

Metering Suite

If your software can handle audio plug-ins, get something like the free T-Racks Metering Suite (www.ikmultimedia.com), shown in Figure 12.18. This nifty utility shows level, perceived loudness, real-time spectrum, and stereo information for any stereo signal you run through it. The level metering is displayed simultaneously both as peak—the kind that gets digital signals into trouble—and RMS, which averages the energy of each wave and approximates loudness.

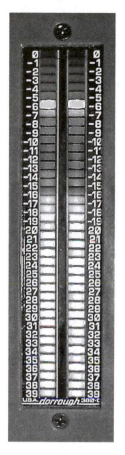

Figure 12.17
A combination peak/average meter, calibrated for digital inputs.

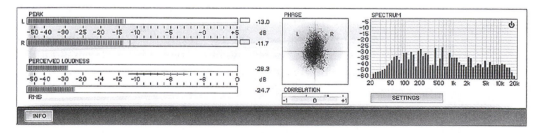

Figure 12.18 IK Multimedia's Metering Suite, a free downloadable plug-in.

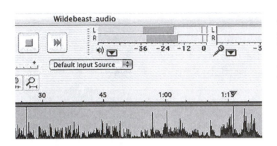

Figure 12.19 The free program Audacity's meters work while you're recording, or when playing an existing file.

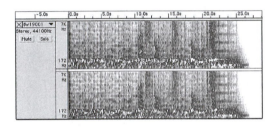

Figure 12.20 A spectrogram in Audacity. This one's zoomed in to show just part of the active spectrum.

Audacity

Audacity is a free, open source audio recorder and editor for Windows, Mac, or Linux. It does some things as well as or even better than commercial programs, but—as discussed in Chapter 10—can take a little getting used to. Its meters, however, are easy to read and reliable. Get the latest version from <u>audacity.sourceforge.net</u>.

Audacity also has a spectrum analysis function that can be useful even for beginners: after you record or open a file in it, you can display its audio as a *spectrogram* (Figure 12.20). This is a three-dimensional spectrum, with frequency shown on the vertical axis, volume as changes of color or intensity, and time on the horizontal. You can spot trends and timbre issues much better than with a constantly jumping spectrum display, and pitched noises stand out as horizontal lines. You can check the entire audio file in one glance, or zoom in to see specific sounds.

Log vs. Linear

All the meters I've shown in this section display volume properly, as a logarithm. Note how their –6 calibrations are very close to the top of their scales. That's because –6 dBFS sounds pretty loud, even though it represents only half the voltage of Full Scale.[6] If the meters were calibrated linearly, like a thermometer, –6 would be at 50%. A proper average level, between –12 dBFS and –20 dBFS depending on the medium, would barely light up a quarter of a linear meter! Three quarters of the meter would be useless, but even worse, beginners would be tempted to record too loudly.

Almost all software meters used to be linear, because desktop computers didn't have the power to compute logarithms fast enough. They looked like Figure 12.21—even though this meter is showing a decent average level, its display has hardly moved. Some current programs still display levels this way. If your program's meters look like this, with their –6 dBFS calibration halfway up the scale, be aware of this

---

[6] If that doesn't make sense to you, glance through the first few chapters again.

✔ TIP

Stereo? Mono? Isolated tracks?

A stereo phase and correlation indication, like the one in the middle of Figure 12.18, can be particularly helpful when working with video tracks. Sometimes, camera files and NLE tracks put identical information on both channels of a stereo pair. The sound is monaural, coming from the phantom center between two speakers. But it wastes resources and takes up twice as much file space when exporting the project's tracks.

If you're not sure whether a signal is true stereo, glance at the phase and correlation meters.

- Real stereo will show a dancing scribble for its phase, like the one in Figure 12.18. The correlation meter will swing between positive and negative, though rarely reaching either extreme.
- Mono signals on two identical tracks will show a vertical line in the phase meter, and a correlation of +1.
- Isolated mics—say, a camera mic on one channel and a lav on the other—will usually show a mostly diagonal blur in the phase meter, flipping orientation depending on whether characters are talking or paused. The correlation will move only a small amount from zero.

Figure 12.21 A meter with a linear audio scale, with –6 at its halfway point, can fool you.

shortcoming. Trust the numbers instead of how much meter is lit up. Or better yet, use one of the other meters available.

Time-averaging meters

If you're preparing material for television, you'll probably also need a time-integrating meter, like the free one in Figure 11.12 on page 303. These are calibrated to US or EBU specs, and read loudness over the entire length of a program or commercial.

You won't need that function until you're ready to mix (Chapter 17), but all of those meters also have peak and averaging functions you can use during ingest or digitizing.

How much is zero?

Traditional VU meters were calibrated to 0 dBm—a precise standard—even though analog circuits could handle a few decibels above that level with no trouble. So engineers got used to the idea of "headroom": they'd run their equipment with loud voices or music going over zero every few seconds. Lineup tones on the tape or over the network would still be calibrated to zero on the meter, but program peaks might hover around +3 VU.

But digital audio levels aren't measured in volts or dBm; they're expressed as a ratio below Full Scale (dBFS). This has led to a confusing state of affairs:

- Analog audio meters start at some negative number, around –40 VU, and then are calibrated through zero to a positive number (usually +3 or +6). Zero is the nominal operating level; lineup tones are set to match it, even though some peaks are expected to be louder than zero.
- But digital audio meters start at a negative number and top out at 0 dBFS. Peak levels have to be held below digital zero, and with a safety factor may be considerably lower. If you record a lineup tone at zero on a digital meter, and use that tone to set up an analog dub with tone equaling 0 VU, the actual track will be too soft.
- Since analog meters read up to +6 VU and digital ones up to 0 dBFS, it would seem logical to make the digital lineup tone precisely –6 dBFS. If you do this, and set the analog meter to zero on that –6 dBFS digital tone, the analog tape will agree with the digital one perfectly—*but only for steady tones*. Remember, analog meters show average levels and don't respond to instantaneous changes. Speech that looks perfectly good on the digital meter may only tickle the analog circuits at –18 VU if the meters are calibrated this way.

While there can't be a one-size-fits-all solution for converting digital tones to analog ones, there are industry standards:

- Professional video and audio media intended for broadcast or theaters have their tone at –20 dBFS. The loudest signal should never go above –10 dBFS for broadcast, or –2 dBFS for film.
- Prosumer video and web media usually put their tone at –12 dBFS. This is the standard mark on most miniDV cameras and consumer recorders. Peaks should never exceed –2 dBFS.

SYNCHRONIZATION

This section is about the technical aspects of sync. There are pointers in the next chapter for manually fixing lipsync problems while you're editing.

Even if audio and video both transfer successfully, they can drift out of sync if you're not paying attention to sample and frame rates. This happens most often when bridging between film and video.

While nonlinear editors have internal databases to keep multiple audio and video tracks in sync, you need a more standardized timing reference when you step out of that closed system. SMPTE timecode—developed by the Society of Motion Picture and Television Engineers, and first popularized as an editing and timing reference in the late 1970s—is the universal language to identify specific frames in a videotape. Analog and digital audio systems use it as well, to keep track of which sounds should play against those frames.

SMPTE code can also be used as a speed reference, by measuring the length of time from one frame to the next, but this usually isn't precise or stable enough for digital audio or even analog color video. Most systems use blackburst (see Chapter 11) to control the speed, once timecode has been applied to get the frames in sync. Better audio workstations give you a choice of what they'll do if timecode and blackburst aren't moving at the same speed: just report the error and continue relying on blackburst, re-sync so that timecode agrees, or stop cold and wait for operator intervention.

But if you're going to intervene, you have to understand what timecode is really doing . . .

Understanding timecode

Prepare to be confused. Of all the techniques we use, SMTPE timecode is the most bewildering. What else can you expect of a system where *29 + 1 = 30* in most cases, but *29 + 1 = 32* about fifty times an hour?

Timecode was invented to help video editing. Each frame gets a unique hour:minute:second:frame address, so you can assemble scenes more predictably. It also serves as a common reference to assure that sound, picture, and animation from different systems all fit together. The one thing it *doesn't* do is keep track of time. A minute of it won't precisely equal a minute on anyone's standard clock. An hour of the stuff might equal an hour on your wristwatch—or maybe it won't. And the last three sentences aren't true in Europe, Africa, or Australia!

Fortunately, all you need is logic—and a little bit of history—to become a master of time(code).

Once upon a time . . . .

The problem started more than 50 years ago. Back in those black-and-white days, U.S. television scanned at 30 frames per second. This number was chosen both because it was easy to derive a sync signal from the 60 Hz power line that ran into every home, and because any hum introduced into the video circuits would be in sync with the picture and not roll around the screen.

When color TV was invented, more information had to be jammed into the picture to keep track of colors. But broadcasters had to keep this more complex signal compatible with older sets, or else they'd lose viewers. So they stretched each frame

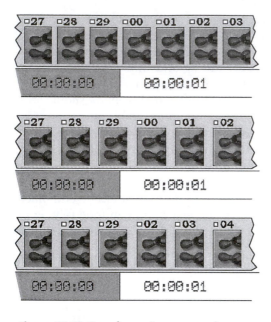

Figure 12.22 Dropframe is necessary because there aren't an even number of frames per second.

a tiny bit longer—1/10th of a percent, to 29.97 fps[7]—and used the extra time to put in a color reference signal. The frame rate was close enough to the older standard that viewers could manually adjust their sets to compensate.

This 29.97 fps system worked fine until timecode was invented. You can see the problem in Figure 12.22. The top filmstrip represents 30 fps black and white video, with a digital wall clock beneath it. At the end of 29 frames, both the video and clock are ready to move on to a new second. But color TV (middle strip) is slightly slower, so it's still playing that 29th frame when it's time for a new second. The timecode numbers can't move until the frame is finished. This tiny error accumulates to the point that an hour's worth of timecode is more than an hour *and three seconds* long. A program that was produced to start at 1:00:00 timecode and end at 1:59:59 would actually finish a few seconds after two o'clock! (To think of it another way: The frame rate was slowed down 1/10th of a percent. An hour is 3,600 seconds, so slowing it down means 3,600 seconds times 0.1%, or 3.6 seconds.)

Broadcasters realized this timecode stuff could cause one-hour shows to bump into the start of a commercial. That could cost them money!

Dropframe

The broadcasters' solution was to periodically skip a few numbers. At the end of most minutes, the number jumps ahead by two. If your tape is parked at 00:01:59:29 (hours:minutes:seconds:frames) and you jog exactly one frame forward, you land on 00:02:00:02. The numbers between those two— ... *00:00* and ... *00:01*—just never happen.

It's important to remember that no frames are ever actually dropped. Just the frame numbers. The bottom strip in Figure 12.22 shows how it counts.

There are 60 minutes in an hour, so dropping two numbers per minute means 120 numbers will be dropped each hour. But the actual error caused by that

---

[7] It actually worked out to 29.97002997 fps. The difference between this number and the commonly accepted 29.97 fps can result in a one-frame error after about ten hours. Unless you're producing *War and Peace* with no commercial breaks, don't worry about it.

¹⁄₁₀th-percent slowdown was 3.6 seconds, or 108 frames. Now our timecode hour is 12 frames too short! So to fine-tune the process, six times an hour—once for every minute that ends in zero—counting reverts to normal. Park at 00:09:59:29 and jog one frame, and you land on 00:10:00:00. This puts back two numbers for every ten minutes, or— *ta-dah!*—12 frames an hour. When you do all this, an hour of dropframe timecode precisely equals an hour of the clock on the wall.

It works, but this crazy counting makes editing more complicated. The duration of a scene frequently doesn't equal the difference between its in-time and its out-time. Editing computers can handle this automatically, but human editors have a hard time getting around it. So television production in NTSC[8] countries uses two timecode formats:

- Non-dropframe timecode counts continuously, so it's easier to use when the running length isn't critical or for short projects. It's usually preferred for TV commercials and non-broadcast media.
- Dropframe timecode is harder to count, but, on average, it agrees with the clock on the wall. It's preferred by broadcast producers and stations.

Both dropframe and non-drop run at the same 29.97 fps rate, so tapes are interchangeable. You can produce your spot using non-drop, and TV stations won't turn it down (they may insist on dropframe for program masters, to make things easier in the control room). Well-designed editing systems even let you mix code formats in the same production.

✳ TIDBIT

Drop kick

I once worked with a producer who insisted his projects were too important to use dropframe timecode. Every frame of his project was vital, and he didn't want any frames dropped into the trash.

You know better.

Those crazy Americans

This nonsense applies only to NTSC countries—North and South America, and parts of industrialized Asia—where color video runs 29.97 fps. In the rest of the world power lines are 50 Hz, so black-and-white TV evolved at 25 fps. This is slow enough that PAL and SECAM countries didn't have to stretch frames to accommodate color.

---

[8] NTSC really stands for National Television Standards Commission, though most broadcast engineers will say it means Never Twice the Same Color.

Audio programs and non-broadcast computer systems sometimes use 30 fps timecode, since it's easier to count, and modern technology has no problem synchronizing it. By definition, 30 fps timecode has to be non-dropframe ... there's no point skipping numbers since it already matches the clock. You may see "30 fps dropframe" on editing equipment, but the name is the mistaken result of confusing frame rate with counting format.

Table 12.1 summarizes the code formats.

Table 12.1 Code formats

Code Type	Frame Rate	Counting Format
24 fps	24 fps (film)	Count to 23, then 1 second 0 frames
25 fps	25 fps	Count to 24, then 1 second 0 frames
29.97 non-drop	29.97 fps	Count to 29, then 1 second 0 frames
29.97 dropframe	29.97 fps	Count to 29, then 1 second 2 frames ... except once every 10 minutes, don't.
30 fps non-drop	30 fps	Count to 29, then 1 second 0 frames
30 fps dropframe	This rate and format combination is rarely used in video or film, but some manufacturers support it anyway.	

Timecode recording and transmission

Timecode in analog studios is usually carried as a bi-phase serial word around 2,400 Hz. The exact frequency depends on the frame rate, but it's always in the middle of the audio range so it can be recorded on standard media. Analog video originally carried it on a track running parallel to the edge of the tape (as opposed to the slanted track that carried picture information). So it's often called longitudinal timecode (LTC)—a term that also refers to that signal as it chirps through the studio wires as a digital serial stream.

Longitudinal tracks can't generate a signal when they're not moving, so an auxiliary code was often encoded as a series of dots above the slant-track picture, where it could be read during still frames. This vertical interval timecode (VITC) can be read whenever the image is visible, but gets disrupted when the image is edited. It can also be carried over a studio's video wiring or transmitted on the air along with the picture.

Most professional analog video decks use both forms of code, choosing the most reliable at any given moment. Digital audio and video decks often keep track of timecode as part of their other timing data. In either case, the frame numbers can be read on the deck's front panel and sent to an edit controller as needed.

Some audio file formats support timecode, but it's not continuous like the code on a tape. Instead, a single *timestamp* in the file's header indicates what time the file should start when it's in sync. If the computer needs to know other timecodes within the file, it computes them on the fly, based on the sample rate and how many samples have been played since the file started.

As far as the next piece of equipment is concerned, there's almost no difference between analog-recorded LTC, video-recorded VITC, or timecode derived from a digital file or tape system.

Using timecode

Timecode, as a string of LTC data, isn't important until you want to synchronize two separate pieces of equipment or an audio tape with a video one. This seldom happens in the world of desktop production, but may be necessary when bringing edited material to a pro facility. Broadcasters frequently specify that commercials begin at exactly the start of a minute (00 seconds, 00 frames), and that programs start at exactly one hour.

Timecode can be used manually as well. If you're transferring an audio or video clip from one project to another, or from NLE to multitrack audio program, you can type its starting code as part of the filename. Plant a marker in the second timeline at that location, and you'll be able to snap the clip to it.

Syncing traditional film with audio

This can get complicated, both because mechanical film cameras often don't have perfect speed stability and because a film's speed actually changes when you convert to most video formats. The last edition of this book had five pages on solving these problems.

These days, very few people shoot actual film. Even Hollywood productions are usually video. So I decided to save a few trees, and move the syncing instructions to the Web. You'll find them at www.GreatSound.info.

CHAPTER 13

Editing Voices

☛ ROSE'S RULES

- Good dialog editing is transparent. The goal is to change a performance or make an interview more concise, but never to sound "edited."
- If you want to edit moving pictures of people doing things, you have to stay aware of how people move in real life. The same thing is true for their voices. You can be a much better dialog editor if you know how people combine sounds to form words.

Being a good video editor doesn't automatically make you a good dialog editor. The principles are different. But if you're good at cutting pictures, you already have one skill that's absolutely necessary for cutting sound: you pay attention to details. It just might not be obvious which details are important . . . particularly if you've spent a long time working with images.

For example, picture editors often let on-screen movements bridge over a cut. If Sue reaches for a doorknob at the end of a mid-shot, you can follow with her hand grabbing the knob in close-up. The continuous motion helps the viewer connect the scenes. We see a single action, even though Sue was shot in two takes.

But you almost never want to edit voices across a continuous sound. If one clip ends with Sue saying *I'm glad to se—*, and the next begins with a different take of *— e you George*, the edit will be disturbing. Even though it's the vocal equivalent of our two separate shots combined to a door knob sequence, it'll sound wrong and destroy the viewer's illusion. Dissolving between those two clips will make things even worse.

This chapter is about the tricks a good dialog editor uses. Want to make Sue's edit work? Edit just before the /t/ in *glad to*, or just before the /s/ in *see*. You can even make the cut before the tiny /d/ that starts *George*.

And yes: there's a /d/ at the start of *George*. Go ahead: say the name slowly. It starts with exactly the same tongue movement, producing exactly the same sound, as

---

✳ TIDBIT

A foreign language?

There's an official way to write these sounds. According to The International Phonetic Alphabet, the /ee/ sound in *see* should be written /i/. It's /t/, /s/, and /d/ symbols mean what you'd think, but the symbols for /zh/ and many other sounds don't even exist in normal typefaces. That's because there are more phonemes than there are letters.

Unfortunately, the phonetic alphabet can look like hieroglyphics to the untrained (see Figure 13.1), so I'll use a simplified version in this book.

ðæts maɪ neɪm dʒeɪ

Figure 13.1 *That's my name, Jay*, in the International Phonetic Alphabet. Each character represents an individual sound.

Figure 13.1 shows 15 separate sounds in a simple four-word sentence. You might find it hard to believe there are this many individual sounds in four syllables, so I'll make it easier: **Sound 13.1** starts with me reading that sentence in a normal voice. Then you hear the same recording, slowed down to 50% of its original speed. Listen carefully and you can hear how my voice slides from one sound to another, even within a single syllable. Or keep playing; the third part of that clip is the recording at 20% of its original speed . . . now the changes are obvious.

My voice is nothing special. These or similar phoneme changes exist in all dialog, and a good editor learns to recognize them while scrubbing through a clip. That's because most of those individual sounds can be used as edit points, or moved around into other words.

Want to get more of a feel for how multiple phonemes go into the words we speak? Go to http://upodn.com. It'll transcribe any text you enter into phonetics, as spoken in Standard English. Their algorithm isn't perfect, and there are always regional variations. So the website might not show a true transcription of how your actors speak in a specific scene, but it'll be close.

the /d/ in *dog*.[1] The science behind this—how mouth movements and breath create specific individual sounds, and how they blend together into the words we recognize—is phonetics. It can be the handiest stuff for a dialog editor to know.

In most of this chapter we'll use *dialog* to refer to any spoken words, whether it's conversations between on-camera actors, talking heads, location interviews, or voice-over. The editing techniques are the same. The only difference is that you've got more freedom during voice-overs or cutaways, since you don't have to worry about lipsync. But even if a scene shows lips, there are dialog-editing tricks you can do to fix the performance.

ESTABLISHING SYNC

Lipsync is easy if you're shooting single-system. Audio and video are part of the same file and get ingested simultaneously. Keep them locked together in your NLE, and they'll stay in sync. If you have to do dialog editing that might upset the sync, work on an unlocked copy. Keep the original on a muted track as a reference, or to let you try again with a fresh copy.

But single system doesn't work for a lot of projects. You might need more than two camera tracks, or better quality than a camera's recording can provide. Fortunately, double-system lipsync is also easy. If you've got a good reference track on the video, you can buy a utility to sync double-system recordings automatically . . . or if you master a few simple tricks, you can sync things yourself more flexibly, and almost as quickly.

One sound, one image

You need an unambiguous place where sync is known to be correct. That is, one frame of the picture has to match one—and only one—moment of the track. Barring technical problems, you only have to do this once for each ingested shot or finished sequence. After that, sync is easy.[2]

Reference track

The simplest reference system is having tracks on both the video and audio that match. This doesn't have to be a perfect match. They'll never be exactly equal, because camera recording circuits aren't as good as separate audio recorders. But they have to be close

---

[1] His whole name is pronounced "d zh ih aw er d zh", where those one- and two-letter figures each represent an individual sound.

[2] It used to be a lot harder. During the days of analog video production, multitrack audio tape speeds weren't reliable. You could match sync, and then lose it later in the same take. Film production had it easier: sprocket holes kept sound and picture locked together. Digital has virtual sprockets formed by the borders of each image frame and audio sample.

enough that you can spot the same words in each. Slide the audio track until its words matches the reference. Then lock them together, and you're done.

Professionals usually go for as close a match as possible, sending a reference signal from the mixer to the camera via wireless. It's a little harder if the camera is using a separate mic, much farther from the action than the boom or lav. Echoes will blur the words you're trying to match. If the distance between camera mic and action is more than a dozen feet or so, acoustic delays will make the camera track late and you have to compensate.[3]

Slates

Hollywood solved this problem long before reference tracks were possible. Film cameras don't record sound. The *slate* with diagonally striped sticks on a small wooden board— an image that says "Hollywood" to almost everybody—was invented for sync!

Using a slate is simple: zoom in, bring the mic close, and clap the sticks together sharply.[4] There'll be a definite frame where the sticks come together, and a definite sound where they hit. Slide them together and you're ready to edit. Specific instructions are below.

A more modern equivalent is the *smart slate* (Figure 13.2). It displays numbers for the camera, simultaneously generating matching timecode for the audio recorder.

Figure 13.2 A smart slate displays timecode, while the matching numbers are recorded with the sound track. (Courtesy Denecke, Inc.)

---

[3] Sound takes about one millisecond to travel one foot . . . or about half a video frame to travel 15 feet, which can result in a noticeable sync error.

[4] Make sure your finger isn't in the way. I got caught on camera smashing my own finger in a slate when I was starting out. A friendly editor gave me the resulting strip of film. I kept it at my desk for years . . .

You don't have to interrupt action to make a slapping noise, and can use multiple cameras that start and stop independently: just be sure to shoot the slate's current numbers at the beginning of each shot.

Syncing with a smart slate can be somewhat automatic—in an ideal editing system, visual numbers are read by Optical Character Recognition and audio clips fly to their proper location—but operator intervention is usually necessary. So smart slates almost always have those old-fashioned striped sticks on top, and most users slap them as a backup.

Two-pop

A third kind of reference isn't possible for the original shoot, but has become almost mandatory during post-production. *Two-pops* are one frame beeps on the sound track, matching either a distinctive flash on the picture or the number 2 on a countdown leader (Figure 13.3). They're added to a sequence while editing, exactly two seconds before the first video frame, and provide a reference both for sync and for program timing. Most network contracts require them, most postproduction engineers appreciate them, and almost all of us have seen them accidentally appear before a broadcast program or commercial.

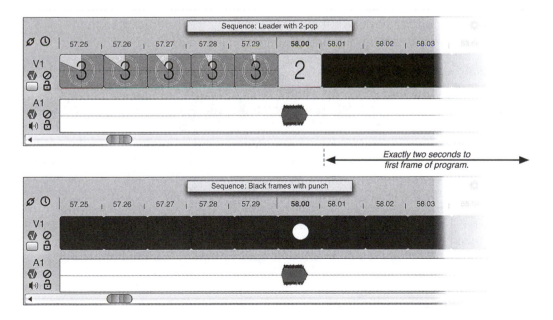

Figure 13.3 Two forms of a two-pop. The top one matches the beep against the "2" frame of a universal leader; the bottom just has a one-frame white circle as the visual sync. Either version is fine.

✔ TIP

Pop off!

The countdown leaders generated in some editing programs can be out of sync, with the beep actually happening a frame later than the number *2*. Check yours by rendering a countdown and viewing it at maximum zoom. It should look like Figure 13.3, with the beep precisely lined up under the *2*.

Two-pops have to be on the audio and video tracks. If you're doing audio post, they should be on at least one exported audio track of each element type (dialog, music, and effects). If there are any potential issues about frame or audio sample rates—which can happen if you're mixing film and video, or producing for international markets—put a *tail pop* at the end of the audio and video tracks as well.

How to sync audio and video

The basic operation is simple. Put both the video and audio clips on your timeline, and slide one until the references match: either the pop or clap gets lined up under the appropriate video frame, or the audio-only clip is in sync with reference audio on the camera's a/v clip. Then lock them together.

A few tricks will make this easier.

How to look at a slate

You can waste a lot of time watching video of a traditional slate closing, trying to mark where the *bang* sound should go. No matter how slowly you shuttle, it's hard to find the exact frame.

Instead, look at individual frames in a viewer or on a zoomed-in timeline. While the upper stick is moving, it'll be slightly blurred. *Find the final frame where it's blurred*, right before the first frame where the sticks are closed. That's as close as you'll get to where the sound should be. Figure 13.4 shows the details.

You can mark even more accurately if your NLE allows subframe editing. If that last blurred frame is blurred a lot, the bang should be toward the end of that frame. If it's blurred only a little, it should be toward the front. In Figure 13.4, the bang could be about a quarter-frame later. Of course for most projects, this kind of precision isn't necessary.

Matching reference audio tracks

The procedure is different if you've recorded reference audio with the picture—either as a feed from the mixer, or with the camera mic—and want to sync a separate audio-only recording to match.

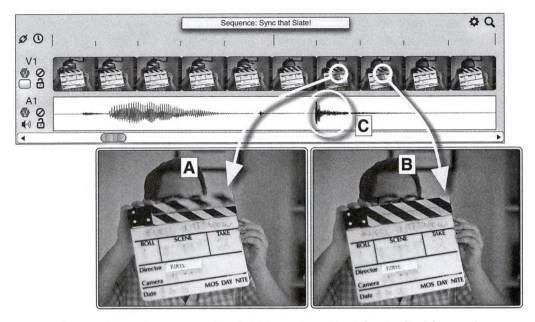

Figure 13.4 The quick way to mark a slate? Zoom in and look for the *final frame* where the upper stick is blurred: that's where the sound goes. Note the blurring in frame A, compared to the steady focus in frame B. The sound (C) belongs in sync with frame A.

1. Place the camera's clip on an audio and video track. Put the audio-only clip on an adjacent audio track. If you've recorded multichannel audio, use additional tracks and link all the multichannel clips so they'll move together. Mute all of those extra tracks, except for the one that's most similar to the camera track. (Usually this will be the top track, and marked *mix*.)
2. Slide the audio-only tracks so the waveforms are approximately matched. Don't worry about perfection; just get the bigger blobs in the same place.
3. Play both the camera track and the audio-only track, set so they're at about the same volume. While they're playing, use the NLE's *nudge* or *bump* command to move the audio-only one until they're in sync. It helps to direct the camera's sound to your left speaker, and the audio-only track to the right, while you're trying to find the exact sync. If audio is late, you'll hear the dialog slightly louder on the left and travelling towards the right. If it's early, this movement will be reversed. As the two clips get closer, they'll start to sound like an echo in the center. When you've achieved exact sync, the echo will disappear or just become slightly metallic.
4. When you've gotten sync, link everybody together and mute the camera's track: you don't need it any more.

PluralEyes

The easy way to achieve the above steps is to use Red Giant LLC's utility *PluralEyes*. It lets you drag a shoot's worth of camera and audio-only clips into a bin, click the *Synchronize* button, and walk away. If the file names and audio are close, PluralEyes will find the proper sync for each pair. Then it sends them, aligned, to your NLE. PluralEyes can get confused, particularly if your reference track is noisy with other voices, or file names and lengths haven't been properly managed. But if you're careful, it's fast and reliable.

☛ ROSE'S RULES

The sin of sound-early

Sync errors are not all created equal. Casual viewers can usually tolerate sound that's a frame or two later than the picture, particularly on very wide shots or if there isn't much dialog. But having the sound early—even a single frame early—can be disconcerting.

That's because we're used to sound taking time to travel through the air. If we see someone talking across a 30' wide road, we expect it'll take a whole frame for their voices to cross the street. If we're watching our kid play soccer from the sidelines, the sound of a kick might not reach us until two or three frames after we see their foot connect.

But we never have to wait for light to reach our eyes. We see things instantly.[5] If a sound reaches us before its matching image, our brains have to assume the sound was before the event happened. And that's weird.

EDITING DIALOG

Once you understand how voices should be edited, you can use these techniques for the rest of your career. The principles are absolutely portable, and they work because of how we listen, not because of special equipment or software. I edit in a computer now because it's faster . . . but years ago, I was cutting ¼-inch tape and 35mm magnetic film. The techniques are basically the same.

However, not all computer programs are equal.

- Most NLEs are organized around frames, and force you to edit audio on frame boundaries. This is actually too wide a margin for effective dialog editing. A /t/ sound lasts less than a third of a frame . . . if you're trying to find it in an NLE,

---

[5] At least, as far as human perception can tell.

you probably won't be able to hone in on it accurately. A few NLEs let you move the in-point of a clip with subframe resolution, but they have to consider the clip itself as a whole number of frames. So the out-point moves as well, even if you don't want it to.

- Audio software has essentially infinite resolution; you can cut from any place to any other place, regardless of frame boundaries.
- Even 35mm film sound is more precise than most NLEs: you can cut from any set of perforations to any other. With four sets of perfs per frame, there's an opportunity to cut every ⅟₉₆th of a second.

If you're going to be doing serious voice or music editing, get a separate audio editing program to use along with your NLE. Many competent programs are often bundled with the NLE, using the same file format and having a way to move clips between them easily. Most also play video within the audio program, so you can know when it's safe to make audio changes without worrying about lip movement.

Program types

Audio editing programs usually follow one of two different models.

They can have multiple audio clips, arranged on tracks on a timeline. If a track is supposed to be silent at any given moment, there either isn't a clip on it, or the clip has been deliberately muted. The look and feel is similar to an NLE, though these programs are often called a DAW (Digital Audio Workstation).

DAWs are designed to handle audio quickly, much faster than you can do it in an NLE. Clips are usually cut or joined on the timeline, rather than having in- and out-points separately marked in a viewer. Cuts and clip lengths don't have to match the frame rate; the program can hold sync even while you're making arbitrary edits. Equalization, reverb, and similar processes are often applied on a track-by-track basis rather than directly to clips, so you can adjust them in the context of a mix. There's more about this kind of editing later in this chapter, and more about the processing in Chapters 16 and 17.

Alternatively, a program can be organized around a continuous audio stream, which lasts from the start of a file to its end. This arrangement is similar to a word processor, where you work on a complete document rather than a string of independent paragraphs. Programs like this are often called Audio Editors. To make an edit, you select a section of sound and then cut or paste . . . the same way you would with words in a text editor. Processing is applied by first selecting areas within the sound file—or the whole file at once—the same way you'd change selected text to italic or bold face.

When you cut a sound in an Editor's track, everything after that sound moves earlier to fill the space . . . just like cutting words out of a text document. When you insert a sound, everything moves later. (Some DAWs offer a *ripple* function that does the same thing, but the results can be confusing if there are unrelated elements on the same track.)

DAWs are usually best for editing sound against picture. The timeline stays in sync with the master video, and audio elements are moved until they match the proper

TIP

There's a trick, of course

Professionals have a shortcut for making DAW edits precisely and quickly. It's not intuitive, but it's very easily mastered. You won't need it for the first editing tutorial in this book, which is trivially easy. But it'll speed up almost every other piece of dialog editing you do. Variations on the technique can help your music and sound effects editing as well.

Instructions appear on page 364, just in time to use them for a more complex tutorial.

---

image. It's easy to replace part of a track with silence or roomtone of the same length, keeping the rest of that track in sync.

Editors are usually best for editing continuous non-sync elements like voice-over and music cues. Operations are fast, and require fewer keystrokes or mouse clicks than in a DAW.

There are exceptions to these distinctions. A few DAWs have fast editing windows where you can cut and paste. A few Editors will support multiple tracks, and sync one of them to a video window. Some we-do-everything programs are bundled with NLEs. But in general, the rule-bending programs just haven't been as powerful as the single-purpose ones. If you're working with video sound and can have only one piece of audio software, choose a DAW.

Scrubbing, jogging, and shuttling

It's unfortunate, but a lot of people edit sound as if it were just blobs on a screen. You'll never do sophisticated editing that way. Anything more complex than assembling paragraphs of text requires actually listening to what you want to edit . . . and you have to listen slowly enough to identify tiny components that make up the sound. Audio folks call this slowed-down listening *scrubbing*. It doesn't take long—in fact, this kind of editing is faster than trying to interpret on-screen blobs for all but the simplest cutting—and it's absolutely necessary.

Normal scrubbing in a DAW is similar to NLE *shuttling*: the sound moves forwards or backwards, either at a constant rate or in response to a mouse being dragged or a knob being turned. It sounds a lot like manually moving an old-fashioned analog tape.

Most NLEs also have a *jog* function, which advances the picture and audio one frame for each press of an arrow key, and then holds a still frame while waiting for the next command. For each jog, you hear one frame's worth of audio and then the sound stops. DAWs usually don't have an equivalent to jogging, because sound isn't frame-based and audio "stills" are silence.

But some audio programs have something more appropriate: *dynamic scrubbing*. As you move the mouse slowly across the audio, you hear short, repeating segments of sound. They can be set in length from about a third of a frame to a half-second. They continue to repeat while you're holding the mouse in place, and then move to the next segments when you move the mouse. The sound is always played at its normal pitch and within the context of that selected scrub length. So it's easy to hear where vowels or musical notes change.

Figure 13.5 is a graphic representation of these two modes. Dynamic scrubbing continuously repeats a short, moving loop so you can hear its natural pitch; tape-like scrubbing slows down each sound, but you can hear their precise beginnings and endings. **Sound 13.2** lets you hear the difference.

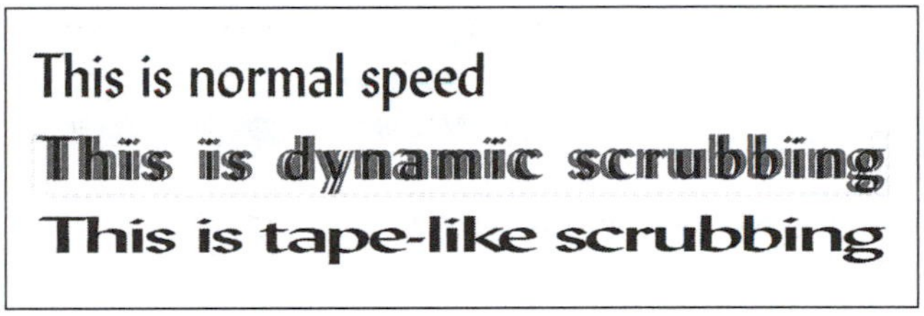

This is normal speed
Thïs ïs dynamïc scrubbïïng
This is tape-like scrubbing

Figure 13.5 Dynamic and tape-like scrubbing modes.

HOW TO EDIT DIALOG

These are the techniques you'll need to know. They might not be intuitive, particularly if you've taught yourself video editing by watching movies and trying to duplicate their effects.

But they're fast and accurate, and based on close to a century of film and radio/TV production. Once you've gotten used to using them, you'll find yourself hitting the *undo* button a lot less: edits will work perfectly the first time, and you'll be able to devote your energies to being creative rather than fighting dialog.

EDITING I: CUTTING IN SILENCES

Nobody . . . talks . . . like . . . this. Speech is made of continuous sound, with constantly changing volume and pitches, punctuated by brief pauses when you breathe. Copy **Sound 13.3** into your editor—or read the preceding two sentences into a microphone—and look at it on a waveform or clip display. It'll probably look like Figure 13.6. Play through the clip, and notice how individual sounds line up with the display. Then save the clip: we'll be editing it a lot, and you'll want to keep coming back to this original version.

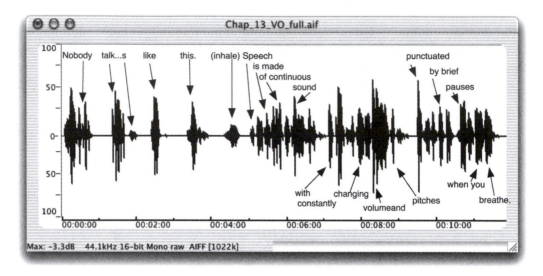

Figure 13.6 The first two sentences of this section.

✔ **TIP**

What, no scrub?

A few audio programs don't let you scrub in the waveform, and their tutorials insist that the only way to edit sound is by eye. Not only are they wrong about the basic premise, there's also a workaround that's almost as good as scrubbing:

1. Select an area around where you think you're going to mark an edit point, of about half a second.
2. Activate the Loop Play command, so the area plays continuously.
3. Grab the left boundary of the loop, and slide it. The start of the loop will move to match, letting you hear more or less of the loop depending on how you moved it. With some programs, you'll have to Stop and restart Loop Play for it to recognize the new boundary.
4. Move the loop boundary back and forth until it starts exactly at the sound where you want to edit. Drop a marker there.

It may seem like a lot of steps, but with practice—and one hand on the mouse and the other pressing keyboard commands—it becomes a fast way to find a precise edit point.

I added callouts to make the picture easier to interpret. The hills and valleys represent where the track gets softer or louder.[6] Notice how some words share a broad hill (like the phrase *volume and*), while other single-syllable words might have two separate hills of their own (*talks*). In that last word, there's one loud burst for the /t/, a quieter stretch for /al/, a short pause while the lower lip closes against the teeth, and then the louder friction of the /ks/.

If you wanted to edit between two takes of that narration, you could mark your cuts any time in the silences before each of the first four words. Or you could cut pauses after *sound* or *pitches*. But if you're cutting in the pause between the first and second sentences, you'll have to be careful: there's a pause, but it's not really silence. That's where the announcer breathes. Try to cut in the middle of that pause, and you'll disturb its natural rise and fall. The edit will call attention to itself, distracting from your message.

If you want to make that edit, you have to cut completely around the breath. Try it both ways, or listen to my version of that sloppy cut on **Sound 13.4**. (There's more about breath editing later in this chapter.)

The point is that it's very difficult to do a smooth edit in the middle of a continuous sound. Sustained vowels and long consonants (such as the /z/ in the middle of *pauses*) are continuous, but so are roomtone and the breath between words. In fact, it's the first rule of editing:

☞ ROSE'S RULES

> **Rule 1:** Never cut away from the middle of one long sound into silence, or into the middle of another long sound.

Like every rule, there are exceptions. If you fool the ear into thinking that the first sound continued, you can get away with this kind of edit. We'll discuss how to do this with music in the next chapter. To do it when you're editing voice, you have to pay attention to how individual sounds start.

EDITING II: SOUNDS WITH HARD ATTACKS

Notice how the left sides of some hills in Figure 13.6 are very steep. These are the beginnings of sounds that get suddenly loud: the /t/ at the start of *talks* and in the middle of *continuous*, the /k/ at the start of *continuous*, or the /p/ in *punctuated* or *pitches*.

---

[6] Read more about these audio envelopes in Chapter 1.

One of the characteristics of sudden loud sounds is that they mask other, softer sounds! You can use this to distract the listener, so they ignore what's technically a wrong sound either at the same time or immediately before the edit.[7] So if you edit from a softer sound to a louder one, the loud sound hides discontinuities caused by the edit itself.

Figure 13.7 shows how sudden loud sounds can distract the ear in an actual edit. The left side of the figure is zoomed in so you can see how the waveform abruptly changes direction; this would normally cause a click. But because it's part of a cut from a softer sound to a much louder one, as you can see when the screen is zoomed out (right), nobody hears the problem.

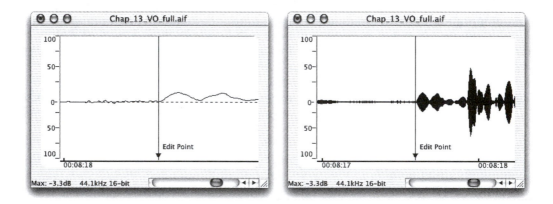

Figure 13.7 There's a jump in this edit (zoomed in on the left), but because the cut is to a louder sound, you'll never hear the problem.

This is the key to the second rule of editing:

☞ ROSE'S RULES

Rule 2: You can generally cut from any continuous soft sound into any other sound with a hard attack.

---

[7] Yes, it's a cheat. But it works. We're making movies here, not running a class in advanced elocution.

✳ TIDBIT

Spelling errors?

Look at the previous page. There's no *z* in *pauses*, and no *k* in *continuous* . . . so why am I spelling them this way in the book?

Phonetics—even our simplified version—depends on accurately hearing and depicting actual sounds. It has nothing to do with letters or spelling.

The letter *s* in the middle of *pauses* has a buzzing to it, just like the /z/ in *zoo*. If you try saying that letter like the /s/ in *Sue*, you get a totally different word: *paw-sis*.[8] Try it.

You can also find cases where the letter *s* turns to /z/, at the end of *boys* and *eggs*.

And why is the *c* in *continuous* written as /k/? It's certainly not the same sound as the *c* in *certainly* (which would be written /s/). In fact, there's no character in phonetics for the letter *c*. That's because it's always sounded like some other consonant.

Again, we're editing sounds, not squiggles on a page or blobs on a screen. So we use a language that talks accurately about these sounds.

An editing exercise: Cutting where there's no pause

You can use that rule to change the material you just put into your NLE, deleting "continuous sound with" so it reads:

```
Narr: Speech is made of |constantly changing volume and
pitches, punctuated by brief pauses when you breathe.
```

The | indicates where the edit should be.

Try it yourself! Load the example **Sound 13.3** into your audio software, and chose one of the following:

If you're using an Editor, do this:

1. Scrub backward and forward in your editor until you hear the sharp /k/ sound at the beginning of "continuous," and make a mark.
2. Continue scrubbing to the /k/ at the beginning of "constantly," and make another mark.
3. Select between the two marks (Figure 13.8) and delete. You're done.

Play it back, and your edit should sound just like my version (**Sound 13.5**).

---

[8] Or: what your dog shouldn't do to your sister.

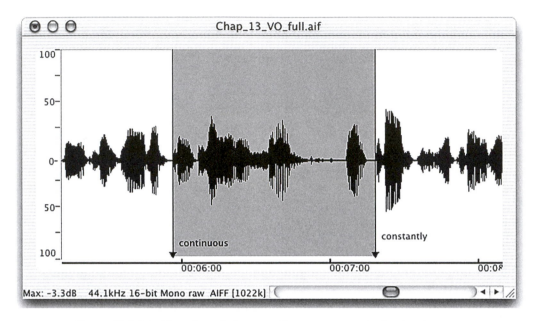

Figure 13.8 Marking the edit in an audio program, and selecting between the marks to delete.

If you're using a DAW, do this:

1. Scrub backward and forward across the clip until you hear the sharp /k/ sound at the beginning of "continuous" (Figure 13.9). Then stop scrubbing.
2. Plant a marker on the timeline, where you stopped. We chose Marker 1 (Figure 13.10).
3. Scrub to find the /k/ in "constantly," and give it a different marker[9] (Figure 13.11).
4. Use the *split*, *cut at cursor*, or *blade* command to split the clip at that point. With most software, this will also select the partial clip to the right of the cut (darkened in Figure 13.12).

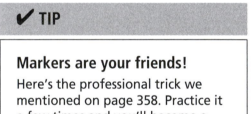

✔ TIP

Markers are your friends!

Here's the professional trick we mentioned on page 358. Practice it a few times and you'll become a much better editor.

---

[9] You don't actually need this second marker; you could just stop scrubbing and leave the cursor there. But marking takes only one keystroke and is a great habit to get into. You'll find these additional markers very handy when start editing music.

5. Without deselecting that partial clip, jump the cursor back to the marker you made in the second step. Most software will make this jump by just pressing the marker number . . . in this case, by tapping the *1* key.

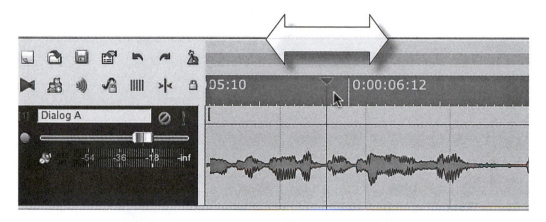

Figure 13.9 Scrub the cursor to find the first edit point . . .

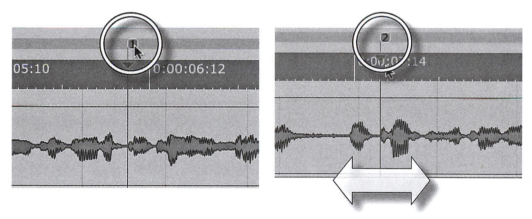

Figure 13.10
. . . plant a marker at that point . . .

Figure 13.11
. . . scrub and mark the second point,
the same way . . .

6. Keep that partial clip selected, and press the command for *move to cursor*. In many programs this will be the *L* key. The partial clip (starting with the word "constantly") will fly to first marker, since that's where we left the cursor in the previous step. Many programs will also apply a fast crossfade where the two partial clips join. It should look like Figure 13.13, and sound like **Sound 13.5**.

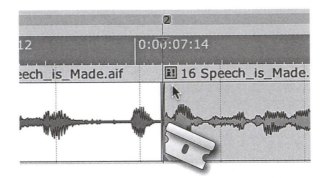
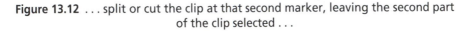

Figure 13.12 . . . split or cut the clip at that second marker, leaving the second part of the clip selected . . .

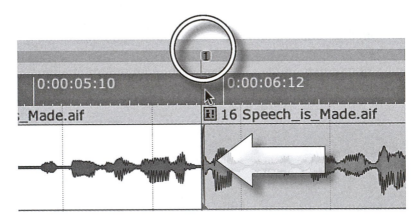

Figure 13.13 . . . jump back to the first marker, move the selection there, and you're done.

Read those steps again!

The above description might seem like a lot of work, but that's only because I've broken it down and included a lot of screenshots. The routine is actually simple: scrub and mark one side of the edit, scrub and mark the other, cut and slide.

Practice it a couple of times . . . and see how much easier dialog editing becomes.

It gets even simpler when cutting music, since scrubbing isn't always necessary. You'll learn that variation in the next chapter.

What we've done

This edit works because we've cut from one phoneme (the /k/ in "continuous") into an identical phoneme in a different word (/k/ in "constantly"). If this were video editing, the equivalent would be what's called *cutting on a matched action*, and would assure a smooth cut. The same rule holds for sound:

☛ ROSE'S RULES

Rule 3: You can almost always cut away from the start of a sound in one word, and into the start of that same sound in another word.

But the cut-into-something-hard rule is more powerful. We could go from virtually anything to a hard sound, and it would be fine.

Here's proof (and a chance to practice another technique), cutting away from a /k/ and into a /p/:

```
Narr: Speech is made of |pauses when you breathe.
```

1. Go ahead. Reload the original clip and mark the /k/ in "continuous."
2. Mark the /p/ in "pauses" for the other side of the edit. If you scrub slowly, you'll be able to hear precisely where the buzzing /v/ in "of" ends, then a tiny break, and then the start of the /p/.

3. Cut them together, and it should be as smooth as my version on **Sound 13.6**.

Practice a few times on other voice tracks, and you'll be ready for truly advanced voice editing.

EDITING III: HEARING PHONEMES

So far, you've made edits by finding and marking hard attacks. But speech is made up of sounds, not just sudden attacks. Once you learn to recognize individual phonemes and can find their beginnings and ends, you've got a lot more flexibility in how you edit.

An even more impressive exercise

We'll start with a slightly more complicated edit, finding the boundary between /z/ and /m/ in "speech is made" so we can turn the line into

```
Narr: Speech is |punctuated by brief pauses when you
breathe.
```

1. Reload the clip, and start scrubbing from the front. You'll hear a recognizable /t ch/ at the very end of "speech."[10] Immediately after that is the beginning of the word "is."

2. Keep scrubbing forward, and you'll hear a hissing or whistling—depending on how fast you're scrubbing—at the start of the /z/ that finishes "is." Scrub some more, very slowly, and stop as soon as that whistle ends. Mark it. That's the end of /z/ and the beginning of /m/ in "made."

3. Now mark the /p/ at the start of "punctuated"—just like you did in the previous exercise—and make the edit between them.

The result will sound like **Sound 13.7**. If it doesn't, you probably scrubbed a little bit too far after the end of the /z/. Undo and try again.

Fooling the ear

If you can't find something hard to cut on, or identical sounds to cut between, you can sometimes fool the ear into thinking an edit is smoother than it really is:

- Cutting away from the start of one sound, and into the start of a *similar* sound, often works.

That's because in normal speech, the end of one sound is often influenced by the sound it's going into. The mouth has to get into the right shape for the next phoneme, and it starts moving slightly before the phoneme actually starts.

Try it yourself:

```
Narr: Speech is made of continuous sound, with constantly
changing volume and pitches |when you breathe.
```

1. Find the /s/ at the end of "pitches." Do this by playing or scrubbing until you hear the word "pitches" start, and then scrubbing very slowly. You'll notice the /t ch/ in the middle of the "pitches," then the /i/, then a hiss as the /s/ starts. It's similar, but not identical, to the buzzing /z/. Continue slowly to the end of the hiss; that's the end of the phoneme. Mark it.

2. Move ahead a few seconds to the word "pauses." Mark the end of the final /z/, just like you did with the word "is."

3. Edit the two marks together. If it sounds a tiny bit awkward, you've probably left a brief pause after the /s/. Trim a tiny bit off that edit, and try again. **Sound 13.8** shows this edit with and without the pause, so you can hear the difference. There's even a science to determining when sounds are similar. Read on.

---

[10] The "ch" sound is actually two separate phonemes, /t/ and /sh/. When two phonemes are frequently said together as a unit, it's called a *diphthong*.

Phonemes come in families

There are 46 phonemes in normal American English, but as an editor you really only need to know about a few categories of them:

- two kinds of consonants and two ways of making them;
- the vowels and a few special consonants that glide between vowels; and
- some common sounds that are really diphthongs of two others (such as the /d/ and /zh/ that make up the letter *j*).

✳ TIDBIT

Why bother with phonetics?

Can't you just make edits by trial and error, undoing the ones that don't sound right? Sure. But you'll do a better job, much faster, when you understand the simple science involved.

Think of it like this: You can light a set by pointing every fixture you have on the subject, looking through the lens, and then moving or turning off instruments when you don't like the shadows or hot spots. But if you're a good DP, you know some rules about light . . . so you'll get that set lit a lot faster, with fewer instruments and less fuss.

Voiced and unvoiced consonants

You've probably noticed that /s/ (as at the end of "tots") and /z/ (at the end of "toys") have similar, but not identical, sounds. In fact, you put tongue behind your upper teeth exactly the same way to make both sounds. The only difference is that /z/ has a buzzing from your vocal cords, while /s/ is made just by exhaling—your throat doesn't buzz at all. /z/ is called a *voiced* consonant; /s/ is *unvoiced*.

Try it: put your hand lightly on your throat, near your collarbone. Say "totsssss" with a long, drawn-out /s/. Now say "toyzzzz" the same way. You'll feel a vibration on the last phoneme of "toys", but not on the /s/ in "tots."[11]

As an editor, it's important to know this distinction:

- Unvoiced consonants have very little to identify who's speaking. Almost none of a specific character's voice is carried in these sounds. This means that except for matters of room acoustics or background noise, you can often substitute one actor's unvoiced consonant for the same consonant from a different actor. Believe it or not, you can take an /s/ from one of Sue's lines and put it into George's mouth, and it'll sound fine!

---

[11] You'll also feel vibration during the vowels of both words. Vowels are always voiced.

- You can sometimes swap voiced and unvoiced consonants when you need to create new words. If George said "boy" when the script required "boys," but the only final *s* you have in his voice is from the word "tots," you might still be able to cut them together. The result will sound slightly foreign, "boysss" with a hissing ending, but may work in context. (You can't use one of Sue's /z/ sounds for a George /s/, because voiced consonants include a lot of the sound of a particular person's voice.)
- Other voiced/unvoiced pairs include

v	(as in "very")	and	f	(as in "ferry")
zh	("seizure")	and	sh	("sea shore")
g	("gut")	and	k	("cut")
d	("dip")	and	t	("tip")
b	("bark")	and	p	("park")
th	("then")	and	th	("thin")

This last pair is hard to notate since English makes no spelling distinction between them. You just have to be aware that the two sounds are different, when you're looking for replacement phonemes in dialog.

Voiced/unvoiced pairs of consonants are very similar; you can sometimes use one, knowing that viewers will fill in the other because of the context. Sounds also come in more general families, based on the physics of how they make noise; knowing this can also help you find a place to edit.

Fricatives or friction consonants

The sounds /z/ and /s/, /v/ and /f/, /zh/ and /sh/, and the two /th/ sounds are all based on hisses. They're made by forcing air through a small opening, formed by your tongue held close to some other part of your mouth. This air friction generates high frequencies. Because they're higher than most other parts of speech, they stand out when you scrub through a track slowly. Learn to identify this hiss (as when you found the end of the word "is"), and you'll be able to spot the start and end of these consonants quickly.

The sound /h/ belongs in the same fricative family, but the mouth is held open. There's less friction; the sound is from air moving against the sides of the throat and mouth. It also hisses, but much more quietly.

Plosives or stop consonants

The sounds /b/, /p/, /g/, /k/, /d/, and /t/ are formed by letting air pressure build up and then releasing it quickly.[12]

---

[12] This burst of pressure can cause a popping sound when it's too close to the mic. The most common symptom is a "popped p," but those other plosive consonants can also pop when conditions are right.

The only way humans can make a plosive while talking, is by shutting off the flow of breath momentarily. This is done either by closing the lips (/b/), or by sealing the tongue against part of the roof of the mouth (/g/, /d/).

Having this simple and consistent recipe for plosives can make life easy for the dialog editor:

- When a plosive starts a syllable, there'll be a tiny pause before it. Listen for that silence, and you've found the exact beginning of the syllable.
- When a plosive ends a syllable, it actually has two parts: the closure, and then the release. Say the word "cat" slowly, and you'll hear two distinct sounds: /kaa/, then a brief pause and a short /tih/. If the same plosive consonant happens twice in a row (as between the words in "that Tom!"), you can almost always *elide* them together (/thah tom/).

✔ TIP

When plosives go bad!
- Some classically trained announcers start their voices buzzing before plosives. You'll hear a frame or two of /m/ before the pop of an initial /b/ or /g/. You can almost always cut this buzzing out without affecting the word.
- Overly formal or nervous speakers will often separate two adjacent plosives more than they need to (/thah . . . t tom/). Cut out one of the two, and the speaker will seem more relaxed.

Glottal and nasals

The sounds /h/, /n/, /m/, and the /ng/ at the end of "ring" are four completely different, long consonants. They can often be shortened by cutting out their middles, but they can't be substituted for anything else.

Vowels and intervowels

While written English has five vowels (and sometimes "y"), there are a dozen in the spoken language. The important thing for an editor is learning to tell them apart, because they can't be substituted for one another. For example, the letter "a" can be five different sounds: "cake," "cat," "tar," "tall," and "alone." If you're looking for alternate syllables to fix a badly recorded word with an *a* in it, don't just search for that letter in the script.

Vowels are, obviously, always voiced. They are always formed by buzzing the vocal cords and changing the resonant shapes of the mouth. They have no unvoiced equivalent.

The consonants /w/ and /y/ always appear with a vowel (though sometimes with an /h/ in between), and their ends are modified by the vowel they're gliding into. If you need to fix a bad /w/ in "wail," chances are the /w/ in "water" won't work . . . the *a*'s are different.

The consonants /l/ and /r/ are always said with a vowel on one side, the other, or both. They're not influenced as much by the vowels next to them, but will be different depending on whether they're leading into one or following it.

Diphthongs or double phonemes

Some common sounds are always made of two phonemes joined together. Learn to listen for them because they give you twice as many editing options as single phonemes.

☞ ROSE'S RULES

Rule 4: You can frequently isolate a single sound from a diphthong to use elsewhere. You can almost always cut from the middle of one diphthong to the middle of another, or to the start of a different sound.

There are two consonant diphthongs, /t sh/ (as in "church") and its cognate /d zh/ ("George"). There are five vowel diphthongs: /aah ih/ ("eye"), /aw ih/ ("toy"), /ah oo/ ("loud"), /ay ih/ ("aim"), and /oo uu/ ("open").

This is advanced stuff. Diphthongs in vowels are often hard to hear, but when you become a good editor, you'll actually be able to cut them separately!

Intonation

Voiced sounds have pitch, and people express emotions by varying this pitch when they speak. As you get more into dialog editing, you'll be amazed how *little* attention you have to pay to this factor. If you're cutting between multiple takes of the same script, the pitch will be remarkably consistent. Any slight variations you cause by editing will probably sound like natural intonation, particularly if the edit is smooth and the viewer is following the content. Wide variations will be immediately apparent, so you can undo the edit and try something else. One of the things you should try is a few percent of pitch manipulation or varispeed, if your editing system has this feature. A small pitch shift—rarely as much as 3%—may be all you need to join two unfriendly phonemes.

Projection levels

A performer's projection affects more than how loud they are. As you raise your voice, the throat tightens. This makes the basic buzz of the voice lose some of its lower frequencies. If the performer has been properly trained, they'll probably also push their voice "into the mask," directing more energy to the resonating cavities in the front of the face. This adds high harmonics.

You can't compensate for these timbral changes by simply adjusting volume. In most cases, you can't compensate for them at all, and editing between two takes of widely varying projection levels can be difficult.

The envelopes of individual words also frequently change as projection levels rise, if the pace is also being slowed down. The beginnings of each word can get stressed more than in normal speech, to make sure they're heard separately.

✔ **TIP**

If you must cut between two takes with different projection, keep the takes on two separate tracks as you move their phonemes around. Then experiment with volume and equalization to make them match. A little reverb on the softer track can also help. Once the sound matches, mix the two tracks to a single composite voice.

EDITING IV: THEATRICAL FILM DIALOG

Most of what's in this chapter applies to spoken words in any project: training video, TV documentary, wedding album, theatrical film. They all usually require some dialog editing, and the rules for that editing are always the same.

But theatrical film deserves an extra level of care. That's partially because when a track is played in a large auditorium through a good system, we can concentrate on it ... and hear minor flaws that would be acceptable on the small screen. It's also because the budgets and traditions of feature film often let you take more time with the dialog editing, and our expectations are higher.

I'm not complaining. I wish we could put this kind of work into every project, no matter what the budget or medium.

Roomtone

Our world has a background track. Unless you're in an absolutely quiet studio,[13] voices you hear or record are constantly surrounded by the sounds of computer fans,

---

[13] Which is unlikely, of course. You'd have to stop all molecular movement, which means either keeping the studio at absolute zero or pumping out the air. But you can build a room where the background noise is only a few dozen dB above the threshold of hearing, and negligible compared to the electronic noise contributed by the mic and preamp.

distant traffic, people's breathing, and other random noise. Most of the time it's not noticeable. But if you suddenly cut the noise out—perhaps because you've added a pause or removed an "um" from the dialog— you'll hear the gap.

If the project will be heard on small speakers or in a noisy environment, you can sometimes use music under the scene to fill the holes and distract from any gaps. Lots of commercials and training videos are cut this way.

But what works with music doesn't work with random noise. Don't make the beginners' mistake of thinking you can fill holes in dialog with continuous traffic or other distraction. For this to work, the added noise would have to be so loud that it distracts from the noise already recorded with voices . . . making the whole scene seem unnatural and badly mixed.

Recorded roomtone

The classic solution is to have everybody on the set hold still for 30 seconds or so, while you record *roomtone*.[14] The mic position and recorder settings should be about the same as they were for dialog, the crew should stay in position, and if the camera has a fan or there are noisy lamp ballasts, they should be left on as well.

This recording of tone is logged like any other take. Pieces of it are then used to fill any holes left by the dialog edit. Fast crossfades—often less than half a frame— smooth the transition between dialog recording and tone.

But getting everyone on a set to stand still for 30 seconds is difficult. And with modern productions being shot primarily at busy locations, instead of on soundstages, the background noise can change a lot from one setup to the next. Fortunately, there's a workaround.

Harvested roomtone

You can often find a few seconds of silence within the take itself. If it's a scripted film, there'll be a moment of quiet between the slate and "action." If it's ad-lib or documentary interviews, there'll be a pause between the setup or question and the response. Splice a few of these together, duplicate them in a *c-loop* (page 436), and you'll have workable roomtone.

Be careful about harvesting tone from pauses in the dialog itself. These often have tiny breaths or mouth noises that aren't noticeable in context . . . but when you start looping or editing them, they stop sounding natural and call attention to the edit (Figure 13.14).

If a scene has already been edited, you can often find good tone right before or after the clip that was actually used! Open up the edit by expanding its handles (Figure 13.15). This will usually uncover a clean pause, which you can isolate and c-loop. Obviously, you should work on a copy of the clip or have some other way to quickly restore the original edit after you've gathered its roomtone.

---

[14] Sometimes called *ambience* or *background tone*, since you need to record the "room" when you're shooting outdoors as well.

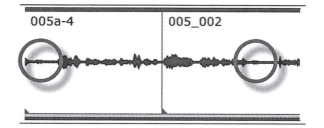

Figure 13.14 Two dialog clips in an edited scene. You can't use their pauses for roomtone because of mouth noises (circled).

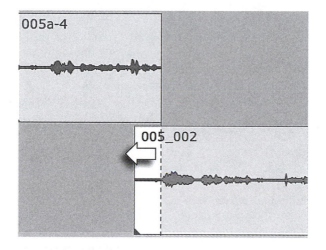

Figure 13.15 Open the handle of one of the clips (shown on an adjacent track for clarity), and you'll often find clean roomtone.

Manufactured roomtone

The problem with looping any short segments of tone, even with a forward and reversed c-loop, is that the repetition becomes obvious. Elements in the tone, whether they're specific noises or just changes in gusts of wind or traffic, get recognizable after the third or fourth time you've heard them. True roomtone is random and never repeats. A music synthesizer can generate somewhat random tones, but it's virtually impossible to program them to sound like the air and natural movement in the room where you shot.

The trick (you *knew* I'd reveal a trick, sooner or later) is to synthesize roomtone without using a synthesizer! Instead, use a fairly new kind of reverb plug-in that works by *convolution* or *sampling*. These reverbs use short samples of real echoes recorded in natural spaces—everything from a phone booth to a concert hall—and then process the incoming sound to match those echoes. They're great for matching studio ADR to production dialog, and there's more about the process in Chapter 16.

If you want to manufacture roomtone, load the convolution reverb with a short sample of actual roomtone from the shoot. It doesn't need to be more than a second or so long, but has to be clean: any breaths, footsteps, or other noises will destroy the analysis. Fortunately, you can usually find a good sample within the handles.

Then, instead of using dialog or music for the reverb's input, use random noise! Most DAWs come with a test generator plug-in (free ones are available from shareware sources). Select its *white noise* option—that's random electronic noise, sounding a lot like circuit hiss—and feed it to the reverb. Set the reverb for 100% processed output and record the result: instant roomtone. It'll probably be too loud, since processors like to run with full resolution. Either use the reverb's output control to match the dialog recording, or apply an appropriate adjustment to the file you just recorded.

Skeptical? Since I came across this trick, I've used it for multiple scenes in some pieces that were shown on large theater systems. It's not quite as elegant or classical as actual recorded roomtone . . . but unless that tone is going to be naked, exposed for a long time without any music or sound effects, it works!

I like this process so much that I threw together a plug-in to simplify it. *Room Tone Generator* (Figure 13.16) contains the noise source and a simple but sufficient convolution reverb: load a short file with clean tone from the actual shoot, adjust the volume, and you're ready to go. It's a free download at GreatSound.info.

The download is in both VST and AU versions for Mac, and also requires the components in an older version of SonicBirth (free at sonicbirth.sourceforge.net, details in Chapter 16). If you want to build and distribute a free version for Windows, be my guest. The incredibly simple circuit is in Figure 13.17.

Figure 13.16 This plug-in synthesizes roomtone, based on a short model you load. It's free at my website.

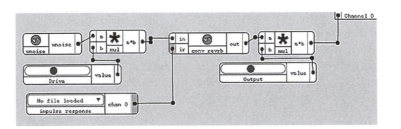

Figure 13.17 How the plug-in of Figure 13.16 works. This schematic is captured from SonicBirth, which is also free. Read the text for details.

Track splitting

The main technique that separates theatrical dialog from other forms is *track splitting*. It serves two primary purposes:

- **Hiding subtle jumps in timbre and background sound:** There can be thousands of these in a film. They're inevitable when you cut from one camera angle to another, because sound changes with each camera setup: boom mics move to a different position, characters might be closer to reflective surfaces, and unless you're in a studio, the background noise keeps changing. Think about it: when you condense a morning's worth of out-of-sequence shots into a single scene, stuff is going to change . . . even if the dialog is supposed to be continuous.
- **Simplifying the mix:** The goal is a single dialog track, coming from the center speaker in the theater. But breaking it up onto a half-dozen or more faders lets you preset levels and processors for each character or mic setup, and crossfade between them as the scene progresses. This is easier and faster than trying to program all those changes into an automation system.

Figure 13.18 shows some of the track splitting in a scant 15 seconds of a fairly simple scene.

- On the bottom (letter A in Figure 13.18) is how the picture editor cut the scene in an NLE, and passed it to audio post as an OMF. This scene actually consists of a master shot and a couple of close-ups.

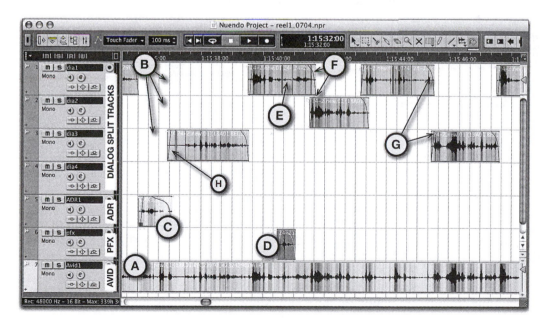

Figure 13.18 Dialog editing in 15 seconds of a simple scene.

- The scene has three different characters. Letter B shows how where individual lines have been copied from the NLE's version, and split among the top three tracks. This lets you apply different volume and equalization settings to each character, or if you want to subtly emphasize one character during the mix.
- One line had to be replaced with ADR and will need completely different processing to match, so it's separated at letter C.
- One sound effect—a door slam—was picked up by the boom during the action. It's not dialog but might be useful in the mix, so it's moved to a production effects track (D). That slam might be replaced with a different one, recorded separately. So a little bit of roomtone is copied from elsewhere in the take, and pasted where the slam was (E). This way, the background will continue if a different slam is used.
- Note how most of the clips on the top three tracks overlap by a half-second or so (such as at F), even though there are hard cuts between them on the original. These clips were extended by grabbing their handles from the OMF.
- The curved lines over the ends of most clips (G) are fades. They work in pairs as crossfades, disguising differences in roomtone. Most good audio programs will add these fades automatically.
- We were lucky mixing this scene. The actors had paused between their lines, so when the editor created overlaps, there was room ambience to cover the crossfades. But you can see (at H) how a small clip of extra roomtone had to be stuck to the front of one dialog clip. We found some clean ambience elsewhere in the take, where no one was speaking, and used it here.

✳ TIDBIT

Why not just process the clips?

Most audio software lets you apply volume, equalization, and other processing to individual clips on a track separately, or apply them to the entire track as a whole. The former is handy for repairs and effects where just one line—or sometimes one word—needs treatment. But the latter is faster, easier to change, and usually leads to a smoother mix.

Processing individual clips locks you into their sound. Depending on the program, restoring the original can be difficult or impossible. It's seldom a good idea to make this decision until all the elements are in place, and you're monitoring in a proper environment.

If you are tempted to pre-process a clip to solve a problem, keep an unprocessed version of it on an unused track. Mute this *mirror* track so it doesn't confuse things. You'll be glad it's there, when the processing doesn't mix quite the way you wanted.

There's another feature film technique that also results in better tracks, the *dialog premix*. We'll cover that in Chapter 17.

EDITING V: THE TRICKS

Breathless

Go back to **Sound 13.3**, one you loaded at the start of this chapter, or look at Figure 13.6. There's a big puff of air in the middle. Most announcers will take a gigantic breath at the start of a paragraph, and grab loud, fast ones between some sentences. These noises really say "I'm reading from a script," because nobody ever takes them during natural ad-lib conversations. They should come out of voice-over tracks.

Breaths before a paragraph are easy to get rid of: just move the in-point a little later. But those catch-breaths during a read are more troublesome. You can't just cut them out—that pulls the surrounding words too close together. You can't just erase them or turn their volume down, that leaves the words too far apart. If the announcer is on-camera, you can't change their timing at all.

Voice-over breaths can usually be replaced by pauses *two-thirds* their length. If it takes one second for the announcer to gasp, replace it with 20 frames of silence or roomtone. The result will be cleaner, more energetic, and completely natural.

I don't know why two-thirds is the magic number, but it's worked for me in thousands of projects with hundreds of different announcers. Even though I edit by ear—erasing the entire pause, playing the line in real-time, and tapping the Mark key where I think the next phrase should start—it almost always turns out to be two-thirds.

If you're starting with a clean voice-over recording and it will be used on a limited medium such as broadcast TV, or be mixed with music, you can replace breaths with digital silence. But if it'll be played at theatrical levels, use roomtone; otherwise, the finished edit will sound choppy.

On-camera breaths are trickier, since the two-thirds trick would destroy sync. Replacing the whole breath with roomtone can also be a mistake: if we see the talent's mouth open, we should hear something. Consider these on-camera breaths as you would any of the other meaningless placeholders in natural speech, like *uh* and *er*: fade them down enough to be unobtrusive, but not so much that you notice the gap. It's easier to do this as a clip edit, rather than trying to move faders quickly during the mix:

1. Split or cut the clip at the start of the breath or noise, and at the start of the following word.
2. Lower the volume of the small clip you've just isolated. A good place to start is 6 dB reduction, but it depends on the talent.
3. Make sure there are crossfades between it and the rest of the original clip.

Simply shocking!

Amateur announcers and real-life interview subjects don't take the big breaths, but often do something worse: they unconsciously let their breath build up, then blast it out when they talk. It causes a little click if the phrase starts with a vowel. These *glottal shocks* are a natural result of nervousness in the throat, so we all get used to associating them with that condition. Your listeners won't know why, but they'll know your track is somehow hesitant and unconvincing.

Glottal shocks often follow long pauses, when a speaker is unsure and looking for "just the right word." If you try to shorten this pause but don't take care of the shock, your editing won't sound natural. It's easy to get rid of the pesky things, but only if you zoom in. Deleting about a hundredth of a second, at the start of a word, is usually enough to turn a speaker from nervous to confident.

Extensions

When cutting documentaries or testimonials, you frequently need to start or end a voice segment on a particular syllable, even though the speaker might have more to say before or after the clip. If they didn't pause exactly where you want to edit, even the most accurate edit will sound abrupt as their voice suddenly stops or starts.

Add a little roomtone or natural background noise, butted right up to the edit. This will make it sound as though the performer—and not your editing system—made the pause.

Snap, crackle . . .

When the clock rolls around to winter, the announcers start ticking. You can hear annoying clicks and snaps in their voices, particularly when they're close-miked and saying sounds that require the tongue to touch the roof of the mouth (like /l/ or /k/). It's caused by central heating! This dries up their mouths, thickening saliva, which starts to stick and stretch and . . . well, the sound is almost as disgusting as the description.

Unfortunately, cutting out the snap entirely can destroy the rhythm of the word. Erasing it—or replacing it with silence—leaves a noticeable hole.

But you can usually replace the snap with a tiny snippet of the vowel immediately before or after it. Locate a snap, select about the same length of audio right next to it— it'll be less than a frame—copy, and paste over the snap. Depending on the program, you may need to use a *Replace* or *Overdub* function; you want the new sound to fit over the snap, rather than move the snap later.

Because these snaps are so fast, it's almost impossible to fix them in a frame-based NLE. Use an audio program. Or hand the announcer a glass of water, and re-record.

Squeezing and stretching

Modern DAWs let you change the timing of a clip, speeding or slowing words without affecting their pitch or timbre. Obviously, it can only be done during cutaways, when lipsync isn't an issue. But it can be enormously powerful, and is worth considering when you need to

- add emphasis to a thought (or to client's name) by subtly slowing it down;
- speed up a "the," "and," or other linking word that an interview subject stretched, to cover silence when they're trying to think of a word; or
- expand an edited interview section to fit its original cutaway, after you've made it more fluent by removing all the "aahs" and stutters.

Always make a backup before doing this kind of operation. It'll be your guide for sync if you get lost. And you can play it for reference if you think the manipulations have gone too far.

Putting it all together

Figure 13.19 shows how these techniques can be combined, to smooth out 30 seconds of a documentary about a musician. The basic dialog, as received from the project's picture editor, is on the bottom track. The edited track that went into the mix is on the top. I've pointed out eight places on the editor's track where a little audio smoothing made things work better; those are the notes in italics. There are also smaller edits where roomtone was pieced together to fit.

You can try some of these things yourself. **Sound 13.9**[15] is track from the original picture edit; **Sound 13.10** is the dialog after it's been cut. **Clip 13.1** is matching video, including the mixed track from that segment.

EDITING VI: KEEPING TRACK OF SYNC

So far all of the voice editing we've talked about has been without pictures. Surprisingly, cutting sync dialog isn't very different. An NLE should take care of synchronization automatically; you can move and mark either sound or picture, and if the software knows the two belong together, they should both stay together. Two rules will keep you out of most trouble:

☞ ROSE'S RULES

- As soon as you import or digitize synced audio and video, lock their tracks together in the software.
- Make an unlocked copy on another track for editing.

Always keep a copy of the original, locked, unedited takes. They'll let you check and restore sync easily, if you accidentally move something or make an edit while a character's lips are visible.

---

[15] This and the related clips are from *Tom Rush: No Regrets.* © 2013 Ezzie Films and BlueStar Media, used by permission and with thanks.

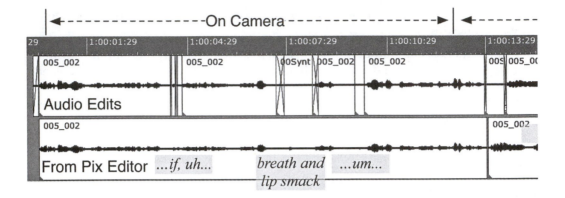

Figure 13.19 Thirty seconds of a 102-minute documentary, showing the dialog edits that made the film work better.

Keeping things in sync in most single-track editing programs is a little trickier. Once you've loaded the audio/video file, the sound portion can be edited any way you want. If you do anything that changes its length—inserting or deleting sounds, or changing their tempo—sync will get lost. Minor changes shouldn't cause any trouble if you keep this in mind:

☞ ROSE'S RULES

> To edit audio-for-video without affecting sync, stick with operations that don't affect overall length: use Replace rather than Insert, or Erase rather than Cut.

It's just a tiny bit more work to delete specific sounds in a sync track, or close up the gaps between words, without affecting sync after the edit. Consider the original audio example from this chapter. If we wanted to shorten the silence between "continuous sound" and "with constantly," we could mark both sides of the silence and then cut between the marks (Figure 13.20). That, obviously, also moves the "punctuated by brief pauses" phrase and could cause us to lose sync.

But if we want to close up those two words without affecting the overall length, we just need to add a third mark at the start of the next phrase.

1. Select between the second and third mark—the phrase that immediately follows the desired edit (Figure 13.21).
2. Use the program's Copy function instead of Cut.
3. Locate to the first mark—the beginning of the edit—and use the program's Replace or Paste Over function. This moves the phrase closer to the one that preceded it, closing up the words.

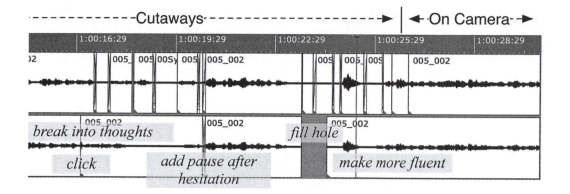

Figure 13.19 continued

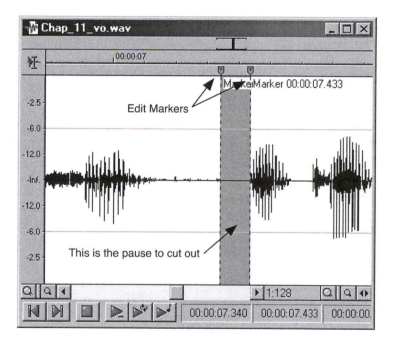

Figure 13.20 Cutting out the pause will slide everything after it.

4. Check the end of the newly replaced region. If there was a long pause after the section you moved, it'll probably be fine. But if there wasn't much of a pause, you may hear the last syllables of the moved section twice. Erase the extra, or paste some roomtone over it.

Some audio programs simplify steps 2 and 3 with a single "move" command.

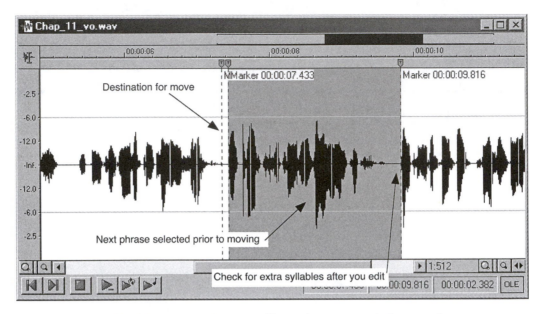

Figure 13.21 To preserve the sync of later elements, mark the next phrase, and move it earlier.

Parallel track operations

Sometimes, it's handy to move an audio element from one track to another without changing when it occurs. NLEs make this easy: you can use the Razor or similar tool to cut into the clip, and then move it to the next track while staying aligned to the frame line. If you want to do the same thing in an audio-only program or workstation, you may need a modifier key (such as holding Shift) before moving the clip. If the software doesn't support this, you can plant a marker at the edit, and use the same marker both as the start of a Cut operation and the destination for a Replace.

Multiple mics

Many documentary interviews are shot with simultaneous boom and lav, routed to separate tracks in the camera. Some features are shot double-system with three or more tracks, isolating individual lavs as well as a mixed or boom track. To handle these kinds of tracks, do something similar to the track splitting you'd use for dialog. Import each mic on its own track in sync with picture. When you want to avoid a noise on the primary mic (clothing rustles on the lav, or off-mic sounds on the boom), use the Razor or similar tool to make cuts on both tracks on either side of the noise. Remove the noisy section of the primary mic's track, and everything up to the noise on the secondary mic's track. Provide a slight overlap to simplify mixing.

Continue through the scene this way. When you reach the end, throw away the last segment on the secondary mic's track. Then when you're mixing, apply whatever reverberation is necessary to make the lav match the boom (Chapter 16), touch up the equalization on one or the other track, and they should play back as a perfect, noise-free whole.

Sync problems

Lipsync sometimes drifts. Mouths will flap, but their sounds get heard slightly earlier or later, making everything seem like a badly dubbed foreign film.

Sync problems are often the result of setup errors in the editing system, either at the board or interrupt level within the editing computer or because blackburst signals aren't being properly used (see Chapter 11). Sometimes these manifest themselves as problems in a rendered output but not during preview, or during long playbacks but not short ones. There are as many possible causes as there are systems, so you'll need a technician or manufacturer's support line to diagnose and fix the problem. But once it's solved, it should stay solved.

Sometimes sync problems are the result of user errors, such as forgetting to lock tracks together or setting the wrong timecode or reference standard. Some NLEs make certain operations, such as L-cuts, difficult and prone to error. If sync seems unstable but you know the system is set up properly, check the manufacturer's FAQ or ask an editor who's experienced with your software.

If you're moving tracks from one program to another within the same computer, or exporting them as files to another computer but bringing them back before the final output, sync should stay accurate down to the sample level. The only times you'll encounter problems are if you're doing something that intentionally changes the file's length (editing it or changing the tempo), or a process adds or subtracts samples inadvertently (badly done sample-rate conversion, re-digitizing, or re-clocking real-time digital audio).

Knowing the cause doesn't help much, however, if you've already lost sync.

Fixing sync

Lipsync can be a strange thing. Before you start sliding things around, verify that they're really out. A few techniques are helpful when checking lipsync:

- Give yourself the advantage of a large picture monitor and smooth movement. It's hard to detect lipsync on a 240 × 320 pixel screen, and almost impossible to spot it at 15 frames per second. Where your monitor speaker is placed can also make a difference: a speaker next to the picture monitor will always sound like it's in better sync than one on the other side of the room.
- Shuttle audio and video at about half speed. This is fast enough that you can understand the sound, while being slow enough to spot lip movements in the picture.
- Look for plosives that build up sound behind the lips (/b/ or /p/). The first frame where the lips are parted should exactly match the first frame of sound.

- Try changing things and see if they get better or worse. Move the audio a frame earlier and watch the sequence. If that doesn't immediately look better, move it two frames later (so it's now one frame later than it originally was). If *that* doesn't help either, the problem either isn't lipsync, or sync is so variable you'll have to dig deeper.

These same techniques can be used for fixing sync on individual words. Slide things until they're better, staying aware that sometimes a whole track may require correction, while, other times, only a few clips will be out. Some performances and shooting situations result in soft or difficult-to-spot lipsync. If a scene seems to be out of sync, but nothing you do makes it look any better, shrug and hope for the best.

Sometimes a track will start in sync, and then slowly drift farther and farther out. This is almost always because sound and picture are playing at slightly different rates, usually because of a setup error. Check the program's or equipment's settings.

If that doesn't fix it, go to the end of the program, and use some of the techniques above to see how far out of sync the track has gotten. Then convert the length of the program into frames. Take a calculator and divide the length of the program *plus* the error into the length of the program. Apply the result, as a percentage speed correction, to the track. This is a slightly Rube Goldberg-ish solution that doesn't address the original cause of the problem, but it works. And believe it or not, for a while, one of the biggest names in NLE software was proposing it on their website as a workaround for a known sync problem in their program!

A FINAL EXERCISE

Okay. You've read this chapter, you've practiced with the examples, and you've gotten pretty good at this voice-cutting stuff. Here's a challenge for fun.[16]

Sound 13.11 is a famous news bite from the final U.S. president of the twentieth century. Using that short bite as the only source—and nothing from anything else he ever said—turn it around so he admits the very thing he's denying here. The second part of the track can serve as a model.

Don't settle for just deleting "not . . . "; that's a lazy edit. If you swap a few phonemes, you can change the "have" to "had" . . . and "I did" to "I've."

I didn't pick this sound bite for partisan reasons—presidents from both parties have been known to misspeak. But it is an impressive demonstration of editing prowess. (At least it was an NAB Convention a few years ago, where I did these edits in front of a live audience, taking less than two minutes not only to do the whole job but also to explain which phonemes I'd moved.)

---

[16] Or maybe not fun, depending on your political leanings.

CHAPTER 14

Working with Music

Was *The Jazz Singer* the first Hollywood movie with a musical score?

Not by a decade. Long before Al Jolson's 1927 hit, producers were making full musical scores for their silent films! Big theaters would get custom sheet music along with the film prints, and live orchestras would play it while the movie was projected.

This was real music, not the tinny piano you might associate with *Perils of Pauline*. For example, the hymn-like theme song that ran for decades on the popular *Amos 'n' Andy* show was originally written for D. W. Griffith's 1915 epic *Birth of a Nation*. (Want to hear it? Search the Web for "The Perfect Song" . . . that's really its title.)

Perhaps you think using pop songs to cross-promote a movie is something new? Back in the 1920s, Hollywood moguls were commissioning Tin Pan Alley lyrics with their movies' names in the titles; they'd plug the songs on early radio broadcasts. This gave us "Ramona" and "Jeannine, I Dream of Lilac Time," ancient hits that are now performed as standards. The insistence on using the movies' titles in love songs also gave us monstrosities like "Woman Disputed, I Love You" and "Red Man, Why Are You Blue?"[1]

The point is, music has always been an essential part of filmmaking.

- It can add the right seriousness, importance, or excitement to a presentation.
- It can tie things together, or delineate sections when the topic changes.
- It can heighten emotions when the images and dialog aren't enough to carry a scene.
- It can provide a driving rhythm for montages, or tug at a sales prospect's heart.
- A grand theme, sweeping to a conclusion, can even let suffering viewers know that a too-long corporate epic or classroom film is about to end . . . so they can start paying attention again.

No matter what kind of project you're producing, chances are you can find effective, interesting music for it without breaking your budget or the copyright laws. That's what this chapter is about.

DECIDING WHAT MUSIC YOU'LL NEED

You don't need a musical education or any particular instrumental chops to use music effectively. You don't have to know what MIDI is, or who sings *altissimo*. Many films and TV series are scored by people who can't read a note. What's needed is the ability to look at a script or roughcut, figure out what music is needed, and then describe it in useful terms. A computer keyboard will be more helpful than a piano's.

Feature film music supervisors usually don't write the score. While there's usually a composer to write a score, most films also include a lot of music from other sources. Some of these *cues* may be pop or classical songs, licensed for the movie, and chosen because their familiarity and style helps set a mood. Other cues—even on big-budget Hollywood features—are often taken from the same low-cost stock libraries you can use for corporate or wedding videos, or for your own indie feature.

- If you want to use music effectively, think like a music supervisor. What they bring, along with musical taste and experience, is an understanding of the emotional flow of the film . . . you've already got that. Then, it's just a question of listing what music is needed, and figuring out where to get it.
- Start with a list of spotting notes. This can be useful even for a project as simple as your sister's wedding album or the CEO's Message to the Troops.
- Read the script or watch a roughcut, and note what kind of music you need and where it belongs (Figure 14.1 shows one form of a spotting list; you can also use a spreadsheet like the one in Chapter 10, or even some scrap paper).

---

[1] Let us review the preceding three paragraphs: a hit movie about a Jew who performed in blackface, a film glorifying the Klan, an incredibly racist radio show, and some random offensiveness against women and Native Americans. Maybe we've made some progress in the past century.

- The most important part of each note will be *what the cue is trying to say*: descriptions like "inspirational," or "building to a limitless future" are more helpful than "music under." Add anything else that strikes you about the orchestration, tempo, or style.
- If you don't know a precise musical term, don't worry. The words *fast* or *sweet* work as well as *allegro* or *dolce*.
- You can also make notes by referring to musical groups, specific songs, classical forms, or anything else that serves as a specific reminder. Even "like the stabbing in *Psycho*" will get your point across.
- For each cue, include how long it'll be on the screen and any internal transitions or builds it'll need. Don't worry about the timing of those internal changes, unless the picture is locked and you're making notes for an original score. It's easy enough to adjust the timing of any music, using some of the editing techniques at the end of this chapter.

Digital Playroom

Custom Productions: Focus, Focus, Focus

Music list v.2   *Times in mm:ss from offline*

TIME	CUE	DESCRIPTION
00:07	m001	*Industrial march.* Stock. Fanfares to approx :03 then under; hit at :15 ("uses of radio") then under again. Music slides up at :26 — sort of the opposite as the effect of a turntable slowing down. Can be done as DSP or use a gliss.
00:43	m002	*I want it all.* Original, almost reverential, orchestral, for BOSS' summary. Must cut into m003. 00:52 punctuate reverse angle: not overdone, just hold rhythm 00:57 after UNDERLING 1. Picks up again. Slight hit patriotic hymn under "every man; woman, child..." 01:03 hold after "want to buy". Keep rhythm, or just sustain chord 01:07 "Monday morning at 9" kicks off rhythm to bridge into m003
01:09	m003	*Research montage.* Stock. Suggest orchestral rag... uptempo, offbeat, but mainstream orchestration to keep it businesslike. 02:05 out.
02:08	m004	*Tension and Resolve.* Original, through dialog. Keep the orch tone of m002

Figure 14.1 A music spotting list. This one is very specific, since some of the cues will be composed to fit . . . and because the client was given a copy.

Having a list is important even if you're the only one who'll be referring to it, or if you'll be getting all the music from a small library. It'll save a lot of time later in the process.

Don't specify one long piece of music when two short ones will do. It doesn't cost extra to change the music according to the dynamics of what we're seeing. A composer will usually ask for a set fee based on how much music you need, not on how many individual melodies there are. If you're getting music from a library, you've probably either paid buyout fees or will be purchasing a blanket license that covers the entire show. So give the viewer a break from time to time—put in a different piece, or even silence. Twenty minutes of endlessly repeating music isn't interesting when you're on hold; why subject your video's audience to the same torture?

If you're listing multiple cues, indicate which should be related ("peaceful theme :45, based on earlier march #7") and which should sound different. Obviously, this will be a big help for a composer you hire. It also can be useful if you're getting stock music from a library, since some library cues are organized into suites of related themes.

"Live" music on-camera

If we're going to see the musicians perform, there's the additional challenge of coordinating the music before you shoot.

Lipsyncing

If the music is complicated or there's dialog or anything else going on in a scene, it's always best to have your musicians just pretend to perform. If a band mimes their playing, you'll be able to record nearby dialog cleanly. If an actor is singing on-camera, have them sing along with playback of their own voice (or someone else's) recorded in a music studio: you'll be able to break the song into shorter shots without worrying about continuity, and they can concentrate on movements and facial expressions while staying on the beat and key.

This technique is standard for scripted musical comedies and music videos, but it also works for other formats, such as having a live band in a bar scene, or street musicians under exterior dialog. Since you don't add the music until post, it's a lot easier to capture clean dialog on the set, and you've got flexibility to edit for story flow without worrying about disrupting the song.

You'll need to get the music before the shoot, of course, so your performers have something they can mime to. They'll also have to be rehearsed with this particular recording. You'll need to arrange equipment and personnel for a playback on-set (see page 140). And you'll need some way to sync the existing music to what you're shooting: standard practice is to simply re-record playback into the camera or double-system recorder on one channel, while live mics are on another. Use the dubbed music as an editing guide until you can replace it with the high quality, stereo version.

It also helps to break the music file down into pieces that are just a little longer than your planned shots, a few musical measures or a few dozen seconds. This makes

✔ TIP

Catch that click!

Click tracks are often prepared as part of multitrack studio pop productions; it's easy to have the music studio prepare playback segments that start with them. But other forms of music, including acoustic and classical, usually don't have a click track. In that case, you can record a verbal "click": count a simple "*1 . . . 2 . . . 3 . . . 4 . . .*" with the segment starting on the next *1*. This takes a little thought: some music counts in *3*s or other numbers, and some segments might start somewhere other than the *1*. We'll cover all that starting on page 411.

<u>**Sound 14.1**</u> is a short musical segment[2] repeated with both kinds of count: first a click, and then a countdown.

Some musical phrases start slightly before or after the "1" count. Make the appropriate adjustment when you're cutting segments. Some music is played with a varying tempo, or doesn't have a constant tempo at all. If that's the case, plan a lot of extra rehearsals . . . or shoot very short takes that are easily edited to fit the song.

✔ TIP

How to count accurately

Ever hear a bunch of young kids try to start a song together? One of them counts "*1 . . . 2 . . . 3 . . .*" And then they all come in at random.

For a count to work, it's got to be exactly in the rhythm of the song that'll follow, and lead exactly to where the real song should start.

Here's the trick: Set up a mic and headphones, so you can hear the actual music while you count. Record your voice only, not the music. Start the song playing, listen to its rhythm, then count *1* through *4* against the next few measures in a row.

Pick your best set of four numbers. Then replace the "*1*" that follows it with the actual musical segment.

---

[2] A couple of bars from "New Opportunities" (Doug Wood, OM201/7) © Omnimusic, Inc.; used by permission.

it easier to do multiple takes without lengthy waiting. Give each segment a separate number and file name, related to the shot breakdown for the scene.

Standard practice is to add one measure of *click track* before each segment. This is a steady metronome, usually counting four beats, before the instruments come in. Roll camera, make sure everybody is ready to perform, and start playback. Let the actors listen to the click. Then they'll all be able to start miming together and on the right beat.

Real live music

Dealing with music that's actually being performed while you shoot is a lot harder than faking it. That's why Hollywood fakes it whenever possible. On-set acoustics and the need for clean visuals aren't compatible with the best music recording.

A few kinds of acoustic music, mostly classical and solo folk, can be successfully recorded by a single mic or stereo pair. You need to be in a room that sounds good for that kind of music. You'll also need to put the mic where it belongs . . . which is usually in the shot. If having an on-camera mic offends your filmmaking, something's going to suffer. It may be best to re-think how you're using music.

If the music requires any electronics—keyboards, amplified instruments, or singers with mics—things get a lot more complicated quickly. You'll need someone at the shoot who can mix the music for you—that can't be the band's mixer at a performance, who's busy with other chores. Ideally, you should do a mix for the camera and any live Web feed, and also record multitrack with every mic isolated. You'll use those separate tracks to refine the mix after the picture is cut. A lot of times I've had to subtly raise a solo instrument or vocalist, even though they weren't mixed loudly in the band's stereo version, to help "sell" close-ups in the picture.

Amplified instruments typically get multiple channels. Each amp should have its own mic, placed where it'll hear just that instrument. It's common to also record a *DI* feed: a direct connection from the instrument, without the coloration an amp adds. For some instruments a third mic is placed next to the player for an acoustic pickup. All three get separate tracks—for each instrument—and are mixed together in post.

Some instruments might not be miked. Drums or brass are often loud enough for the venue without an amp. But you need to record them, and their mics should be close enough that you don't hear the other instruments or audience.

Vocal mics should also be sent to isolated tracks. And if there's an audience, you probably want a stereo pair of mics picking up their reactions and the room ambience.

It's a lot of tracks and a lot of mics. Many of the mics can be shared between the band's PA system and your recorder, using special transformers that feed both without interaction. Some house mixing consoles also have taps for isolated mics you'll need. But this is not a place to experiment. There are technical challenges that should be handled by someone who knows sound and is dedicated to your film. That person will have to coordinate in advance with the band's or venue's engineer. Some house engineers refuse to allow any connection to their equipment.

Most PA system consoles have a stereo "recording" output, with an isolated version of the mix they're sending to the speakers. Don't expect it to sound good for

☛ **ROSE'S RULES**

Music requires preparation

Shooting live music requires coordination between the band, the venue, their house engineer, and your production sound mixer or audio post supervisor. Don't expect to show up, point a mic or plug into their system: you might get some sound, but it won't be any better than the tubby and unmusical mess you sometimes hear as b-roll under an evening news story about the performance.

your film. The band's mixer is trying to create an experience for the live audience. This has to work properly with any unamplified instruments, any standalone amps, the room's acoustics, and how the audience is behaving at any moment. What comes out of the recording jack won't sound like the band you remember from the performance.

Source music

Source, or *diegetic*, music is part of the scene rather than the underscore (Chapter 4). But it still has to be spotted and specified. So this is the time to also make notes on music that should be coming from on-screen performers or props like TV sets.

Additional scoring

Most films have a lot of music that will never end up on a soundtrack album. These additional cues can include montages, main- and end-titles, quick stabs under dialog to heighten a dramatic or comic moment, and transitions between scenes. They add a richness and professional finish to your project. Watch some films, notice how many cues there actually are, and plan for them.

SOURCES OF MUSIC

Finding really great music isn't hard—all you need is time or money. Here are some ways to save both.

Original music

The easiest way to get music is to hire a composer. While John Williams[3] doesn't come cheap, you may find a Williams wannabe at a local music school, recording studio, or over the Internet. There's been an explosion of low-cost, high-quality musical and

---

[3] Neither the Hollywood composer nor the English classical guitarist.

digital recording equipment over the past two decades, and skilled musicians can turn out a fully professional score without a major investment in facilities or session players. Good original scores can now be had for anywhere from a couple of hundred to just under a thousand dollars per finished minute, depending on the level of production required. Episodic TV dramas are often done on a contract basis for under $10,000 per show.

A lot of composers maintain websites, and an Internet search for "original music" with "video" will turn up hundreds of qualified sites. Unfortunately, ownership of a website—even one with fancy graphics and a picture of a studio—is no guarantee of quality. Neither is a long list of projects at the Internet Movie Database (imdb.com).

So once you've found likely candidates, you have to evaluate their work. Ask to hear some of their past scores, both as excerpts from the finished films and as the clean music tracks supplied to the producer. You want both versions so you can judge their musical and production abilities, without being distracted by the movie. If they don't have access to clean music, it might be because they didn't create it.

There are several things to listen for when evaluating a music demo:

1. Was it composed well? Is the music appealing and does it match the mood of the film? If a piece is supposed to be something other than electronic instruments, does it sound real? Making artificial strings or horns sound real requires serious composing and arranging skill—the composer has to know what those instruments *should* be playing—as well as good software.
2. Does it stay interesting for its entire length? Some libraries publish longer pieces that are the same 90 seconds repeated multiple times; you could do that just as easily by copying and pasting. Having some variation in the music shows the composers' skills, and also gives you more options for editing.
3. Was it produced well? Play it in stereo on good speakers. Noises, badly tuned instruments, and a lack of clarity in the mix are signs of amateur production. This can indicate the composer doesn't have real-world experience or lacks the necessary equipment to do a good job for you. If the music wasn't produced at all—if the composer is providing self-playing MIDI files—you're going to be saddled with the chore of turning them into usable music. It can be expensive to do this well.
4. Was it performed well? Music software makes it easy to fake an acceptable performance by fixing wrong notes, evening out the tempo or dynamics, and even adding an artificial "human" randomness. But there's a big difference between acceptable and good performances, particularly in how expressively a line is played on acoustic instruments. Listen particularly to solos. Do you get a sense of a personality in the performance? Or does it sound played by a machine?
5. Is the style of music appropriate for your project? I put this last both because it's probably the easiest for you to evaluate—you know what you like—and also because it can be the least important. An experienced professional with good scoring chops can usually master a number of styles. I'm continually amazed at the flexibility of many of the composers on films I've done.

Formerly original music

Stock music used to be a curse. When I started out, using a music library often meant you gave up quality to get economy. Selections were heavily weighted toward small pop and dance bands because they were cheap to produce. If you did hear an orchestra, it was frequently small and unrehearsed, and occasionally out of tune. The few good cuts that did exist tended to be overused—I've judged business film festivals where three entries had the same theme song. Furthermore, it took a skilled music editor to blend and customize stock music, when the only tools we had were ¼" tape and mag film.[4]

But despite its limitations, stock music was often the only option. Back when I had a downtown studio, we kept a library of over a thousand licensable LPs on hand . . . and a full-time librarian to keep track of them. Then the business changed entirely.

Modern music libraries

Digital recording, computers, and *samplers*[5] created the revolution. Composers could write and arrange full scores on their computers, review and change what they'd written while listening to desktop versions, and then walk into a studio and combine a few live players with better-quality synthesizers and sampled backup groups.

Soon it wasn't even necessary to walk into a studio at all; you could do the whole project in your living room. Now lots of people could create music, and this raised the standards for all libraries. Bigger ones could combine these techniques with studio sessions, and supply full orchestras with acoustic or vocal textures that can't be synthesized. Smaller ones could fill the gap with smaller music, created entirely within computers but sounding perfectly appropriate for their styles.

At the same time, the explosion of media—all those cable channels and high-end videos—meant a lot more music was being created. The composers often retained the right to sell remixed or generic versions of their works to a library after a period of exclusivity passed, or to start a library of their own.

> Bottom line: there's a ton of good, new stock music. A lot of what you can get today is excellent. You'll hear it in national commercials, network programs, and Hollywood features. There's also a lot more music to choose from. The biggest houses release as many as a hundred new cues each month. A Web search seems to turn up more than a hundred smaller libraries.

---

[4] It's a lot easier now that you can preview and adjust edits on a computer. You'll still need some skills, and instructions start on page 416.

[5] Instruments that play recordings of other instruments—even choirs—from their keyboards while remaining responsive to subtleties in the playing style. Kurzweil made the first successful studio version in the mid-1980s. Software versions are now considered a standard sound design and composition tool.

There's also a ton of not-so-good music. Many of the smallest libraries are one-person operations. Their work can suffer from the same limitations as low-end original scoring, so you should evaluate their libraries with the same criteria.

Paying for library music

Library publishers make their money by selling the same recording over and over. You buy the rights to use it in your project, paying a fraction of what the cue cost to create; the library sells the same music to other producers and recoups their investment. Fortunately, there's a lot of good music to choose from, and editing it properly against your picture can make the music sound like it was written for your film. So there's not too much chance anyone will recognize your scoring on a competitor's film.

Library music is sold two different ways. The rates depend both on how the publisher chooses to do business and how you plan to use the music, but they're surprisingly consistent within those two categories.

✳ TIDBIT

From the library's point of view

Doug Wood is President of Omnimusic, a production music library that's been around since 1977. It now has about 25,000 tracks that can be licensed for film and video.

"Most people don't realize how music can reach into the subconscious. But think about it: people don't say 'I like this melody or harmony' . . . they say 'I *love* this song.' How powerful does something have to be to make an adult say, spontaneously, that they love something?

"Unfortunately, there's been an explosion of producers who don't know what music can do for them. They think of it as just something that fills the empty space when the announcer stops.

"We try to focus on *what nails the particular thing they're trying to communicate.* For example, sports isn't just rock and roll . . . it's about teamwork, or perseverance, or reaching a goal, depending on the story. You can make the music convey that, depending on how you structure the piece.

"So the challenge, particularly with a large library, is finding just the right choice. Our website (www.omnimusic.com) lets you search by style, mood, tempo and other factors. Or you can call us. Our people know the libraries, and we love to help clients find music that absolutely meets their needs."

Needle-drop music

The better libraries usually work on a needle-drop basis. The term comes from the original payment scheme, where a fee was charged each time a technician dropped the tone arm onto a disk, to dub the song onto mag film for editing. A really good piece may be licensed thousands of times in its life, so publishers find it profitable to create quality product. (Digital media doesn't use needles, of course, so these are often called *laser-drops*, *drops*, or just *uses*.)

Needle-drop libraries charge minimal prices for CDs or let established customers download for free from their websites. They make their money by charging for each use: $75–90 per song for a business video, up to $1,000 or so for unlimited use in broadcast media and productions for sale, and a few thousand for feature films. Rates can be negotiable, depending on your standing with the publisher. You don't pay anything until you decide to use a particular piece.

Most needle-drop libraries have a special low price for festival rights. You can put their best music into your theatrical feature, but show it only at festivals and within the industry. If a distributor or network picks up the film, you can then upgrade to the necessary rights for theatrical or broadcast.

These libraries also offer "production blankets"—you can use their entire catalog, in as many snippets as you want—based on the total length of your project and how it'll be shown. A blanket for a ten-minute corporate video may cost about $400. It typically buys about half a dozen different pieces, but you can use hundreds if you want. Blanket licenses from larger publishers usually cost more because the music selection is wider. You can also buy annual blankets from some libraries, covering all your productions that year. Prices vary widely, depending on the size of the library and what media you produce for, but can be an incredible bargain for busy producers.

When you use a needle-drop selection, you're responsible for reporting the usage—including details about the song, the project, and the medium—to the publisher. They'll supply you with forms or an online site for this purpose, and then issue an invoice and license covering specific nonexclusive rights for your film. Even if you're on an annual blanket with the library, they'll still want the reports. It's how they evaluate their music and compensate the composers.

Buyout music

Many of the newer libraries sell their music on a *buyout* basis. You pay to purchase their CD or download individual songs, but have the right to use the music any time, in almost any of your productions. Prices vary, but are usually around $20 per download or $60–160 for a disc with eight or ten different songs, and there are discounts for quantity. License terms also vary, but in general allow any kind of production except network TV, paid theatrical, or products for sale.

Essentially, you're making an investment that you will actually use the songs in your film. As with any investment, you can get burned; there is absolutely no correlation between price and quality. So you have to be very sure the music will fit your film before you buy.

TIP

Buyout or needle-drop?

In general:

- The needle-drop libraries often have much deeper selections with higher creative and production values.
- The buyout libraries are more reasonably priced, if you're doing more than one production that will use a particular cue or style of music.

I tend toward the needle-drop libraries for my own productions. I'd rather pay a few dollars more and have a much bigger choice of good candidates for any particular cue. But remember: I'm selling a *sound* service, and this is part of my product.

I know some perfectly respectable producers who prefer buyout music, and have found favorite cues they can amortize over multiple productions. As far as they're concerned, music is just an accessory to the films they sell.

Two different business models. Both have their advantages. Take your pick.

Listen to the full cue at the library's website. If possible, play your picture at the same time. Watch out for cuts that sound like they were padded out with loops of the same chords and rhythm, with a single keyboard ad-libbing over them . . . many buyout libraries are built this way, but it limits your options while editing. It also sounds boring.

The best cues will have an internal structure with a definite build (as appropriate) or a secondary melody, and real variations that you can edit and move around. Some buyout libraries are incredible bargains. If you do a lot of projects and don't need Hollywood production quality, they may be the right choice.

Don't purchase buyout CDs from a library you haven't worked with before, unless you've had a chance to evaluate the actual discs. A five-minute demo may sound impressive as a montage, but it could be hiding the fact that there's only five minutes of usable music in the entire CD. Reputable music houses will provide evaluation copies on short-term loan to reputable producers, or let you listen to the entire CD online.

Performing rights organizations (PROs) and cuesheets

Most American music is covered by the American Society of Composers, Authors, and Publishers (ASCAP), Broadcast Music, Incorporated (BMI), or the Society of European Stage Authors and Composers (SESAC) which, despite its name, is headquartered in New York. These organizations see that composers and lyricists get paid when members' songs are performed for the public.

☞ ROSE'S RULES

Make sure your client knows the rules

Get this straight, because a lot of producers have it wrong: a TV station's annual fee to ASCAP or BMI does *not* cover using any music as scoring in films, commercials, or even short promos. It doesn't matter if the production was made in-house; it's still not covered. And it can't cover using a commercial recording: rights to recordings aren't granted by PROs.

Do stations regularly violate this rule, and use music without getting proper permission? Yes. Do copyright owners sometimes wink at this violation? Yes, again. Are you feeling lucky?[6]

The PROs work on the basis of annual fees, charged to anyone playing music for the public: broadcasters, theaters, theme parks, convention centers, and even restaurants. They're also trying to assert control over webcasts.

When you use music in a film that'll be broadcast or released theatrically, you'll probably have to prepare a *cuesheet*: a list of what music is included, who wrote and published it, and how it's used in the film (as foreground, background, main title, or other function). The PROs pay the creators based on this information. For more details and downloadable forms, check www.ascap.com and www.bmi.com.

While TV stations usually pay an annual fee to the PROs for broadcast licenses, *this does not mean you can use that society's music without paying additional fees.* The annual licenses are for composers and lyricists only, and only for the words and music of songs performed as entertainment. The licenses don't cover using the song in any kind of produced video, and don't cover any recorded performance of the song.

At present, nobody insists on cuesheets for videos shown at conventions, point-of-purchase at retail stores, inside restaurants, or at other casual public exhibitions. This might change in the future.

If you're getting music from a library, the necessary rights are included in their license fee. (You'll still have to fill out cuesheets if an exhibitor wants them.) If you're commissioning music from a composer or music house, rights will be specified in their contract.

---

[6] If you're *not* feeling lucky, but your broadcast client insists they have the right to use music because of their annual ASCAP or BMI license, just ask them to put it in writing. Have them specify that they'll cover your losses if a copyright owner decides to sue. (A lawyer can give you precise but friendly wording; you might want to hide it as boilerplate on your production contract.) For what it's worth: I have *never* had a client walk away because I insisted on that indemnification.

Other forms of stock music

MIDI music

You may also buy music as MIDI files, that can be played at low quality through internal synthesizers in most computers, or through high-end samplers or synths. You can also find plenty of free MIDI versions of public domain melodies on the Web. MIDI can be cheaper and a lot more flexible to edit, but the burden is on you to turn it into usable music tracks for your film. You'll need additional software and equipment, and also some skills with music creation and mixing. But if you know what you're doing, you can create acceptable tracks—certainly as good as the basic buyout libraries.

Loop-based libraries and software

Today's computers are fast enough that another kind of music creation software is possible: the *looping* program. Most pop music is made up of repeating patterns—a two-bar drum riff, an eight-bar bass, a snippet of melody that repeats twice—that play simultaneously and then alternate with variations. It takes chops to create and perform these patterns, but it also requires some respect for musical rules to get everyone playing them in the right key and on the beat. Loop-based software uses pre-recorded snippets of solo instruments and sections to satisfy that first requirement, and then manipulates the recordings in real-time—changing pitch and tempo as necessary—to take care of the second.

In other words, you select chunks of music played on instruments you like, and the program turns them into a musically reasonable song. Since you can choose the chunks based on mood and feel, and change them in response to actions on the screen, it's a fast and relatively versatile way to create a film or video score.

Sony's Acid was the first practical software of this type, and vast quantities of usable loops for it were created by third-party publishers and hobbyists. Apple's GarageBand simplified the interface and popularized it for non-musicians; it can also read Acid loops. There are now a variety of programs available with features for professional songwriters and filmmakers. There are also a large amount of books, DVDs, and Web tutorials on how to use them. So we won't go into the techniques here.

Most loops are sold with the understanding they'll go into derivative works: you can use them to score your film or TV show, in conjunction with original melodies or other loops, without paying a royalty. It takes some musical judgment to turn a pile of loops into an interesting song, but no particular training or practice. And loop music can also be a scratchpad to try out different ideas against your picture: when you find something that works, hand the composition to a composer or studio producer and have them refine the sound.

Loop music has limitations. It lends itself only to certain styles—dance and pop are easy; true jazz or classical are virtually impossible—and compositions tend to fade out rather than end. But if you need a quick, no-cost underscore and aren't looking for that major label or big studio sound, it can be perfectly viable.

WHAT'S THIS MIDI?

MIDI (Musical Instrument Digital Interface) is a local area network standard that's been around since the early 1980s. It works like other LANs, in that messages are constantly flowing across the network and each device pays attention only to the ones addressed to it. Unlike most modern computer wiring, MIDI is usually set up as a single-direction daisy chain: keyboard to computer, and then computer to synth A, synth A to synth B. But its data can also be carried on USB cables or Ethernet, and software synthesizers can get the required messages through the operating system.

The messages themselves are primarily musical instructions: *Play middle C, turn C off and play the E above it*, and so on. Obviously, enough messages equals a tune. Other MIDI messages may control volume, pitchbend, continuous pressure on sustained notes, what sound is assigned to each address (such as *piano on channel one, trumpet on channel two*), and special messages reserved by the manufacturer.

Addressing can get convoluted. The original MIDI specification called for only 16 unique addresses, called "channels." Today's synths make different sounds simultaneously, and each may need up to a dozen channels to sort them out. This doesn't leave many for the next instrument down the line. On the other hand, multiple synths can listen for the same address, so you can hook up additional instruments to play simultaneously and thicken the sound.

For this reason, many MIDI music studios use multiple networks. MIDI interfaces connect each of the controlling computer's serial or USB ports to as many as eight separate networks, called "cables." A computer with two ports can then control up to 16 simultaneous sounds on each of 16 cables. Sequencer programs control what messages are sent, and also let you edit melodies, create their own harmony or rhythmic variations, and even print sheet music. Most modern programs also carry digital audio tracks and will sync to video.

Since MIDI data represents just the note commands, rather than the actual sounds, files and communication can be very efficient. A MIDI version of a 60-second theme might need only 16 kilobytes, while a CD-quality recording of that same theme would eat more than 10 megabytes. Of course, the audio version can also include hot session players, studio mixing effects and human vocals—things impossible to encode in a MIDI file. The smaller MIDI file also doesn't include the software and equipment, and serious production expertise, needed to get a great sound.

While I usually work with excellent composers and buy music from top needle-drop libraries, I'll use loop music when appropriate.[7]

Non-library recordings, or How copyright is gonna get ya

As a producer, what are your rights regarding music from commercial CDs you or clients already own, or songs you've bought from an Internet service like iTunes?

Basically, you have the right to remain silent.

Only three choices are guaranteed to keep you out of trouble: compose and perform the music yourself, get permission from the people who did—which usually requires separate negotiation with those who composed the work, and with those who recorded it—or don't use the music. Copyright is a fact of life.

- Virtually any use of a music recording in any video requires written permission. Any video. In fact, dubbing a pop song onto your own home movies is technically an infringement, though there's little chance of your being sued over it.
- When you buy a commercial CD or pay for a music download, you get the right to play it for yourself and immediate friends. You also get the right to make a personal digital copy for protection and listening convenience. So putting it on your iPod *is* legal. Putting it on YouTube isn't.
- It doesn't matter whether you work for a charitable or educational institution, have no money, don't charge admission, or intend that the piece will "be good publicity for the recording artist." You need permission.
- It doesn't matter whether the song itself is classical or in the public domain—the recording is probably protected by a separate copyright. You need permission.
- It doesn't matter if you used less than eight bars: brevity was never a reliable defense in copyright cases, and was specifically eliminated by Congress more than 30 years ago. You need permission.
- It doesn't matter if "My clients will buy a copy of the CD, and I'll use that copy in the wedding album I produce." They may be a lovely couple, but when they paid for the disc, they didn't buy the right to synchronize it. You need permission.

Get the message? The doctrine of "fair use" has very limited application. Unless you're quoting a brief selection in a legitimate critical review of the performance, it probably doesn't apply. Check with a lawyer before making any assumptions about it.[8]

You *can* assume any music written after the first two decades of the twentieth century is under copyright, and recent changes in the copyright laws will protect newer pieces a lot longer. Classical works and pop standards may be old enough for their

---

[7] That is, when I want something generic-sounding and inconsequential, for no money, with a clean copyright.

[8] I can't give legal advice. I can tell you that, as someone who writes about this industry, I've heard of videographers being put out of business after using a pop song in a wedding album. One of the happy couple's neighbors happened to work for a giant copyright holder.

copyrights to have expired, but newer editions and arrangements of those works are still protected.

Even if you stick to 100-year-old songs, the recording most likely has its own copyright. You used to be able to tell by looking for a soundrecording copyright symbol, the letter P in a circle, somewhere on the disc or printed label. These days music is sold without labels, but it's still protected. Publishers and record labels have large and hungry business departments, and they almost always win in court.[9]

There's another reason to play by these rules, if you're aiming at TV or the festival circuit. Most broadcasters and exhibitors won't touch a film until the producer guarantees that copyrights have been cleared, and indemnifies them against suits for infringement. Many DVD replication houses have a similar policy.

It's entirely possible you'll sneak under the publishers' radar. Despite urban legends about lawyers coming after Boy Scouts for singing protected songs at a campfire, many casual uses are never spotted by the copyright owners. But that doesn't make it legal, it doesn't reduce an owner's right to come after you in the future, and the fact that some other producer didn't get caught for using the same music isn't a defense.

The perils of pop

Even if you're not afraid of lawyers or bad karma, be careful about using pop music under a video. Songs are powerful memory triggers, and psychologists have found that people will pay more attention to the tune they already know than to what's in your film. They'll also be thinking about what happened the last time they heard it . . . which might not have anything to do with your characters or sales message.

National advertisers can get away with using pop songs in their spots because they run the ads so many times that their message can overpower the memories. Similarly, movies can get away with pop tunes because the film experience is so strong . . . when done right, you get involved in the characters and plot, and the music contributes rather than detracts. Obviously, both the advertisers and film studios also are careful about paying for the music and getting permission.

If you honestly believe a commercial recording might be appropriate for your project, don't be afraid to ask for it. Sometimes, copyright owners can be surprisingly generous—particularly if good causes are involved. I worked on a PBS network promo that got permission to use a Beatles recording, and on a music school documentary that had the rights to use Leonard Bernstein conducting the New York Philharmonic. In both cases, those rights were contributed.[10]

---

[9] Publishers and record labels often have the same parent corporation, and their giant legal departments look out for all the different kinds of rights that can apply. (Occasionally the money they collect actually goes to the composers and performers, but that's a different issue.)

[10] I also worked on a theatrical feature that paid an obscene amount for a pop song, shot the sequence that used it in playback . . . and then had the director cut the whole scene during previews. The music was never used, but the contract still demanded payment. So be sure that you really want to use the cue, and consider hiring an entertainment lawyer to take care of the details.

Even if the cause is less than noble, you may be able to secure limited-audience rights for a reasonable amount. Some copyright owners want to support independent filmmakers: if they like your work and think the film has a chance, they'll let you use their song for a reasonable fee, sometimes less than $1,000 for festival exhibition. They also figure they'll be able to collect much bigger fees if a major studio decides to pick up your film and distribute it theatrically.

Rights to the song itself—the notes on paper and the printed lyrics—belong to the writers and are usually assigned to a publishing company; you can search the PROs' websites to find them. If you're going to record a new version of the song yourself, and then edit it into your movie, the creators can sell you the rights you need. (As noted above, PROs like ASCAP or BMI can not sell you those rights.)

If you're using an existing recording, you still need the writers' or publisher's permission from the previous paragraph. But then things get murkier: you also need permission from whoever owns the recorded master. That may be the band, or the record label; it depends on their contract. Bands sometimes like to help filmmakers, but they're sometimes offended by them. Record labels sometimes like to make the band happy, but they also sometimes want to make as much money as possible. Ask the wrong person for permission, and that might offend the person who would have given it to you. Confusing? Hire a pro who knows the industry and how to negotiate. Search the Web for "music clearance agency."

If it turns out that rights to a commercial recording are too expensive, most large music libraries have a good selection of "soundalikes" you can use at their regular rates. These won't sound *exactly* like the original recording—that could also be a violation of copyright—but are close enough to get the message across.

Sources for source music

Some of the music libraries carry both good contemporary and generic "era" music—such as big band, swing, or classic rock—designed to be coming from on-screen radios and TVs. If you want an authentic older style for a documentary or period piece, check the archive sections of the larger needle-drop houses. Some of those companies were around in the 1940s and 1950s; they can license you the same recordings they sold on vinyl back then. Those houses also often have appropriate music for period elevators and supermarkets; between the 1950s and 1970s, a lot of background music came from the same sources.

You can also get authentic period music for free on the Internet. Search sites like loc.gov, internetarchive.org, and commons.wikimedia.org. They have recordings of public domain pieces; many of them carry the notice that the recordings are public domain as well, or have been made available for non-commercial use under various schemes. Some recordings are so old the master copyright has expired, some were contributed, and some were made by military bands and other government employees and are therefore public domain.

Need something more modern? A few of the buyout libraries have vocal cuts with the same musical and production values as current pop styles. They possibly *were* failed pop songs that the composer is trying to recoup an investment from, but we don't care. You can put them on a character's TV or music player and they'll sound perfectly real.

Needle-drop libraries are frequently very good with solo piano, jazz combo, and big band sounds for a restaurant or club. But it's harder to get authentic music that sounds like the nightly entertainment at a bar or the amateurs at a school dance. Most library music is too well performed, or has too much of a studio sound, to be convincing. Ask the library if they have any demo or scratch tracks they'd be willing to license. Or find a local band, and ask if they have any tapes of live performances of their original music you can use.

It almost always helps to start a scene in the middle of a source cue, rather than at the front. Unless your characters are psychic, they wouldn't have turned on their radios at the start of a song, or walked into a club at the precise beginning of a set.

Source music always needs equalization and reverb—often with drastic settings—to make it match the ambience of a scene (see Chapter 16).

Mix and match

You can use Hollywood's trick of mixing original and library music in your own limited-budget film or video, hiring a composer for specialty pieces but blending them with stock elements where it will save money. For a ten-minute humorous film about advertising, I needed (and couldn't afford) an almost continuous score. Parts of it had to be precisely timed to on-screen actions and specific words of the script, but could use a small group or sampled chamber orchestra. Other cues required a full orchestra or styles of playing that are difficult to synthesize. Still others were just to set a background or location, and could be easily found in a library.

We created a spotting list (part of it is shown in Figure 14.1) detailing 25 different musical elements, ranging from a few seconds to slightly less than a minute. Each was designed for a particular part of the video. We selected 18 of the cues from a good needle-drop library and made sure they could be edited to fit picture. Finally, I gave the edited cues and the spotting notes to a local composer, along with reference video. She wrote and recorded the other pieces, fitting precise word or visual cues and being sure to match into the key and tempo of the existing music. She didn't have to charge us for ten minutes of original music, and everything blended into a seamless whole.

SELECTING MUSIC FROM A LIBRARY

Grab your notes, the script, and—if possible—the rough video edit, narration tracks, or anything else that will have to work with the music. Then head for the library.

In a lot of cases, "the library" will be a website. Most music libraries have some online search facility, and will let you listen to short samples or low-resolution versions while you select. If you've established a relationship with the library, they might also let you download high-resolution copies for auditioning. (Of course, you're obligated to pay for any music you use.)

Searching strategies differ depending on the music company. Some let you enter desired characteristics as text; some make you pick from a list; most let you select a genre; some let you also pick specific instruments or tempi. Unfortunately, it seems like no two definitions of characteristic, genre, or tempo are the same: until you've gotten used to how a specific library has organized its search, expect to spend a lot of time pursuing dead ends. Figure 14.2 shows a typical online library search engine, and the cues it found.

Because of these differences in how libraries are organized, expect your first few searches at any supplier to be inefficient. Don't judge the library by how long it takes you to find a particular cue; this gets faster as you get used to their system.

Or ask an expert. The bigger libraries (and even some pop publishers) often have licensing offices in major production cities, with expert librarians on tap; the service is free or very inexpensive because it helps them sell licenses.

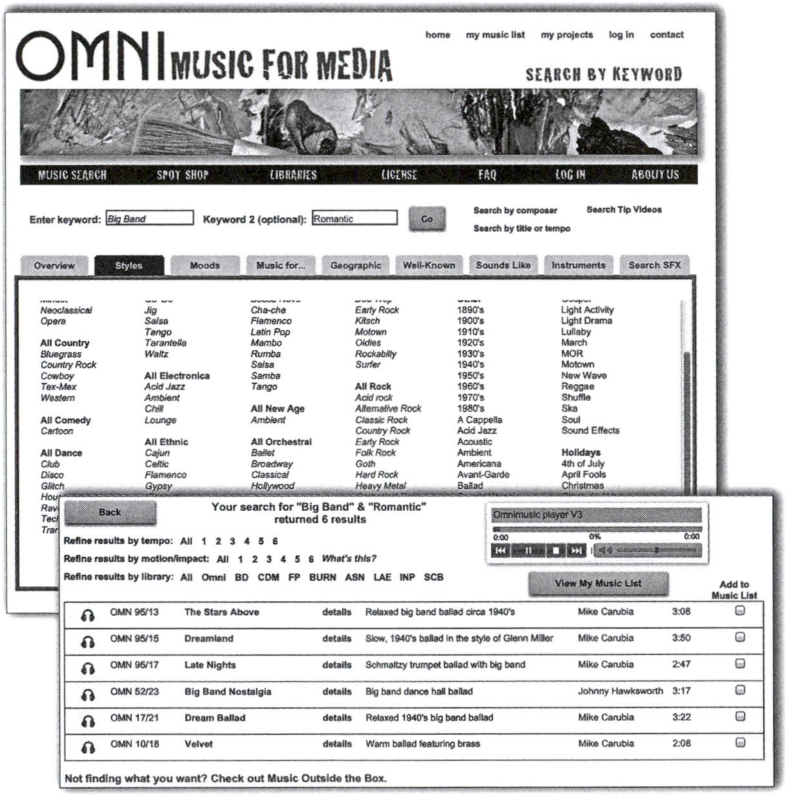

Figure 14.2 An online music search. This one's from Omnimusic.

Obviously, you'll want to listen to the songs you're considering. (Maybe it isn't obvious. Some libraries expect you to select—and pay for—cuts based on their text descriptions. Avoid them.) But before you listen, look at the labels. The titles won't tell you much—"Our Wedding" could be Mendelssohn or Wagner, a medley of waltzes, or even slapstick—but the descriptions can be useful. The better libraries use wordings like "brooding strings; panic stabs at :19 and :23." Some more marginal libraries describe everything as "Great! The perfect music for financial, high tech, extreme sports, and retail" . . . uh-huh.

Check the composer, too. Bigger libraries have stables of freelancers with different styles. Two or three pieces by the same composer, even if they're on different discs, might fit perfectly as a suite. You may also find yourself enjoying the style of one particular composer and look specifically for that name.

Once you've found some cuts, start listening, and make notes on which music is best for each place in your video. Then turn *off* the sound the moment you've gotten a feel for a potentially usable cut, and make some notes.

✔ TIP

Silence is golden!

Not listening is an important part of choosing music. Use the pause control a lot, and take frequent breaks.

Human brains turn to oatmeal after extended library-music sessions—remember, most of this music was never designed to be in the foreground—so stop every 15 minutes or so, and do something else. This will make it easier to distinguish and evaluate individual pieces.

Selective listening is an important part of the process as well. The melody of a library cut often starts some ten seconds after the intro, but there may be variations later on. If you think a piece has some merit but you don't like precisely what you're hearing, skip forward and listen for the change in texture. Include, in your notes, what parts you liked and which you'd rather avoid.

Once you've got a shortlist, go back and explore those pieces again. Mix the voice with music while you're listening, or play the cut while you watch video. If you don't have a way to mix online music with narration or picture playback inside your computer, run two computers at the same time: having the video on a nearby tablet, laptop, or even phone can be a useful reference.

If the library allows, make copies of your potential selections, and bring them back into the NLE or video suite for previewing. It's important to try the music under real circumstances.

✔ TIP

The take-away test

When you think you've found the right music, keep playing the video or narration *and turn the music off!* You should immediately feel, in your gut, that something's missing. If you don't, the music isn't contributing anything to the project.

This may sound trivial, but it will tell you a lot . . . even if you're an experienced music user.

Don't worry too much about synchronizing specific hits or meeting a particular length while you're auditioning. You'll be able to do all that when you edit.

No matter what you do, don't forget that music is an artistic element. No set of rules, catalog descriptions, or software can replace your best directorial judgment. Don't be afraid to go against type—I once scored a PBS documentary about jogging by using Bach fugues—and don't be afraid to make a statement. Just be sure it's the same statement your client wants to make.

MUSIC EDITING

What was once a major difference between library and original music—precise fit to the picture—isn't a big consideration any more. Once you master the techniques of music editing, you'll be able to blend existing music tracks to fit picture as perfectly as most of the classic Hollywood scores. Even if you can't carry a tune, you can trim pieces smoothly and quickly at your desktop: the only musical skill you need is the ability to tap a finger in time with the beat. You probably do that already when you hear a song you like. I'll show you the other steps in a couple of pages.

Solution 1: Ignore the problem

It pains me to hear this, but many otherwise respectable producers end their music cues by fading them out when the next scene starts. This is as sloppy as bad lighting, letting talent mispronounce words, cutting movements together that don't match, or leaving typos in the titles. We have easy, low-cost ways to make every piece of music sound like it was written for the film . . . or at least performed by people who were watching the scene.

Your film will be more effective when every part of it works together. That includes the music. Make a music edit or two, and your production will be more professional.

Solution 2: Automate it

If you're totally scared of music editing, you can get tools that cut their own music automatically to a specific running time. You select the cue, specify how long it should run, wait a few seconds, and import the finished product back to your NLE. Smart Sound's Sonicfire Pro (Figure 14.3) is the main app in this category.

Figure 14.3 A self-editing music library, Sonicfire Pro.
You pick a song and adjust specify its length and how it's mixed (lower left part of the screen).
You can then rearrange the song's blocks (lower right) to fit your project.

Sonicfire uses proprietary files from their own music library. Each file includes a multitrack recording of the cue, split into voices for harmonies, melody, and so forth; plus a database of edit points that break the song into blocks. You choose a cue, pick from a few pre-built style variations, specify a "mood" and running length, and the program assembles blocks of music to fit your spec. Blocks are pre-set phrases of music that can be strung together freely, though some are marked specifically for intro or ending. You can move blocks around, if you want, to fit cues within the song.

In Sonicfire's world, mood means how the music is mixed, not its emotion. You can hear just the rhythm and chords for an underscore, bring up a few instruments for light activity, mix in the whole band for a main theme, or use only effects and percussion for an abstract mood. What mixes will be available depend on the song. There's also a mixer panel where you can fine-tune each group of instruments.

When you're happy with the result, you render the result and send it as a stereo track to your NLE. Sonicfire integrates with some NLEs so that you can go back and refine the music edits when the picture changes.

The downside of a program like this is that it works only with music that's been encoded for the system, and you pay a premium for the encoding. The selection is severely limited compared to standard buyout libraries, and the cues are about twice as expensive. But if you need quick edits to specific lengths and don't mind reusing the same cues—say, in wedding videos for different clients or different episodes of a continuing TV series—an automatic editor can be a good idea.

Solution 3: Learn the easy way to edit music

No book will ever turn me into a good video editor. I lack the visual design skills. But, over the years, I've learned some rules of thumb (cut on motion, respect the axis . . . oh, *you* know) that make my rare video sessions a less painful experience.

It's the same thing with music editing. Unless you're born with musical sensibilities and have learned how chords and beats go together to make a song, you'll never be a truly brilliant music cutter. But there are a couple of easy-to-learn rules that'll make anybody's editing faster and more professional. Practice these, and while you might not be brilliant, you'll certainly be able to cut music with network TV proficiency.

Most of the time, what makes bad music editing sound so horrible has nothing to do with chords or melody. It's simply a broken rhythm. Every mainstream piece of music since the late Renaissance has a constant heartbeat, with accents in a regular pattern. The tempo might change, or different beats might get accented, but only according to specific rules. We learn those rules subconsciously, starting with the first lullaby our mothers sing us. If an edit breaks a rule, we know something is wrong— even if we don't know precisely what.

On the other hand, the rules about that heartbeat are simple. You can learn them even if you can't carry a tune in an iPod. Use some simple techniques and you'll soon be cutting like a pro—and making generic library pieces fit like a custom score.

First: Trust your ears

Music editing is not visual. *Forget anything you've been told about matching the big lumps on a waveform.* Music editing requires knowing exactly where the beat is. But there's nothing in a visual waveform—no matter how tightly you zoom in—guaranteed to help you find it. All you'll see is where things get loudest, usually because somebody has hit a drum. If you're cutting classical music, there might not be any drum beats. If you're cutting world music, there are too many (Figure 14.4).

Second: Learn to count

The key to music editing is being able to count while you listen . . . usually all the way to four, and then you start with one again. If you can count in rhythm, you know where the edits belong without ever having look at waveforms! The technique works just as well on programs that can't zoom in, and even on non-visual systems like online edit controllers.

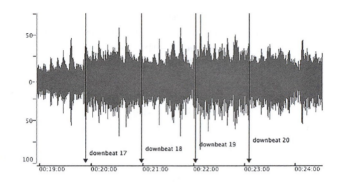

Figure 14.4 Beat it!
You'd never find these downbeats by eye. I was able to mark them quickly,
but only while listening to the music in real time.

✳ TIDBIT

TAPPING WITH THE STARS

Tap your finger on your desk, in time to some music. If you can do that and count to four, you can edit accurately by ear.

This tapping technique is how I've cut music for network TV and major film studios. It's how every other music editor I've ever known does their job: with simple finger taps. But for some reason, NLE tutorials insist you look at blobs on a screen instead.[11]

Blobs can be useful . . . but only when it's time to fine-tune an edit that you've already marked by tapping. With a little practice, the edits you make by tapping will be good enough that you'll never have to bother with fine-tuning.

Here's what you'll be counting

Most of the music you'll ever use—or hear—is made up of evenly spaced beats organized into groups. Usually there are four of them in a group, though occasionally there may be two, three, or six.[12] For now, let's stick to four.

- Four beats make up a *bar* or *measure*.
- There is always a strong emphasis on the first beat of the bar. That's the *downbeat*.
- There is usually a slightly weaker emphasis on the third beat.

---

[11] Probably two reasons: 1) It's easy to show blobs on a screenshot; and 2) They haven't hired someone like me to write their tutorials.

[12] And sometimes five, seven, or other numbers, but those are extremely rare in production music. Once you master the more common four-beat system, you'll find even this oddly counted music easier to edit.

This four-beat pattern keeps on ticking no matter what the melody or lyrics are doing; most melodies are based on groups of four or eight of these bars. Rock traditionally hits a drum on beats *2* and *4*—that *backbeat* is what made it so daring, when the music first appeared—but its lyrics and melodies still emphasize the *1* at the start of measures.

The pattern can change tempo, speeding up or slowing down, but it does so smoothly and without breaking the pattern. Melody lines might start slightly ahead or behind the *1*, but the pattern still holds, and you still base your edit on the downbeat. We'll get into how you roll that edit to include a melody, without disturbing the beat pattern, in a couple of pages.

The trick is to learn to count those four beats at the same time you're deciding where to edit. It isn't hard. All you need is enough eye–hand coordination to tap your edit system's marking buttons at the right time. It's like dancing with your fingers instead of your feet.

☛ ROSE'S RULES

If you don't respect the four-beat pattern, your music edits will probably sound wrong. If you *do* respect it, there's a good chance the chords and melody will fall into place without any extra effort.

Hands-on music editing

We'll start with a little Stephen Foster ditty: Everybody sing!

Camptown ladies sing this song, Doo-dah! Doo-dah! Camptown racetrack five miles long, oh the doo-dah-day!

 If you don't know the song or hate to sing along, listen to **Sound 14.2**.[13]

Step 1: Tap your finger

While you're singing, tap your finger along with the beat. Short syllables get one tap each. The word *song* is held twice as long, so it gets two taps. The *dah*s are held longest of all, three taps. If we print a dot for each finger tap, it looks like Figure 14.5. Notice how no matter what the words are doing, the dots are evenly spaced. The tapping should have a similarly constant rhythm.

---

[13] Vocalist Frank Luther, from a wax cylinder recorded about 90 years ago. The song itself was published in 1852. Both are early enough to now be in public domain. (Digitized version found at internetarchive.org.)

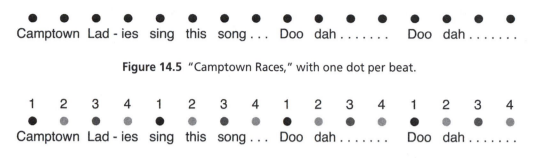

Figure 14.5 "Camptown Races," with one dot per beat.

| 1 | 2 | 3 | 4 | 1 | 2 | 3 | 4 | 1 | 2 | 3 | 4 | 1 | 2 | 3 | 4 |

Camptown Lad - ies sing this song . . . Doo dah . . . . Doo dah . . . .

Figure 14.6 The same song, counting 1–4 with the beat.

Step 2: Count

Now sing it again, but this time count out loud, from one to four, while you're tapping. The loudest syllable will always be "one," like in Figure 14.6.

Think about the pattern of stresses in the "Camptown Races" lyric:

- The strongest syllables in the first line are *Camp-*, *sing*, and the *doo*s; they're always on the one-count. I made their dots darker in the figure, to call attention to these stresses.
- The next strongest are *Lad-* and *song*, on the three. I made their dots a dark gray.

We counted to four because it's the most common musical structure; musicians even call it *Common Time*. Even if a song is written with two beats to the measure—as Camptown actually was—it can usually be counted as four; that'll be how most people sing its melody. The one-and-three stress pattern holds for almost all music in common time. Practice counting along with songs you hear, and it'll become second nature.

Step 3: Find the downbeat

Listen for the most accented syllable of the melody; that's where you put the number *1*. Stay with the melody, and don't be fooled by the loudest drum hit: pop styles often accent the second and fourth beats of each measure to make them more danceable. (If you want to sing "Camptown" in hoe-down style, clap your hands on 2 and 4. Try it!) *If you sing along with the melody, you'll always be able to find the downbeat.*

The downbeat, on 1, gets its name because this is where a conductor's hand moves down when leading an orchestra. That movement, and the ones that follow, are a centuries-old tradition. (There's a specific direction for each beat of the measure, depending on how many beats there are overall. Experienced music editors often follow the same hand patterns when marking a song, so they can feel the structure instead of having to count aloud.[14])

---

[14] My clients sometimes think it looks silly for me to be "conducting" my editing software . . . but it really helps.

Some songs don't start on their loudest syllable, so you have to start counting on a different number. Others can have a few short notes sharing a beat. Figure 14.7 is another Stephen Foster song to illustrate both situations. The *Oh I* shares one beat, the fourth in this measure. The syllables *come* and *bam–* are much louder than any others around them, and they're on the downbeat.

A few songs move in threes instead of fours. The principle's the same, as you can see in Figure 14.8. The three fast syllables in *Beautiful* occupy just one count—the same way that *Dream* does. *Beau–* and *Wake* are definitely the accented syllables, on the downbeat. A very few songs count in other numbers; once you're comfortable in four and three you'll be able to adapt.

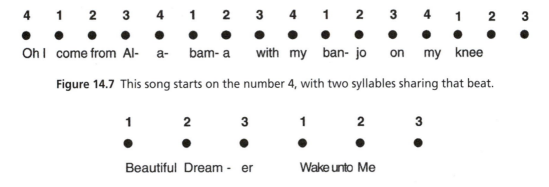

Figure 14.7 This song starts on the number 4, with two syllables sharing that beat.

Figure 14.8 This song uses patterns of three syllables. Sometimes all three syllables are on the same beat, but there's also always three beats to a measure.

Cutting by counting

Once you've learned to count accurately with the music, the editing part is simple. All you have to do is match the numbers. Start by loading **Sound 14.3**[15] into your editing system. This is a modern light corporate or magazine TV theme. It counts in four.

On your mark . . .

1. Open the music in a clip window, start playing it, and count along. You might want to play it a few times before proceeding, to get used to the tempo.

2. Start tapping the marking button very lightly on each count, so lightly that the keyboard doesn't respond. When you get to each *1*, tap just hard enough to

---

[15] First 60 seconds or so from "Syncopation" (Dave Hab, OM205/9) © Omnimusic. This and the other cues in this section are short excerpts from much longer pieces. Omnimusic is letting us post them on our website, and gives you permission to copy them into your editing system for the tutorials. If you want to hear the full-length versions, license them for a production, or explore the thousands of other pieces in this large and respected library, go to www.omnimusic.com or call (800) 828–6664.

actually make a mark. When you're done, you should have a bunch of marks looking something like the square flags in Figure 14.9. The number on each flag is merely an ID assigned by the software; each flag represents a *1* that we tapped along with the song's rhythm.

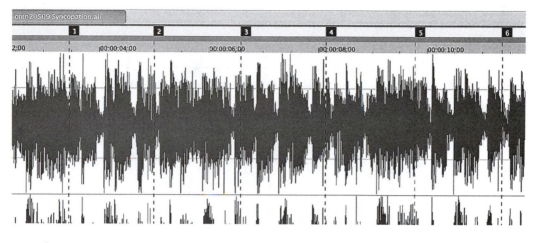

Figure 14.9 Tap just hard enough to make a mark each time you count the number 1.

. . . and edit!

Move the clip to a timeline, and you're ready to edit. If you want to shorten the piece, cut out the space between two marks and butt the pieces together. In Figure 14.10, we've selected from Marker 3 to Marker 5, about three seconds of time. (Because of the way chords flow in most music, it usually sounds better to cut from an even number to another even one, or from an odd number to another odd one.)

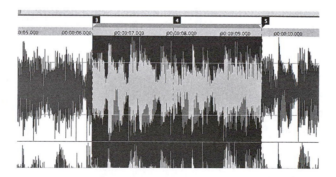

Figure 14.10 Selecting between two marks, so we can shorten the cue.

For Figure 14.11, we merely tapped the *Delete* key. The result? Music flows smoothly across the deletion without any clicks, hiccups, or stutters. There was no need to zoom in, undo, trim, or waste time.[16] **Sound 14.4** lets you hear the result.

If your first attempt doesn't sound as good as mine, chances are you tightened up. Your fingers were a little too stressed to move smoothly, or you were trying to "tap-and-not-tap" from too high over your keyboard. Relax, rest your index finger on your software's marking key, and try again.

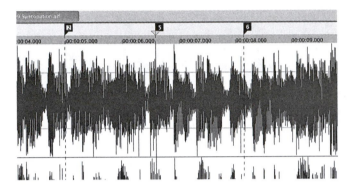

Figure 14.11 Press *delete*, and your edit is done!

This is a very short edit—there's only about three seconds between the markers—but the technique works for edits of any length. If you need to edit longer stretches of music, make the marks farther apart—say, every fourth *1*. If we wanted to extend the music, we could have taken that stretch between marker 3 and marker 5 and copied it into the timeline again.

We did this in an audio editor (Sony Sound Forge) rather than an NLE because it made for a clearer screenshot. The process is almost exactly the same in any timeline-based video or audio program, except you cut at the marks and then drag the pieces together.

Editing off the beat

Sometimes you want to make an edit on the start of a melody, which in many songs isn't exactly on the downbeat. The best way to do this is to mark downbeats, just as you would for any other music. Line up the downbeats for an edit, but then roll the edit point as needed to catch the melody. This is easiest to do in an NLE or multitrack DAW, rather than an audio editor.

---

[16] Really! Sound 14.4 is exactly the way the edit came out, right after tapping and deleting as described in the text. Okay: I've been doing this kind of editing for a long time; your first attempt might not be as smooth. Or it might. You'll never know until you try.

Listen to **Sound 14.5**, a mid-tempo small group romantic piece.[17] There's an oboe melody starting at twenty seconds in. Let's repeat that melody to extend the music.

1. Play the clip and mark its downbeats, as we did in Figure 14.12. Note where a melody starts ahead of the barline, and split the clip at the marker immediately after. You can see that in the color change at marker 9.
2. Note the barline immediately after where you'd like the melody to start again. In the figure, that's at marker 16. We made another split there in Figure 14.12, just to make things easier to see. The part we've isolated by splitting doesn't have a complete melody yet. Don't worry about that.
3. Paste a copy of the isolated part so it starts at that second barline you noted. Figure 14.13 shows it pasted in at marker 16. We've set up our editor so the remainder of the song moves later: you can see that part now starting around 45 seconds. If you play the edit now, you'll hear a hiccup at marker 16. That's because we've started the repeat of the melody *after* the oboe started playing. So we'll adjust the edit.

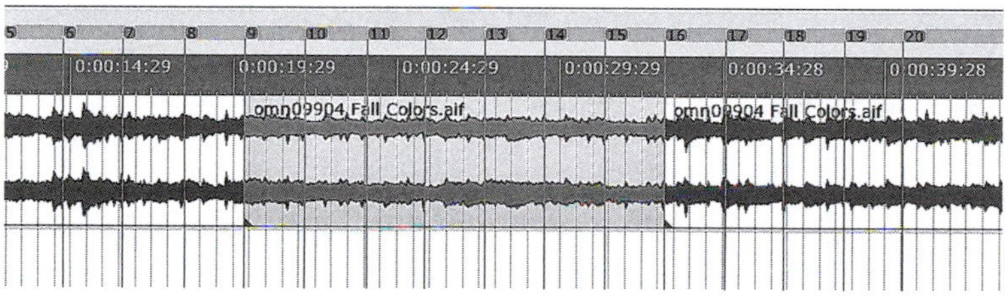

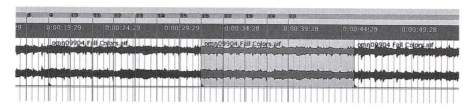

Figure 14.12 The melody actually starts ahead of our marker 9.
We want to repeat it, ahead of marker 16.

Figure 14.13 Partial melody from previous figure, now repeated at marker 16. Note how the previous music from marker 16 has moved down to around 45 seconds.

---

[17] A minute from the middle of "Fall Colors" (Frank Catanzaro/Doug Wood, OM99/4) © Omnimusic and used by permission.

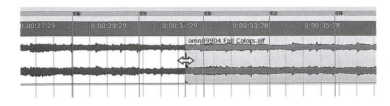

Figure 14.14 Rolling the edit earlier to catch the start of the melody.
Since we're moving the out-point of the previous clip at the same time, the musical
meter or heartbeat stays constant.

4. Roll the edit point, moving the line between original and repeat earlier until it catches the start of the oboe. Figure 14.14 shows our rolling the edit, moving the start of the oboe's clip to just ahead of 35 seconds. Now it catches the start of the oboe, but since we're exiting the previous clip earlier as well, the other instruments will keep playing on the proper beats.

You can do a similar edit across two tracks, sharing a barline but crossfading into the new melody earlier or later than that line. The important thing is that, no matter where you make the edit, you still preserve that constant heartbeat—the length of time from one downbeat to the next has to stay the same.

When it doesn't sound good . . .

If you hear a little hiccup at the edit, chances are you didn't mark the downbeat accurately. This is usually because you were too conscious of tapping the marking button and stiffened your hand up slightly when it was time to press. Editing is like a lot of other physical activities: it helps to stay loose and relaxed. Practice counting aloud as you make the lighter and heavier taps.

If you want to verify that you've made the marks accurately, put copies of the clip on two adjacent tracks, with the first marker on one track lined up to a later marker on the other. Play them both simultaneously: if the marks were correct, you won't hear any stuttering in the drums.

Practice counting along with the beat while you're reviewing an edit as well. If the edit is accurate, your *1* should line up perfectly before and after the cut. If you have to adjust slightly while you're counting, one or both of the edit points were off the beat.

An edit can also sound odd because the chords or melody doesn't match. Try moving one of the points an odd number of measures earlier or later. For example, if you cut marker 3 to marker 6 and don't like the result, you may have much better luck coming in on marker 5, 7, or 9.

As you cut more music, you'll develop a better feel for how chords change and melodies develop, and you'll have fewer awkward edits. But don't expect to ever outgrow the idea of counting along with the rhythm. It's one of the most powerful techniques you can use.

Adapting to other systems

If your system edits sound by cutting or pasting sections, the process is very similar. Plant markers on the downbeats, then stop the playback and select an area from one marker to another. Use the cut command if you want to shorten the cue. If you want to lengthen it, use the copy command. Then place the insertion point on another marker, and paste.

If you're using a traditional multi-machine online editor with keyboard-controlled in- and out-points, you just have to mark more carefully. Copy the first part of the cue, at least past the edit point, onto the master tape. Play it back, tapping the Record-in button on downbeats, until you mark the desired record-in point. Now play back the source tape, marking the source-in the same way. Preview the edit, and the beat should be constant. Then, if you want, multi-trim to pick up the melody.

More practice

Not every cue is going to be as straightforward as the previous exercises. But the principles stay the same. Here are a few more cues to practice with.

Sound 14.6[18] is a modern jazz baroque vocal (*what does that mean? Think Swingle Singers*). The soprano scat soloist always starts her phrases after the bar line. But despite this being jazz, and not having any drums to make nice spikes in the waveform, it marks just like the example in Sound 14.5. Your downbeats should look like Figure 14.15; the soloist enters just after marker 7.

Sound 14.7[19] is a French waltz. Waltzes, of course, count in three rather than four. You'll still tap on every beat, strong enough to mark on *1*, lightly on *2* and *3*, and then repeat with a strong *1* again.

Sound 14.8[20] is the opening of a large cinematic piece for orchestra and chorus. The melody here is carried by the strings. Because string instruments start their envelopes slowly (Chapter 1), it's difficult to edit into them by cutting. However, making a short crossfade at the edit point usually creates a good match for how strings

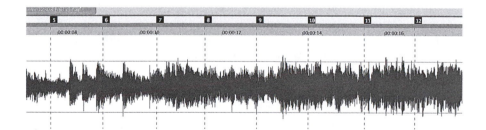

Figure 14.15 No drums in this jazz baroque piece, but it's still easy to mark by tapping.

---

[18] "Firelight" (Doug Wood, OM123/3) © Omnimusic and used by permission.

[19] "French Kiss" (Bernd Schoenhart, OM162/3) © Omnimusic and used by permission.

[20] "Reverence" (Tom Rice, OM217/2) © Omnimusic and used by permission.

would have played. Figure 14.16 shows a crossfade, circled, where two bars have been cut out. The fade is only one frame long, too short to be meaningful in a video edit but long enough to make the audio cut work.

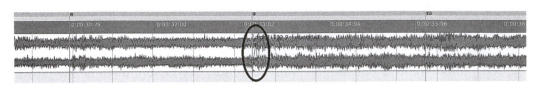

Figure 14.16 A one-frame crossfade (circled) makes this edit in the string section of an orchestra sound good.

Matching music to picture

Once you get comfortable editing this way, each individual cut will take very little time to execute. Then you'll be ready to create custom scores, adding or subtracting measures so that musical climaxes and changes match changes in the video. A few things will help you achieve that perfect marriage of music and picture:

- If a downbeat is almost lined up with an important visual cue, try shifting the entire music track a few frames. The earlier edits may still appear to be in sync after they've been moved slightly, and it'll be easier to catch that golden moment.
- Don't be afraid to speed up or slow down the entire piece slightly, even it means changing the pitch. Acoustic instruments can be shifted about 3% faster or slower before their timbre sounds wrong, but synthesizers can be shifted as much as 10% and still sound reasonable.
- If your software can change the tempo without affecting the pitch, you can do more radical manipulation—as much as 20% either way in the best audio programs. You can also change the tempo for just part of a cue, or squeeze or stretch only a couple of bars to fit a video sequence, if the pitch doesn't change.
- If a piece has prominent drums, don't worry about matching the video perfectly. When there's an important visual hit, add a matching drum sound effect on a different track. It'll sound like the drummer was deliberately playing ahead of or behind the beat to match picture. This works with orchestral percussion as well as with jazz and rock.

A final tip

Reverberation can cause problems with sound pickup when you're shooting, but it's great stuff to have when you're editing music. A little reverb, faded up right before a cut and out right after, can make up for sounds that got lost because they extended over the barline. And if you have to fade the end of a piece quickly to match a visual fade, a little reverb can help make it sound like the musicians stopped playing on cue. In fact, sometimes a very fast fade—on a single beat—and reverb is the only way to create an ending with loop music.

CHAPTER 15

Sound Effects

SILENCE IS NOT GOLDEN

Just like music, sound effects have been a part of movies since the earliest silent blockbusters. Theater organs often included a "toy counter"—bells, bird whistles, car horns, ratchets, pieces of wood that slapped together (gun shots), sirens, and anything else that could be rigged to a button on the organ console.[1] These effects thrilled audiences because, as rough as they were, they still could be heard as adding realism to a film. Of course, realism has more to do with convention than reality. While it's tempting to laugh at early audiences being thrilled by bird whistles accompanying grainy black-and-white panoramas, today's practices aren't much more realistic.

For example, when Gene Roddenberry first tested the opening of *Star Trek*, the

---

[1] Want to spend a joyful two minutes? Listen to Bill Coale demonstrating a modern digital theater organ's simulation of a classic toy counter, at http://youtu.be/QqYsXOFfkdA.

Enterprise didn't make a sound as it flew past the camera. It wasn't supposed to: space is a vacuum as well as a final frontier. But by the time the series got to television, the ship's engines had a satisfying *whoosh*. Roddenberry rewrote the laws of physics to make a scale-model spaceship more exciting. Today, Hollywood rockets scream by in six or more digital channels . . . but the sound isn't any more realistic than those original toy-counter bird whistles.

In Hollywood, reality often means, "If you can see it, you must hear something." Feature films have teams of sound editors, often spending a week on effects for each ten-minute reel. Everything is foleyed (Chapter 9) or has effects cut to it. Sound effects supervisors will walk into a mix with synchronized tracks for what seems like every buzzing fly in a scene,[2] along with the expected laser swords or giant explosions. It's overkill—many of these sounds never make it to the final track—but still follows the "see it, hear it" rule.

If your budget is somewhat smaller than those Hollywood blockbusters, sound effects can be even more important: when properly chosen and applied, they add realism to stock footage or scenes shot on a limited set. They can heighten drama, provide comic relief, and command attention. A good stereo ambience, played through properly placed speakers, can even capture the space around a computer screen or kiosk and isolate the user.

The trick is planning how to use effects most efficiently. If you don't have the armies of technicians necessary to edit a specific sound for every possibly motion, it makes sense to invest your time only on the effects that'll make a difference.

Silence can be golden

In fact, the first step in creating a good effects track is to ignore the effects entirely. Concentrate on the dialog first. Make it sound real. Then worry about the music! In some kinds of films, scenes that were crying out for effects will be completely covered by the score. Or as one re-recording mixer points out, "They call the stems 'D/M/E,' not 'D/E/M' . . . because Dialog and Music are the higher priority."

Pioneer sound designer Tony Schwartz once told me sound effects are a waste of time. According to him, those footsteps and rattles never sounded like real life, and would get in the way of the story rather than help. His preference was *effective sounds*—noises that might be even unrelated to the storyline, but trigger the audience's own memories.

Dr. Shwartz' rule certainly holds for commercials, and also for most corporate and training films. Those media exist to communicate specific messages. Narrative films, on the other hand, are about stories. Those work best when we can identify with the characters and believe in their worlds. Sound effects become an important part of the characters' reality.

---

[2] I've seen an effects supervisor walk in with a track that had nothing but a couple of buzzing flies, designed to play very softly in the middle of an otherwise busy scene. It was a mood-setting reality effect to go with the camera's panning past a pail of old vomit. The director decided not to use that track.

In your face or in the background?

You can reconcile these two points of view by dividing a film's sound effects into two different roles:

- **Punctuation effects** say "hey, listen to me!" They're supposed to call attention to themselves, and trigger a reaction on their own or because of how they comment on the visuals. Viewers accept that these effects were added during the production process—we know Stooge heads doesn't really go *bonk!* when you hit them—and accept the sounds as entertainment. Comedy rim shots, slide whistles when a clown falls over, auditory icons (like those Intel chimes), and possibly even the whoosh of the Enterprise[3] in space fall into this category. Punctuation effects have to be carefully considered and placed, but they can be sparse. You don't have to use a lot, or build a complete world.
- **Reality effects** never call attention to themselves. They should sound like they were captured at the same time as dialog. They're part of the characters' world. These effects are there to sell the idea that what we're seeing is a slice of real life ... even though we know intellectually it was pieced together from multiple takes. They might also be there to emphasize a scene's emotion, as real-life sounds that just happen to complement what we're feeling. For example, an off-screen dog might start barking just before that little kid on the screen is getting threatened by the villain. Or we might hear a distant train whistle, along with the sparse crickets and quiet campfire, just as our hero is bedding down for the night in the middle of a lonely prairie. Reality effects help us suspend disbelief. Since the real world is never completely quiet, a reality effects track should never be quiet either. If the camera is showing something that normally makes noise, we should hear it as well. If the scene doesn't have machines or footsteps or anything else noisy, we should still hear the normal background of the characters' environment: traffic, birds, or soft wind outdoors; maybe a ticking clock or the quiet hum of a refrigerator indoors.[4]

Many sounds can fit into either category, depending on how you place them. Small chimes have been an abstract logo for a TV network, a representative icon for a home-delivery cosmetic company, and a cartoon "idea!", while still serving as real-world clocks or doorbells.

---

[3] Here's a sound effects question for Trekkies: what makes the Enterprise go whoosh? Its engine doesn't burn gasses. Its hull doesn't rub against air molecules, no matter how fast it's going. And being science fiction rather than fantasy, you can't blame the sound on wizards.

[4] The real-world sound of many interiors does include traffic, at least in developed countries. Urban and suburban rooms will have street traffic just outside their windows. Even quiet farms, in many places, will have the distant sound of a highway as part of their background. Since there's nothing visual to support these sounds, most film tracks ignore them. But some British TV series do include traffic-through-windows as part of their suburban interiors.

✳ TIDBIT

No rules, just right

The only important characteristic of a sound effect is how it makes the viewer feel. It doesn't matter where you get it,[5] what the file's name was, or what frames it's synced to. If an effect feels right, it *is* right.

If the effect doesn't feel right, lose it. It's not helping your movie.

Choosing sound effects can be a much more casual process than choosing music. Music selection usually involves a separate auditioning session, so you can concentrate on individual cues and select them without the distractions of trying to edit them together. It's almost always more efficient to grab sound effects as you need them. That's because sound effects aren't presented in the abstract. Until you've placed one against picture and all the other sounds in the scene, you can't tell if it's going to work. So if you're going to the trouble of auditioning it with all the other tracks, you might as well put it on the timeline and move onto the next.

But of course, some planning is always necessary.

Planning reality effects

It's important to look over the entire sequence while you're getting an idea for effects, so you can respect the dramatic arc of the scene. The effects that are part of the plot—explosions, screams, or even off-screen gasps—are most important and can help viewers forget that other sounds may be missing.

Don't make sound effects compete with each other. There's been a trend in Hollywood action pictures to mix a continuous wall of sound, with everything at maximum volume. This is wearing even in a theater. Home viewing, even on good equipment, has a more limited range.

Don't expect your audience to pay attention to two different sounds, at the same volume and timbre, at the same time. A simultaneous gunshot and car crash may sound great on large studio monitors when you know what you're listening to, but an audience will have a hard time sorting them out. Even some soft combinations, such as a cricket background mixed with a campfire, are similar enough that they turn into indistinguishable mush on smaller screens.

Unfamiliar sounds work best when we know what they're supposed to be, either because we can see what's making the noise or because a character refers to it.

---

[5] Assuming a healthy respect for copyright, of course.

It's best to approach this kind of issue when you're first planning the film. Chapter 4 has some tips.

Using backgrounds to simplify effects

It's a good idea to plan or edit background tracks first. A lot of times, they'll eliminate the need for more elaborate effects work. Since the mind associates what it hears with what it sees, random sounds in a stock background recording can appear to match specific on-screen actions. I usually find a few clunks and rattles in a background that serve as perfect foley or hard-effect replacements just by sliding them a few frames.

Backgrounds are also easiest to put in, since you can spot their approximate start and end points just by looking at the timeline. Most sound editors extend their backgrounds slightly past the video out-point, so they can be faded during the mix to cover abrupt picture transitions.

Planning punctuation effects

This is a chance to get creative, since these sounds are not slaves to the picture. Have fun.

I've always found planning abstract sounds to be a two-step process. The first step is going through the script or storyboard, thinking about what effects could heighten the message or entertainment, and making notes. Sometimes I've filled pages, almost like a musical score, showing how each sound will lead into the next. **Sound 15.1**[6] is a brief excerpt from a long-form project I mapped out that way: an exploration of forests and people using wood, through music and sound effects only. It was played as a background loop on hidden stereo speakers throughout Weyerhaeuser's travelling trade show exhibits, to subtly capture the space while not interfering with conversations.

Feel free to write lots of notes for effects while you're planning. Don't worry about there being too many or confusing the viewer: at this point you're brainstorming, and these are merely notes on paper. When you're done, select the best ones, present them to the director (or make the decisions, if you're the director), and note any that'll require setups at the shoot or time in the edit.

The second step in planning takes place after the picture is cut. Revise your plans based on the actual picture. Be prepared to cut and add based on what you see: the actors might have ad-libbed business, or the editor made some visual puns. Sometimes these visual extras mean you can delete planned sound effects, but sometimes they cry out for aural sweetening.

---

[6] From *Lifeforms*, © Weyerhaeuser Company, designed and executed by yours truly. This was an environmental background developed to aurally capture Weyerhaeuser's display space at trade shows, and it's intended to subtly grow on the listener. So it's okay to play it in the background. The first two minutes are mostly introduction. The really good stuff doesn't start to happen until about 3:30.

SOURCES FOR SOUND EFFECTS

While audio professionals spend thousands of dollars for immense sound collections on audio CDs or networked hard drives, it's easy to start more modestly. In fact, you can get started right now, thanks to the Hollywood Edge's giveaway (see box).

Consumer sound effects discs

You may find sound effects CDs for a few dollars at discount stores and online general retailers. These frequently aren't a bargain, for both copyright and technical reasons.

Prior to 1978's changes in copyright law, there was no general protection for sound recordings. Dishonest publishers could buy sound effects LPs at retail, transfer the sounds to their own masters, and sell them as their own. Some of those effects are still circulating today on retail CDs, with all the noise and even some of the record scratches you'd expect on multi-generation copies. They're nothing you'd want in your own film, unless you're doing a parody of a really bad mid-twentieth-century production.

Today almost all recordings are protected by copyright. While the professional libraries discussed below include a license for you to use them in productions, the retail discs might not. Some of the retail CDs carry warnings that they're for home use only. Others don't have that notice . . . but lack of a warning isn't a defense when you get sued for infringement.

Professional CD libraries

Most of the prerecorded sound effects used by professionals come from a few specialized publishers like Hollywood Edge. Their sounds are recorded digitally, without echo whenever possible, with a minimum of processing so that you've got the most flexibility to tweak them in your mix. Some are even recorded 24-bit or in surround, though the latter is of limited usefulness when you're mixing anything other than an ambience.

The effects are organized into libraries and published on CDs, DVD-ROMs, or hard drives. A specialized library might have four or five discs of nothing but foley footsteps or wind. Other libraries are organized by categories, such as Old West, War, or Sci-Fi. The general libraries might include a few dozen discs or Gigabytes of drive space, with enough different sounds to cover most production needs.

Depending on how specialized a library is, how easy the sounds were to record, and how many discs are in a set, professional sound effects will cost between $30 and $75 per CD's worth (about half an hour's worth of longer sounds, or as many as 100 short ones). These include the right to use the sound in any way other than resale as sound effects, and usually include catalog files that will integrate into databases. Hollywood Edge's main competitor is Sound Ideas (www.sound-ideas.com). Both those companies publish their own libraries and also represent a large number of independent libraries. Both also frequently have sales and special deals. If you're serious about building a library, get to know both companies.

✳ TIDBIT

A great freebie

Want a doorbell, crowd cheer, airplane fly-by, gunshots with and without silencer? You can have these and other effects for your library, free, from Hollywoodedge.com. Go to the Free Sound Effects tab on their main page (Figure 15.1). After you register (no fee or credit card required, and they don't spam) you'll be able to download a zipped archive of 99 well-recorded and useful effects, with the rights to use them in your productions.

It's good advertising on their part, since the site introduces you to their immense selection of commercial sound effects libraries. There are online catalogs and demo compilations. The selection is so big that they frequently have clearance sales: full libraries for half the normal price.

Hollywood Edge sells their effects on hard drive or as CDs to rip into your computer. These free files are mp3, but they're high enough quality to use in a theatrical track . . . and you can't beat the price.

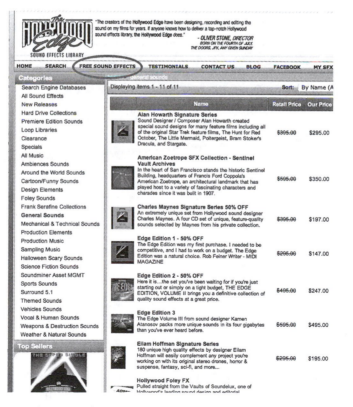

Figure 15.1 A catalog page from Hollywoodedge.com, a professional supplier of effects for sound designers. Click the circled tab to download 99 useful effects.

Sound Dogs online library

Sound Dogs (www.sounddogs.com), a division of a large Hollywood effects company, posts a catalog of their own and other professional sounds (Figure 15.2). You search and audition from a very large selection of sounds. When you find one you like, enter a credit card number—the cost varies with file size, but most of the shorter effects are under a couple of dollars—and, within a few minutes, the system sends back a link to where the sounds are waiting. The effects come with full license to use in your production, and you can add them to your library for future productions without further payment.

Sound Dogs is great when you need a couple of specialized effects during a late-night editing session. But it does take time to search and download the effects, and it costs more to buy them this way than in a published collection. It's best to use them as a supplement for a larger collection you've bought on CD or hard drive. (The Dogs also deal in buyout music, but I've found their selection limited compared to other sources.)

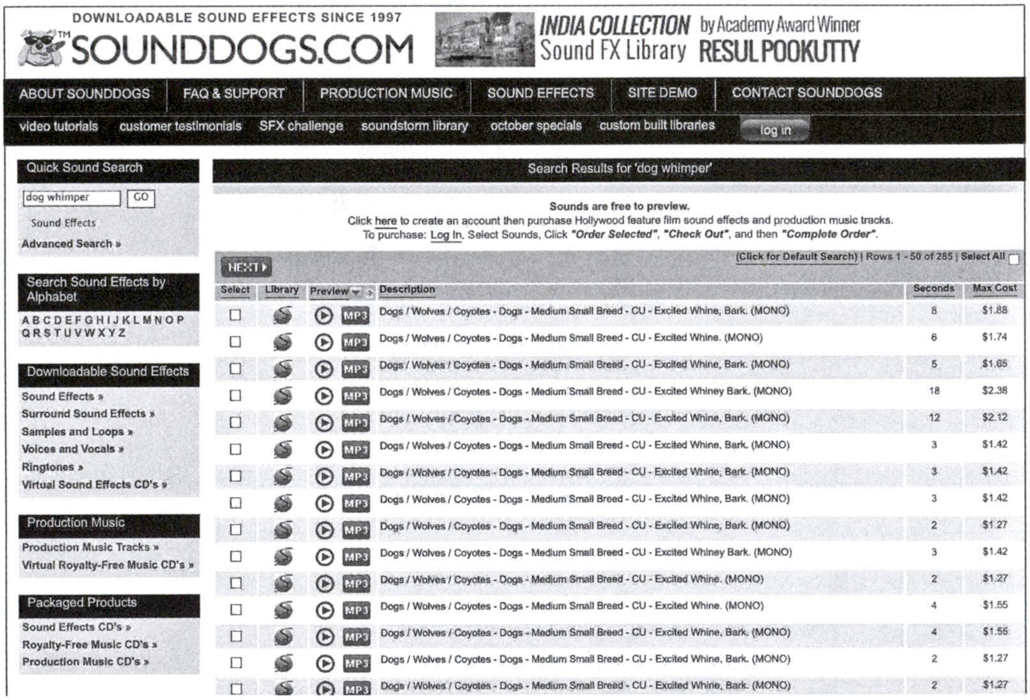

Figure 15.2 You can buy high-quality sound effects as you need them from www.sounddogs.com.

Free sound effect websites

A Google search for "free sound effects" turns up more than a hundred million listings! You'll find a few vendors who have posted free samples from their commercial libraries, and these can be worth downloading . . . but they're apt to be short, and require separate searches and downloads for each effect. Their terms can vary—some are for web or non-commercial use only; others are licensed for film and TV—so check the sites' wording carefully.

Many of the listings, however, are from hobbyists who have put up pages of effects they've captured from movies and TV shows. Sound quality is poor to awful, and using the sounds will almost certainly violate someone's copyright.

BUILDING A LIBRARY

On the other hand, sometimes you have to leave the editing room to get the effects you want. If you don't want to use library effects or your needs are very specialized, you'll have to plan for and record custom effects.

Pocket recorders

Those digital recorders in the $150 range, which are so handy for low budget film dialog (see page 183), are also great for gathering effects. The trick is to remember that your ears are a lot more directional than the mics on those recorders.

- If you're recording ambiences, the recorders' wide pickup won't be a problem: almost anything you hear in the environment will get recorded. So will any handling noise when you rub fingers against the recorder, any clothing noise if it's in your pocket, and of course anything you say or even whisper while you're holding it. So stand still and quiet. Let the environment happen around you for a minute or so. If you've got a pair of earbuds or small walkman-type phones, they can be a psychological help as well as a technical one. Wear them while you're recording the ambience. People will assume you're listening to music while waiting for someone. They won't mind that you're standing there seemingly doing nothing, and they won't try to talk to you.
- If you're trying to record specific sounds that would be difficult to capture inside a studio—changing a tire, perhaps, or playing pinball—directionality becomes an issue. Ambient noise will be a lot louder in the file than you remember from real life, and may make it impossible to edit the effect or add it to your mix. If you can't bring a more directional mic, let the inverse-square law be your friend: get a lot closer to the noise source than you'd think necessary. You'll get a much cleaner and more usable recording.
- Of course level control is an issue any time you record. If environments are too soft, they'll be buried in noise. If real-life construction sounds are too loud, they'll turn into useless crackle. But don't use the recorders' automatic level control!

That will destroy the natural dynamics of the sound, as well as increase apparent noise during pauses. Keep an eye on the meter and adjust the volume control for the best recording.

Using props

The key to getting good specific effects is gathering props or finding a real-world object that makes the noise you want. Handle and listen to everything.[7]

Once you've found something that makes the right sound, over-record! Do as many takes of that effect as you think you'll need, and then do some more. Remember, it doesn't cost any extra to keep recording. What you don't use on this film might come in handy on the next.

While you're making multiple takes, vary how you make the noise. For example, a coffee mug can *clink* or *clunk* or *thud* or make a dozen other sounds, depending on where you hold it, how hard you grip it, and how you hit it against some other object.

Wild effects at the shoot

If an effect has to match an on-screen action, the best way to get it may be recording on set, right after you finish shooting. You'll have the microphone, recorder, and all the necessary props right there . . . though budget and time constraints might make

✍ TRY THIS

Make some (small) noise!

Grab some object near you, right now. It could be a pen, a cup, your tablet, your keys . . . anything you can comfortably hold and move around. See how many different sounds you can make by hitting it in various ways.

Varying how you hold the object (tighter or looser, with open fingers or closed fist) and *where* you hold it (handle, side, around the middle) will make a difference in the sound. So will whatever you're hitting it against.

Now think about how you'd categorize the different sounds you've made: by timbre, by what they sound like, by verbal approximation, or any other way that'll let you find the sound when you need it.

(If you're reading this book for a film class, propose that you prepare a fully detailed report on all the noises you just made. Now turn on your recorder, and capture the instructor's laughter.)

---

[7] I won't repeat here how Ben Burtt turned antenna guy wires into *Star Wars*' lightsabers. If you've read anything about film sound, you've heard the story. If not, go to filmsound.org/starwars, or any of a dozen other sites.

this strategy impossible. You can also record usable effects in a studio, in your editing suite, and out in the real world. Chapter 10 has specific tips for this kind of recording.

Keep an index

Whatever sound effects you record, it helps to make a few notes about them. Then, when you get back to your computer, isolate and file the individual sounds with names that'll help you remember what they're supposed to be. As you gather an archive of files, you'll be building a searchable custom library.

When you've got only a few effects in your sound folder, you can find the one you want with a simple directory or finder search. As the library grows, it's worth building an index. Any basic directory-organizing tool will work for a start. A simple database or spreadsheet index will let you add columns for descriptions, how you got the effect, and key places where you used it.

As their libraries get bigger, professionals use a specialized audio manager like Soundminer (Figure 15.3) or Basehead. These let you search with multiple terms and

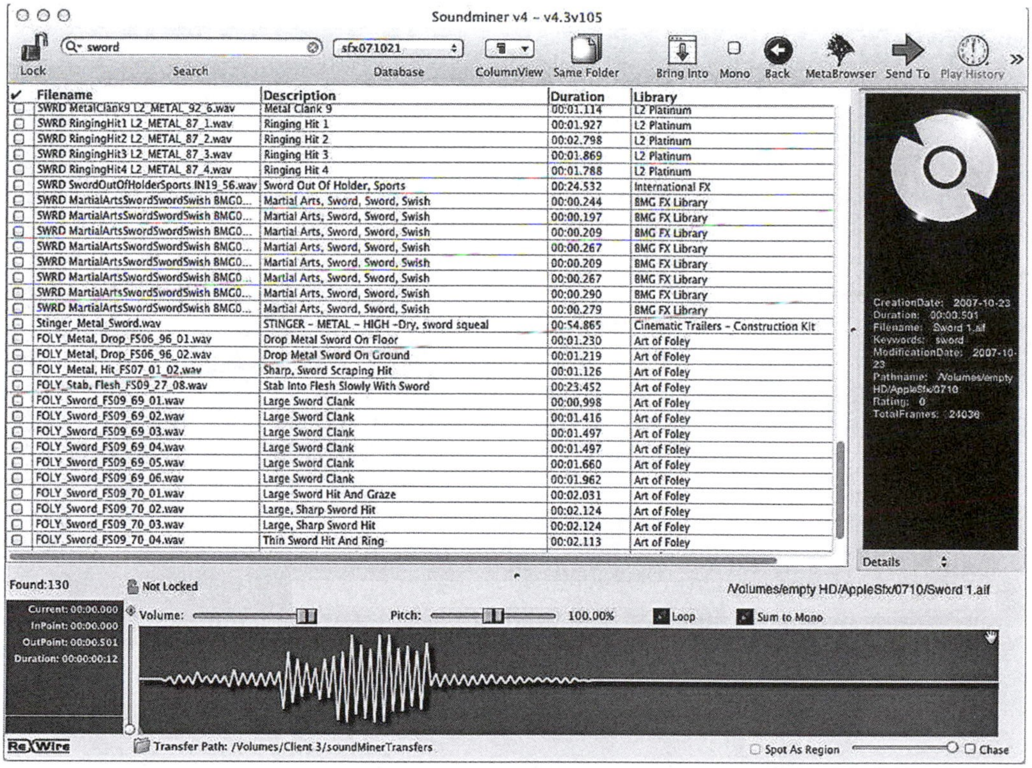

Figure 15.3 A specialized program like Soundminer lets you search, modify, and apply sound effects from a single window.

automatic synonyms, audition and select all or part of a sound, and apply some effects or speed variation, all from their main window. Then you press a single key, and the program drops the desired sound directly onto your DAW's timeline, in sync and on the proper track!

Vocal and synthesized effects

Most audio programs include basic synthesis, and free VST synthesizer plug-ins are available from shareware sources. Creating usable electronic sound effects takes more steps than we can go into here, but there are plenty of books dedicated to the subject.[8] The bigger problem, I've found, is that they all sound electronic: great for lasers and sci-fi, but limiting if you're trying to build a real world. Depending on the kind of synthesis involved, they can also be hard to mix in the final track: the sounds from certain techniques tend to merge together, becoming one unexpected sound rather than the two distinct effects you needed for the story.

Vocal effects can be more versatile than electronic ones. See the section on Mr. Sound Effects, at the end of Chapter 9.

CHOOSING THE RIGHT EFFECT

So you've got 100 or 1,000 effects in front of you, in a collection of discs or on the screen. Here's how to choose the right ones.

- Try to hear them in your head before you look. This is a reality check to make sure the sound can actually exist.[9]
- It can also help if you break the sound into easily found components. A "Cellblock Door" can be just a jingling key ring and a sliding metal gate, slowed and mixed with a heavy echo.
- Hard sounds (Chapter 4) are caused by physical actions. So if you can't find something in the catalog that's a perfect match, look for something else that moves in the same way. A golf club, arrow, and leather whip make a very similar *wsssh* in the air. An electric car window motor may work perfectly as a robot arm, laser printer, or spaceship door. You can occasionally make outlandish substitutions if the sound you're using isn't immediately identifiable, and there's enough of a visual cue to suggest what it should be. When a network ran the movie *Mouse Hunt*, I sweetened its trailer with a toy balloon! Rubbing a finger against the balloon, in various pressures and rhythms, gave me a full vocabulary for the star rodent.

---

[8] And there's an extensive section in my own *Audio Postproduction for Film and Video*.

[9] A major ad agency once asked me for the sound of a flashing neon sign, as heard from across a busy street. I resisted the temptation to ask what color.

- Don't rely too much on the name; you actually have to listen before deciding. "Police Car" could be an old-fashioned siren or a modern electronic whooper, near or far, with or without an engine; or it could be a high-speed chase, or even a two-way radio. The better libraries use long, detailed descriptions, but details are no substitute for listening.
- Pay attention to what's around the effect while you listen: not just other noises, but also the acoustics. A car door has a lot of different slams depending on whether it's outdoors or inside a parking garage, how much of a hurry the slammer is in, and how far away we are from the car. Exterior sounds can often be used for interiors if they're clean and you add echo . . . but it's almost impossible to make an interior sound match an outdoor shot. You can add distance to an exterior sound by using an equalizer to roll off the high midrange (Chapter 16).
- You can loop or repeat relatively short backgrounds to cover longer scenes. About 20 or 30 seconds' worth of original sound is usually sufficient, but see the note about looping backgrounds later in this chapter.
- Sound effects don't have to be in the right language. Foreign street scenes or crowds can work fine in an English-speaking video, if you edit out any identifiable phrases. Mixed properly, they'll fill out a scene without interfering with principal dialog, and it's a lot harder to tell when they've been looped. This trick works on the small screen but can be risky in a theatrical feature, because it's so much easier to hear details of the track on a big system.

✳ TIDBIT

Scream time

Sometimes, sound effects become an in-joke among sound editors. The Wilhelm Scream is a notable one. Recorded more than a half-century ago for a minor Western, this male scream has snuck into more than 200 movies including *Star Wars* and *The Hobbit*. It's been heard in video games, radio shows, and anywhere else a sound designer can find a meaningful place to apply it: the joke works only if most viewers assume it's a natural part of the story. Meanwhile, my colleagues and other film aficionados can say, "yup . . . another Wilhelm."

I even managed to place Wilhelm in a short film about a computer screen technology! **Sound 15.2** lets you hear a section from the mix, with a few other effects accompanying Wilhelm. The full video is at www.dplay.com/movies/EinkAgcy.mov.[10]

Google "Wilhelm Scream" to find the latest websites and YouTube compilations devoted to this vocal icon.

---

[10] You might recognize the setting for this film. I used a short piece to demonstrate mic positions in Chapter 7. Again, thanks to Captains of Industry for its use.

Sound effects palettes

Hard effects generally fall into one of three categories: those made by mechanical actions (usually wood or metal, but also such things as rock scrapes); those from organic sources (crowd noises, animals, fantasy monsters); and those from electronic circuits.

It may seem strange, but I've found that montages and mixed effects seem to work best if you stay within the same source category, making exceptions only for accents. It's a lot like an artist staying in a single palette of earth tones or cool pastels.

PLACING SOUND EFFECTS

Track layouts

Give some thought to track layout also, before you place effects. Leave some dead space between effects on the same track; if they're butted up against each other, they'll be difficult to keep track of on a timeline and almost impossible to control during the mix. If you keep similar sounds on the same track, you won't have to be constantly changing global echo or equalization settings.

After you've done this a few times, you'll evolve a few standard track layouts. I usually put dialog splits on the top tracks, hard-effect tracks below them, then background effects, and finally music tracks on the bottom. It makes mixing faster because the same kinds of sound always appear in the same place on my screen and on the same channels of my mixing console. It also makes life simpler when the producer asks for dialog, effect, and music *stems*—separate, synchronized mixes with just one category of sound—for foreign-language release.

- The easiest way to simplify sound effects placement is to ignore a lot of it. In Hollywood, almost every action is matched by an effect, down to the tiniest foley. But they've also got armies of sound editors building the track. On the small screen, you can often limit your efforts to just those sounds that advance the plot.
- Place the music before you worry about effects in a small-screen project. TV mixes aren't very subtle, and if the music's going to be loud, you might not be able to hear anything else.
- No matter what size project it is, you can save time by placing ambiences before you worry about hard effects. Often a random movement in a background sound will work perfectly for an on-screen action if you merely move it a few frames.
- Don't worry about the little sounds—clothing rustles or pencil scratches—until you're sure they're necessary.
- For video projects, it can save time to do effects spotting with the narration or dialog tracks up. Television is driven by dialog, and words have to take priority over other sounds. If you're working on a big screen film, this becomes a question of how much time you've got to spend: any scene might benefit from effects, but you may have to decide if a particular scene is worth the effort.

- Sometimes it's important to hear an effect, for plot or sound-design reasons, but there's simultaneous dialog. In these cases, be prepared to lower the dialog. If the words are also important, the best solution is often to re-edit the picture so they don't compete.

Looping

If a background sound isn't long enough to cover a scene, put it in more than once. You might hear a slight break in the sound where two copies are spliced together, but there are ways to disguise where the "loop"[11] joins:

- Place the splice under a hard effect or loud dialog line.
- Slide the splice to where the camera angle changes.
- Put the repeats on alternate tracks, and let them overlap for a few seconds, with a cross-fade between them (Figure 15.4). This will usually make the splice imperceptible.

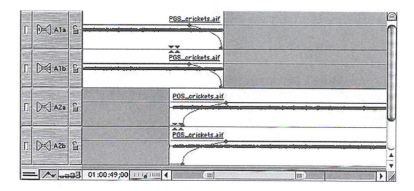

Figure 15.4 The same sound repeated on alternating tracks. Note the crossfade where they overlap.

   Track 98 of the Hollywood Edge free effects ("Wind Gusts Heavy Howling") is a good sample for you try this technique with. Even though that sound changes through its 30 seconds, an overlap will let you extend it. If it's being extended for so many repeats that viewers would get used to the pattern of wind gusts, you can try the next trick:

- Some backgrounds, such as traffic, change pitch or timbre as they develop. Others, such as sea wash, have a definite rhythm. In either case, a repeating loop would be obvious because the sound is different at each end of the loop, and crossfading

---

[11] The term came from the practice of cutting film background sounds into long loops—often dozens of feet long—that would continuously pass through the player. In this way, the term is related to *looping* for dialog replacement.

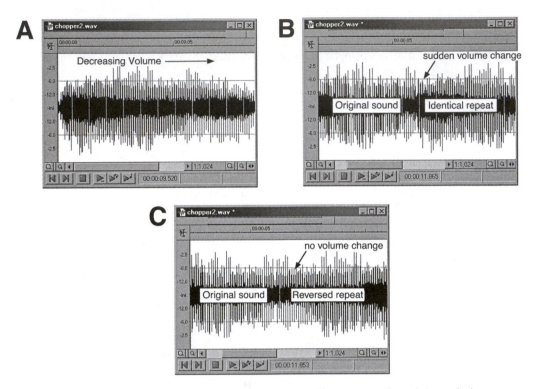

Figure 15.5 When looping an effect that sounds different at each end, it can help to reverse the second copy.

would mean we hear the different parts simultaneously. Hollywood's trick for that is the *flip loop* or *c-loop*, shown in Figure 15.5. At the top is an original helicopter background. Note how its volume decreases slightly over time. Looping it (Figure 15.5B) makes an obvious jump, because we've joined the loud start to the softer ending. To fix this, take the original sound and reverse it[12]—instead of going from loud to soft as the original did, the copy will go from soft to loud. Then copy that after the original (Figure 15.5C). Since there's no change in volume, we're not aware of where the pieces are joined. The new combined version starts and ends at the same level, so it can be looped as a whole. You'd be amazed how many background sounds can be played backwards and still sound right. Try it with ocean waves or city traffic—even a car horn might work backwards, depending on the reverb from nearby buildings. Or make a c-loop of the "Prop Plane Tiger Fly By" in the Hollywood Edge free collection, and turn it into a plane that's circling us.

---

[12] In some programs, you do this by applying a speed of –100%; in others, apply a "Reverse" effect.

Adding hard effects

After the backgrounds are in place, play back the sequence and see what effects still seem to be missing. This might not be too long a list. Television can ignore most foley, which gets lost through a small speaker anyway. Theatrical scenes with music and a background track can often ignore foley as well. You'll probably also find that some hard effects were picked up with dialog and just need to be boosted in the mix.

Usually you can insert a hard effect right on the same frame where you see an action. Jog to the single frame where the action starts, and plant a marker. Then drag the start of the effect to that marker. Some effects can be placed intuitively (it doesn't take much imagination to find the exact frame where a punch lands or a car crashes). You may be surprised how easy it is to place other effects, once you scan at the single-frame level. Guns, for example, almost always have a one-frame barrel flash exactly when they're fired, like the one in Figure 15.6. Mark the frame, then snap the front of the sound to it.

Figure 15.6 Only one frame has a barrel flash. That's where the *bang!* belongs.

Don't worry about compensating for the speed of sound: as soon as something happens, viewers expect to hear it. Who cares if the collapsing building is a few hundred feet away, and the crash would take half a second to reach us? If a sound is big enough, convention dictates that it will travel instantly. That's why when a laser death-cannon destroys a rebel home planet, we hear the explosion immediately ... even though the planet is a few thousand kilometers away, through the soundless vacuum of space.

Figure 15.7 This fast-cut sequence didn't leave room for the start of the explosion sound, so put it a frame or two ahead of the cut.

Sometimes, the editing rhythm is so fast, you can't find an appropriate frame. Consider the movie promo in Figure 15.7. We see an explosion at 9:03—but it's already started when we cut to it. There's no frame where the sound should start! This also happens frequently in fight scenes, with a cut from one shot with a fist flying, to a reverse angle where the punch has already landed. If this is the case, place the sound a frame or two ahead of its visual (starting the explosion sound around 9:01). The sound can even help smooth the visual discontinuity.

If the video is moving very quickly, there may not be enough time for big effects to die out, either. Perhaps the explosion was followed by a hospital interior, a second or so later. That's too short for the sound of an explosion to register. Keep the explosion over the cut while you add a hospital background; then fade it under the first dialog so the background shows through.

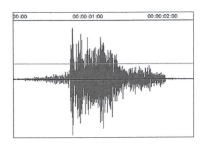

Figure 15.8 Waveform of an explosion. Things don't really start happening until almost a second has gone by.

As you're placing effects, consider that many should be cued to their middle instead of their front. Figure 15.8 shows a typical explosion. There's a rumble at the start of the sound, before we hear the big crunch. But you'd want the crunch to sync with the first frame of fireball. Plant a marker on the big sound, in this case about 24 frames in. Line the marker up with the visual frame, and let the front of the effect fall where it will. If the scene doesn't have enough time to fit the entire intro before the part you've marked, trim the sound's in-point.

Many sounds are based on multiple actions, and an effect may need some internal editing to fit picture. For example, "closing a door" can consist of a hinge squeal, a latch strike and release, and a rattle against the frame. While you might be able to place the strike and release as one edit, timing of the squeal and rattle depend on how the character closed the door. Use the razor tool to separate those sounds onto separate clips. Then slide them on different tracks to match the door's movement.

MAKING EFFECTS SOUND MORE EFFECTIVE

Hollywood loves big percussive effects: car crashes, explosions, gigantic guns. Many times, realistic sounds just don't cut it: you've cut in a sound that matches the picture exactly, but it isn't dramatic enough. You need to make it bigger.

In the next chapter, we'll talk about how compression and other processes can hype an effect. Those processes are best reserved for the mix. Here are a few things you can do while you're still editing.

Layering effects

Many sounds can be improved by layering. Putting multiple elements on different tracks, and then mixing them, can make some sound effects work better in the mix.

Layered backgrounds

Backgrounds and steady sounds can be made richer by combining elements that complement each other. Pick separate effects that sound different in terms of timbre or rhythm, and they'll work together to build the characters' world.

If a background is going to be mixed with dialog, any midrange sounds in it will compete with the voices. Since most background recordings—and real-world environments—have a lot of midrange in them, you'll have to turn the track down during the mix, or equalize it so it almost disappears.

A good solution is to find two different backgrounds—one predominantly high-pitched, the other low—and use both under a scene. For example, instead of using a single busy street background, combine rumbling start-and-stop traffic with pedestrian footsteps. The result can sound bigger without interfering with dialog. If you want to add some midrange honking horns, do it during pauses or unimportant words. I'll sometimes walk into a mix with "choirs" of sound effects tracks under a scene—separate bass, alto, and soprano ranges—so we can constantly adjust them based on the dialog and action.

Other examples

- Add some children playing to a city park or a carnival background. The staccato higher voices will add interest and brightness while not interfering with adult dialog.
- A few birds can turn a lightly sloshing lakeside into a pretty outdoor scene. Or use some crickets to make it a lake at night.
- Complex machines can be built out of simpler conveyor belts, rhythmic grinders, and gears. For effects that last the length of a scene, copy a short section of all the tracks at once and loop it for as long as you need. The repeating loop will simulate a happily running machine.

Layered hard effects

Gunshots and explosions lend themselves to layering. But you can't just mix two shots together and expect the result to be twice as loud; we won't hear it that way. Instead, do a little manipulation so each new layer actually adds something. **Sound 15.3** demonstrates this. All five of the *bang!* sounds in that file are at the same volume.

- The first shot is a single gunshot, taken from Hollywood Edge's *SuperSingle* disc. It's big and accurate ... but in some dramatic situations, you might want it bigger.
- The second shot adds another gun from the same disc. Even though two different guns are firing simultaneously, the effect isn't any more powerful than a single one. The initial bang vibrations are so chaotic that adding any more chaos doesn't help.
- The third shot starts to feel bigger. All we've done is added a second copy of the first sound effect, but slowed it down to 80% of the original speed. The lower pitch adds a nice bass richness to the long decay, and the slower waves extend the initial shot.[13]
- The fourth shot adds a third copy. This copy has been slowed to 50% and a chorus effect (page 471) has been added to give the reverb some extra movement.
- The fifth one adds stereo! The original shot is in the center, an 80% slower version is on the left, and a 53% slower version is on the right. The brain hears all three as a single gunshot ... but one with an extra dimension.

Spreading effects to make room for dialog

Let's push that last gunshot trick a little more: stereo effects can seem much wider if you spread their tracks apart, and get rid of the middle. Delay one side of the stereo signal several seconds, but fade both sides in and out together. This is easily done in an audio workstation; in an NLE, you may have to use two separate stereo pairs, one greatly offset from the other. Use the Take Left command on one pair, so it turns into a mono signal from just the left track; and Take Right on the other. Pan one about 40% to the left, the other 40% to the right, and put matching fades on both. Or try phase-inverting software, included in some audio programs as a "solo eliminator" for eliminating the vocalist in commercial recordings. It removes sounds from the center of a stereo field though may turn the result into a mono file that has to be treated with other processing.

If you've done any stereo trickery, check the result in mono when you're done. Make sure you haven't introduced something that will sound hollow if the track goes on the Web or a mono home setup.

---

[13] Obviously, I used a slowing effect that doesn't try to maintain the original pitch. This is a user selection in most software: you can maintain the pitch when changing the speed of dialog or music; or you can let both pitch and speed change (the way they would with analog tape), which is useful for effects.

Some random sound effects wisdom

A few additional things can help while you're working with effects.

- Effects should be digitized at full volume, even if they're from actions that don't make much noise. You can lower their level with a rubber band while you're previewing, but don't do anything that lowers the level of the sound file itself. This prevents noise buildup, and prevents problems if you want to add echo or other processes at the mix.
- Don't be afraid to vary the speed. A small increase can add excitement to a sound. A large decrease can make a sound bigger. If you're slowing a sound down in an audio program with a Preserve Pitch option, try it both ways and see which you like better. If you're lowering pitch by more than an octave, try it in multiple programs: a badly designed algorithm can add aliasing distortion, which sounds bad on music or dialog but can make effects seem brighter.
- You can add a *feeling* of speed to steady sounds like auto engines by applying a flanging effect (Chapter 16). If you don't have a flange processor in your software, put the sound on two tracks, delay one track a few frames, speed the delayed one up so it ends in sync with the other, and mix both tracks together.
- Use pitch shift on just one channel of a stereo effect to make it bigger. You'll usually want less than a 3% change, but the right amount depends on the sound. Try different settings and check the result on mono speakers as well as in stereo.

. . . and a warning

Don't expect to make effects bigger by "turning up the bass." If an effect was properly recorded, boosting the lows with an equalizer will usually just make it muddier. It won't add frequencies that weren't in the original sound.

Instead, use one of the speed-varying tricks above.

CHAPTER 16

Processing

Few audio tools are as useful or abused as effects processors. A professional studio will have thousands of dollars invested in these units or equivalent plug-ins. They'll use them to change the tonal balance of a sound, alter its dynamics, manipulate its apparent environment, or even change the sound into something totally different. In every case, the real goal is to make the track easier to understand or a dramatic premise easier to accept.

But for these processors to do any good at all, you have to know what's going on inside them. You can't just grab a knob and twist until it sounds good . . . that's as likely to harm one aspect of the track as improve another. Learning how to use processors properly isn't difficult. All it takes is a little knowledge of how sound works, some imagination, and the next few pages.

✳ TIDBIT

What's in a word?

The previous chapter was about sound effects—recordings you add to a track to heighten its realism. This one is about effects processors like equalizers and compressors. In a busy studio both the recordings and the processors are referred to simply as *effects*. Which kind you mean should be obvious from the context.[1]

HOW ANY EFFECT CAN WRECK A SOUND

A few warnings before we begin. These apply to every kind of processor, from hardware-based analog units to NLE plug-ins, but are particularly important in the desktop environment.

Watch out for overloads

Somewhere, inside virtually any effects processor, the signal level has to get boosted. If it boosts things too high, the system will distort—adding fuzziness to an analog signal or crackling to a digital one. Unfortunately, the amount of boost usually isn't obvious from a volume knob or even a meter, and the distortion might not show up until the loudest part of a track. It can be easy to cause serious damage without noticing.

Pay attention to any OVERLOAD or CLIP indicators on the front panel or control screen, and listen for distortion or crackling on loud signals while you preview an effect. If you see or hear a problem, turn down the input volume control until the distortion goes away. Then adjust the output volume control until the output meter reads correctly.

If you're working with a plug-in that lets you hear only a limited-length preview, select the loudest part of the track while you're making these adjustments. Save the settings, select the entire section you want to process, go back to the plug-in and process with the settings you've saved. Then review the section to listen for problems. After a while, you'll get used to your software and won't need to do this previewing.

In most NLEs, you can't easily select just the loud part of a clip. Fortunately, most NLEs apply effects by just storing their settings along with the clip. They're applied when you preview or render, but the original files are never changed. If you're mixing in a system like this, don't panic if you hear distortion: effects that aren't sounding good can be removed or changed before the final output.

---

[1] Many NLEs refer to all of their audio effects as *filters*. To an audio person, a filter is just a specific kind of equalizer.

Watch out for sounds that are too soft

Any time you do anything more complicated than turning a sound on or off, there's math involved. Compression, equalization, and reverb are really just long, complicated strings of steps like multiplication and division. If these steps result in a higher number than the system is designed for, you hear the distortion noted above.

But remember, digital audio is always a fraction of Full Scale. The smallest fraction is determined by the number of bits: in a 16-bit system, it's roughly 1/32,000 of Full Scale.[2] Anything smaller than that—and believe me, it's pretty easy for a subtle sound to have details that small—gets rounded to the nearest available number. Any time you round off a signal, you replace details with random noise.

The division, square roots, and other math involved in effects processing can get very complicated. Answers almost never work out to an exact number of bits. So there's potential for a lot of rounding . . . and a lot of subtle noise.

You can reduce the noise by working at 24 bits instead of 16. That gives the system smaller fractions to work with, for less rounding. If you've recorded 16 bits in the field, bump the files up to 24 bits when you start mixing or processing. This won't do anything about noise that's already on the files, but will keep you from adding more due to rounding. If you're delivering 16-bit final masters, convert back down to that standard as a final step. Use dithering (page 43), and the result will be much cleaner than had you stayed at 16 bits throughout the postproduction process.

Use good monitors

You can't adjust a processor unless you know what it's doing. That takes good monitors (see Chapter 11 for some tips on choosing them). If you don't have good speakers at your editing setup, save the processing decisions until you're someplace that does.

A set of very good headphones can be useful for adjusting an equalizer or noise-reduction software, but headphones affect how you perceive volume. So you can't use them for adjusting compression or reverb.

Presets . . . friend or foe?

Most third-party NLE plug-ins, and many of the effects built into audio-only programs, come with a library of pre-built settings. These often have names like "vocal enhance" or "small room reverb." They're written by people who know the software. Load

---

[2] A 16 bit word can describe 65,535 possible values. But audio signals are bipolar (in the electrical sense), so those values have to be distributed evenly: half of them are negative, and half positive.

[3] There is one exception: if you know your viewers will be watching with particular poor speakers, and you have a chance to mix on *exactly* the same speakers: the exact same models, with the exact same amplifiers. They have to be exact, because no two bad speakers sound bad in the same way. There is no such thing as an "average" cheap speaker.

✳ TIDBIT

There's no way around it

If you can't afford good speakers, and have no way to move your mix to some place with adequate monitors, your processing and mix decisions will suffer.

It's like trying to do color-correction while wearing cheap sunglasses. Even if you've gotten used to how those glasses affect what you're seeing, there are some colors that'll never make it to your eyes. You can't color-correct for what you can't see, and you can't equalize or adjust the mix for what you can't hear.[3]

---

them, listen to how they affect your tracks, and see what happens when you change each knob.

Unfortunately, they're rarely written by people who know how to mix films! If the presets make sense at all, they're probably designed for music.[4]

So once you learn how to use an effect, think of the built-in presets merely as a start. Load them, but modify the setting until they work best for your elements, then save the result as your own new preset. (Also, save the settings you come up with for one-time situations like correcting a particularly noisy location. You'll need them if you have to remix the project, and you'll find them a handy starting place for the next noisy location.)

Presets in NLEs

The effects built into many video editors don't have presets, and some don't even have a way to store your settings. Until you get very familiar with processing, keep notes and write down or take screenshots of how you've adjusted the effects for each clip. Or, if your software allows this, use the Copy Filters function to save settings to a dummy clip—any short soundfile—with a name that'll help you remember the effect. Keep these clips in a separate bin labeled *effects presets*, and copy their filters to new clips as you need them. Either method will help you keep a consistent sound throughout your projects, and make it easier to match the processing if you have to re-edit.

WHEN TO APPLY PROCESSING

If you're making a feature film in Hollywood, the answer is obvious: *don't do anything* until you get to the dub stage. The re-recording team are the only people who should

---

[4] Frequency ranges are much wider in music than in film tracks, but the music crowd doesn't care as much about the midrange as we do. Music reverbs are almost always bigger than the interior spaces where dialog is recorded. Software companies invest more time developing presets and effects for music, because the music-making market is much bigger than the film-mixing one.

adjust equalizers or processors. This is the most practical way to handle a feature film's track, and is probably first time the film has been in a room with calibrated monitors, properly designed acoustics, first-class processing tools, and experienced operators. It's also the most efficient workflow: a small army of editors and engineers has worked on different elements of the track, and keeping all the processing in one place saves confusion and having to undo each others' work. If there's a special audio effect—a monster voice, or point-of-view soundscape—it may have been pre-processed, but will still have plenty of room for variation in the final mix.

Smaller projects—corporate and event videos, and personal films—don't have to follow this scheme. But it's still a good idea: resist the temptation to apply processing while you're editing. Instead, wait until everything is in place and you're doing the mix. That way you can process in context, won't do more processing than is necessary, and aren't stuck trying to reverse an effect if you took it too far.

You can make an exception, on smaller projects, for dialog tracks that need repair. It can make sense to apply corrective equalization or noise reduction when you're first deciding if a take is usable. Just don't do too much—these processes leave their own objectionable fingerprints—and always keep the dialog sounding natural. You can add more processing later if needed.

And if you do any processing at all before the final mix, keep an unprocessed version on an adjacent track. Mute the track, but lock it to the processed one so that any subsequent edits happen to both. This will be your insurance when you discover that the effects don't make sense in the mix, or the better speakers at the sound studio reveal annoying artifacts from the processing.

Avoiding commitment

Standalone software and most of the effects in single-track audio editing programs are usually *destructive*. That's not a value judgment. It refers to how the file is changed, and the original unprocessed version is lost. So before you apply a destructive effect, make sure there's a clean copy elsewhere on your hard drive.

Most of the effects in NLEs are applied to single clips but in a non-destructive way: they leave the source material intact and apply the processing to a temporary file before you mix or preview. With non-destructive processing, you can change settings or try different combinations of effects while you develop the mix.

Good multitrack DAWs often let you apply effects either destructively to a specific clip, or non-destructively to an entire track. Since you have virtually unlimited tracks in good audio software, with flexible routing and grouping, it's reasonable to create a new track just to hold one or two clips that need specific processing.

Processing takes processor power

The downside of non-destructive processing is that a lot of simultaneous effects can load down the CPU. This can cause problems with playback during previews, so many NLEs build a temporary file just for previewing.

TIP

Let a hard drive make life easy

Before doing any destructive processing, make sure you've kept an unprocessed version. If you're going to edit the file after processing it, lock the unprocessed version to it so that edits happen to both simultaneously. Then keep two unprocessed versions—one with the edits and one as originally recorded. Keep these backups in the same directory as the working files, with names that'll make them easy to identify.

A $100 hard drive holds about 3,000 *hours* of raw audio, which comes down to a tiny fraction of a penny for each 30-second clip you save. Compare that to the time—and anguish—of trying to recover and edit a new version if you discover the processing isn't what you want.

If you're going to be doing a lot of cutting and don't want to spend time on renders each time you check an edit, look for an Ignore Audio Filters setting in the project's Render or Preview panel.

Each effect affects the next

If you're applying multiple effects to a track, the order in which you use them can make a major difference. We'll discuss how to take advantage of this at the end of this chapter.

EQUALIZERS

These ubiquitous audio processors were invented to boost the highs that got lost over long telephone lines, and their name comes from the idea that they made the phone system *equally efficient* at all frequencies. Some brilliant sound engineer brought them into an early film mixing suite, using them to equalize the sound from multiple microphones. Another genius had them compensate for the boomy acoustics of early theaters. They're now considered an essential part of any audio production facility.

What an equalizer does is the same whether it's a multi-knob wonder in a recording studio, a couple of on-screen sliders in your NLE, or the tone controls on your car radio: it emphasizes or suppresses parts of the audio spectrum, picking out the elements of the signal that will be most useful, and changing the harmonic structure of a sound. The only difference between them—other than the noise or distortion a specific model introduces—is how precisely they let you specify a frequency or how much it's boosted or lowered. Precision is important because sounds you want to keep can be close to ones you want to affect. But precision requires complexity, both in the algorithm and in the load on your CPU.[5]

You can use the equalizer to do the following:

- Increase intelligibility of a voice track.
- Make music more exciting under a montage.
- Tailor both the voice and the music so you can make each of them seem louder at the same time.
- Change the character of background sounds and some hard effects.
- Fix some types of distortion, and correct for boominess or some on-set noises.
- Improve intelligibility on badly miked sequences. This doesn't make the audio actually sound better, but may make it easier to understand.
- Simulate telephones, intercoms, and awful multimedia speakers.

But equalizers have their limits:

- They can't pick out one voice from a crowd.
- They can't eliminate complex or harmonically rich noises like traffic or power-line buzzing.[6]
- They can't generate parts of the band that were never recorded. If you turn up the treble on a track that has no highs because of a low sample rate, all you'll do is boost noise.
- They can't turn lightweight voices into deep-voiced giants.
- They can't compensate for bad monitors in your NLE setup or bad speakers in a viewer's set.

Equalizer types

There are dozens of different equalizer types in equipment catalogs and software specs, but they're really just combinations of three basic functions.

Peaking equalizers

Peaking equalizers affect the volume of the sound around a particular frequency. They'll always have a level control, most of them have frequency controls, and a few also let you adjust the bandwidth (or Q). The Q determines how sharply the equalizer chooses its frequencies. A very high Q can emphasize a single note while ignoring notes next to it, and you can definitely hear the equalization effect. A low Q lets you control an octave or more at once, and can be subtle enough to sound like a characteristic of the original sound. Figures 16.1 and 16.2 show the response curve of a typical

---

[5] Very precise equalization also adds a unique distortion. This is the result of mathematical compromises that have to be made, and exists even on the best plug-ins.

[6] A comb filter, which is actually a delay technique rather than an equalizer, can be effective on power-line buzzes. Details later in the chapter.

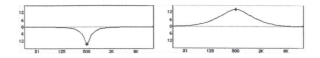

Figure 16.1 Equalizers set for 12 dB loss *(left)* and boost *(right)* at 500 Hz, with a low Q.

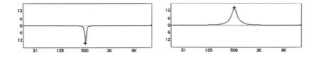

Figure 16.2 The same equalizers with a high Q.

✴ TIDBIT

Hearing an equalizer

Even with trained ears, it can be difficult to spot that a clip has been equalized you're very familiar with an unequalized version. Some instruments or harmonics might be emphasized and others reduced, but the question always arises: *Did it sound this way in the original clip?* Differences in miking, acoustics, and performance can change the "apparent equalization" of a recording before any effects are applied.

So to demonstrate equalization, I prepared a montage with instrumental music, male and female dialog, vocal music, and pink noise.[7]

Sound 16.1 is our basic test montage, unprocessed, for reference. Keep it handy for comparison with the equalized versions.

Sound 16.2 is the montage run through the equalizer in Figure 16.1, set for boost. **Sound 16.3** has that equalizer set for loss. You may notice that dialog seems to be affected more than the music. That's because we spend most of our time listening to unprocessed voices in the real world. Music can be equalized more than dialog, because we're used to recorded versions where playing styles and recording techniques vary.

---

[7] Pink noise is a test signal that has equal power in every octave. It sounds like a constant *sssh*, almost like ocean surf without the back-and-forth motion. It's good for these demos because it's sure to have something going on at each frequency we're equalizing.

peaking equalizer. (All the equalizer curves in this chapter are from screenshots of Waves' Renaissance plug-ins. You can see what the program's full screen looks like in Figure 16.8.)

As the Q gets higher and the equalizer gets more selective, it will add a small amount of distortion to frequencies just outside its range. This is a fact of equalizer life and has nothing to do with the particular brand or design.

- A very high-Q boost can be so sharp it resonates, ringing like a bell when its exact frequency is sounded. **Sound 16.4** shows this, with a Q of 30 on a 24 dB boost at 300 Hz.
- A similarly high Q, set to cut instead of boost, can pick out some kinds of noises and eliminate them completely from a dialog track. This is most effective if the noise doesn't have many harmonics or starts at a very high frequency.
- A peaking equalizer, set for a low Q and moderate cut, can help dialog recordings that have too much boominess because of room reverb.
- A low Q of .5 for a boost of 6 dB around the 6 kHz range can increase the perceived brightness of a track without increasing the noise. **Sound 16.5** lets you hear this effect.

Some NLEs don't let you listen to an equalizer while you're adjusting its frequency. But you can use a workaround. Set keyframes on the frequency adjustment, so it will sweep the range you're interested in while the clip plays (Figure 16.3). Preview the effect. When you hear the sound jump out, stop and note the exact frequency; this may require jogging back or forth a few frames to find where the sound is the loudest. Remove the keyframes, and set the equalizer to that frequency.

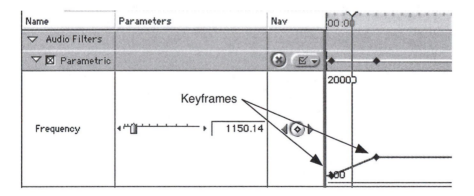

Figure 16.3 Using keyframes to find a frequency for equalization. These settings will sweep from around 500 Hz to 2 kHz over about ten seconds.

✔ TIP

How to tune an equalizer to fix problems

If you want to use a high Q and large cut to eliminate a pitched noise, or a lower Q and moderate cut to remove boominess, it's important to find the precise frequency. Not even a trained engineer can listen to a problem and immediately dial up the right frequency. But there's a trick professionals use:

1. Set the equalizer for maximum Q and maximum *boost*, even though you're intending to eventually cut.
2. Start the track playing, and sweep the frequency control slowly around the area where you think the problem might exist. For room boominess, try 100–300 Hz. For whistles, try 1–3 kHz. Mechanical and other noises can live almost anywhere, so just start sweeping from 100 Hz; you'll find their exact frequency in the next step.
3. At one point while you're sweeping, you'll hear the noise or room resonance jump out at you. It may even burst into crackling distortion. Move the frequency control up and down very slowly, around this point, to find the exact frequency.
4. Turn the decibels control from maximum boost, which you set in the first step, down to maximum cut.
5. Now, fine-tune the amount of correction you'll want. Try reducing the amount of cut if something important is also being affected. If you're removing a single whistle or other tone, leave the Q high. If you're trying to compensate for room acoustics, lower the Q until things sound good.
6. If the offending sound has been lowered but there's still some remaining, we're probably hearing harmonics at a higher frequency. Repeat steps 2–4, paying particular attention to the frequency exactly twice as high as the one you found on the first pass.

Sound 16.6 shows this technique. It's a factory workroom with some unidentified machine. There's a low frequency of a motor starting at around two seconds, and then a whine that lasts about three seconds. This repeats throughout the clip. The whine fights dialog, so we want to get rid of it without significantly changing the factory sound or the rhythmic motor startup.

The first part of Sound 16.6 is the workroom as originally recorded. In the second part, I'm sweeping a very high Q boost to identify the whine's frequency. I start getting near it about 33 seconds into the soundfile, then I hunt more slowly to fine tune the equalizer. (The Q is so high that after the clip ends, at 43 seconds, you can hear the equalizer ringing.) The third part of Sound 16.6 is our processed factory; the only thing I've changed is dialing the equalizer to dip instead of boost. We hear all the details of the original clip, including the motor start. But the whine is gone!

✔ TIP

Beware of Mr. Smiley!

Graphic equalizers are often set to a "smiley" curve by beginners (and boom box owners), boosting the extreme highs and lows as much as 12 dB, but leaving the mids untouched.

   This is rarely a good idea for soundtrack production.

- Dialog lives in the midrange, so equalizing a mixed track with a smiley will make it hard to understand.
- Applying the smiley to music tracks in a film isn't much better: the extreme boosts can add noise and distortion, and the extra level can cause TV processors turn down the entire track . . . making any dialog even harder to understand.

Graphic equalizer

A graphic equalizer is really just a bunch of peaking equalizers with fixed frequencies and overlapping bandwidths (Figure 16.4 shows the one in iTunes). Graphics are the easiest kind of equalizer to use, since the knobs draw a graph of the volume at different frequencies. But they're also the least useful: the factory-set frequencies are seldom the best for a specific use, and the Q can't be adjusted.

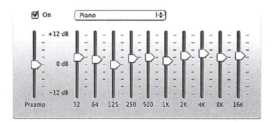

Figure 16.4 A graphic equalizer is no big deal, just a bunch of peaking equalizers with their frequency and Q preset at the factory.

Shelving equalizer

Shelving equalizers (Figure 16.5) apply a controllable amount of boost or cut to sounds above or below the specified frequency. They always have a level control and may have frequency and Q

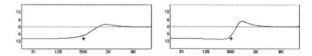

Figure 16.5 Low-frequency shelving equalizers set for –10 dB below 500 Hz, with low Q *(left)* and high Q *(right)*.

controls. The bass and treble controls on your stereo are fixed-frequency shelving equalizers. Shelving equalizers are most useful when you want to apply a broad, gentle correction. However, too much of a shelf can run the risk of boosting noises at the extremes of the spectrum. **Sound 16.7** lets you hear the high-Q shelf in Figure 16.5.

Filters

Cutoff filters, also known as high- or low-pass filters (Figure 16.6) are extreme shelving equalizers, throwing away any sound above (i.e., low-pass) or below (high-pass) the cutoff frequency. Their design lets them have much sharper slopes than shelving equalizers, without the disadvantages of a high Q. In fact, most cutoff filters don't have level or Q controls;[8] they can be used only to reject sounds beyond a desired frequency.

Cutoffs are useful for noise control or removing parts of a sound that can interfere in the mix. Low-pass filters above 8 kHz or so can be helpful for removing distortion from acoustic instrument recordings.

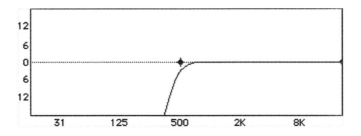

Figure 16.6 High-pass filter (also known as low-cut) at 500 Hz.

The cutoff filters in most NLEs are fairly gentle, reducing 6 dB per octave (as opposed to the 18 dB/octave filters I used for the diagnostics in Chapter 1, Sounds 1.9–1.14). If you're using one to reject a sound, this gentle slope can affect desired sounds as well.

You can increase the slope of a gentle filter by using multiple passes: each time though the filter adds 6 dB/octave. If you're using an audio program, apply the process multiple times (but keep a backup of the original audio in case you go too far). Some programs let you assign multiple filters to the same clip. Figure 16.7 shows how this looks with three high-pass followed by a low-pass. (The frequencies shown will simulate a telephone conversation.) Be aware that multiple filters can stress a program's real-time capacity. You might not be able to hear the effect until you render a preview.

Parametric equalizer

A parametric equalizer gives you complete control, usually with three or more peaking sections, and individual controls for frequency, level, and Q. A software-based

---

[8] A few cutoff filters have a Q control. Leave it at 1 or below for filtering; anything higher can cause boxy or peaky resonances.

parametric like Waves' Renaissance (shown in its entirety in Figure 16.8) lets you change the function of each section, so you can have cutoffs, shelving, and peaking at the same time.

Automatic equalizer

Since a spectrum analyzer (Chapter 12) can tell you how much energy a signal has in each frequency band, you could set one up to control an equalizer and—theoretically, at least—make the timbre of one sound match another. You'd run an ideal track through the analyzer to capture its "soundprint," analyze your own material with it, and the have the equalizer boost or cut your signal in each band to compensate for the differences. Logically, this would be a good way to make ADR match a production recording, or process an entire mix to make it match the latest Hollywood opus of the same genre.

Equalizers with this feature are sometimes used by music producers in hopes of turning their assembly-line pop song into a chart-buster. They don't work very well because lyrics, melody, arrangement, and performance are a lot more important to liking a piece of music than its spectral distribution.

Automatic equalizers have limited value in film production. The amount of energy at a particular frequency depends on the content, not just the recording technique; two different words from the same line of dialog will have different patterns, and so will two different scenes from the same movie. So there's no such thing as an ideal timbre to match, even for production dialog.

In theory, you could use a matching equalizer make one shot in a scene match another, reducing any discontinuity at the

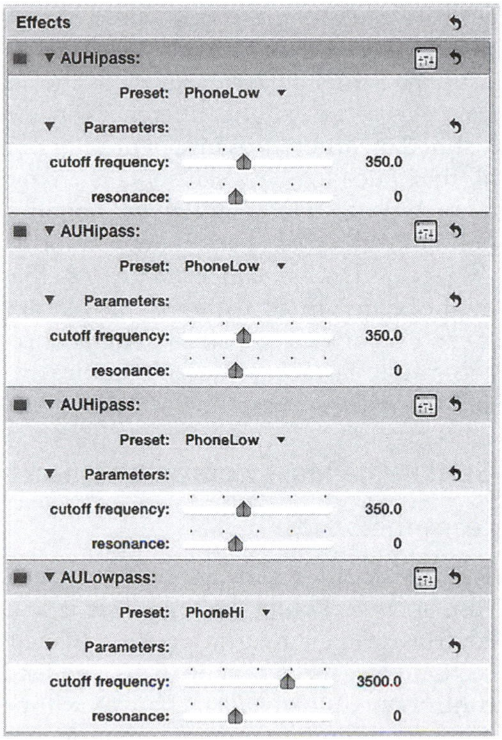

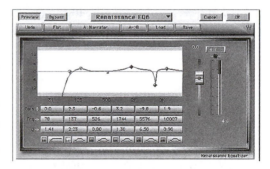

Figure 16.7 You can stack multiple high-pass filters for a sharper effect. This setup makes a good telephone effect.

Figure 16.8 A parametric equalizer set for one cut and five peaking sections.

cut between them. But this would work only if the actors delivered both lines exactly the same way. Some friends have reported using them for ADR—where the goal is to have the actors perform exactly as they did at the shoot—but still have to trim by ear.

We accept slight differences in timbre as a scene develops, particularly if it's justified by differences in shot or actor projection. If dialog is recorded properly, usually all that's needed between shots is a crossfade and level adjustment.

A new style of automatic equalizer couples the above analysis with a neural network, which has been trained to recognize normal speech and music. Programs like Zynaptiq's Unfilter can listen to a less-than-perfect recording, analyze what deficiencies might be due to acoustics or mic placement, and adjust its equalizers to compensate. It can't do anything a skilled engineer couldn't match with conventional plug-ins, but is certainly faster and doesn't require an experienced ear. Keep an eye on user groups and magazines to see how this category of processor develops.

Getting the most from an equalizer

Learn the bands

The best tool for learning how to equalize is the equalizer itself. Grab a short voice clip, such as **Sound 13.2**, and set it to play continuously. Start with all of the level controls in their neutral position (usually marked 0 dB) and the Q around 7. Pick a section, raise its level about 6 dB, and listen to the audio while you sweep the frequency control very slowly. The changes will be subtle as you move from one frequency to the next, but try to give a name to what you hear: *boomy, powerful, harsh, bright*— whatever comes to mind. Then turn the section's level as far down as it'll go, and sweep through its frequencies again. Lowering a few frequencies can make some signals sound better. Then try the whole thing again with some music (**Sounds 14.3** through **14.6**). You'll hear different effects depending on the type of material.

Ears get used to equalization very quickly, so keep going back to the unequalized sound as a reference, and don't spend more than 10 or 15 minutes at a time on this exercise. Do this a few times, and you'll start to learn exactly where to set those equalizer knobs for the sound you want.

✍ TRY THIS

Another way to learn

I've prepared a Web page that teaches you to identify frequency ranges. Sample male and female voices, and music in various genres, are broken into octave-wide bands. Each band is explored with spectrograms—graphic representations of time and frequency—and specially prepared sound files.

Go to www.dplay.com/tutorial/bands.

Overequalization

Once you learn how to hear subtle differences, you can avoid the most common equalizer mistake: setting the knobs too high. Equalizers are volume controls, and too much volume causes problems—particularly in digital systems. Check volumes along the entire equalized track. A 12 dB boost at 5 kHz may help the strings at the start of a piece of music, but it'll cause an awful clatter when the cymbal comes in. (Far better to use a 6 dB boost around 10 kHz.)

- As a general rule, don't raise any control higher than 6 dB—that's a one-bit boost, in digital terms—and remember that overlapping bands have their levels added together. Save the more radical settings for special effects, or to rescue badly recorded tracks.
- You usually shouldn't turn all the knobs in the same direction. If everything's boosted, the signal won't sound better—just more distorted.

Unless you're fixing specific noises at the extremes of the band, almost all equalization takes place between 200 Hz and 10 kHz . . . with most of it under 3 kHz. If you're equalizing much beyond these frequencies, you're probably adding noise.

Equalizer tips

If you're in a hurry, these ideas can help you get started. But don't treat the settings as gospel. Every track is slightly different, and every equalizer contributes its own sound.

- **Strengthen an announcer.** Cut off everything below 90 Hz—those frequencies are just wasting power. Then try a gentle peak (3 dB, Q = 7) around 240 Hz for warmth, and a similar boost around 1.8 kHz for intelligibility. A sharp dip (–18 dB, Q = 100) around 5 kHz can help sibilance.
- **Help fix muddy dialog** with a cutoff below 150 Hz, and a 3–6 dB boost (Q = 7) around 2 kHz.

✔ TIP

Turn the knobs counterclockwise!

Remember, equalizers can be turned *down* as well as up. If a voice is getting lost under the music track, don't look for a way to boost the voice. Instead, dip the music a few decibels, around 1.5–2 kHz.

Doing it this way lets the music show through without changing the voice timbre, so the overall mix continues to sound natural.

- **Make music more intense.** If there's no singing or spoken words that'll be affected by the equalizer, try boosting the bass notes (6 dB, Q = 3) around 100 Hz, and add a 6 dB high-frequency shelf around 3 kHz.
- **Simulate a telephone conversation** with the setup in Figure 16.7.
- **Tune out hum or whistles** with multiple sections of a parametric. Turn on just the lowest frequency section, and tune it using the technique explained under "Peaking equalizers." Then turn on the next higher section and tune it the same way, starting around twice the frequency you found for the first. Continue until the sound is fixed or you run out of sections.
- **Reduce distortion.** If a natural sound doesn't have many harmonics (Chapter 1), you can often clean up bad recordings by applying a sharp high-frequency cutoff filter. This not only eliminates hiss; it also reduces the artificial harmonics that a bad analog recording can generate. Start with the equalizer as low at 5 kHz, and then slowly raise its cutoff frequency until the recording doesn't seem muddy.

COMPRESSORS

In the real world, the difference between loud and soft adds excitement to what we hear. But in the electronic world of a film or video track, loud causes distortion and soft gets lost in electronic noise. Used properly, a compressor can control those pesky level changes—and make a track sound louder—without affecting its dynamic feel. But used the wrong way, a compressor turns tracks into bland, unlistenable mush.

It's easy to misuse these things. That's because the best compressors have a daunting array of knobs with relatively non-intuitive names. Experts need this much control to properly shape the sound, because every element has its own dynamic footprint and should be handled differently. When you finish this chapter, you'll be on the way to expertise . . . and will know how to reach for the right knob every time.

What happens inside a compressor

You can understand how a compressor works with a couple of simple graphs. There's no calculating or complicated numbers involved, just tracing your finger up a line on the page or screen.

Compressor input and output

The graphs starting with Figure 16.9 show how volumes can be affected by a compressor. Sounds coming in are displayed on the vertical axis: loud is at the top, soft is at the bottom. The signal travels to the black diagonal line, and reflects down to the horizontal axis. That horizontal line shows the output: soft on the left, loud on the right.

Ratio

Just about every compressor has a knob marked RATIO. In Figure 16.9, the ratio is set to 1:1. What comes out is the same as what went in. But in Figure 16.10, we've set the ratio to 3:1. The angle is steeper. If you trace the dotted lines, you'll see that loud sounds still come out, just about as loud as they went in . . . but soft sounds have been amplified! They're now louder than they were. What was a large volume range going in becomes a small one coming out. Ratios can get as high as 100:1 when a compressor is being used to control peak levels.

Threshold

There's a problem, unfortunately. If you look at Figure 16.10, a very soft signal—say, around 5% on the input axis—also gets boosted. This could easily be stuff you wanted to keep soft, like room noise or camera hiss.

We fix the problem by putting a little kink in the ratio line. Figure 16.11 shows how it works. Below the bend, the ratio is still 1:1 . . . and soft sounds aren't affected. The location of this bend is usually set by a THRESHOLD control, and its abruptness may be adjusted by a KNEE control. Some compressors have a fixed threshold and let you adjust the overall INPUT level around it. The effect is the same.

Gain and gate

You'll notice that the outputs of Figures 16.10 and 16.11 don't get very loud. They've been lowered by the action of the ratio slope. We compensate with an OUTPUT or MAKEUP GAIN control (Figure 16.12). This acts like a simple amplifier on the output, and lets us apply compression while making the entire signal louder.

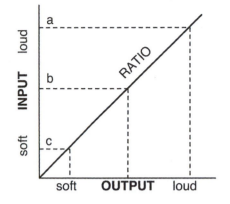

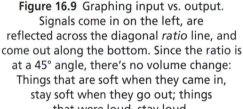

Figure 16.9 Graphing input vs. output. Signals come in on the left, are reflected across the diagonal *ratio* line, and come out along the bottom. Since the ratio is at a 45° angle, there's no volume change: Things that are soft when they came in, stay soft when they go out; things that were loud, stay loud.

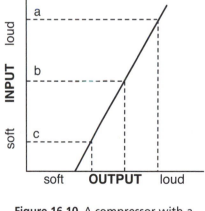

Figure 16.10 A compressor with a ratio of 3:1.

You might also have a GATE adjustment to control noise. Signals softer than its setting are totally cut off. You can see this in Figure 16.13, where a very soft signal doesn't make it to the output at all. (A noise gate is a processor with this function only.)

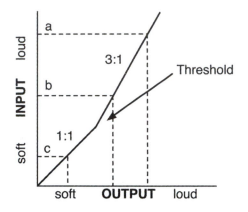

Figure 16.11 Adding a threshold control, so soft sounds aren't affected.

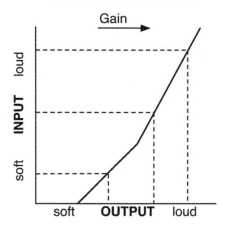

Figure 16.12 Adding makeup gain, so loud sounds stay loud.

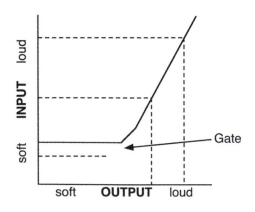

Figure 16.13
A gate turns the signal off, when the input goes below a threshold.

The gate works like a fast on-off switch, totally silencing a signal when it falls below the threshold, but turning on when the signal gets louder. Total silence can sound unnatural, so noise gates often have BYPASS or THROUGH controls to let a little signal through when they're in the off condition.

Some compressors have a "gated compression" feature, which isn't the same as a noise gate. In a real compressor circuit, the slope of our drawings is replaced by an amplifier with continuously variable gain. Gated compression freezes the gain of that amplifier whenever the input drops below a preset level, so soft sounds can pass through it without being boosted unnaturally.

Using the compressor

- The best way to adjust a compressor is by ear, with a sample of the actual program material. If you can, keep looping the same five- or ten-second section so you can be sure you're hearing differences in the compression rather than changes in the source. Adjust only one knob at a time, until you're sure of its effect.
- Good compressors also have a GAIN REDUCTION meter. These tell you how much the signal is being lowered, and usually look like a volume meter that stays at full level when there's no input, but then goes down as the input gets louder. (It's measuring how much we're

controlling the volume, so *loud* inputs make the compressor turn its internal volume knob *down* . . . get it?) Keep an eye on the Gain Reduction meter. It should be bouncing in time with the input. If the meter stays at a fixed value, the threshold or time constants (see below) are set wrong, or you're overloading the input. In either case, the compressor isn't doing much to the signal other than providing distortion.

- If you set a high THRESHOLD (or low INPUT), a high RATIO, and sharp or hard KNEE, the compressor will just regulate extreme peaks to avoid overloads. This setting preserves most of the dynamic range, and is often used during original recording. **Sound 16.8** is an example: listen carefully because the effect is subtle; about the only place you can hear a slight volume reduction is on the word "Acme".
- On the other hand, a lower THRESHOLD and RATIO squeezes the volumes together, making a narration stronger or music easier to mix. Since this affects the overall feel of a track, it's best left until the final mix. You can hear this kind of compression on **Sound 16.9**.
- High ratios tend to emphasize any distortion in the sound. Even the distortion of an extra analog-to-digital conversion can become audible in a heavily compressed track.
- Don't obsess about MAKEUP GAIN while you're adjusting other knobs. After you've got things set the way you want, fine-tune the makeup to get a good level on the compressor's output.
- Compressors exist to make volume ranges smaller, which can be an essential function for broadcast, Web, or home-video projects. That's because the track often has to compete against a narrow range playback system and high ambient noise. On the other hand, theatrical film tracks are generally played on high quality systems in large, soundproof rooms—and the fact that these rooms are darkened, except for the screen, makes it even easier for a viewer to pay attention. So compression is used a lot more gently on film mixes, usually just as protection against sudden overloads.

Compression in the fourth dimension

Those graphs can't illustrate one important aspect of compression: time. Remember *envelopes* from Chapter 1? A compressor has to be set so it responds to the volume of a sound (black wavy line in Figure 16.14), but not be so fast that it reacts to individual waves.

Attack and decay controls

A compressor can be taught the difference between envelopes and individual waves, sort of, if you tell it how slowly the slowest wave is in your signal. Then it assumes changes that are slower have to be an envelope.

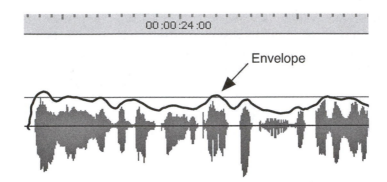

Figure 16.14 A has to be able to respond to an envelope but not individual waves.

This requires two additional controls: ATTACK determines how long it takes to pull the volume down when the input crosses the threshold; DECAY sets how long it takes to recover normal volumes after the input goes down. If there's a gate, it might have its own time controls.

- A fast ATTACK will protect you from momentary distortion or digital overloads, particularly with percussive sounds or sharp consonants. But too fast an attack can destroy the impact of these sounds.
- A fast DECAY can extend echoes and other sustained sounds by making them louder as they're fading out. (A guitarist's sustain pedal is really a compressor with a fast decay.) You can often increase the effect of reverberation in a recording by compressing it and changing the decay time.
- If both settings are too fast, low-pitched sounds will distort as the compressor tries to smooth out waves instead of the envelope. The fundamental frequency of a male narrator's voice—around ten milliseconds—is within the range of most compressors.
- A slow ATTACK lets the initial hit of a musical instrument show through in a mix, while keeping the overall track under control. Too slow an attack on a voice track can result in a spitty sound because vowel sounds will be lowered more than initial consonants.

Figure 16.15 shows how these time settings can change a sound effect. The first envelope (A) is a .357 Magnum shot at medium range, with no compression. B is the same shot with a slow attack and decay; only the initial sound gets through, so the result is more of a pile-driver clank than a bang. C has a very fast attack and decay; the hit is suppressed and the reverb emphasized, making it sound more like a big explosion. **Sound 16.10** lets you hear all these changes: when you listen, remember that all three were from the same original recording.

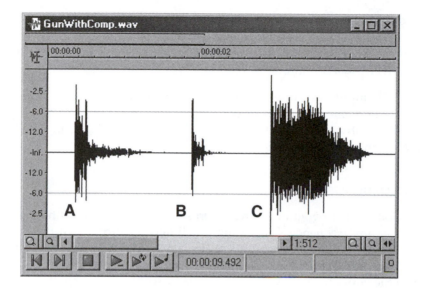

Figure 16.15 Changing the attack and decay controls can completely change a sound.

Sidechains

Compressors adjust their timing by applying filters to a control voltage, which is just a version of the input signal.[9] The timed version's circuit is called the *sidechain*. How we hook up that sidechain lets us do some useful things:

- The left and right sidechains of a stereo compressor can be linked together, so both channels are controlled identically and the stereo image is preserved. Or they can be unlinked to make the whole image swing away from any loud off-center sounds.
- The sidechain can be filtered to make the compressor react more to specific frequencies. Tuning it for sibilance turns a compressor into a de-esser.
- The sidechain can be patched to a different signal entirely. Put a compressor on a music track, while its sidechain is listening to the narrator, and the music will automatically fade down whenever the narrator talks.
- You can even make a compressor predict the future, by putting a delay in the main signal path but none in the sidechain. The sidechain hears things before

---

[9] The only difference is that the input is *rectified*, which means its negative voltages are turned positive. (The positive voltages aren't affected.) Since audio tends to move equally in both directions—negative and positive voltages, or compression and rarefaction of air pressure—averaging the movements usually gives you zero. No matter how loud or soft the audio, its negative and positive voltages cancel each other out. This is fine for representing vibrating molecules, which shift back and forth. But it's useless for measuring a sound's loudness or controlling a compressor.

they hit the main signal input, so it can adjust for sounds that are coming up. This is particularly useful for sudden loud sounds like gunshots, where a compressor's slow attack time might let some of the initial *bang!* through and cause overloads.

Sidechain inputs are often found in hardware compressors, but are almost impossible to implement in an NLE plug-in because they require extra signal paths. Some high-end software compressors include separate equalizers in the sidechain; a few DAWs support assignable sidechains.

Multiband compression

A compressor reacts to volume changes across the entire bandwidth of the signal; a loud sound at any frequency, low or high, will make it turn down the volume. This works fine for many applications. But imagine a mixed track with a narrator speaking over music that has a strong bass drum beat. Each time the drum is hit, a compressor would turn the entire track down and the narrator would get momentarily softer. This is what happened when radio stations first started playing disco! The transmitter compressors would ride the bass notes properly, but the strings and other sustained high notes would be put on a rollercoaster ride . . . down when a bass note played, back up when the bass let go.

The solution is to break the audio signal into multiple bands using filters. Each band gets its own compressor, usually with different timings, and then the multiple outputs are mixed together. When stations started using multiband compressors for disco, they started seeming louder overall because the midrange wasn't bouncing around. Advertisers liked this, so non-disco stations adopted them too. Soon, broadcasters were using more sophisticated multiband processors to sound louder than their competition.

Following the same principle, hardware- or software-based combination equalizers and multiband compressors are sold as final "loudness" generators in music production. These can be effective in video mixes, with a couple of warnings:

- Every other part of your signal chain has to be absolutely clean. The extreme processing emphasizes noise and distortion that would be normally hidden by midrange signals.
- You must build your own presets. The factory-set frequency bands and compression characteristics are designed for rock music, not for soundtracks where the midrange is most important.

Multiband compression can destroy many of the masking cues used by data reduction algorithms like mp3 and AAC (Chapter 2). If you're going to be combining these techniques, plan to spend a lot of time fine-tuning how they interact.

REVERBERATION

Real rooms have walls that bounce sound back to us. Recording studios don't, because the walls have been treated to reduce reflections. In real rooms, very close mics like lavs tend to ignore the reflections because they're so much closer to the actors' mouths. In both cases, the reverb-free sound can seem artificial.

This may be a good thing, if a spokesperson is talking directly to camera or a narrator lives in the nonspace of a voice-over. But reverb is essential if you want dramatic dialog to sound like it's in a real room: if you can't capture the real reverb of a practical shooting set, you'll have to add your own reverb to simulate it.

Real reflections

Light is the fastest thing in the known universe; at normal distances, its speed is so fast it appears instantaneous. Sound is a slowpoke by comparison: it travels about 1,100 feet per second, depending on air temperature.[10] A video frame is roughly $\frac{1}{30}$th of a second. So it can take a couple of frames for a drumbeat to reach the back of a large concert hall. If you're sitting in that hall, the drum's sound can reach you over multiple paths: directly from the drum skin, bounced off a side wall, bounced off the ceiling, and even bounced off that rear wall. Each path takes a slightly different length of time. And since the sound doesn't stop when it reaches your ear, each path's sound is then reflected over the other paths ... taking other lengths of time. Mix all those delayed drums together, and you've got reverb.

Figure 16.16 shows how it works. Imagine a concert hall roughly 45 feet wide by 70 feet deep. You're about 20 feet from the drum. There's no way you can hear that drum sooner than 20 milliseconds after it's played—two-thirds of a frame —because it takes that long for the first

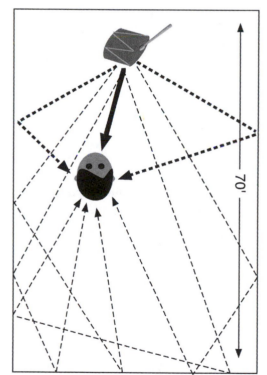

Figure 16.16 Reverb paths in a concert hall. It's the longer (dashed) paths that give the room its rich sound.

---

[10] There was an exhaustive discussion of this in Chapter 1.

sound to reach you. I drew that direct 20-foot path as a heavy black line between the drum and you.

But sound also bounces off the side walls and then to your ears. I've drawn two of those possible paths as heavy dashed lines. The one on the left is about 40 feet long, and the one on the right is almost 60 feet. You hear a second drumbeat at 40 milliseconds, and a third at 60 milliseconds. If these were the only paths, you'd hear a drum and two distinct echoes—it could sound like a giant stadium. A well-designed concert hall has plenty of other relatively direct paths, so these early echoes are mixed with others and you hear a richer sound instead.

Sound fills the room. Reflections bounce off the back wall, off the side to the back and to the ceiling, from one side to another, and so on. All of these paths—the dashed thinner lines—eventually reach your ears, but you hear so many of them that they merge into a barrage of late reflections. The longer the path, the softer the sound gets; in a well-designed hall, it can take many seconds to die out.

Of course, there are other factors. A concert hall, a gymnasium, and a hotel lobby can all have the same size and shape but sound completely different. That's because multiple surfaces determine how far apart the reflections are when they reach you. Also, the shape and the material of each surface affect the tone of the reverb. Hard surfaces reflect more highs. Complex shapes focus the highs in different directions.

Artificial reverb

Soundtrack producers have had a long struggle trying to create natural-sounding reverbs. Early film mixers set aside a hard-walled room as an echo chamber: they'd put a loudspeaker at one end and a mic at the other, play dialog through the speaker, and move the mic until it sounded like the concert hall or other room they were trying to simulate.[11] Then they discovered it was cheaper and more flexible to use a metal plate, suspended on springs, with a speaker on one end and mic on the other. As a logical (and even cheaper) extension, some later echo devices replaced the plate with a spring suspended in rubber. These spring reverbs were often included in guitar amps, and sold for home stereos.

Traditional (algorithmic) reverb

The first digital reverberators revolutionized recording. They generated reverb by building the delays in memory, and were cleaner and more controllable than anything mechanical. Digital reverb can have dozens of delays, each representing a different reflecting surface in an imaginary room. Since real surfaces reflect highs and lows

---

[11] Very early talkies would apply this reverb to exterior shots, because "everybody knows there's an echo outdoors." But the single slap of a voice off a distant canyon wall or building is nothing like the rich reverb of an echo chamber. These mixes sounded very strange. I guess people were thrilled that the movies could talk at all, so they excused this obvious artificiality.

differently—a thin windowpane may reflect highs and absorb lows, while a bookcase does the opposite—equalizers are included for the delays. To adjust the sound of a reverb, you control these delays and equalizers.

These reverbs are called *algorithmic* because they use a defined process of delays and mixing. A good algorithmic reverb lets you adjust the signal flow, letting you set:

- the timing and number of early reflections (up to about $\frac{1}{10}$th of a second);
- the density of late reflections and how quickly they build;
- the relative bass and treble of late reflections;
- how long it takes late reflections to die out;
- the relative levels of initial sound and early and late reflections.

By controlling those factors, you can simulate just about any acoustic space. Figure 16.17 shows some of the controls in one popular software reverb, Waves' TrueVerb plug-in. You can see individual early reflections over the first 50 milliseconds, and then a fairly fast decay of late reflections in this relatively small but rich-sounding room. (A separate panel lets you equalize the late reflections and control the overall mix.)

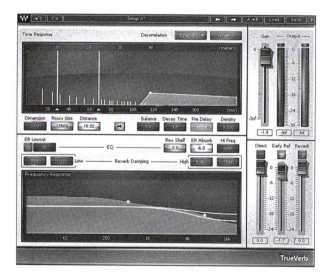

Figure 16.17 Waves' TrueVerb includes a graph of the reflections it generates.

Sampling (convolution) reverbs

Artificial reverb is a compromise: no practical computer has enough power to model all the reflections in a real room. So the softer reflections are simulated with a mix of random, cross-fed delays. It's a tribute to the cleverness of the early reverb inventors that they could sound good while using less computational power than a modern telephone. But even today's algorithmic reverbs are a simulation, mathematical tricks to do what acoustics accomplish in a real room.

Within the past few years, a totally different approach has become possible. Rather than simulate the reflections mathematically, *convolution* or *sampling* reverbs use actual recordings (called *samples* or *Impulse Responses*) of how physical spaces react to specific test sounds. They analyze how the spaces respond, and then duplicate the most recognizable parts of that response on your tracks. It takes a lot of math, but with a powerful enough computer, they sound almost like your clip has been recorded in the room that was originally sampled. Additional trims let you fine-tune the sound to complete the illusion. They can make a clean ADR line or foley effect sound like it belongs to the original production track.

There are a lot of sources for reasonably priced, high quality sampling reverbs now. One low-cost plug-in is LiquidSonics' Reverberate (Figure 16.18). There are also free plug-ins with more limited controls, and many DAWs now include sophisticated convolution reverbs as part of their basic package.

You'll need samples as well. Most plug-ins come with a good selection of halls, churches, and other rooms suitable for music mixing. The better ones also include offices and living spaces. Many sites offer free samples, and you can also record your own to exactly match a shooting situation. Search the Web for details on both.

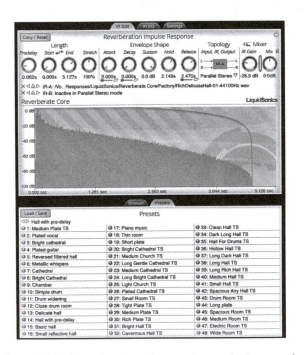

Figure 16.18 Reverberate, a low-cost convolution reverb.

Both kinds of reverb are important tools. Algorithmic ones have a lot more flexibility, and can be tuned for simulated environments and sound design. Convolution reverbs are more natural for real spaces. They can also simulate random noise in a sampled space, handy when you need roomtone for dialog editing. See page 375.

Practical reverb

The first place to control reverb is at the original recording, using the tips in Chapter 6. A good boom operator will strive for just the minimum natural reverb to convey a sense of space, knowing that we can add more reverb at the mix. ADR and foley recordings—and some tracks picked up by lavs—will have very little reverb at all.

To adjust an algorithmic reverb for normal dialog situations, turn its MIX control to about 75% reverb. That's far more than will sound natural, but is usually necessary to hear the effect for fine-tuning. If you have a choice of algorithms, choose Small Room. Then start Previewing. Adjust the REVERB TIME for something fairly short that doesn't interfere with intelligibility. Set DIFFUSION fairly high for most rooms, but a large totally empty room—say, a new house with no furniture—will have lower diffusion. Set the EQUALIZER or BRIGHTNESS toward the middle, with more highs in a room with plaster walls and fewer in a room with lots of curtains or wooden walls. Then lower the MIX until it seems right for the room and matches a boom sound; usually this will be around 20% reverb. A convolution reverb may have slightly different controls, but their overall effect is the same.

Many people believe reverb doesn't belong in voice-overs. Reverb implies a room around the voice, and a voice-over exists in limbo where it can talk intimately to us. That's an aesthetic judgment, of course—though it's one I agree with—and you can certainly try other treatments for voice-over.

Be careful when applying reverb to individual clips in an NLE or DAW. With most software, it can last only as long as the edited clip—which means the effect could cut out abruptly after the last syllable. Add some silence at the end of the clip so late reflections have time to die out. This may require exporting a new audio element that includes the silence, and then replacing the clip with the new version. If your program lets you apply reverb to an entire track instead of just to clips, this won't be a problem. Most audio software lets you send a track to a reverb effect, and then bring the unprocessed track up on one fader and just the reverb on a separate one. This is the most flexible way to work.

Be aware of the sound field when applying reverb. If you're applying it to a mono clip, or patching it into a mono track, the reverb will be one-dimensional and in the center of the screen. This is appropriate when matching ADR to mono dialog, since the production mic picked up the real room's reverb in mono. But it might not be what you want if you're using reverb to make an environment bigger, or smooth out a piece of music—those normally have stereo reverb effects. With most audio programs, you can either insert a mono reverb on a mono track, or send the mono track to a stereo reverb.

Algorithmic reverbs often have separate controls for the early reflections. Set them longer and farther apart to create very large spaces. (If your reverb lacks this feature, you can simulate it by putting the same clip on two separate tracks. Apply an echo effect to one track for the early reflections. Slide the second track later—about six frames for every 100 feet[12] from us to the farthest wall—and apply a long reverb.)

✳ TIDBIT

Hello . . . lo . . . lo . . .

Reverb and echo are different things. Reverb (at least in a good program) is a complex simulation of all the reflections in a real space, with various timings. Echo is a single or multiple repeat of a sound, with a fixed timing. The only time an echo effect can sound natural is in a large exterior setting with only one reflective surface—a canyon wall or a large building—or in hard-walled, perfectly cube-shaped rooms with no furniture or other features.

Removing reverb

Figure 16.19 Unveil, one of the new programs that actually reduce reverb in a recording. But they're not automatic, and can't perform miracles.

Real reverb is a complicated sound, and artificial reverbs add to the complication with random elements. No software can listen to a recording, decide what part of the sound was caused by acoustics and what was the naked sound coming from someone's voice, and remove the reverb part. But recent plug-ins come close. They use neural networking and large databases of what things should sound like, and are able to make reasonable guesses at what's signal and what's reverb. Figure 16.19 shows one of the first, Zynaptiq's Unveil.

Unfortunately, these programs can't go back and test the original room. So you have to adjust their analysis in various ways. Be prepared to spend some time with the software manual and critical listening. All of the processors have a BYPASS control and most have a button to let you listen to just the reverb; use these while you're experimenting.

They also can't eliminate echoes (as opposed to reverb; see box above) because that sound is too similar to the original, and can distort the sound if you try to remove

---

[12] Three frames for the sound to get there; three to come back.

too much reverb. On the other hand, Unveil can also control some audio gremlins that aren't reverb.

> <u>Bottom line</u>: don't expect miracles, and do read the plug-ins' documentation. If you're willing to work a little, the new de-reverberators can clean up recordings that otherwise might not be usable.

Old-fashioned reverb reduction

You can also reduce reverb *during pauses* with an expander. Set its threshold just below the program level, and let it reduce the volume when the input gets softer. When the source pauses, the expander will fade down the remaining reverb.

This effect can sometimes rescue sudden percussive sounds in reverberant spaces, for example turning an indoor parking lot car-door slam into one outdoors. But it won't rescue dialog, because any reverb stays at full volume whenever the actor is talking. If you need to clean this kind of continuous source, use a neural network de-reverb processor like Unveil.

Beyond reverb

Reverb isn't just for simulating rooms. Add it to sound effects and synthesized elements to make them richer. If you have to cut the end of an effect or piece of music to eliminate other sounds, add some echo to let it end gracefully. Reverb can also help smooth over awkward edits within a piece of music.

One classic studio production trick is "preverb": echoes that come before an element instead of after it. Add some silence before a clip, and then reverse the whole thing so it plays backwards. Apply a nice, rich reverb. Then reverse the reverberated clip. The echoes will build up magically into the desired sound, which lends an eerie sound to voices and can be interesting on percussive effects. (**Sound 16.11** lets you hear this effect on voice, and on the splash of a dive into a swimming pool.)

Always think about why the reverb is there. Does it match the room we see? Remember Hollywood's early mistake of adding reverb to exteriors . . . the studio executives just weren't *listening*.

Similarly, don't expect a reverb to necessarily make something sound bigger. In the real world, we associate reverb with distance, not size. Sure, we usually stand farther away from very big objects . . . so a large machine in the background ambience of a room would probably have reverb. But adding reverb does not make a voice-over sound bigger. It just makes it sound farther away, destroying intimacy.

Other delay-based effects

The same digital delays that are at the heart of reverb units can also be used for special effects. Multiple short delays, with constantly changing delay times, can be combined to make one instrument or voice sound like many; this is called a *chorus* effect. Chorus can be used to thicken a crowd or background sound, but keep the effect subtle.

A single longer delay, with a slower change in its delay time, can be combined with the original signal. As it does, different frequencies will be canceled or reinforced based on the delay time. This *flanging* effect imparts a moving whooshing character to a sound, and is often heard in pop music production. It can add a sense of motion to steady sound effects, increase the speed of automobile passbys, and is a mainstay of science fiction sound design.

Pitch shifters use the same memory function as a delay, but read the audio data out at a different rate than it was written. This raises or lowers the pitch by changing the timing of each sound wave, just like changing the speed on a tape playback. Unlike varispeed tape, however, the long-term timing isn't affected. Instead, many times a second, the software repeats or eliminates waves to compensate for the speed variation. Depending on how well the software is written, it may do a very good job of figuring out which waves can be manipulated without our noticing.

Comb filtering

Dimmer noise and other power-line junk can be very hard to eliminate from a track because it has so many harmonics. But one delay technique, *comb filtering*, is surprisingly effective. You need to know the precise frequency of the noise's fundamental. Divide one by it to get the period of the wave (if the noise is based on 60 Hz, then the period is 1/60, or 0.01666 seconds, or 16.666 milliseconds). Then combine the signal with a delayed version of itself, exactly half that period later (for 60 Hz that would be 8.333 milliseconds). The delay will form nulls in the signal, very deep notches that eliminate many of the harmonics. The nulls are so deep and regularly spaced, that if you drew a frequency response graph, they'd look like teeth of a comb.

The numbers in the previous paragraph are actually repeating decimals (such as 0.0166666666 . . .); I cut them off to save space on the page. Very few audio programs outside the lab let you set a delay this precisely. But you can simulate the delay in an audio program that supports multiple tracks, by putting a copy of the original clip on a second track and sliding it the right amount. For the most accurate setting, locate the actual noise waveform during a pause in dialog, measure its length, and slide the copy to the halfway point. Oftentimes, there'll be an inverted noise spike halfway across the wave. This visual adjustment can be better than trying to calculate the delay, since small sample-rate differences between camera and NLE can change the noise frequency from exactly 60 Hz.

The delay necessary for comb filtering can make a track sound slightly metallic. Reduce this effect by lowering the level of the delay around 3 dB.

Vocal elimination

In pop music production, the vocalist and most instruments are usually recorded with a individual mics, rather than in stereo, and then distributed from left to right electronically. The main vocal is put in the center of the stereo image, meaning its sound is identical on both the left and right channels.

If you invert the polarity of just one channel of the stereo pair, the vocal energy of this centered solo will produce a negative voltage on one side while producing a positive one on the other. If you then combine the channels equally into mono, positive and negative will cancel each other—eliminating the vocalist. Radio stations often use this technique when creating song parodies. It can also be used to lower the melody line in pre-produced music so dialog can show through.

This technique has limitations. It's useless on acoustic recordings such as live performances, or if pop music studio tricks like double-tracking have been used. It doesn't eliminate a soloist's reverb, which is usually in stereo, so the result can be a ghostlike echo of a voice that isn't there.[13] And it also eliminates anything else that was centered in a studio recording, which often includes critical parts of the drum kit and the bass line. Still, it's an amazingly effective trick when used with the right material.

Meanwhile, those neural network plug-in designers are working on ways to isolate soloists in mono and acoustic recordings.

NOISE REDUCTION

While comb filtering can reduce power-line noises, it's not effective against most other forms of noise found at a shooting location. Fortunately, there are other techniques.

Noise reduction by masking

Noise gates and expanders can make noise a lot less annoying, by turning everything down when there's nothing important going on. When there are meaningful sounds, the volume comes back up, but listeners' ears pay attention to the important stuff and ignore the noise. This is very similar to reducing reverb with an expander, described a few pages ago.

Noise gate as noise control

Noise gates got their name because this very simple circuit was the first available to control noise. Multitrack music and film studios would put them on every track, turning off electronic noise and tape hiss until their track had something useful.

You can still use a noise gate to clean up a recording. But unless the noises are very soft to begin with, you'll hear those sounds clicking in and out as the gate operates. For a lot of people, the on and off action is more distracting than constant noise.

One solution is to give the noise gate a slow decay setting, similar to the one on a compressor. When dialog stops, the background noise slowly fades down. Coupled with a FLOOR or RANGE control—to let some of the noise through at all times—this can be effective.

---

[13] A reverb elimination program (page 470) can help a little, if you apply it before trying to remove the soloist.

Expander

A better solution is an expander, which works like a backwards compressor: signals below the threshold are turned down, by an amount inversely proportional to their volume. The expander's threshold is usually set just below dialog level. Prop noises and footsteps are loud enough that they don't get affected very much. Background noise, during the pauses, gets lowered.

Multiband noise reducers

Gates and expanders only work well when the main signal has about the same timbre as the noise. If dialog has a high-frequency hiss, we'll be aware of those high frequencies even while somebody is talking: the frequencies in a normal voice aren't enough to distract us. (If we were trying to clean up a noisy piccolo recording, it would probably work fine.)

This problem can be solved by splitting the signal into bands, and expanding each one separately. In the dialog case above, a high-frequency expander wouldn't open at all because there wouldn't be enough highs in the voice to trigger it. But midrange sounds would control a midrange expander: when the actor pauses, any midrange noises get stopped; when she talks, her voice has enough midrange energy to distract us from the noise that's getting through.

This process of expanding individual bands to hide noise relies on *masking*, the same effect behind mp3 and other encoders. See Chapter 2 for more details.

Hardware-based noise reducers usually settle for a limited number of bands. One Dolby unit, popular in Hollywood during analog days—and still used—had only four bands; a multi-thousand digital unit now found in film studios has only a few dozen. But software can have hundreds of bands. Each band consists of a sharp bandpass filter and a downward expander. To use one of these programs, select a chunk of audio that has just noise and no dialog. The software measures the noise volume for each band (this takes only a few seconds) and sets the threshold just above it. Then process the entire clip.

Soundness' SoundSoap (Figure 16.20), a plug-in for Mac or Windows, is typical of powerful but easy to use noise reducers. There's also a totally free but effective version in Audacity (Chapter 12).

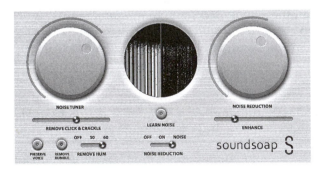

Figure 16.20 SoundSoap, a typical noise reduction plug-in.

Learning the noise
This kind of software sets itself using a sample of the offending noise. Generally, you play some noise that doesn't have dialog or other useful content mixed in, and

press a LEARN button. But the program doesn't actually record the noise, and doesn't try to subtract that learned signal from the recording.[14]

Instead, it analyzes how loud the noise is in each of the program's bands. Then it sets the band's thresholds slightly above the noise level. The assumption is that anything *louder* than the threshold is desirable signal. And there's the catch: if the noise is almost as loud as the dialog, the software can't control it at all. And if it's slightly softer, but still loud enough to be heard over dialog in a particular band, the processing will leave ugly artifacts.

Spectral noise reducers

There's an old joke about a man who needs surgery. The broken bones show clearly on his x-ray, but he can't afford a hospital. So he asks the doctor "Can't you just touch up the x-ray?"

A few programs have developed over the past decade that let you control noise by looking at an acoustic "x-ray," a spectrogram of frequency and level over time. You use various tools, including Photoshop-like brushes and magic wands, to select the offending noise.

If the noise is continuous, the program applies very sharp filters to remove it over the length of the clip.

If the noise is sporadic—say, a car horn in the middle of an exterior scene—it applies the filters only when needed. Then it fills in the filtered section with artificial sound, synthesized from what came before and after. **Sound 16.12** lets you hear an exterior clip, first before and then after this processing.

✳ TIDBIT

Smoke and mirrors

Most noise reducers don't.

Instead, they turn down the entire signal within a frequency band, when there's nothing interesting in the band you'd want to keep. If there *is* something interesting—perhaps because the frequencies are in the speech range, and someone is talking—that band's noise isn't stopped at all in that band. It shows through at full volume . . . but your ear locks onto the meaningful parts of the signal, and ignores the noise.

When the dialog pauses, the program turns that band down . . . lowering the noise, as well as anything else at those frequencies.

---

[14] It would be nice if it did. But real-world noise has too much random variation . . . and the slightest difference between the sample and the actual noise would make things worse, not better.

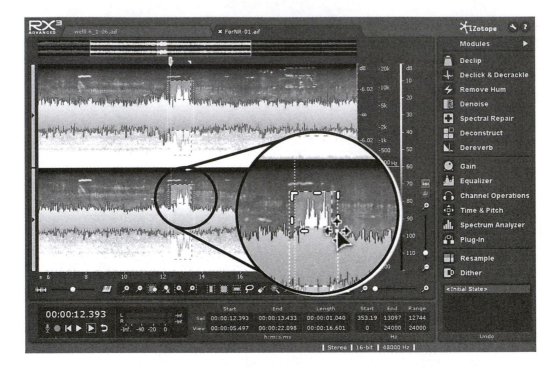

Figure 16.21 iZotope RX3, set for the car horn in Sound 16.12. I added the magnifying circle so you could see how just the horn is selected.

The leading program in this category is currently iZotope's RX3 (Figure 16.21). It can be daunting (and expensive) for casual users, but is impressive when used correctly.

Noise reduction strategies

Noise reduction works best when it doesn't have too much to do. The closer noise levels get to dialog, the more the algorithms are likely to introduce metallic whooshes and other artifacts. These can be controlled by fine-tuning the software—read the manual; these adjustments are never intuitive—but it's better to start with as little noise as possible.

- Don't assume that any on-set noise can be reduced in postproduction. Use the techniques in Chapter 6 to lower it as much as possible before shooting.
- Remove as much pitched noise as possible before processing, with a parametric equalizer, cutoff filter, or comb filter.
- To a noise reduction program, reverb can sound like noise. If the mic distance is too great, the reverb will contribute to those metallic artifacts. Use good boom technique or a lav (Chapter 7), and consider running a program like Unveil instead of a noise reducer.

- In general, two gentle passes will work better than one aggressive one. You'll have to re-learn the noise for the second pass, since it's been reduced. But this strategy can reduce chirps and other artifacts.
- Settle for some noise. A low-artifact, slightly noisy track is better than an artifact-filled quiet one.
- If you're prepping dialog tracks for a film mix, always bring an unprocessed version of the same track. Some of the processing artifacts get much nastier when you hear them on a good monitoring system or in a theater. Having an unprocessed version gives you some options.

COMBINING EFFECTS

It takes a lot of processing to make a really good soundtrack. Voices are usually equalized and then compressed, even in dramatic scenes, so they're easier to understand. Hard effects are almost always equalized to give them more impact, and then compressed to control their overall level; a gate may be added so they begin or end cleanly. Backgrounds are usually equalized so they don't interfere with the voice, and compressed to a constant level so they'll be easier to mix. A whole dramatic scene may have reverb added, or individual elements might get their own reverb so they match better.

Music should be equalized so it doesn't interfere with voice, but while compression on a music track can make it easier to mix, it can also destroy the dynamic rhythm of the score. Sometimes a little additional reverb, following the equalization, is all a music track needs to be mixable.

Source music, on the other hand, usually needs a lot of processing before it belongs to a scene. If a song is supposed to be heard through a radio or other speaker, use a high-pass at 200 Hz and a low-pass somewhere around 7 kHz, followed by some heavy compression and then reverb with very fast early reflections and a quick decay. This may be more radical than many real-world radio speakers, but the point is to sound *more* like a speaker than the scene's dialog—which, of course, the viewers are already hearing through their own speakers.

If a broadcast mix includes dialog and music, I usually add a little low-midrange peak to bring out the voices, followed by a multiband compressor with fast attacks and decays to bring up the lower-level sounds.

In general, it's most efficient to apply equalization before compression. The equalizer affects how loud the signal will be at various frequencies, which compression can then control. If you compress before equalizing, the compressor might be reacting to extreme high-or low-frequency sounds that'll never make it to the final mix. It's usually best to apply gating—if any—before the compressor so the gate has a wider range of levels to work with.

Reverberation can be added before or after the other processes. Equalizing before a reverb will affect the source sound without changing the acoustics of the simulated room; equalizing afterwards will make the room's walls harder or softer. Low-frequency sounds can travel greater distances, so shelving out some of the highs can make a long reverb seem slightly bigger. If you compress after a reverb, it'll change how long it takes late reflections to decay and make the reverb last longer.

Helping the effects along

While today's desktop computers are very powerful, the kind of processing necessary for a complicated mix can stress even the best system. The symptoms can be failure for plug-ins to load, a stuttering sound, or even a total crash. Serious mixers beef up their systems by adding chips specially dedicated to audio processing. These add-on digital signal processors (DSP) live either as a PCI card inside the computer, or a separate box connected by FireWire or Thunderbolt. Often they include some desirable plug-ins that would be too complex for a normal CPU to handle.

Learning more

Processing is a special category of mixing, and both the skills and the practical folklore go very deep.[15] Even though I've worked to keep this chapter as meaty as possible, there's a limit to how much I can fit in these pages. One of the best ways to improve your skills is practice, particularly with good speakers. It can take years to become a really good broadcast or film mixer.

You can speed up the process somewhat by using David Moulton's training CDs (moultonlabs.com). Moulton is a noted audio educator, Grammy-nominated engineer, and speaker designer. He put these discs together based on his experience training a generation of highly respected music mixers. While the course is oriented toward music production, the ear training is valuable to a filmmaker.

You might also want to check my other book, *Audio Postproduction.* It includes six separate chapters just on processing, with lots of audio demonstrations and cookbook recipes for common video and film situations. Since that book has so much more room to explain things, there are more practical examples and visual analogies for the technical concepts. It's available at the big online bookstores; details and downloadable samples are at my site www.dplay.com.

---

[15] I'm considered something of an expert, having designed the effects in a couple of big-name studio products. But my knowledge is nothing compared to some of the folks I've learned from.

CHAPTER 17

The Mix

There's a series producer who likes to come to my studio to finish her projects. Well, actually she likes to stand outside the studio, and watch me through a half-open doorway. She figures if a mix sounds good under those circumstances, it'll work well on the air. Considering how most people hear TV—with all the distractions, poor equipment, and random acoustics in the viewing room—she may be right.

If her shows were only for theatrical distribution, this technique wouldn't work. You watch theatrical films in a quiet room with a good sound system.[1] The darkened room and big screen help you concentrate. (Of course if your movie is successful in the theater, lots of people will eventually see it on broadcast and via streaming or DVD. So a good, clear small-screen track is still important.)

Unfortunately, no two consumer TVs, soundbars, or home theaters have the same sound quality. Even identical models can sound different, depending on their

---

[1] Well, *usually* it's a good sound system.

placement in the room and nearby furnishings or other absorbers. A TV track also has to be strong enough to fight air-conditioners, vacuum cleaners, crying babies, and other distractions.

Tablet and smartphone viewing has fewer acoustic problems, since the viewer is in the nearfield (Chapter 11). That's about the best that can be said for these gadgets: the speakers are unpredictably bad, with limited frequency response and high distortion. This is for physical and economic reasons: even if manufacturers could fit good speakers in devices that small, there's no profit in doing so. People don't buy these things for their sound.

It's a paradox, but the only way to make sure a track can survive one of these bad listening situations, is to mix it in a situation where you *can* hear everything. You can't fake it by mixing on an iPad or tiny computer speakers. Trying to optimize a mix while listening to one bad system, usually means it'll sound worse on any other bad systems. And it guarantees the film won't sound great best on a good system.

The best solution—and the one preferred by TV professionals—is straightforward:

- Do the mix on high-quality speakers, where you can hear even the tiniest variation in the sound. You should understand how poorer systems and lower listening volumes will affect your mix, so it's okay to use them for checking. Broadcast and music control rooms often have small speaker systems just for this purpose. You don't mix on these speakers, but they're there for playback. Theatrical dub stages almost never have this kind of speaker . . . you can listen large, or not at all.[2]
- Mix in a room with good acoustics, or keep the speakers so close that room acoustics aren't an influence.

☞ ROSE'S RULES

Don't touch that dial!

Once you've set monitor levels, *don't mess with them.*

Get your ears used to what a standard level sounds like on your monitors. The ear hears dynamics and low frequencies differently as the volume changes. That's why you have to stay consistent.

Mix with the key element—usually dialog—around that level on a meter. Dialog is relatively steady, so once you've gotten used to the right volume, you won't need to be looking at the meter very often. Adjust other elements by ear—not by meter—until they sound right for the mix and the story.

---

[2] I mix on small theater speakers in a controlled acoustic space, but also have a pair of classic Auratone 5" soundcubes to keep ad clients happy. I never turn them on unless requested.

- Control the monitor levels so your ears don't get fooled. Perceptions change with volume: when things are louder, your ears are more sensitive to extreme highs and lows, and it's easier to distinguish differences in envelope. On the other hand, loud mixing can mask some kinds of distortion ... a track that sounds good at high Sound Pressure Levels might be unintelligible for normal listening. Professionals generally set theatrical and broadcast monitors to SMPTE[3] standard: –20 dBFS equals 85 dB SPL at the listening position, when a single speaker is playing pink noise. That's for large dub stages; in smaller rooms, 83 dB SPL is generally considered appropriate. If you're mixing only for desktop or DVD use, make the same kind of measurements but look for 83 dB SPL at –10 dBFS. Whichever standard you choose, stick with it for the length of the film ... and ideally, for every other project you mix.

Mixing is a physical activity as well as a mental one. Your fingers are constantly tweaking the faders, and your eyes constantly darting between picture monitor, level meter, and tracks. It can be a little stressful. But it's worth the effort, because the mix is our last chance to get things right.

HOW TO MIX

Since mixing can be an intense experience, it makes sense to organize things to let you work as efficiently as possible. This requires the right tools and preparation. Most of the necessary hardware or software—monitor speakers, level meters, and effects processors—has been covered in Chapters 11 and 16.

Edit first, mix second, really *listen* third

Try to do all the editing and track building before you start the mix. When you're editing, you deal with short time spans, and concentrate on the same sound over and over. Mixing works best in long sweeps. It should be done as continuously as possible. That's how viewers will see your film.

It's inevitable that you'll be stopping during the mix as well, to change fader levels and refine how they move. But you'll still be thinking in terms of mix continuity. If you stop to edit, you'll be thinking about individual moments ... and continuity suffers. Besides, you'll get another chance to fix the edits, after reviewing the whole thing.

When you think the mix is finished, take a break. Then come back (ideally, after a meal or the next day) and review it without stopping. Sit comfortably in a darkened room, and equip yourself with paper or a tablet for notes, and a timecode reader on the screen. This is also a good time to invite the director, producer, or others for a review.

---

[3] The Society of Motion Picture and Television Engineers sets standards for a lot of things, including monitor levels. SMPTE is more than just timecode.

Start playing from the top. But if you hear something questionable, *don't stop*. Make a note with the approximate timecode, and keep going. It's amazing how many little things you can spot in a full length film, even if you've been working on the track for weeks: levels that aren't quite perfect become more obvious when you're watching the scene in context; dicey edits and random digital clicks are easier to spot because you're not concentrating on some other part of the same sequence.

After it's done, go back to each noted spot and fix as appropriate. (If there are other people at this review, you may have to play some politics. Fix the director's notes first, then the producer's. Finally you can address your own notes, as sound supervisor or re-recording mixer.)

Use your faders

Most film and TV mixes are done either on digital consoles playing multiple outputs of a DAW, or on a console-like controller for the DAW's software mixer. Both kinds of hardware look the same: there's a panel with sliding faders for each track, some knobs to control effects, and a few computer screens. They're both used the same way, too: the beginning of each scene is previewed while equalizers and other processors are adjusted, faders are preset to a good starting mix, and then everything is re-cued and played. The levels are then adjusted as the scene plays through. If there's a mistake or improvement, you back up and fix it.

Mixing for video or film is dynamic. A sound's envelope is constantly changing, so you have to constantly tweak those faders to keep the important sounds on top, without pushing other sounds so low that they get lost. It's typical for a mix engineer to keep one finger on each of the important faders, twitching them up and down a few decibels for individual sounds as necessary.

Even if you've got an arsenal of processing plug-ins or rack equipment, moving that fader is the most important part of mixing. It gives you the most control over how the story is told. So the one thing that's almost never done to a soundtrack is to leave the faders in one position for the length of a film.

Making pre-dubs

A film mix can have more than 50 tracks of dialog, music, and effects. Even with three mixers sitting at a giant console, it's too much to deal with efficiently. So similar elements are usually *pre-dubbed* or *pre-mixed*. Multiple dialog tracks that have been split by character or mic setup are individually processed, and then smoothly blended into a single track of continuous dialog for the scene.

There's another reason to pre-dub dialog. In any dramatized film, we're trying to create the illusion that this really happened to the characters, exactly as it's shown on the screen. The most important way to keep that illusion is *continuity*. We shouldn't be aware of how acoustics and background sounds change with each new camera setup, even though they're sometimes shot on different days. If the action is supposed to be continuous, hearing a change in sound quality is as distracting as a wardrobe or makeup change from one shot to the next.

Continuity is also important in a narrated or reality film, but intelligibility is even more important. Pre-mixing the narrator's tracks with any on-camera dialog makes it easier to keep these voices clean and understandable, even when other elements are added.

Sound effects are sometimes pre-mixed, depending on their complexity, to simplify things at the final mix. Music is almost always pre-mixed in music studios. It's supplied to the film as a finished master, or as pre-mixed groups of rhythm, melody, harmony, or other musical elements.

There may be more than one pre-dub within a category. Often, production dialog and ADR will be separated for ease of mixing, or plot-critical hard effects might be dubbed separately from foley effects.

This kind of mixing has to be done in pieces, stopping to reset processors and going back to see whether a different blend of tracks will work better. The idea is to take care of all the detail work first. It's like cleaning up all the branches and trees first, then stepping back to organize the forest.

A much smaller production might not have as many tracks. Projects with just a narrator or on-screen host and a few pieces of music, perhaps with a couple of isolated sound effects, are simple enough to mix at once. Pre-dubs won't be necessary.

✳ TIDBIT

What's in a name?

In a sound studio, "dub" means *duplicate*. Re-recording individual sounds into a finished track originally meant copying the combined sounds onto a new piece of film.[4] That's why a re-recording facility is called a dub stage, and the combining of tracks to prepare for a final mix is called pre-dubbing.

The term has stuck, even for projects that don't make intermediate copies. Many productions are mixed entirely within software. In this case, a dialog pre-dub is actually the process of writing automation for all the dialog tracks. Then automation is written for the other tracks. These pre-dubs are strings of numbers, representing fader and knob settings at different times.

Automation and pre-dubs

Pre-dubs were invented because the alternative—trying to mix everything at once on a big film—is virtually impossible. That would have taken an army of engineers at a gigantic console, each paying attention to their special area of the track, while a

---

[4] Optical soundtrack film in the early days, then replaced by magnetic film similar to that used in tape recorders. Both forms of film had perforations on the sides, so sprocketed gears could keep them in sync with the picture.

supervisor coordinated the overall sound. If one person made a mistake, everybody would have to back up and start again.

Pre-dubs let the mixing team concentrate on one category of sound at a time. It was a technical compromise, since the analog dubs always had more distortion or noise than the originals. But it gave filmmakers the ability to create more complex soundtracks . . . and studio owners the ability to produce tracks without hiring armies of technicians or investing in hundred-channel consoles.

The digital revolution made two big changes in this process. Digital recording, of course, doesn't lose quality with each generation. So the pre-dubs could be technically perfect. But a bigger change was computerized automation. Before automation you had to move all the faders in just the right way, at just the right time, to make a scene work. Forget one fader or miss a cue by a couple of frames, and you'd have to start over. It was a performance that required time-consuming rehearsals.

But automation records and repeats a movement forever. You can concentrate on just a handful of faders, get them right, and then let the computer recreate those moves while you deal with other tracks.

The first automated mixes literally replaced engineers' fingers with robots. Tiny motors in the mixing console moved fader knobs up and down, changing the volume in real-time. The motor assemblies were complicated and prone to breakdown, and the faders themselves could introduce noise. Today's consoles control the volume by manipulating digital samples in a CPU, but the motorized sliding knobs have been kept as a convenient user interface. It's noise-free and if a motor breaks, the CPU still does the right thing.

Mixing in the box

A digital console is really just a specialized computer with lots of knobs. If you didn't need the knobs, you could do the same operation in a modern desktop computer. Many projects today don't use a mixing console. Each track's audio samples are read from hard drive, multiplied by a stored value representing the fader position, and then added with the other tracks. All this—and the more specialized math required for equalization and reverb—takes place in real-time or faster, in the same computer. The computer then writes an audio file representing the final mix.

This process is often called *mixing in the box*.[5] All popular NLEs and DAWs include some form of it, though some are easier to use than others.

While the mix takes place in the CPU, the external controller is still important. Sliders and knobs make a great user interface for mixing, and if the sliders are automated with small motors, you can see their settings at a glance. But there's no audio in that controller. The sliders and knobs are just a sophisticated replacement for mouse and keyboard. There's more about mixing in the box, and these control surfaces, in Chapter 11.

---

[5] The name was originally intended as an insult, for no-budget films that couldn't get mixed on a dub stage. But computers keep getting more capable, and today many big dub stages are designed for this kind of mixing.

Mixing without knobs

If your setup limits you to using "rubber bands" or volume handles superimposed over tracks in a timeline, it's going to be difficult—or at least very time-consuming—to do a good mix. Figure 17.1 shows 20 seconds of a work in progress. While there's a lot of movement in those volume lines, it isn't anywhere near finished. We need to trim the background so it doesn't interfere with other effects, swell the music at the climax, and then fine-tune the whole thing so we're not aware of the mix when we concentrate on the drama. What takes the most time is the mouse-to-ear connection; each adjustment requires you to find or create a keyframe, click near it, drag, and then play over the section to decide if you like the result.

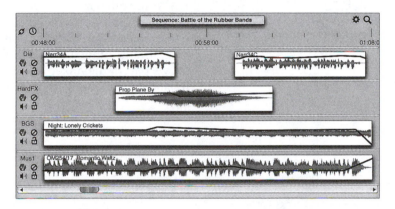

Figure 17.1 It can take a long time to fine-tune all those rubber bands.

✔ **TIP**

Try mixing in chunks

If you must mix with rubber bands and a mouse, you'll save time by working on a whole screen's worth at a time. Play back, change every track that needs adjustment, check your changes, and move on.

Virtual mixers

On-screen mixing consoles like the one in Figure 17.2 are an improvement over rubber bands. The fader knobs are a bigger target for your mouse than a keyframe or volume line, so you can grab the right control faster. But from the program's point of view, it's just a different interface for the same actions: as you move the virtual faders with automation turned on, the software plants keyframes and manipulates rubber bands on the timeline. If you go back to the timeline, you'll see each of your movements on

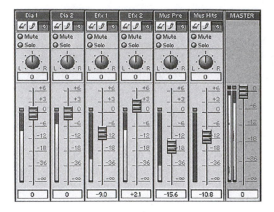

Figure 17.2 An on-screen mixing console in an NLE. You can move the drawings of knobs with a mouse.

the track and can edit them rubber-band style.

Virtual mixers are easier to understand visually than rubber bands in a timeline, and show at least how volumes and stereo panning are being manipulated in a mix. All have controls for the program's mix automation, usually on a track-by-track basis so you can read the fades on some tracks while writing new moves on the selected one. The virtual mixers in DAWs are often more powerful than those in NLEs; most add equalizers and audio effects on each track, and buttons to control routing and other functions. Figure 17.3 shows part of the mixer in Nuendo, a professional DAW used for post-production.

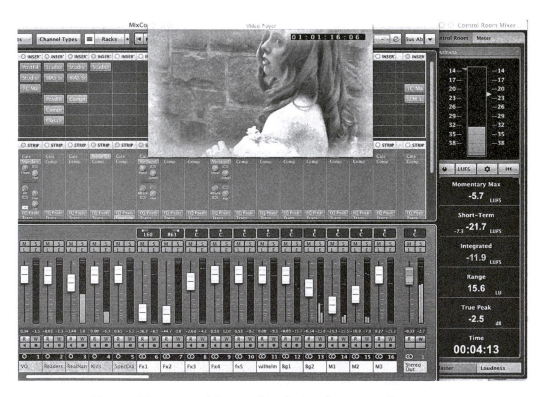

Figure 17.3 A more elaborate virtual mixer from an audio program.

On-screen mixers can work for music producers, where tracks tend to stay at the same setting, but they're less useful in film or video production. Mouse-based mixing can move only one fader at a time, and a film mix usually involves lots of moves at once—that's why there are two or more engineers at big film mixing consoles, even when dialog has been pre-mixed and presumably all its moves are done. As virtual mixers get more elaborate, they get even harder to use: you have to find the right point on the screen and get the mouse over it, while under the pressure of mixing a movie.

Not mixing

Many producers choose a middle ground, using their mouse-based NLEs for the simplest mixes and taking the complex ones to a separate audio facility. This can give you the advantages of better monitoring, higher-quality effects, and an experienced engineer.[6] There are some tips for getting the most from out-of-house mixes later in this chapter.

Scheduling

A two-hour feature can take a month or more to mix. At least half that time is spent creating pre-dubs, with most of those days devoted to dialog work. In a big film, backgrounds and other effects get their own pre-dubs as well. About a third of the time is used for mixing the film itself, combining the pre-dubs into realistic scenes and then adding music. A couple of days are reserved for reviewing and making final changes, and then technical operations.

Smaller projects can't take that long, of course. You can mix low-budget features in a week and a half, and ten-minute indie shorts in half a day. But the proportions of time spent stay about the same. If a project isn't using pre-dubs things will go a little faster, though it's still important to set aside time for getting the voices right before worrying about other elements.

Before you mix, don't

Wine tasters rinse their mouths out with water between critical sips, so they can detect every subtle aspect of the vintage they're examining. You should cleanse your ears for the same reason. Don't listen to anything at all for a while before starting a mix.

You may have spent hours or even weeks editing individual elements against the picture. It's only natural that you'll be hyper-aware of each of those editorial gems, and want them to sparkle in the finished product—even if they get in the way of the story. Plan for some time between building the track and mixing it. Even on short projects it makes sense to wait overnight, take a meal break, or at least go for a walk. Don't begrudge the extra minutes this takes; it can save you from having to come back for a remix. (Even though I charge for these projects by the hour, I'll stop the clock—and lose a few bucks—for a break. It always results in a better mix.)

---

[6] And pays my salary when I'm not writing books.

After you mix, listen

The review process discussed on page 272 is important. Don't ignore it. The film isn't done until you've listened to the whole thing, top to bottom, without stopping.

TECHNIQUES OF MIXING

Tracks and panning

The first challenge is figuring out what goes where. Most NLEs don't make this obvious. Mono elements, like narration or dialog, don't need two separate tracks. If you want to hear them on a pair of stereo speakers, use the PAN control to split the signal to both. If both speakers carry the same signal at the same volume, they mix together in mid-air. Your ear hears them as if they were coming from a speaker in the middle, even though there's no speaker there.[7] Engineers call this the *phantom center*.

✳ TIDBIT

What's left?

Don't confuse *stereo* with *dual mono*.

- Music tracks and ambiences are usually stereo, which means there are slightly different signals going to the left and right speakers. Violins on the left of the orchestra are louder on the left speaker, but may still be heard a little softer and later in the right one. Basses are primarily on the right; trombones, in the center, come out of both speakers equally. When you play both speakers, the ear interprets the level and timing differences as a continuous area filled with instruments . . . and the trombones sound like they're in the middle, even though there's no speaker there.
- Narrators and dialog are usually mono. The signal sent to left and right speakers will be identical. Put them on a single track and set the track's PAN to the middle.
- Theatrical surround mixes have a separate center channel, primarily for dialog. Its speaker sits behind the middle of the screen. If you're mixing theatrical surround, send dialog to that channel. If you're mixing stereo, split it to both left and right: if the film ever gets played on a surround system, the system's logic will route it to the center.

---

[7] If you don't hear it coming from the center, reflections in the room may be interfering. If you're in the nearfield so reflections don't matter, and you hear the sound distinctly coming from both sides but not from the center, chances are the speakers aren't wired with the same polarity. Fix this before you attempt any mixing.

The phenomenon works for mixes as well as solo sounds. You can have stereo music with different instruments on the left and right, and a mono narrator panned to the middle. When you play back, the music will occupy the full width between the two speakers, with each instrument in the right place. But the narrator will still come from that phantom center.

Things get complicated when you add stereo or surround elements. Some programs make you treat stereo as separate tracks for left and right, taking twice as much space on the timeline. A music cue mixed in surround might need five or more tracks. Each normally uses a separate fader, making the whole mix more difficult to deal with. If that's the case, look for some way to group the tracks to a single fader, or to link the tracks so they fade simultaneously.

Additional controls

Most mixers have MUTE and SOLO controls for each fader, like the ones near the top of Figure 17.2. These can be invaluable when setting up a mix, or tracking down problems. Their meaning is fairly obvious: muting a track turns it off temporarily; soloing a track leaves it turned on but mutes all the others. You can solo more than one track at the same time, if you want to hear that combination while muting everything else. Some programs let you record the muting action into automation, to eliminate a particular word or sound from the mix.

Protecting the center

As noted above, the center channel of a surround setup is for dialog. This is for dramatic reasons rather than technical ones. Dialog is assumed to be mono, coming from the center of the screen whenever its person talking is on-camera. There are good reasons for this.

Why not match characters' voices to their on-screen positions?
Panning voices as people moved across the screen could be a perceptual mess—what do you do when somebody jumps from the side of a two-shot to the center of a close-up? Does their voice jump? We accept a shift in point of view, during a scene, as part of the natural flow of film editing. But this kind of sudden shift in acoustic perspective only confuses things, and takes people away from the story.

Moving voices off-center can also cause exhibition problems. Depending on where you sit in the theater, subtleties of the story could get distorted.

Imagine two characters arguing in a two-shot. Mr. Lefty, on the left side of the screen, has his voice coming from the left speaker. Ms. Righty is on the right side of the screen and her voice comes from the speaker on the right. The director wants both characters to be equally loud and intense. That's how the actors perform the scene, and that's how someone in the middle of the theater hears it.

But what if you're sitting on the right front of the theater? You'll be much closer to Righty's speaker. Thanks to inverse-square, her voice will seem much louder than her friend's. If you're on the left, you'll hear Lefty's voice louder. In either case, what you hear isn't what the director intended.

Why not use the phantom center for dialog?

We could mix both voices to a single channel, route it to both speakers, and let the phantom center effect keep those voices in the center of the frame. But this works only for someone in the middle of the theater. If you're on the left side of the theater, that left speaker appears much louder to you. It's got both voices, but they appear to come from the left side of the screen instead of between the two characters.

Solution: A speaker in the middle

That's why we mix the mics together and route them all through a center dialog speaker, usually located behind the screen. No matter where you sit in the theater, voices come from the center of the screen. Dialog might seem softer for people sitting along the sides of the house than it does for those in the middle, but at least it always comes from the right place.

In fact, a 5.1 mix can have dialog in the center channel at the same time it's using the phantom center for effects or music! Pan the effects to left and right sides equally. The center-channel signal will often seem to be "in front" of the phantom center material, though this depends on the level and nature of the sound.

There are problems, of course. Anyone on the side of the theater will think those panned effects are coming from the side while dialog stays in the center. And if the film is ever be released with a stereo track instead of a surround one, or broadcast for home consumption, the phantom and center-channel material will fight each other. To avoid these problems, experienced mixers usually pan or otherwise spread non-dialog mono elements so they're not in the center of the screen.

Why we move the knobs . . .

A soundtrack can be thought of as a physical space, with mixing being the process of putting everything in its place. Things can be close to you or far away, and they can spread (to a limited extent, depending on the final delivery medium) across the left-to-right axis. If you're mixing for surround, sounds can even be behind you. But if two sounds try to occupy the same space, both will suffer.

Mix engineers use four specific ways to place sounds in acoustic space.

Volume

Obviously, louder sounds are closer. Just remember that only one sound can predominate at a time. Don't try to make *everything* close.

Don't try to make things very far, either, unless your project will be shown only in theaters. TV and Web video are not subtle media. If a sound effect or music cue seems to work best when it's very soft, try turning it off entirely. You might discover it's not needed. If you miss it, try to find some way—using effects or timing changes—to bring it forward slightly. Don't just leave it soft: there's a chance most viewers won't ever hear it.

Equalization

Music engineers frequently call the midrange equalizer a "presence" control. It makes a big difference in how close a sound appears.

Boosting the midrange, particularly between around 1.2 kHz to 2.5 kHz, tends to bring voices forward. If you turn a music track down in these frequencies, it'll leave more room for the dialog. Mid-low frequencies, between 100 Hz and 250 Hz, can add warmth and intimacy to a voice. Be careful about adding too many extreme low frequencies; they just add muddiness in most video tracks.

While you can't use equalizers to move individual instruments forward or back in a piece of mixed music, you can control groups of harmonics. Dipping the frequencies noted in the previous paragraph will make a piece of music work better with dialog, letting you bring the entire music track forward. This works for sound effects as well.

High frequencies get absorbed as sound travels through the air. It's not enough to be noticeable in interior spaces, but turning down the highs can add distance to exterior sounds.

Reverberation

It's an advertising cliché: the announcer shouts BIG – BIG – BIG SALE!!! with a heavy reverb. But reverberation doesn't make things bigger; it just makes them farther away.[8] That's because in the real world, as we get farther from a sound source, we hear more reflections and less direct sound. It's the opposite of the reflection-free sound from a nearfield speaker or a lav that's close to the mouth.

Use reverb as another tool for placing a sound in the imaginary space of a mix: more reverb sends it back, less reverb (but more volume) brings it forward. This applies more to interiors than exteriors. When you go outdoors, reflecting surfaces tend to be much simpler and farther away than the sound source, so you might hear one or two quick slaps . . . but not the rich reverb you'd get in a concert hall. In general, using a reverb on exteriors sounds artificial.

There is much more about equalization and reverb in Chapter 16.

Panning

Music and film mixers can also *pan*—adjust the relative left/right position in a stereo field, or surround position in more complex tracks—to help define physical space. It's most powerful when placing mono sound effects, to spread all the elements across a scene. (It's also essential when mixing music, to keep instruments separate while they're playing together, but that's a subject for many other books.)

Unfortunately, you don't have as much freedom for panning when mixing broadcast: even if a viewer has a stereo receiver, chances are they're not sitting exactly

---

[8] Well, if something is far away and we still hear it as loud, it's probably pretty big. But the primary effect is still one of distance, not size or immediacy.

centered between the speakers.[9] Most people keep their TV sets off to one side of the room, a position where they might as well be mono. On top of that, channels sometimes get flipped or even lost at a TV station or when a local cable retransmits it.

Many "stereo" TV shows are actually glorified mono. All the dialog and any important sound effects are strictly center stage. Only the music, background sounds, and audience reactions are mixed in stereo. This keeps the sound consistent and avoids disconcerting situations if channels are lost or flipped.

If you're mixing video for an environment where the playback system can be controlled, such as a theatrical release or corporate meeting video, you can do more with stereo. (But remember to keep dialog in the center, for reasons we discussed a few pages ago.)

Kiosk mixes don't even have to worry about putting dialog in the center. With a kiosk, you know exactly where the viewer will be: standing in front of the screen, centered between the speakers. Using stereo here can help capture the space, defining an area that's separate from the museum or office lobby where the kiosk exists. Just be careful not to create an image that's much wider than the screen itself.

Panning in surround

Volume, equalization, and reverb work essentially the same way to define 5.1 spaces as they do for stereo. Panning, on the other hand, picks up an additional direction.

There are two philosophies for surround panning. One is to keep all the action in front of us, and let the surround carry just the environmental background and reverb. This is the traditional position of an audience at a live dramatic performance. The other is to put the action all around you. It can be more exciting. But it can also be disorienting, since the image still comes only from the front. A reasonable compromise is to keep the action up-front, but let the musicians and large effects surround us.

If you're mixing surround on a project that might be used for broadcast, be wary of panning important sound only to the rear. Older sets and smaller cable systems might collapse your track to stereo. Depending how they do this, sounds in the rear might completely disappear! Most surround TV shows keep the important things front and center, just like a stereo TV mix . . . only the ambiences, audience reactions, and reverb from music are directed to the rear.

The time dimension

A mix's acoustic space also uses the fourth dimension, and every element should have its own place in time. Music isn't the only audio element with rhythm; dialog and effects have patters of stress and relaxation as well. If two stresses happen at the same time, they'll interfere with each other.

---

[9] I have a friend who produces corporate extravaganzas for a major company, often involving 5.1 mixes on film plus live dancers and elaborate sets. His home setup has a 50" screen . . . and all five speakers on one side of the room! (That's the only way they'd fit his décor.)

Watch out for voice rhythms that match the music exactly; this can happen during long stretches of narration. It makes the track sound dull, and detracts from both voice and music. The same thing can happen in a song, if the vocalist is a slave to the metronome.[10] Pop singers solve this by singing some words slightly ahead of the beat, and some slightly behind, depending on the emotions in the lyric. You can do the same with a narration track, sliding paragraphs when they land too squarely on the beat.

Tiny time

Traditional movie mixing used 35mm magnetic film for the individual tracks. It had four sets of perforations per frame, just like the picture did. But if a single sprocket slips in a film projector, you'll see the top of the frame cut off and applied to the bottom of the screen ... a clichéd comic effect for early movies, or cartoons where Daffy Duck looks up to his own feet and says "What are *you* doing up there?"

But audio doesn't have frame lines. If the mag film slips a sprocket or two, things will still sound fine ... just a little earlier or later. Engineers sometimes intentionally slipped music this way, to make it work better with dialog. Often a quarter- or half-frame works well, when a full frame just sounds out of sync.

Most DAWs let you slip tracks earlier or later while they're playing, without being constrained by frame lines; the better ones also have preset jumps of a quarter or half frame. Often you can set a keyboard shortcut for these jumps. Start things playing, tap the shortcut button, and try shifting in both directions to see if it improves things.

Video programs usually don't have subframe capability, though a few will let you stop, bring the audio clip up in a viewer, and nudge its in-point by less than a frame. It's a complicated process that makes before-and-after comparisons impossible. But there's a workaround:

1. Open the timeline, and slide the music track two frames earlier than you had it.
2. Apply a delay plug-in to the music clip. Set it for a 60 millisecond delay, with no modulation or feedback. Sixty milliseconds is close enough to two frames that the music will sound like it hasn't been moved at all.
3. Start things playing with the delay effect's panel showing. Adjust the delay time. Anything less than 60 milliseconds will make the music earlier than it originally was. Anything more than 60 milliseconds will make it later. You can jump in 15-millisecond increments if you want to respect the old quarter-frame tradition ...

If sliding the music disturbs a carefully panned hit against picture, copy the music onto two tracks and slide only one of them. Crossfade between the two during a sustained note and you get the best of both placements.

---

[10] In fact, I'll often refer to dialog that exactly lines up against music as being *square*, in a musical sense. Producers always seem to know what I mean.

Separating by distance

Humans have an amazing ability to follow multiple sound streams based on how close they are to the listener. While this function probably evolved so we could keep track of predators in the jungle, you can use it to separate individual sounds that fall in the same left-right position in a track. Since it uses basic presence cues, this trick works equally well in mono, stereo, or surround.

The trick is to simulate distance using timbre and reverb. You'll have the most flexibility if you start with two sounds that don't have reverb of their own, and share a common timbre: perhaps two narrators, both recorded in a studio.

Decide which should be pushed behind the other; that's the track we'll work on. Apply cutoff filters below 300 Hz and above 9 kHz. Lower the level very slightly, and add just a little bit of room reverb.

Now listen to both simultaneously. Chances are, they'll both be easier to follow than if you'd mixed them equally. Your brain can now sort out the voices, so it can process them separately!

Want an example? **Sound 17.1** has two studio announcers, one selling a car and one selling rocket sleds.[11] **Sound 17.2** plays them simultaneously . . . and is hard to understand. **Sound 17.3** has the processing applied to our sled salesman: chances are, you'll find it easier to understand than the previous example.

You can use this presence phenomenon in documentaries to separate an over-lapping narration from the interview without having to lose either. Use it to push crowd walla further into the background, so it doesn't interfere with dialog, or to layer two sound effects. One handy trick is to patch a single track to two different faders in a mixer, or copy it to two tracks in software. Apply the equalization and reverb to only one of them, and then crossfade between faders to move the sound closer or farther away.

Mix distortion

When two tracks are mixed together, the result is usually slightly louder than either one of them alone.[12] As you add more tracks to the mix, things get even louder. If you let them get out of hand, they'll be louder than the system can handle. If your system hasn't been set up with proper gain-staging (Chapter 12), there's very little margin for error.

When things get much too loud because you've combined a lot of loud tracks, you hear gross distortion and know to stop mixing. But the distortion can be subtle, occurring only on momentary peaks. Your eyes—and a calibrated digital level meter—are the best way to spot this. Don't rely on your ears alone because you can fool yourself into thinking that distortion has gone away by raising the monitor level . . .

---

[11] That's two Warner Brothers cartoon references in as many pages. It's the end of the book, folks, and I'm getting a little silly.

[12] How much louder depends on the individual waveforms and their relationship to each other.

☞ **ROSE'S RULES**

Six quick rules for better mixes

These apply whether you're the producer, director, or hands-on mix engineer. Ignore them at your peril.

Saving time on the mix wastes time

If you can't afford the hours to do it right, take shortcuts while you're editing individual tracks; a good mix will hide them. But don't take shortcuts while you're mixing, or else you'll have to remix it tomorrow

Pump down the volume!

Working with the speakers very loud may be exciting, but probably has nothing to do with what your audience will hear. Follow the rules on page 481, and don't raise the monitor levels just because "it feels good."

All distortion hurts

Listening at reasonable levels also helps you track down fuzziness in the sound. The ear expects—and forgives—distortion in loud sounds. Turn down the volume, find the distortion, and fix it. Otherwise, subsequent broadcasting or compressing will only make things worse.

It's never too soon to fix a problem

As soon as you hear something you don't like, back up and remix. Do this while you're still conscious of the overall flow. If you finish a scene and then go back, the new section may not blend in so well. You'll also run the risk of forgetting some of the places you wanted to touch up.

This, of course, doesn't apply when you're doing the final top-to-bottom review (page 272).

Don't be seduced by stereo or surround

It may sound impressive in the mixing suite, but unless you're headed for a theater, most of listeners will never hear things that big.

Watch TV with your eyes closed

If you're working on short-form projects like commercials, listen to the finished mix at least once *without* picture. You may hear a lot of rough spots that were easy to ignore while the images were distracting you.

Figure 17.4 Both mixes have the same overall level, but the one on the left won't sound as good. This works in software-based mixers as well as hardware ones.

another reason to never touch the monitor volume control when you're mixing. If you're working in a clip-based NLE, you might not even know there's distortion until you play the final rendered mix or look for clipped waveforms on it.

The best way to avoid distortion during the mix is to remember that faders go down as well as up. Build your final track by lowering some sounds as you boost others. While the two mixers in Figure 17.4 have the same output level on their meters, the one on the left is probably seriously overloaded; the fact that its master fader is set very low should be an immediate giveaway. Besides, lowering some of the levels gives you a wider physical range in which you can set the faders, for a more subtle mix.

Working with automation

Basic concepts

When you get right down to it, the most sophisticated automated in-the-box mix is based on rubber-band control lines, just like those in a basic NLE. If you move a fader while recording automation, the system creates points on a rubber-band line. During playback, the software adjusts the track's volume based on the line. Meanwhile, on-screen or motorized faders move up and down to match the line's position. There's more about this process in Chapter 11.

What makes automation so powerful is that the computer can play back fades you've already recorded, while you're perfecting the ones on other tracks. In effect, you can be moving as many faders, with as many virtual "fingers", as there are tracks in your project. Figure 17.5 shows the whole process graphically. I'm pushing a fader up for dialog, on channel 5, so it plays louder. As I do, the automation writes a point on the timeline to set that dialog's rubber band higher. Meanwhile, the fades I've already written on tracks 7 and 8 are playing back. While this particular console has only eight faders, they can be assigned as needed. Tracks that don't show up on a

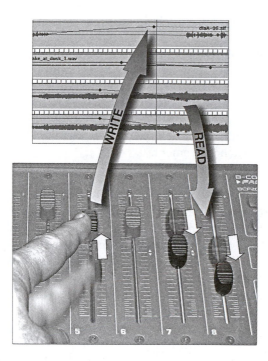

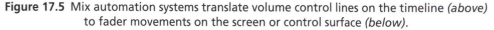

Figure 17.5 Mix automation systems translate volume control lines on the timeline *(above)* to fader movements on the screen or control surface *(below)*.

fader will still sound right, because the automation system still reads their rubber bands on the timeline.

Automation modes

Most software is pretty smart about deciding when to play and when to record, even if you're making changes on a track that's almost perfect. Better programs give you a choice of how they make these decisions, even when tracks are nominally set to write new automation data.

- **Touch mode** keeps a track in play mode until you actually grab a fader. If you leave a fader alone, it will move up and down according to the track's volume line. But when you click and hold your mouse button over a virtual fader, or touch a sensor built into the control surface's knob, it redraws the line based on your current movements. If you let go of the fader, the volume goes back to any level you might have previously written. This makes it easy to record small changes.
- **Latching mode** works like Touch mode, except after you've moved a fader the volume stays where you left it. You can then move other faders, without worrying about losing the setting you just applied. The changes are written to the tracks,

but only for the area between where you first touched the fader and when you stopped.

- **Overwrite mode** replaces existing data as soon as you start the transport. You can preset an entire scene with the transport stopped, and then record all its faders at once.
- **Trim mode** scales any existing fader movements based on where you've set the fader. Use this if you've recorded a complex automation sequence with a lot of fades, and then want to make a particular element louder or softer without having to remake each movement.

Mouse mixing

Even if you've got a control surface and lots of responsive faders under your fingers, there will be times your fingers haven't moved exactly the way you want them. You might have done an elaborate transition between two scenes perfectly, but missed where the picture dissolves by a few frames. Or you might want to adjust the level of just a single word or note. That's when it pays to remember that your software is really using control points on rubber-band volume lines, even if you're accessing them with virtual or real faders.

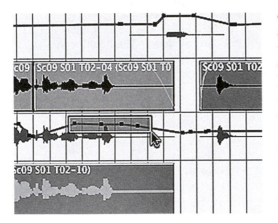

Figure 17.6 Selecting just a few control points with a mouse.

Almost every program lets you select control points or keyframes that have already been written, and move them without disturbing their relationship to each other or moving other points on the line. You can slide the selected points up or down to change the volume precisely, or sideways to change their timing. Figure 17.6 shows a group of points about to be selected on part of a dialog line. Sliding all those points to the left will make the same fade happen, but a few frames earlier.

The operation is sometimes called *mouse mixing*. It's easily the most efficient way to make precise changes, particularly when you're happy with the rest of the mix.

Automating other processes

Your software might let you automate panning, amount of reverb, muting, and other processes. Good DAWs even automate functions on any plug-ins that have been inserted in a track. In each case, the program creates a new control line for the function, similar to rubber bands used for volume. You can edit its points the same way, too.

If you're using a hardware control surface, look for ASSIGN and FLIP buttons. The former let you set exactly what the rotary encoder above each fader will adjust—usually, it's panning, but you can assign other functions. The latter exchanges the fader and rotary encoder functions, so you can use the large fader to precisely adjust things like panning and equalization.

LOUDNESS AND BROADCAST STANDARDS

This section applies to TV mixes only, and will tell you how to comply with new US and European broadcast regulations.

It's interesting. But if your project isn't going to be broadcast, you can safely skip it.[13]

You'd think it would be simple. For decades, TV viewers have complained that commercials were much louder than the programs they interrupted. You'd be straining to hear dialog, and then hoping your ears didn't bleed while someone bragged about toilet bowl cleaner. On top of that, it seemed no two stations were set to the same loudness; change the channel and you had to change the volume. Remote controls were getting a workout.

In fact, a lot of high-priced engineers[14] were busy keeping things that way. Stations used sophisticated processors—combination multiband compressors and equalizers, with some other tricks thrown in—to make sure their transmitters stayed as loud as possible. Ad agencies hired audio post specialists based, in part, on how much louder their mixes sounded without being distorted.

The transition to digital helped, a little. The absolute maximum was −10 dBFS[15] and sounded the same no matter whose transmitter was sending it. So at least two stations, broadcasting the same commercial, would sound the same. At the same time, −20 dBFS was adopted as nominal level for dialog and lineup tone. Those numbers still appear in most network production contracts.

Unfortunately, actual average program levels—usually the meter readings for dialog—could be almost anywhere from a few dB above nominal to way below it. This depended entirely upon the director, and often had to do with the intimacy of a scene plus how many explosions or car crashes there were. Average commercial levels, when the agency was looking for LOUD and the engineers knew their job, would hover

---

[13] Unless your instructor has said it'll be on a test.

[14] And at least one moderately priced one: me.

[15] You'll remember from Chapter 2 that 0 dBFS is the digital maximum. The other 10 dB got lost when Sony decided −10 should be the working maximum for their gear. At the time, they made the bulk of TV audio equipment . . . so the standard was adopted by everybody else.

somewhere above nominal; there were frequent peaks at –10. So the commercials were still annoyingly loud.

ITU-R BS.1770, EBU R128, and ATSC A/85

These tongue-twisters are loudness standards from the International Television Union, the European Broadcast Union, and the Advanced Television Systems Committee. They were developed over the first decade of this century, and pretty much carry the force of law for broadcasting now. If you're mixing for TV, you have to follow them.

They're actually not too scary. BS.1770 defines a way to measure the perceived loudness of a TV signal. It takes into account how different channels in a surround mix will get played, how the ear responds to different frequencies at different volumes, and how this all gets perceived during the length of a program or commercial. The math is complicated, but it all boils down to Loudness Units. These are usually expressed in decibels as LUFS (Loudness Units relative to Full Scale); or LKFS (Loudness *K-weighted*), named for an algorithm used in the process. For practical purposes, both units mean the same thing.

The CALM Act

The Commercial Advertisement Loudness Mitigation Act, which became US law in 2010, requires the FCC to standardize a way of measuring loudness, and stop TV stations from broadcasting commercials that measure louder than the surrounding program. The FCC adopted A/85 as described above, and stations installed equipment to monitor and control loudness using that standard.

You don't have to do anything to comply with this law; that's up to the stations. But they can reject material that doesn't meet their published standards. So it makes sense to measure any programs or commercials you mix, using one of the meters described below. Otherwise you'll find yourself mixing it again.

How to use the new numbers

There are lots of free or low-cost meters to analyze your program, and give you a measurement on that scale. Figure 17.7 shows two of the free versions, Steinberg's free SLM 128 (steinberg.net), and Melda Productions MLoudnessAnalyzer (meldaproduction. com). These are both plug-ins that you insert in a mixer output; they display values while you're mixing or playing an existing mix. Orban has a free standalone app that measures any audio played into your computer and will also generate log files; details are on page 302.

PBS's contract is typical of the major networks: it specifies an average loudness of –24 dB LKFS ± 2 dB for each segment, with momentary peaks as high as –2 dBFS. (It also warns you that peaks above –10 dBFS may distort on older equipment.) Read your mix's numbers, make the final file a little louder or softer if necessary to reach –24 dB LFKS, and you're ready to go.

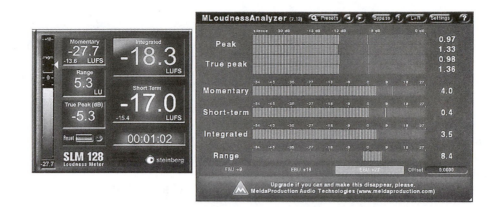

Figure 17.7 Two free meters that help you comply with European and US TV loudness standards. Steinberg's is on the left; Melda Productions' on the right.

✳ TIDBIT

The actual state of the art

I talked to David Moulton, *TV Technology Magazine*'s long-time audio columnist and a Grammy-nominated engineer, about actual loudness on the air. He's been measuring it on a regular basis since the days of analog TV, and writing about its problems.

"Going back to when I started, thinking back to the articles I wrote then, things were really messed up. It was discouraging. When things went all-digital, it got better. But the big difference has been the CALM Act. I don't think anyone's been charged with violating it, but it's been a social force. It seemed to get the production houses and the distribution chains to start paying attention to what they were really doing.

"I was surprised and really pleased. It seemed as soon as the CALM act passed, people started getting their act together. Now I no longer feel the need to change the level as I'm switching channels. Two years ago[16] I had to.

"I'm happiest with the networks. Some local stations are still sloppy with their commercial breaks, and low-rent cable channels are all over the map. But even that is getting better."

---

[16] Interviewed in 2013.

Dialnorm

This is a Dolby Laboratories standard that embeds a code number into the audio, based on the average loudness of an *anchor element*. The anchor is the most important type of element in the program. It's usually dialog, but a musical program might set Dialnorm by reading the music.

When the code number reaches a playback device, including most digital cable TV set-top boxes, it adjusts the output volume based on both the anchor's loudness and any viewer settings. Most viewers ignore those settings. Most stations don't insist that their program suppliers measure it, and instead leave the station's Dialnorm encoder set to an average value for everything.

In practical terms, mix your TV programs to A/85 and R128, and you'll be fine.

PREPARING FOR SOMEONE ELSE TO MIX

If you don't have good monitoring and mixing equipment, or the mix is particularly tricky and will require special skills, it makes sense to take your tracks elsewhere. This can be an outside studio that specializes in postproduction audio, a local general-purpose music studio, or your company's sound specialist down the hall. Most of the preparation will be the same.

Ask the expert

Large facilities try to standardize their operations by assigning pre-production to account executives or scheduling managers, but this makes sense only for standard situations. If your project is anything out of the ordinary (of course it is—who wants to do an ordinary film?), you should talk to the engineer who'll actually do the work. Five minutes with the right person, a few days before the session, will save an hour of scrambling for equipment or experimenting with special setups.[17]

Start with the basics. How long does the piece run? Is it dramatic, talking heads, vérité, or voice-over? Discuss how it will be shown, since mixing for a desktop is very different from mixing for a theater or hotel ballroom. And don't forget subsequent uses, such as cutting the show into modules or a foreign-language version. These considerations affect what kind of equipment and procedures will work best.

Then talk about specific elements. If dialog or voice-over is simple, you've probably already cut them in your NLE. But fine-tuning sounds may be faster, more precise, and possibly cheaper on an audio workstation. Obviously, let the engineers know if you're planning to record a new voice-over or ADR. Warn them if you want to record narration while watching pictures, in case they need to set up monitors or a playback

---

[17] Besides, we engineering types love to solve problems. Get us thinking about your project ahead of time, and we'll be more committed to doing it creatively.

deck. You might have to arrive a few minutes earlier than the talent, so video can be transferred to a hard-disk playback system.

Interchange

While most of the audio programs used in a mixing suite can accept files from most NLEs, there are exceptions and strangenesses, and standards keep evolving. Check Chapter 10 for some details and suggestions to keep this process working properly.

You'll also need to provide picture. Tape is virtually obsolete for this function, and a lot of studios haven't turned on their tape decks in years. But there are differences in file formats and standards, and in the amount of data compression you apply. Talk to the studio to see what format they accept; to find the best compromise between data rate, file size, and image quality; and to decide the best way to get these large interchange and video files to them.

There isn't as much variability on the files they'll give back. Mixes will either be stereo AIFF or .wav, surround poly-channel .wav, or separate mono .wav tracks with suffixes to denote their channel. Files with a 24 bit depth and a 48 kHz sample rate are considered standard, though TV and Web mixes have a limited enough dynamic range that 16 bits will work fine. If something is going only to the Web, 44.1 kHz can be an acceptable rate; it's friendlier for Web compression.

Sync should always be verified by two-pops on the reference video, OMF and other tracks coming from your editing system to the sound studio; these will also be put on on the finished mix. Long-form programs should have a tail-pop as well.

It's a lot of variability. Unless you've used a particular workflow before, it makes sense to do a test from your NLE to the sound house, and from them back to you. Most professional sound people do not charge for this kind of test.

What to bring to a mix

Obviously you should bring your edited tracks and video when you're mixing at an outside studio, in the file formats you've all agreed on. Many facilities will let you send these elements ahead of time, so they can preload or dub them.

But there are a few other things you should also bring. If there's any chance you'll need to rebuild dialog or grab effects, bring the original video or sound files and logs. In the unlikely case you're working on videotape, bring the master for them to lay the final mix onto.

You may also need some paperwork. Bring contracts or a purchase order if necessary to keep the studio manager happy. Don't forget cellphone and email of anyone you might need to reach during the session for changes or approvals. The one thing you probably *won't* need used to be an essential: a track layout chart. These were necessary when you went into a mix with reels of tape or mag film. But they're never looked at in most DAW mixes, since the same information is displayed in sync on the screen.

AFTER THE MIX

If you're mixing in an NLE, check the final rendered version carefully for sync and distortion. It may help to open the finished mix in a waveform viewer or clip window, to verify there is sufficient level and no overloads. It should look similar to the properly digitized files in Chapter 12.

Mixing in a separate system, or at an outside studio, requires a couple of extra steps. If you haven't rendered a final NLE output, the best plan is to put the finished mix back into your editing system. Have the studio make a compatible file with the same sync pops you gave them in the edited tracks, load it into your editor, and line up the pops. Once you've done that, you can move the mix's in- and out-points so the pops don't make it to the final render.

Print masters

Theatrical films usually go through a *print mastering* stage as well. This is primarily a technical operation to make sure the final mix conforms to standards for Dolby or other systems, but is also a final opportunity for both intentional tweaks and accidental changes. If your project is going through this step, it can be a good idea to hang around and keep an ear on things.

Of course you should also make backups of all the computer files used in your mix. Large projects often devote two separate hard drives or data tapes for identical backups: one stays with the producer, and one goes in a vault.

THE LAST THING YOU SHOULD DO

Put the tape on a shelf. Come back to it a month later, listen to it, pat yourself on the back for a job well done . . . and figure out what you'd do differently next time.

CHAPTER 18

"Help! It Doesn't Sound Right!"

If you're hearing a specific problem in your project and need to find out how to fix it in a hurry, this chapter of Frequently Asked Questions is for you.

Of course, I'd rather you read the whole book. That way you'll learn how sound really works, and be able to get the best possible tracks with the least effort. But as a pragmatist—and someone who's lived with years of project deadlines—I understand this may not be possible right now.

So flip through this section until you find the specific problem that's bothering you. If it can be repaired easily, you'll find the instructions right here. If the fix is slightly more complicated, I'll point you to a specific part of this book or a website with updated information. One of these will probably be enough to get you back on track.

But please . . . when you have time, read the rest of the book. It'll save you from this kind of panic on your next film.

GENERAL PRODUCTION ISSUES

Camera and mic operation

Can I shoot single-system on camera X?

Some of today's digital cameras are good enough to record broadcast-quality sound while you're shooting. A very few are good enough for theatrical-quality dialog . . . but even the best have sound issues, including noises and dropouts. You'll get a better, more flexible track by using a separate recorder with someone to control it. See the discussion and lab measurements of specific cameras, starting on page 231.

☞ ROSE'S RULES

The simple way to avoid problems

Use good isolating earphones while you're shooting.

They have to surround the ear and block outside sounds.[1] Most audio problems can be prevented, but only if you know what's being recorded. This is particularly true if you're feeding a camera: connections can break or knobs can get nudged; sometimes a camera will even change its own settings without telling you.

Since many cameras have poor quality headphone outputs, sound operators often prefer to monitor through their mixers instead. This is fine for adjusting mics and mixing during the take . . . but you should check a playback as well, to make sure the camera recorded what you're hearing. You'll find connections for this on many pro mixers; if your mixer doesn't have that function, plug the headphones directly into the camera and check at the end of each setup.

If you're shooting single-system, you have to check the take for quality as well as for signal level. Cameras can distort even if their meters say everything is fine.

Do I need a license to use a wireless?

The wireless world has changed over the past few years. There are fewer available frequencies, and many more microphones competing for them. Not just film crews, but also stage shows, churches, athletic events, and convention centers use wireless. If there isn't much activity where you're shooting, you probably can get by without a license. But if you are shooting where there are a lot of other mics, an FCC license can help guarantee your slot. See page 208.

How can I find usable wireless frequencies at location X?

Easiest way is to ask the rental company to check when you're getting the mics for that shoot. If you already own the mics, see the instructions on page 208.

---

[1] But don't use headphones with active noise-reduction or noise-cancelling circuits. These are great on airplanes, but they'll distort what you're trying to hear at a shoot.

Too much background noise

Too much machinery, traffic, footsteps . . .

Environmental noise and echo problems can have similar solutions. They're almost always improved by moving the mic closer to the actors' mouths.

The most common noises in interior shots are caused by machines that you might forget are running, such as air-conditioners, refrigerators, computer fans, or hidden ones like air pumps in fish tanks. Turn them off. If that's absolutely not possible, get the noise-making device as far from the action as possible, and throw some sound-absorbing blankets around it. Don't forget to turn the machines back on after the shot; we're not here to ruin food or suffocate fish.

The fans and compressors in large HVAC systems are often far from your shooting location, but the systems still make noise. Most of what you hear from big systems comes from the vents, because of air turbulence around the grills. If you can't turn the system off, try removing the grill where the duct comes through the wall or ceiling.

If actors' footsteps are a problem, throw down a blanket for them to walk on, put foam pads (available from film sound suppliers) under their shoes, or let them work in socks. If prop-handling noises are a problem, block the scene so the noises occur during dialog pauses, so you can reduce them in postproduction. Use foam core board or a foam placemat to dampen the sound when a prop gets put down on a table.

If traffic noises are a problem in an interior, make sure all the windows are closed tightly. Then hang sound blankets over the windows. Low-frequency traffic rumbles can be controlled by a mic's low-end rolloff switch, and further filtered in post.

There's not much you can do about traffic or pedestrian noise outdoors, unless your production is big enough to shut down the street. But try not to add your own noises. Generators and other noisy machinery should be as far from the shooting area as possible. If you can, put them on the other side of existing buildings so the walls can block some noise.

If these noises are already on your track, see "Noise Reduction" on page 473. But don't expect a perfect cure . . . electronic processing is no substitute for careful recording.

Noise in a radio mic

These things can be unpredictable, so always bring a wired alternative. This can be as simple as an adapter that'll let you plug the mic into a mixer or camera, instead of into the transmitter.

Before you give up on a radio mic, make sure you're using fresh batteries: it's not unusual to have to replace the batteries two or even three times during a long shoot day. Get the receiving antenna as close to the mic as possible while maintaining line-of-sight (large metal objects can disrupt the signal), and orient it in the same direction as the transmitter's antenna.

If the signal fades or distorts as talent walks around, the radio waves are probably bouncing unpredictably because of metal elements in the building walls. Moving the receiver closer can help, and so can a technique called *diversity reception.* There's a lot more about getting good results from wireless in Chapter 7.

Electronic hum during the recording

Hum can be introduced by the mic cable, particularly when you're using small digital cameras with mini-jack mic inputs. If your camera connects that way, get an XLR balancing adapter (page 223): the improvement, with a good mic, will amaze you.

Even with a balancing transformer, a microphone's tiny signal is easily polluted by electronic noise. Keep all mic cables away from AC power- or video-lines. If the cable must cross one of these noisy wires, do it at a right angle; this minimizes the area where pickup can occur. Star-Quad, an inexpensive upgrade to standard XLR mic cables, can reduce noise pickup.

If you're borrowing signals from a computer, PA system, or playback device and things start to hum, you may have a voltage mismatch . . . but a ground loop is more likely. The best solution is an isolation transformer in the audio line. If one isn't available, you might be able to get a clean signal by running the camera on a battery instead of AC supply. Disconnect the camera from monitors or anything else plugged into an AC outlet. Try to arrange things so that the only item plugged into the wall is the house sound system.

We often refer to ground loop noise as "60-cycle hum," but its effects extend throughout the audio band, and are almost impossible to eliminate with standard filters.

Problems with on-camera dialog

Don't feel bad; this happens all the time in Hollywood. Unfortunately, often the only way to fix a bad dialog track is to re-record it. The actors go into a studio, and speak in sync with their pictures. This is standard practice in big-budget projects. It's also time-consuming, annoys the actors, introduces problems of its own, and can cost a bundle. And it's not usable in documentaries and other talking-head productions.

You can avoid the need to replace dialog by listening carefully during the shoot, either on a good speaker in a separate control room or with high-quality headphones. Play back the first and last take as well, so you can catch equipment or tape troubles. Then follow the steps below to fix any problems you hear.

It's not easy to remember during the heat of production, but "wasting" a couple of minutes on the set, to move a microphone or hide its shadow, or to hang a sound blanket over a window, can save you hours in postproduction. It may just keep a day's shooting from ending up on the scrap heap.

If you've already got bad tracks and reshooting isn't an option, you may have to live with the problems. Or re-record the dialog, using the tips in Chapter 9 (at the book's website, GreatSound.info).

"It's hard to understand the words!"

If the actors are mumbling, send them to acting school. Mics often pick up things that untrained ears miss, but they can't guess what a mumbled word should be.

If you can hear them clearly in person but have to strain to hear them during playback, and the problem isn't one of the noise or electronic ones listed above, check these situations:

Echoey rooms

Too much room echo around their voices

This is the most common problem with dialog tracks, particularly those done by beginning filmmakers. You need to treat the room with sound-absorbing material (Chapter 6), or get the mic closer to their mouths (Chapter 7). For best results do both.

A camera-mounted shotgun mic will almost always be too far away for effective dialog recording indoors. It may be usable outdoors, but only if the camera is close to the subject and there isn't too much background noise.

If you can place a shotgun on a boom, in front of and no more than a foot or so above the talent's head, you'll get the most realistic dialog. Where you put the mic and how you aim it is critical: it has to be close to the actors' mouths and pointed toward them, without getting close to or pointing toward reflective surfaces. See the section on booming, starting on page 179.

If you don't have the time or resources to use a boom mic effectively, a lavaliere or "tie tack" mic can be appropriate. Get the mic as close as possible to the talent's mouth, hiding it in their clothing or hair if necessary. Don't worry about it being so close you lose a sense of the room around the actors: you can make it sound more distant in postproduction. (Do worry about it being too far. There's no way to fix that in post.)

There's a lot of information about using boom mics and lavalieres in Chapter 7.

Too much echo and random room noises, but voices seem okay

Your camera's Automatic Level Control (ALC) may be lowering the recording volume while the actors talk, and raising it whenever they pause. Turn it off.

If you can't defeat the automatic control, try lowering the microphone signal level with a simple attenuator or mixer. You may have to experiment to find a level that doesn't make the automatic control work so hard, but still avoids electronic noise. Don't attempt to defeat ALC by moving the mic farther from the talent. That just increases room echo. There's more about this starting on page 236.

More echo on one actor than on another

If you're using a single mic, make sure it's aimed properly. If it's on a boom, someone has to pan it between the actors. If that doesn't help, try adding some strategically placed absorption (Chapter 6).

Hollow sound from multiple lavs

If you're using more than one body mic, things can get strange. Sue's mic can start picking up George's voice and vice versa. If this is the situation, you might hear echoes when they're across the room—that depends on the room's acoustics. But you'll definitely hear a hollowness when they come close together.

Don't just combine the mics in a mixer and walk away. You need someone actively controlling the mixer during the take, lowering each actor's mic when the other is talking. Or save the mix for later: send each mic to a separate channel in your recorder or camera, and sort them out in postproduction.

Dialog problems introduced by the recorder

Playback doesn't sound like the recording

Make sure the camera or recorder is properly adjusted. Set digital recorders to 16-bit, 48 kHz mode or higher. If you're using an analog recorder, the heads must be clean or you'll hear a muffled sound.

Adjust the recording volume very carefully (page 235). Prosumer cameras have a limited range between noise and distortion.

Background noises seem to jump around with each take

If the actual noise level on the set keeps changing while you shoot, it's a production management problem. Shut down the noise, or hope to minimize its effect by getting the mic very close to the actors. Record a couple of seconds of extra background noise at the head and tail of each take; it'll be handy when you're editing.

If noise levels stay relatively constant during the shoot, but jump around between takes when you play back, either the camera's Automatic Level Control or some production assistant's fingers were too active.

Track splitting and L-cuts can smooth out some of these jumps when you edit the track; see Chapter 13.

Audio is too quiet in the editor: When I boost it, I hear hiss and buzzing

If you've transferred from the camera using FireWire, this was most likely a problem in the original footage. MiniDV cameras have to be set very carefully to make sure they're not generating electronic noise. See Chapter 8.

If you've transferred via an analog connection, even from a digital tape, check the original for noise. It may have been recorded properly but the settings were wrong when you transferred it to the computer. See Chapter 12.

No matter which kind of transfer you did, check the computer's system-level input volume controls. They can override the settings in your NLE software.

POSTPRODUCTION AUDIO ISSUES

If your system uses an analog audio connection into the editor, it's essential that you set digitizing levels properly. Don't trust an on-screen meter until you've calibrated your system using the tips in Chapter 12.

Lipsync problems

If the track is largely in sync but you see errors only on specific clips, it's probably an operator error. Some desktop systems are notoriously unintuitive for anything other than straight cuts. If this happens only once or twice in a project, just nudge the track until it's in sync; tips are on page 385. If it happens a lot, be prepared to upgrade your software or take a training course.

How do I sync double-system with camera X?

The easiest way to sync a single camera and recorder is to have matching audio on both. Take a feed from the line out or headphone jack of your recorder and send it to the camera. Even a cheap consumer wireless link will work for that. Ingest audio from both the camera and the separate recorder, slide the recorder's track until it matches, delete the camera's track, and you're done. PluralEyes (page 356) can automate the process.

If you're using multiple cameras or for some reason can't get audio to the camera, you'll need to use slates (Chapter 13) or timecode (Chapter 12). Slates are easier and cheaper.

Don't take anything for granted: test your whole workflow, far enough in advance that you can make changes if necessary. Some cameras handle timecode in non-intuitive ways. See the individual camera forums at dvxuser.com for advice and user experiences.

Sync drift

If it's impossible to get stable sync—if you can get the first line to look right, but other lines in the scene vary between early and late—it's probably a software problem. If the track stays in sync for the first five minutes or so, but then jumps wildly out and never comes back, you've most likely got hardware issues. Either way, contact the editing system manufacturer. There may be an update or workaround. You may have to reconfigure your computer and restart. It's also possible you're using audio and video boards the manufacturer didn't qualify to work together.

If a track starts out in sync but seems to jump earlier from time to time, suspect dropped video frames. Check the settings, defragment the hard drive, quit any other programs, and turn off all network services.

Sync gets progressively worse
If a track drifts out of sync at a constant rate, getting worse over time but never making any obvious jumps, you've probably got incompatible references between audio and

video software. Is video sync or blackburst distributed everywhere it's supposed to go? Do timecode or frame rate settings agree throughout your system? Manually sync the front and back of the video and measure how much it's drifted over time: this can help you or the manufacturer diagnose the problem. If nothing else, finding out how big the error is lets you apply a speed correction to fix it.

A constant drift of just under two frames per minute is almost always related to differences between 30 fps audio and 29.97 fps NTSC video. It can be the result of mixing film and video in the workflow. If you're shooting film and editing as video, or shooting video at special speeds for eventual film release, you have to take extra precautions with sync. See Chapter 12.

Some NLEs automatically apply film-to-video speed conversion when you change timecode formats or rates, regardless of whether it's appropriate. If you've sent clips that were in sync to an audio program for finishing, but the resulting mix is out of sync by roughly two frames per minute, suspect this bug. The best solution is to revert to a version of the NLE timeline before you changed timecode, and import the mix there. Then you can do whatever changes are necessary to both sound and video simultaneously. Or marry the finished picture and final mix in some other program. As a last resort, you can change the mix's sample rate by 0.1% in a sophisticated audio program . . . and then let the NLE's bug change it back. This compromises the sound, but at least gets the project finished.

Some prosumer cameras are built with their audio sample rate a tiny bit off-speed to take advantage of cheaper components. This can cause sync errors when the material is transferred to a properly designed NLE. A few NLEs have switches to compensate; check the manual. Re-digitizing through an analog connection will eliminate this problem, though it will also lower the quality.

Many of these errors are cumulative and don't show up until the middle of a film. If so, try breaking the project into shorter pieces. Export each as a QuickTime or .avi. Then string those finished (and properly synchronized) pieces together in the editor.

Problems with double-system

If you recorded double-system, you may have to go back to the original footage and use the slate to re-sync the takes. Generally, once a take has been synchronized, digital equipment will hold it steady for at least 15 minutes.

If you're shooting events with long continuous takes, even high-end digital gear can drift. The sound recorder can drift from the camera, and one camera can drift from another one. The only reliable solution is to wire the devices together with a video sync signal (Chapters 8 and 11).

If you recorded without a slate, or used a totally non-sync medium like analog audio cassettes or many film cameras, you're in for a nightmare of manual re-syncing and trimming. A sound engineer with lipsync experience and a good DAW may be able to save time and money. Rethinking the film with narration rather than dialog can save a lot of heartache.

Single-system sound is consistently early

If picture seems late at the start, and stays out by the same amount, suspect your equipment. Many cameras have inherent video delays because of scanning and processing, but don't delay their onboard audio to match. Many large-screen LCD displays or projectors also introduce a picture delay.

You can measure camera delays by slapping a slate and checking how many frames there are between the last blurred frame of the stick and the start of the sound. This may vary depending on camera settings, particularly if the camera is trying to achieve a film look. Once you know what the specific error is, you can slide the tracks in your NLE to compensate.

If the picture monitor in your editing suite has a delay, either because of issues with the video card or because of processing for a large screen, you might have to live with it. Don't try to adjust for this by manually sliding picture against sound, because the offset will change depending on whether you're looking at a still frame or running at speed. A few editing programs have a function to properly compensate for monitor delays.

Delays in the picture are likely to get much worse if your project is broadcast, bounced around satellite systems, and shown on home theaters. There's nothing you can do about this as a producer. Sorry.

Original takes seem slightly late compared to NLE version

If you're replacing clips in an OMF or AAF export with the original production files, and sync seems off by a frame or less, suspect padding: some NLEs extend clips to the nearest frame line when exporting, even though it changes the length of the clip. This problem is easiest to notice when you mix the exported version with the new one.

Check the NLE settings to see if this feature can be turned off; otherwise, you'll have to sync those clips manually.

Hum and noise

If a track gets noisy in your NLE but is clean when you play it in the camera, check the connections and re-digitize. Make sure your NLE is set for 16-bit or higher resolution, and the same sample rate as your footage (usually 48 kHz). Even if your final goal is a low-resolution medium like Web or cellphone video, always import at the original bit depth or higher.

How to fix noises that couldn't be eliminated at the shoot

If you're willing to sacrifice realism for intelligibility, get a good filter and start with settings like these:

- Sharp rolloff (at least 12 dB/octave) below 200 Hz and above 8 kHz
- Consonant peak, 6 dB around one octave wide, at 1.75 kHz
- Optional warmth boost around 2 dB at 250 Hz

Fine-tune the settings with a good audio monitor, always listening for distortion. If you're not sure what things like dB and Hz are, check Chapter 1. If you're not sure how to use a filter, check Chapter 16. If you don't have good monitor speakers, don't do anything. You'll have to go to a sound studio for the final mix. It's impossible to do a good mix without accurate speakers, and it's wisest to put off any corrections until then.

Power-line hum is seldom just at power-line frequencies and can't be fixed with a standard filter. A comb filter, with mathematically related notches like the teeth of a comb, can help a lot (see Chapter 16) . . . but it can also leave things sounding hollow or metallic.

Hum and hiss that don't obscure the dialog, but are annoying during pauses, can be eliminated with sliding filters and multiband noise gates. That's in Chapter 16 also.

There's a separate chapter devoted to noise reduction in my book *Audio Post-production*. It also has sections on using equalizers and expanders for noise control, and cookbook examples with CD samples of various kinds of noise. It was far too much material to include here.

Narration issues

Radio and TV have conditioned us to expect voice-overs to be cleanly recorded, disembodied voices speaking directly to us from limbo (hey, I don't make the rules). You can't record them in the kind of real-world reverberant spaces that are appropriate for dramatic dialog, or even music recording. Read Chapter 9 for some tips on recording them properly.

Voice-over recording lacks clarity

If you've gotten this recording from another studio, chances are it was delivered as a file. If the file was sent over the Internet, there may have been a problem with the compression algorithm. Check the original recording, and if it sounds okay but is too big to download, have the studio send you an uncompressed file on CD-ROM. Or it may be a problem with how your NLE converts file formats; try converting in an audio program.

Obviously, narration recordings are also subject to the same issues as production dialog. Check the first part of this chapter.

If you've recorded narration by pointing a camera mic directly at the speaker's mouth, try using just one channel of the stereo pair. Use the Take Right or Take Left command in your NLE's audio clip options.

And take heart: when I wrote the first edition of this book about 15 years ago, narrations were often delivered on tape. There were a lot more things, back then, that could go wrong.

Voice-over sounds fine by itself, but is weaker than other elements

A little processing is a good thing. See Chapter 16 for advice on using equalization and compression to make a voice punchier.

Computer doesn't play audio well

If you hear skipping, pops, or brief silences when you play from hard disk but not from the original track, suspect data-flow problems. Don't assume that because the video looks good, the system can handle "simpler" audio data. The eye can ignore uneven picture more easily than the ear can ignore uneven sound.

If this is the problem, start by looking for solutions at the editing system's website and user forum. You may need to change your computer's startup configuration and reboot. As a last resort, lower the sample rate or use mono instead of stereo.

Problems with data flow

It's possible the hard disk isn't accessing audio quickly enough, or the CPU is trying to do too many other things at the same time. Try defragmenting the hard disk or copying the audio file to a faster drive. Optical drives and USB "thumb drives" can be much slower than internal hard disks.

External FireWire and USB drives can be slowed down if the same bus is also handling video or accessing accessory drives. If you don't actually need a particular device at the moment, disconnecting it from the chain can sometimes let the audio devices communicate better. USB hubs can also slow things down, compared to plugging the devices directly into your computer.

Problems after upgrades

Reports with some newer system and software upgrades suggest that things get better if you totally reformat and reload your system. This operation will shut you down for a while, so save this fix until you're desperate.

If individual clips sound fine but playback stutters or distorts when you try to play from the timeline, there's probably a sample rate issue. Check Clip Info to make sure every clip is at the same rate as the overall project. If not, export those clips to an audio program and convert their sample rate.

Problems in some software but not others

Check your Flash install. It might need an update, or have problems with specific browsers and other software. It can help to delete all site data and settings in the Flash player. If you have to re-install, use Adobe's uninstaller first; manually removing elements or using Windows' Add/Remove panel might not do the job.

Lots of wasted time for renders

Some NLEs will accept a variety of audio formats, but don't actually convert their data until you try to view the sequence. If you then change the sequence, they have to convert the data all over again. If you're encountering delays while working with multiple sample rates or compressed files, open the files in an audio program before importing. Convert them to standard AIFF or .wav, at a rate and bit depth that matches your NLE's project, and import the converted version instead.

Noises during playback

Periodic clicking in a file

This is almost always the result of digital audio being out of sync with the hardware or other audio elements. Check that your sound card and software settings match. If you copied the audio digitally from a real-time audio source such as DAT, CD, or MiniDisc, make sure the sound card and the source shared the same sync reference. Both should be locked to a blackburst generator, or the card must be set to use its own input as the reference.

Random squeaks, whistles, or edginess mixed with some sounds

This is almost always aliasing distortion. The file was recorded at a sample rate that the sound card doesn't properly support (no matter what the manufacturer printed on its box). See Chapter 2.

Maybe you're lucky and the problem is in the card's playback filters. Try playing the file on a different computer. If it sounds okay, get a different brand of sound card.

But it's more likely the problem was created during the original recording, and the file can't be repaired. Try re-recording at the highest sample rate your software will support. If that results in a cleaner file, you may then convert to a lower rate in software and avoid this problem. The best solution is to get a card that was properly designed in the first place.

Aliasing can also occur when very bright sounds are captured in devices with consumer-level audio circuits, which includes (unfortunately) many semi-pro DV cameras and pocket recorders. The only solution is to use a better recorder at the shoot.

You may be able to make aliasing less annoying, by sacrificing clarity. Try a sharp low-pass filter, set around 7 kHz. This will muffle the sound as well as controlling the squeaks and whistles. If there are only a few squeaks and whistles, you might be able to control them in a spectral editor like RX3 (page 475).

PROBLEMS THAT SURFACE DURING EDITING

Dialog seems uneven from shot to shot

If you're using a lavaliere, this probably won't happen unless you changed the wardrobe or your actors changed their projection on different shots. If you're using a boom that had to be pulled too far away for the long shot, try using audio from a close-up take. If you can't, try using an L-cut (audio and video cut on different frames) to disguise the changes.

If your project will have a proper dialog edit and mix in a DAW, don't worry too much: you'll be able to split these edits to multiple tracks, and crossfade them to smooth out the differences (page 377). If things really sound ragged, check with the sound supervisor before completing the edit: the only fix might be ADR.

If you're mixing yourself in the NLE, you'll need to overlap and equalize and process individual clips to smooth out these variations. Resist the temptation to do this during the editing process. Wait until the mix, where you'll have better monitors and be able to concentrate more on the track. If you have a lot of clips to be processed, you'll probably save time by moving to a DAW that lets you apply equalizers to entire tracks at once.

Music edits don't sound smooth

While there's an art to music editing (one you can learn easily; see Chapter 14), the problem may be mechanical. If you've followed the instructions in that chapter and edits still sound a little jumpy, you're probably running into frame-line issues. NLEs usually insist that edits can happen only between frames—even on audio tracks—and ⅓₀th of a second can be an eternity in music. Export the music to an audio program, cut it to length, and import the finished version.

MIX PROBLEMS

First, make sure you're being realistic. If you don't have good monitor speakers in a well-designed environment, plug-ins that can be tuned in real time, and a system that lets you adjust multiple tracks simultaneously, you really can't do a complicated mix . . . or even be confident that a simple mix will sound the way you intended, when it goes on TV or is played in a theater. Talk to a sound studio that specializes in film and video.

An experienced engineer with the right equipment can save you time, fix problems that aren't repairable on your desktop, assure a polished overall sound, and comply with current loudness regulations for broadcast.

Besides, it's how a bunch of us make our living.

When good mixes go bad

It sounded great on the desktop, but bad on TV / in the theater / in the conference room

Music got too soft / too loud

If the music is softer than expected but dialog sounds okay, chances are you're using home speakers optimized for pop music, or small multimedia speakers supplemented by subwoofers. The speakers emphasized the extreme highs and lows, so while you were mixing you didn't make the music loud enough. This problem can also result from too reverberant a mixing room: since reverb is more obvious on voice than on music, you may have turned down the music so it wouldn't interfere.

This problem can also occur if one of the stereo speakers in your mixing setup is mis-wired and has reversed phase. Stereo elements like music may sound okay, while mono ones get suppressed acoustically . . . so you make those mono elements louder to compensate. This usually affects bass notes more than midrange, so you may have also added too much low-end equalization to the voice. Fix the speaker wiring and remix.

If the dialog seems too soft compared to the music, your speakers probably emphasized the midrange. This is common with midsized multimedia speakers, and also with the cube speakers often placed on top of professional mixing consoles.

The solution for both problems is to remix using good speakers and acoustics. Tweaking an equalizer during playback, to compensate for an original mix's weaknesses, can provide a temporary fix. It can also generate distortion that fights intelligibility, so treat this just as a last-minute option if you discover a problem at the presentation venue. Applying extreme equalization to your badly designed speakers, as a substitute for getting better speakers or treating the room's acoustics, will have the same distortion issues . . . and often just uncovers other deficiencies in the speakers.

The proportions were right, but the whole mix was too soft / loud / distorted on the air . . .

If you're mixing a show for US or European broadcast, you'll have to provide LKFS or similar measurements.

The Good News: new US and European broadcast regulations use a measurement system that makes this kind of problem much more unlikely than it was a few years ago. Average levels for a show are strictly defined, and the broadcasters respect those levels. The Bad News: you need standardized measurements for this system, something that the level meters in most NLEs and many DAWs won't provide. Broadcasters may reject shows or commercials that don't comply.

The other Good News: you can do the measurements yourself using free or low-cost meters, and adjust the program to comply. See page 500.

. . . or has similar loudness problems in non-broadcast media

Basic cable channels, local cable systems, and internal networks generally don't use the newer measurement system. Theatrical film has a different standard. DVDs and Web video might not use a standard measurement at all.

Cable TV and internal networks

Make sure the line-up tone at the head of your tape is accurate. Not only should it match the standard zero setting on your recorder, it also has to match the "average loud" level of your program. Most system operators and dub houses rely on the tone exclusively when setting levels, and they won't try to compensate if program audio doesn't match.

Broadcast audio on digital videotape is standardized with tone and average program level at –20 dBFS (decibels related to Full Scale; defined in Chapter 2), and no peaks higher than –10 dBFS. MiniDV cameras and some NLEs use a –12 dBFS average standard, which can cause distortion if the system operators or dub house isn't used to it. Best to check with them, and see which level they expect.

Broadcast audio on analog videotape is usually standardized with tone at the magnetic level represented by 0 VU on the recorder's meter, with peaks no higher than +6 VU. The average-to-peak difference appears smaller on analog rather than digital meters, because analog meters can't respond to fast peaks as well.

If you're having trouble keeping the average level in the right place while peaks stay below the maximum, try moderate compression on individual elements in your track as well as peak limiting on the overall mix. Tips for using these processors appear in Chapter 16.

Theatrical film

Movie theaters and large dub stages have speakers that are calibrated to a standard level, where –20 dBFS on the tape or file equals 85 dB SPL under specific conditions (page 481). Smaller rooms are frequently calibrated with –20 dBFS = 83 dB SPL. Make sure your system and volume controls match one of these settings. Then mix with normal on-screen dialog around that –20 dBFS level and occasionally glance at a meter for verification.

DVDs and Web videos

There is no official level, but dialog is usually about 10 dB hotter than in the theaters. This gives you much less headroom for explosions and other sounds that are louder than dialog, so watch for distortion on those sounds.

Some elements sound fine in stereo, but disappear on TV / Web / etc.

Something is out of phase. The signal on the left channel is pushing while the one on the right is pulling by exactly the same amount. (If that doesn't make sense to you, you'll either have to trust me or re-read Chapter 1.) When the two channels for that element are combined, they cancel each other out.

In a pinch, you can play the mixed project in mono by using just one channel of your original stereo mix. It won't sound as good, but at least all the elements will probably be there.

The underlying problem can be caused by a wiring error, in studios that move analog signals on balanced cables. It can also happen when the monaural balanced output of a mixer appears on phone jacks, and a stereo-to-mono phone plug adapter is used to split its signal to two channels. The problem almost never occurs when you're editing and mixing entirely in a computer, but if any of your signals go through analog equipment on the way to the computer, check the wiring.

Some low-cost synthesizers and effects processors, hardware or software, reverse the phase of one channel intentionally. This is bad design. Don't use them in a project that might be heard in mono, unless you know how to deal with stereo phase.

If you can't trace the problem to wiring or an external effect, it may be that one of your stereo source recordings had a phase issue. Listen to the problem clips in mono. If their sound disappears, open them in an audio program and invert the phase of one channel.

Entire mix sounds very wide in stereo, but disappears in mono

This is a variation of the above problem, but much easier to fix. It probably occurred when you dubbed the output of your editing system to a final master, because one of the stereo cables was wired wrong. Redub, using two correctly wired cables.

If you can tolerate the generation loss, make a submaster by copying the original master with one correctly wired cable and one mis-wired one. It doesn't matter which channel you reverse when making the submaster.

How loud should music / dialog / sfx be in the mix?

Loud enough to make you happy. That's not a wise-guy answer: there is no recommended meter reading for any elements, other than the theatrical and broadcast standards for average dialog noted above. Get the dialog right, and then mix the other elements so they complement the story and have the emotional effect you want.

You need good monitoring and acoustics to make mix decisions properly, and experience helps you avoid mistakes that sound clever in the mix suite but not in a theater or on the air. Other than that, "how loud things should be" is purely an artistic decision. Mix by ear, not by meter.

How can I make my film Dolby / THX / etc.?

Dolby Digital is a compression standard. It's used to pack multiple channels of reasonable quality audio on a DVD or film track. You can compress your project using plug-ins bundled with some video and DVD authoring software, available from Dolby and others. Mix in stereo or surround, render the individual channels at full resolution (at least 16 bits, 48 kHz), and run them through this software. Your mix will be Dolby . . . but you won't be able to advertise that fact.

The Dolby Digital name and logo are protected. Even if you've encoded your show to their standard, you can't put their trademarks on your film, packaging, or marketing materials without permission. There are application forms in the Professional Services section at Dolby.com. They'll get back to you with information about their fees, which can also include technical evaluation and processing.

You can't make a film THX. This is a set of standards for the mixing suite, theater, and home equipment, not something you do to a track. If a film has been mixed on a stage that's THX certified, you may be able to use their logo or audio/video header. For more information, see the Professional Sound Engineer section at THX.com.

OTHER COMMON QUESTIONS

Where can I find cheap talent / music / sound effects?

Voice-over casting advice is in Chapter 9. Music scoring is Chapter 14. You usually get what you pay for, but there are some strategies for stretching the budget.

Sound effects are free if you record them yourself or create them on a synthesizer. But even professionally recorded, fully licensed ones are cheap—often only a few dollars per minute—if you buy them individually over the Internet. Check www.sound-ideas.com and www.sounddogs.com.

Some music recordings and a few sound effects may be in the public domain if they're old enough, were recorded by the government, or have been specifically released by the owners. Check the Appendix (page 533) for some good sources.

Is it a violation to use copyrighted recordings in an educational or nonprofit video?

Yes. It doesn't matter how noble the intended use. Even if the underlying song is in the public domain, any recording (other than a few historical ones) is likely to have a separate copyright.

Only an attorney can give legal advice, but as a general rule "fair use" applies only to private viewing at home or brief excerpts in a critical review of the music itself. It doesn't include the use of commercial recordings in a professionally produced video, even if the client already owns the CD.

Well then, can I use copyrighted music in my temporary mix?

This is more a question of nobody stopping you. It's technically an infringement, but you're unlikely to get noticed if the project is played for only a few close associates. Hollywood editors regularly use *temp scores* of existing music as placeholders, to give the director a feel for what kind of music could go in a scene. But they replace these songs before the movie is seen by the public. See page 271.

Be aware that festivals are considered public, and usually require you to guarantee copyright clearance before they'll accept a film.

What software should I use? What brand of sound card? Mac or PC or Linux?

The techniques of the soundtrack—what this book is really about—have had nearly a century to develop and are well understood. Digital recording hasn't been around as long, but radical developments take many years to make it from lab to studio. So it's my expectation that you'll be able to use this book for a while.

On the other hand, new software and computer systems are being introduced every few months. Rather than risk outdated information, I've avoided specific recommendations in this book. If you want to keep up, check the user and manufacturer websites listed in the Appendix. If you want to know what tools I'm using this week, check my studio's site or drop me a note.

HOW DO I GET STARTED IN THE FILM / VIDEO SOUND BUSINESS?

If you have a passion, you're probably already doing sound on your own for friends or school productions. Network with the people making those movies. Also hang out at the production and postproduction sound sites listed in the Appendix. Start as a visitor, getting used to how the conversations flow. Then, when you feel it's appropriate, contribute or ask questions. Be patient, take opportunities as they come along, and you'll eventually find a niche in the business.

I don't recommend buying equipment until you've taken the above steps. If you get a gig before you own the necessary gear, you can rent. If the production doesn't have enough money to support the rental, use cheaper equipment, borrow from a friend, or improvise. Don't be fooled by wannabe directors who insist on lengthy equipment lists but pay in "experience."

If you've built a career in studio music recording or live sound, be prepared to re-learn a lot. While the science is the same, the techniques and philosophies are different. This book will help. Then follow the advice in the previous paragraphs.

If you want to do sound because you love it, you'll succeed. If you want to do it as an easy way to make money, you'll be disappointed.

APPENDIX A

Glossary

Every specialty creates its own jargon, verbal shortcuts to express precise situations quickly. Audio jargon can be confusing, particularly if you're coming from the more visual world of film or video.

Jargon is also sometimes used to create an aura of mystery, keeping outsiders from knowing what's going on. But that's not what this book is about, so here's a practical guide to what we audio engineers are talking about. If you don't find a term here, check the index.

A/85: Set of recommendations from the Advanced Television Systems Committee, adopted as the basis for the CALM Act in the United States.

AAF: See *interchange format*

A/B/C-weighting: Filters applied to a sound pressure measurement or loudness meter, in an attempt to mimic the ear's sensitivity to different frequencies at different loudnesses.

ADAT: Alesis Digital Audio Tape, an eight-track format using S/VHS cassettes and named for the company that invented it. ADATs were the first practical, low-cost digital multitracks and became a favorite of scoring composers. A similar but more robust eight-track format, Tascam's DTRS (also known as DA8 or DA88), uses Hi-8 cassettes, was adopted by Sony, and became a standard in Hollywood and at TV networks. Both formats are largely obsolete, replaced by multichannel files.

ADR: Automatic (or Automated) Dialog Replacement, also sometimes known as "looping." Production audio can be noisy and, even if recorded on a quiet sound stage, can be inconsistent from shot to shot. ADR systems let actors go into a sound studio, hear short pieces of their own dialog repeated over and over in a constant rhythm, and then recreate the performance—line by line—in sync with picture. See Chapter 9.

AES/EBU: Literally, the Audio Engineering Society and European Broadcasting Union. But the combination of initials almost always refers to a standard for interconnecting digital audio devices, developed by those two organizations. It uses balanced wiring on special 110 Ω cables. See Chapter 3.

AIFF: Audio Interchange File Format, the standard for Macintosh audio- and video-editing systems. The order of bits is different from Microsoft's .wav format, but both are capable of the same quality sound. Most programs are smart enough to open either, and there are plenty of free converters for both platforms.

Anchor element: The consistently most important element in a specific mix, used in loudness measurement. This is usually dialog, but might be music in some programs.

ATTC: Address Track Time Code. LTC recorded on a special track of an analog video tape or down the center of an analog audio tape. Mostly obsolete.

Auto-conform: In the dark days of analog video and film, each generation of editing would add noise to the soundtrack. Important productions considered the edited version just as a reference, and an automatic conforming system (or hapless audio engineer) would rebuild the sound from the original production recordings. This is still done on many features. Modern workflows often edit full-resolution copies of the production audio along with the picture, and pass perfect clones of it to the sound department, so conforming can often be skipped if you do everything else right. Today, auto-conforming is also sometimes used to synchronize existing DAW projects with last-minute picture edits.

Bag, bag work: Location sound kit that can be operated while worn over your shoulder. The bag usually includes a mixer and recorder, a few wireless receivers, possibly a transmitter for the camera link, and an extra battery supply. Everything is wired together and controls face the top of the bag for easy operation.

BGs: Background sounds (the term is pronounced like the disco group). Usually a track or two of recorded environments, such as crowds or traffic noises, edited to fit the length of a scene. Careful choice of BGs can eliminate the need for a lot of foley.

Box, in the: Slang for film mixes done entirely within a DAW's computer, rather than having multiple signals routed through a large mixing console. Even though audio signals are digitally combined inside the computer for an in-the-box mix, a console-like controller with faders and knobs is usually provided as the user interface.

BS.1770: International standard for measuring loudness, based both on how we perceive different frequencies and on how that perception changes depending on what's gone before. The standard is incorporated in most of the broadcast loudness regulations.

Bump: To adjust the timing between sound and picture in precise frame or subframe units, while both are running. This is most often used to fine-tune lipsync, but bumping a piece of music a frame or two can have amazing results in how it feels against picture.

Burn-in: Video picture with timecode numbers superimposed on the picture. Originally referred to a videotape made with these numbers. Today the numbers might be added to the file, or provided by the playback system.

BWF: Broadcast Wave Format, an audio interchange format standardized by the European Broadcasting Union. It's similar to Microsoft .wav and can be read by most audio programs, but it also lets you embed timecode and other information, and supports multichannel files.

CALM Act: The Commercial Advertisement Loudness Mitigation Act, US law that attempts to regulate the perceived loudness of each element in a TV broadcast, so that commercials aren't much louder than the program and different channels all seem to be at the same volume. Its implementation relies on the A/85 measurement.

Cat-5: Category 5 cable, designed for Ethernet data connections. Its construction makes it also usable for balanced analog and digital audio signals, even though it's not shielded. Because so much of it is manufactured for the computer industry, it's a lot cheaper than conventional audio cables.

CD-quality: Properly speaking, a digital audio signal or device capable of 20 Hz–20 kHz bandwidth with little deviation, very low distortion, and a 96 dB dynamic range. Many manufacturers use the term improperly to imply a quality that isn't justified by a system's design. Unless you can verify specifications using some of the measurements in Chapter 8, the term is meaningless.

Click track: An electronic metronome played into headphones, or a track on a tape with that signal, so that musicians can perform to precise timing.

Codec: Any system for encoding a signal on one end of a transmission, and decoding it at the other. AAC, mp3, and Dolby Digital are common codecs used in film and video sound. Some people insist that the digital audio process itself is a codec, even without data reduction: analog mic voltages are sampled in bits for processing and transmission, and then converted back to analog for the speaker.

DA8, DA88, DTRS: See *ADAT*.

Dante: Computerized networking protocol that puts as many as 1,024 audio channels on a Gigabit Ethernet connection. Uses packet technology, so multiple devices can be connected through routers, cables are bi-directional, and individual channels can be separately addressed.

DAW: Digital Audio Workstation, software or integrated software and hardware for editing, processing, and mixing sound. Most DAWs include a way to play video in sync.

dBA/dBB/dBC: Decibels measured with A, B, or C-weighting.

dBFS: Decibels, referred to Full Scale in a digital system. Full Scale is the level that results when all of the bits in a digital word are turned on. The system can't conceive of any signal bigger than that, since there wouldn't be any bits left to express it.

dBm: Decibels, referenced to 1 milliwatt. Used as a measurement for microphones and transformer-connected pro audio equipment.

dBu: Decibels, referenced to 0.775 volts. Used as a measurement for modern pro audio equipment that doesn't use transformers.

dBV: Decibels, referenced to 1 volt. Used as a measurement for consumer audio equipment.

Decibel: A precise measurement of the ratio between two signals. Its use is often misunderstood, possibly because there are so many variations in how it's referenced. Chapter 1 explains it all.

Dialnorm: Dolby's licensed system for regulating broadcast volume at the viewer's set, so that the same program can have appropriate loudness in home theaters, on standard TVs, and on mobile devices.

Dialog channel: The center channel in a theatrical surround mix, and a derived center in some stereo mixes, designed to play through a speaker centered behind the screen. This channel is almost always reserved just for dialog.

Dialog pre-mix: A step taken in almost every film mix, where split dialog recordings from the original shoot are combined and crossfaded to make a smooth, continuous voice track before the sound effects and music are added. The production audio is often split into a dozen channels or more, so that different characters and shooting situations can be adjusted separately.

Distortion: Anything that changes the output of an audio system so it no longer reflects the input signal. Strictly speaking, reverb or equalization are also forms of distortion, though the term is usually reserved for unintentional, gross changes in the waveform.

DIT: Digital Imaging Technician, a computer video expert at a large digital film shoot.

Dither: Specially shaped random noise added to a digital signal to improve its perceived quality at low levels.

D/M/E: Dialog, music, and effects stems, separate tracks carrying only one kind of sound, used for foreign translations. More flexible than an *M&E* mix.

Double-system: Recording production sound on a separate audio tape recorder while a video or film camera is running. This is often looked at as a way to improve the sound of digital camcorders, but Chapter 8 suggests other things you should try first.

Dropframe: A way of counting timecode so that frame numbers stay, on average, in sync with real-world time. No actual frames are dropped in the process. See Chapter 12.

DSLR: Digital Single Lens Reflex, a movie camera configuration based on sophisticated digital still cameras, using conventional 35mm film lenses and accessories. These cost much less than full digital cinema cameras, but aren't as flexible and frequently lack high-quality sound recording.

Dynamic range: The range between the loudest signal a system can carry without distortion, and its low-level noise that would obscure any softer signals, expressed in decibels. In a purely digital signal, each bit is worth just about 6 dB dynamic range. But when you start involving analog circuits, dynamic range gets harder to pin down: low-level noise gets contributed by the electronics itself, and high-level distortion sets in gradually as the volume increases.

Earwig: Slang for a concealed, in-ear receiver worn by talent for cueing and music playback. Known more formally as IFB (Interruptible Foldback, a term dating from live TV).

EDL: Edit Decision List. A database file, usually in plain language, describing all the edits in a production. Used for interchange among NLE and DAW systems.

Foley: Generating sound effects by duplicating the actors' on-screen movements in a sound studio. A team of good foley artists can watch a scene once, gather armloads of props, and then create everything from footsteps to fist fights in perfect sync. *Digital foley* refers to the process of matching those little sounds in an audio workstation (usually because good foley artists are expensive). The name honors Jack Foley, a Hollywood second-unit director and sound guru of the 1940s, who popularized the technique.

Hard effects: Also known as spot effects. Sounds that are impractical to foley (such as telephone bells, explosions, and space-pirate laser guns) and usually important to the story. These are often drawn from large digital effects libraries, but may be created for the project. In feature-film production, the term often refers to *any* sound effects that are in sync with picture.

High fidelity: An ambiguous term. Traditionally, it referred to somewhere near a 20 Hz–20 kHz frequency range with less than 2 dB variation between sounds of different frequencies, and a dynamic range of at least 70 dB with less than 0.3% distortion—but the bar keeps rising as technology improves. Has nothing to do with whether a system is analog or digital, or even whether it'll be good for dialog recording.

Hitting a post: Audio people use this term to refer to the cues within a long sound effect or music track. It's not enough to make a sound begin and end in sync with the picture; you also have to make sure that internal elements match ("hit") the on-screen actions ("posts"). A good sound editor will make lots of tiny edits and use other tricks to hit as many posts as possible.

House sync: In large facilities, a single video signal (usually an all-black picture in color TV format) is distributed to just about every audio and video device. House sync is not the same as timecode. The former is a precise heartbeat, accurate to microseconds. It keeps signals compatible, but can't tell one frame from another. Timecode identifies frames for editing but is only precise to a few dozen milliseconds. It's usually a mistake to control critical audio- or videotape speeds with it.

IFB: See *earwig*.

Interchange format: A standard method of passing audio elements and editing instructions between audio and video editing software. Usually a file—or bunches of files—carried on an optical disc, hard drive, or download. OMF and AAF are the most popular forms. While those formats are standardized, there can be problems between different manufacturers' implementations. See Chapter 10.

IR Sample: Impulse Response recording. A clean recording of how a room reverberates when a test signal is sounded. Specialized plug-ins can analyze the sample and apply its acoustics to continuous audio, simulating the room's natural reverb.

ISDN: Integrated Services Digital Network. A way of combining standard telephone wiring with special equipment to create high speed digital dial-up connections as needed. In the world of audio, the term usually refers to real-time transfers and remote recording sessions using ISDN wiring. Still used in many situations, including voice-overs for advertising and movie trailers, though being replaced by broadband internet.

Layback: Copying a finished mix from an audio workstation or separate audiotape back to a videotape master.

Layup: Transferring production sound from edited videotape to an audio medium for further manipulation. Networked editing systems can make both layback and layup unnecessary, and send audio directly between DAW and NLE.

LFE: Low-Frequency Effects channel. The "dot-one" in a 5.1 surround system, dedicated to extreme lows in sound effects and music. Only one channel is needed for LFE, because these sounds aren't particularly directional. In home theater setups, the LFE is often combined with low frequencies from the main channels as well.

LKFS: Loudness Units, K-weighted. This is a modern version of the traditional A, B, and C weighting, attempting to make a voltage meter respond to loudness like a human ear does.

LTC: Longitudinal Time Code. SMPTE timecode data is actually a biphase digital stream in the audio range, sounding something like a fax machine signal. When it's recorded on an analog audio track, it's called "longitudinal," since it runs parallel to the tape instead of slanting like a videotape track. While the analog video version is mostly obsolete, LTC also refers to the biphase signal itself, and the wire that plugs into a timecode input or output. This is often distributed at complex or multi-camera shoots. See Chapter 12.

LUFS: Loudness Units referenced to Full Scale. Measurement system, similar to decibels, but based on how people perceive loudness over the long term. Defined in *R128*.

M&E: Music and effects, a submix of a production's soundtrack with no dialog to make foreign translations easier.

MADI: Multichannel Audio Digital Interface, a computer-aided method of putting as many as 64 simultaneous audio streams on a single video cable or glass fiber. Unlike computer networks, MADI does not rely on packets. Cables run from a single multichannel output to a single multichannel input, and are then separated by the equipment. There are no routers or addressing involved.

Masking: A phenomenon where sounds at one frequency make it difficult or impossible to hear other simultaneous (or, in the case of *temporal* masking, closely occurring) sounds at a nearby frequency. The basis behind every system of perceptual encoding. See Chapter 2.

Mid-side (M-S): Stereo microphone technique with excellent control of width and mono compatibility. See Chapter 6.

MIDI: Musical Instrument Digital Interface, a common language and electrical standard for describing events such as the turning on or off of a note. See Chapter 14.

Mono: Short for *monaural*, literally "one ear." An audio signal with no directional information, frequently recorded with a single mic. In most systems, mono signals are automatically placed in the center of a stereo field. Dialog is almost always recorded and mixed in mono.

MOS: Scenes that are videotaped or filmed without any audio, usually because the camera setup or location makes sound impractical. The expectation is that a track will be created using foley and other effects. While it can make sense in traditional film production, it's often a bad idea with projects shot on video, since having *any* track—even one from a camera-mounted microphone far from the action—is better than nothing and may be usable for sound effects or a sync reference. Rumor has it, the term MOS originated when an early German-speaking film director wanted to work "mit out sound."

MP3: MPEG II Layer 3, an international standard devised by the Moving Picture Experts Group. It's the most common file format and data-reduction scheme for delivering audio over the Internet.

NLE: Non-Linear Editor, a computer program or integrated hardware and software for editing and finishing video.

Noise, pink: Electronic noise with an equal likelihood of a signal in each octave. Since any octave has twice as many frequencies as the octave below it, pink noise is created by filtering white noise so there's less energy as the frequency gets higher. Unlike *white noise*, it reflects how we hear and is used for acoustic testing.

Noise, white: Random electronic noise with an equal likelihood of a signal at any frequency. This is the kind of noise commonly generated by analog circuits.

Octave: The musical interval of 12 semitones, or a frequency ratio of 2:1.

Offset: The difference in timecode between any two tapes or elements. Video editors typically start their programs at 1:00:00:00 (one hour; no minutes, seconds, or frames) to allow for color bars and slates. If an audio operator decided to start that same program at 00:01:00:00, the sound would have a –59 minute offset. Some digital audio processors introduce delays to handle the sound more intelligently, so small offsets are sometimes necessary.

OMF: See *interchange format*.

Pan: To move a mono audio signal across the stereo field, or place it in a specific left/right position.

Print Master: Final stage of mixing a theatrical film. Quality is checked, and signal is conditioned or compressed for Dolby or other distribution formats.

Production audio: Sounds recorded in the field while the picture is being shot, usually dialog. May be recorded in the camera, or as *double-system*.

R-DAT: Exactly the same as a standard or timecode DAT tape; the R stands for the rotary heads (like a video deck). Now mostly obsolete.

R128: Recommendation 128 of the European Broadcast Union, released in 2011, to control loudness when switching channels or between programs and commercials.

s/pdif: A standard for interconnecting stereo digital audio devices, similar to AES/EBU but using video-style cables and carrying information that's appropriate for consumer audio. The same data may appear on optical fibers as *Toslink*. See Chapter 2.

SMPTE: Short for SMPTE timecode, the frame-accurate time data recorded on video and audio tapes to control editing and keep elements together. It stands for the Society of Motion Picture and Television Engineers, who invented the format.

Sound cart: Small mobile cart with permanently installed sound equipment, designed to be rolled to an appropriate position on a film set. Usually includes at least a recorder and mixer, wireless receivers and camera link transmitter, keyboard for logging, video monitor, power distribution, and storage for accessories.

Stem: Partial film mix including only the dialog, music, or sound effects elements. Used in various combinations for translated versions of the film and promos. When all the stems are combined, the result should sound like the full mix.

Stereo: An audio signal that includes two distinct channels of information, one intended for the left ear and one for the right, to help the listener locate sound sources across an imaginary line in front of them. This is not the same thing as two channels of identical information, which is just a mono signal with redundant data.

Timbre: A characteristic of a sound wave that has to do with the number and strength of a wave's harmonics (Chapter 1), often referred to as its *brightness* or *richness*. Timbre is different from volume or pitch, though an untrained ear can easily be tricked into confusing these characteristics.

Toslink: Standard for carrying digital audio between devices as light pulses on an optical fiber. Named for Toshiba, which invented it.

Tri-level sync: A form of video sync used in high-definition production. See *house sync*.

VITC: Vertical Interval Time Code. Time data encoded as a series of dots at the top of each video field. Unlike LTC, it can be read when an analog tape is paused. This makes it easier to jog a tape to find a specific action, and then match a sound to it. Now mostly obsolete.

Walla: Voices of people in a crowd, recorded at an event or studio or taken from a sound effects CD. On-camera crowds are usually told to mime their conversations to make dialog pickup easier; walla is then added in post. Walla can also be used to simulate an off-camera crowd to make a scene larger.

Wet/dry: Refers to reverberation. Most foley, hard effects, and ADR are recorded dry, without any natural reverberation. Appropriate echoes are then added during the mix, to make the sounds appear to belong to the on-screen environment. But some effects are recorded wet—that is, with natural (or artificial) reverb. These have to be chosen carefully so the quality matches the scene, and they can be harder to edit because you can't cut into the reverberations.

Wild: Recorded without synchronization. Sound effects are usually gathered this way and matched up in an editing system. But some things are wild by mistake and have to be carefully re-synced. This can happen when a timecode generator or low-end audio workstation isn't locked to house sync, or when audio has been stored on an unstable medium such as audio cassette.

XLR: The standard connector for high-end analog and digital audio, originally known as Cannon's XLR product line. It was universally accepted and is now supported by most other connector manufacturers. It's rugged and has low contact resistance, but its primary advantage is that it can carry balanced wiring (Chapter 3). This makes its cables more immune to noise and hum.

Zero level: Means two different things depending on whether you're working in analog or digital. Analog zero is a nominal volume near the top of the scale, and loud sounds are expected to go above it. Digital zero is an absolute limit, the loudest thing that can be recorded. Depending on the facility and style of audio mixing, analog zero is equivalent to somewhere between 12 dB and 20 dB below digital zero. See Chapter 12.

APPENDIX B

Resources

WEB

Many companies, organizations, and individuals maintain websites where you can learn more about our industry and its technologies. These resources are free except where noted, though registration might be required. Since the Web is ever-changing, these sites may also contain links to other resources that evolved after I wrote this book. Of course, some of them may also have disappeared by the time you read this.

American Radio Relay League (www.arrl.org)

This amateur radio organization publishes many books about electronics, including an excellent primer, *Understanding Basic Electronics*, for $30. Their *ARRL Handbook* ($60 hardcover, including CD-ROM) is a 1,300-page technical encyclopedia, updated every year.

Cinema Audio Society (cinemaaudiosociety.org)

Organization of production sound mixers and boom operators, with an informative online journal, an active discussion board, and links to other film sound technical societies.

Digital Playroom (dplay.com)

My website. It has a large tutorial section, reprints of some of my *DV Magazine* and *ProVideoCoalition* articles, a two-hour video presentation on film sound, some spoofs of our industry . . . and information on my studio (which is how I pay for the whole thing).

Epanorama.Net

Engineer Tomi Engdhal's website: an immense database of contributed articles, circuit diagrams, and tutorials about audio and electronics.

Equipment Emporium (filmtvsound.com)

Educator and sound recordist Fred Ginsberg's site, with lots of articles about soundtrack production, and downloadable manuals for some common gear.

FilmSound.org

Immense library of articles devoted to all aspects of film sound design. The site also includes discussions of more than 150 specific films, and essays by noted sound designers Randy Thom and Walter Murch.

Gearslutz.com

Busy forum (more than 10,000 members and guests) for people who love audio and its equipment. Most of the topics are about music recording, but there are active subgroups devoted to film/video post, studio acoustics, and equipment classified ads.

Internet Movie Database (imdb.com)

Cast, crew, and occasional trivia for just about every movie ever made—Hollywood features, made-for-TV, low-budget indies, the works.

JWSoundGroup.org

Very active discussion group, managed by veteran Hollywood mixer and Oscar nominee Jeff Wexler, and populated by film professionals. Lots of topics (primarily about location and production sound), question-and-answer threads, and both technical and philosophical discussions. Free registration required to post, but anyone can read and search the threads.

Quantel Limited (quantel.com)

This film and video equipment manufacturer has assembled a large downloadable library on digital audio and video, workflows, and interchange systems.

Rane Corporation (rane.com/tech.html)

Rane makes equipment for commercial sound installations. Click the "Reference" tab on this page for a library of downloadable booklets, and a complete technical dictionary.

Rycote's Microphone Database (microphone-data.com)

Published specifications for thousands of professional and semi-pro microphones, sponsored by this manufacturer of professional shock mounts and windscreens.

Video University (videouniversity.com)

This site has a few basic articles on audio, plus a lot of information about the technology and business of video.

SOURCES FOR PUBLIC DOMAIN MATERIALS

Just about any usable audio or video clip you find on the Web is protected by copyright, and can't be put into your film without permission. But a few sites specialize in material that's *mostly* free to use . . . read each clip's page or description to see if there are restrictions.

Internet Archive (archive.org)

Fascinating searchable repository of electronic media including more than a million video clips, close to two million sound recordings, and an almost countless collection of archived Web pages. Some of the material is designated public domain, some available with restrictions, and some currently protected but with contact information for the owners.

Library of Congress (loc.gov)

Among other things, this vast national library includes historic voice and music recordings whose copyright has expired, performances recorded by the government,[1] and a lot of other material useful for filmmakers. Much of the collection has been digitized and is downloadable. The Library of Congress also runs the U.S. Copyright Office: their website has text and multimedia presentations on how copyright affects us, and is where you go for forms and filing when you want to copyright your own work.

Wikimedia Commons (commons.wikimedia.org)

Close to 20 million files, images, and videos that have been contributed for public use. Restrictions for use are posted with each file: while some of the material has no restrictions at all, much of it requires that you credit the original creator or add a note that this was public domain content; some pieces are only for non-commercial use; a few also ask that you contribute your final project to the commons.

---

[1] If tax money paid for the microphones, the recording is usually public domain. But be aware some of the music might be protected by its own copyright.

PROFESSIONAL ORGANIZATIONS

I've separated these organizations from the sites above, because their primary value is promoting a profession and networking, rather than serving as an online resource. But many of them do have useful publications and online information.

American Society Of Composers, Authors, and Publishers (ASCAP), Broadcast Music Incorporated (BMI)

Performing Rights Organizations, see Chapter 14.

Audio Engineering Society (AES)

60 East 42nd Street, New York, NY 10165 (212) 661–8528 Fax (212) 682–0477
www.aes.org

Media Communications Association (formerly ITVA)

9202 North Meridian Street, Indianapolis, IN 46260 (317) 816–6269 Fax (800) 801–8926
www.mca-i.org

National Association of Broadcasters (NAB)

1771 N Street, NW Washington, DC 20036 (202) 429–5300 Fax (202) 429–4199
www.nab.org

Screen Actors' Guild – American Federation of Television and Radio Artists

Talent guild; see Chapter 9.

Society of Motion Picture and Television Engineers (SMPTE)

595 West Hartsdale Avenue White Plains, NY 10607 (914) 761–1100 Fax 914/761–3115
www.smpte.org

Index

Note: Page numbers with w prefix refer to Chapter 9, available on the Web as downloadable pdf file. See Page 250 or go to www.GreatSound.info for password and access details.